KU-604-842

July Crisis

This is a magisterial new account of Europe's tragic descent into a largely inadvertent war in the summer of 1914. T. G. Otte reveals why a century-old system of Great Power politics collapsed so disastrously in the weeks from the 'shot heard around the world' on 28 June to Germany's declaration of war on Russia on 1 August. He shows definitively that the key to understanding how and why Europe descended into world war is to be found in the near-collective failure of statecraft by the rulers of Europe and not in abstract concepts such as the 'balance of power' or the 'alliance system'. In this unprecedented panorama of Europe on the brink, from the ministerial palaces of Berlin and Vienna to Belgrade, London, Paris and St Petersburg, T. G. Otte reveals the hawks and doves whose decision-making led to a war that would define a century and which still reverberates today.

T. G. Otte is Professor of Diplomatic History at the University of East Anglia.

July Crisis

The World's Descent into War, Summer 1914

T. G. Otte

CAMBRIDGE UNIVERSITY PRESS

CAMBRIDGE
UNIVERSITY PRESS

University Printing House, Cambridge CB2 8BS, United Kingdom

Cambridge University Press is part of the University of Cambridge.

It furthers the University's mission by disseminating knowledge in the pursuit of
education, learning and research at the highest international levels of excellence.

www.cambridge.org
Information on this title: www.cambridge.org/9781107064904

© T.G. Otte 2014

This publication is in copyright. Subject to statutory exception
and to the provisions of relevant collective licensing agreements,
no reproduction of any part may take place without the written
permission of Cambridge University Press.

First published 2014

Printed in the United Kingdom by Clays, St Ives plc

A catalogue record for this publication is available from the British Library

Library of Congress Cataloguing in Publication data
Otte, Thomas G., 1967–
July Crisis : the world's descent into war, summer 1914 / T. G. Otte.
    pages   cm
Summary: "Definitive new account of the catalytic events that led to the outbreak of
war. Thomas Otte argues that neither martial culture nor the alliance system played
a decisive role for much of the crisis. Instead he reveals the fatal flaws, failings, and
miscalculations of those who led Europe into war" – Provided by publisher.
ISBN 978-1-107-06490-4 (Hardback)
 1. Europe–History–July Crisis, 1914.   2. World War, 1914–1918–Causes.
I. Title.
D511.O83 2014
940.3'11–dc23   2013047702

ISBN 978-1-107-06490-4 Hardback

Cambridge University Press has no responsibility for the persistence or accuracy of
URLs for external or third-party internet websites referred to in this publication,
and does not guarantee that any content on such websites is, or will remain,
accurate or appropriate.

In memory of
August S., killed in action, 1 September 1916,
Henry S., missing in action, presumed killed,
12 April 1918,
two great-grandfathers, who fought on opposite sides.

CONTENTS

ILLUSTRATIONS

MAPS

PREFACE AND ACKNOWLEDGEMENTS

'And so they've killed our Ferdinand', said the charwoman to
Švejk ... 'Which Ferdinand, Mrs Müller?', he asked ... 'Oh no,
sir, it's His Imperial Highness, the Archduke Ferdinand, from
Konopište, the fat churchy one ... They bumped him off at
Sarajevo, with a revolver, you know. He drove there in a car
with his Archduchess.'

JAROSLAV HAŠEK[1]

The First World War has cast a long shadow over the twentieth
century, and beyond. One hundred years on, the horror of the conflict still
commands attention, and will probably never cease to do so. How and why
the civilized world, seemingly so secure in its material and intellectual
achievements, could have descended into a global conflict has continued
to intrigue not just historians, but also the general public. It has certainly
puzzled me ever since I first developed an interest in the past. And the more
I studied the period of the long nineteenth century, the more it became clear
to me that the answer, in so far as there can be one, is not to be found in *les
forces profondes*, the vast impersonal forces, that some think shape historical processes, but, rather, that the reasons, in so far as they can ever be
fathomed, may be glimpsed in the doings of men (and they were all men in
1914), their flaws and failings, their calculations and miscalculations. It
would be difficult to improve on Marx's insight that people make their own
history, if not under circumstances of their choosing. Politics more especially are subject to the ambiguities of free will and the play of the contingent. In that lies hope for the future; but it is also a reminder of man's
shortcomings. What follows here is an attempt to make sense of the events
of Europe's last summer.

People also matter in a less abstract sense. In the course of
researching and writing this book I have incurred debts of gratitude to
various people, and it is a great pleasure to acknowledge this debt. Anyone
working on the origins of the First World War will be acutely conscious of
the immense intellectual debt that is owed to those who have laboured in

---

[1] J. Hašek, *The Good Soldier Švejk* (London, 1973 [orig. 1921]), 4–5.

this particular vineyard before. To an extent the footnotes bear testimony to my debt to the wider scholarly community. A number of friends and colleagues, however, need to be singled out for special thanks. Keith Neilson once more proved a trusted source of advice and help. He made time during his own busy schedule to read the whole manuscript of this book, and it is immeasurably better for it. There was little that escaped his hawkeye. I am grateful to Bruce Menning, who generously shared with me his thoughts and ideas about the late imperial Russian military, and who patiently answered my many questions. Chai Lieven kindly sent me a copy of Basil Strandtmann's unpublished memoirs, and was the source of invaluable insights into the nature of the Russian state. Pursuing the Russian theme, my colleague at UEA, Peter Waldron, offered various thoughts and suggestions, for all of which I am grateful. I owe a special debt also to Roy Bridge, who volunteered his services as my very own 'k.u.k. Erz-privilegierter Haus-, Hof-, und Staatskopist', and from whom I have learnt so much about the Habsburg Empire over the years. I also greatly benefited from discussing Berchtold and Austro-Hungarian diplomacy with Sam Williamson. Lothar Höbelt, as always, came up trumps when I was stuck for an answer. I am grateful to Alma Hannig for sharing with me her thoughts on the Archduke Franz Ferdinand. My colleague Jan Vermeiren provided insights into Ambassador Tschirschky and his entourage. Guenther Roth very kindly provided me with a copy of one of Kurt Riezler's letters. Zara Steiner and Erik Goldstein have been constant sources of encouragement and constructive criticism, and for that I am more grateful than they can know. Similarly, Vernon Bogdanor has kept me thinking about Asquith, Grey and the nineteen men around the Cabinet table in Downing Street. His judicious comments ensured that I was not satisfied with the obvious answers. It is a pleasure to acknowledge my gratitude to Simon Kerry for his thoughts and material on Lord Lansdowne. Sven Bergmann, as ever, was ready to pinprick my carefully formed ideas, and for that I thank him, too. Researching 1914 meant reading innumerable numbers of old books, and pulling yet another weighty tome off my shelves all too often reminded me what a gap my friend and fellow bibliomaniac Hans Seelig has left. I am grateful to Arnold Rosen for letting me talk about a subject about which I care so much. Over the years I have benefited also from conversations with Holger Afflerbach, Chris Clark, Laurence Cole, Mark Cornwall, Günther Kronenbitter, Andrew Lambert, Margaret Macmillan, John Maurer, Annika Mombauer, William Mulligan and David Stevenson. I am grateful to all of them.

I am immensely grateful to Michael Watson, prince of editors. He and his team at Cambridge University Press have helped me to see this project through to fruition with their customary courtesy, efficiency and patience. I must also acknowledge my gratitude to Stuart Proffitt, who took an early interest in this work and who has greatly helped me to refine my thinking, as did Bill Hamilton.

Whatever may be worthwhile in this book has enormously profited from the assistance of my friends and colleagues. Whatever its failings, omissions and shortcomings, they are mine alone.

My greatest debt, as always, is to Joanna and Gwendolen. Between them, they somehow managed to keep me sane and made sure that there was no July crisis in the summer of 2013.

T. G. O.
North Norfolk, September 2013

ABBREVIATIONS

AHR	*American Historical Review*
BayD	*Bayerische Dokumente zum Kriegsausbruch*, ed. P. Dirr (Munich, 1922)
BBBP	*Bescheiden Betreffende de Buitenlandse Politiek van Nederland* 3rd ser., *1899–1919*, ed. C. Smit (8 vols., The Hague, 1957–74)
BD	*British Documents on the Origins of the War, 1898–1914*, ed. G. P. Gooch and H. W. V. Temperley (11 vols., London, 1928–38)
BDS	*Graf Benckendorffs Diplomatischer Schriftwechsel*, ed. B. von Siebert (3 vols., new edn Berlin and Leipzig, 1928)
BelD	*Belgische Dokumente zur Vorgeschichte des Weltkrieges, 1885–1914* (5 vols., Berlin, 1919)
BIHR	*Bulletin of the Institute of Historical Research*
BJIS	*British Journal of International Studies*
BL	British Library, London
BMH	*Berliner Monatshefte zur Kriegsschuldfrage*
BN	Bibliothèque Nationale, Paris
Bodl.	Bodleian Library, Oxford
CEH	*Central European History*
CJH	*Canadian Journal of History*
CSH	*Cultural and Social History*
CUBA	Columbia University, Bakhmetiev Archive, New York
CUL	Cambridge University Library, Cambridge
DA	*Diplomatische Aktenstücke zur Vorgeschichte des Krieges 1914: Ergänzungen und Nachträge zum Österreichisch-Ungarischen Rotbuch, 28 Juni bis 27 August 1914*, ed. Republik Österreich, Staatsamt für Äusseres (3 vols., Vienna, 1919)
DD	*Die Deutschen Dokumente zum Kriegsausbruch*, ed. K. Kautsky, M. Montgelas and W. Schücking (4 vols., Berlin, 1919)
DDF	*Documents Diplomatiques Française*, 3rd ser., *1911–1914*, ed. Ministère des Affaires Étrangères (11 vols., Paris, 1929–36)

DDI	*Documenti Diplomatici Italiana*, 4th ser., *1908–1914*, ed. Ministero degli Affari esteri (12 vols., Rome, 1964)
DDS	*Documents Diplomatiques Suisses*, v, *1904–1914*, ed. H. Lüthy and G. Kreis (Berne, 1983)
DGB	*Deutsche Gesandtschaftsberichte zum Kriegsausbruch*, ed. A. Bach (Berlin, 1937)
DSI	*Der Diplomatische Schriftwechsel Iswolskys*, ed. F. Stieve (4 vols., Berlin, 1924)
DSP	*Dokumenti o Spolojnoj Politici Kraljevine Srbije*, ed. V. Dedijer and Ž. Anić (7 vols., Belgrade, 1980)
ECE/ ECE	*Eastern and Central Europe/Europe Central et de l'Est*
EEQ	*East European Quarterly*
EHR	*English Historical Review*
ESR	*European Studies Review*
FA	*Foreign Affairs*
FH	*French History*
GP	*Die Grosse Politik der Europäischen Kabinette, 1871–1914*, ed. J. Lepsius, A. Mendelssohn-Bartholdy and F. Thimme (40 vols., Berlin, 1922–7)
GR	*Germanic Review*
GWU	*Geschichte in Wissenschaft und Unterricht*
HHStA	Haus-, Hof- und Staatsarchiv, Vienna
HJ	*Historical Journal*
HZ	*Historische Zeitschrift*
IBZI	*Internationale Beziehungen im Zeitalter des Imperialismus*, 1st ser., *1911–14*, ed. O. Hoetzsch (5 vols., Berlin, 1931–6)
IHR	*International History Review*
IWM	Imperial War Museum, London
JBS	*Journal of British Studies*
JCEH	*Journal of Central European History*
JCH	*Journal of Contemporary History*
JK	*Julikrise und Kriegsausbruch 1914*, ed. I. Geiss (2 vols., Hanover, 1963–4)
JMH	*Journal of Modern History*
JMilH	*Journal of Military History*
KA	*Krasny Arkhiv*
LN	*Un Livre Noir. Diplomatie d'avant-guerre d'après les documents des archives russes, novembre 1910 – juillet 1914* (2 vols., Paris, s.a.), ed. R. Marchand
LSE	London School of Economics
LUR	*Laurentian University Review*

MAE	Ministère des Affaires Étrangères, Paris
MGM	*Militärgeschichtliche Mitteilungen*
MÖStA	*Mitteilungen des Österreichischen Staats-Archivs*
NLS	National Library of Scotland, Edinburgh
NRO	Northamptonshire Record Office, Northampton
OGD	*Official German Documents Relating to the World War*, ed. Carnegie Endowment for International Peace (2 vols., New York, 1923)
ÖUA	*Österreich-Ungarns Aussenpolitik von der Bosnischen Krise 1908 bis zum Kriegsausbruch 1914*, ed. L. Bittner, A. F. Pribram, H. Srbik and H. Uebersberger (9 vols., Vienna and Leipzig, 1930)
PA	Politisches Archiv, Haus-, Hof- und Staatsarchiv
PAAA	Politisches Archiv, Auswärtiges Amt, Berlin
PAL	Parliamentary Archive, House of Lords, London
PCC	*Paul Cambon: Correspondance, 1870–1924*, ed. H. Cambon (3 vols., Paris, 1940–5)
P&P	*Past & Present*
P&S	*Politics & Society*
RGVIA	Rossiiskii Gosudarstvennyi Voenno-istoricheskii Arkhiv, Moscow
RH	*Revue Historique*
RHD	*Revue d'Histoire Diplomatique*
RIS	*Review of International Studies*
SEER	*Slavonic and East European Review*
SocR	*Sociological Review*
SR	*Slavonic Review*
SSEES	School of Slavonic and East European Studies, London
TNA (PRO)	The National Archive (Public Record Office), Kew, London
WiH	*War-in-History*

PRINCIPAL *DRAMATIS PERSONAE*

The Sarajevo assassins

Nedeljko Čabrinović, Vaso Čubrilović, Trifko Grabež, Danilo Ilić, Mehmed Mehmedbašić, Cvijetko Popović, Gavrilo Prinčip.

Austria-Hungary	
Kaiser Franz Joseph	Emperor of Austria, King of Hungary
Archduke Franz Ferdinand of Austria-Este	Heir to the Habsburg throne
Sophie, Duchess of Hohenberg	Wife of Franz Ferdinand
Ludwig, Freiherr Ambrózy von Séden	Embassy Counsellor, Rome
Leopold, Graf Berchtold von und zu Ungarschitz	Common Foreign Minister
Leon, Ritter von Biliński	Common Finance Minister
István, Freiherr Burián von Rajecz	Hungarian Minister at the imperial court
Franz, Freiherr Conrad von Hötzendorf	Chief of the General Staff
Otto, Graf Czernin von und zu Chudenitz	Embassy Counsellor, St Petersburg
Ottokar, Graf Czernin von und zu Chudenitz	Minister, Bucharest
Johann, Graf Forgách von Ghymes und Gács	First Section Chief, Foreign Ministry
Georg, Freiherr von Franckenstein	Embassy Counsellor, London
Major-General Wladimir, Freiherr Giesl von Gieslingen	Minister, Belgrade
Franz, Freiherr von Haymerle	Embassy Counsellor, Berlin
Alexander, Graf Hoyos	Section Chief, Foreign Ministry
Admiral Carl Kailer von Kaltenfels	Deputy Chief, Naval Staff
General Alexander Ritter von Krobatin	Common War Minister
Karl, Freiherr von Macchio	Section Chief, Foreign Ministry
Albert, Graf von Mensdorff-Pouilly-Dietrichstein	Ambassador, London
Kajetan Mérey von Kapos-Mére	Ambassador, Rome
Franz, Freiherr von Matscheko	Counsellor, Foreign Ministry
Berthold Molden	Viennese journalist
Alexander, Freiherr Musulin von Gomirje	Section Chief, Foreign Ministry
Johann, Markgraf von Pallavicini	Ambassador, Constantinople
General Oskar Potiorek	Governor of Bosnia-Herzegovina

(cont.)

Austria-Hungary

Josef Redlich	Professor of Law and *Reichsrat* Deputy
Ivan Skerlecz von Lomnicza	*Ban* (Viceroy) of Croatia
Wilhelm, Ritter von Storck	Legation Counsellor, Belgrade
Major-General Karl Graf Stürgkh	Austrian Prime Minister
Friedrich, Graf Szápáry von Szápár	Ambassador, St Petersburg
Nikolaus, Graf Szécsen von Temerin	Ambassador, Paris
Ladislaus, Graf Szögyény-Marich	Ambassador, Berlin
István, Graf Tisza de Borosjenő et Szeged	Hungarian Prime Minister

France

Raymond Poincaré	President of the Republic
Camille Barrère	Ambassador, Rome
Philippe Berthelot	Political Director, Foreign Ministry
Jean-Baptiste Bienvenu-Martin	Minister of Justice (acting Foreign Minister)
Jules Cambon	Ambassador, Berlin
Paul Cambon	Ambassador, London
Charles Pineton de Chambrun	Embassy Counsellor, Paris
Pierre Descos	Minister, Belgrade
Alfred Dumaine	Ambassador, Vienna
Abel Ferry	Under-secretary, Foreign Ministry
Marshal Joseph Joffre	Chief of the General Staff
Gustave Henri Benoît, Comte de Manneville	Embassy Counsellor, Berlin
Pierre de Margerie	Director of Political Affairs, Foreign Ministry
Adolphe Messimy	War Minister
Maurice Paléologue	Ambassador, St Petersburg
René Viviani	Prime Minister and Foreign Minister

Germany

Kaiser Wilhelm II	German Emperor, King of Prussia
Prince Heinrich of Prussia	Kaiser's brother
Albert Ballin	German shipping magnate
Claus von Below-Saleske	Minister, Brussels
Dietrich von Bethmann Hollweg	Embassy Secretary at Vienna
Theobald von Bethmann Hollweg	Chancellor
Lieutenant-General Oskar von Chelius	Military Plenipotentiary, St Petersburg
Clemens Ernst Gottlieb von Delbrück	State Secretary of the Interior and Vice-chancellor

(*cont.*)

Germany	
General Erich von Falkenhayn	Prussian War Minister
Hans von Flotow	Ambassador, Rome
Hugo Ganz	Vienna correspondent, *Frankfurter Zeitung*
Julius Adolf, Freiherr von Griesinger	Minister, Belgrade
Gottlieb von Jagow	State Secretary, Foreign Ministry
Karl Max, Fürst von Lichnowsky	Ambassador, London
General Moriz, Freiherr von Lyncker	Chief of Kaiser's Military Cabinet
General Helmuth von Moltke, the Younger	Chief of the General Staff
Victor Naumann	Journalist
General Hans von Plessen	Kaiser's Adjutant-General
Friedrich, Graf Pourtalès von Cronstern	Ambassador, St Petersburg
Kurt Riezler	Aide to the Chancellor
Wilhelm Eduard, Freiherr von Schoen	Ambassador, Paris
Wilhelm von Stumm	Political Director, Foreign Ministry
Grand Admiral Alfred von Tirpitz	Navy Minister
Heinrich, Freiherr von Tschirschky und Bögendorff	Ambassador, Vienna
Hans Wilhelm, Freiherr von Wangenheim	Ambassador, Constantinople
Theodor Wolff	Editor, *Berliner Tageblatt*
Arthur Zimmermann	Under-State Secretary, Foreign Ministry

Great Britain	
King George V	King of Great Britain and Ireland, Emperor of India
Herbert Henry Asquith	Prime Minister
Sir Henry George Outram Bax-Ironside	Minister, Sofia
Sir Francis Leveson Bertie	Ambassador, Paris
Sir George William Buchanan	Ambassador, St Petersburg
Sir Maurice de Bunsen	Ambassador, Vienna
John Elliot Burns	President of the Board of Trade
Hon. Winston Spencer Churchill	First Lord of the Admiralty
Dayrell Montague Crackanthorpe	Chargé d'Affaires, Belgrade
Charles Louis Des Graz	Minister, Belgrade
Sir Eyre Alexander Crowe	Assistant Under-secretary, Foreign Office
Sir (William) Edward Goschen	Ambassador, Berlin
Sir Edward Grey	Foreign Secretary
Richard Burdon Haldane, Viscount Haldane of Cloan	Lord Chancellor
Lewis Harcourt	Colonial Secretary

(*cont.*)

Great Britain

David Lloyd George	Chancellor of the Exchequer
William Lygon, 7th Earl of Beauchamp	First Commissioner of Works, Leader of the House of Lords
Edwin Samuel Montagu	Financial Secretary to the Treasury
John, Viscount Morley of Blackburn	Lord President of the Council
Sir Arthur Nicolson	Permanent Under-secretary, Foreign Office
John Albert Pease	President of the Board of Education
Hon. Arthur Ponsonby	Liberal MP
Sir James Rennell Rodd	Ambassador, Rome
Sir Horace George Montague Rumbold	Embassy Counsellor, Berlin
Walter Runciman	President of the Board of Agriculture
Hon. (Odo William) Theophilus Villiers Russell	Embassy Counsellor, Vienna
Herbert Louis Samuel	President of the Local Government Board
Sir John Allsebrook Simon	Attorney-General
John Alfred Spender	Editor, *The Westminster Gazette*
Sir William George Tyrrell	Private Secretary to Sir Edward Grey

---

Italy

Giuseppe, Duca di Avarna di Gualtieri	Ambassador, Vienna
Ricardo Bollati	Ambassador, Berlin
Andrea, Marchese Carlotti di Riparbello	Ambassador, St Petersburg
Guglielmo, Marchese Imperiali di Francavilla	Ambassador, London
Antonio Paterno-Castelli, Marchese di San Giuliano	Foreign Minister
Antonio Salandra	Prime Minister
Nicola, Barone Squitti di Palermiti e Guarna	Minister, Belgrade

---

Russia

Tsar Nicholas II	Tsar of All the Russias, King of Poland, Grand Duke of Finland
Pyotr Lvovich Bark	Finance Minister
Nikolai Aleksandrovich Basili	Deputy *chef de cabinet*, Foreign Ministry
Aleksandr Konstantinovich, Count von Benckendorff	Ambassador, London
Arkadi Nikola'evich Bronevski	Embassy Counsellor, Berlin
Konstantin Yevgeni'evich von Bützow	Head of Second Department, Foreign Ministry
General Yuri Nikoforovich Danilov	Quartermaster-General

(*cont.*)

Russia	
General Sergei Konstantinovich Dobrorolski	Director, Mobilization Section, General Staff
Baron Vladimir Borisovich Fredericksz	Minister of the imperial household
Mikhail Nikola'evich de Giers	Ambassador, Constantinople
Ivan Loginovich Goremykin	President, Council of Ministers
Rear-Admiral Ivan Konstantinovich Grigorovich	Navy Minister
Nikolai Genrikovich de Hartwig	Minister, Belgrade
Aleksandr Petrovich Izvolsky	Ambassador, Paris
Alexander Vasilevich Krivoshein	Agriculture Minister
Anatoli Nikola'evich Krupenski	Ambassador, Rome
Nikolai Aleksandrovich, Prince Kudashev	Embassy Counsellor, Vienna
Vasili'i Alekse'evich Maklakov	Minister of the Interior
General Nikolai Avgustovich Monkewitz	Staff Officer
Anatol Anatolevich Neratov	Assistant Foreign Minister
Sergei Dmitrievich Sazonov	Foreign Minister
Moritz Fabianovich, Baron von Schilling	Head of Department I (Western Europe), Foreign Ministry
Nikolai Nikola'evich Shebeko	Ambassador, Vienna
Vasili'i Nikola'evich von Strandtmann	Legation Counsellor, Belgrade
General Vladimir Aleksandrovich Sukhomlinov	Chief of General Staff
Sergei Nikola'evich Sverbe'ev	Ambassador, Berlin
Prince Grigori'i Nikola'evich Trubetskoy	Head of Near Eastern Department, Foreign Ministry
General Nikolai Nikola'evich Yanushkevich	Chief of Staff

Serbia	
King Petar Karadjordjević	King of Serbia
Prince Aleksandr Karadjordjević	Crown Prince and Regent
Mateja Bošković	Minister, London
Milan Ciganović	Railway clerk and intelligence agent
Colonel Dragutin T. Dimitrijević ('Apis')	Head of Military Intelligence Section
Slavko Gruić	Secretary-General, Foreign Ministry
Velizar Janković	Trade Minister
Jovan Jovanović	Minister, Vienna
Ljuba Jovanović	Minister of Education
Milutin Jovanović	Legation Secretary, Vienna

(*cont.*)

Serbia	
Lazar Paču	Finance Minister
Nikola Pašić	Prime Minister
Stojan Protić	Minister of the Interior
Field Marshal Radomir Putnik	Chief of Staff
Miroslav Spalajković	Minister, St Petersburg
Dušan Stefanović	War Minister
Captain Voja Tankošić	Military intelligence officer
Milenko Vesnić	Minister, Paris

Note to Readers: To retain some of the period flavour I have followed the custom of the time and used the following shorthands for the foreign ministries of the Powers: Ballhausplatz (Austria-Hungary); Choristers' Bridge (Russia); Downing Street (Great Britain); Quai d'Orsay (France); Quirinale (Italy); and Wilhelmstrasse (Germany).

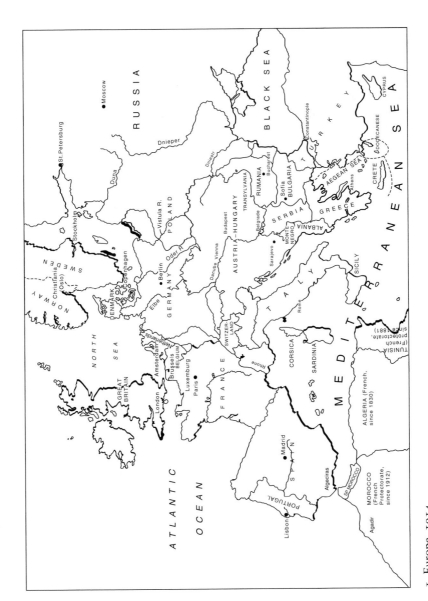

1. Europe, 1914

2. The Balkans, 1914

INTRODUCTION

Do not despise the diplomatic documents.

GILBERT MURRAY (1915)[1]

It appears to me to be from its very nature an impossibility even to determine from documentary evidence the question of who was responsible for the outbreak of the war.

VICTOR NAUMANN (1919)[2]

At the end of June 1914, the young Oxford historian E. L. Woodward was spending part of his summer vacation at a resort in the Black Forest. In the late afternoon of Sunday, 28 June, the polite tinkling of cosmopolitan teacups on the long terrace of the Badenweiler spa hotel was interrupted by some startling news: the Archduke Franz Ferdinand, heir to the Habsburg throne and future ruler of some forty-five million people in central and south-eastern Europe, had been assassinated in Sarajevo. The hotel crowd excitedly dispersed to form separate groups according to nationality: 'I knew that something very grave had happened', Woodward reflected many decades later.[3] Something grave had indeed happened, though Woodward was perhaps reading back into the past a fancy of foresight.

When viewed at the distance of a century, there is a paradox about 1914: it should have been an unremarkable year. After years of turmoil, especially in south-eastern Europe, the short-term indicators pointed towards peace. European diplomats spoke of a new era of détente. But the two recent Balkan conflicts in 1912 and 1913 had left unexploded ordnance in their wake, one being Albania, now independent but without agreed frontiers. Under the rule of a German princeling, the Prince of Wied, the country was on the verge of becoming a failed state: 'les caisses sont vides, le thrône est Wied, tout est vide [the coffers are empty, [on] the

---

[1] G. Murray, *The Foreign Policy of Sir Edward Grey, 1906–1915* (Oxford, 1915), 122.
[2] Statement Dr V. Naumann [1919], *OGD* I, no. 8.
[3] E. L. Woodward, *Short Journey* (London, 1942), 72–3; for similar observations on that day see S. Zweig, *Die Welt von Gestern: Erinnerungen eines Europäers* (Frankfurt, 1981 (pb), [1st edn 1944]), 248–51.

throne is Wied, everything is empty]',[4] as some unkindly soul put it in the spring of 1914. But whilst there were problems in the periphery of Europe, relations between the Great Powers appeared relatively free of friction, especially when compared with previous years. To explain how and why the Powers found themselves in a world war, then, poses a significant challenge to the student of the past.

To say that the First World War transformed the modern world is to state the obvious. The conflict was, as George F. Kennan observed, 'the great seminal catastrophe' of the twentieth century:[5] from it flowed many, if not all, of the vicissitudes of that century. Even outwardly, it has left its scars on the surface of Europe's landscape and social fabric. In Britain, but also in many Commonwealth countries, this war, the bloodiest in these nations' histories, has remained something of a national obsession. Commemorated sombrely and formally once a year, it continues to provide a stimulus for soul-searching. And no-one can drive through the flat fields of Flanders or the rolling hills of the Champagne and not be struck by the endless rows of white tombstones and crosses in the Commonwealth war cemeteries, or in the *jardins de funèbre* and the *Heldenhaine* that pockmark those landscapes.

Countless participants in the war wrote on the profound impact of the conflict; legions of later writers have amplified on it and have reflected on the origins of the war. The 1914–18 conflict has never ceased to attract the attention of scholars and the wider public alike. Its origins have furnished enough nutritious matter for generations of historians to feed on. The debate surrounding the origins is, as John Langdon's aptly named historiographical study suggests, 'the long debate'.[6] This prolonged preoccupation with the immediate, and the longer-term, structural origins of the war is easily understandable. Three considerations help to explain it. For one thing, as the Swiss historian Werner Näf observed in 1930, for all the loose pre-1914 talk of a 'coming war', the reality of the world war

---

[4] As quoted in *JK* 1, 216.

[5] G. F. Kennan, *The Decline of Bismarck's European Order: Franco-Russian Relations 1875–1890* (Princeton, NJ, 1979), 3.

[6] J. W. Langdon, *July 1914: The Long Debate, 1919–1990* (Oxford, 1991); see also J. Droz, *Les causes de la Première Guerre mondiale. Essai d'historiographie* (Paris, 1973); for further studies with special emphasis on the debate in Germany see J. A. Moses, *The Politics of Illusion: The Fischer Controversy in German Historiography*; W. Jäger, *Historische Forschung und politische Kultur in Deutschland. Die Debatte um den Ausbruch des Ersten Weltkriegs, 1914–1980* (Göttingen, 1984); A. Mombauer, *The Origins of the First World War: Controversies and Consensus* (London, 2002); see also the articles on the Fischer controversy in the special issue of *JCH* XLVIII, 2 (2013).

shook European civilization.[7] There it was, noted the Austrian novelist Arthur Schnitzler in his diary: 'The world war. The ruin of the world. Tremendous and frightful news.'[8] The war rocked the sense of security, prosperity and progress that had sustained the confidence of the nations of Europe. Until the summer of 1914, most Europeans, certainly those of the comfortable middle and upper classes, led a 'relatively privileged life ... confident that ... frontiers would always be open, that intellectual and scientific progress would continue, without disturbing the habitual course of life'.[9] After 1919, confronted with the realities of war, and with the many limbless and otherwise mutilated ex-soldiers a daily reminder of its horrors, the European and North American publics were driven by an almost psychological need to come to terms with what had occurred.

The profound transformation of European society and culture, indeed of world politics, is the second consideration that helps to explain the enduring fascination with the First World War. In many ways, that conflict ushered in the short twentieth century. It is a pleasant diversion to speculate that, without the war, the balmy summer's afternoon of 1914, so powerfully invoked in the novels of Henry James and others, could have been perpetuated and the later horrors averted. Without the war, one Vladimir Ilyich Ulyanov may well have been destined to eke out a meagre living as an abstruse dialectician in the emigré circles of Zürich. A certain, moderately talented, postcard painter might well have continued to dream dreams of improbable greatness in the dank dosshouses on the banks of the Danube, never to develop his mesmeric evil powers. And he and Messrs Dzhugashvili (better known by his *nom de guerre* Stalin), Bronshtein (Trotsky) and Broz (Tito), all living within a few streets of each other in the Habsburg capital in early 1913, would have remained habitués of the city's coffee houses, four faceless fringe figures among the polyglot crowds of the city, of no great concern to later generations. And the idea of an 'iron curtain' might have been something dreamed up by very avant-garde interior designers. But the after-effects of the war continue to reverberate to the present day, nowhere more so than in the Middle East. Thus, Osama bin Laden sought to justify the 9/11 terrorist attacks on the United States with reference to the Muslim community 'tasting this humiliation and contempt for more than eighty years', by which he meant the dissolution

[7] As quoted in M. Rauchensteiner, *Der Tod des Doppeladlers. Österreich-Ungarn und der Weltkrieg* (Graz, 1993), 11.

[8] Schnitzler diary, 5 Aug. 1914, W. Welzig (ed.), *Arthur Schnitzlers Tagebuch, 1913–1916* (Vienna, 1983), 129.

[9] F. Stern, 'Historians and the Great War: Private Experiences and Explications', in his *Einstein's German World* (London, 1997), 202.

of the caliphate in the aftermath of the First World War.[10] If this statement betrayed a somewhat uncertain grasp of history, it nevertheless highlighted the continued political relevance of the First World War and its outcomes.

The third factor helping to explain the longevity of the debate about the origins of the war is political. For the half-century after 1919, much of the debate surrounding 1914 was influenced by political considerations. The Paris peace treaties, foisted on the vanquished Central Powers, all contained a 'war-guilt clause' that attributed joint or, in the case of Germany, sole responsibility for the war.[11] The clause justified the stipulations of the peace treaties which were imposed on the defeated nations. From the perspective of the vanquished, disproving individual war guilt or asserting some form of collective, and thus individually exculpating, responsibility on the part of all the Powers had a political point to it: it was meant to knock aside the intellectual props on which the 1919 peace settlement rested.[12] Thus in the aftermath of the peace conferences, historians – many government-appointed – began to fill the trenches barely yet vacated by the exhausted troops. On the war itself there now followed what the German staff officer-turned-historian Bernhard Schwertfeger called the 'world war of the documents'.[13] Governments published pre-war despatches and telegrams in an effort to refute their 'war guilt' or any share in it. The wave of weighty document collections soon unleashed a revisionist tide. This was especially marked in Germany, anxious to prove her innocence, but also in the United States, aggrieved at having been dragged into a seemingly senseless overseas conflict. Political passions had by no means evaporated by the middle of the century, as was demonstrated by the vitriolic controversy triggered by Fritz Fischer and his disciples in the 1960s. They placed the sole responsibility for both world wars squarely on

[10] Bin Laden statement on Al Jazeera TV station, 7 Oct. 2001, *FBIS Report: Compilation of Usama Bin Ladin Statements 1994 – January 2004* (Washington, DC, 2004), 183, at www.fas.org/irp/world/para/ubl-fbis.pdf.

[11] They are art. 231 Versailles Treaty (Germany), art. 177 Treaty of St Germain (Austria), art. 161 Trianon Treaty (Hungary), art. 231 Treaty of Sèvres (Turkey) and art. 121 Treaty of Neuilly-sur-Seine (Bulgaria), in United States Senate, *Peace Treaties* (Washington, DC, 1921).

[12] See the thoughts offered by H. H. Herwig, 'Clio Deceived: Patriotic Self-Censorship in Germany after the Great War', K. M. Wilson (ed.), *Forging Collective Memory: Government and International Historians through Two World Wars* (Oxford, 1996), 87–127, and K. A. Hamilton, 'The Pursuit of "Enlightened Patriotism": The British Foreign Office and Historical Researchers during the Great War and its Aftermath', *ibid.*, 192–229; see also S. Zala, *Geschichte unter der Schere der politischen Zensur: Amtliche Aktensammlungen im internationalen Vergleich* (Munich, 2001), 47–91.

[13] As quoted in C. Clark, *The Sleepwalkers: How Europe Went to War in 1914* (London, 2012), xxiii.

Germany, while orthodox revisionists sought to absolve her from at least the responsibility for the 1914 conflict. To no small extent the explosive nature of this debate was rooted in a wider debate about a German 'Sonderweg', a special, abnormal path of development since the nineteenth century, a faintly masochistic, Teutonic variant of A. J. P. Taylor's controversial *Course of German History*.[14]

Much of the poison has been drained from not just that particular debate, but also the debate surrounding 1914. Even so, the origins of the Great War still have the potential of generating intense passions, as was underlined by the often heated discussions in the United Kingdom in the summer of 2013 on the appropriate ways of commemorating the centenary of the war.[15]

Historians have continued to shine their torches into the many nooks and crannies of pre-1914 Great Power relations. The immediate origins of the war have been examined meticulously and so have been its presumed longer-term causes, what Harry Hinsley once referred to as 'the impersonal and the man-made' forces, or in more recent nomenclature 'structure versus agency'.[16]

The first point to make is that much of the debate about 1914 continues to be focused on Germany and her role in pre-war international politics. At the same time, the focus has shifted away from decision-making processes in the various European capitals. Instead, historians have tended to concentrate their attention on underlying, structural forces. In the 1970s, some scholars sought to recast the debate in terms of vast socio-economic forces that drove the politics of the period.[17] Few historians today would subscribe to some of the cruder notions of a *Primat der Innenpolitik*, which accords foreign policy a subservient function. Even so, the notion of

---

[14] A. J. P. Taylor, *The Course of German History* (London, 1945); for the problems of 'continuity' see the perceptive comments by J. Droz, 'L'Allemagne est-elle responsable de la Première Guerre mondiale?', A. Prost (ed.), *14–18: Mourir pour la patrie* (Paris, 1992), 74–80; for the Fischer controversy see Moses, *Politics of Illusion*, esp. 107–32; Mombauer, *Origins*, 127–65; and the articles in *JCH* XLVIII, 2 (2013).

[15] Ben Macintyre's thoughtful piece 'One Last Battle over How We Mark the First World War', *The Times*, 27 Apr. 2013, triggered a prolonged discussion of the subject.

[16] F. H. Hinsley, *Power and the Pursuit of Peace: Theory and Practice in the History of Relations between States* (Cambridge, 1967 (pb)), 290; see also K. J. Holsti, *Peace and War: Armed Conflicts and International Order, 1648–1989* (Cambridge, 1992), 3–24; and B. F. Baumoeller, *The Great Powers and the International System: Systemic Theory in Empirical Perspective* (Cambridge, 2012), 3–10.

[17] Illustrative of the neo-Kehrite strand, V. R. Berghahn, *Germany and the Approach of War in 1914* (London, 1973), and I. Geiss, *German Foreign Policy, 1871–1914* (London, 1979).

Europe's ruling élites on the eve of the Great War as being beleaguered continues to command much support among scholars. These élites, so the argument runs, were ill-suited to cope with the demands of the age of the masses. More especially, they were unable to contain the genie of hyper-nationalism, which they themselves had let out of the bottle. The forces of nationalism, demographic pressures and more intense economic competition pushed the Powers towards confrontation. The situation was compounded by the now far less flexible nature of international politics. The straitjacket of a near-rigid system of power blocs, which pitted aggressive and ambitious Germany and her allies against a defensive, status quo-oriented, so-called 'Triple Entente', curtailed the freedom of manoeuvre of the chancelleries of Europe. Finally, heightened arms races since around 1904 raised the stakes yet further. Colonel House, Woodrow Wilson's confidential aide, is often cited in support of such interpretations. Writing to the President during his European sojourn, he observed that the situation there was 'extraordinary': 'It is militarism run stark mad ... There is some day to be an awful cataclysm'.[18] Thus, the dictats of railway timetables, the inherent logic of arms races and the mechanisms of the existing alliance system forced the actions of the Powers in 1914.[19] Underlying much of the extant literature, indeed, is an implicit, quasi-teleological assumption: a concatenation of crises and the confluence of diverse structural forces made war in 1914 inevitable.[20]

There is nevertheless scope for a fresh examination of the July crisis of 1914. For one thing, recent interpretations have tended to move away from the sources, and the latter warrant a much closer inspection. Re-examining them helps to highlight a question that ought to be central to all discussions of the events of 1914. The Sarajevo crisis was not the first such international dispute the Powers had had to confront. There had been

[18] House to Wilson, 29 May 1914, C. Seymour (ed.), *The Intimate Papers of Colonel House* (4 vols., London, 1926), I, 255.
[19] The *loci classici* are G. W. F. Hallgarten, *Das Wettrüsten. Seine Geschichte bis zur Gegenwart* (Frankfurt, 1967) and A. J. P. Taylor, *War by Timetable: How the First World War Began* (London, 1969); for further studies see G. Barraclough, *From Agadir to Armageddon: Anatomy of a Crisis* (London, 1982); J. Snyder, *The Ideology of the Offensive: Military Decision Making and the Disasters of 1914* (Ithaca, NY, 1984); S. D. Sagan, '1914 Revisited: Allies, Offense, and Instability', S. E. Miller, S. M. Lynn-Jones and S. Van Evera (eds.), *Military Strategy and the Origins of the First World War* (Princeton, NJ, rev. edn 1991), 59–108; D. G. Herrmann, *The Arming of Europe and the Making of the First World War* (Princeton, NJ, 1996); and D. Stevenson's magisterial and nuanced *Armaments and the Coming of War: Europe, 1904–1914* (Oxford, 1996).
[20] For some thoughts on this see T. G. Otte, *The Foreign Office Mind: The Making of British Foreign Policy, 1865–1914* (Cambridge, 2011), 21–2.

several Balkan stand-offs within the eighteen months or so before July 1914, and yet none of them escalated into a full-blown war. What historians ought to ask themselves is, what made the summer of 1914 so different?[21]

But the move away from the sources that accompanied the focus on impersonal forces also diminishes too much the role of individual decision-makers. In turn, this has tended to mask a much more complex political reality, one that cannot be reduced to a handful of impersonal, structural forces. The same is also true of more recent attempts at a cultural and social turn in international history, one which seeks a safe haven from the disturbed past and present by genderizing 'Britannia' or reconstructing 'ornamentalist' representations of identity through imperial regalia and exotic finery. All of these distract from the 'diplomatic twitch' that lies at the heart of governmental decisions for peace and war.[22] But they also have a distorting and oddly distancing effect on posterity's perspective on the problems facing the decision-makers of 1914, with the insinuation that their plumed hats, stiff collars and elaborate court rituals somehow reflected their antiquated attitudes.[23] In the end, the decisions to mobilize millions of men and to send them to 'do and die' on the battlefields were not made by anonymous 'factors', but by real people. They were made by small circles of advisers and officials around the crowned heads in Vienna, Berlin and St Petersburg. There was nothing illegitimate in this. Within the existing constitutional arrangements, the two Kaisers and the Tsar had the power to decide over war and peace. But in France and Britain, too, the number of people involved was small. Their perceptions and calculations were essential; their miscalculations and eventual decisions would ultimately prove catastrophic.

Their concerns about the present and fears for the future thus hold one of the keys to a deeper understanding of the events of the summer of 1914. These men could not know the future, any more than we can today. It is, therefore, important to appreciate the elements of risk and risk calculation that their deliberations contained. All of this becomes more

---

[21] See also the pertinent observation by W. Mulligan, *The Origins of the First World War* (Cambridge, 2010), 3–22.

[22] See the cogent reassertion of the importance of the traditional focus of international history by D. Reynolds, 'International History, the Cultural Turn and the Diplomatic Twitch', *CSH* III, 1 (2006), 75–91; and also T. G. Otte, 'Diplomacy and Decision-Making', P. Finney (ed.), *International History* (Basingstoke and New York, 2005), 36–57.

[23] The most eloquent expression of this is D. Cannadine, *Ornamentalism: How the British Saw their Empire* (London, 2001); for observations on the distorting and distancing effects of such approaches see Otte, 'Diplomacy', 38–9; Clark, *Sleepwalkers*, xxv.

intelligible only if one takes a closer look at who took decisions, how they took them and why. Similarly, the often haphazard, frequently chaotic nature of decision-making in the capitals of the Great Powers belies assertions of Europe's ineluctable progress towards war.

At the heart of this book lies that strange dialogue between the broader system of Great Power politics and the actions of individuals. Debates about the interaction between individual agency and systemic constraints are, of course, the staple diet of much of the extant literature on international relations and international history. All too often, the default position of systemic scholars is to assert the complexity of the 'system' and then to stipulate 'correct' – that is system-appropriate – policy choices against which the actual policy decisions are then measured (and subsequently approved or dismissed).[24] Such an approach is not only ahistorical; it also fails to elucidate the more variegated nature of the relations both between the Powers and within the decision-making élites. The conceptual framework for the book, then, is different. Although it places the events of 1914 in the context of the existing alliance structures, accepted norms of international behaviour and notions of national 'honour', its focus is on the role of the individual decision-makers. The staccato of the July crisis drives forward the analysis of the perceptions, misperceptions and deliberate deceptions of the 'doves' and 'hawks' in the chancelleries of Europe as they struggled to control a complex international situation and to master its escalating dynamic.

[24] See e.g. P. W. Schroeder, 'Old Wine in Old Bottles: Recent Contributions to British Foreign Policy and European International Politics, 1789–1848', *JBS* xxvi, 1 (1987), 9–10; for a critique see T. G. Otte, 'A Janus-like Power: Great Britain and the European Concert, 1814–1853', Wolfram Pyta (ed.), *Das europäische Mächtekonzert. Friedens- und Sicherheitspolitik vom Wiener Kongress 1815 bis zum Krimkrieg 1853* (Cologne and Vienna, 2009), 125–54.

1 PRELUDE: THE ROAD TO SARAJEVO

> The summer of 1914 did in fact begin well, better than so many
> earlier summers ... After ten years or so of troubles and commotion,
> the people hoped at least for a lull and a good year which would
> recompense in every way for the harms and misfortunes of
> earlier years.
>
> IVO ANDRIĆ[1]

Great historical events require a trigger moment. The occurrence
that set in motion the chain of events which culminated in the First World
War was the assassination of the Archduke Franz Ferdinand. The preparations for his visit to Bosnia-Herzegovina encapsulate the essential
characteristics of that ancient empire whose throne he stood to inherit,
the Habsburg Empire, just as the plot to kill him throws a revealing light
on the currents and countercurrents of the Balkans, Europe's most disturbed region in the years before 1914. But the chaos, confusion and
coincidences at Sarajevo on 28 June 1914 also set the tone for the crisis
that preceded the first general war since the defeat of Napoleon Bonaparte nearly a century earlier.

The Bosnian visit

The Archduke's visit to the provincial capital of Bosnia-Herzegovina,
administered by Austria-Hungary since 1878 and formally annexed in
1908, had long been planned. It originated with the Habsburg military
commander and governor of the province, General Oskar Potiorek, who
suggested in the late summer of 1913 that Franz Ferdinand might wish to
attend the manoeuvres of the local XVth and XVIth Army Corps to be held
in central Bosnia towards the end of June the following year.[2]

---

[1] I. Andrić, *The Bridge on the Drina* (London, 1994 [orig. 1945]), 266.
[2] The precise date of Potiorek's invitation is in some doubt; for the background see
F. Conrad von Hötzendorf, *Aus meiner Dienstzeit* (5 vols., Vienna, 1921–5), III, 445–7
and 700–2.

The high-profile visit by a member of the imperial dynasty was meant to 'show the flag'. Potiorek considered such a demonstration of Habsburg commitment to the province, with its volatile ethnic composition, all the more necessary since Austro-Hungarian rule there was troubled. Attempts since 1908 to establish a functioning administration, supported by the local population, had run into the quicksand of ethnic politics. The province's constitution, proclaimed in February 1909, was in parts liberal, guaranteeing minority rights unheard of elsewhere in the Balkans, and in parts regressive in that it limited the powers of the provincial parliament. Like the seventeenth-century Holy Roman Empire, it was *monstro simile*. The seventy-two deputies of the *Landtag* or *Sabor*, the provincial parliament, were elected through an electoral college system (*curia*) that reflected the different religious and ethnic groups of Bosnia-Herzegovina, topped up by twenty senior religious representatives who were appointed members. The legislative process was prolix even by Habsburg standards. Any bill required the approval of the governments at both Vienna and Budapest, in whom, in contrast to other parts of the Habsburg Empire, sovereign power was jointly vested. Ultimate responsibility for administering the provinces lay with the common Austro-Hungarian finance minister, one of only four common ministers in the Danube Monarchy, the others being the foreign, war and navy ministers. Reconciling the positions of the Austrian and Magyar governments was a fraught and laborious process. As Leon von Biliński, the finance minister since 1912, later reflected, Vienna's approval was easily obtained, that by Budapest less forthcoming and dependent on commercial and other advantages for the Hungarian half of the empire being secured first.[3] The day-to-day running of the provincial administration was in the hands of the military commander, who acted as *Landeschef* or governor, assisted by a *Ziviladlatus*, a senior civil servant appointed directly by the Emperor to head the civilian departments at Sarajevo.

If the imperial context of Bosnian politics was complex, the local situation was even more so. Nearly half the inhabitants were ethnic Serbs, who were to varying degrees hostile to Habsburg overlordship, and indeed

[3] L. [von] Biliński, *Wspomnienia i dokumenty, 1846–1922* (2 vols., Warsaw, 1924–5), I, 237. For the constitutional arrangements see J. Brauner, 'Bosnien und Herzegowina. Politik, Verwaltung und leitende Personen vor Kriegsausbruch', *BMH* VII, 4 (1929), 316–19; see also R. W. Seton-Watson, 'The Role of Bosnia in International Politics, 1875–1914', L. S. Sutherland (ed.), *Studies in History: British Academy Lectures* (Oxford, 1966), 263–5; P. F. Sugar, *Industrialization of Bosnia-Hercegovina, 1878–1918* (Seattle, WA, 1963), 79–80; N. Malcolm, *Bosnia: A Short History* (London, 1994), 151–5.

had fallen increasingly under the sway of pan-Serb nationalism. Indeed, attempts by Potiorek in 1912 to win over the Serb bloc in the *Landtag* to support his administration came to nothing when its radical section torpedoed the governor's programme 'because Belgrade did not concur with it'.[4] The rest of the province's population was made up mainly of Catholic Croats and Muslim Bosniaks. The former were divided between those who saw their future within the Habsburg Monarchy, albeit with greater autonomous rights, and a smaller, but vociferous group, who favoured union with the Serbs in a Southern Slav (or Yugoslav) state. The Muslim minority, meanwhile, were the Emperor's most loyal subjects, but they were politically the least significant of the three main ethnic groups. Their leaders, the larger landlords who had controlled the province in Ottoman days, were more concerned about their class interests and showed a marked reluctance to defend Muslim sectional interests. Upon such foundations no functioning, let alone lasting, political structures could be built.[5]

Young Bosnia and its discontents

If Potiorek thought an official visit necessary to demonstrate Habsburg resolve and to encourage the province's loyal elements, inviting the Archduke was nevertheless risky. This is not a matter of hindsight, but was appreciated at the time, including by Franz Ferdinand and many in his entourage. The secret police had warned against the visit, and more especially against scheduling it for Sunday, 28 June. For that day marked *vidovdan*, St Vitus's Day, the anniversary of the historic Battle of Kosovo Polje in 1389. The defeat of the mediaeval Serb kingdom at the hands of the encroaching Ottomans, and the assassination of the Turkish Sultan Murad I by Miloš Obilić, a Serbian knight, in the aftermath of the battle, had acquired a quasi-mythical importance to Serbian identity and was central to the nationalist revival in Serbia in the second half of the long nineteenth century.[6] The arrival on that day of the future ruler of the Habsburg

---

[4] Biliński, *Wspomnienia*, I, 265. The public avowal of this by Gligorij Jeftanović, one of the leaders of the Bosnian-Serb intelligentsia, was treasonable, of course, but such was the situation in the province that Potiorek and Biliński chose to conciliate rather than to prosecute.

[5] For some of the background see V. Dedijer, *The Road to Sarajevo* (London, 1967), 78–87 and 130–2.

[6] T. Judah, *The Serbs: History, Myth and the Destruction of Yugoslavia* (New Haven, CT, 2nd edn 2000), 29–46. Tellingly, Serbia's most distinguished military decoration was named after Miloš Obilić, who had slit the Sultan's throat before being captured and beheaded by the Turks.

Empire, widely regarded as the roadblock to fulfilling the Yugoslav dream, was therefore likely to be resented by many Bosnian Serbs. The fact that that Sunday in 1914 happened to be the 525th anniversary of Kosovo Polje added yet further piquancy.[7]

There were further concerns. The political situation in the province and in neighbouring Croatia and Dalmatia was disturbed. At Agram (now Zagreb), the *ban* (or Viceroy) of Croatia, Baron Eduard Cuvaj von Ivanska, ruled with an iron fist. His quasi-absolutist régime provoked a violent backlash. Cuvaj himself was the target of an unsuccessful assassination attempt in August 1913; and so was his successor, Baron Iván Skerlecz von Lomnicza, in May 1914. These acts of violence were a prelude to the Sarajevo plot. For Cuvaj's Croatian commissariat had a destabilizing effect also on Bosnia-Herzegovina, where Potiorek, *Landeschef* since 1911, had ruled with emergency measures since May 1913.[8] And here, too, there had been a surge in politically motivated murders. On 15 June 1910, after the opening ceremony of the Bosnian provincial parliament, a Serb from the Herzegovina, Bogdan Žerajić, fired five shots at Potiorek's predecessor, General Marijan Varešanin. Each one missed, and with the final bullet remaining Žerajić killed himself. Intriguingly, the incident occurred on the Appel Quay, along the Miljačka river near the Lateiner Bridge, where Franz Ferdinand's murderers would wait four years later. It was only after the would-be assassin's suicide that Austrian investigators uncovered that his original target had been the Emperor Franz Joseph, who had visited Sarajevo a fortnight earlier, on 3 June. On that occasion, however, for reasons that have never been satisfactorily explained, Žerajić missed his opportunity of shooting the Emperor. Certainly, during the monarch's visit security had been very tight. The streets of the Bosnian capital were lined with soldiers two-men deep, and the police had taken over two hundred suspects into custody prior to the Emperor's arrival.[9]

More significant than the Emperor's escape on that day in 1910 was the effect of Žerajić's attempt on Cuvaj's life and his subsequent suicide on the disaffected nationalist youths of Bosnia. The effect was twofold, and shows a chilling parallel with a twenty-first century newly

---

[7] Hartwig to Sazonov (no. 40), 17/30 June 1914, *IBZI* iv, no. 35. Conrad, the Chief of Staff, had disapproved of the visit: see A. Urbański von Ostrymiecz, 'Conrad von Hötzendorf und die Reise nach Serajewo', *BMH* vii, 5 (1929), 463–71.

[8] See Brauner, 'Bosnien und Herzegowina', 319–20; also V. Bibl, 'Österreich-Ungarns innenpolitische Lage bei Ausbruch des Weltkriegs', *BMH* xxi, 7 (1934), 597.

[9] Dedijer, *Road to Sarajevo*, 240–1; H. Uebersberger, *Österreich zwischen Russland und Serbien. Zur Südslawischen Frage und der Entstehung des Ersten Weltkrieges* (Cologne and Graz, 1958), 254–5; J. Remak, *Sarajevo: The Story of a Political Murder* (London, 1959), 36 and 116–17.

accustomed to the phenomenon of disaffected young men self-radicalizing. Žerajić's attack on the Viceroy focused attention more sharply on terrorist tactics, and it created a 'martyr cult' around the failed assassin. Fiery pamphlets glorifying Žerajić's deed and death circulated widely. One of them, 'The Death of a Hero', called on young Serbs to avenge that hero.[10]

Its author, and an associate of Žerajić, Vladimir Gačinović, was a leading light of '*Mlada Bosna*' ('Young Bosnia'), a pan-Serb ultra-nationalist organization that espoused terrorist means. Among its members were also the seven young men who lay in wait for the Archduke at Sarajevo – Gavrilo Prinčip, Nedeljko Čabrinović, Trifko Grabež, Vaso Čubrilović, Cvijetko Popović, Danilo Ilić and Mehmed Mehmedbašić. They were a motley crew. Čubrilović and Popović, at seventeen the youngest of them, were schoolboys still. Two of the others, nineteen-year-old Prinčip and Grabež, who was eighteen, had been expelled from their high schools in Bosnia but were now students in Belgrade. Their family background was that of the province's impoverished peasantry. Ilić, a twenty-four-year old schoolteacher from a poor family in central Bosnia, was very much the organizational brains behind the plot. Čabrinović hailed from a prosperous but dysfunctional family of Sarajevo coffee merchants. Now nineteen, he was a high-school dropout who had eventually settled down as a typesetter at the government printing works in Belgrade, but who also nurtured quasi-philosophical and literary ambitions. Aged twenty-seven, Mehmedbašić was the oldest of the seven, and the only Muslim. He was a trained carpenter, but was the son of an impoverished Ottoman feudal landlord. Indeed, he had allowed his father's last *kmets* (serfs) to purchase their freedom, to raise funds for his political activities.[11]

The Sarajevo Seven had little in common, except their youth and inexperience, their ardent nationalism and their willingness to become martyrs to their chosen cause. Žerajić and the mediaeval knight Obilić were frequent points of reference for them once they had become radicalized in the cafés of Sarajevo and Belgrade. They were a mixture of 'primitive rebels' and coffee-house terrorists, inspired by romantic nationalist poetry, fantasies of violence and half-digested dollops of Kropotkinean anarchism.[12] For all that, or perhaps because of it, they were clean-living. They did not drink, they did not gamble and they did not consort with women.

[10] Remak, *Sarajevo*, 36.
[11] Dedijer, *Road to Sarajevo*, 175–234, offers detailed insights; see also the more popular account by D. J. Smith, *One Morning in Sarajevo: 28 June 1914* (London, 2008).
[12] For the concept of 'primitive rebels' see E. J. Hobsbawm, *Primitive Rebels: Studies in Archaic Forms of Social Movement in the 19th and 20th Centuries* (London, 1959).

Apis and 'Black Hand'

If they appeared to be little more than a bunch of misguided and hot-headed amateurs, they had nevertheless made important connections with more powerful forces. The 'Young Bosnians' were loosely affiliated with a secretive organization in Serbia proper. Popularly known as '*Črna Ruka*' ('Black Hand'), its full name was '*Ujedinjenje ili Smrt*' ('Union or Death'). Founded in May 1911, it was one of a multitude of similar organizations that penetrated the Serbian military apparatus and politics. The most significant of these was *Narodna Odbrana* ('National Defence'), a mass organization formed in 1908 following Austria-Hungary's annexation of Bosnia-Herzegovina. It was organized in local committees throughout Serbia, and advocated the unification of all Serbs through militant policies. A revolutionary organization that aimed at the destruction of Habsburg power in the Balkans, it provided for guerilla training for young volunteers under the leadership of Voja Tankošić, a militant army captain who had come to specialize in covert military operations.[13]

    Narodna Odbrana generated much public activity. Its propaganda certainly caused a good deal of unease in the neighbouring Habsburg Empire. And yet it had few concrete achievements. Its bark was ferocious, but it did not bite. Into this void stepped 'Black Hand'. Its seven founder members, of whom Tankošić was one, were mostly army officers, even though army regulations forbade any political activities. The organization's secretive nature, its convoluted statutes and elaborate initiation rites, replete with daggers and blood symbolism, might have come straight from the pages of one of Baroness Orczy's ripping Scarlet Pimpernel yarns. But its purpose was deadly serious. It was intended as a nationalist-revolutionary avant-garde designed to foment revolutionary activities outside Serbia proper with the aim of bringing about the unification of all Southern Slavs. Captain Čedomir Popović, one of the 'Black Hand' founders, cultivated close ties with border officials to reconnoitre the Austro-Serb and Serbo-Turkish frontiers and to facilitate operations in Habsburg and Ottoman territories. Popović developed the idea of prioritizing militancy over the propaganda activities of *Narodna Odbrana*. At the same time, Popović ensured that 'Black Hand' used the latter's prestige among the Southern Slavs in the Habsburg territories as cover for its activities. Indeed, he engineered the appointment of Major

---

[13] D. MacKenzie, *Apis: The Congenial Conspirator. The Life of Colonel Dragutin T. Dimitrijević* (Boulder, CO, 1989), 64–75.

Milan Vašić, a member of the 'Black Hand' central committee, as Secretary of *Narodna Odbrana*.[14]

The degree to which the new organization managed to infiltrate *Narodna Odbrana* helps to explain why, after Sarajevo, the Austrian investigations wrongly blamed the latter for the murder. Indeed, although Belgrade was soon awash with rumours about a secretive society of officers, Habsburg diplomats were uncertain about its ultimate aims. The Monarchy's envoy in the Serbian capital until 1913, the usually well-informed Istvan von Ugron zu Ábránfalva, asserted that its real purpose was domestic, and that it was aimed at removing the ruling Radical party from power.[15]

The 'Black Hand' did not, in fact, confine itself exclusively to clandestine operations. It also ran a newspaper, *Pijemont*, which was at least part-financed by members of the Serbian court. Its title was programmatic, and reflected a frequently recurring theme in Serbian nationalist literature of the long nineteenth century. Just as the Kingdom of Piedmont-Sardinia had united all of Italy half a century earlier, so it was the historic mission of Serbia to spearhead the liberation and unification of all Southern Slavs currently living under the yokes of the Ottoman and Habsburg Empires. Indeed, the statutes of the 'Black Hand' referred to 'Serbia as Piedmont'.[16]

Three of the Sarajevo plotters – Prinčip, Čabrinović and Grabež – came into contact with the 'Black Hand' through Tankošić, who trawled the cheap coffee houses of Belgrade for potential recruits among the disaffected Bosnian youths who frequented such places in the Serbian capital. Having identified them as likely operatives, Tankošić kept himself in the background and left it to one of his underlings, Milan Ciganović, to instruct the three in the use of weapons.[17] Ciganović was a twenty-six-year-old Bosnian who had fought as a partisan under Tankošić against the Bulgarians during the Second Balkan War in 1913, and who had now found employment on the Serbian state railways.

Using a go-between was important to protect Tankošić against being identified should the three be arrested and interrogated by

---

[14] C. A. Popović, 'Organizacija "Ujedinjenje ili Smrt"', *Nova Evropa* xv, 12 (11 June 1927), 398–9; Remak, *Sarajevo*, 43–9.

[15] Ugron to Aehrenthal (nos. 94A and 95), 12 and 13 Nov. 1911, HHStA, PA XIX/62; see also the post-war reflections by F. von Wiesner on Austro-Hungarian misreading of the respective roles of the two organizations, 'Die Schuld der serbischen Regierung am Mord von Sarajewo', *BMH* vi, 4 (1928), 329–30.

[16] Uebersberger, *Österreich*, 240 and 243–4; D. MacKenzie, 'Serbia as Piedmont and the Yugoslav Idea, 1804–1914', *EEQ* xxviii, 2 (1994), 153–82.

[17] Testimony Grabež , A. Musset (ed.), *L'Attentat de Sarajevo. Documents inédits et texte intégral des sténogrammes du procès* (Paris, 1930), 162–3.

Austro-Hungarian security forces. But it was even more important to shield the man behind Tankošić himself. In the former ambition he failed, in the latter he succeeded. The man in the background was Colonel Dragutin T. Dimitrijević, the charismatic head of the military intelligence section of the Serbian general staff, better known to posterity by his nickname Apis, after the Egyptian bull-god, on account of his massive physique and his ruthlessness.[18] A national revolutionary, Dimitrijević was also one of the founder-members of the 'Black Hand'. Although many aspects of his life and career remain shrouded in mystery, there can be little doubt that he was the moving spirit behind the plot to kill Franz Ferdinand. Indeed, Apis was uniquely experienced in this respect, having played a prominent part in the unsuccessful attempt to depose the then King of Serbia, Aleksandar Obrenović, on 11 September 1901, and the subsequent successful coup d'état of June 1903.[19]

The gruesome murder of the King and his Queen, Draga Mašin, and the subsequent mutilation of their bodies, was remarkable for its barbarity even in the bloody annals of regicide. There was widely felt revulsion at the deed in Europe; and most of the Powers severed relations with Serbia for a number of years on the grounds that, as one British diplomat quipped, they 'had ideas which [the Serbs] might think peculiar with regard to assassination'.[20] But while the new Karadjordjević régime in Belgrade was shunned internationally, Apis, who had received near-fatal injuries during the coup, had made a name for himself at home. By 1913, at the young age of thirty-seven, he was made head of military intelligence, and, with the resources thus available to him, he plotted the murder of Archduke Franz Ferdinand.

Apis's rationale for the killing cannot now be reconstructed with absolute certainty. Apis himself and those involved in the plot left behind very little contemporaneous documentary evidence. This is not in the least surprising. Trained up in the arts of secrecy, subterfuge and skullduggery, they were not likely to produce a paper trail. Good tradecraft, after all, demands that no traces be left that might later incriminate anyone associated with an operation. And to survive in the murky underworld of Serbian politics, it was perhaps even more necessary to observe the strictest secrecy.

[18] It is often asserted that his nickname stemmed from the Greek απις (bee), but his most recent biographer confirms that this is based on an erroneous assumption: MacKenzie, *Apis*, 1.
[19] *Ibid.*, 31–50. It is possible that the idea of killing Franz Ferdinand originated with one of Apis's agents, Rade Malobabić: *ibid.*, 258–9. An attempt had also been made on the life of Aleksandar's father, King Milan, in 1900; for some contemporary reflections see V. Georgevitch, *Das Ende der Obrenovitch. Beiträge zur Geschichte Serbiens, 1897–1900* (Leipzig, 1905).
[20] Bertie to Lansdowne, 25 Dec. 1904, Lansdowne MSS, TNA (PRO), FO 800/142.

In consequence, historians have had to rely on not always entirely reliable materials in their attempts to unravel the skeins of the Sarajevo plot. The witness statements and depositions made during the Sarajevo trial conceal as much as they reveal, not least because the captured assassins were little more than Apis's 'useful idiots', zealous but ignorant and so deniable.[21] Apis's own trial at Salonika in 1917 before a kangaroo court arraigned by his internal enemies in the Serbian government served only one purpose – to remove him for good as a potential political liability at a critical moment during the First World War. Post-war memoirs were often coloured by considerations other than a quest for historical truth. It is little wonder, then, that Sarajevo has proved such a cornucopia of conspiracy fantasies. Such is the nature of the deed, and the circumstances surrounding it, that it will perhaps never be possible to unravel it completely, as Sir Edward Grey surmised in the 1920s: 'Probably there is not, and never was, any one person who knew all that there was to know.'[22]

All of this notwithstanding, the extant evidence has been sifted extensively, and the background to the plot has been examined with attention to the minutest details. Stripping away the impossible and excluding the improbable – and leaving to one side Jews, freemasons, the *Okhrana* and all the other staple items of conspiracy theories – it is possible to make a number of deductions that, whilst not conclusive, have the benefit of plausibility.

The young Bosnian assassins had originally intended to murder Potiorek rather than the Archduke.[23] Popular discontent with the General's emergency régime made him an obvious target for an act of terrorism, as Danilo Ilić argued during the Sarajevo trial in October 1914, as a 'means of protest'. There had been the earlier attempt on Varešanin's life in 1910, and the murder of his successor now might destabilize Habsburg control of Bosnia-Herzegovina. At the same time it would have the appearance of an entirely local affair, a violent, thus regrettable but possibly understandable reaction against regional misrule. Political murder was not entirely unknown in the Habsburg lands. Indeed, at the turn of 1913–14, Mehmedbašić was assigned the task of stabbing the Governor. He duly

---

[21] While the assassins revealed the Ciganović and Tankošić connection, they seemed entirely ignorant of Apis and 'Black Hand': see e.g. testimony Čabrinović, 12 Oct. 1914, Musset (ed.), *L'Attentat*, 90–1.

[22] [E.] Viscount Grey of Fallodon, *Twenty-Five Years, 1892–1916* (2 vols., New York, 1925), I, 298; for some insights into the 1917 Salonika trial see also S. Gavrilović, 'New Evidence on the Sarajevo Assassination', *JMH* XXVII, 4 (1955), 410–14.

[23] Testimony Čabrinović, 12 Oct. 1914, Musset (ed.), *L'Attentat*, 77. Grabež later recalled that they were uncertain whether to choose Franz Ferdinand or Potiorek: testimony Grabež, *ibid.*, 157.

headed for Sarajevo, but seems to have lost his nerve and disposed of the dagger and the poison into which the implement was to have been dipped.[24]

By now the decision had been taken to assassinate Franz Ferdinand rather than the provincial governor. It seems that there were two strands to Apis's thinking. Both centred not so much on the Archduke's person as on what he was thought to represent. Of course, in deciding to murder the Archduke Apis raised the stakes significantly. Franz Ferdinand's murder could not be dismissed as an act of communal garden militancy, regrettable, no doubt, but of no wider significance. Removing the heir to the throne at a moment when the Francisco-Josephinian régime was moving towards its inevitable biological conclusion – the octogenarian Emperor was frequently ill now – was meant to shake the very foundations of the Habsburg Monarchy.

Cross-examined during the trial, Franz Ferdinand's assassin, Gavrilo Prinčip, revealed something of Apis's thinking. The Archduke was dangerous, he asserted, because '[h]e would have prevented, as a future ruler, our union by realizing certain reforms which would evidently have been against our interests'.[25] This touched on the Archduke's well-known preference for solving the Monarchy's nationality problems by offering its Southern Slav subjects major concessions. Anti-Habsburg, pan-Serb agitation fed on the grievances of disaffected Serbs within the confines of the Austro-Hungarian Empire. By contrast, Franz Ferdinand's 'trialist' scheme of reorganizing the Dual Monarchy as a federal state, allowing for the creation of a prosperous and autonomous Southern Slav kingdom within the Empire, threatened to blunt the appeal of pan-Serbism or Yugoslavism. It might well have killed off the latter, and deprived Serbia of her self-appointed mission. The Piedmont of *Yugoslavia irredenta* would instead have become an appendix of a revived Habsburg Empire. If anything, union with an Austro-Hungarian-Slav trialist federation might have a considerable appeal for many in the Kingdom of Serbia itself.[26] It also

---

[24] Testimony Ilić, 13 Oct. 1914, *ibid.*, 189; L. Albertini, *The Origins of the War of 1914* (3 vols., London, 1953), II, 79. In April 1908, a Ukrainian student had assassinated the governor of Ruthenia, Count Potocki: see F. Fellner (ed.), *Schicksalsjahr Österreichs, 1908–1919. Das Politische Tagebuch Josef Redlichs* (2 vols., Graz and Cologne, 1953), I, 237, n. 30.

[25] Testimony Prinčip, 12 Oct. 1914, Musset (ed.), *L'Attentat*, 131; for some further reflections on this see also Z. A. B. Zeman, 'The Balkans and the Coming of the War', R. J. W. Evans and H. Pogge von Strandmann (eds.), *The Coming of the First World War* (Oxford, repr. 1991), 19–22.

[26] For this argument see Remak, *Sarajevo*, 54–7; Albertini, *Origins of the War*, II, 86–8; and also C. Clark, *The Sleepwalkers: How Europe Went to War in 1914* (London, 2012), 49.

helps to explain why the more radical Bosnian Serbs sought to kill off Potiorek's earlier attempts to co-opt moderate Serbs. If such a thing worked in Bosnia, it might well furnish the basis for constitutional reform of the Habsburg Empire as a whole.

There was another consideration that seems to have weighed with Dimitrijević, one that was linked to his fears of the Archduke's trialist reform programme. The two, in fact, reinforced each other. In Apis's assessment, Franz Ferdinand was the head of the 'war party' at Vienna, the only Habsburg leader capable of re-energizing the seemingly decaying Dual Monarchy. His reforms would reverse the recent decline of Austro-Hungarian power in the region, envelop Serbia and so force her to gravitate towards her Habsburg foe. There is evidence to suggest that Dimitrijević was genuinely convinced that Austria-Hungary might attack Serbia in 1914, at a time when the latter had still not recovered from the two rounds of fighting in the Balkans in 1912 and 1913. 'We still need several years of peace', Apis explained to Svetozar Pribičević, a senior Serbian politician in Croatia, in 1913: 'Then after that we will come to you [in Croatia].'[27]

That Serbia required a period of international calm in order to consolidate her position after the Balkan wars was not a contentious view at Belgrade. But opinions differed on how best to achieve this. While the government sought salvation in a conciliatory policy towards Vienna, Apis, the national revolutionary, favoured decapitating the Habsburg 'war party'. Eliminating the Archduke would buy Serbia the time she needed to recover from the recent wars and prepare for the next, possibly final, phase of the irredentist struggle against Austria-Hungary. By then, moreover, Russia would be ready to support Serbia in a war.[28]

For all his skills as an intelligence operative and bureaucratic brawler at Belgrade, Dimitrijević was a man of limited political experience and even more limited political intelligence when it came to the world outside Serbia. For far from being the head of the militant elements in the Habsburg leadership, Franz Ferdinand, as will be seen later, was the one restraining element at Vienna. The fact that Apis misjudged the Archduke is of less importance than the fact that he acted on that misjudgement. It was, moreover, a common misjudgment.[29] Even so, in initiating the Archduke's

[27] As quoted in MacKenzie, Apis, 124; see also C. A. Popović, 'Das Sarajewoer Attentat und die Organisation "Vereinigung oder Tot"', BMH x, 11 (1932), 1113.

[28] MacKenzie, ibid., 125–31.

[29] On hearing of the assassination, the Italian foreign minister commented, 'The crime is abhorrent, but world peace will not complain', Krupenski to Sazonov (private), 17/30 June 1914, IBZI IV, no. 29.

murder, Apis helped to bring about the Austro-Serb war which he had sought to defer.

There is some evidence to suggest that, sometime in May 1914, both Apis and Tankošić had second thoughts about the planned assassination. It was not so much the enormity of the contemplated deed that made them hesitate but the inexperience of the immature youths who had volunteered their services. Ironically, it was above all Prinčip's refusal to abort the plan that ensured that the operation was carried out after all.[30]

Under the guidance of Tankošić's underling Ciganović, Prinčip, Čabrinović and Grabež had practised shooting in the woods around Belgrade and in the park of Topčider, the royal palace outside the capital. On 27 May, they received their weapons from Ciganović, though it was Tankošić who had procured the four revolvers and six bombs. The guns were Belgian-made Browning automatics. These had been delivered to a Belgrade arms dealer in December 1913, and were apparently purchased by Apis. The bombs were of Serbian make, manufactured at the state arsenal at Kragujevac, and were remainders from the recent Balkan wars. Rectangular in shape and small in size, they could easily be concealed in a jacket pocket. The detonator was hidden underneath a cap at the top, which had to be removed so that the device could be primed. This was done with a sharp knock, for instance by hitting it against a wall or lamppost. Once primed, the bomb would explode after about twelve seconds, and the assassins were advised to count to ten before launching it at the target in the expectation that the missile would then explode on impact. These were not precise weapons, and there was considerable room for error, as the events of 28 June would show. Finally, the three were also supplied with vials of cyanide. They were instructed that, on completing their mission, they were to shoot themselves; and, if this were not possible, they were to swallow the poison.[31] In this way their martyrdom was assured, and the wirepullers at Belgrade were to remain in the shadows.

The journey from Belgrade back to Bosnia was planned with considerable attention to detail. Ciganović, in his official capacity as a railway clerk, supplied Prinčip and his two companions with free tickets for the state railways and steps were taken to ensure that their luggage was not inspected – in the best Baroness Orczy style the three carried with them a card bearing the letters M. C., Ciganović's initials, in case they needed to identify themselves along the route. They left early, precisely a month

---

[30] For a discussion of the evidence see Popović, 'Sarajewoer Attentat', 1114; MacKenzie, *Apis*, 135–7.

[31] Remak, *Sarajevo*, 68; for technical details of the weapons see Smith, *One Morning*, 82.

before the Archduke's official visit to Sarajevo. No passports were required in those days, but simply taking the train from Belgrade to Slavonski Brod and on to Sarajevo, or crossing at one of the official border posts, was considered too risky. When they reached the Austro-Serbian frontier along the Drina river, the group split, Prinčip and Grabež crossing into Bosnia further north while Čabrinović struck out on his own. The frontier itself was well guarded by local gendarmes and six companies of Austrian *Gebirgsjäger* (mountaineer sharpshooters), organized in twenty-three platoons at forty men each. There were also two infantry battalions and one company garrisoned at places near the Drina. It was nevertheless impossible to protect the whole of the over 160 mile-long Drina frontier against clandestine crossings. Even during the war, with Serbia under Austro-German occupation, smuggling across the river proved difficult to suppress. The three assassins and their handlers, moreover, had chosen well. Along its lower reaches the Drina was some 250 to 450 yards wide, its course often changed by flooding, and its rocky eastern (Serbian) bank dominated the low-lying Austrian side. In many places the river was fordable, and dense undergrowth and many smaller islands provided good cover. Once they had crossed the Drina, the three made their way to Tuzla where they reunited, and thence to Sarajevo, mostly avoiding the main roads.[32]

The Archduke inspects his troops

While the three met up with the other local plotters and went to ground to await the arrival of the archducal party in Bosnia, Franz Ferdinand prepared for his journey. The various autobiographical accounts of members of the Archduke's entourage later stressed his sense of foreboding as he set off for Bosnia from his Bohemian castle at Konopište, once Wallenstein's refuge, on 23 June. It is difficult to verify any of this. There was certainly no shortage of ominous signs for those who later looked for them. As the Vienna express train headed towards the Habsburg capital, part of the undercarriage of the Archduke's private saloon carriage overheated and smoke poured out from underneath it, and he had to continue his journey in an ordinary compartment. His onward journey from Vienna to Trieste

---

[32] Testimony Grabež, 13 Oct. 1914, Musset (ed.), *L'Attentat*, 164–6; Remak, *Sarajevo*, 79–90. For a detailed discussion of the arrangements along the frontier and a description of its geography see L. Schnagl, 'War der Grenzübertritt der Mörder des Erzherzogs Franz Ferdinand auf eine Nachlässigkeit der österreichischen Grenzbehörden zurückzuführen?', *BMH* XII, 11 (1924), 957–66. Schnagl served with the 3rd battalion of the Infantry Regiment No. 49 in Bosnia in 1914.

was disrupted because the replacement carriage made available for him at Vienna's Südbahnhof had developed an electrical fault. Franz Ferdinand had to make do with candles for lighting, leading him to make flippant observations about the funereal gloom inside the carriage.[33] 'You see', his chamberlain later recalled him saying, 'this is how it starts, first an overheated carriage, then a murderous attempt at Sarajevo, and if nothing else helps an explosion aboard the steamer [sic] Viribus'.[34] But there was something of the stubborn Bourbon in his character – an inheritance from his mother, the daughter of 'Re Bomba', King Ferdinand II of Naples. Always impatient with the restrictions imposed by his security detail, he had earlier dismissed suggestions of additional measures to provide for greater personal security: 'I shall not allow myself to be placed under a glass cloche. We are always in mortal danger. One has to trust in God.'[35]

Appropriately for someone who had always taken a keen interest in naval matters, the Archduke continued the final part of his journey by crossing the Adriatic Sea, aboard SMS Viribus Unitis, one of the Habsburg navy's recent dreadnought-type battleships. Off the Dalmatian coast, at the mouth of the river Narenta, he boarded the navy yacht Dalmat. Now in the company of Potiorek, he continued his journey upriver to Metković and thence by train via Mostar to the spa town of Ilidža, where he was reunited with his wife, Countess Sophie Chotek of Chotkow and Wognin, the Duchess of Hohenberg, who had travelled by the overland route.[36] From there, the Archduke attended the army manoeuvres on 26 and 27 June in the mountainous terrain between Konjic and Tarčin. Four infantry divisions, two cavalry squadrons and twenty artillery batteries took part in the exercises; some 22,000 troops, about half the force under Potiorek's command. Security in the manoeuvre area had been stepped up significantly. This had less to do with the presence of the Habsburg heir than with the strong fear of Serbian military spies. For his part, Franz Ferdinand delighted in shaking off the twenty gendarmes detailed to protect him. The manoeuvres were not without incident in this respect. At least one man was arrested, lurking in the undergrowth, only to be released when the

[33] P. Nikitsch-Boulles, Vor dem Sturm (Berlin, 1925), 210–13. Nikitsch-Boulles was Franz Ferdinand's private secretary; see also T. von Sosnosky, Franz Ferdinand, der Erzherzog-Thronfolger. Ein Lebensbild (Munich, 1929), 202–4, for similar accounts.
[34] Baron A. von Morsey, 'Konopischt und Sarajewo. Erinnerungen', BMH XII, 6 (1934), 490.
[35] C. von Bardolff, Soldat im alten Österreich. Erinnerungen aus meinem Leben (Jena, 1938), 132.
[36] P. G. Halperin, Anton Haus. Österreich-Ungarns Grossadmiral (Graz, 1998), 141–2.

Archduke identified him as the court photographer and the long black rod he carried turned out to be part of his photographic equipment.[37]

The Archduke's nonchalant attitude towards his personal security during the manoeuvres stood in sharp contrast to the sense of foreboding to which some in his entourage later attested. Indeed, at the end of the first day of the military exercises, Friday 26 June, he and the Duchess visited Sarajevo in an open-top motorcar. It had been a spontaneous decision, spurred by the Duchess's wish to purchase an oriental carpet in the famed bazaar of the Bosnian capital. No security had been provided, and the visit passed without incident. The shopping trip to Sarajevo and the successful conclusion of the manoeuvres on 27 June evidently left Franz Ferdinand in an expansive mood. The state of the troops, he wired to the Emperor, 'their training and performance were quite excellent, above all praise … Everything fresh and lively. Tomorrow I shall visit Sarajevo and travel back in the evening.'[38]

The positive impressions of the day may well explain why the Archduke, well known for his mood swings, decided against the suggestion of his court chamberlain, Baron Karl von Rumerskirch, to cancel the remainder of the programme and to return to the *Viribus Unitis* off the Dalmatian coast and thence to Trieste in time for the archducal couple's fourteenth wedding anniversary on 1 July. What may have prompted Rumerskirch is not entirely clear. It may have been a conversation between the Duchess and one of the pro-Habsburg leaders of the *Sabor*, Dr Josip Sunarić, at a post-manoeuvre reception. The Duchess referred to Sunarić's earlier warnings against a visit, and enthused about the warm and friendly reception she had received during her visit. Sunarić replied, 'I pray to God that when I have the honour of meeting you again tomorrow night, you can repeat these words to me. A great burden will be lifted from me.'[39] To abort the visit to Sarajevo now, argued Lieutenant-Colonel Erich von Merizzi, Potiorek's adjutant, would be a snub to the *Landeschef* and an affront to the Habsburg loyalists among the local population, and might undermine Potiorek's efforts to secure the support of the more moderate Serb elements.[40] And with that decision began the end of Austria-Hungary.

[37] See the eyewitness account by L. Schnagl, 'Die Manöver in Bosnien im Jahre 1914', *BMH* VI, 9 (1928), 873–81.

[38] Tel. Franz Ferdinand to Franz Joseph, 27 June 1914, Schnagl, 'Manöver', 879; here also for the story of the shopping trip.

[39] As quoted in Dedijer, *Sarajevo*, 10.

[40] Rumerskirch made the suggestion after dinner on 27 June, see Nikitsch-Boulles, *Vor dem Sturm*, 214; and Morsey, 'Konopischt', 491. Conrad, who disapproved of the political part of the visit, contrived to leave Ilidža in the evening of 27 June: see Conrad, *Dienstzeit* IV, 16.

St Vitus's Day at Sarajevo

Whatever the many might-have-beens of Sarajevo, one thing is beyond doubt: security measures were remarkably casual. This was especially so when compared with the heavy military and police presence during Emperor Franz Joseph's visit to the city in June 1910. There had been no police sweeps on ultra-nationalist militants, as there had been on that earlier occasion. Security arrangements were left in the hands of the local police force, no more than 120 men all told; and, again in contrast to 1910, no soldiers lined the streets of the capital. The troops that had attended the manoeuvres during the previous two days were confined to barracks and camps outside Sarajevo, and they were under strict orders not to enter the city during the archducal visit. The insufficient security measures were the more remarkable, as Potiorek, who was a fluent Serbian-speaker, was considered to be well attuned to the mood of the local population.[41]

If no sufficient security arrangements had been made prior to the visit, matters did not improve on the day, and no additional measures would be taken. The proceedings of the day commenced uneventfully enough. The morning was bright and sunny, the first such day after several days of rain. At 9.30 a.m., the archducal couple left Ilidža by special *Hofzug* (court train) for Sarajevo, where they were formally received by Potiorek. Having inspected the guard of honour drawn up in the station forecourt, the imperial party got into the six waiting motorcars, the last of these being kept in reserve. The first car, meanwhile, had been designated for the plainclothes special-branch detectives who had accompanied the Archduke on the train from Ilidža and who were to act as his security detail for the remainder of the visit. But owing to some confusion – the first of several on the day – they were left behind at the station, and only their commanding officer travelled in the motorcade along with three local gendarmes.[42] In the second car were the mayor of Sarajevo, Fehim Effendi Čurčić, resplendent in a fez and official sash, and the Sarajevo police chief, Dr Edmund Gerde. On them followed the archducal car, a Viennese Graef & Stift sports car, its grey canvas top folded back, its black leather seats and walnut steering wheel and dashboard shining. Attached to its side was the imperial standard, with a yellow and black border and the double-headed Habsburg eagle in the centre. Travelling with the couple was

---

[41] For the orders see Schnagl, 'Manöver', 881; Remak, *Sarajevo*, 116–17; see also the vignette by E. von Glaise-Horstenau, 'Feldzeugmeister Potiorek', *BMH* XII, 2 (1934), 144–8. The rank of *Feldzeugmeister*, unique to the Habsburg army, was equivalent to that of General of Artillery.

[42] Morsey, 'Konopischt', 492; Biliński, *Wspomnienia*, I, 282.

Potiorek, sitting on the folding seat opposite them. In the front, next to the chauffeur – a Czech by the name of Leopold Sojka – was Colonel Count Franz Harrach, the car's owner.[43] The Archduke could easily be picked out amongst the other officials, in a full-dress cavalry uniform with pale blue tunic, *Generalsbinde* (a silver braided band with a 'patent' clasp), black trousers with red stripes down the sides and a cocked hat with glossy green cockerel feathers. The Duchess Sophie stood out equally among the uniformed men, in her wide-brimmed and veiled hat and white dress.

Their first destination was Sarajevo's city hall, like so many official buildings of the period in Bosnia a massive, pseudo-Moorish monstrosity. The municipal dignitaries had gathered here to welcome their future ruler. The route down Appel Quay, a long street that stretches along the embankment of the Miljačka, the river that runs through the centre of Sarajevo, may well have been chosen for its picturesque scenery. From the Quay and the four bridges across the river open up vistas over the skyline of the Bosnian capital with its tall poplar trees, minarets and domes, reminders of the not-too-distant Ottoman past. Beyond lie the hilly slopes that surround Sarajevo, covered in lush greenery and dotted with orchards. The houses to the left of Appel Quay were the low, red-roofed buildings typical of the region; beyond them was the bazaar, a maze of wooden stalls and booths. Across the Quay was strung bunting in the Habsburg black-and-yellow or the Bosnian yellow-and-red. Many houses were bedecked in the same colours; many were decorated with flowers and oriental rugs; and some shops and houses displayed the Archduke's portrait in their windows. A twenty-four gun salute rang out across the valley, and as the motorcade rolled slowly along the Quay occasional shouts of '*Vivat!*' and '*Živio!*' ('Long may he live!') could be heard from a meagre crowd that stood in the shade of the houses on the north side. The opposite side, along the Miljačka embankment, lying in the sun, was practically deserted.

Amongst the thin crowd there were the seven assassins, lurking and expectant, hopeful and yet worried, resolute but also uncertain. They had divided into two groups, and had taken up positions along Appel Quay, their various weapons concealed under their jackets. In this way, if one of them failed in their deadly mission, another member of the group would step forward. Only Ilić, the organizer of the mission, had no fixed position. Instead he moved along the Quay from one member of the group to the next to issue last-minute instructions and stiffen their resolve. All of them carried a packet of cyanide to be ingested on completion of the deed. Not far from here was the grammar school where Prinčip, Popović and

---

[43] Baron A. von Morsey, 'Der Schicksalstag von Sarajevo', *Reichspost*, 28 June 1924.

Čubrilović had sat on the benches under the benevolent eyes of the hated Habsburg Emperor. Their target, the future Emperor, was not far away now.

At about 10 a.m., as the procession of cars made its stately progress down the Quay, on the approach to the narrow, wooden Čumurja bridge, it passed the first of the conspirators standing on the riverside. This was Mehmedbašić. But as the archducal party drew level, just as in January 1914 when he aborted the attack on Potiorek, he lost his nerve. He later claimed that, at that precise moment, a policeman hove into view. To produce the bomb from underneath his coat and to prime it now would have meant to reveal the plot, without the chance of actually throwing his bomb, as he later rationalized his failure to act. And so the cavalcade rolled on.[44]

A little further up from Mehmedbašić, Čabrinović had taken up position, also on the sunny and largely deserted riverside, and conspicuously clad in a buttoned-up, black jacket and hat. Among the Sarajevo group, this high-school dropout, who had in turn become an anarchist, a socialist and now an ultra-nationalist, was considered unsteady and unreliable. Yet, where Mehmedbašić froze with terror, Čabrinović showed great calmness. He unwrapped the bomb, primed it, stepped forward, and then hurled it at the Archduke's car. To set the fuse, he broke, as instructed, the detonator cap by knocking it against a metal lamppost by the parapet of the embankment. The action of priming the bomb alone produced a sharp cracking noise. Whether alerted by the report or whether he had seen the missile hurled at the car, Sojka, the driver, accelerated. The bomb passed between Harrach at the front and Potiorek on the folding seat at the back. Eyewitnesses later disagreed whether it was deflected by Franz Ferdinand's arm, stretched out to protect his wife, or whether it bounced off the folded canvas top of the car, or whether it was a combination of the two. Whatever may have been the cause, the bomb missed its target, and exploded under the left front wheel of the next car. The crater it left – some 11 by 12½ inches wide and 6½ inches deep – gives some impression of the explosive force of the Kragujevac bombs. Some ten to fifteen spectators suffered injuries of varying degrees. The Duchess, too, had been grazed by a splinter. The second car itself was badly damaged. Among its occupants, Count Reinhold Boos-Waldeck, the vehicle's owner, suffered shrapnel wounds. Potiorek's aide-de-camp, Merizzi, who the night before had warned against abandoning the Sarajevo part of the Archduke's visit, was badly injured in the head and bled copiously.[45]

---

[44] Remak, *Sarajevo*, 118–19.
[45] Testimony Dr Max Bernstein, 5 July 1914, Sosnosky, *Franz Ferdinand*, app. I, 215–18; Morsey, 'Konopischt', 492–3; Bardolff, *Soldat im alten Österreich*, 182–3.

As for Čabrinović, as instructed, on throwing the missile he swallowed the cyanide powder, and hurled himself over the embankment wall into the river. Yet martyrdom was denied him. The river, despite the recent rain, was low so that the would-be assassin merely fell some twenty-odd feet to land on the exposed riverbed. And the poison, the ultimate insurance of martyrdom, also failed to work and merely scorched his throat and oesophagus. The powder given to the Sarajevo Seven turned out to be too old and had begun to degrade. Thus, sprawled on the Miljačka mud and writhing in agony, Čabrinović was arrested by several bystanders who had scrambled after him, among them a barber, who nearly shot him, a shopkeeper, and two gendarmes who carried him off to the police station.[46]

In the meantime, Franz Ferdinand reacted to the incident with remarkable calmness. Rather than ordering the driver to leave the scene and follow the first two cars, whose passengers were unaware of what had happened, he halted the motorcade and saw to it that the injured were looked after and the passengers redistributed among the remaining cars. During the commotion, two of the officers in the Archduke's party, Baron Andreas von Morsey, his second chamberlain, and Captain Pilz, who had travelled in the fourth car, crossed the next bridge, the Lateiner bridge – so named because it was the shortest route to the Roman Catholic cathedral – to ensure that the failed assassin was taken away to the police station. On the bridge they passed a young man, who had also hurried along to watch the spectacle on the riverbed below. This was Gavrilo Prinčip, though of course they did not know it then. Prinčip later stated during the trial that it had been his initial idea to shoot Čabrinović, before shooting himself, to ensure that his co-assassin did not reveal the full extent of the plot under police interrogation.[47]

By now the Archduke had decided that it was time to move on. 'The fellow must be mad. Gentlemen, let us proceed with our programme', he could be heard saying.[48] As the archducal motorcade nosed its way through the debris and smouldering wreckage of Boos-Waldeck's car, the remaining conspirators were still at their chosen positions. Yet they all failed to act. Vaso Čubrilović, the youngest of the group, was the next along the route. He had seen Čabrinović throw the bomb, but what he did next is not entirely clear. Prior to his arrest he boasted of having fired his revolver at Franz Ferdinand. During the trial, he changed his story and claimed not to have shot at the car because he took pity on the Duchess

---

[46] Remak, *Sarajevo*, 124–5; Clark, *Sleepwalkers*, 371.
[47] Testimony Prinčip, 12 Oct. 1914, Musset (ed.), *L'Attentat*, 128–9; Morsey, 'Konopischt', 494.
[48] *Neue Freie Presse*, 29 June 1914; also in Dedijer, *Sarajevo*, 13.

sitting next to the hated Habsburg heir.[49] On the opposite side of the Quay, the shady town side, near the Austro-Hungarian Bank, Cvijetko Popović had taken up his position. By the time the procession of cars lurched forward again, he was no longer there. 'I lost courage', he later confessed. Having heard the explosion of Čabrinović's bomb, and realising that he could not easily cross the road now, he retreated to the building of '*Prosvjeta*' (Instruction), a charitable institution for educating the rural Serbian youth in Bosnia, and hid his bomb in its cellar.[50]

There were now only Princip and Trifko Grabež left. The latter, whose nineteenth birthday this was, was searching for Princip along the embankment between the Lateiner bridge, with its ancient Turkish stone arches, and the modern Kaiser bridge. As he later testified, their original arrangement had been for him to detonate his explosive device as the cavalcade approached, and for Princip then to shoot the Archduke in the ensuing commotion. Unable to spot his co-conspirator, and clearly nervous now, Grabež shifted his position to the Kaiser bridge, where Žerajić had tried to assassinate governor Varešanin four years earlier almost to the day. But by now the mass of spectators was so large that he could make no further progress and returned towards the Lateiner bridge. Here, too, a swelling crowd had begun to surge along the Quay, and when the Archduke's party passed Grabež, he froze. Why he did so is not clear. He later claimed that the heaving mass of spectators had been so tight that he was unable to free the bomb from under his clothing. But like Čubrilović he changed his account, and stated during his trial that he lost courage at the moment the car passed.[51]

Princip, meanwhile, had lost sight of the Archduke's cavalcade, and took up a new position near the Lateiner bridge, opposite the corner of Appel Quay and Lateiner Street, on the assumption – correct as it turned out – that Franz Ferdinand and his party were likely to return along the officially designated route. By this time, the procession had reached its intended destination at the city hall. Here the Archduke and his wife were received by Mayor Čurčić, surrounded by other municipal notables – the Muslim Bosniaks in their local costumes, with fezzes, open waistcoats and baggy Turkish trousers, and the Croats and other Christians in tailcoats and top hats. Čurčić began to read from his prepared text, but he had

[49] Testimony Čubrilović, Musset (ed.), *L'Attentat*, 205–15. There is a degree of confusion in the witness statements, with some placing Čubrilović before Čabrinović, see e.g. Sosnosky, *Franz Ferdinand*, 210.
[50] Testimony Popović, Musset (ed.), *L'Attentat*, 223–4. For the '*Prosvjeta*' institution see 'Introduction', *ibid.*, 36.
[51] Testimony Grabež, *ibid.*, 172–4; Remak, *Sarajevo*, 127–8.

hardly begun when Franz Ferdinand, visibly irritated by the incongruous words of joyous welcome, snapped: 'Herr Bürgermeister, we come here to pay a visit and bombs are thrown at us. Altogether this is an amazing indignity.' The Duchess then stepped into the embarrassed silence and whispered in her husband's ear, which placated him, and he motioned the mayor to continue with his speech. Čurčić stumbled through the remainder of his speech, replete with expressions of the most loyal devotion to the Habsburg dynasty and Bosnia's glorious future in the Empire.[52]

However inappropriate, surreal even, the mayor's oration may have appeared under the circumstances, Franz Ferdinand's speech was gracious. Having expressed his satisfaction with Bosnia-Herzegovina's progress in recent years, he then switched to Serbo-Croatian to conclude with a few appreciative remarks about Sarajevo and its inhabitants. The visiting party meanwhile had split up, with the Duchess holding a separate reception for the wives of the Muslim dignitaries, so that they could remove their veils. Downstairs, in the foyer, Franz Ferdinand was overheard making comments on the events of the morning, laced with the heavy sarcasm to which he was prone: 'Just you wait! In true Austrian fashion, instead of rendering him harmless, the scoundrel will be decorated with the order of merit!'[53]

He then turned to Potiorek to enquire whether any further incidents had to be expected. The governor admitted that, 'despite all security measures', this possibility could not be excluded. He suggested that the party ought to return to the train station via a different route from that advertised publicly (down Appel Quay before turning right into Lateiner Street and then onto Franz Josef Street towards the Catholic cathedral). Two routes were possible, either along the Quay or via the Konak, the governor's official residence on the other side of the river, where Potiorek lived as Vienna's satrap shielded from his surroundings by its high white walls. Franz Ferdinand expressed his wish to visit Merizzi, the governor's wounded adjutant, who had been taken to the garrison hospital on the outskirts of the city. Major Paul Höger, who served in the Archduke's military cabinet, then argued that the visiting royalty should be kept at the city hall until the major thoroughfares had been cleared of all bystanders. This was rejected by Potiorek. Any such measure would have meant calling up the troops recently returned from the manoeuvres and now encamped outside Sarajevo; and this, the governor decided, was impossible. The soldiers, after all, were kitted out in field grey, and did not have their

---

[52] Reuter's report, as quoted in *The Times*, 29 June 1914; Morsey, 'Konopischt', 494.
[53] Nikitsch-Boulles, *Vor dem Sturm*, 215; Dedijer, *Sarajevo*, 13–14.

full-dress uniforms with them, as required for all official functions involving members of the imperial family.[54]

After some further discussion the Archduke decided that the return journey was to take the party down the length of the Appel Quay, without having to touch the inner city of Sarajevo. The alterations were then summarized by the head of Franz Ferdinand's military cabinet, General Carl von Bardolff. One further change was made. The Duchess, who was originally supposed to travel separately to the Konak, insisted on accompanying her husband for the remainder of their visit to the Bosnian capital. It was then left to Gerde, the Sarajevo police chief, to brief the drivers and security personnel on the new arrangements. For good measure, Harrach insisted on standing on the running board of the archducal car. On the, perhaps natural, assumption that any assassin would fire at the heir to the throne rather than his wife, Harrach decided to stand next to the Archduke, that is on the left-hand side of the car, facing towards the river.[55]

The Archduke and his party left the city hall at around 10.45 a.m. It is not clear whether Gerde had failed to carry out his task, or whether his explanations were misunderstood by the drivers, or whether he himself had not fully grasped Bardolff's summary. Whatever the case might be, as the procession of cars made its way down the Quay, the lead vehicle, with the mayor and Gerde, turned right into Lateiner Street in accordance with the original itinerary. The second car, Harrach's Graef & Stift which conveyed the archducal couple, was about to follow when Potiorek called out: 'Stop. What is this? We are going the wrong way.' Sojka, the Czech driver, braked and made to reverse the car. In so doing he stopped in front of Moritz Schiller's delicatessen, close to the crowded pavement and right in front of Prinčip, who had moved there after the earlier mishaps. Unable to extract the explosive device from underneath his jacket, he drew his Browning revolver and fired from close range. He could scarcely miss. In the long chain of thought-lessnesses, ignored warnings, misguided ambitions and sloppiness, Prinčip was but the last link.

There are conflicting reports as to how many shots were fired. Morsey, who travelled in the following vehicle, recalled hearing three shots, while Harrach, looking on in horror as Prinčip fired from the unprotected right-hand side, attested to two shots being fired.[56] Potiorek could later not recall whether Prinčip had fired two or three or, indeed, four times. He also

---

[54] Nikitsch-Boulles, *ibid.*, 216; deposition Potiorek, Musset (ed.), *L'Attentat*, 441.
[55] For further details see Morsey, 'Konopischt', 495.
[56] *Ibid.*, 496–7; testimony Harrach, Sosnosky, *Franz Ferdinand*, 220–1.

spoke of a powerful sense of unreality: 'At the moment when the assassin fired, he was at about my level. I stared at him ... I saw neither a flash nor smoke as he fired. The detonation was very faint.'[57]

Initially, the archducal couple appeared unharmed; both sat upright in the car, and neither moved. In fact, both had been fatally injured. The first shot had torn through the car door and lodged in the Duchess's abdomen; the second had hit the Archduke in the neck, severing his jugular vein. As the Duchess slumped forward, lying with her head on her husband's knee, Harrach managed to keep Franz Ferdinand in an upright position by grabbing him by his collar. A stream of blood had begun to pour from his mouth, and he could be heard muttering 'Sopherl, Sopherl! Don't die! Stay alive for my children!' On Harrach's enquiry as to whether he was in any pain, Franz Ferdinand whispered repeatedly, 'It is nothing', before losing consciousness.[58] The car then sped off towards the Konak, where the Duchess was pronounced dead on arrival. Franz Ferdinand was carried inside, and Morsey, his chamberlain, who had followed the car on foot, had to cut open the Archduke's prized *Generalsbinde* with its patent clasp, which had jammed, and his tunic. But there was nothing anyone could do now. A little before 11 a.m., the attending medical doctor pronounced Franz Ferdinand dead. He and Sophie would be the first casualties of the First World War.[59]

As for Princip, he had succeeded where the others had failed. But he, too, was denied the martyrdom all seven had craved. As the Archduke's car headed across the river, the surging crowd enveloped his attacker. In the melée, his pistol was knocked out of his hand, and the cyanide, which he managed to swallow, proved as ineffective as Čabrinović's had. He was beaten and kicked by bystanders around him, and was only saved from being lynched by one of the gendarmes, who dragged him away to the police station. There he arrived bruised and dishevelled, bleeding from his many cuts and vomiting from the degraded poison.[60] It is interesting to speculate that, had the cyanide ingested by Princip and Čabrinović worked, the Austro-Hungarian authorities might have remained in ignorance of the murderers' Belgrade connections, and the subsequent crisis might well have played out quite differently.

---

[57] Deposition Potiorek, Musset (ed.), *L'Attentat*, 441–2.
[58] Testimony Harrach, Sosnosky, *Franz Ferdinand*, 220.
[59] Morsey, 'Konopischt', 498–9.
[60] Remak, *Sarajevo*, 138–9. Princip was to die in 1918, incarcerated in the Bohemian fortress of Theresienstadt (Terezin).

The Belgrade connection

The young Bosnians' links to members of the Serbian military intelligence apparatus was to be the keystone of Austria-Hungary's official case for war; and, in consequence, it has attracted the attention of historians. That the plot to kill the Archduke originated with Apis, the head of the intelligence section of the general staff, and his underlings in the 'Black Hand', is now widely accepted by scholars of the period. In turn, this raises the question of what prior knowledge, if any, of the planned assassination Serbian government ministers and officials had. As with the Sarajevo plot itself, this matter has generated a good deal of obfuscation and speculation. Even so, whilst some details may be debatable, the broad outlines of Belgrade's foreknowledge can be established with certainty. Of equal, if not greater importance, however, are the domestic constraints under which the Serbian government had to operate.

To begin with the latter, Serbia's domestic political scenery was in turmoil. The prime minister of the day was Nikola Pašić, leader of the Radical party and a wily survivor of the vicissitudes of Serbian politics. Through adroit manoeuvring and skilful manipulations he had carved out a powerful position for himself; and, in one position or another, he dominated the affairs of Serbia and her post-1919 successor, the Kingdom of the Serbs, Croats and Slovenes, between 1903 and 1926. But he was not all-powerful. At the time of the Sarajevo assassination, he had extricated himself and his administration with some difficulty from a prolonged power struggle. This was no mere party-political jockeying for office, and went beyond the ordinary 'cut and thrust' of exchanges on the floor of the Skupština, even though the parliamentary opposition sought to exploit Pašić's predicament for its own purposes. It was rather the culmination of a constitutional crisis that had long been simmering. Its origins lay with the officers' coup of 1903. What triggered the constitutional crisis in May 1914 was the so-called 'Priorities question', that is whether the territories, newly acquired in the two Balkan wars, were to be administered by the army or the civilian authorities in Belgrade. In April, Stojan Protić, Pašić's right-hand man and minister of the interior, had issued a decree affirming the priority of civilian officials over military officers in 'New Serbia'. On the surface of it, it had the appearance of a largely administrative problem. But in reality it touched on a fundamental constitutional issue, and the outcome of the struggle would shape Serbia's future development. In essence, it revolved around the position of the army within the state and the extent to which it was able to control the civilian government.[61]

---

[61] M. Cornwall, 'Serbia', K. M. Wilson (ed.), *Decisions for War, 1914* (London, 1995), 56–8, offers a most incisive account; for further details see Dedijer, *Sarajevo*, 366–400;

Emboldened by the military successes during the recent regional conflicts, a group of army officers, loosely affiliated with Apis and the 'Black Hand' and largely led by him, used the 'Priorities question' to prepare a ministerial coup against the Pašić government. Their object was to entrench military influence over the civilian government and to advance their pan-Serb political programme. Pierre Descos, the French envoy in Belgrade, reported on the 'moral disturbance' which the wars had caused, especially among army officers, who formed 'a silent opposition against the old-Radical cabinet'. In this struggle, which pitted the armed forces against the civilian government, the officers were 'in turmoil [*s'émeuvent*] and hold meetings; the police keep a watch on them and this surveillance irritates them'. Protić, the minister of the interior, spoke of the officers' 'praetorian tendencies', while *Pijemont*, the army paper linked to Apis, fuelled the fire by conjuring up memories of the 1903 putsch and forecasting 'fresh turmoil'.[62] Baron Wladimir Giesl von Gieslingen, the new Habsburg minister at Belgrade, observed: 'The antagonism between the government and the conspirator party (*Črna Ruka*), which has existed for a number of years ... has become so aggravated on account of a series of incidents in the last few weeks that violent clash between the enemies vying for power and influence does not seem impossible.' The government seemed determined to take up the fight. There were even rumours that Protić was to head the military administration in an effort to break the power of the conspirators. The King, Giesl argued, owed his throne to the ultra-nationalist officers, and did not dare to support them openly. His sympathies, however, belonged to the *Črna Ruka*, and as the organization 'is not especially fastidious in its choice of means to attain its ends ... the possibility of violent eruptions, possibly even the fall of the government or an armed *coup d'état*, cannot be excluded, unless, as has been the case so far, the government surrenders to the military party'.[63]

As the crisis reached its climax in early June, Giesl warned that there was only one conclusion to be drawn from the power struggle at Belgrade, 'that the army is and will remain for many years the most powerful factor in Serbia'. At the same time, he averred, it mattered little which political party was at the helm. Pašić's old-Radicals were far from pro-Habsburg and the current opposition was likely to overcompensate for

Petrovich, *Modern Serbia* II, 610–11; also D. Djordjević, 'Serbian Society, 1903–1914', D. Djordjević and B. Király (eds.), *East Central European Society and the Balkan Wars* (Boulder, CO, 1987), 233–4.

[62] Descos to Doumergue (no. 139), 7 May 1914, *DDF* (3) X, no. 207; see also MacKenzie, *Apis*, 105–22.

[63] Giesl to Berchtold (no. 67A), 8 May 1914, HHStA, PA XIX/66.

its lack of government experience by pandering to ultra-nationalist sentiments: 'The decisive factor in Serbia, the army, is inspired by Southern Slav
chauvinism and hatred for Austria-Hungary and will force the policy of any
government in a nationalist-chauvinist and Austrophobe direction.'[64]

Giesl underestimated the political skills of the canny Serbian prime
minister as much as he overestimated the staying power of the ultra-
nationalist army officers. Ultimately, the anti-Pašić putsch came to nothing,
although the Protić decree was withdrawn. In part, this was because Apis
and the *Črna Ruka* were far less effective political operators than their own
propaganda suggested. More important still, perhaps, the ultra-nationalists
ran into the opposition of the influential Russian minister to Serbia, Nikolai
Genrikovich Hartwig, who threw the weight of his prestige and influence
behind Pašić. The prime minister had also garnered the support of Crown
Prince Aleksandr, who, in a surprise move on 24 June 1914, assumed the
position of Regent in place of his aged and sick father, King Petar.[65]

If Pašić prevailed in May and June of 1914 it was because of royal
and Russian support. But Apis and the ultra-nationalist officers' clique in
the army had not been broken yet. Fresh elections, scheduled for 14
August, Pašić hoped, would strengthen his position before the final showdown with his army opponents. Sarajevo and the July crisis thus erupted in
the middle of an election that, for Pašić, was about far more than the
composition of the next government. It also meant that, whilst he wished
to destroy the influence of the army officers as an alternative centre of
political gravity, he could not afford to be outflanked by the ultra-
nationalists during the election campaign. Playing the patriotic card at
home to maximum electoral effect and conciliating the powerful Austro-
Hungarian neighbour involved a near-impossible tightrope walk.

Domestic considerations also constrained Pašić in his handling of
internal intelligence relating to the activities of young Bosnians based in
Belgrade. In early June, Protić had informed him that at least two Bosnian
students had crossed the Drina frontier into Bosnia with the assistance of
Serbian border officials; that they were armed; and that they were planning
an operation in Bosnia. There is no evidence to suggest that Pašić or Protić
had detailed knowledge of the plot against Franz Ferdinand. They nevertheless instituted an investigation into the activities along the border with a
view to preventing similar crossings in the future. The two also understood
the connection between the border guards and Apis and his underlings in
Belgrade. Towards the end of June, therefore, Pašić ordered another

---

[64] Giesl to Berchtold (no. 82A), 6 June 1914, HHStA, PA XIX/66.
[65] Giesl to Berchtold (no. 108), 6 June 1914, *ibid.*; see also Cornwall, 'Serbia', 57–8.

investigation into Apis's clandestine activities. Protić and he appreciated that the latter's nationalist-revolutionary agitation in Bosnia-Herzegovina 'could provoke a war between Serbia and Austria-Hungary with logical consequences'.[66]

In the aftermath of Sarajevo, then, Pašić was caught in an awkward situation. He himself had already ordered an internal investigation at Belgrade into some of the connections of the assassins. In consequence, he was fully alive to the fact that 'official Serbia' was implicated in the murder to some extent. It explains why Pašić's response to Austro-Hungarian representations in the matter was less than straightforward.

This also extends to the question of whether Pašić had warned Vienna of some plot against the Archduke while in Bosnia. Rumours to that effect began to circulate soon after the assassination. On 30 June, the French acting consul-general at Budapest reported that the Serbian minister at Vienna, Jovan Jovanović, had made some sort of representation at the Ballhausplatz 'to intimate the dangers which might attend the archduke in Bosnia'.[67] The Serbian envoy at Paris, Milenko Vesnić, was even more forthright and asserted that Belgrade 'had warned the Austrian government that it got wind of a plot'.[68] These rumours were certainly taken seriously at Vienna, where an official denial of any such warnings was issued on 2 July; and on 7 July Pašić himself, in an interview with the Hungarian newspaper *Az Est*, denied any prior knowledge of the plot and having warned the Habsburg government.[69] The story of Belgrade's secret warning was revived in the 1920s by Jovan Jovanović and others, and generated a vigorous polemic at the time.

It is difficult, even at the distance of a century, to establish whether a warning was sent. It was in Austria-Hungary's obvious interest to deny that this had been the case, lest Vienna be accused of unconscionable negligence. Similarly, anxious to protect his patriotic credentials during the election campaign, Pašić could not very well admit to having warned the Habsburg government, considered by many Serb nationalists to be their

---

[66] Protić to Pašić, 24 June 1914, as quoted in Cornwall, *ibid.*, 57. In the mid-1920s, Pašić's erstwhile ally and recent political foe, Ljuba Jovanović, involved the premier in a lengthy dispute in which he argued that Pašić had had detailed knowledge of the plot. Politics was a stronger motivation, it seems, than the quest for historical truth; for some details see A. von Wegerer, 'Der Anlass zum Weltkrieg. Ausschnitte zum Attentat von Sarajewo', *BMH* III, 6 (1925), 393–8. Jovanović's book was published in English as *The Murder of Sarajevo* (London, 1935).

[67] D'Apchier le Maugin to Viviani (no. 79), 30 June 1914, *DDF* (3) x, no. 463.

[68] Note Ferry, 1 July 1914, *ibid.*, no. 466; also Clark, *Sleepwalkers*, 60.

[69] 'Die Warnungen des serbischen Gesandten', *Neue Freie Presse*, 3 July 1914; for the *Az Est* interview see Albertini, *Origins* II, 99.

country's arch-enemy. By the same token, it served the interests of neither side after the war to admit to any kind of foreknowledge, with its implication of direct involvement or indirect culpability on account of negligence.

According to Jovanović's recollections, he acted on his own initiative. He was, however, severely constrained in his ability to communicate with the government to which he was accredited. Jovanović undoubtedly agreed with Pašić that, after the two recent bouts of fighting in the Balkans, Serbia required a period of tranquillity to consolidate her regional position and that therefore some sort of conciliation with Austria-Hungary was necessary. Yet with his nationalist past and rumoured connections to the *Črna Ruka*, the envoy's official relations with the Habsburg foreign ministry were strained. Count Berchtold, the minister, had made a habit of not seeing him. Indeed, at various times, the Ballhausplatz had been on the verge of declaring him *persona non grata* to force the Serbian government to send a more agreeable diplomatic representative to Vienna. Under the circumstances, Jovanović decided to see Biliński, the Austro-Hungarian finance minister. He had always found the Polish Count and fluent Russian-speaker a more congenial interlocutor than the *grands seigneurs* at the Ballhausplatz. Besides, as Biliński was the minister responsible for Bosnia-Herzegovina, Jovanović could legitimately claim the need to see him.

Thus, on 5 June, he went to see him at the finance ministry, once the palace of Prince Eugene of Savoy. He raised with Biliński the forthcoming Bosnian manoeuvres, which he assumed would take place along the Drina river and which he understood would be attended by Franz Ferdinand:

> I said to minister Biliński: 'If this is true, then I can assure Your Excellency that it will arouse the greatest discontent among the Serbs, who must regard it as an act of provocation. Under such circumstances manoeuvres are dangerous. Among the Serb youths there may be someone who will put in his rifle or revolver not a blank but a real cartridge, and he may fire it. And that bullet may strike the challenger. Therefore it would good and sensible if the Archduke Franz Ferdinand did not go to Sarajevo and that the manoeuvres did not take place on *Vidovdan* and not in Bosnia.

Jovanović claimed to have returned to the finance ministry a few days later, only to find that his 'surely clear words' had not had the desired effect.[70]

---

[70] J. Jovanović, 'Meine Warnung an den Erzherzog Franz Ferdinand', *Neues Wiener Tageblatt*, 28 June 1924; see also K. von Macchio, 'Momentbilder aus der Julikrise 1914', *BMH* XIV, 10 (1936), 764.

According to the testimony of Paul Flandrak, head of the press department of Biliński's finance ministry, the Serbian envoy had indeed paid a visit to his chief in June 1914. But he used the occasion to speculate whether the Archduke's visit might not give rise to tensions on either side of the frontier. He urged Biliński to treat his observations as of a private nature; it was his desire to prevent anything that was liable to complicate Austro-Serbian relations. For his part, Biliński shared some of Jovanović's misgivings at the Archduke's planned visit to Sarajevo. These were not rooted in security concerns, however. Rather, Biliński thought that the intended political gesture, implied in the Bosnian trip, was premature while the internal affairs of the province remained in their current unsettled state. In consequence, he paid little attention to Jovanović's words. But it was this conversation that later gave rise to the legend of a Serbian warning.[71] Although Biliński did not later explicitly refute Jovanović's version of events, he nevertheless observed that the 'rumour that I had warned the emperor against the journey does not conform with the truth. For I had no cause to involve myself in this military trip.'[72]

The extant evidence is sufficiently strong to suggest that some attempt was made to dissuade the Habsburg authorities from allowing the Archduke to visit Bosnia. But whether this constituted a warning is far less clear. For one thing, even according to his own recollection, Jovanović's words were deliberately Delphic, and scarcely constituted a clear warning. For another, he had emphasized the provocative nature of the manoeuvres because the military exercise was to take place 'on the Drina'. As the manoeuvres were actually held in central Bosnia, this diminished the force of Jovanović's observations. Given the state of affairs in the early summer of 1914, it would have been difficult for Biliński – or any other Habsburg minister – not to conclude that Jovanović's initiative was little more than an attempt to persuade Vienna to abort the Archduke's visit altogether. Cancellation at such short notice would have been seen as a sign of weakness, further evidence of the Dual Monarchy's decay. As Franz Ferdinand's visit was intended precisely to reverse this impression and to underscore Austria-Hungary's commitment to Bosnia, Jovanović's comments could not but be construed as a fairly obvious political stratagem.

The date of the Serbian minister's private conversation with Biliński is also problematic. If the interview took place on 5 June, as Jovanović asserted, it seems unlikely that he acted on Pašić's instructions. For it was only around that time that Protić, the minister of the interior,

---

[71] P. Flandrak, 'Bilinskis Eingreifen in die auswärtige Politik', *Neues Wiener Journal*, 26 Apr. 1925; see also Albertini, *Origins* II, 103.
[72] Biliński, *Wspomnienia* I, 277–8.

became aware of the recent border crossings; and it was not until 15 June that Pašić and the cabinet discussed the matter. It would not, of course, have been impossible for such a subtle and wily tactician as the Serbian prime minister to act with such subterfuge. It might even have been possible for him to issue a more direct warning. At the same time, there was little incentive for him to do so. It was not difficult to foresee that any warning, be it indirect through Jovanović or more explicit through other channels, would invite the sort of diplomatic offensive that was to unfold in the aftermath of Sarajevo. The adverse consequences for Pašić's domestic position were equally easy to discern. It was better, then, to do nothing. There was no way of knowing whether an attempt on the Archduke's life would be made, and if it was made, whether it would be successful. After all, as was seen earlier, even Apis harboured doubts about the suitability of Prinčip and his associates.[73]

However amateurish the deed and its perpetrators might have been, the provocative – incendiary even – nature of the murder of the archducal couple was beyond question. For the better part of the past decade, Austro-Serbian relations had deteriorated sharply, and the tensions between the two countries had been at the heart of recent international crises. No government could have ignored the assassination of its future monarch. Much, however, now depended on how precisely the Habsburg leadership would react to the events of 28 June. In the end, far from postponing a conflict by decapitating what Apis considered to be the war party at Vienna, the assassination of Franz Ferdinand unleashed the belligerent elements in the Habsburg capital.

[73] See p. 33 above; MacKenzie, *Apis*, 135–7.

2 SARAJEVO AND ITS ECHOES: 28 JUNE TO 5 JULY

> Voices from the crowd: Bravo! That's it – *Serbien muss sterbien* [Serbia must die] – Whether she wants to or not.
>
> KARL KRAUS[1]

The news of the Archduke's assassination burst on a political scene at Vienna that was seemingly quiescent. In 1914, Sunday, 28 June marked the end of the 'season' in the Habsburg capital. Society and political leaders had already dispersed, or were about to leave for the country for the remainder of the summer. But underneath the impression of a capital in holiday mood there was a barely suppressed febrile atmosphere that made officials and their political masters susceptible to suggestions of a military confrontation with the troublesome southern neighbour. They were ever ready to react to the latest provocation with force.

'Music everywhere': the reaction in Vienna

The violent death of the Archduke appalled all Europe. This, after all, was a civilized age. 'An agonized cry of horror resounds across five continents', wrote the semi-official *Pester Lloyd*, Hungary's leading paper.[2] Europe's monarchs died peacefully in their beds; they were not gunned down in the street. Even *The Times* carried no fewer than seven news items on the murder at Sarajevo in its issue of 29 June. For a brief moment, the events in far-away Bosnia superseded the grim news from Ireland and attracted the attention of the British press and public.[3] Franz Ferdinand and his consort had made a great impression during their visit to Britain in November 1913, and the Archduke enjoyed a degree of popularity here: 'It is less than a year since many of us saw the Archduke and his wife enjoying their visit to Windsor seeming to be so happy here, and this too quickens our

[1] K. Kraus, *Die Letzten Tage der Menschheit. Tragödie in fünf Akten* (Vienna and Leipzig, 1922), act I, scene i, 32.
[2] *Pester Lloyd* (29 June 1914, morning edn).
[3] *The Times*, 29 June 1914. For some instructive comments see D. C. Watt, 'The British Reactions to the Assassination at Sarajevo', *ESR* 1, 3 (1971), 233–47.

sympathy.'[4] King George V himself called on the Habsburg ambassador, Count Albert Mensdorff; the Royal court was in official mourning; and on 5 July, there was a requiem mass at the Roman Catholic Westminster Cathedral, which was attended by several Cabinet ministers.[5]

If there was sympathy abroad, in Austria-Hungary the public reaction to 'la lugubre catastrophe ... à Sarajevo' was muted, as the Swiss envoy at Vienna reported. The heir to the throne had lacked the popular touch; nor had the truculent Archduke ever been very popular with the court, chiefly because of his morganatic (non-Royal) marriage to a mere countess. Among the powerful Magyar magnates in the Hungarian half of the Dual Monarchy, meanwhile, he was detested on account of his leaning towards a 'reactionary and clerical policy'. His undisguised preference for constitutional reforms that were to convert the current arrangements into something akin to a federation, with greater autonomy devolved to the Slav areas of the Empire, merely deepened Hungarian hostility. Monday, 29 June was a public holiday (St Peter and St Paul), and the capital felt deserted and quiet.[6] And yet, as if to underline the murdered Archduke's unpopularity, the giant ferris wheel in the Prater meadow kept turning: 'music everywhere', the well-connected Viennese lawyer and *Reichsrat* deputy Josef Redlich noted with dismay. Everyone, recorded Lady de Bunsen, wife of the British ambassador, in her diary, 'seemed very gay and not the least upset by such a terrible event'.[7] The murdered archducal couple, moreover, were buried quickly and without much ado at his country estate at Artstetten near Linz; it was 'a state funeral third class'.

'Opportunity for a destructive strike'

If the public at large ignored the Archduke's demise, official statements at Vienna were equally reserved. An inspired article in *Neue Freie Presse*, one of the leading Viennese papers, emphasized that the assassination was not

---

[4] Mensdorff to Grey (private), 29 June 1914, Nachlass Mensdorff, Karton 11; see also the adulatory piece by E. Sellars, 'The Murdered Archduke', *The Nineteenth Century* LXXVI, 450 (Aug. 1914); for further thoughts see F. R. Bridge, *Great Britain and Austria-Hungary, 1906–1914: A Diplomatic History* (London, 1972), 214–15.

[5] Mensdorff diary, 2 and 5 July 1914, Nachlass Mensdorff, HHStA, Karton 4.

[6] Choffat to Hoffmann, 29 June 1914, DDS VI, no. 1; tel. Franklin to San Giuliano (no. 5783/23), 29 June 1914, DDI (4) XII, no. 12.

[7] Redlich diary, 29 June 1914, I, F. Fellner (ed.), *Schicksalsjahre Österreichs. Das politische Tagebuch Josef Redlichs, 1908–1919* (2 vols., Graz and Cologne, 1953) I, 235; and Berta de Bunsen diary, 28 June 1914, C. H. D. Howard (ed.), 'The Vienna Diary of Berta de Bunsen, 28 June – 17 August 1914', BIHR LI, 2 (1978), 212; see also Shebeko to Sazonov (no. 42), 23 June/6 July 1914, IBZI IV, no. 104.

the work of a deluded individual but of 'hired murderers', recruited from amongst Bosnia's 'stirred up youths'; and it pointed the finger at Belgrade. It was in the 'highest interest of the state' to establish their connections with Serbian officials. The article also asserted, however, that there would be 'no policy of wrath' against Serbs within the Monarchy or without it. But it concluded with a warning addressed to the suspected wire-pullers at Belgrade: 'they will be caught and uprooted from Bosnian soil. Those concerned should remember Dante's words that ought to be engraved on the Monarchy's border markers: Woe betide him who touches it.'[8]

The Austro-Hungarian foreign minister, Count Leopold von Berchtold, who had hastily returned to the capital from his Moravian castle at Buchlau (Buchlovice),[9] was no more forthcoming in his first encounters with foreign diplomats. But he left them in no doubt that the 'threads of the conspiracy ... came together at Belgrade'. The assassins had travelled, armed and equipped with explosives, from there, and 'he spoke bitterly about Serbian intrigues'.[10] No firm decisions, indeed, had as yet been taken, as the former Austro-Hungarian ambassador at Rome recorded on 29 June, even if he himself thought that 'we were on the eve of great events'.[11]

Behind the scenes, however, Austrian officials were far less restrained. Legation counsellor Wilhelm Ritter von Storck, then in charge of the Habsburg mission at Belgrade, posited an explicit link between the murder of the Archduke and the official celebrations in Serbia of the anniversary of Kosovo Polje. For years government-sponsored, pan-Serb propaganda had inculcated into ordinary Serbs the conviction that Austria now was the 'hereditary enemy' of their nation. Such press agitation had 'sown hatred for years, and has now harvested murder and violence'.[12]

[8] 'Erzherzog Franz Ferdinand', *Neue Freie Presse*, 30 June 1914 (morning edn).
[9] Tel. Kinsky to Berchtold (urgent), 28 June 1914, HHStA, PA I/810, Liasse XX Attentat auf Erzherzog Franz Ferdinand. Kinsky was in charge of Berchtold's *cabinet*; see [A.] von Musulin, *Das Haus am Ballplatz. Erinnerungen eines österreichisch-ungarischen Diplomaten* (Munich, 1924), 214; H. Hantsch, *Leopold Graf Berchtold. Grandseigneur und Staatsmann* (2 vols., Graz, 1963) II, 551–2.
[10] Tschirschky to Bethmann Hollweg, 30 June 1914, *DD* I, no. 8; and tel. Avarna to San Giuliano (no. 5772/881), *DDI* (4) XII, no. 14.
[11] H. Graf von Lützow, *Im diplomatischen Dienst der k.u.k. Monarchie*, ed. P. Hohenbalken (Vienna, 1971), 218. Lützow's informant was the influential *Sektionschef* of the Foreign Ministry, Count Johann von Forgách.
[12] Storck to Berchtold (no. Z 97/P A-B), 29 June 1914, HHStA, PA I/810, Liasse XX, Attentat auf Erzherzog Franz Ferdinand; for some of the background see H. Hantsch, 'Die Spannungen zwischen Österreich-Ungarn und Serbien-Russland, 1908–1914', Institut für Österreichkunde (ed.), *Österreich am Vorabend des Ersten Weltkrieges* (Graz, 1964), 8–18.

Two days after the assassination Storck's conviction of a Serb connection had hardened, and he urged the Ballhausplatz to adopt a firm line. During previous Balkan crises Vienna had tolerated Serbian pinpricks. But matters bore a different aspect now. The Habsburg leadership had 'to seize the first advantageous opportunity for a destructive strike against the kingdom [Serbia]'. This was necessary so as 'to secure the Monarchy a few decades of tranquil internal development and to preserve undiminished for the crown the empire, which the dynasty of Habsburg-Lorraine gathered under its sceptre in the course of centuries'. Belgrade, he concluded, 'must learn to be afraid of us again; otherwise not only the annexed provinces [Bosnia-Herzegovina] but also our older border districts shall be endangered'.[13]

Such a strongly worded suggestion by a middle-ranking official might seem surprising. But Storck's language reflected widely held views at the Ballhausplatz, the white, stuccoed late-Baroque mansion next to the Hofburg palace, restrained by Viennese standards, where once Kaunitz and Metternich had directed the affairs of Europe. To the left of its vestibule there was a suite of offices, and here were to be found some of the key players at Vienna: the foreign minister's *chef de cabinet*, Count Alexander ('Alek') Hoyos; the influential head of the first section of the ministry, Count Johann Forgách; and Baron Alexander von Musulin, ostensibly in charge of religious affairs at the foreign ministry, but in reality the department's leading Balkan expert. All three were convinced of the need to eliminate the Serb threat to the Habsburg dominions. Forgách, one of the foreign minister's closest political advisers, had served as Austro-Hungarian minister at Belgrade from 1907, but had to be recalled from there in 1911 on account of his involvement in the so-called Friedjung forgeries – an attempt by Vienna to compromise Serbo-Croat politicians in the Habsburg lands on trumped-up treason charges. Forgách left his post a confirmed Serbophobe. During the winter of 1913–14 he had grown more alarmed at the 'plans which are being spun in the Balkans originating in Serbia and under Russian aegis'.[14]

Musulin, a Croat imbued with a deep sense of hostility towards pan-Serb, Southern Slavism, was convinced of the need to contain the Serbian threat.[15] The fear that the growth of Slav nationalism would

[13] Storck to Berchtold (no. Z 98/P A-C, strictly confidential), 30 June 1914, HHStA, PA I/810, Liasse XX, Attentat auf Erzherzog Franz Ferdinand; also Griesinger to Bethmann Hollweg, 30 June 1914, *DD* I, no. 10.

[14] Forgách to Mensdorff, 5 Feb. 1914, Nachlass Mensdorff, HHStA, Karton 9.

[15] For a detailed assessment of Forgách see J. A. Treichel, 'Magyars at the Ballplatz: A Study of the Hungarians in the Austro-Hungarian Diplomatic Service, 1906–1914' (Ph.D. thesis, Georgetown, 1971), 123–68; see also F. Würthle, *Die Spur führt nach*

accelerate the centrifugal forces in the multi-ethnic Austro-Hungarian Empire was real enough. The leading diplomats at the Ballhausplatz, moreover, had all gained their formative professional experiences in the Balkans and eastern Europe, more especially during the Bosnian annexation crisis of 1908–9, in many respects a forerunner of the events of the summer of 1914.[16] Habsburg diplomacy suffered from 'tunnel vision' during the final years before 1914. Austro-Hungarian foreign policy was essentially *Balkanpolitik*. This explains also why the wider Great Power constellation played no significant role in Austro-Hungarian decision-making during the Sarajevo crisis. That senior officials at Vienna had plumped for some form of coercion immediately on receiving news of the assassination was not lost on the German ambassador, Heinrich von Tschirschky: 'Here I frequently hear the wish, even among serious people, for a proper settling of accounts with Serbia.'[17] Musulin later reflected on the sombre mood prevailing at the Ballhausplatz: 'That means war.'[18] This was the audacity of despair.

The extent to which Vienna's field of vision had narrowed to the Balkans and to which political analyses there were infused by a considerable element of wishful thinking was underlined by a memorandum by Berthold Molden, a political commentator with close contacts at the Ballhausplatz. The question before the Habsburg Empire now was whether or not to deal with Serbia's persistent provocations. There could be no question of any 'responsibility towards Europe at all, because there is no Europe', Molden argued. A limited campaign might achieve little more than to replicate the Austrian campaigns against Piedmont-Sardinia in 1848, militarily successful but leading to no lasting political settlement.

Belgrad (Vienna, 1975), 186–92. Musulin advocated a federal, Croat-dominated Southern Slav union under Habsburg aegis: see Musulin, *Haus am Ballplatz*, 204–10. For the Friedjung affair see H. and C. Seton-Watson, *The Making of the New Europe: R. W. Seton-Watson and the Last Years of Austria-Hungary* (London, 1981), 76–9; for Forgách's involvement, see also R. Leslie, 'Österreich-Ungarn vor dem Kriegsausbruch. Der Ballhausplatz in Wien im Juli 1914 aus der Sicht eines österreichisch-ungarischen Diplomaten', R. Melville, C. Scharf, M. Vogt and U. Wengenroth (eds.), *Deutschland und Europa in der Neuzeit. Festschrift für Karl Otmar von Aretin* (Stuttgart, 1988), 664.

[16] M. Rauchensteiner, *Der Tod des Doppeladlers. Österreich-Ungarn und der Erste Weltkrieg* (Graz and Vienna, 1993), 68; W. D. Godsey, Jr, *Aristocratic Redoubt: The Austro-Hungarian Foreign Office on the Eve of the First World War* (W. Lafayette, IN, 1999), 177–93.

[17] Tschirschky to Bethmann Hollweg, 30 June 1914, *DD* I, no. 7.

[18] Musulin, *Haus am Ballplatz*, 214; also K. von Macchio, 'Momentbilder aus der Julikrise 1914', *BMH* XIV, 10 (1936), 765–6; E. U. Cormons [pseud. E. Urbas], *Schicksale und Schatten. Eine österreichische Autobiographie* (Salzburg, 1951), 158.

Molden speculated that Serbia had to be reduced in size, and that the annexation of Serbian territory would offer something 'tangible and visible' – an indication that Hoyos's *ex tempore* comments on 5 July at Berlin were no such thing after all. Austria-Hungary's international position, Molden noted, was increasingly exposed, and a reassertion of Habsburg power would not only destroy 'Serbian imperialism' but also be a blow to Russian pretensions. If St Petersburg did not interfere, all notions of Russia's 'protector role' would stand revealed as 'vain grandiloquence'. Then the 'Balkan spectre' would have been banished, and Romania and even Serbia would gravitate towards Austria-Hungary again. Britain, too, would welcome the end of the Russian-sponsored conspiracy against the Monarchy.[19]

The internal deliberations at Vienna were shaped by a combination of diplomatic, strategic and domestic considerations. Recent experience, the Bosnian crisis of 1908–9 and the Austro-Serb stand-off in October 1913 at the end of the Second Balkan War, suggested that, faced with a determined Austria, Belgrade would yield. The assumption that a third Habsburg-Serbian crisis would follow a similar pattern was reinforced by Austrian perceptions of Russia. There was no doubt as to Russia's latent potential. The Russian armaments programmes of 1912–13, indeed, created some unease among Habsburg diplomats.[20] But, at the same time, Russia's apparent financial and domestic weakness featured prominently in the reports from the St Petersburg embassy. Count Otto Czernin, the chargé d'affaires at St Petersburg, and the two previous Habsburg ambassadors to Russia, Counts Duglas Thurn and Friedrich von Szápáry, all stressed the fragile financial underpinnings of Russia's military programme, as well as the country's latent domestic instability.[21] Czernin, moreover, emphasized 'Russia's current weakness'. Russian policy pursued no 'aggressive ideas of encircling ... the Monarchy'. Indeed, her diplomacy was 'weak and fickle'. Only the further deterioration of Austria-Hungary's own internal situation would stimulate 'the destructive tendencies of the

---

[19] Memo. Molden, 'Memorandum des Herrn Molden über die Situation', 6 July 1914, HHStA, PA I/811. A copy was passed to Forgách; for further thoughts see S. Wank, 'Desperate Counsel in Vienna in July 1914: Berthold Molden's Unpublished Memorandum', *CEH* xxxvi, 2 (1993), 281–310.

[20] See e.g. Otto Czernin to Berchtold (no. 40F, confidential), 24/11 Oct. 1913, HHStA, PA X/139; for further thoughts see also S. R. Williamson, 'Military Dimensions of the Habsburg-Romanov Relations during the Era of the Balkan Wars', D. Djordjević and B. Király (eds.), *East Central European Society and the Balkan Wars* (Boulder, CO, 1987), 317–37.

[21] Tel. Thurn to Berchtold (no. 285), 19 Aug. 1913, and Otto Czernin to Berchtold (no. 42D), 8 Nov./26 Oct. 1913, HHStA, PA X/139; Szápáry to Berchtold (no. 23B), 21/8 May 1914, PA X/140.

Tsarist empire'.[22] Szápáry argued that the Russian government still saw 'the internal economic and national strengthening of the [Russian] empire as its most immediate task' for the foreseeable future.[23]

There were, however, also reasons for concern. One of these was Russia's active wooing of Romania. The prospect of Romania abandoning her traditional Habsburg alliance for either the Tsar's warm embrace or neutrality was viewed with some unease at the Ballhausplatz. The principal factor in Romanian calculations, Czernin argued, was the strained relations between Russia and Austria-Hungary: 'Only in creating such conditions can Romanian megalomania continue to blossom and produce fruit.'[24] That Romania 'was indeed lost today' as a strategic partner in regional politics shaped Austro-Hungarian foreign policy thinking in the first half of 1914. Bucharest's renewed adhesion to the old Habsburg alliance, argued Czernin's elder brother, Ottokar, the minister at Bucharest, was to be had only at the price of guaranteeing Romania against Bulgaria, recently defeated by the other Balkan states in the second war in the region:

> If this price is too high, then one does not have to close the bargain. If you believe it is to be had more cheaply, then the future will surely prove that you are wrong. And the future will prove something else – and this I wish to emphasize again and most strongly – that it is impossible to bring together the current Bulgaria (without Macedonia) and Romania and that we will have to decide whether we wish to have a Romanian or a Bulgarian policy; for otherwise we shall fall between two chairs.[25]

The tension between these two options considerably complicated decision-making at Vienna in July 1914. For now, recent developments

[22] Otto Czernin to Berchtold (no. 46F), 6 Dec./23 Nov. 1913, HHStA, PA X/139; Leslie, 'Österreich-Ungarn vor dem Kriegsausbruch', 668–9.

[23] Szápáry to Berchtold (no. 10B), 22/9 Feb. 1914, PA X/140. Berchtold marked this passage of the dispatch; see also J. Angelow, *Kalkül und Prestige. Der Zweibund am Vorabend des Ersten Weltkrieges* (Vienna, 2000), 400–3.

[24] Otto Czernin to Berchtold (no. 14G), 14/1 Mar. 1914, HHStA, PA X/140; B. Jelavich, *The Habsburg Empire in European Affairs, 1814–1918* (Hamden, CT, 1975), 158–60, and 'Romania in the First World War: The Pre-War Crisis, 1912–1914', *IHR* XIV, 3 (1992), 441–51.

[25] Ottokar Czernin to Berchtold (private and secret), 14 May 1914, ÖUA VIII, no. 9668; memo. Sazonov, 11 June 1914, *LN* II, 377–84; for Austro-German concerns about Romania see also the post-war reflections of the German minister at Bucharest, F. Rosen, *Aus einem diplomatischen Wanderleben*, II, *Bukarest, Lissabon* (Berlin, 1932), 69–73.

foreshadowed a further deterioration of Austria-Hungary's international position. By implication, a more assertive policy in the region might force Bucharest back into the Habsburg orbit, and possibly also solve the Bulgarian problem into the bargain.

A more pressing consideration still was the state of the *Zweibund*, the alliance with Germany, and the *Dreibund*, the Triple Alliance with Italy. A month before Sarajevo Szápáry delivered himself of a lengthy and scathing analysis of German policy towards Russia. Berlin had appeased St Petersburg, ready to sacrifice vital Austrian interests in the Balkans. Even the recent crisis over the appointment of the German general Otto Liman von Sanders to a senior position in the Ottoman army came to an 'inglorious end'. It was a picture of 'a sad diplomatic decline'. German reluctance to stand up to Russia, the ambassador warned, would encourage the latter to be more assertive, and would weaken Italy's adherence to the triplice. At the same time, in light of the uncertain situation in the Balkans, Austria-Hungary was unable to loosen her own ties with Berlin.[26] Again, a more assertive Austrian policy would galvanize Germany and bolster the Triple Alliance.

In the Austrian military, too, the conviction had hardened that a war with Serbia was desirable. At the time of Serbia's rapid advances against the Ottomans during the First Balkan War, the Chief of the General Staff, Baron Franz Conrad von Hötzendorf, pressed for a pre-emptive strike against the Monarchy's southern neighbour. There was no other option, he warned the Emperor Franz Joseph, but 'to move against Serbia now and to seize the leadership of the Southern Slavs before it is too late'. For now, Italian and Romanian support could be relied on, but any further delay would merely strengthen Serbia and drive Rome and Bucharest away from Austria-Hungary.[27] Perhaps more than any other Habsburg officer, Conrad was imbued with a sense of an inevitable, almost fated, conflict with Serbia, as he explained to Berchtold: 'I still count on a military

[26] Szápáry to Berchtold (no. 21D), 25/8 May 1914, HHStA, PA X/140. Szápáry had long been critical of what he regarded as Germany's insufficient support; see memo. Szápáry, 7 Oct. 1912, ÖUA IV, no. 3991; see also Angelow, *Kalkül und Prestige*, 301–3.

[27] Conrad notes on audience, 3 Feb. 1913, F. Conrad von Hötzendorf, *Aus meiner Dienstzeit* (5 vols., Vienna, 1921–5) III, 84–6. Tellingly, the Emperor replied: 'Yes, but it is the duty of a ruler to preserve peace.' When compiling his memoirs, Conrad had access to the official files at the *Kriegsarchiv*; a few trivial omissions apart, the documents reprinted in the memoirs are correct; see N. Stone, 'Moltke-Conrad: Relations between the Austro-Hungarian and German General Staffs, 1909–1914', *HJ* IX, 2 (1966), 206, n. 9. See also I. Deák, *Beyond Nationalism: A Social and Political History of the Habsburg Officer Corps, 1848–1918* (Oxford, 1992), 70–7.

operation by the Monarchy against Serbia because I see in the growth of that state a critical danger for the Monarchy, which it will be more difficult to address the longer we leave it.'[28]

After the October crisis of 1913, Conrad returned to the charge and pressed for war: 'Mobilising one more time without acquiring a piece of territory, the army would not stand it.'[29] This was not merely a question of army morale or the *amour propre* of general staff officers. It was above all a question of finance. During the First Balkan War, in the autumn of 1912, Vienna had increased the peacetime strength of the Habsburg forces from 415,000 to 620,000 men, at an additional cost of Kr 309m, three-quarters of the entire Austro-Hungarian defence budget.[30] The money was raised through a two-year loan, secured in New York on not altogether favourable terms. The political risks of mobilization aside, the financial costs were prohibitive, not least in view of the precarious situation of the Habsburg economy in the three years before 1914.[31] Mobilizing or augmenting the armed forces could therefore not be replicated ad infinitum. Largely for that reason, the then war minister General Moritz Baron Auffenberg von Komarów argued, in December 1912, that 'one should fix the summer of 1914 as the moment of attack [on Serbia]'.[32]

'War, war, war': the 'war party' unleashed

There was an ironic twist to the debates at Vienna during the Sarajevo crisis. The assassination of Franz Ferdinand had also removed the one man who on previous occasions had restrained the 'war party'. The slain

[28] Conrad to Berchtold, 8 Feb. 1913, *Aus meiner Dienstzeit* III, 106–8; also in ÖUA V, no. 5725; for a balanced analysis of the misguided policy towards the Southern Slavs, see J. Remak, 'The Healthy Invalid: How Doomed the Habsburg Empire', *JMH* XLI, 2 (1964), 136–7.

[29] Conrad, *Aus meiner Dienstzeit* III, 420 and 463; J. H. Maurer, 'Field Marshal Conrad von Hötzendorf and the Outbreak of the First World War', T. G. Otte and C. A. Pagedas (eds.), *Personalities, War and Diplomacy: Essays in International History* (London, 1997), 40–2.

[30] D. Stevenson, *Armaments and the Coming of the War: Europe, 1904–1914* (Oxford, 1996), 279–85; S. R. Williamson, *Austria-Hungary and the Origins of the First World War* (London, 1991), 126–32.

[31] *The Economist*, 7 Dec. 1912; H. Benedikt, *Die wirtschaftliche Entwicklung der Franz-Joseph-Zeit* (Vienna, 1958), 176; E. März, *Austrian Banking and Financial Policy: Creditanstalt at a Turning Point, 1913–1923* (London, 1984), 26–35.

[32] Memo. Friedjung (on interview Auffenberg), Dec. 1912 (after 12 Dec. 1912), F. Adlgasser (ed.), *Heinrich Friedjung: Geschichte in Gesprächen. Aufzeichnungen, 1898–1919* (2 vols., Vienna, 1997) II, 375.

Archduke was a 'gifted but authoritarian' future ruler, who espoused reform schemes that were 'superficially radical, yet in essence profoundly Catholic-conservative'.[33] In life he had not been an advocate of peace at any price, but he understood that there were good reasons for avoiding conflict. Franz Ferdinand's thinking revolved around the likely consequences of a war for the internal conditions of the Habsburg Empire and the alliance with Germany. Serbia's defeat in a 'separate war [*Spezialkrieg*]' was never in doubt, 'but what then?' The Monarchy would be ostracized in Europe as a disruptive element; 'and may God prevent that we should annex Serbia, a totally debt-ridden country full of regicides and scoundrels'. Controlling it would be a considerable drain on Austria-Hungary's military and material resources: 'We could chuck billions at it, and we should still have a ghastly irredenta to deal with.' Like any of the autocrats of the period, Franz Ferdinand was concerned about the destabilizing effects of foreign complications on the internal development of the Monarchy, which he thought was threatened by 'anti-dynastic, Jewish, masonic elements'. He did not rule out a more forceful policy at some stage, but for now domestic consolidation was imperative and that meant 'peace abroad. That is my *credo*; for it I shall labour and fight for my whole life.'[34]

Another consideration weighed on the future ruler's mind. Any military campaign in the Balkans, whatever its course and outcome, would increase Austria-Hungary's dependence on the German ally. The unequal nature of the relations with Berlin was brought home to him during a brief visit to Kaiser Wilhelm II's hunting lodge at Springe in November 1912 at the beginning of the First Balkan War. Although reaffirming Germany's commitment to the alliance in the event of Russian interference in any Austro-Serb dispute over Serbian access to the Adriatic, Wilhelm made it

[33] R. J. W. Evans, 'The Habsburg Monarchy and the Coming of War', in R. J. W. Evans and H. Pogge von Strandmann (eds.), *The Coming of the First World War* (Oxford, repr. 1991), 35. For an authoritative study of the Archduke see R. A. Kann, *Erzherzog Franz Ferdinand Studien* (Munich, 1976).

[34] Franz Ferdinand to Berchtold, 1 Feb. 1913, in Hantsch, *Berchtold* I, 388–91; and R. A. Kann, 'Erzherzog Franz Ferdinand und Graf Berchtold als Aussenminister', *MÖStA* XX (1969), 259–60. Franz Ferdinand was strongly influenced by arguments developed by the lawyer Heinrich Lammasch; see S. Verosta, *Theorie und Realität von Bündnissen: Heinrich Lammasch, Karl Renner und der Zweibund, 1897–1914* (Vienna, 1971), app. VII, 631–3; for his restraining influence see S. R. Williamson, 'Influence, Power, and the Policy Process: The Case of Franz Ferdinand, 1906–1914', *HJ* XVII, 2 (1974), 417–34; F. Fejtö, *Requiem pour un empire défunt. Histoire de la destruction de l'Autriche-Hongrie* (Paris, 1993 (pb)), 174–82; and A. Hannig, '"Wir schauen in der Loge zu". Thronfolger Franz Ferdinand und die Aussenpolitik Österreich-Ungarns vor dem Ersten Weltkrieg', *Etudes Danubiennes* XXVII (2011), 51–66.

clear that Germany would not be dragged into a European conflict over that issue. Delivered with his customary back-slapping bonhomie, as the Belgian envoy reported, the Kaiser stressed the need for moderation: 'Above all, don't do anything stupid [surtout pas des bêtises]'.[35] Indeed, the Kaiser was soon reported in German papers to have told his friend 'Franzl' as the train pulled out of Springe station: 'I find you rattle too much – with my sabre.'[36]

Whether the German Emperor had used precisely those words or not, his warnings had made an impression on Franz Ferdinand. The German leadership, meanwhile, continued to urge restraint, using Duke Albrecht von Württemberg, the Archduke's brother-in-law, as an intermediary. During a private meeting at the end of January 1913, just before fighting resumed in the Balkans, Albrecht hinted that 'in a war of conquest [by Austria-Hungary] the *casus foederis* would not arise for us [Germany]'. The Archduke replied that he had pondered this problem for several weeks and had concluded that 'the only correct policy is to let the Balkan peoples settle matters among themselves and to watch ... as they smash each other's skulls'. Indeed, there was 'not a single reason' for opening a military campaign against Serbia now.[37]

Franz Ferdinand turned to the issue of the German alliance in a letter to Berchtold two days after the Württemberger's visit. 'Persons close to me', he intimated, 'have confirmed me in my peace idea'. War had to be avoided for now: 'If we were to aim for the great war with Russia, then that would be a misfortune, and who knows whether our left and right flanks will be protected. Germany has to deal with France, and Romania will use the Bulgarian danger as an excuse.'[38] When Conrad pressed for a preventive strike against Serbia, the notoriously short-tempered Archduke

---

[35] Beyens to Davignon, 30 Nov. 1912, *BelD* suppl. I, no. 97; Wilhelm II to Kiderlen-Wächter, 21 Nov. 1912, *GP* XXXIII, no. 12405. F. Fischer, *Der Krieg der Illusionen. Die deutsche Politik von 1911 bis 1914* (Düsseldorf, 1969), 289–323; U. Trumpener, 'German Military Involvement in the First Balkan War', Djordjević and Király (eds.), *Balkan Wars*, 346–62.

[36] As quoted in H. Kanner, *Kaiserliche Katastrophenpolitik. Ein Stück zeitgenössischer Geschichte* (Vienna, 1922), 120; the papers in question were close to the Auswärtiges Amt.

[37] Albrecht to Fürstenberg, 2 Feb. 1913, *GP* XXXIV/1, no. 12788. Prince Maximilian Egon II of Fürstenberg was a prominent member of Wilhelm II's entourage; see I. V. Hull, *The Entourage of Kaiser Wilhelm II, 1888–1918* (Cambridge, 1982), 34–5 and 147–57.

[38] Franz Ferdinand to Berchtold, 1 Feb. 1913, in Kann, 'Franz Ferdinand', 259; G. Kronenbitter, *'Krieg im Frieden'. Die Führung der k.u.k. Armee und die Grossmachtpolitik Österreich-Ungarns, 1906–1914* (Munich, 2003), 441–2.

exploded, as the head of his military chancellery, Carl von Bardolff, recorded: 'Conrad's idea is madness. A war with Russia will finish us. If we move against Serbia, then we shall have war with Russia. Should the Kaiser of Austria and the Tsar knock each other off their thrones and clear the way for revolution? Tell Conrad that I categorically reject any further suggestions in that direction.'[39] As Berchtold assured the German ambassador, 'if people knew how pacific the Archduke Franz Ferdinand was, certain diplomats would be amazed'.[40]

If Franz Ferdinand had known of no single reason for attacking Serbia, his violent death now furnished it. He and his wife would be the first casualties of the world war. A force for peace during his life, noted Josef Redlich, 'his death ... has helped *us* to find the energy that he would never have found as long as he lived'.[41] The assassin's bullet had thus also freed Conrad, so long frustrated in his quest for a pre-emptive strike against Serbia by the ruler-designate at the Belvedere palace. The chief of staff appeared at the Ballhausplatz and urged Berchtold to move at once: 'On 1 July we ought to mobilize without any further talks with Serbia. If you have a poisonous adder at your heel, you stamp on its head, and you do not wait for the lethal bite. With a far-away look of melancholy on his fine-featured face, he concluded emphatically with three words – war, war, war.'[42] And for good measure, he left the foreign minister in no doubt that, from a military perspective, war would have been preferable in 1912 or 1913, implying that, like his predecessor, the rumbustious Count Aehrenthal, Berchtold was about to miss a strategic opportunity.[43]

[39] C. von Bardolff, *Soldat im alten Österreich. Erinnerungen aus meinem Leben* (Jena, 1938), 177.

[40] Tschirschky to Bethmann Hollweg (no. 50, confidential), 5 Feb. 1913, *GP* xxxiv/1, no. 12797.

[41] Redlich diary, 24 July 1914, *Tagebuch* I, 239.

[42] Berchtold, 'Die ersten Tage nach dem Attentat vom 28. Juni', unpubl. MS, Nachlass Berchtold, as quoted in Hantsch, *Berchtold* II, 558. The original seems to have disappeared. The MS memoirs cover the period up to 28 June 1914; see Nachlass Berchtold, HHStA, PA I/524a, Karton 1 ('Berchtold I–IV', 1909–1912), and Karton 2 ('Berchtold V–VIII', 1912 – 28 June 1914'). For Conrad see J. H. Maurer, *The Outbreak of the First World War: Strategic Planning, Crisis Decision Making and Deterrence Failure* (Westport, CT, 1995), 53–9; L. Sondhaus, *Franz Conrad von Hötzendorf: Architect of the Apocalypse* (Boston and Leiden, 2000), 99–100 and 121–30.

[43] Interview Berchtold, in H. R. Madol [pseud. Gerhard Salomon], *Gespräche mit Verantwortlichen* (Berlin, 1933), 13. Berchtold repeated the 'war, war, war' outbreak; for Madol see O. B. Pollak, 'The Biography of a Biographer: Hans Roger Madol, 1903–1956', *GR* lxxviii, 1 (2003), 74–85.

There were other voices joining the clamour for war. The war minister, General Alexander Ritter von Krobatin, returned from an inspection tour in the Tyrol and struck a hawkish tone from the outset. A military strike, he urged, was the only viable option now.[44] Potiorek, whose bungling had contributed more than anything else to the current situation, advocated a military solution. In so doing he may well have sought to salve his conscience over his own negligent culpability.[45] Whatever his motivations, Potiorek repeatedly emphasized that 'only by means of energetic action in the sphere of foreign policy can tranquillity and normal conditions be established in Bosnia'.[46] It was imperative for the stability of the province and its further development, he impressed upon the authorities in Vienna, that 'the Monarchy adopts decisive and to all the world visible measures once and for all to eradicate the campaign of sabotage [*Wühlarbeit*] that originates at Belgrade'. If this were not done, the confidence of the local population in the strength of the Habsburg Empire would be shaken: 'In the Orient only the forceful deed impresses people, and it alone is considered testimony of strength.' He also noted, not entirely logically, that an 'open and visible intervention at Belgrade' was necessary because capital punishment could not be applied to the apprehended terrorists given their youth.[47]

That professional soldiers showed a preference for a military solution should not come as a surprise. A more unexpected advocate of war emerged in the person of Leon Ritter von Biliński, the Austro-Hungarian finance minister. A Polish nobleman, he was one of the three common ministers, the others being the foreign and war ministers, who together constituted what little central government the Habsburg Empire had. In this role, and as the minister responsible for the administration of Bosnia, Biliński was to play a significant role in Habsburg decision-making during the July crisis. As a Pole, he shared none of the animosity of the Austro-Germans and Magyars towards the Monarchy's Slav subjects. If anything, in the affairs of Bosnia-Herzegovina he had shown himself accommodating and considerate, anxious to reconcile the various ethnic groups of the province with each other and with Habsburg overlordship.[48] Nor did he

---

[44] Hantsch, *Berchtold* II, 559.

[45] See the speculation by the Russian ambassador at Vienna, Nikolai Nikola'evich Shebeko, *Souvenirs. Essai historiographique sur les origines de la guerre* (Paris, 1936), 185.

[46] Tel. Potiorek to War Ministry (no. 5012), 29 June 1914, *ÖUA* VIII, no. 9948; N. Stone, 'Army and Society in the Habsburg Monarchy, 1900–1914', *P&P* no. 33 (1966), 110.

[47] Tel. Potiorek to Biliński, 1 July 1914, *ÖUA* VIII, no. 9974.

[48] Biliński, *Wspomnienia* I, 238–9, gives a flavour of the deals over cigarettes and coffee; for an instructive pen portrait see Clark, *Sleepwalkers*, 392–3.

veer from his conciliatory line in Bosnian affairs in the aftermath of Sarajevo, when Potiorek sought to impose repressive measures that threatened to punish the whole population of the province 'for the crimes of a faction'.[49]

Biliński had never been especially close to the murdered Archduke, but their thinking ran on parallel planes. Accommodating in his dealings with the Monarchy's Slav subjects, he had also so far advocated a cautious foreign policy and opposed Conrad in his quest for a pretext to launch a preventive war.[50] Sarajevo changed all that. As the head of the Bosnian administration, he may well have felt personally responsible for the security failures in the provincial capital which had cost the archducal couple their lives, even though these were the result of Potiorek's incompetence. But above all he was a loyal Habsburg subject, and he was convinced that the final struggle with Serbia was now inevitable. With a view to the situation in Bosnia-Herzegovina, he argued that diplomacy had run its course. Already Serbia's earlier setback in the autumn of 1913 had created tensions in the province. Making Potiorek's arguments his own, Biliński asserted that '[t]he Serb responds only to violence; a diplomatic success would make no impression in Bosnia and would be more damaging than anything else'.[51]

Count Berchtold declares for war

The vociferous clamour for a robust military response to Sarajevo in the upper echelons of the Habsburg government may well have reflected the widely held view at Vienna that the foreign minister, Count Leopold Berchtold, was not a strong minister, especially when compared with Aehrenthal, his predecessor. Berchtold had not been close to the murdered Archduke. Nor had he been close to his entourage, the latter generally regarded at the time as a form of parallel government at the Belvedere palace. His position as a Hungarian magnate – his German ancestry, name and education notwithstanding – alone prevented that. But there was more to it than Franz Ferdinand's profound disdain for the Hungarian nobility.

---

[49] Biliński to Potiorek, 3 July 1914, and to Krobatin, 4 July 1914, ÖUA VIII, nos. 10029 and 10030.

[50] Conrad, *Aus meiner Dienstzeit* III, 464–6.

[51] Minutes of Ministerial Council, 7 July 1914, M. Komjáthy (ed.), *Protokolle des Gemeinsamen Ministerrates der Österreichisch-Ungarischen Monarchie, 1814–1918* (Budapest, 1966), no. 1, 145–6; for the notion of personal guilt see Clark, *Sleepwalkers*, 373.

Ottokar Czernin, a close confidant of the Archduke, then envoy at Bucharest and later the last Habsburg foreign minister, offered a scathing assessment of Berchtold as foreign minister: 'poor Berchtold finds so often that others really understand so much more than he. He asks too much, [and] feels his way forward too much.'[52]

The blasé *grand seigneur* Berchtold was something of a dilettante. Refined and reserved, a charming cavalier and altogether a reluctant minister, he was seen as a man of conciliation and moderation who lacked steadfastness and a sense of direction. And yet Berchtold had, in fact, pursued a harder line before, for instance during the stand-off with Serbia over Scutari and northern Albania, which culminated in an Austro-Hungarian ultimatum in October 1913.[53] In the immediate aftermath of Sarajevo, indeed, he swiftly resolved to deploy the military option. When Conrad pressed for immediate mobilization on 29 June, the foreign minister admitted that 'the moment for the solution of the Serb Question had indeed arrived'. He still insisted, however, on the proper political preparation of any move against Serbia, possibly fearing Conrad's impetuosity.[54] If Lützow is to be believed, Berchtold did not wish it to be said of him, 'as of Aehrenthal, that I missed the right moment to wage war'.[55]

That Berchtold had decided to outdo Aehrenthal and resort to force became clear at his audience with Franz Joseph at Schönbrunn palace on 30 June. No decision, of course, could be taken without the Emperor's

---

[52] Czernin to Franz Ferdinand, 18 July 1913, Nachlass Franz Ferdinand, HHStA, Karton 13; also in Kann, 'Franz Ferdinand', 249; S. Wank, 'The Appointment of Count Berchtold as Austro-Hungarian Foreign Minister', *JCEA* XXIII, 2 (1963), 143–51. Berchtold was a hereditary member of the Austrian *Herrenhaus* and the Magyar House of Magnates. Under Hungarian law, such dual membership was not permissible, and Berchtold, unlike his father, opted for Magyar nationality; see Hantsch, *Berchtold* I, 8–9; Treichel, 'Magyars at the Ballplatz', 106–22.
[53] For detailed discussions see Williamson, *Austria-Hungary*, 121–63; F. R. Bridge, *From Sadowa to Sarajevo: The Foreign Policy of Austria-Hungary, 1866–1914* (London, 1972), 355–72; I. Diószegi, *Hungarians in the Ballhausplatz: Studies on the Austro-Hungarian Common Foreign Policy* (Budapest, 1983), 222–34; M. A. Faissler, 'Austria-Hungary and the Disruption of the Balkan League', *SR* XIX, 53 (1940), 141–57.
[54] Conrad, *Aus meiner Dienstzeit* IV, 34; see also Berchtold interview in Bernadotte E. Schmitt, *Interviewing the Authors of the War* (Chicago, 1930), 28; F. R. Bridge, 'The Foreign Policy of the Monarchy, 1908–1918', M. Cornwall (ed.), *The Last Years of Austria-Hungary: Essays in Political and Military History, 1908–1918* (Exeter, 1988), 20.
[55] Lützow, *Im diplomatischen Dienst*, 218. The conversation took place on 13 July. This was the charge made against him by Conrad on 29 July: see interview Berchtold, in Madol, *Gespräche*, 13; R. C. Hall, *The Balkan Wars, 1912–1913: Prelude to the First World War* (London, 2000), 130–5.

consent. The aged and ailing monarch had left the capital for his summer residence at Ischl on 27 June. His sojourn in the Salzkammergut commenced ominously – his train carriage nearly caught fire – and it was to be of short duration. On receiving the news of Franz Ferdinand's murder, he returned to Schönbrunn without delay, and was back in Vienna on 29 June. But he took his time in forming any firm decisions. He refused to see Berchtold, let alone Conrad, whose views were all too familiar to him. Two days after Sarajevo he could no longer delay receiving his foreign minister.

As Berchtold later reflected, the Emperor appeared composed at the audience. He had never been close to his nephew and heir, and if he felt any emotion, it may well have been a sense that, troublesome as Franz Ferdinand had been in the past, he would be even more so dead. The monarch agreed with his minister that 'our policy of tolerance had been badly rewarded' and that Austria-Hungary's position in south-eastern Europe had suffered considerable damage. The future of the Monarchy was at stake, Berchtold explained, all the more so since its neighbours to the south and east would be encouraged in their 'work of destruction' by any sign of Habsburg weakness. He therefore suggested the urgent need for a 'clear programme of action', a euphemism for war, if ever there was one, as the Emperor undoubtedly appreciated. The monarch hesitated, and instead requested that Berchtold confer with the prime minister of the Hungarian half of the Dual Empire, Count István Tisza, knowing full well that the latter was opposed to a military strike.[56]

Franz Joseph's reply was in keeping with the slow and methodical habits of the Habsburg ruler. Having plunged his empire into three unfortunate wars over the past half-a-century, he had good reasons for caution. On 2 July, he decided against any immediate punitive expedition against Serbia. The Emperor neither restrained those clamouring for war, nor did he push for it himself. He did not have to. It was sufficient not to reject Berchtold's scenario – either Serbia's complete subjugation or war. But for now, Belgrade's responsibility needed to be established, and the support of the German ally secured. On that latter score Franz Joseph may well have had doubts. 'The future looks bleak', he confided to the German ambassador, Heinrich von Tschirschky. He hoped that the German Kaiser appreciated the extent of the Serbian threat to the Habsburg Empire. Russia's

[56] Hantsch, *Berchtold* II, 559–60; F. Herre, *Kaiser Franz Joseph von Österreich* (Cologne, 1983 (pb)), 443–4; for general reflections on Franz Joseph's relations with his foreign ministers see H. Hantsch, 'Kaiser Franz Joseph und die Aussenpolitik', F. Engel-Janosi and H. Rumpler (eds.), *Probleme der Franzisko-Josephinischen Zeit, 1848–1916* (Vienna, 1967), 25–39.

planned trial mobilization, scheduled for the autumn, was cause for concern, especially if the current crisis had not been resolved by then. He repeatedly emphasized the 'growing danger "down there" [in the Balkans]'. The only 'ray of light in the otherwise gloomy political situation' was the marked improvement in Anglo-German relations, which, he hoped, would have a beneficial effect on Austria-Hungary. Before dismissing the ambassador, the monarch returned to the Serb problem: 'The Belgrade intrigues are intolerable. One could not possibly do anything good with these people.' It was important to consider the future and the preservation of the position of the *Dreibund* Powers.[57]

The Emperor is not quite sure of Germany

Franz Joseph's lack of confidence in Germany's support was evident. On 5 July, the Emperor at last received Conrad, who once more, and predictably, argued forcefully that war against Serbia was now inevitable. The monarch accepted the proposition, but noted that Russian intervention would make any such expedition well-nigh impossible: 'I [Conrad:] "But we have the support of Germany." His Majesty gave me a searching glance: "Are you quite sure of Germany?"'[58]

But seeking German assurances was necessary on several counts, one of which was the palpable dissatisfaction with that ally, as Szápáry's earlier comments in June indicated. The Margrave Johann Pallavicini, the Monarchy's seasoned envoy to the *Sublime Porte*, reinforced this point. The ambassador enjoyed the reputation as one of the most capable Habsburg diplomats, and his views carried weight. A man of undoubted intelligence, he possessed a good conceptual grasp of Austria-Hungary's foreign policy problems, unlike so many of his colleagues; and he freely and frequently submitted his policy suggestions to the Ballhausplatz. The days immediately after Sarajevo were no exception. Germany had to be confronted with a choice: acceptance of Russia's ultimate hegemony in the Balkans or 'cutting the Gordian knot ... by means of an energetic action, whereby I do not necessarily mean war'. Faced with such a situation, he predicted, Berlin would opt for the latter, 'leaving us a free hand in Oriental affairs, [and] go with us

[57] Tel. Tschirschky to Bethmann Hollweg (no. 81), 2 July 1914, and despatch (secret), 2 July 1914, *DD* I, nos. 9 and 11.
[58] Conrad, *Aus meiner Dienstzeit* IV, 33–4; for a discussion of the *Zweibund* see J. Angelow, 'Vom "Bündnis" zum "Block". Struktur, Forschungsstand und Problemlage einer Geschichte des Zweibundes, 1879–1914', *MGM* LIV, 1 (1995), 129–70.

through thick and thin'.[59] Thus, energetic action now was to reassert Habsburg influence in the region and revive the *Zweibund* alliance, and so tilt the balance of influence within the alliance in Austria-Hungary's favour.

Throughout the spring and early summer, Vienna had indeed planned a major diplomatic offensive in south-eastern Europe to redress the Monarchy's declining influence. A memorandum, drawn up a few days before Sarajevo by Baron Franz von Matscheko, a counsellor at the Ballhausplatz, crystallized the key aspects of official thinking at Vienna. The extrusion of Turkey from Europe, the territorial expansion of Serbia and the growth of Franco-Russian influence in the Balkans challenged Austria-Hungary's position in the region. But the main focus of Matscheko's analysis was on the uncertain state of Austro-Romanian relations. If Bucharest were to succumb to Russia's active wooing and abandon its traditional Habsburg alliance, a counterpoise would be necessary, preferably in the form of a combination with Bulgaria, possibly joined by Turkey. In the event of a European war, certain military measures along the Transylvanian salient would then be necessary.[60]

As was seen earlier, the cooling of the traditionally close relations with Romania and the country's apparent drift into the Russian orbit had been the source of some concern amongst Habsburg diplomats.[61] If Romania were to seek closer ties with Russia, ambassador Szápáry warned, 'we shall see for how much longer Italy will remain convinced that being tied to the *Dreibund* would guarantee a successful Mediterranean policy rather than renewed compromise with other Powers'.[62] Ironically, while Szápáry and Ottokar Czernin, who had been despatched to Bucharest to secure Romania's adhesion to the Habsburg alliance, suggested some sort of diplomatic offensive, Czernin's mentor, Franz Ferdinand, had urged caution. Further enquiries would merely make Bucharest demand a higher price: 'The Romanians are *realpolitiker*; they want to have two irons in the

---

[59] Pallavicini to Berchtold (private), 6 July 1914, ÖUA VIII, no. 10083; for some of the background see G. E. Silberstein, *The Troubled Alliance: German-Austrian Relations, 1914–1917* (Lexington, KY, 1970), 14–30; F. R. Bridge, 'Austria-Hungary and the Ottoman Empire in the Twentieth Century', *MÖStA* XXXIV (1981), 264–5. Pallavicini's views carried weight; he had briefly been acting foreign minister in 1911: see Godsey, *Aristocratic Redoubt*, 195–6.

[60] Draft memo. Matscheko, n.d. [before 24 June 1914], ÖUA VIII, no. 9918. Matscheko had originally failed his diplomatic entrance examination; see Godsey, *Aristocratic Redoubt*, 45–6.

[61] See Otto Czernin to Berchtold (no. 14G), 1/14 Mar. 1914, HHStA, PA X/140.

[62] Szápáry to Berchtold (no. 21D), 8/25 May 1914, *ibid*.

fire and will wait to see whether, in the far future, [Russian] Bessarabia or [Hungarian] Transylvania will fall to them.'[63]

Whatever the future might hold for Austria-Hungary's position in the Balkans, the real target of the planned diplomatic offensive was her German ally, as Matscheko's memorandum made clear. The ultimate aim of Russia's attempts at encircling the Habsburg Empire was to make it impossible for Germany to resist Russian political and economic predominance in eastern Europe. Berlin, therefore, had to be made to understand 'that it was a common interest of the Monarchy no less than of Germany, in the current phase of the Balkan crisis, early and energetically to block the development carefully planned and directed by Russia, that might possibly be irreversible later'.[64] In essence, Germany was to be recruited to force Romania to reorientate her policy and to seek closer ties with the *Dreibund* alliance. Any doubts that the diplomatic offensive was intended to coerce Germany to take a more active role in the Balkans were removed by a private letter from Hoyos to his close friend Pallavicini at Constantinople: 'a long memorandum is being drafted, which will be dispatched soon, and the minister [Berchtold] is doing his utmost to open Tschirschky's eyes'.[65]

In a further ironic twist, in a story already rich in such turns, Matscheko's *Denkschrift* of late June, hastily redrafted, was to furnish the strategic rationale for a war against Serbia after Sarajevo. From Vienna's perspective, Germany appeared an unsatisfactory, somewhat semi-detached ally, not sufficiently attuned to the strategic interests of the Monarchy. As seen, Wilhelm II's warnings had made a lasting impression on Franz Ferdinand. They also had an effect on Berchtold. For the Kaiser's counsel of caution was repeated by the German chancellor, Theobald von Bethmann Hollweg. In February 1913, at a time of mounting Austro-Russian tensions, he had sought to restrain Vienna's policy. Pan-Slav forces would gain the upper hand at St Petersburg and swamp the moderate elements there 'if Austria-Hungary drifts into a conflict with Serbia'. A neutral observer, he suggested, would have to conclude that it would be 'impossible for Russia, with her traditional relations with the Balkans states, to watch passively a military campaign by Austria-Hungary against

---

[63] Franz Ferdinand to Berchtold, 12 Apr. 1913, Kann, 'Franz Ferdinand', 274. Czernin's first interview with King Carol of Romania remained predictably inconclusive: Ottokar Czernin to Berchtold (nos. 38A and 38C, secret), 23 Apr. 1914, ÖUA VII, nos. 9600 and 9601.

[64] Memo. Matscheko, n.d. [but before 24 June 1914], ÖUA VIII, no. 9918; cf. F. Stieve, *Die Tragödie der Bundesgenossen. Deutschland und Österreich, 1908–1914* (Munich, 1930), 166–7.

[65] Hoyos to Pallavicini, 26 June 1914, ÖUA VIII, no. 9926.

Serbia without enormous loss of prestige'. Italian support could not be taken for granted, while Germany herself would have to carry the burden of a continental war. Thus, *sub rosa*, he made it clear that Austria-Hungary was not to move without consulting Berlin. The chancellor also placed great stress on the recent change in British policy: 'Today England is a mediating element, through which we have always been able to exercise a calming and restraining influence on Russia.' Indeed, he was convinced that what he called Britain's *Ententepolitik* had passed its high-water mark, and that a further reorientation of British policy was likely, 'if we succeed in getting through the current crisis without conflict'. For good measure, he impressed on Berchtold the need for the utmost caution:

> I should regard it as a mistake of incalculable consequences to bring about a military solution – even if some interests of the Austro-Hungarian Monarchy point towards it – at a moment when there is for us a prospect, though distant, [of a reorientation of British policy] to wage the conflict under significantly more advantageous circumstances.[66]

Bethmann's attempts to counteract the bellicose tendencies at Vienna were thrown into sharper relief by the Chief of the General Staff, General Helmuth von Moltke (the younger). The Habsburg leadership had no clear sense of strategic priorities, he observed to the state secretary at the Auswärtiges Amt, Gottlieb von Jagow. There were two parties at Vienna, a war and a peace party, which kept each other in check: 'Hence the schizophrenic [Austro-Hungarian] policy ... For us it is undoubtedly extremely awkward to have become dependent on Austria to a certain degree on account of *our treaties* and of the necessity of having to preserve Austria.'[67]

Moltke's use of the plural in reference to German treaty commitments to Austria-Hungary is suggestive. The existing *Zweibund* alliance treaty was defensive in nature, and did not entail any obligations on Berlin's part to assist the Habsburg Empire in an offensive war. But the treaty was complemented by an arrangement between the two chiefs of staff, Moltke and Conrad, of 1909, which pledged Germany to support

---

[66] Bethmann Hollweg to Berchtold (private), 10 Feb. 1913, *GP* XXXIV/1, no. 12818. Prince Stolberg of the German embassy duly urged the Ballhausplatz 'to avoid if at all possible a breach on account of border questions that are insignificant in comparison to a general conflagration': daily report Macchio, 14 Feb. 1913, *ÖUA* V, no. 5792.

[67] Moltke to Jagow (private), 6 Feb. 1913, *GP* XXXIV/1, no. 12793 (my emphasis); for some of the background see A. Mombauer, *Helmuth von Moltke and the Origins of the First World War* (Cambridge, 2001), 145–53.

Austria-Hungary if the latter had 'no alternative but to march into Serbia' to put an end to Belgrade's provocations. In such an event, Moltke averred, 'active intervention by Russia' was likely: 'This would be the *casus foederis* for Germany.'[68] The operational arrangements made between the two staffs were confirmed in talks between Moltke and Field Marshal-Lieutenant Blasius Schemua, briefly Conrad's successor, in November 1912. Moltke thus assured Schemua 'not of any hesitant offensive, but a powerful one parallel with ours [Austria-Hungary] ... he said repeatedly that we can rely upon Germany's support, in complete loyalty to the alliance, if we are threatened by Russia'.[69]

For Moltke, being 'dependent on Austria to a certain degree' was a price worth paying for the sixteen Habsburg army corps in the event of a continental war. But this made it all the more important to check the war party at Vienna politically. There was to be no automaticity. As he explained to Jagow, the 'principal task' of German policy would be, 'if possible, to prevent Austrian acts of folly – no pleasant and no easy task'.[70] It was for Berlin to determine if and when war was necessary, something illustrated by Moltke's marginal comment on one of Conrad's letters: 'We have no interest in bringing about a European war merely to fight for Austria. It would be different if war was forced on us. Then, in God's name, at 'em [*drauf*].'[71]

Moltke continued to assure Conrad of German support. To an extent, his thinking reflected some of the racialist tropes then prevalent among some senior German military officers: 'I still remain of the view that before long a European war must come, which will be a struggle between Germandom and Slavdom ... But the attack must come from the Slavs.'[72]

[68] Moltke to Conrad, 10 Jan. 1909, Conrad, *Aus meiner Dienstzeit* I, 379–84. The initiative came from the Austrian side, and the talks had been arranged by the then German chancellor, Prince Bülow, and the Habsburg foreign minister, Count Aehrenthal; for an examination of the talks, see Stone, 'Moltke-Conrad', 201–28; for the previous lack of cooperation see L. Höbelt, 'Schlieffen, Beck, Potiorek und das Ende der gemeinsame deutsch-österreichisch-ungarischen Aufmarschpläne im Osten', MGM XXXVI, 2 (1984), 7–30.

[69] Memo. Schemua, 22 Nov. 1912, as quoted in Stone, 'Moltke-Conrad', 212; for Schemua see J. Mann, 'Feldmarschalleutnant Blasius Schemua, Chef des Generalstabes am Vorabend des Weltkrieges' (Ph.D. thesis, Vienna, 1978). Conrad returned as chief of staff in December 1912.

[70] Moltke to Jagow (private), 6 Feb. 1913, GP xxxiv/1, no. 12793.

[71] Marginal note Moltke, n.d., on Conrad to Moltke, 11 Jan. 1913, in T. von Schäfer, 'Generaloberst von Moltke in den Tagen vor der Mobilmachung und seine Einwirkung auf Österreich-Ungarn', BMH IV, 8 (1926), 546.

[72] Moltke to Conrad, 10 Feb. 1913, Conrad, *Aus meiner Dienstzeit* III, 14407; also GP xxxiv/1, no. 12824, encl.

However reassuring in some respects, Moltke's prognostication of an inevitable racial struggle, pitting Slavs against Teutons, was less than tactful, indeed rather stupid, given the multi-ethnic nature of the Habsburg dominions – and Conrad was not slow in spelling the facts of political life in the Monarchy.[73] Indeed, as Conrad later reflected, he himself 'had no confidence in Germany's policy, but absolute confidence in Germany's military might'.[74]

The diplomatic and staff communications between Berlin and Vienna during the First Balkan War had touched on an element of uncertainty at the core of the Austro-German alliance, an element that generated a degree of friction between the two sides. In essence, implicit in the Moltke/Conrad understanding was a German 'blank cheque' to Austria-Hungary. In practice, however, both Moltke and the civilian leadership in the Wilhelmstrasse were anxious to prevent any sort of dependence on the smaller partner and to restrain the hotheads at Vienna. As for the Austro-Hungarian side, the implicit 'blank cheque' strengthened the war party, and Conrad's position in Habsburg decision-making especially. At the same time, the Monarchy's leadership was reluctant to act unilaterally on the assumption of automatic German support. The end result was a balance of tension within the *Zweibund* alliance that left neither side satisfied.

If Conrad was frustrated at the restraining influence exercised by Berlin,[75] then so were senior Habsburg diplomats. On the eve of Sarajevo, Szápáry, at St Petersburg, offered a searing critique of German diplomacy laced with a heavy dose of scathing sarcasm. Berlin's previous '*Drang nach Osten*' had culminated in the 'new German policy of conflict without struggle [*streitlose Auseinandersetzung*]'. As for Bethmann Hollweg's efforts in 1913 to restrain Vienna's policy towards Serbia, they had been, he observed, 'the first step towards sacrificing Austro-Hungarian interests in the Orient'.[76]

---

[73] Conrad to Moltke, 15 Feb. 1913, Conrad, *Aus meiner Dienstzeit* III, 149–50; for some further thoughts on this see S. B. Winters, 'The Impact of the Dual Alliance upon the Slavs of the Austro-Hungarian Monarchy: A Centennial Reappraisal', *ECE/ECE* VII, 2 (1980), 326–44.

[74] Conrad, 'Private Aufzeichnungen', K. Peball (ed.), *Conrad von Hötzendorf. Private Aufzeichnungen* (Vienna, 1977), 65; see also S. R. Williamson, 'Austria-Hungary and the Coming of the First World War', E. R. May, R. Rosecrance and Z. S. Steiner (eds.), *History and Neorealism* (Cambridge, 2010), 112.

[75] Conrad was frustrated in more ways than one. He wished for war and victory so that he could marry Gina von Reininghaus: see Sondhaus, *Conrad*, 103–38.

[76] Szápáry to Berchtold (no. 21D), 8/25 May 1914, HHStA, PA X/140. The ambassador's sneering comment was a reference to a book by the political commentator Hans Plehn, *Deutsche Weltpolitik und kein Krieg!* (Berlin, 1913), which had caused some stir in Germany.

Count Tisza calls for calm deliberation

Against this background, Berchtold now turned to Berlin to convert the implicit 'blank cheque' into hard political currency. German support was also required other than for diplomatic and military reasons. There was also a domestic aspect to Habsburg decision-making, and this vitiated against the swift action demanded by Conrad and some of the diplomats. Since the Empire's demise, scholars have obsessed about its nationality problems to an extent that would have been quite incomprehensible to most contemporaries. Far more important to them were the relations between the twin partners in the Dual Monarchy, the Austrian *Kaiserreich* and the kingdom of Hungary. Both the Cisleithanian (Austrian) and the Transleithanian (Magyar) halves of the Empire had their separate governments, but were united under the Habsburg dynasty. Under the Empire's dualist constitutional structure the consent of the Budapest government had to be obtained before any military measures could be taken against Serbia. The 1867 *Ausgleich*, the constitutional compromise that established the Dual Monarchy, was a 'marvellous machinery which through a multitude of wheels and levers made one of the smallest nations in Europe [Hungary] into a Great Power'.[77] Without Budapest's approval, there could be no military campaign against Serbia. And here lay a potentially very serious obstacle. For the Hungarian prime minister, Count István Tisza, was a dour and dogged defender of Magyar hegemony and aristocratic government in the Hungarian half of the Monarchy – and he opposed war.

If the slain Archduke had been the fiercest opponent of a Balkan war, Tisza came a close second. He had acquired a dominant position in Budapest politics through a mixture of guile, intimidation and skilful electoral bribery. There was nevertheless something hard and unbending about the austere Calvinist magnate; he was a Cromwell type, as one contemporary observed.[78] Tisza was a Magyar nationalist, but one firmly

---

[77] L. B. Namier, *Vanished Supremacies: Essays on European History, 1812–1918* (London, 1962 (pb)), 147; see also O. Jászi, *The Dissolution of the Habsburg Monarchy* (Chicago, repr. 1971), 106–18; C. A. Macartney, 'The Compromise of 1867', R. H. Hatton and M. S. Anderson (eds.), *Studies in Diplomatic History: Essays in Memory of David Bayne Horn* (London, 1970), 287–300; J. Galántai, *Der österreichisch-ungarische Dualismus, 1867–1918* (Vienna, 1985), 42–9 and 108–41. The river Leitha separated the two halves of the Empire.

[78] R. Sieghart, *Die letzten Jahrzehnte einer Grossmacht. Menschen, Völker, Probleme des Habsburger Reiches* (Berlin, 1932), 172; see also the contemporary criticism of Tisza's Magyarization policy in T. von Sosnosky, *Die Politik im Habsburgerreiche. Randglossen zur Zeitgeschichte* (2 vols., Berlin, 1913) I, 223–90; on Tisza also N. Stone, 'Constitutional Crises in Hungary, 1903–6', *SEER* xlv, 1 (1967), 168–9.

wedded to the dynastic union with the Habsburgs as the bearer of the crown of St Stephen. He was by no means an advocate of peace at any price. In October 1913, for instance, he had urged Berchtold to adopt a harder line against Serbia. Even so, he was irrevocably opposed to anything that might lead to the extension of Habsburg control over yet more Slav territories, so diluting Magyar dominance in the Transleithanian half of the Empire. In fact, how to deal with the Monarchy's Slav population had been a bone of contention between Tisza, who favoured their ruthless suppression and subsequent Magyarization, and the Archduke, whose trialist reform projects had a strong anti-Hungarian tendency that was both personal and political. Sarajevo thus brought blessed relief to Tisza. Even if he could not, of course, condone the method, Prinčip's bullet had freed him from the incubus of a major constitutional showdown with Franz Ferdinand once the latter had succeeded to the throne.

For Tisza, in sharp contrast to Berchtold and Conrad, there was no urgency to the situation after Sarajevo. And, again unlike the foreign minister and the chief of staff, he had a coherent foreign policy programme. In March 1914, he had limned a new approach to the Monarchy's Balkan problems, which now required 'calm deliberation, *sang froid* and a quiet, yet determined and persistent approach on our part'. It was a *politique de longue main* which he envisaged. Instead of relying on the alliance with Romania, always covetous of Transylvania, he suggested pivoting towards Bulgaria, carefully avoiding anything that might push her into renewed conflict with Greece or Turkey. In turn this would help to neutralize Romania and so force her to revert to her traditional Austrian mooring. Crucially, preparing a combination with Bulgaria required close cooperation with Germany: 'we must determine the aims of our Balkan policy together with Germany and harmonize our action with Germany's moves'. Tisza's *Denkschrift* was infused with a sense 'that we are passing through difficult times, [and] moving towards great events and dangers; but we need not give up hope of a successful fight against these dangers if we gather strength and prepare the development of affairs jointly with Germany'.[79]

Like most Magyar magnates, Tisza was a staunch supporter of the German alliance, as indeed he was an admirer of Bismarck.[80] Berlin's support for any action against Belgrade was thus necessary also to

---

[79] Memo. Tisza, 15 Mar. 1914, ÖUA VII, no. 9482; also H. Marczali, 'Papers of Count Tisza, 1914–1918', *AHR* XXIX, 2 (1924), 303–6; Fejtö, *Requiem*, 41–3; G. Vermes, *István Tisza: The Liberal Vision and Conservative Statecraft of a Magyar Nationalist* (New York, 1985), 211–2.

[80] See G. Vermes, 'The Impact of the Dual Alliance on the Magyars of the Austro-Hungarian Monarchy', *ECE/ECE* VII, 2 (1980), 317 and 322–4.

overcome the internal obstacles in Habsburg decision-making. That Tisza would not easily be moved was well understood at Vienna, as Franz Joseph's request that Berchtold arrange a meeting with the Hungarian premier underlined.[81] For his part, Tisza was influenced by the views of Baron István Burián von Rajecz, a career diplomat, one-time joint finance minister and now the Hungarian representative at the imperial court, who was his closest foreign policy adviser. Burián had consistently argued for developing closer relations with Bulgaria as a counterpoise to the one-sided dependence on Bucharest; and in the early summer of 1914 he still thought that some form of accommodation with Russia in south-eastern Europe was in the realm of the possible.[82]

This was very much the line that Tisza developed when he met with Berchtold in the afternoon of 30 June. He demanded a calm and measured response. Belgrade ought to be given time to demonstrate good behaviour: 'Further, it ought to be considered whether the international situation might not in future be developed in a more advantageous direction for the Monarchy.' In this context, he reverted to the notion that Bulgaria should become the pivot ('*Stützpunkt*') of Austria-Hungary's Balkan policy. Berchtold dismissed this scenario as hypothetical. Remaining passive now, he warned, would call into question the alliance-worthiness of Austria-Hungary for Bulgaria. He also deployed Conrad's argument: 'Once mobilized, we need to persevere. The army would not stomach a third mobilization [after 1912 and 1913] which did not lead to action.'[83]

No decision was arrived at at the meeting between the foreign minister and the Magyar premier, however. On the following day, 1 July, Tisza was received by the Emperor at Schönbrunn. The prime minister spoke out against Berchtold's idea of 'making the abominable deed of Sarajevo a pretext for settling scores with Serbia'. It would be 'a fatal mistake' to do so, and he refused to share responsibility for it – an implicit

---

[81] Berchtold, 'Die ersten Tage', in Hantsch, *Berchtold* II, 560; S. R. Williamson, 'Leopold Count Berchtold: The Man who Could have Prevented the Great War', G. Bischof, F. Plasser and P. Berger (eds.), *From Empire to Republic: Post-World War I Austria* (New Orleans, 2010), 30–1. There was an element of rivalry between the two men; rumour had it in April 1914 that Tisza would succeed Berchtold: *ibid.*, 25.

[82] Burián diary, 20 and 30 June 1914, I. Diószegi, 'Aussenminister Stephan Graf Burián. Biographie und Tagebuchstelle', *Annales universitatis scientiarum budapestinensis de Rolando Eötvös nominatae, Sectio historicorum* VIII (1966), 203–5; Vermes, *Tisza*, 219–20.

[83] Berchtold, 'Die ersten Tage', Hantsch, *Berchtold* II, 560–1; J.-P. Bled, *François-Joseph* (Paris, 1987), 667–8.

threat of resignation if Hungary's constitutional right to be consulted was ignored. If Berchtold's plan were acted upon, the Monarchy would be internationally isolated. It might 'unleash a great war under unpropitious circumstances', now that Romania was as good as lost and Bulgaria was exhausted from the latest round of fighting in the Balkans. Tisza returned to the idea of a fresh diplomatic initiative to pivot towards Sofia. There were two options: either combined Austro-German pressure to coerce Romania to remain wedded to the *Dreibund*, or a combination with Bulgaria to force Bucharest back into the fold. To a large extent this was the familiar Magyar scenario already outlined in Tisza's March memorandum, albeit now adapted to a dramatically altered context. Tisza emphasized the need for 'energetic action', though this was clearly not meant to be a unilateral strike against Serbia. Indeed, as before, he urged that Austro-Hungarian diplomacy seek closest coordination with Germany to 'secure active support for our Balkan policy'.[84] At the time, Tisza assumed that Wilhelm II would attend the archducal funeral, thus allowing for some form of funereal diplomacy to prepare a more active Balkan policy. This was not to come to pass.

Berlin counsels moderation

Following Tisza's meetings with Berchtold and the Emperor one thing was beyond doubt: there was divided counsel at Vienna. The Habsburg Empire had, in effect, two foreign ministers, each with very clear and distinctly different views. Whatever else would happen, Austria-Hungary would not move any time soon. The attitude of Germany thus acquired critical importance.

At this point, it was by no means certain how Berlin would react. Anti-Serb recriminations and pro-Habsburg protestations in the German press were only to be expected. But the initial response by German officials was more ambiguous. The situation was complicated by the fact that the German capital was practically deserted. Many of the leading civilian and military officials were absent from Berlin; some of them would remain so for much of July. The state secretary at the Auswärtiges Amt, Gottlieb von Jagow, was on his honeymoon in Switzerland until 7 July, and Wilhelm von Stumm, the influential head of the ministry's 'Political Department', was also on furlough. Moltke, the chief of staff, was on sick leave, taking

---

[84] Memo. Tisza, 1 July 1914, ÖUA VIII, no. 9978; M. Schiavon, *L'Autriche-Hongrie dans la première guerre mondiale* (Paris, 2011), 69–70.

the waters at the Bohemian spa town of Karlsbad (now Karlovy Vary) in search of relief from his acute liver disease. Chancellor Bethmann, meanwhile, was only intermittently present in the capital. What response there was thus came from middle-ranking officials, deputizing for department heads.

The day-to-day running of the Auswärtiges Amt lay in the hands of Arthur Zimmermann. A former state prosecutor from eastern Prussia and originally in the separate consular service, he was a career civil servant, bluff, jovial and popular with the foreign diplomats at Berlin, and not without ambitions. The United States ambassador, indeed, thought him 'one of the ablest men in Germany today'.[85] Zimmermann's initial comments to foreign representatives were circumspect. He was in no doubt, he told the British chargé d'affaires, Sir Horace Rumbold, that the murder was 'the outcome of a plot hatched by partisans of a greater Servia'. At the same time, he dissociated the authorities at Belgrade from 'this dreadful crime', but suggested that it was for them now openly to condemn the murder.[86]

This was also the line he took with other foreign diplomats. Zimmermann agreed with the Russian ambassador, Sergei Nikola'evich Sverbe'ev, that there could be no question of collective Serb responsibility for the assassination. Yet it was incumbent on the Serbian government to help to solve the crime, and if the trail led to Serbia proper, 'the guilty had to be subjected to severe punishment'.[87] Zimmermann stuck to this position and impressed upon the French chargé, Gustave Henri Benoît, Comte de Manneville, that he expected Belgrade to comply with any demands for prosecuting those implicated in the crime. If it acted otherwise, it would have against it the 'opinion of the whole civilized world'.[88] In conversation with Riccardo Bollati, the Italian ambassador, he confessed that 'the principal danger' of the current situation was that Austria-Hungary's 'legitimate indignation' might lead to 'very vigorous and provocative measures against the neighbouring kingdom'. It was 'continuous labour' for Berlin to prevent Vienna from taking 'compromising decisions'.[89]

---

[85] As quoted in B. Tuchman, *The Zimmermann Telegram* (London, 1958), 115.

[86] Rumbold to Grey (no. 265), 30 June 1914, *BD* XI, no. 22. Zimmermann was 'supposed to be rather against war': Rumbold to Drummond, 1 Aug. 1917, Rumbold MSS, Bodl., Ms. Rumbold dep. 22.

[87] Sverbe'ev to Sazonov (no. 44), 2 July 1914, *IBZI* IV, no. 62. The conversation took place on 30 June.

[88] Tel. Manneville to Viviani (no. 169), 4 July 1914, *DDF* (3) X, no. 472. Here, Zimmermann did not dissociate Belgrade from the plot. This may have been an omission by de Manneville; it may have reflected Berchtold's assertion that the 'threads ran together at Belgrade'.

[89] Tel. Bollati to San Giuliano (no. 5828/490), 30 June 1914, *DDI* (4) XII, no. 25.

There are no notes by Zimmermann on any of the conversations in those early days after Sarajevo, but the tone and arguments attributed to him in the reports by foreign diplomats are remarkably similar. Zimmermann, in fact, made much the same observation to the Habsburg envoy at Berlin, Count Ladislaus Szögyény-Marich. A desire for energetic steps against Serbia was understandable. The 'general sympathies of the whole civilized world', after all, were on the side of Austria-Hungary. And yet he emphasized the need for 'great caution' and warned 'against addressing humiliating demands to Serbia'.[90]

The reports by the envoys at Berlin of two of the smaller German states throw a revealing light on Zimmermann's thinking at that time. They are significant also because the chancellor had sought the under-secretary's advice during the week after Sarajevo. The Bavarian representative in the imperial capital, Count Hugo Lerchenfeld, sensed a degree of apprehension at the Wilhelmstrasse. If the ongoing murder investigations established any connection with persons close to the Serbian government, 'tensions may arise between Serbia and Austria-Hungary that would have considerable effect on the affairs of the entire Balkans'.[91] In reporting Zimmermann's views to the Dresden court, the Saxon envoy, Baron Ernst von Salza Lichtenau, was more explicit. The murdered Habsburg heir, the under-secretary explained, had been 'an uncertain factor' in Austro-Hungarian affairs, and his removal from the scene might have a stabilizing effect in the longer term. Zimmermann was by no means sanguine, however, about the more immediate future: 'The main difficulty for German policy was caused by the alliance with Austria-Hungary; but we could not now back off and had to ensure that the allied empire did not drive us into a too difficult situation.' This was a prescient observation. At one and the same time, it marked the continuity of German diplomacy since the Balkan wars, but accentuated the sharp break with previous policy that was to occur within a matter of days. For now, Zimmermann reiterated the observation already made to Sverbe'ev. Belgrade ought to show willingness to accommodate Austro-Hungarian demands. In that case all would be well, as Salza

[90] Tel. Szögyény to Berchtold (no. 236), 4 July 1914, ÖUA VIII, no. 10039; A. von Wegerer, *Der Ausbruch des Weltkrieges 1914* (2 vols., Hamburg, 1939) I, 129.

[91] Lerchenfeld to Hertling (no. 356), 29 June 1914, *BayD*, no. 2; see also L. Meyer-Arndt, *Die Julikrise 1914. Wie Deutschland in den Ersten Weltkrieg schlitterte* (Cologne, 2006), 16. As constituted in 1871, the German Empire was not a centralized state, but a federation of princes, with most of the state governments sending permanent envoys to the other German courts, in which roles they exercised a partly diplomatic and partly legislative function (in the *Bundesrat* or Federal Council); for an impression see H. von Lerchenfeld-Koefering, *Erinnerungen und Denkwürdigkeiten, 1843–1925* (Berlin, 2nd edn 1935), 176–80.

Lichtenau reported: 'At the Auswärtiges Amt they think that a war between Austria-Hungary and Serbia could thus be avoided.' If it could not, Greece and Bulgaria would enter the conflict, 'Russia would mobilize and a world war could no longer be prevented'. Even so, Zimmermann repeatedly stressed his conviction that there would be no Austro-Serb war. Moreover, neither France nor Russia was in a position to join a major military conflict. France's complicated domestic politics militated against it. As for Russia, Zimmermann observed that she 'rattles her sabre, but this only in order to obtain the promised 500 millions [Fr] from France'. Britain, meanwhile, was thoroughly pacific.[92]

Intrigues at the German embassy in Vienna

The initial German preference for moderation was also reflected in the advice proffered at Vienna by the German ambassador there, Baron Heinrich von Tschirschky. This Saxon nobleman, a former state secretary, was well connected at Berlin. Somewhat highly strung and nervous, he was nevertheless well-liked in the Habsburg capital, despite his marriage to the daughter of a Hungarian Jewish 'sugar baron', a considerable social handicap for any foreign ambassador at the conservative imperial court, dominated as it was by an exclusive aristocratic coterie.[93] In retrospect, indeed, the ambassador was one of the principal actors on the German side during the July crisis. His attitude towards Austria-Hungary was not free of ambivalence. He had often been plagued by doubts as to 'whether it is really worth it to tie ourselves to this creaking political entity and to continue the laborious effort of pulling it along'. On the other hand, the only logical alternative to the *Zweibund* alliance would be the partition of the Dual Monarchy, followed by the incorporation of its German-speaking (but Catholic) provinces in a Greater Germany – not an alluring prospect to the Protestant, Prussian-dominated Wilhelmine leadership. Yet Tschirschky was certain that if an attempt to consolidate 'the disparate forces' of Austria-Hungary failed, 'decomposition would advance swiftly and we

[92] Salza Lichtenau to Vitzthum (no. 1045, confidential), 2 July 1914, *DGB* no. 2.
[93] De Bunsen to Grey (no. 31, confidential), 13 Feb. 1914, TNA (PRO), FO 371/1899/6900; Lützow, *Im diplomatischen Dienst*, 219–20; L. Cecil, *The German Diplomatic Service, 1871–1914* (Princeton, NJ, 1976), 90–2; see also T. G. Otte, '"Outdoor Relief for the Aristocracy"?: European Nobility and Diplomacy, 1850–1914', M. Mösslang and T. Riotte (eds.), *The Diplomats' World: A Cultural History of Diplomacy, 1815–1914* (Oxford, 2008), 52.

would have to adapt our policy accordingly'.[94] In the face of such a prospect, even Conrad's idea of a preventive war seemed preferable.[95]

Tschirschky had committed the original sin of professional diplomacy – he had 'gone native' and identified himself completely with Austria-Hungary. For now, however, he counselled caution. At his first meeting with Berchtold after Sarajevo, on 30 June, he advised 'calmly, but emphatically and seriously', against any hasty action. Vienna had to take into consideration the interests of its ally, the 'general European situation' and 'the attitude of Italy and Romania in all questions relating to Serbia'.[96]

At the first official interview, on 2 July, Tschirschky stuck to this line. There was, however, an important qualification. He assured Berchtold of Germany's continued support in Balkan matters. On the foreign minister's observation that such support had been more apparent than real in the recent regional crises, the ambassador specified, as a private suggestion, the terms on which German assistance was to be had. Many an idea had emanated from Vienna, but never 'a clearly defined plan of action'. Berlin could only 'engage fully and wholly on our [Austria-Hungary's] behalf' on the basis of such a plan. It was all very well, Tschirschky observed, to wish 'to settle accounts with Serbia', but how far was Vienna prepared to go, and what did it intend to do after accounts had been settled?

These were pertinent questions. But German support was conditional on a second point, Tschirschky suggested. Relations with Italy and Romania had to be placed on a firmer footing. He explicitly warned against starting a war against Serbia without having received prior assurances of Italian and Romanian neutrality. Berchtold reacted with some irritation to this. It was for Germany to influence the government at Bucharest in the desired direction. As for an approach to Rome before a move against Serbia, this would only whet Italy's appetite for compensation, possibly in Albania or elsewhere along the Adriatic coast, which was anathema to Habsburg diplomacy.[97] If the interview had brought no clarity concerning Germany's likely stance, it had nevertheless underlined the need for a clear statement of intent to be communicated to Berlin.

After his interview with Berchtold, Tschirschky was received by the Emperor. The ambassador's observations to the monarch were couched

[94] Tschirschky to Jagow (private), 22 May 1914, *GP* XXXIX, no. 15732.
[95] See Conrad's notes on a conversation with Tschirschky, 16 Mar. 1914, Conrad, *Aus meiner Dienstzeit* III, 597.
[96] Tschirschky to Bethmann Hollweg, 30 June 1914, *DD* I, no. 7; min. Berchtold, 3 July 1914, *ÖUA* VIII, no. 10006.
[97] Daily report Berchtold, 3 July 1914, *ÖUA* VIII, no. 10006. The interview took place on 2 July. There is no corresponding report by Tschirschky.

in more reserved language than that used in his conversation with the foreign minister in the morning. In substance, however, there was little difference. Vienna could rest assured that it should 'find Germany resolutely behind the Monarchy as soon as it was a question of defending its vital interests. The decision whether and where such interests existed had to be left to Austria herself.' Yet he warned that 'moods and wishes' could not furnish a sound foundation for 'a responsible policy'. He emphasized that 'with every significant step the general political situation had to be considered and the likely attitude of the other Powers and states to be taken into account and the ground carefully to be prepared'.[98]

Tschirschky's statement to the Emperor and his minister was not without problems. It was certainly not entirely coherent. For all the repeated emphasis on the need for a carefully calibrated and circumspect response to Sarajevo, his assurance that it was for Vienna to define what constituted vital Habsburg interests, which would then be supported by Germany, contained the essence of the 'blank cheque' of 5 July. In proffering these 'private' suggestions, Tschirschky had acted off his own bat; he had not been authorized to make any such statement. The fact that he did not, contrary to established practice, report his conversation with Berchtold would tend to support this. Indeed, it seems unlikely that the German chancellor, technically the minister responsible for the Auswärtiges Amt, ever saw Tschirschky's despatch on his audience with Franz Joseph.[99]

A follow-up despatch later that same afternoon cast some further light on Tschirschky's analysis and helped to crystallize German concerns. The full consequences of the Archduke's murder, he suggested, could not yet be assessed. Franz Ferdinand's reform scheme had always aimed at creating a 'stable basis for an active foreign policy'. His removal from the scene would weaken the Germanic element in the Monarchy. The aged Emperor, 'who had never felt himself to be a German', was not likely to act decisively now. His heir-presumptive, the young Archduke Karl, lacked the necessary experience and was surrounded by an 'even by Austrian standards egregiously incompetent entourage'. Tschirschky thus arrived at the gloomy prognosis that in all likelihood Austria-Hungary would persist in her 'laissez faire and laissez aller' ways. And yet he had not given up hope entirely that a strong man might emerge: 'For, as things are, a strengthening

---

[98] Tschirschky to Bethmann Hollweg (no. 214, secret), 2 July 1914, *DD* I, no. 11.
[99] The file bears the note 'Personally answered by the under-secretary [Zimmermann]'. No such reply is extant. Possibly this is the letter Zimmermann claimed to have written to Tschirschky, but which was then mislaid in the office: see statement Zimmermann, *OGD* I, 31–2.

of the Monarchy would under all circumstances be more in our interest than its continued slow decline that must in the end lead to dissolution.'[100]

It is difficult to avoid the conclusion that Tschirschky was pursuing his own private, twin-track diplomacy. Possibly, he even thought that it was for him to stiffen Austria-Hungary's resolve. Having urged caution upon Vienna, and having intimated to Berchtold that Germany's stance was largely dependent on Vienna formulating a strategic plan, he then pressed the Habsburg government for immediate action. He did so through a backchannel to the Ballhausplatz in the person of Hugo Ganz, Vienna correspondent of the liberal-leaning *Frankfurter Zeitung* and a well-known confidant of the German embassy.

On 4 July Ganz appeared at the press department of the Ballhausplatz. He had come straight from Tschirschky, who had 'stated emphatically and repeatedly ... that Germany would support the Monarchy through thick and thin', whatever course of action Vienna might decide upon. For good measure, the ambassador had added, 'the sooner Austria-Hungary moved, the better. Yesterday would have been better than today, but today [is] better than tomorrow.' Tschirschky's message, transmitted through Ganz, did not fail to make a strong impression on Forgách and Berchtold, who passed the information to Tisza and the Emperor. Ganz's concluding observation, that 'one Great Power could not speak more openly to another than that', needs to be taken with the proverbial grains.[101] After all, Tschirschky's pressing for immediate action was not made by him personally, and so had plausible deniability. For on that same day Zimmermann had still warned Austria-Hungary against 'addressing humiliating demands to Serbia'.[102]

The Kaiser intervenes

Tschirschky was not alone in pressing Vienna to act with dispatch. As Zimmermann hinted to the Saxon representative at Berlin, some in the German military argued that war now, while Russia was not ready, would

---

[100] Tschirschky to Bethmann Hollweg (no. 213), 2 July 1914, PAAA Österreich 103, Band 7; also *JK* I, no. 10.

[101] Daily report Forgách (no. 3117), 4 July 1914, and mins. Forgách and Berchtold, *ÖUA* VIII, no. 10038. Intriguingly, Tschirschky reported to Berlin that an article in the *Frankfurter Zeitung*, 3 July 1914, urging 'calm and collectedness', would be misunderstood at Vienna: Tschirschky to Bethmann Hollweg, 4 July 1914, *DD* I, no. 14a.

[102] Tel. Szögyény to Berchtold (no. 236), 4 July 1914, *ÖUA* VIII, no. 10039.

be preferable to a later contest. Even so, the Saxon envoy was optimistic that the Kaiser 'would not let himself be seduced' by the siren calls of the war party.[103] That the volatile German monarch was liable to be pushed and pulled in different directions by competing influences at Berlin was nothing new. The Saxon minister's confidence in Wilhelm II's peaceable disposition, however, was somewhat misplaced. On 4 July, Tschirschky's despatch of 30 June, which reflected Berlin's official moderation, crossed the Kaiser's desk. Superlatives were that monarch's natural form of expression. Tone-deaf to nuances and colour-blind to the shades of grey that dominate political life, he was given to exuberant outbursts. He was incensed by the ambassador's words of warning to Berchtold:

> Who authorized him to do this? This is very stupid! [It] does not concern him as it is solely Austria's business what she wants to do. Later, if things go wrong, they will say Germany was not willing!! Tschirschky should stop this nonsense. The Serbs need to be sorted out [*mit den Serben muss aufgeräumt werden*], *and soon*.

On Tschirschky's reference to Austro-Hungarian demands for settling scores with Serbia, he commented: 'now or never'. The ambassador's suggestion that Vienna ought to consider the wider European situation, he dismissed as 'commonplace sentiments' ('*Binsenweisheiten*').[104]

The Kaiser's explosive eruption was to establish a harder line in German policy, with profound implications for the course of events in July 1914. What it did not do, however, was to influence Tschirschky's secret dual-track diplomacy in the Habsburg capital. By the time Wilhelm II caught sight of Tschirschky's first despatch, the ambassador had already urged Berchtold to define Austria-Hungary's objectives, and had already sent the journalist Ganz to the Ballhausplatz to urge it to make haste.[105]

---

[103] Salza Lichtenau to Vitzthum (no. 1045, confidential), 2 July 1914, *DGB* no. 2.

[104] Marginal comment Wilhelm II, 4 July 1914, *DD* I, no. 7 (original emphasis); F. Fischer, *Der Griff nach der Weltmacht. Die Kriegszielpolitik des kaiserlichen Deutschland, 1914–1918* (Düsseldorf, 3rd rev. edn, 1964), 61.

[105] For the view that Tschirschky was influenced by Wilhelm's outburst see Hantsch, *Berchtold* II, 566, and Clark, *Sleepwalkers*, 412. However, this is based on a misreading of the evidence. For one thing, Tschirschky's pressing for a definite Austrian programme was made on 2 July; for another the Kaiser did not see the despatch of 30 June until 4 July. Although his marginalia were undated, the date can be deduced from the Emperor's well-documented habit of reading and returning documents promptly. The despatch was returned to the Auswärtiges Amt on 4 July: *DD* I, no. 7 n.; also B. W. von Bülow, *Die Krisis. Die Grundlinien der diplomatischen Verhandlungen bei Kriegsausbruch* (Berlin, 3rd edn 1922), 44. Tschirschky was warned that his 'lukewarm attitude' ('*Lauheit*') was

Count Hoyos goes to Berlin

Although they could not know of the German Emperor's outburst, Austro-Hungarian officials appreciated that Wilhelm's stance would be vital to the success of their efforts to canvass German support. On 1 July, after the meetings between Berchtold and Tisza, and the latter and Emperor Franz Joseph, Alek Hoyos received a visit by yet another of Tschirschky's journalistic go-betweens, the writer and commentator Victor Naumann, who was well-connected in official circles at Berlin. The latter spoke in general terms of the danger posed by the Russian armaments programme, and hinted at the desirability of some sort of preventive war. In reply, Hoyos suggested that such an eventuality would not be unwelcome to Vienna, especially if Austria-Hungary were forced 'to do something against Serbia'. This was the opening that Naumann may well have been waiting for. It had become an 'existential question for the Monarchy that the crime [Sarajevo] was not left unpunished, but also that Serbia should be destroyed'. More significantly, he added that the German Emperor was 'aghast at the bloody deed of Sarajevo', and that 'if one spoke to him in the right manner ... he would give us every assurance and would this time persevere', even if it meant war. War now, he asserted, would be a 'liberating deed': 'Austria-Hungary would be lost as a monarchy and a Great Power if she did not exploit this moment.'[106]

No doubt, much of Naumann's exposition contained little more than could be gleaned from the better class of Berlin newspapers, but it concentrated Ballhausplatz thinking on the need to appeal to the German Emperor. This had become all the more pressing because, on 2 July, on the advice of Chancellor Bethmann, Wilhelm had decided against attending the funeral of the archducal couple in person, officially because of a 'slight indisposition' or because of 'lumbago', but in reality because of a rumour, reported by the German consul at Sarajevo, that a dozen assassins had been despatched from Belgrade to Vienna as part of a conspiracy to murder the Kaiser.[107] Until then, Austro-Hungarian officials had assumed that the

not welcome around 8 July, i.e. after Jagow's return to Berlin: see tel. Szögyény to Berchtold (no. 243), 8 July 1914, ÖUA VIII, no. 10127.

[106] Note Hoyos, 1 July 1914, ÖUA VIII, no. 9966; see also Naumann's memoirs, in which he portrays Hoyos in a more belligerent mood: *Dokumente und Aufzeichnungen* (Berlin, 1928), 6–7; Fischer, *Krieg der Illusionen*, 686.

[107] For the official justification see tel. Rumbold to Grey (no. 80), 2 July 1914, BD XI, no. 24, and de Manneville to Viviani (no. 391), 5 July 1914, DDF (3) X, no. 475. For the report on the alleged plot see tel. Eiswaldt to Auswärtiges Amt (no. 11), 1 July 1914, and tel. Bethmann Hollweg to Tschirschky (no. 107), 2 July 1914, DD I, nos. 6a and b; also statement Eiswaldt, OGD I, no. 17.

Kaiser's presence in Vienna would furnish an opportunity to win German assurances of support for some action in the Balkans.[108]

Some form of diplomatic mission to Berlin, then, was necessary, one that involved a direct appeal to the Kaiser. Its preparation was left in Berchtold's hands, and he, in turn, instructed Hoyos, his *chef de cabinet*, to draft a personal letter from Franz Joseph to Wilhelm II, along with a lengthy memorandum on Austria-Hungary's position in the Balkans. Both documents were originally meant to be despatched, in the normal way, by diplomatic messenger. But late on Saturday, 4 July, the embassy at Berlin was informed that Hoyos would deliver them personally to Berlin, where they were to be handed to the Kaiser and the chancellor by ambassador Szögyény, while Hoyos himself was to call on the Auswärtiges Amt.[109]

The selection of Hoyos for the secret mission to Berlin was in part dictated by his position at the Ballhausplatz. As the head of the foreign minister's private office he was in daily contact with Berchtold and so cognizant of his concerns and thinking. Although still relatively young – he had only just turned thirty-eight – he was an experienced official who had established for himself a position of influence. The son of a Habsburg ambassador to France, he followed family tradition and entered the diplomatic service himself. After the obligatory postings abroad, which included Paris, Belgrade and Berlin, he was recalled to the Ballhausplatz in 1911. His sister having married into the Bismarck dynasty, he had excellent contacts at Berlin, even though the Wilhelmstrasse suspected his reliability on account of his English mother (a Whitehead of torpedo fame) and his French wife. Hoyos knew Zimmermann well – they had first met in 1901 in northern China, at Tientsin, where Zimmermann had been vice-consul – and he was friendly with Dietrich von Bethmann Hollweg, a cousin of the chancellor, then posted to the German embassy at Vienna. Such contacts made Hoyos the ideal choice for the confidential exchanges with the German ally. He had, in fact, been sent on such a mission to Berlin before, during the Bosnian annexation crisis; and he was convinced that, as in 1908–9, German support was to be had. Indeed, it was Hoyos himself who suggested to Berchtold the idea of another mission.[110]

---

[108] See e.g. memo. Tisza, 1 July 1914, *ÖUA* VIII, no. 9979.

[109] Tel. Berchtold to Szögyény (no. 212), 4 July 1914, *ibid.*, no. 10037.

[110] F. Fellner, 'Die Mission "Hoyos"', in F. Fellner, *Vom Dreibund zum Völkerbund. Studien zur Geschichte der internationalen Beziehungen, 1882–1919*, ed. H. Maschl and B. Mazohl-Wallering (Munich, 1994), 124–6; for a pen portrait see Cormons, *Schicksale*, 124.

From the minister's perspective as well, Hoyos was the right man for this task. His *chef de cabinet* was well-known for his hawkish views, and some historians have suggested that he, along with Forgách and Szápáry, exercised a strong influence over the weak-willed Berchtold.[111] Whatever his hesitations during earlier crises, as seen, Berchtold had already made up his mind in favour of some form of coercive action immediately after Sarajevo. Indeed, his oral instructions to Hoyos were unequivocal on this point. He was to explain to Szögyény that 'the moment had come to settle the score with Serbia'. Certain guarantees of good conduct would be demanded from Serbia. If these were rejected, 'a military action would be contemplated'. Before this could be done, however, the attitude of Berlin had to be established.[112] In choosing the hawk Hoyos, he despatched to Berlin one of the most articulate advocates of aggressive action against Serbia. Berchtold could thus be sure that Berlin would receive the assurances of Austria-Hungary's determination to act that Tschirschky had suggested would be necessary in order to secure German assistance. Sending Hoyos on a personal mission also had two pleasing side effects. Firstly, it helped to keep Szögyény in line; although deeply committed to the alliance with Germany and a reliable professional, the 73-year-old ambassador, who had represented his Emperor at Berlin since 1892, was perhaps not the man to convey firmness of purpose and intent. Secondly, using an informal channel reduced the risk of Tisza interfering in the diplomatic process. Hoyos's personal preference for a preventive strike is beyond doubt. He had taken an increasingly gloomy view of Habsburg prospects in the Balkans.[113] And yet, if Lützow is to be believed, there was a certain insouciance in Hoyos's militancy: 'What could possibly happen to us? If it goes badly, then we will lose Bosnia and a piece of Eastern Galicia!'[114]

Indeed, the two documents he prepared for the mission to Berlin bore the hallmark of a blasé belligerence. Both leave an impression of studied vagueness. Neither offered a clear perspective, let alone a clearly defined policy programme. However the two documents were not a random assembly of baroque metaphors and empty rhetorical devices, as a casual glance might suggest. Hoyos's memorandum was, in essence, Matscheko's *Denkschrift* composed a few days before Sarajevo. Then it

---

[111] *Inter alios* Verosta, *Theorie und Realität*, 391; J. von Szilassy, *Der Untergang der Donau-Monarchie. Diplomatische Erinnerungen* (Berlin, 1921), 253–4.
[112] Berchtold, 'Mission Hoyos', 57, Hantsch, *Berchtold* II, 573.
[113] See, e.g., Redlich diary, 8 Jan. 1914, *Tagebuch* II, 214.
[114] Lützow, *Im diplomatischen Dienst*, 219. Lützow merely referred to him as Berchtold's 'intimate adviser', but that was as good as naming him.

had been intended as preparation for a more decisive diplomatic initiative in the Balkans. Now, in its redrafted form – the third revision – it was to justify the use of force against Serbia, except that it did not do so unequivocally.

The Hoyos memorandum developed the same meandering account of the increasingly beleaguered position of the Habsburg Empire in the Balkans as found in Matscheko's original draft. It emphasized repeatedly the deleterious effect of the 'great tremors of the last two years' on the *Dreibund* as a whole. While the alliance had steadily worked towards conservative and defensive ends, France and Russia pursued offensive aims in the region. Moreover, the memorandum alleged that Paris and St Petersburg were actively engaged in an attempt to forge a renewed league of the Balkan states. Such a combination 'could only be poised against Austria-Hungary and could only be brought about on the basis of a programme that, in the last consequence, offered its members the prospect of territorial expansion at the expense of the territorial integrity of the Monarchy and through the gradual moving of frontiers from East to West'.

The main emphasis of the Hoyos memorandum, however, was on the cooling and increasingly strained relations with Romania. Whereas Matscheko's draft had envisaged a firm policy towards Bucharest, tempered by conciliation, the revised document wrote off Romania as a potential ally: 'A categorical *aut-aut* [either or] on the part of the Monarchy could thus only lead to an open breach.' The original *Denkschrift* had developed a two-pronged Austro-German move, with German pressure intended to bring Bucharest to its senses. There was nothing left of this in the Hoyos memorandum. On the contrary, the likely result of German efforts in parallel with a Habsburg initiative was judged to be 'likewise doubtful'. Therefore, it was practically impossible 'to develop the alliance with Romania so reliably and durably that it might furnish the pivot of Austria-Hungary's Balkan policy'.

The consequences of this shift in Vienna's position were far-reaching, but they were not made explicit in the document. In Matscheko's memorandum, and also in earlier plans during the spring of 1914, a rapprochement with Romania was meant to prepare a rapprochement with Serbia, using Bucharest as an intermediary.[115] This was no longer contemplated. Both Matscheko's original and the revised Hoyos version dealt at length with the military aspects of Austria-Hungary's Romanian problem. There was an important difference, however. The pre-Sarajevo memorandum had stressed the strategic significance of Romania in the event of an Austro-Russian war in order to underscore the urgent need for a fresh

---

[115] For this consideration see memo. Flotow, May 1914, ÖUA VIII, no. 9627.

approach to the south-eastern neighbour. By contrast, while Hoyos incorporated some of the original sections dealing with the military dimension of the problem, he rearranged the sequential order so that the matter of Romania's likely attitude to a conflict in the east was now discussed after the hint that the existing alliance with Romania was practically defunct. Instead, the revised Hoyos memorandum suggested re-orientating Habsburg policy towards Bulgaria, Serbia's implacable enemy, without, however, stating that Romania was irrevocably lost.

With a view to the German position, many of the relevant comments in the Matscheko version were given a sharper edge. While the former had admitted that the Balkans were of secondary importance to Berlin, no such qualifying admission was made in the Hoyos memorandum. Russia's armaments programme, it asserted, was aimed more against Germany than against Austria-Hungary. The realization of Russia's expansionist aims was at the expense of Germany's interests and would therefore 'have to meet with the latter's inescapable resistance'. Russia's 'manifest encircling tendencies' against the Habsburg Empire were also aimed at making it impossible for Germany to resist 'those ultimate aims of Russia and her political and economic supremacy'. In the draft version there was also a reference to French revanchism.

If the Hoyos memorandum lacked the inner coherence of Matscheko's *Denkschrift*, it was not without its own logic. But whereas the latter developed a longer-term perspective, the final version was clearly intended for the here and now. It left unanswered the question of the Monarchy's future relations with Romania. But the implied move away from reconciliation with Bucharest and the suggested pivoting towards Bulgaria implied a firmly anti-Serb policy. Any doubts on that score were removed by the postscript, added, it was stated, after Sarajevo: 'The full implications of the shameless murder can scarcely be judged today. But it has at least produced incontestable proof, if such were still needed, of the irreconcilable nature of the antagonism between the Monarchy and Serbia as much as of the danger and intensity of the reckless pan-Serb movement.' Vienna had demonstrated goodwill and forbearance in the past, but had met with nothing but the 'obdurate, irreconcilable and aggressive hostility of Serbia'. Under these circumstances, the memorandum concluded with more pathos than elegance, 'necessity demands all the more peremptorily of the Monarchy that it tears asunder the threads which its enemies are weaving together as a net above its head'.[116]

---

[116] Memo. [Hoyos], n.d. [*c*. 1 July 1914], *ibid.*, no. 9984. The revised draft, with amendments in Matscheko's and Hoyos's hands, is in HHStA, PA I/1091; for further insights see M. B. A. Petersson, 'Das österreichisch-ungarische Memorandum an Deutschland vom 5. Juli 1914', *Scandia* xxx (1964), 138–90.

Hoyos's memorandum contained a surfeit of pomp, pathos and purple prose, of the kind which perhaps only the Ballhausplatz was capable of producing. But it did not lack its own logic; and its implications were clear. Any conceivable doubt as to what these were was removed by Franz Joseph's private letter to Wilhelm II that accompanied the memorandum. Of the two documents this was the more important one. Not only was it a direct appeal to monarchical solidarity – and a not-so-subtle attempt at emotional effect – it could also confidently be expected that the Kaiser would pay greater attention to it than to the long and somewhat dense *Denkschrift*. Having dwelt on the fate of his 'poor nephew' and having praised Wilhelm as his one 'true, reliable friend', Franz Joseph asserted that the assassination was a direct consequence of a pan-Slav agitation 'whose sole aim is the weakening of the *Dreibund* and the smashing of my empire'. Sarajevo was part of 'a well organized conspiracy, the threads of which extend to Belgrade'. Although the Emperor was careful not to accuse the Serbian government of complicity in the murder, he certainly implied as much. The present situation, therefore, was 'a standing menace to my dynasty and my countries'. The Emperor's letter dwelt at some length on the now more distant relations with Romania before returning to the Serbian problem. Austro-Hungarian policy had in future to work towards 'the isolation and diminution of Serbia'. To that end, a rapprochement with Bulgaria was desirable. Only 'if Serbia, which is currently the pivot of pan-Slav politics, is neutralized as a factor of political power in the Balkans' would Austria-Hungary be safe and could the region be reorganized 'under the patronage of the *Dreibund*'. Franz Joseph concluded with a direct appeal to the Kaiser that left no doubt about the direction of Austro-Hungarian policy: 'After the latest terrible events you, too, will be convinced that there can be no reconciliation of the antagonism that separates us from Serbia, and that the conservative policy pursued by all European monarchs will be imperilled for as long as this furnace of criminal agitation at Belgrade carries on unpunished.'[117]

If the two documents lacked precision as to the nature of the planned next steps, they could leave no doubt in their recipient's mind that they were meant to frame the case for war. In terms of the internal dynamics of the Habsburg leadership, moreover, by including the idea of rebalancing Austro-Hungarian policy towards Bulgaria, the July memorandum went some way towards meeting Tisza's concerns. The difference, of course, was that the Magyar leader hoped to use an Austro-Bulgarian

---

[117] Franz Joseph to Wilhelm II, n.d. [2 July 1914], ÖUA VIII, no. 9984 and *DD* I, no. 13; Bled, *François-Joseph*, 668–9.

combination to contain Serbia, while the Ballhausplatz viewed it as part of a war strategy aimed at the Serbian neighbour.

Szögyény and Hoyos perform a double act

The German Kaiser's hawkish comments on Tschirschky's earlier counsel of moderation guaranteed that Hoyos would meet with a sympathetic reaction at Berlin, though he himself could not have known it as he travelled north on the night express from Vienna. When he arrived in the early hours of Sunday, 5 July, the German capital was practically deserted. The chancellor had returned to his Hohenfinow country estate on the previous day, and Wilhelm II himself was to depart for his long-planned yachting trip to the Norwegian fjords on the following day. Any audience with the Kaiser, then, had to be arranged for that same day, as had already been requested by Szögyény.

On Hoyos's arrival the seasoned Habsburg ambassador received his instructions from Berchtold's emissary before setting off for Potsdam. At 11.30 a.m., Hoyos, accompanied by Franz von Haymerle, a counsellor at the Berlin embassy, went to the Auswärtiges Amt to call upon Zimmermann, his old acquaintance from their days in China. The Count treated Zimmermann by no means as an equal. A sense of aristocratic superiority over the bourgeois lawyer and boisterous '*Kraftmensch*' was one factor; Zimmermann's lowly professional origins in the consular service may have been another.[118] Whatever his social disdain for the middle-class bureaucrat, and whatever textual ambiguities may have been left in the two documents, copies of which he presented to Zimmermann, Hoyos made Vienna's intentions abundantly clear. In the course of their conversation, he suggested 'a surprise attack against Serbia without prior diplomatic action' as the 'right modus procedendi'. Austria-Hungary 'had to strike and present Europe with a fait accompli. In Austria a complete partition of Serbia was contemplated.'[119]

Unfortunately for the historian, neither man made a record of the conversation at the time. What documentary evidence exists is of a later date and thus liable to have been influenced by subsequent events. The evidence, however, agrees on one point: that Hoyos advocated military

[118] Hoyos noted that the under-secretary was no proper diplomat: see A. von Hoyos, 'Meine Mission', Fellner, 'Mission "Hoyos"', 137.
[119] Berchtold, 'Mission Hoyos', 62, Hantsch, *Berchtold* II, 572. This was later confirmed by Hoyos: see K. Jagow, 'Der Potsdamer Kronrat. Geschichte und Legende', *Süddeutsche Monatshefte* XI, 25 (Aug. 1928), 782.

action. In 1919, Zimmermann testified before a parliamentary enquiry that Berchtold's emissary had explained that on this occasion Austria-Hungary 'was going to act energetically on the Serb question. According to his view, Serbia must be destroyed.'[120] Berchtold later commented on this as 'a regrettable extempore by my otherwise reliable *chef de cabinet*', with the implication that Hoyos had expressed merely his personal views and that he had not been authorized.[121] No doubt, Hoyos had aired his own opinion. But the foreign minister protested too much. For, as seen earlier, he himself had fastened upon a military solution as soon as the news of Sarajevo broke.

There is also some uncertainty as to Zimmermann's reaction. According to his post-war testimony, he replied to Hoyos's forthright statement 'I, too, considered an energetic communication to Serbia ... a matter of course in view of the provocation'. The other Powers would also respond sympathetically 'considering the revolting character of the deed at Sarajevo'.[122] Zimmermann's deposition did not elucidate the shape that such 'energetic communication' might take; nor did he touch on another aspect of Hoyos's statement. As Berchtold's aide later recollected, he had emphasized Austria-Hungary's determination to act 'even at the risk of a war with Russia', and that Vienna appreciated 'that such a policy might bring about a world war'.[123] He also recalled that, bearing in mind Tschirschky's advice that Vienna needed to present a firm and definite plan, he had explained to the under-secretary that, 'once we had beaten Serbia, we intended to partition her territory among Austria-Hungary, Bulgaria, and Albania. Zimmermann replied with a smile of satisfaction that this was a question concerning only ourselves and that he would raise no objections.'[124] Zimmermann further stated that there was a '90% probability of a European war, if you [Austria-Hungary] took steps against Serbia'.[125]

It is not at all clear whether Zimmermann really ventured such a prognosis. If he did, it was not grounded in any facts. As will be seen, no serious attempt was made at Berlin to assess the broader consequences of an escalating Balkan crisis. A competent, conscientious and diligent administrator, Zimmermann had nevertheless a reputation for shooting from the

[120] Statement Zimmermann, *OGD* I, 32.
[121] Berchtold, 'Mission Hoyos', 62, Hantsch, *Berchtold* II, 572.
[122] Statement Zimmermann, *OGD* I, 32.
[123] Hoyos to Mérey, 20 July 1917, Nachlass Mérey, HHStA Karton 10; repr. in 'Der Brief des Grafen Hoyos an den ehemaligen k.u.k. Botschafter in Rom, Graf Mérey', *BMH* x, 1 (1932), 66.
[124] Hoyos interview, Nov. 1933, L. Albertini, *The Origins of the War of 1914* (3 vols., London, 1953) II, 144.
[125] Hoyos, 'Meine Mission', Fellner, 'Mission "Hoyos"', 137.

lip. Indeed, Jagow later commented that on occasions 'Zimmermann did not know what he said'.[126] What is clear, however, is that Zimmermann, along with other senior officials at Berlin, was left under the impression that Austria-Hungary would act without delay. On that assumption, any military conflict was likely to remain confined to the two belligerents.[127]

Whatever Zimmermann may or may not have said, the undersecretary's statements were at best suggestive of the views generally held in Berlin circles at that moment. Far more significant for the course of events was Szögyény's private audience with Wilhelm II at the Neues Palais, Frederick the Great's opulent, domed late-Baroque pile in the park at Potsdam, at 1 p.m. on that same day. The aged Habsburg envoy, with his amiable eccentricity, exotic Magyar costume and heavily accented German, formed a striking contrast to Berchtold's elegant, fluent and belligerent aide Hoyos. Yet underneath that colourful and guileless exterior there was a shrewd and intelligent diplomatic professional. Indeed, Szögyény occupied a special position at Berlin. Well-connected in German official circles, and well-liked by his fellow foreign representatives, the doyen of Berlin's diplomatic corps was considered to be one of the best informed yet most discreet ambassadors there. He was tolerant of the German monarch's many personal foibles. If anything, he played up to them and submitted to being teased as 'my gypsy' or being made the butt of the Kaiser's invariably appalling practical jokes.[128] For his part, Wilhelm II liked the harmless Hungarian, and he trusted him. And with his seeming simplicity and naïveté, Szögyény was better placed than Hoyos to accomplish the object of his mission.

The Kaiser received the ambassador at the Neues Palais, where he had spent a rainy Sunday morning, after the obligatory early morning service, examining the latest works by Georg Schöbel, a historical genre painter.[129] The interview commenced shortly before 1 p.m., and Szögyény handed to the Emperor Franz Joseph's letter and the accompanying memorandum. No-one else was present at this first encounter. Neither the chancellor nor a representative of the Auswärtiges Amt were on hand to offer advice or guidance, though Bethmann Hollweg had been ordered to attend later in the evening. In some respects, it was typical of the chaotic and

---

[126] G. von Jagow, 'Zimmermann', unpubl. MS, Nachlass Jagow, TNA (PRO), GFM 25/3.

[127] Zimmermann to Albertini, 17 June 1938, Albertini, *Origins* II, 145.

[128] Goschen diary, 19 Aug. 1911, C. H. D. Howard (ed.), *The Diary of Edward Goschen, 1900–1914* (London, 1980), 243; F. Kern, *Skizzen zum Kriegsausbruch im Jahre 1914*, ed. H. Hallmann (Darmstadt, 1968), 60–1.

[129] Diary Aide-de-Camp Major von Hirschfeld, 5 July 1914, Jagow, 'Kronrat', 780–1.

disjointed Byzantinism at the imperial court that none of the relevant ministers or officials were present.[130] At Berlin, many vied for influence; few, however, were prepared to accept responsibility. At another level, the interview would determine not only the course of events during July 1914 but, arguably, the shape of the twentieth century.

Wilhelm II studied both documents 'with the greatest attention', though how closely he read the twenty-seven-page *Denkschrift* can only be speculated. His initial comments were brief and general. A 'serious action' against Serbia was only to be expected, he conceded, but warned that the plans outlined in the two communications from Vienna contained the risk of 'a serious European complication'. He could therefore give 'no definite answer' until he had consulted with the chancellor. The Kaiser then invited Szögyény to join him at the déjeuner laid on next door.[131]

So far, so responsible – his outburst on the previous evening about Tschirschky notwithstanding, Wilhelm II's reply to Szögyény was as cautious as the ambassador and Zimmermann had been. There were some ten persons gathered around the luncheon table, and it seems unlikely that Sarajevo and matters of state were discussed.[132] After lunch, Szögyény returned to the charge and impressed upon the Kaiser the 'severity of the situation'. From Wilhelm's response, it may be deduced that the 'gypsy' pushed the person of his imperial master into the foreground and made much of the monarchical principle. Austria-Hungary, the Kaiser assured him, could count on Germany's full support. He reiterated that he would have to consult with Bethmann Hollweg, but explained that the chancellor would 'completely agree with his views'. This would be especially the case in so far as any move against Serbia was concerned. In his view, however, Austria-Hungary 'should not wait with this action'. St Petersburg was likely to be hostile, 'but he had been prepared for it, and were it to come to a war between Austria-Hungary and Russia, we might be convinced that Germany would stand by us with the tried loyalty of an ally'. As for Russia's attitude, the Kaiser was confident that, 'as things stand today, she was in no way prepared for war, and would surely think carefully whether to resort to force'. He noted that, given the ongoing anti-Habsburg agitation in the Balkans, even Emperor Franz Joseph, 'with his renowned love of peace', would find it difficult not to move against Serbia.

---

[130] For authoritative examinations see J. C. G. Röhl, *The Kaiser and his Court: Wilhelm II and the Government of Germany* (Cambridge, 1996), and I. V. Hull, *The Entourage of Kaiser Wilhelm II* (Cambridge, 1982).

[131] Tel. Szögyény to Berchtold (no. 237, strictly secret), 5 July 1914, ÖUA VIII, no. 10058. The two documents are also in *DD* I, nos. 13 and 14.

[132] Diary *Hoffurier*, 5 July 1914, in Jagow, 'Kronrat', 781.

Significantly, he added that 'if we [Austria-Hungary] had really recognized the necessity of a military action against Serbia, he would regret it if we failed to exploit the current, for us so advantageous moment'. Regarding the scheme of a reorientation of Habsburg diplomacy in the Balkans towards Bulgaria, the Kaiser expressed some reservations, largely on account of his suspicions of the mercurial King Ferdinand of Bulgaria. Even so, he did not reject the Bulgarian option, provided that any arrangement with Sofia did not entail a poise against Romania.[133]

The ambassador had achieved more than he could possibly have hoped for. Indeed, it was something of a major diplomatic triumph, albeit one that had made liberal use of *léger de main* in pursuit of undiplomatic ends, and one that was to have appalling consequences. For one thing, Szögyény had left the German monarch under the impression that the Habsburg leadership was united in its determination to strike against Belgrade, when in reality nothing could have been further from the truth. Given that, prior to his present post at Berlin, Szögyény had been the Hungarian minister *ad latere*, i.e. the Magyar representative at the Vienna court, and given his overtly Magyar public persona at Berlin, his sin of omission is even greater. But his earnest post-prandial representation on the 'severity of the situation' had also enticed the Kaiser to commit Germany to Austria-Hungary without any conditions. It is true that ever since succeeding to the throne in 1888, Wilhelm II had been wont to affirm his personal loyalty to the *Zweibund* ally in Vienna in invariably demonstrative language.[134] In practice, however, Berlin had tended to restrain Austria-Hungary, most recently during the Austro-Serbian crises in 1913. If the Kaiser intimated any concerns about possible European complications before lunch, there is no evidence of them afterwards.

The chancellor confirms the 'blank cheque'

Later that same day, at 5 p.m., the Kaiser met with a small number of his military entourage in the gardens of the palace. The war minister, General Erich von Falkenhayn, had been ordered by telephone to attend at the Neues Palais, where he found General Hans von Plessen, the Kaiser's adjutant-general, and General Moriz Baron von Lyncker, the chief of his

---

[133] Tel. Szögyény to Berchtold (no. 237, strictly secret), 5 July 1914, ÖUA VIII, no. 10058; Fischer, *Krieg der Illusionen*, 691–2.

[134] See, e.g., W. J. Mommsen, 'Kaiser Wilhelm II and German Politics', *JCH* xxv, 2–3 (1990), 309–10; H. Afflerbach, *Der Dreibund. Europäische Grossmacht- und Allianz-politik vor dem Ersten Weltkrieg* (Vienna, 2002), 366.

military cabinet, already gathered. Wilhelm then read out excerpts from the two documents transmitted by Szögyény. The assembled officers were left under the impression that 'the Aus[trians] were preparing for a war against Serbia'. As Plessen recorded in his diary: 'Here the view prevails that the sooner the Austrians strike against Serbia, the better, and that the Russians – although friends of Serbia – would not join in after all.'[135]

One hour later, at 6 p.m., Wilhelm received Bethmann Hollweg and Zimmermann in the park of the Neues Palais. The chancellor had returned from his country estate some three hours earlier, and was at once briefed by the acting head of the Auswärtiges Amt about Hoyos's communications. There is no record of their meeting at the chancellery or their conversation en route to Potsdam. At the Neues Palais they experienced once more what befell so many officials commanded to report to the Kaiser to offer advice – they had matters expounded to them. After Bethmann had briefly sketched an outline of the international situation, the monarch 'spoke without waiting to hear the Chancellor's propositions'. He emphasized 'quite calmly and positively' the imperilled position of Austria-Hungary in the Balkans, and approved of the idea of an Austro-Bulgarian compact as long as the Romanian alliance was maintained intact. The Kaiser concluded: 'Whatever the measures taken by Austria-Hungary against Serbia as a result of the Serajevo crime might demand, we should refrain from all suggestions or incitement in this regard. It was Austria's affair for her to settle in her own way, and it was not our business.'[136]

Germany would not abandon Austria-Hungary in her hour of need: The 'undiminished preservation of Austria' was a vital German interest. Significantly, both Bethmann and the under-secretary concurred with the Kaiser's views, especially with his observation that 'we should refrain from direct suggestions and advice, all the more as we should work with all our means against the danger that the Austro-Serb quarrel might escalate into an international conflict'.[137]

With that the two men were dismissed, and the Kaiser set off for the Norwegian fjords early the next morning.[138] Later that afternoon, the

[135] Plessen diary, 5 July 1914, *DGB*, 14; diary Hirschfeld, 5 July 1914, Jagow, 'Kronrat', 781 and 784; also statement Falkenhayn, *OGB* I, no. 17; H. Afflerbach, *Falkenhayn. Politisches Denken und Handeln im Kaiserreich* (Munich, 1994), 151.

[136] Statement Zimmermann, *OGD* I, no. 3.

[137] T. von Bethmann Hollweg, *Betrachtungen zum Weltkriege* (2 vols., Berlin, 1919) I, 134–5. The statements by Zimmermann and Bethmann on the 5 July meeting are remarkably similar and are suggestive of a degree of later collusion; see also K. H. Jarausch, *The Enigmatic Chancellor: Bethmann Hollweg and the Hubris of Imperial Germany* (New Haven, CT, 1973), 155–6.

[138] Diary *Hoffurier*, 6 July 1914, Jagow, 'Kronrat', 786.

chancellor received Szögyény and Hoyos at the chancellor's palais in the Wilhelmstrasse, with Zimmermann in attendance. In essence, Bethmann ratified the commitment made by his monarch; he gave it an official imprimatur. He dwelt on the dangers for Austria-Hungary and the *Dreibund* arising out of Russia's Balkan intrigues. He accepted that Bulgaria's eventual adhesion to the triplice had now become desirable, but cautioned against alienating Romania. German diplomacy would make the necessary supportive noises. He then turned to the matter of Austro-Serb relations. It was for Vienna to judge what needed to be done to place them on a new footing. But whatever course of action was decided upon, 'we could count upon it with confidence that Germany would stand by us as an ally and a friend of the Monarchy'. Bethmann's explanations left Szögyény in no doubt: he wired to the Ballhausplatz that both chancellor and Kaiser favoured 'an immediate intervention by us against Serbia as the most radical and the best solution of our difficulties in the Balkans'. Indeed, Bethmann had pressed the point that, viewed from an international perspective, 'the present moment [was] more advantageous than a later one'. Neither Italy nor Romania ought to be alerted to the planned move against Serbia, he urged, before returning to the subject of Bulgaria, *Dreibund* relations and the future of Albania.[139]

Leaving aside the fact that Szögyény's report was composed by Hoyos, who, in line with his and Berchtold's wishes, no doubt sharpened Bethmann's exposition, the chancellor's statement was nevertheless peculiar. Only a small portion of the conversation dealt with the Serbian question, arguably the most pressing problem and the reason for Hoyos's secret mission to Berlin. The issue was thus framed in a narrow Balkan context. Possible international complications were not touched upon. No mention was made of Russia, let alone any of the other Powers. And yet, there could be no doubt that the German chancellor had confirmed the commitment Szögyény had elicited from the Kaiser.[140] The precise nature of the contemplated action was a matter for Vienna to determine, Bethmann Hollweg confirmed. But 'Kaiser Franz Joseph could rest assured that H[is] M[ajesty, Kaiser Wilhelm II] would stand loyally by Austria-Hungary in accordance with his duties as an ally and in old friendship'.[141]

[139] Tel. Szögyény to Berchtold (no. 239), 6 July 1914, ÖUA VIII, no. 10076; statement Zimmermann, OGD I, no. 17.

[140] For Hoyos's authorship of the telegram see Albertini, *Origins* II, 147–8; on the 'oddities' of Bethmann's explanations see also Clark, *Sleepwalkers*, 415.

[141] Tel. Bethmann to Tschirschky (no. 113), 6 July 1914, DD I, no. 15. Intriguingly, the German summary of the conversation also focused primarily on the relations with

This, then, was the so-called 'blank cheque'. Implicit in the earlier military convention between Moltke, Conrad and Schemua, the Habsburg government had so far been reluctant to ask for it to be endorsed by the civilian leadership at Berlin. This had now been done, and it was for Austria-Hungary to fill in the cheque. Germany had surrendered her ability to restrain Vienna; the direction and pace of developments would now be determined there.

The motives behind the 'blank cheque' have been the subject of an extensive and often heated debate, which started almost as soon as the First World War broke out. To this day, the matter remains controversial, the extant evidence being partial at best, and so open to divergent interpretations. Most analyses of German decision-making in July 1914, indeed, are problematic to varying degrees. One such interpretation is the argument that, in committing to Austria-Hungary, Berlin had somehow exceeded what Vienna had asked for; and that it had, in fact, pushed its ally into war. Somewhat ironically, the argument was first made by Hoyos three years into the war. Berlin, he then opined, had been at liberty 'to say "No" to us and stop us from making a move against Serbia; we might have felt aggrieved but the German government would certainly not have been influenced by our good or bad mood'.[142] The argument, albeit somewhat toned down and more nuanced, has reverberated down the decades since then.[143]

As was seen earlier, Szögyény's skilful handling of the Kaiser undoubtedly elicited a more unconditional promise than could reasonably have been expected, given Germany's cautious stance during the recent Balkan crises. But neither the two documents presented on that occasion nor Hoyos's hawkish *ex tempore* at the Wilhelmstrasse left much room for doubt. Vienna wanted war, and the German leadership understood as much. They could have restrained the Austrians, and chose not to do so. But certainly they did not frogmarch a reluctant Habsburg Empire to war.

This, then, raises the question of how the Germans assessed the situation in the aftermath of Sarajevo and the likely international ramifications. Some scholars have argued that Berlin took the 'calculated risk' of an Austro-Serb quarrel in the Balkans escalating into a continental war; and

---

Bulgaria and Romania. Only the concluding paragraph dealt with Serbia, six out of twenty-four lines of printed text.

[142] Hoyos to Mérey, 20 July 1917, Nachlass Mérey, HHStA Karton 10; see also A. von Hoyos, *Der deutsch-englische Gegensatz und sein Einfluss auf die Balkanpolitik Österreich-Ungarns* (Berlin and Leipzig, 1922), 81–6, a somewhat ineffectual effort.

[143] E.g. Albertini, *Origins* II, 79–80; implicit also in F. Fellner, 'Austria-Hungary', K. M. Wilson (ed.), *Decisions for War 1914* (London, 1995), 9–26.

that the aim of German policy was either a diplomatic success or a preventive continental war.[144] Much of the scholarly debate also centres on the personality of Bethmann Hollweg. Such interpretations are not without problems either. The documentary evidence, indeed, would suggest that the notion of a 'calculated risk' ought to be modified.

The first point to make is that there was no proper policy coordination at Berlin at all. Neither the Kaiser's entourage nor his ministers had prepared the monarch for the meeting with Szögyény. The chancellor was absent from the capital and, as seen, was unaware of the ambassador's audience with the Kaiser until he was ordered to return to Berlin in the course of 5 July. Zimmermann, who had a clear appreciation of Austro-Hungarian ambitions following his conversation with Hoyos, also took no steps to forewarn the Kaiser. The monarch had spent the morning strolling among the rose bushes in the Potsdam park and then examining Professor Schöbel's pictures. He cannot have had any doubt as to the significance of Szögyény's request for an audience, and his own intemperate comments on Tschirschky's despatches from Vienna are strongly suggestive of his personal preference for some form of coercion of Serbia. Yet his initial response to Szögyény's communications had been measured and reserved. It was only after lunch, during their second conversation, that the German monarch offered his and his country's unequivocal support after the ambassador's explicit appeal to the Kaiser's sense of monarchical solidarity. This shift in Wilhelm's attitude lends even greater force to Avner Offer's argument that his decision 'was taken impetuously, almost casually', driven more by moral outrage at the attack on the monarchical idea than by cold calculation.[145]

There was also a personal dimension to this. In Austria-Hungary no-one had lost an ally or a friend in the unloved and unpopular Archduke – not the Emperor, not Berchtold and certainly not Conrad or Tisza. But Wilhelm II had lost a friend and an ally. If relations between the

[144] See, for instance, F. Stern, 'Bethmann Hollweg and the War: The Limits of Responsibility', in F. Stern and L. Krieger (eds.), *The Responsibility of Power: Essays in Honor of Hajo Holborn* (New York, 1967), 252–85; K. D. Erdmann, 'Zur Beurteilung Bethmann Hollwegs', *GWU* xv (1964), 527; E. Zechlin, 'Motive und Taktik der Reichsleitung 1914', in E. Zechlin, *Krieg und Kriegsziele. Zur deutschen Politik im Ersten Weltkrieg* (Düsseldorf, 1979), 95–102; A. Hillgruber, 'Riezlers Theorie des kalkulierten Risikos und Bethmann Hollwegs politische Konzeption in der Julikrise 1914', *HZ* ccii (1966), 333–58; K. H. Jarausch, 'The Illusion of Limited War: Chancellor Bethmann Hollweg's Calculated Risk, July 1914', *CEH* ii, 1 (1969), 48–76, and 'Revising German History: Bethmann Hollweg Revisited', *ibid.* xxi, 3 (1988), 224–43.
[145] A. Offer, 'Going to War in 1914: A Matter of Honour?', *P&S* xxiii, 2 (1995), 222.

mercurial monarch at Berlin and the stiffer and heavily clerically influenced Habsburg heir had initially been somewhat awkward, they had ripened to something akin to friendship. The Kaiser regarded 'Franzi', four years his junior, as a close friend, and the Archduke equally warmed to the 'splendid chap' ('*Mordskerl*') Wilhelm. In sharp contrast to the imperial court at Vienna, with its stiff Spanish ceremonial etiquette, and unlike much of the Austro-Hungarian aristocracy, the Kaiser also extended his friendship to Franz Ferdinand's morganatic wife, Sophie Chotek.[146] There was a further ironic twist to this. As seen earlier, Prinčip's two fatal bullets removed from the scene one of the restraining influences at Vienna. Conversely, the assassination of the archducal couple acted as a powerful impulse on Wilhelm II, who, on previous occasions, had sought to reinforce Franz Ferdinand's cautious approach to Balkan affairs.[147]

It would be an absurd simplification, of course, to assume that the German Kaiser was entirely subject to violent personal impulses. As his initially reserved response to Szögyény indicated, he was not at all blind to the risks entailed in Vienna's plans. In turn, this raises the question whether, and, if so, how Wilhelm II assessed the situation and its likely broader ramifications. What is striking here is the disjointed nature of decision-making at Berlin. It was only after Szögyény had left Potsdam that the Kaiser sought out his military advisers. According to Falkenhayn, Wilhelm emphasized that 'very serious consequences' might arise from Austria-Hungary's evident determination 'to put an end at last to the Greater-Serbia propaganda'. In conclusion, he enquired whether the army was 'ready for all contingencies'. The war minister replied 'briefly and unconditionally' in the affirmative. On asking whether any preparations were to be made, the Kaiser 'answered just as briefly that they were not, and dismissed me'.[148] And with that, Germany's military posture had been determined for the entire July crisis.

The Kaiser might well have expected such a positive reply from his war minister. Even so, his cursory, almost perfunctory, treatment of the matter would suggest that he did not anticipate an escalation of any Austro-Serb conflict. This is not to suggest that there were not voices in military circles at Berlin advocating a pre-emptive war before Russia's military might grew yet further. As Salza Lichtenau, the Saxon envoy at the Berlin court, reported to his government on 2 July, officials at the

---

[146] See R. A. Kann, 'Emperor Wilhelm II and Archduke Franz Ferdinand in their Correspondence', *AHR* LXVIII, 1 (1952), 323–51; F. Weissensteiner, *Franz Ferdinand. Der vehinderte Herrscher* (Munich, 2nd edn 1999 (pb)), 195–7.

[147] E.g. Wilhelm II to Franz Ferdinand, 26 Feb. 1913, Kann, 'Correspondence', 345–6.

[148] Statement Falkenhayn, *OGD* I, no. 17.

Auswärtiges Amt were confident that there would be no war between Austria-Hungary and Serbia. However, senior military officers argued 'that we should let it come to a war now, when Russia is not yet ready'. But he added that the Kaiser would not be tempted in that direction.[149] The Saxon military plenipotentiary at Berlin, Major-General Traugott Baron Leuckart von Weissdorf, came to a similar assessment following a conversation with the Quartermaster-General in the General Staff, Major-General Count Georg von Waldersee. Much would depend on how Russia reacted to a war in the Balkans, Waldersee suggested, and hinted that a European war now would be preferable to one at a later stage: 'circumstances and prospects would certainly not improve'. At the same time, he noted that Wilhelm II had 'declared himself for the preservation of peace'.[150]

The leading biographer of Wilhelm II, John Röhl, has emphasized the monarch's frequently bellicose rhetoric in the years before 1914 and his ideological propensity to view world politics in terms of an impending racial struggle between Teutons and Slavs.[151] Already earlier, at the so-called 'war council' on 8 December 1912, the Kaiser had suggested that Austria-Hungary ought to deal vigorously with Serbia before it was too late. On that occasion, Russia's intervention and the subsequent escalation of an Austro-Serb conflict were also discussed. Indeed, the tenor of the meeting was very much that war was inevitable, though various considerations, such as the widening of the Kiel Canal, made it desirable to postpone any conflict for at least eighteen months.[152] And yet for all the ominous rhetoric deployed so liberally on that occasion, '[t]he result was practically zero', recorded Admiral Georg von Müller, head of the Kaiser's naval cabinet.[153] There had in fact been no systematic preparation for a conflict in the aftermath of the 'war council'. Indeed, Bethmann Hollweg, on hearing of the meeting which he had not attended, wearily commented on 'the Kaiser playing war again'.[154] Nor was there any systematic analysis of the post-Sarajevo situation in July 1914. Moreover,

---

[149] Salza Lichtenau to Vitzthum (no. 1045, confidential), 2 July 1914, *DGB* no. 2.

[150] Leuckart to Carlowitz (no. 73/3472), 3 July 1914, *ibid.* no. 3.

[151] J. C. G. Röhl, *Wilhelm II* (3 vols., Munich, 1993–2008) III, 1080–6.

[152] John Röhl has written extensively about this meeting; see, e.g., *Kaiser and his Court*, 162–89; also Fischer, *Krieg der Illusionen*, 232–41.

[153] Müller diary, 8 Dec. 1912, W. Görlitz (ed.), *Der Kaiser. Aufzeichnungen des Chefs des Marinekabinetts, Admiral Georg von Müller über die Ära Wilhelms II* (Göttingen, 1965), 125; for further comments see J. C. G. Röhl, 'Admiral von Müller and the Approach of War, 1911–1914', *HJ* XII, 4 (1969), 651–73.

[154] See also tel. Bethmann Hollweg to Wilhelm II (no. 125), 18 Dec. 1912, *GP* XXXIX, no. 15560; for the lack of preparations see D. Stevenson, *Armaments and the Coming of War, 1904–1914* (Oxford, 1996), 287–98.

when faced with the growing risk of war at the end of the month, Wilhelm was prepared to back down.

There is a further complication. Eyewitness accounts of the Kaiser's brief meeting with his military are contradictory. As seen, Hans von Plessen, his chief aide-de-camp, recorded in his diary that Vienna was preparing for war, that an early Austro-Hungarian strike against Serbia was desirable, 'and that the Russians – though friends of the Serbs – will not join in'.[155] Falkenhayn, meanwhile, had formed a very different view. The two documents that Szögyény had handed to the Kaiser, and which the war minister was shown later that afternoon, did not suggest to him that Vienna had come to 'a firm decision' yet, he explained to Moltke, then absent from Berlin on sick-leave. Indeed, he noted that the Habsburg government had not spoken of 'a military solution', but had merely intimated '"energetic" political steps, for instance the conclusion of a treaty with Bulgaria, for which they wanted to be assured of German support'. The chancellor, too, Falkenhayn observed, did not 'seem to believe that the Austrian government are in earnest with now more decided language'. There was no reason for alarm, therefore; and the Chief of the General Staff could safely remain at Karlsbad.[156]

Whatever else Falkenhayn's comments might suggest, they underscore the fact that there was no proper assessment of the political and military situation on that fateful 5 July. The absence of proper, intellectually rigorous strategic planning was typical of the Byzantine nature of the Wilhelmine state, and it was replicated at the political level. There were few institutional checks on the Kaiser's powers.[157] His habit of surrounding himself with sycophants exacerbated the situation.

'The dancing bear' takes stock

Bethmann Hollweg was not a member of the Kaiser's inner circle. The tall, stooping, quiet and a little professorial chancellor was as unlike the brash Prussian *Junker*-types in Wilhelm's entourage as was possible. Of largely middle-class descent – his family were Frankfurt bankers – and with a Franco-Swiss mother to boot, he was little attuned to the braying officers'

[155] Plessen diary, 5 July 1914, H. Afflerbach (ed.), *Kaiser Wilhelm II als Oberster Kriegsherr im Ersten Weltkrieg. Quellen aus der militärischen Umgebung des Kaisers, 1914–1918* (Munich, 2005), no. P4.
[156] Falkenhayn to Moltke (very secret), 5 July 1914, *JK* I, no. 23.
[157] See J. C. G. Röhl's penetrating analysis of the nature of policy-making in the *Kaiserreich*, *The Kaiser and his Court*, 107–30.

mess tone that prevailed around the Kaiser. Yet Bethmann Hollweg did not act as the necessary check on the monarch's volatility. A cultured, thoughtful and well-meaning man, the sphinx-like chancellor impressed many who met him. Britain's Lord Chancellor, the German-educated lawyer and philosopher Viscount Haldane, thought him the 'Lincoln of Germany'. Yet with Bethmann, thoughtfulness often gave way to melancholy introspection and quiet despair. Ultimately, he lacked both the drive and guile necessary in politics. By training and instinct he was a bureaucrat, not a political leader. He executed the Kaiser's will; he did not offer advice. Indeed, in Berlin court circles he was known as the 'dancing bear' on account of his habit of nervously shifting from one foot to the other when addressing the Kaiser.[158]

The events of 5 July were all of a piece in this respect in that Bethmann was not consulted prior to Wilhelm's meeting with Szögyény.[159] Wilhelm had undoubtedly broken with constitutional propriety in offering Germany's unconditional support. But Bethmann did not counsel against it: 'The views of the Kaiser were in accordance with my own thinking'.[160] The chancellor's later reflections on the interview in the park of the Neues Palais are suggestive of his motivations in early July 1914, but they offer no conclusive proof. Bethmann was certainly more apprehensive of the external and internal risks inherent in the current crisis than the Kaiser and his military entourage. With such complications in view, he diluted the assurances to Austria-Hungary by excising the words 'under all circumstances' in the relevant passages in Tschirschky's instructions after the interview with Szögyény and Hoyos on 6 July.[161] In substance, however, German policy had not altered.

---

[158] For Bethmann's sphinx-like character see K. Hildebrand, *Kanzler ohne Eigenschaften? Urteile der Geschichtsschreibung* (Düsseldorf, 2nd edn 1970), 64. Fritz Fischer also characterized him as a 'puzzling chancellor': see 'Theobald von Bethmann Hollweg', W. von Sternberg (ed.), *Die deutschen Kanzler. Von Bismarck bis Schmidt* (Frankfurt, 1987), 87 [87–114]. Given Bethmann's ponderousness, Berliners christened one of the star attractions at Berlin zoo, a giant tortoise, 'Theobald': Lerchenfeld-Koefering, *Erinnerungen*, 392.

[159] A. Zimmermann, 'Fürst Bülows Kritik am Auswärtigen Amt', F. Thimme (ed.), *Front wider Bülow. Staatsmänner, Diplomaten und Forscher zu seinen Denkwürdigkeiten* (Munich, 1931), 231; W. von Rheinbaben, *Kaiser, Kanzler, Präsidenten* (Mainz, 1968), 108–9.

[160] Bethmann Hollweg, *Betrachtungen* I, 125. For a penetrating analysis of the inscrutable chancellor see F. Stern, 'Bethmann Hollweg and the War: The Bounds of Responsibility', in F. Stern, *The Failure of Illiberalism: Essays in the Political Culture of Modern Germany* (New York, 1992), 77–118.

[161] See *DD* I, no. 15, n. 5.

The chancellor's laconic post-war observation that the views expressed by Wilhelm to Szögyény 'were in accordance with my own thinking' remained the cornerstone of Bethmann's position in July 1914. It rested on concerns about Austria-Hungary's future stability and the further growth in Russian power. The two were linked, of course. For the past two years the chancellor's views on Russo-German relations had veered from profound pessimism to genuine optimism and back. In the summer of 1912, on his return from a visit to Russia, he was satisfied with the prospects for improved relations with St Petersburg, even though he accepted that 'Russia loves us no more than she loves any other Great Power. For that we are too strong, too much of a parvenu and just too disgusting.'[162] At that time he thought a *modus vivendi* with Germany's eastern neighbour a realistic proposition. Although Russia's recovery from defeat in war and revolution at home in 1905 had been speedier than might have been expected, the country's need for further financial consolidation and sustained economic reform seemed to vitiate against an adventurous foreign policy. Senior diplomats and financiers, Bethmann was told, 'fear [ed] major internal complications as a consequence of a war; their interest in the Balkans was not so great that they would want to run such an immeasurable risk'.[163] The notion of the latent fragility and instability of the Tsar's rule was a recurring theme in German diplomatic reporting. There could be no doubt, observed the German ambassador at St Petersburg, Bethmann's cousin Count Friedrich Pourtalès, in early 1914, 'that even if the current [domestic] tranquillity may last for years, one has to reckon with the possibility of a new revolution breaking out'.[164]

If fear of revolution was expected to act as a brake on Russian policy, there were, however, countervailing tendencies. The most pressing of these was the political force of pan-Slavism. In the spring of 1913, '*Purzelchen*' Pourtalès had commented on the official toleration of the often strident tone of the pan-Slav papers as a sign of weakness. The truth was, he suggested, 'that many influential and key circles see in this nationalist

[162] Bethmann Hollweg to Pourtalès, 30 July 1912, Nachlass Pourtalès, GFM 25/3; Jarausch, 'Illusion of Limited War', 52–3.
[163] Mendelssohn to Bethmann Hollweg (private), 10 Apr. 1913, PAAA Russland 61, Allgemeine Angelegenheiten, Bd. 121; for his hopes of a *modus vivendi* see Rathenau diary, 25 July 1912, H. Pogge-von Strandmann (ed.), *Walther Rathenau. Tagebücher, 1907–1922* (Düsseldorf, 1967), 168–9.
[164] Pourtalès to Bethmann Hollweg (no. 34), 31 Jan. 1914, PAAA Russland 61, Allgemeine Angelegenheiten, Bd. 121; see also T. G. Otte, '"A Formidable Factor in European Politics": Views of Russia in 1914', J. S. Levy and J. A. Vasquez (eds.), *The Outbreak of the First World War: Structure, Politics, and Decision-Making* (Cambridge, 2014), esp. 100–2.

movement a panacea against revolutionary propaganda and that therefore this movement is generally favoured and supported'.[165] The ambassador consistently warned that, whilst the Tsar and his closest advisers were pacific, in the event of an Austro-Serb conflict 'nothing can be guaranteed'. A Slavophile emotional spasm ('*Gefühlspolitik*') would sweep away all other calculations and would even 'affect those circles that only yesterday made fun of the exaggerated sympathy with the Slav brethren'.[166]

Russia's accelerated rearmament certainly weighed on Bethmann's mind in the summer of 1914. He had left Berlin immediately after the meeting with the two Habsburg diplomats at the Wilhelmstrasse, returning to his Hohenfinow estate accompanied by Kurt Riezler, a young official at the chancellery who had become his confidant. Neither the chancellor nor his young aide were much given to the usually loose and often bellicose talk prevalent in the Kaiser's entourage, with its overt display of manly and martial virtues. If anything, both tended towards introspection and philosophical reflections – Riezler was to become one of the founder-members of the New York New School. Certainly, his diary entries captured something of the chancellor's gloomy disposition:

> Yesterday with Reich chancellor. The old chateau, the wonderful enormous trees, the avenue like a vaulted gothic ceiling. Everywhere the deep impression of the wife's [Bethmann's] death. Melancholy and restraint in landscape and people.
>
> In the evening on the verandah, under the night sky, long conversation of the situation … Russia's military power growing rapidly; following strategic build-up of Poland situation untenable; Austria continually weakening and more immobile; the undermining [of Austria-Hungary] from North, South East far advanced. At any rate incapable of going to war for a German cause.

The conversation soon turned into a monologue. Bethmann spoke of 'difficult decisions': 'Official Serbia implicated. Austria wants to bestir herself. Franz Joseph's missive to Kaiser with enquiry about casus foederis.' And he spoke of the danger of losing Austria-Hungary, 'our last decent ally'. The chancellor acknowledged the risk of escalation. Any European war would lead 'to a revolution of existing conditions. The status quo has very much outlived itself, bereft of ideas. "Everything has grown very old".'

[165] Pourtalès to Bethmann Hollweg (no. 118), 12 Apr. 1913, PAAA Russland 61, Allgemeine Angelegenheiten, Bd. 120.
[166] Pourtalès to Jagow, 6 Feb. 1913, Nachlass Pourtalès, TNA (PRO), GFM 25/3.

Pace his many vociferous critics among Prussia's conservatives, war would not rejuvenate the established order but overthrow it: 'In general wilful blindness all around, a thick fog over the people ... The future belongs to Russia, who grows and grows, and who becomes an ever more oppressive nightmare for us.'[167]

While some of Riezler's notes may have been amended in later years, the mounting concern at Berlin about the growth of Russia's military power is well documented. A little over a month before the chancellor delivered himself of this gloomy prognostication under night skies of Hohenfinow, the Bavarian envoy at Berlin discussed the ongoing French and Russian armaments programmes with Bethmann: 'But no-one in France wants war. Russia was more dangerous. There the Slav enthusiasm could turn people's heads so that Russia would one day do something stupid.'[168]

In mid-June an article in the St Peterburg financial journal *Birshevi'ia Vedomosti* added fuel to such worries. Russia, the article asserted, had made 'colossal sacrifices' for the Franco-Russian alliance. She now had an army of some 2.3 million men and 'proceeded towards further reforms, the construction of a whole network of strategic railways, [and] the swiftest concentration of the army in the event of war'. In truth, the article was probably aimed more at reminding the ally – and paymaster – at Paris of Russia's importance than at alarming the Germans. But alarmed German officials certainly were, the more so as it transpired that the article had been inspired by the Russian war minister, General Vladimir Sukhomlinov.[169]

---

[167] Riezler diary, 7 July 1914, K. D. Erdmann (ed.), *Kurt Riezler. Tagebücher, Aufsätze, Dokumente* (Göttingen, 1972), 181–3. For the complex nature and history of the diaries, the controversy surrounding them and their abiding value see H. Afflerbach, 'Einleitung', to the second edn (Göttingen, 2008), i–xix; for Riezler see L. Strauss, 'Kurt Riezler, 1882–1955', *SocR* XVIII, 1 (1956), 3–6; W. J. Mommsen, 'Kurt Riezler, ein Intellektueller im Dienste Wilhelminischer Machtpolitik', *GWU* IX (1973), 236–41; I. Geiss, 'Kurt Riezler und der Erste Weltkrieg', in I. Geiss and B. J. Wendt (eds.), *Deutschland und die Weltpolitik des 19. und 20. Jahrhunderts. Festschrift für Fritz Fischer* (Düsseldorf, 1973), 398–418; W. C. Thompson, *In the Eye of the Storm: Kurt Riezler and the Crises of Modern Germany* (Iowa City, IA, 1980).
[168] Lerchenfeld to Hertling (no. 328), 4 June 1914, *BayD* no. 1.
[169] Pourtalès to Bethmann Hollweg, 13 June 1914, and article in *Birshevi'ia Vedomosti*, 13 June 1914, *DD* I, nos. 1 and 2. Sukhomlinov was in the habit of using the paper to air his views: see tel. Jagow to Pourtalès (no. 41), 12 Mar. 1914, and reply (tel. no. 53), 13 Mar. 1914, *GP* XXXIX, nos. 15845–6; for a summary of contemporary press commentary see H. von Kuhl, *Der deutsche Generalstab in Vorbereitung und Durchführung des Weltkrieges* (Berlin, 1920), 70–5; see also D. W. Spring, 'Russia and the Franco-Russian Alliance, 1905–1914: Dependence or Interdependence?', *SEER* LXVI, 4 (1988), 590–1.

The Kaiser covered the article with his habitually intemperate marginalia: 'Well! At last the Russians have put their cards on the table. He in Germany who still does not believe that Russo-Gaul is working at high pressure towards a war with us soon ... deserves to be sent to the Dalldorf lunatic asylum.'[170]

Bethmann had read the article, too. His response was more measured than that of his imperial master; and he was not slow in discerning its intended target. Yet he did not disguise his concern at the 'bellicose tendencies of the Russian militarist party' revealed in the article. If previously only figures on the raffish pan-German fringe of German politics had speculated about Russian plans for a war against Germany, 'even more sober-minded politicians were beginning to incline towards that view'. Since the Kaiser had recently warmed to such ideas himself, the chancellor feared a fresh bout of 'armaments fever' in the second half of 1914. In contrast to the sentiments attributed to him by Riezler in July, Bethmann was by no means prepared to accept bellicose articles in the St Petersburg press as prima facie evidence of Russia's intentions: 'Little as the uncertainty in Russian affairs makes it possible to discern the real aims of Russia with some confidence, and as much as, in our political disposi-tions, we have to take account of the fact that of all the European Great Powers Russia is the one most inclined to run the risk of military adven-ture, I still do not believe that Russia is planning a war against us soon.' On the contrary, he speculated that Russia's recent and reinvigorated military build-up was largely a political tool to enable Russian diplomacy to interfere more forcefully in another round of Balkan crises that had to be expected. Nor, in fact, did the chancellor consider such ambitions illegitimate for a Power such as Russia. The preservation of peace, how-ever, depended entirely on the attitude of Germany and Great Britain: 'If we [Britain and Germany] then firmly appear as guarantors of the European peace, as long as we pursue this aim from the start in accord-ance with a common plan – which neither the *Dreibund* nor the entente obligations prevent – then war can be avoided.' Otherwise, he added ominously, 'any minor odd clash of interest between Russia and Austria-Hungary may set alight the torch of war. A prudent policy has to keep this eventuality in view.'[171] These were wise words, indeed; and Bethmann would have been the wiser had he adhered to his own prescrip-tion when the final Balkan crisis broke.

[170] Marginal note Wilhelm II, 15 June 1914, *DD* I, no. 2.
[171] Bethmann Hollweg to Lichnowsky (no. 893, strictly confidential), 16 June 1914, *GP* XXXIX, no. 15883; for the opposite view that Bethmann was alarmed, see Clark, *Sleepwalkers*, 421.

If the chancellor's tone was on the whole confident, his observations on the need for joint Anglo-German crisis management nevertheless touched a critical point. Throughout the two recent Balkan conflicts, Berlin and London had cooperated closely and had so ensured that the turmoil did not escalate beyond the region. But now the German chancellor was no longer optimistic that such cooperation with London was to be had in the event of further problems in south-eastern Europe. In his talks with Riezler under the starry skies of his north Brandenburg home, he referred to insights provided by 'secret intelligence': 'He takes a serious view of Anglo-Russian negotiations on a naval conversation, amphibious landing in Pomerania, last link in the chain.'[172]

Theobald von Bethmann Hollweg was not the first senior politician to be taken in by misleading or partial intelligence data, nor would he be the last. In the context of the events of 1914, the 'intelligence dimension' was of some significance. Through Benno von Siebert, a Baltic German nobleman in the Russian diplomatic service, then posted to the London embassy, the authorities in Berlin were aware of Russia's desire for a naval convention with Britain, with the object of strengthening Anglo-Russian ties. For Sir Edward Grey, the British Foreign Secretary, a joint Franco-Russian initiative in that direction was 'a very delicate matter'.[173] For reasons that will be discussed later, neither Grey nor the British Cabinet was keen on the scheme, and the Foreign Secretary did his best to throw cold water on it. Any talks 'could not amount to very much', and there could be no question of the Royal Navy operating in the Baltic at the sufferance of, let alone in combination with, the imperial Russian fleet.[174]

While Grey hoped to kick the matter into the long grass of diplomacy, his replies to German enquiries about rumours of naval talks with Russia appeared evasive and obfuscating when compared with the more decided language of the Russian despatches provided by Siebert. The impact of such intelligence cannot, of course, be quantified, but Bethmann had certainly come to doubt Grey's reliability, indeed his honesty. He appreciated that London did not wish for war 'and would not join a war

---

[172] Riezler diary, 7 July 1914, Erdmann (ed.), *Riezler*, 182.
[173] Min. Grey, n.d., on min. Nicolson (secret), 17 Apr. 1914, TNA (PRO), FO 371/2092/17370; for some of the background see T. G. Otte, '"Détente 1914": Sir William Tyrrell's Mission to Germany', *HJ* LVI, 1 (2013), 190–3 [175–204]; for the German background see E. Hölzle, *Der Geheimnisverrat und der Kriegsausbruch 1914* (Göttingen, 1973), 10–15 *et passim*; and more balanced M. Rauh, 'Die britisch-russische Marinekonvention von 1914 und der Ausbruch des Ersten Weltkriegs', *MGM* XLI (1987), 37–62.
[174] Grey to Buchanan (no. 249, secret), 1 May 1914, TNA (PRO), FO 371/2092/19288; Harcourt diary, 13 May 1914, Harcourt MSS, Bodl., no accession no.

instigated against Germany. But that would not prevent that, if it came to war, we would not find England on our side.'[175]

No doubt, like any educated and patriotic Prussian, the chancellor will have recalled that Frederick the Great started the Seven Years' War as a pre-emptive strike after his spy in the Saxon chancellery had obtained a copy of a planned grand coalition against Prussia. If this made Bethmann more susceptible to suggestions of a preventive war, the overall impression of the German chancellor's attitude is one of hesitation and irresolution. Lack of trust in Grey, in turn, reinforced his concerns about maintaining the Habsburg Empire as Germany's only reliable ally. As he suggested to Riezler on 8 July: 'A "fait accompli" and then friendly [attitude] towards the entente, that way the shock can be absorbed.' He even speculated that, if no war ensued – either because the Tsar was unwilling or France was unwilling – the entente grouping might yet be pulled apart.[176]

To an extent this last consideration represented an element of continuity in German diplomacy in general but also in Bethmann's policy, both of which had been aimed at driving a wedge between the other Powers. Even so, the chancellor's suggestions in this direction were based on vague hopes; they were not the product of clear political thinking. Bethmann's comments in the summer of 1914 reflected his concerns and his hopes; they reflected his general appreciation of the likely risks and his awareness of future potentialities. But they did not reflect coherent, strategic calculations. For the chancellor there was no 'calculated risk', for he had no clearly defined political objectives; and in consequence he had no notion of a crisis strategy. Well-intentioned passivity was no substitute for it.

'The little misunderstanding' returns from his honeymoon

The chancellor's role during the early phase of the July crisis was marginal rather than central. He was away on his Hohenfinow country estate for much of the month, and remained remarkably aloof from events at Berlin on 10, 15 and 18 July.[177] What is striking is the extent to which German

---

[175] Lerchenfeld to Hertling (no. 328), 4 June 1914, *BayD* no. 1. There had been leaks in the French press, and Bertie had been instructed to remonstrate with the French government: see Bertie to Grey (private), 28 June 1914, Bertie MSS, BL, Add. MSS. 63033.

[176] Riezler diary, 8 July 1914, Erdmann (ed.), *Riezler*, 183; E. von Vietsch, *Bethmann Hollweg. Staatsmann zwischen Macht und Ethos* (Boppard, 1969), 183.

[177] Vietsch, *ibid.*, 197.

decision-making was compartmentalized. As chancellor, Bethmann was also the political head of the Auswärtiges Amt, the low, rambling eighteenth-century building at 76 Wilhelmstrasse, a little down at heel now, where once the Russian envoy at the Prussian court had resided and later Bismarck wove his web of alliances. Now it was in the hands of Gottlieb von Jagow. He was 'on duty practically day and night all through the crisis'.[178] He withheld key information from the chancellor and only consulted him very infrequently during the early stages of the crisis. Much of the diplomatic decision-making in 1914, in fact, went through Jagow, aided by Stumm and Zimmermann.

Jagow, 'the little misunderstanding' as he was known as on account of his non-confrontational manner, was no warmonger, but neither was he an ideal foreign minister. Imperial Germany's last peacetime occupant of the Auswärtiges Amt is also the least well-known of the Kaiser's senior diplomats. Although his relative obscurity reflected his bland and unassuming personality, this diminutive and impecunious Brandenburg *Junker* was not especially enigmatic. His political views reflected an 'ultra-conservative way of thinking ... that was as trimmed and symmetrical as the box hedging in the park of Sanssouci'.[179] Jagow was no nonentity, however. Contemporaries thought him an intelligent and cultured man, though of limited professional experience and even more limited physical robustness.[180]

A protégé of Bethmann's predecessor, Prince Bülow, and aided by his membership of the exclusive 'Borussia' student fraternity and his brother's regimental connections with Bülow, he entered the diplomatic service in 1897, eventually becoming ambassador to Italy in 1909. Four years later, and very reluctantly, he accepted the post of state secretary at the Auswärtiges Amt, the least coveted portfolio in the imperial German government. If at the time many doubted Jagow's 'remaining long Secretary of State, his health being indifferent and determination not strong', the 'little man' was soon 'splendidly seasoned' at the Wilhelmstrasse.[181] As a Berlin-based British journalist put it, 'Jagow does not look as if there was a

---

[178] Rumbold to de Bunsen (private), 15 Apr. 1918, Rumbold MSS, Bodl., Ms. Rumbold dep. 24.

[179] T. Wolff, *Der Krieg des Pontius Pilatus* (Zürich, 1934), 338.

[180] See for instance O. Hammann, *Zur Vorgeschichte des Weltkrieges. Erinnerungen aus den Jahren, 1897–1906* (Berlin, 1919), 1; O. zu Stolberg-Wernigerode, *Die unentschiedene Generation. Die konservativen Führungsschichten am Vorabend des Ersten Weltkriegs* (Munich, 1968), 15 and 382–3.

[181] Quotes from Bertie to Grey (private), 30 Jan. 1913, Bertie MSS, BL, Add. MSS. 63030; and Müller diary, 1 Feb. 1913, Görlitz (ed.), *Der Kaiser*, 1–2.

Bismarck within him, but he has all the virtues which count in modern diplomacy – urbanity, industry and loyalty.'[182]

As state secretary, Jagow shared Bethmann Hollweg's pessimism about the future prospects of the Habsburg Empire. Concerns about the inherent fragility of the Danube Monarchy ran like a red thread through Jagow's eighteen months at the Wilhelmstrasse before July 1914. '[T]he time is not so very far off when it may go the way of the Ottoman Empire', he confided to his friend, the British ambassador at Rome, shortly after taking up the reins at the Auswärtiges Amt. Such eventuality would force Germany to annex the German-speaking parts of the Habsburg Empire, a prospect that filled Jagow with dread: 'Germany had already too many Catholics ... Merged with the German Empire, the Austrian Catholics would enable that party to swamp the progressive Protestant elements.'[183] If anything, such a prospect heightened Jagow's determination to support Austria-Hungary. His sense of foreboding, however, had become more acute. He could 'not unpack his mind of the fear that it was now a race between the two empires [Austria-Hungary and Turkey] as to which would go to pieces first'.[184]

The growth of the centrifugal forces inside the Dual Monarchy was one source of concern for Jagow; another was a growing political reckless-ness among the Habsburg leadership. At the time of the Austro-Serb stand-off in early 1913, he noted with alarm:

> it is argued that ... it is high time to 'dish the Serbs [*mit den Serben abzuräumen*]' ... They [the Austrians] are contemplating an invasion of Serbia and her partition between Romania, Bulgaria and Austria, in order to render the Serbs completely 'harmless'. Indeed, they even contemplate swallowing Montenegro. It is not necessary to lose a single word about the fantastic nature of such plans; this would lead Austria to trialism and therefore most probably to complete paralysis and dissolution ... *Il y a des bêtises que seule l'Autriche est capable de faire* [It is the kind of nonsense only Austria is capable of producing].

Worse still was Vienna's utter disregard for the Great Power dimension of any regional conflict: 'they also imagine that, even if Russia were to move,

---

[182] F. W. Wile, *Men around the Kaiser: The Makers of Modern Germany* (London, repr. 1914 [1st edn 1913]), 216.
[183] Rodd to Grey (private), 6 Jan. 1913, Rennell of Rodd MSS, Bodl., box 15; for his friendship with Rodd see also J. R. Rodd, *Social and Diplomatic Memoirs* (3 vols., London, 1922–5) III, 164–7.
[184] Nicolson to Bunsen, 30 Mar. 1914, De Bunsen MSS, Bodl., box 11.

France and England would remain passive. I cannot share this belief.'[185] Indeed, Jagow had formed a low opinion of the political élite in the Habsburg capital, where 'Imperial and Royal sloppiness merchants [k[aiserlich] u[nd] k[önigliche] Schlampigkeitskrämerei]' reigned supreme.[186]

As with Bethmann, Jagow's pessimism about Austria-Hungary ran in parallel with concerns about the continued growth of Russian military power. Moltke had warned him in early 1914 that 'Russia's war-readiness has made tremendous progress since the Russo-Japanese War and has now reached unprecedented levels', and Jagow himself had operated with the notion of a possible 'world war' during the budget negotiations with the *Reichstag*.[187] It would be tempting to see in such pronouncements a predisposition towards preventive war ideas. But, like Bethmann, Jagow viewed Russian rearmament primarily in a Balkan context and as preparation for a more energetic policy in the region in the near future. This could be countered effectively only if Germany's defensive posture contained a credible element of deterrence. The two German army laws of 1912 and 1913 were, at least in part, designed to achieve that, and conjuring up the spectre of war was a tried and tested means of successive *Reich* governments to force the *Reichstag* deputies to loosen the purse strings.[188]

The converse of all this was Jagow's attempts to bring about a rapprochement with Britain. This had been a principal part of his programme on assuming the office of state secretary, and he steadily worked towards that end until the summer of 1914.[189] Improved Anglo-German relations were desirable in their own right, not least because of the stabilizing effect these would have on international relations in general. But Jagow was not blind to the further advantages of a rapprochement. The two Balkan wars, he noted, had alerted London to the 'dangers, which Russian pretensions and the advance of the Slavic tide in the Balkans entail for

[185] Jagow to Pourtalès (very secret), 6 Feb. 1913, Nachlass Pourtalès, GFM 25/3. He also spoke of a possible 'world war': see F. Fischer, *Der Griff nach der Weltmacht. Die Kriegsziele des kaiserlichen Deutschland, 1914–1918* (Düsseldorf, 3rd edn 1964), 44–5.

[186] Jagow to Pourtalès, 26 July 1913, Nachlass Pourtalès, TNA (PRO), GFM 25/3. As R. W. Seton-Watson observed, 'no English word can fully render the idea of incurably bungling and haphazard methods which this conveys [i.e. *Schlamperei*] characteristic of the old régime in Austria': 'The Murder at Sarajevo', *FA* III, 4 (1924–5), 495.

[187] Moltke to Jagow (no. 3035), 24 Feb. 1914, *GP* XXXIX, no. 15839; F. Fischer, *Griff nach der Weltmacht*, 44–5.

[188] S. Förster, *Der doppelte Militarismus. Die Deutsche Heeresrüstungspolitik zwischen Status-Quo-Sicherung und Aggression, 1890–1913* (Stuttgart, 1985), 208–32.

[189] Jagow to Rodd, 1 Feb. 1913, Rennell of Rodd MSS, Bodl., box 15.

Europe'. He was convinced that this insight would 'mature and lead to a further – already latent – alienation of England from Russia'.[190]

These two considerations were linked. Cooperation with London helped to contain the Austro-Russian antagonism in south-eastern Europe; and an Anglo-German exchange of views might prepare the ground for a joint effort 'to preserve Turkey in her present configuration for as long as possible', the best means of safeguarding German commercial interests in Asia Minor and Mesopotamia.[191] At the same time, Russia remained a disturbing element in the wider region, '[a]nd a reopening of the Asiatic Question would be highly inconvenient', Jagow argued.[192] Indeed, the Anglo-German convention of June 1914 on the Baghdad railway and other such enterprises in Asiatic Turkey testified to the reciprocal wish of the two governments 'to prevent all causes of misunderstandings between Germany and Great Britain', and so seemed to prepare the ground for future cooperation.[193]

For much of 1913 and early 1914, Jagow had been working for a rapprochement with Britain, and publicly spoke of a détente in Anglo-German relations in February 1914.[194] At the time of the Sarajevo murders, Jagow was on his honeymoon in Switzerland and still absent from Berlin during Hoyos's visit. Indeed, he returned to the capital only later on 6 July, but was not present at Bethmann's meeting with Szögyény and Hoyos. Privately, he summed up his assessment of the situation:

> The catastrophe of Sarajevo is terrible; the house of Habsburg-Lorraine truly is an Atridite dynasty, moving from catastrophe to catastrophe. The political impact is difficult to calculate, because one knows too little about what sort the new heir to the throne is and what he promises. The life of the old emperor is drawing to a close ... and the successor is very young. In the meantime, the empire is disintegrating more and more and loses coherence and

---

[190] Jagow to Tschirschky, 17 Mar. 1913, GP xxxiv/2, no. 12982; for some of the background see also R. J. Crampton, *The Hollow Détente: Anglo-German Relations in the Balkans, 1911–1914* (London, 1979), 75–96.

[191] Jagow to Lichnowsky, 31 May 1913, GP xxxviii, 15317; G. von Jagow, 'Richtigstellungen', E. von Steinitz (ed.), *Ring um Sasonow. Neue dokumentarische Darlegungen zum Ausbruch des grossen Krieges durch Kronzeugen* (Berlin, 1928), 136.

[192] Jagow to Pourtalès, 26 Sept. 1913, Nachlass Pourtalès, GFM 25/3.

[193] 'German-British Convention', 15 June 1914, BD x/2, no. 249 encl. After the war, Jagow reflected that since the two countries had come to far-reaching understandings on colonial and commercial questions, 'it would, without doubt, gradually have led to a political détente': *Ursachen und Ausbruch des Weltkrieges* (Berlin, 1919), 63.

[194] Goschen to Grey (no. 48), 5 Feb. 1914, TNA (PRO), FO 371/1857/5608.

prestige. It needs a strong hand to gather strength again; does the young prince have that?[195]

At this stage, it seems, Jagow had not been fully apprised of the conversations at Potsdam and the chancellor's palais on 5 and 6 July. Later, in an unpublished essay on the July crisis, he reflected that, on hearing of the conversations, he had entertained 'serious concerns about the possible consequences' of the commitment to Austria-Hungary. He would not have sought to retract the promise made, but noted that 'I would have warned the Viennese, whilst acknowledging our alliance obligations, not to let it come to a great war because that entailed too serious a danger for both Central Powers.' His assertion, then, that he never regarded the commitment made as 'carte blanche', and that he expected Vienna to consult with the German ally before taking any further steps, was somewhat disingenuous, as the course of events would show.[196]

There was no proper strategic guidance in German foreign policy in July 1914. If there was a 'calculated risk', it was based on individual calculations, not on collective deliberations and decisions. Finally, if German policy sought to deploy deterrence and 'bluff', seemingly threatening a continental war in order to secure a diplomatic success, then this would have required close diplomatic and military coordination with Vienna. Nothing of the kind happened. Decision-making in the two *Zweibund* capitals ran along parallel lines but remained separate. Imbued with a vague sense of German military superiority, the Kaiser and the civilian leadership had embarked on a policy, the course and consequences of which they had not calculated. Germany was a giant with a brain made of clay. But nor was there proper strategic guidance at Vienna. Berchtold and his advisers were determined to have a war with Serbia, the aims and ramifications of which they had not considered either. The Habsburg Empire was a lesser giant than its northern ally, but its head, too, was made of clay. And this empire now set the direction and pace of events.

---

[195] Jagow to Blücher, 6 July 1914, Nachlass Jagow, TNA (PRO), GFM 25/16.
[196] Jagow, 'Juli 1914 und Kriegsausbruch', n.d., unpubl. MS, *ibid.*, fos. 97–8. Jagow also confirmed here that he did not make any notes during those days.

3 THE TRIUMPH OF TACTICS OVER STRATEGY: 6 TO 21 JULY

> There, in Kakania, this misunderstood and since disappeared state, yet in so many ways exemplary without being so recognized, there was also tempo, just not too much tempo.
>
> ROBERT MUSIL[1]

The talks at Potsdam and Berlin on 5 and 6 July marked an important turning point during the events of the summer of 1914. In securing the 'blank cheque', the suave hawk Hoyos and the faux 'gypsy' ambassador Szögyény had achieved a remarkable diplomatic triumph, albeit one for entirely undiplomatic ends and one that was to remain well-concealed until war was imminent. The promise of unconditional German support gave the Ballhausplatz the assurance it had sought before any firm action against Serbia could be contemplated. For Berchtold the 'blank cheque' opened the road towards a swift and decisive move against the intractable southern neighbour. Its speed and decisiveness, and the specific circumstances of the Sarajevo regicide, created the chance of deterring intervention by the other Powers. Above all it offered the hope of circumscribing Russia's room for interference, as German support had done in the Bosnian annexation crisis in 1908–9. Berlin's support thus ought to ensure that the contemplated move against Serbia would not escalate into a wider conflict. If it did, then Germany would provide cover along the Monarchy's long and vulnerable Galician frontier in the north. As was seen earlier, the notion of 'settling accounts' with Serbia set the tone of the discussions at Vienna in the days immediately after Sarajevo. The 'blank cheque' reinforced the belligerent attitude of senior Habsburg officials. It guaranteed that Austria-Hungary's final reckoning with Serbia would be a military one. A diplomatic solution was now the least favoured option for Vienna.

It is difficult to conceive of the Habsburg leadership opting for a military solution had it not been for Berlin's unequivocal promise of support.[2]

---

[1] R. Musil, *Der Mann ohne Eigenschaften* (2 vols., Reinbek bei Hamburg, 1987) I, 32.
[2] See S. R. Williamson Jr, *Austria-Hungary and the Origins of the First World War* (London, 1991), 197, on which the following is based.

True, the Austrians had been close to striking against Serbia in October 1913 without much prior consultation with Berlin. No doubt also, Vienna's determination was greater now than it had been in the previous autumn. At that time, the Chief of the General Staff, Baron Conrad, had once more pressed for action 'to inflict on Serbia a diplomatic, and possibly even a military, defeat'. The latter had always been to the fore of his thinking: 'one had to fight a war as soon as the circumstances were propitious. Most wars were lost by those who missed their chances.'[3] It would not have been beyond the wit of Conrad to stage a border incident that would have furnished a convenient pretext for a preventive strike against Serbia. Failing that, seizing some spot along the frontier might have been an option with a view to pressurizing Belgrade into making diplomatic concessions. Whatever other options might have been available to Austria-Hungary, the 'blank cheque' now enabled Berchtold and Conrad to overcome the Magyar government's opposition to war; and here lay the crucial difference with earlier Balkan crises.

There was a further difference. In leaving it to Vienna to decide the nature of any measures to be taken against Serbia, Germany had surrendered her ability to restrain Austria-Hungary. With the 'blank cheque' Berlin had abdicated any kind of influence, indeed. The course of events would be determined by the Ballhausplatz. But a rapid decision in Vienna was unlikely. In an empire in which bureaucratic customs, constitutional arrangements and dualist reticencies had conspired to make dilatoriness into a high art form, the notion of swift and decisive action was a tall order. Bethmann and the Wilhelmstrasse would have done well to remember Jagow's earlier complaint of Habsburg 'Schlampigkeitskrämerei' (sloppiness).[4] Indeed, it would take Austria-Hungary almost another three weeks to move. The delays, the motivations behind them and their effects form the next phase of the July crisis.

At Berlin, senior officials clearly anticipated a swift Austrian move that never materialized. Arthur Zimmermann, the under-secretary at the Auswärtiges Amt, for instance, concluded that the current moment was advantageous for an Austro-Hungarian preventive strike, what he called a 'campaign of revenge', and that any ensuing conflict could be localized. Yet he was doubtful 'that they in Vienna will decide to do it'.[5] Zimmermann

[3] Protocol of Ministerial Council, 3 Oct. 1913, F. Conrad von Hötzendorf, *Aus meiner Dienstzeit* III, *Der Ausgang des Balkankrieges und die Zeit bis zum Fürstenmord in Sarajevo* (Vienna, 1922), app. 5, 730–1; L. Sondhaus, *Franz Conrad von Hötzendorf: Architect of the Apocalypse* (Boston and Leiden, 2000), 131–4.

[4] Jagow to Pourtalès, 26 July 1913, Nachlass Pourtalès, TNA (PRO), GFM 25/3.

[5] Schoen to Hertling (no. 373), 9 July 1914, *BayD* no. 8.

and others at the Wilhelmstrasse, reported Szögyény, were urging Vienna to seize the moment to deal with Serbia. Berlin, he added, did not believe that Britain, particularly, would enter a conflict in south-eastern Europe. Not only had Anglo-German relations improved so much in recent months, but Britain 'was not at all willing to pull the chestnuts out of the fire for Serbia or, ultimately, for Russia', senior officials at the Wilhelmstrasse reasoned.[6]

When viewed in the context of events later in July, there is a terrible irony about Habsburg tardiness. It is difficult not to conclude that, if Vienna had struck immediately after the murder of the Archduke, no world war would have ensued. Militarily, it would have entailed an element of risk in that it would have precluded full mobilization of the Habsburg armed forces. But the odds in such an operation were still in Austria-Hungary's favour. There would have been a political risk, too, because an immediate armed response meant dispensing with the usual diplomatic formalities of issuing an ultimatum and declaring war. But that risk, too, was small and manageable – none of these niceties had been observed when Japan attacked Russia ten years earlier. The other European Powers would have deplored the resort to military force, but, given the nature of the provocation, would have been not unsympathetic to Vienna's action. It was for the representative of a smaller Power, the Romanian prime minister, Ion C. Brătianu, to spell this out on 24 July, one day after the Austro-Hungarian ultimatum was delivered. He strongly regretted the note to Belgrade, 'for it proved that we [Austria-Hungary] *willed* war'. If only Austria-Hungary had acted immediately after the assassination, then she 'would have had the sympathies of Europe on [her] side'.[7] Indeed, years later, Berchtold was ready to concede that 'the only mistake of which we can accuse ourselves is that we struck *too late*', though what he meant was that the Monarchy should have sought a military confrontation with Serbia before 1914.[8]

The ponderous political apparatus moves

No such swift response, however, was possible. Not the least obstacle remained Tisza's strong opposition to war. Armed with the 'blank cheque' Berchtold now set about overcoming the Hungarian leader's resistance. For nothing had yet been decided, nor could it be for as long as he remained

[6] Szögyény to Berchtold (no. 60P), 12 July 1914, HHStA, PA I/1091.
[7] Tel. Czernin to Berchtold (no. 241), 24 July 1914, HHStA, PA I/810, Liasse XX.
[8] Berchtold diary, 4 Sept. 1918, Nachlass Berchtold, HHStA, Karton 5.

intransigent. Tisza, as Berchtold observed to Conrad on 6 July, opposed war because he feared a Romanian incursion into Transylvania while the bulk of the Habsburg army was preoccupied with the campaign against Serbia.[9] That, of course, was the traditional Magyar perspective on the Habsburg Monarchy's regional position, one dominated by concerns about Transylvania's exposed position at the easternmost extremity of the Monarchy.

A meeting of the joint ministerial council, scheduled for the afternoon of 7 July, gave Berchtold an opportunity to tackle the Hungarian premier. He prepared the ground immediately he received Szögyény's telegram on his audience at Potsdam, the essence of which Berchtold transmitted to Tisza: '[W]e should not wait with an action against Serbia. We should not leave unexploited the present advantageous moment. Russia was not ready for war now and Germany stood loyally on our side.'[10] In a further, separate move Berchtold sought to influence Tisza before the ministers' conclave, dispatching Baron Wladimir Giesl, the envoy to Serbia recently returned from leave in the south of France, to see the Hungarian leader privately at his Vienna palais. The prime minister was not for turning. He rejected any move that might infringe Serbia's sovereign rights and might lead to war: 'But if they want that, then the Emperor (Tisza said King) will have to look for a new minister.'[11] This was a serious threat, adding to the current crisis in the Empire's external relations the prospect of a constitutional crisis within it.

Berchtold himself had a first opportunity to test Tisza's position just before the ministers convened in the late morning of 7 July, when Tisza called on the foreign minister at the Ballhausplatz. He was accompanied by Count Karl Stürgkh, the prime minister of the Austrian half of the Dual Monarchy, a nullity of no great political weight and little influence during the July crisis, whose only achievement was to be assassinated in 1916. Also present were Hoyos, who reported on his mission to Berlin, and Tschirschky, the German ambassador. Berchtold, his hand forced by Tisza,

---

[9] F. Conrad von Hötzendorf, *Aus meiner Dienstzeit* IV, *Die politischen und militärischen Vorgänge vom Fürstenmord in Sarajevo bis zum Abschluss der ersten und bis zum Beginn der zweiten Offensive gegen Serbien und Russland* (Vienna, 1923), 39–40; J. H. Maurer, 'Field Marshal Conrad von Hötzendorf and the Outbreak of the First World War', T. G. Otte and C. A. Pagedas (eds.), *Personalities, War and Diplomacy: Essays in International History* (London, 1997), 44–5.

[10] Tel. Berchtold to Tisza, 6 July 1914, *ÖUA* VIII, no. 10091. The telegram was sent at 1.30 p.m., well before Hoyos's second telegraphic report on the meeting with Bethmann and Zimmermann arrived at 8 p.m.

[11] W. Baron Giesl, *Zwei Jahrzehnte im Nahen Orient. Aufzeichnungen*, ed. [E.] von Steinitz (Berlin, 1927), 256. For the Magyar nationalist Tisza Franz Joseph was His Apostolic Majesty, the King of Hungary.

underlined that Hoyos's comments at Berlin had been of an entirely personal nature, especially in so far as his suggestion that Serbia would have to be partitioned afterwards was concerned. This was a remarkable statement to make. At the same time, the foreign minister sought to regain some ground by expressing the gratitude of the two prime ministers for Berlin's unequivocal indication of support.[12]

According to Berchtold's notes, Tisza admitted that recent evidence of official Serb involvement in the murder of the archducal couple had made an impression on him. Thus far he had refused to accept the possibility of Belgrade being implicated in the crime. If he had erred in that respect, however, he still insisted on the need to avoid war. A diplomatic success was practically guaranteed, whereas the resort to armed force entailed the grave risk of European complications.

As elsewhere during the July crisis, personalities mattered. The German ambassador seems to have played a significant role at the meeting. Berchtold described him as having had 'a clear head and strong will, with clearly defined ideas'. As always, such men made an impression on Berchtold, though in July 1914 Tschirschky's exhortations merely reinforced his own predilection for a pre-emptive strike:

> Tschirschky believed ... that a policy of action by the Vienna cabinet was in the interest of both parties [Germany and Austria-Hungary]. Only through a manifestation of strength could Austria-Hungary be prevented from collapsing, whilst being maintained as an ally for Germany. Now it was still possible to preempt the threatened general war. If Russia and France were to intervene after all, then the current military balance was more advantageous for the Triple Alliance than later.

The ambassador's urgent representations on that day, the Kaiser's promise of 5 July and Bethmann's further explanations of the 6th all amounted, as Berchtold reflected, to something akin to 'Napoleon III's "*fate presto*" [Make haste!] to the Sardinian delegates [in 1859]'. But encumbered with 'our ponderous political and military apparatus we were not in a position to emulate the examples of Cavour and Cialdini right to the end'.[13]

---

[12] Tel. Tschirschky to Auswärtiges Amt (no. 83, secret), 7 July 1914, *DD* I, no. 18. The telegram was despatched at 3.25 p.m., but it is clear from its contents that the meeting took place before the ministerial council later that morning.

[13] Berchtold, 'Die ersten Tage nach dem Attentat vom 28. Juni', as quoted in H. Hantsch, *Leopold Graf Berchtold. Grandseigneur und Staatsmann* (2 vols., Graz and Vienna, 1963) II, 575–6.

As the morning meeting at the Ballhausplatz indicated, Tisza had changed his stance somewhat. But on the key question of war and peace he remained unyielding. The meeting of the ministerial council later that morning confirmed this. The ostensible purpose of the meeting was to decide on law-and-order measures in Bosnia-Herzegovina in the wake of sporadic outbursts of inter-ethnic violence there following Franz Ferdinand's assassination.[14] In the event, the ministers swiftly turned to the issue of the Monarchy's general strategic position.

What is striking about the proceedings of that day is the sombre tone of quiet and calm deliberation. There was none of that 'gung-ho' bellicosity that had reverberated down the corridors of the Ballhausplatz in the days immediately after Sarajevo. Different options were raised, weighed and given due consideration. Even so, the balance of opinion was heavily tilted in favour of a military solution. As Samuel R. Williamson has pointed out, with the notable exception of Tisza, the ministers gathered around the cabinet table that day had faced the question of peace and war on three previous occasions during the last twenty months.[15] Given the weight of their collective experience, peace stood little chance.

The meeting was presided over by Berchtold, with Hoyos taking the minutes. It was attended by the two prime ministers, Stürgkh and Tisza, and by the Monarchy's only other two joint ministers, Leon Ritter von Biliński (Finance) and General Alexander Ritter von Krobatin (War). Later in the afternoon they were joined by Conrad and the deputy chief of the naval staff, Vice-Admiral Carl Kailer von Kaltenfels.[16] Berchtold opened proceedings by informing the ministers of Berlin's unequivocal promise of support in the event of military complications with Serbia. The moment had come, he noted, when they had to decide whether Serbia ought 'to be rendered harmless for ever'. A decisive move against Belgrade brought with it the risk of a Russian intervention and might whet Italy's and Romania's appetite for compensation. As to the former eventuality, Russia's current policy aimed at uniting the smaller Balkan nations against the Monarchy. Austria-Hungary's position in the region could only deteriorate over time. To delay firm and decisive action now would be an indication of vacillation and weakness, and would strengthen the gravitational pull of Russia on the smaller states in the region. The logical solution, he reasoned, was 'to pre-empt our enemies and, by means of a timely settling of accounts with Serbia, to halt developments already in train'.

[14] Krobatin to Berchtold, 7 July 1914, HHStA, PA I/810, Liasse XX.
[15] Williamson, *Austria-Hungary*, 198.
[16] P. G. Halperin, *Anton Haus. Österreich-Ungarns Grossadmiral* (Graz, 1998), 141–3.

In response, Tisza conceded that he, too, now thought that 'the possibility of a military action against Serbia had moved closer'. He justified his change of view with reference to the growing body of evidence of the assassins' links to military circles at Belgrade and the hostile attitude of the Serbian press. Yet Tisza still held out against war. Under no circumstances would he support a surprise attack on Serbia. To do so would isolate Austria-Hungary diplomatically and very likely unite the Balkan states against her, while Bulgaria was still in no position to offer effective support. The Magyar prime minister insisted on the proper diplomatic preparation of any move against Serbia. Austria-Hungary ought to make demands on Belgrade, 'and only issue an ultimatum if Serbia did not fulfil them. These demands had to be hard but not unacceptable.' What Tisza envisaged was, in essence, a repetition of the policy pursued in October 1913 during the stand-off over Serbia's access to the Adriatic in the aftermath of the Second Balkan War. Now, if Serbia yielded to Vienna's demands, 'we could point to a stunning diplomatic success and our prestige in the Balkans would rise'. If, on the other hand, Belgrade refused, 'then he, too, would be for military action'. The object of any such campaign, however, had to be the 'diminution but never the complete annihilation of Serbia'. The latter would make Russian intervention inevitable. A formal declaration renouncing any intention to annex Serbian territory was thus a vital means of preventing foreign intervention in the stand-off.

There were also domestic considerations. No Hungarian prime minister could accept the annexation of Serb territory given the likely negative impact of such a move on the internal stability of the Magyar half of the Dual Monarchy. There could be no doubt that Tisza would only submit to the military option *in extremis*. He dismissed Berchtold's suggestion that Berlin's unconditional support afforded the Monarchy a unique opportunity to strike at Serbia. It was not for Germany, he asserted, to 'judge whether we should now move against Serbia or not. Personally, he was of the view that at the present moment a war need not necessarily be fought.' In the event of war now, significant reserves would have to be kept to protect Transylvania against a Romanian invasion – the old Magyar concern about the exposed Carpathian salient.

The outcome of these exchanges was a partial success for Tisza. He was able to persuade the other ministers to reject Krobatin's idea of a surprise attack, which the latter had sought to justify by reference to the Russo-Japanese and the recent Balkan wars, none of which had been preceded by a formal declaration of war. Instead, the council agreed on the need for the proper diplomatic preparation of any military move.

In substance, however, Tisza was defeated on the key question of war and peace. For the other ministers expected that a strongly worded ultimatum would be rejected by Belgrade, and that a localized war would then ensue. Berchtold argued that previous diplomatic successes against Serbia had yielded no lasting positive results, and that 'a radical solution ... was only possible by means of energetic intervention'. In this the foreign minister was seconded by Stürgkh, who pointed to the Monarchy's tenuous hold over Bosnia and Herzegovina and suggested that 'the internal crisis in Bosnia could only be resolved through a manifestation of force against Serbia'. Biliński, who combined the finance portfolio with administering the two provinces, supported that view: 'a diplomatic success would make no impression on Bosnia and would be more damaging than anything else'. Similarly, whilst the annexation of Serb territory was ruled out, the ministers accepted Stürgkh's suggestions that, after a war with Serbia, the ruling Karadjordjević dynasty ought to be removed, the Serb crown be offered to a European prince, and 'a certain dependency of the reduced kingdom [Serbia] to the Monarchy be established in regard to military matters'. Thus, when the assembled ministers broke up for lunch, all but Tisza had decided upon a diplomatic confrontation with Belgrade that was meant to lead to an Austro-Serb war. Tellingly, indeed, there was no discussion as to what demands should be made of Belgrade.[17]

The afternoon session, with Conrad and the naval representative in attendance, turned to the military aspects of the current situation. Conrad was called upon to examine three different scenarios. He explained that it would be possible to mobilize against Serbia first, and only later, if necessary, against Russia, though the decision for the latter would have to be made by the fifth day of mobilization. Some time was spent on discussing Magyar concerns about the defence of Transylvania. On this point Conrad gave assurances that sufficient troops were kept in readiness there to act as an effective deterrent against a Romanian incursion. As for the third scenario, a war with Russia, the chief of staff explained that the bulk of the armed forces would be thrown against Russian Poland, and only two armies would take to the field against Serbia and possibly Montenegro. On Tisza's persistent probing he had to concede that parts of Galicia might well have to be evacuated at the beginning of operations. Conrad concluded his exposition by trotting out the line, all too familiar to Tisza and the other ministers, that any further

---

[17] Minutes of Meeting of Ministerial Council, 7 July 1914, M. Komjáthy (ed.), *Protokolle des Gemeinsame Ministerrates der Österreich-Ungarischen Monarchie (1914–1918)* (Budapest, 1966), no. 1; M. Rauchensteiner, *Der Tod des Doppeladlers. Österreich-Ungarn und der Erste Weltkrieg* (Graz, 1993), 73–5; G. Vermes, *István Tisza: The Liberal Vision and Conservative Statecraft of a Magyar Nationalist* (New York, 1985), 222–3.

delay in seeking a military solution to the Monarchy's Balkan problems would merely shift the balance of forces against it.[18]

At the conclusion of the meeting, Tisza reiterated his warnings against war, and even hinted that he might resign if his views were not respected. Even so, Berchtold, in summing up the meeting, touched on a crucial point. While the divergence of opinion between Tisza and the other ministers remained, the differences had narrowed considerably. Even the Hungarian prime minister's diplomatic route, Berchtold observed, would 'in all probability lead to the warlike confrontation with Serbia deemed necessary by him [Berchtold] and the other ministers'.[19]

That Tisza had shifted his position is beyond doubt. Hoyos's talks at Potsdam and Berlin had made an impression on the Hungarian leader, and so had the hardening suspicions of an official Serb connection with the Sarajevo plot.[20] As for the meeting itself, a number of points are worth noting. The first of these is the now firm conviction shared by all ministers present that there was a chain of evidence linking Belgrade to the murder of the Archduke. They had no detailed knowledge; their conviction of a link to Belgrade rested largely on brief summaries of the ongoing investigations at Sarajevo. Secondly, there was no clear, guiding principle to their deliberations beyond the now all-powerful notion of 'settling accounts with Serbia'. That her planned humiliation was likely to be achieved only by means of a war, Hoyos himself privately admitted to a fellow diplomat.[21] But what demands were to be made of Belgrade, and how it was to be treated after the war, were issues that were scarcely touched upon. The third point relates to Austria-Hungary's ally at Berlin. Whilst German support was welcomed, it mattered primarily in terms of the internal

---

[18] Conrad had requested that his explanations not be recorded officially: see minutes, 7 July 1914, Komjáthy (ed.), *Protokolle*, 148; for his exposition see Conrad, *Aus meiner Dienstzeit* iv, 53–6. Conrad attended ministerial council meetings from March 1911: see O. Regele, *Generalstabschefs aus Vier Jahrhunderten. Das Amt des Chefs des Generalstabs in der Donaumonarchie. Seine Träger und Organe von 1529 bis 1918* (Vienna, 1966), 66.

[19] Minutes of Council of Ministers, 7 July 1914, Komjáthy (ed.), *Protokolle*, 149; J. Angelow, *Kalkül und Prestige. Der Zweibund am Vorabend des Ersten Weltkrieges* (Vienna, 2000), 454.

[20] N. Stone, 'Hungary and the Crisis of July 1914', *JCH* i, 1 (1966), 153–70; F. R. Bridge, *From Sadowa to Sarajevo: The Foreign Policy of Austria-Hungary, 1866–1914* (London, 1972), 375.

[21] L. von Andrian-Werburg, 'Der Kriegsbeginn', appended to R. Leslie, 'Österreich-Ungarn vor dem Kriegsausbruch. Der Ballhausplatz in Wien im Juli 1914 aus der Sicht eines österreichisch-ungarischen Diplomaten', R. Melville, C. Scharf, M. Vogt and U. Wengenroth (eds.), *Deutschland und Europa in der Neuzeit. Festschrift für Karl Otmar von Aretin* (Stuttgart, 1988), 679.

dynamics of the Habsburg leadership. *Pace* Hoyos's later assertions in 1917, Franz Joseph's ministers did not consider themselves driven into a war by Germany.[22]

Connected to this is a fourth point, the scant consideration paid to the other ally, Italy. Under the existing *Dreibund* treaty, Rome could expect to receive compensation in the Balkans, most probably in Albania, for any gains made by Austria-Hungary in the region.[23] The assembled ministers were clearly aware of the problem – hence their initial suggestion of a swift strike against Serbia to create a fait accompli before Rome could make demands. However, since, at Tisza's insistence, the meeting had decided against a surprise attack, Austria-Hungary's Italian problem had not been resolved; it had merely been deferred, and it would be the root cause of the later Austro-German difficulties with their Italian ally once war had broken out. As for the final point, Russia's likely reaction to an Austro-Serb conflict, the problem had been recognized but no practical steps had been considered. The ministers clearly appreciated the risk of escalation. Yet the consideration given to the Russian factor was cursory and casual. If anything it underscored the extent to which Habsburg decision-making was now afflicted by tunnel vision. Settling accounts with Belgrade overrode all other considerations.

Count Tisza is isolated

The meeting had left Tisza somewhat isolated. As the prospect of war hove into view his concerns about the always-fragile internal cohesion of the Habsburg Empire and Magyar dominance in the Trans-Leithanian half were rekindled. Tisza was no pacifist. His reluctance to embrace the military option was rooted in domestic calculations. His stance was shaped by a form of primacy of domestic politics, albeit with the difference that domestic concerns made the preservation of peace preferable to the alternative of war. The inclusion of further Slav elements in the Monarchy had been anathema to the ruling Magyar magnates ever since the dualist compromise of 1867. Any further growth in the number of ethnic Slavs had the potential of diluting Magyar power and of undermining the political status quo in the Monarchy. For that reason Tisza had dug in his heels over the annexation of Serb territory, and the other ministers had yielded to him on that point.

[22] See Hoyos to Mérey, 20 July 1917, Nachlass Mérey, HHStA, Karton 11.
[23] See H. Afflerbach, *Der Dreibund. Europäische Grossmacht- und Allianzpolitik vor dem Ersten Weltkrieg* (Vienna, 2002), 218–27.

On the central question, however, he did not prevail. He therefore set out his opposition in a memorandum drafted for the Emperor's benefit. Current circumstances made war a highly risky venture, he averred. An attack on Serbia now would lead to Russian and probably also Romanian intervention, and according to his calculations there would not be sufficient forces available to defeat the Serb army and to halt any Romanian incursion into Transylvania.[24]

Tisza conceded that delay might shift the military balance further against Austria-Hungary, but this would be more than made up for by his projected diplomatic offensive, supported by Germany, with the aim of forging new ties with Bulgaria, Greece and Romania. A war with Serbia under such circumstances need not be feared. For now, the precarious state of the Empire's finances and the deleterious effect on its fragile economy were further reasons for caution.

At the meeting of 7 July, the Hungarian prime minister had accepted the need for a démarche directed at Serbia. With that he also accepted that war would ensue if Belgrade rejected the demands made of it. At the same time he continued to insist that the Serb government had to be given the opportunity to avoid war, albeit at the price of a diplomatic humiliation. The 'serious denting of Serb arrogance' would be satisfactory enough, and would allow for a reinvigorated diplomatic offensive in south-eastern Europe. For all his preference for a diplomatic solution, Tisza accepted the possibility of war. And here the démarche was meant to ensure that, if the Serbs rejected Austria-Hungary's demands, they would incur the odium of having provoked another Balkan war. It would prove that, 'even after the Sarajevo outrage, [Serbia] refused loyally to fulfil the duties of a decent neighbour'. Tisza went further. Unlike his ministerial colleagues the previous day, he had given thought to the broader international setting of any showdown with Serbia: 'To avoid complications with Italy, to secure England's sympathy and to enable Russia to remain a spectator in the war at all, a declaration on our part ought to be issued, at the appropriate time and in the appropriate form, that we do not wish to annihilate Serbia, let alone annex her'. After the successful conclusion of the war, Serbia should be forced to cede the territories won during the two Balkan wars to Albania, Bulgaria and Greece. As for Austria-Hungary, she might demand 'certain strategically significant border rectifications'. More importantly, Belgrade would be compelled to indemnify her

---

[24] Note Tisza, 8 July 1914, ÖUA VIII, no. 10146. The figures were provided by Conrad at the ministerial council on 7 July.

for the costs of the war, 'which would give us leverage to keep Serbia in a lock-hold for a long time'.[25]

Tisza's opposition caused a considerable headache for Berchtold and his officials at the Ballhausplatz, who were adamant that there was no alternative to war. Baron Giesl, who called on Berchtold before returning to his post at Belgrade, was left in no doubt what was expected: 'However the Serbs react, you must break off relations and leave; it must come to war.'[26] For his part, the foreign minister had come to view the head of the Magyar government as 'a retarding element', as he observed to Tschirschky after the council meeting of 7 July. Berchtold was determined that if demands were addressed to Belgrade, they had to be such 'that their acceptance could be ruled out'.[27]

It was imperative for Berchtold to overcome Tisza's opposition. Constitutionally, and in terms of practical politics, no decision for war was possible without Magyar consent. The aged Emperor moreover, always mindful of Magyar sensibilities and sentiments, was not likely to accept a military solution if the Hungarian government were opposed to it. And Berchtold had been requested by the monarch to report to him at his summer residence at Ischl, where he had returned after the Archduke's hurried funeral. As Berchtold was determined that the diplomatic route, which the ministers had accepted on 7 July at Tisza's insistence, should be merely the prelude to war, it was important to soften Tisza's opposition further.

To that end, Berchtold once more played the German card. Tschirschky, he informed Tisza, had assured him that Germany was exercising pressure on Bucharest so as to ensure Romanian neutrality. The ambassador had stated emphatically that Berlin expected a decisive Austro-Hungarian action against Serbia, and 'that it would not be understood in Germany if we let the given opportunity pass, without striking out'. Such a decision would be interpreted at Berlin as 'a confession of weakness', and this, Berchtold warned, could not be 'without effect on our position in the *Dreibund* and Germany's future policy'.[28]

---

[25] Memo. Tisza, 8 July 1914, ÖUA VIII, no. 10146; I. Diószegi, *Hungarians in the Ballhausplatz: Studies on the Austro-Hungarian Common Foreign Policy* (Budapest, 1983), 237–8.

[26] As quoted in Rauchensteiner, *Doppeladler*, 75. In his memoirs, by contrast, Giesl suggested that Berchtold had assured him that nothing would happen: see Giesl, *Orient*, 256.

[27] Tel. Tschirschky to Auswärtiges Amt (no. 84, secret), 8 July 1914, *DD* I, no. 19.

[28] Berchtold to Tisza (private), 8 July 1914, ÖUA VIII, no. 10145; see also tel. Szögyény to Berchtold (no. 244), 9 July 1914, *ibid.*, no. 10154, for German representations at Bucharest.

As with Hoyos's secret mission to Berlin, so now with Tschirsch-ky's statements, the attitude of Germany was important primarily in its effect on the internal dynamics of Austro-Hungarian decision-making. The emphatic nature of the ambassador's explanations, Berchtold hoped, would sway Tisza. The foreign minister was to leave Vienna for Ischl in the evening of 8 July to report to Franz Joseph on the council meeting of the previous day. Given Tisza's opposition to war, and knowing that the premier was about to finalize his memorandum for the Emperor, Berchtold wished to give the monarch the impression of unanimity amongst the upper echelons of the Habsburg leadership. This was the more pressing now as Berchtold had set his officials to work on drafting the demands to be made on Serbia. A meeting took place just before Berchtold's departure for Ischl, attended by the foreign minister, Conrad, the belligerent troika of the senior section chiefs at the Ballhausplatz (Forgách, Hoyos and Macchio) and the representative of the Hungarian government at the imperial court, Baron István Burián, a close confidant of Tisza's. Burián occupied a mediating position between Berchtold and his prime minister in Budapest, but had begun to gravitate towards a more hawkish line, as he recorded in his diary:

> Instead of forcing a war – which all want except István Tisza – an ultimatum containing demands that Serbia can scarcely be willing to fulfil. Then either war or such a humiliation for Serbia that she is eliminated as a factor for some time ... The *correct* diplomatic move is thus not *worthless* as they like saying here [at Vienna]; naturally it is necessary that István Tisza agrees to *very harsh* demands ... Germany assures us of full support and urges us to exploit the advantageous moment.[29]

According to Conrad's private notes of the meeting, various campaign scenarios were discussed. But there was unanimity on the means and the ultimate objective. The ultimatum was to have the shortest possible time-frame, no more than twenty-four to forty-eight hours; and the outcome of

[29] Burián diary, 8 July 1914, I. Diószegi, 'Aussenminister Stephan Graf Burián. Biographie und Tagebuchstellen', *Annales Universitatis Scientiarum Budapestinensis de Rolando Eötvös nominatae. Sectio Historica* VIII (1966), 205; see also J. A. Treichel, 'Magyars at the Ballplatz: A Study of the Hungarians in the Austro-Hungarian Diplomatic Service, 1906–1914' (Ph.D. thesis, Georgetown, 1971), 179–89; R. Leslie, 'Österreich-Ungarn vor dem Kriegsausbruch. Der Ballhausplatz in Wien im Juli 1914 aus der Sicht eines österreichisch-ungarischen Diplomaten', R. Melville, C. Scharf, M. Vogt and U. Wengenroth (eds.), *Deutschland und Europa in der Neuzeit. Festschrift für Karl Otmar von Aretin* (Stuttgart, 1988), 664.

the campaign was to cripple Serbia financially and militarily, and to make her politically dependent on Austria-Hungary. Conrad himself, however, resisted any notion of mobilizing the armed forces until the decision for war had been taken.[30]

And yet, Tisza was not to be swayed. Germany's support was welcome, he replied to Berchtold, but it was not for Berlin to issue directives nor for a Hungarian prime minister to follow them. Moreover, when in Berlin, Hoyos had made 'a colossal mistake' by suggesting that Austria-Hungary aimed at the elimination of Serbia as a state. Any misapprehensions at Berlin should be corrected forthwith. For his part, Tisza still rejected the idea of an attack on Serbia without prior diplomatic preparations, but intimated that Romania's reaction to German pressure would be decisive.[31]

Tisza remained opposed to war. Yet he had begun to shift his position, and to an extent this helps to explain why the Ballhausplatz continued along the path it had already mapped out. Berchtold, meanwhile, arrived at Ischl in the early hours of 9 July and was ushered into the Emperor's study at 9.30 a.m. Franz Joseph agreed that there was 'no way back' now. The demands on Serbia should be such that, if accepted, Austria-Hungary had the means of enforcing Serbia's continued compliance with them in future.[32] Berchtold had every reason to be satisfied with the outcome of his audience at Ischl. The Emperor had consented to a diplomatic démarche which should satisfy Tisza. He had also agreed to harsh demands to be addressed to Belgrade, thus ensuring their rejection. Finally, he had accepted that there should be no mobilization unless war was certain, so accommodating Conrad's demands.

In its own peculiar, consensual and ponderous manner, Habsburg policy thus moved at the pace of an arthritic snail. The Emperor, Berchtold observed to Conrad on his return to the capital on 10 July, 'appeared to be in favour of action against Serbia … We could not now retreat not least because of Germany. Tisza counselled caution, was against war; but Baron Burián was in Budapest for talks with Tisza.'[33] In the end it was Burián who would persuade Tisza of the case for war.

---

[30] Conrad, *Aus meiner Dienstzeit* IV, 61–2.

[31] Tisza to Berchtold, 9 July 1914, J. Galántai, *Die österreichisch-ungarische Monarchie und der Weltkrieg* (Budapest, 1979), 261–2. This important letter was not included in ÖUA.

[32] Berchtold, 'Am Vorabend des Weltkrieges', Hantsch, *Berchtold* II, 588–9; see also tel. Tschirschky to Auswärtiges Amt (no. 85, very secret), 10 July 1914, *DD* I, no. 29.

[33] Conrad, *Aus meiner Dienstzeit* IV, 70.

The view from St Petersburg

The focus so far has been entirely on the Central Powers – with good reason, for the key decisions had been taken in Vienna and, after a fashion, in Berlin. No comparable momentous events took place in the other capitals of Europe in the days immediately after Sarajevo. The reaction by the other Powers was varied, reflecting their respective interests and current preoccupations. The events in faraway Bosnia affected them in quite different ways. A number of common themes, however, emerged from their reactions. How the decision-makers at St Petersburg, Paris and London framed the murder of the archducal couple also shaped the decisions they were to take during July and early August 1914.

If the German leadership considered their country to be affected by the assassination, they did so on account of the *Zweibund* ties with Austria-Hungary. On no other Power did Sarajevo have such an immediate impact, albeit one refracted here through a series of alliance concerns. But after Germany Russia was the country most likely to feel the effects of any complications in the Balkans. A confluence of different developments and factors helps to explain why this should have been so.

Following the double setback of military defeat abroad and revolution at home in 1905, Russia had pursued a policy of consolidation. In external affairs the alliance with France, signed in its current form in 1894, remained the cornerstone of Russian policy. With the east Asian outlet for her expansionist drive blocked by Japan, now the dominant regional force, a general Asiatic compromise with Great Britain, Russia's traditional competitor in the region, became both possible and desirable. The 1907 Anglo-Russian convention settled longstanding quarrels between the two Powers and, at least for the moment, halted their struggle for mastery in Asia, one of the dominant themes of Great Power politics since the 1830s. To balance the ties with France and the implicit leaning towards Britain, Russia's foreign minister, Aleksandr Petrovich Izvolsky, and his successor after 1910, Sergei Dmitrievich Sazonov, sought improved relations with Germany. However, such a balancing act was difficult to perform. Ultimately, it failed, partly because of French suspicions, partly because Germany overestimated the strength of her own position vis-à-vis Russia, and partly because Russian policy had begun to gravitate towards the Near East and south-eastern Europe. And there it clashed with Austro-Hungarian interests.[34]

---

[34] For some insights into this see D. C. B. Lieven, *Empire: The Russian Empire and its Rivals from the Sixteenth Century to the Present* (London, 2003 (pb)), 182–98.

The latter development was the more significant as it affected Russian policy in a longer-term perspective. It was to shape the perceptions and the general attitude of Russian decision-makers in the summer of 1914. Already the Bosnian annexation crisis of 1908–9 had given a foretaste of the potential for Balkan complications to cause international disturbances. The crisis had foreshadowed the scenario that would become a horrible reality in 1914: an Austro-Serb dispute escalating into a general European war. Then it had underscored the extent to which Russia's military weakness had diminished her international position, something that was confirmed by subsequent international crises, such as the renewed Franco-German stand-off over Morocco in 1911 and the two Balkan wars of 1912–13. The events of those years showed that St Petersburg was not prepared to resort to armed force in the first instance. For the moment, it was understood in the chancelleries of Europe that 'Russia cannot do much if Austria is backed by Germany'.[35] Necessity had forced Russia to show restraint. But the experience of nearly a decade of foreign setbacks generated a good deal of irritation in official circles at St Petersburg and among the pan-Slavs in Moscow.[36]

In 1914 Russia was in an altogether different position than in 1908–9, and this was to shape Russian assessments of the unfolding crisis. For one thing, the country's economy had recovered from the effects of, first, the global downturn around 1900 and then the problems caused by domestic turmoil after 1905. The notion of Russia's general economic backwardness has long lost its scholarly lustre. If anything, Russia's economic development was typical of the fast-expanding late-nineteenth-century economies in Europe. In the years before 1914, her economy grew on average by 3.25% and, by 1913, her national income was almost on a par with that of Britain (97.1%) and exceeded that of France by a substantial margin (171.5%).[37] True, Russia's economic development, with its dependence on peasant agriculture, foreign technologies and capital, and state promotion of industry, was 'peculiarly Russian in flavour',[38]

[35] Paget to Barclay, 6 Aug. 1912, Barclay MSS, LSE Archives, Barclay 4/1.
[36] K. Neilson, 'Russia', in K. M. Wilson (ed.), Decisions for War 1914 (London, 1995), 97–120, offers a succinct survey.
[37] See the reflections by A. J. Rieber, 'Persistent Factors in Russian Foreign Policy: An Interpretative Essay', H. Ragsdale (ed.), Imperial Russian Foreign Policy (Cambridge, 1993), 322–9 [315–59]; P. Gatrell, Government, Industry and Rearmament in Russia, 1900–1914: The Last Argument of Tsarism (Cambridge, 1994), 161–96; P. R. Gregory, Russian National Income, 1895–1913 (Cambridge, 1982), 153–65. See also the invaluable statistics in A. P. Korelin (for Rossiskaya Akademi'ia Rossiskoi Istori'i) (ed.), Rossi'ia 1913 god. Statistiko-dokumental'nyi Spravochnik (St Petersburg, 1995), here 152–65.
[38] Clive Trebilcock's felicitous phrase, in his The Industrialization of the Continental Powers, 1780–1914 (London, repr. 1994), 281.

stimulated and constrained in equal measure by a restrictive state, and it still contained pockets of real backwardness, most notably in so far as advanced technology and productivity per capita were concerned. Nonetheless, the Russian economy was the fourth largest in the world in 1914. The many pre-modern aspects of the Russian state and Russian society notwithstanding, on the eve of the war Russia was no longer a backward country, and her 'economy ... was sufficient to support Russia's status as a Great Power'.[39]

Russia's economic recovery ran in parallel with the consolidation of state finances. These were always dependent on the caprice of 'His Excellency the Harvest', but in the years before 1914 bumper-crop yields had brought in increased revenues, and so helped to stabilize Russia's budget. But the ingenuity of two finance ministers, Sergei Yulevich Witte and Vladimir Nikola'evich Kokovtsov, moreover, had done much to stabilize Russia's finances and to engineer additional revenue for debt reduction and defence expenditure.[40] With the financial underpinnings of Russian power in better shape, the government in St Petersburg was in a position to pursue ambitious rearmament programmes. Defence expenditure as a percentage of government spending overall rose from 23.2% to 28.3% in the six years before 1913.[41] Increased spending on the armed forces, indeed, fuelled industrial production, as was illustrated by St Petersburg's famous Putilov Works.

The growth in defence spending was only one aspect of Russian military policy after 1905. Especially during the term of the current war minister, General Vladimir Aleksandrovich Sukhomlinov, wide-ranging reforms were launched to overcome the existing shortages in officers and non-commissioned officers, and to enhance the overall professionalism of the Russian army, with the pleasing side-effect of filling his own pockets through a series of profitable stock exchange speculations. He also reorganized the cumbersome reserve system, re-equipped the army with modern field artillery pieces of the most advanced type, and redeployed Russian

---

[39] Neilson, 'Russia', 102; W. E. Mosse, *An Economic History of Russia, 1856–1914* (London, 1996 (pb)), 249–65.

[40] The so-called 'free balance' of the Imperial Treasury was something of an accounts conjuring trick and thus controversial. But it was the 'trump card' of the Russian state, making substantial additional sums of money available, to be spent free of Duma control and entirely at the finance minister's discretion; for a discussion of this, see M. Miller, *The Economic Development of Russia, 1905–1914, with Special Reference to Trade, Industry and Finance* (London, repr. 1967), 132–6.

[41] Gregory, *National Income*, 252; Mosse, *Economic History*, 255; W. Dowler, *Russia in 1913* (De Kalb, IL, 2010), 44–9.

forces from the Polish salient to more defensible positions to the east of the Vistula river under the revised war plan, Plan 19.[42]

Sukhomlinov's main achievement, however, was a four-year military programme, starting in 1914 and to be completed by 1917. The so-called 'Great Programme' was intended to raise the army's peacetime establishment from 1.3 million men to 1.75 million by increasing the annual draft contingent to 585,000. It also envisaged the near doubling of artillery batteries. This was combined with steep increases in the numbers of heavy guns, especially fortress artillery. Field artillery was strangely neglected, especially of the light-howitzer variety that would stand the German army in such good stead during the war, and so was the shell reserve, in line with the premise of the 'Great Programme' that any war would be a short one.[43] Even so the pointers for the future were indisputable. The changes in Russia's defence posture were not limited to the army. The navy also underwent large-scale modernization and reconstruction programmes, and by 1914 the Russians were laying down eight capital battleships in the Baltic and another three in the Black Sea. The latter, the *Ekatarina II* class of vessels, were of the most modern type and easily matched the most advanced ships afloat at the time.[44]

The numbers, impressive though they were, were not in themselves an indication, let alone a guarantee, of the combat effectiveness of Russia's armed forces. But by 1914 it was beyond doubt that Russia had recovered from the nadir of her military power in 1905. Since then, the Tsar's government had spent substantial sums of money on rearmament programmes, and these had yielded impressive results. Whatever else they meant, they certainly enabled St Petersburg to back up its diplomatic moves by armed force.

If the Russian government had any pressing foreign policy concerns in the first half of 1914, these were concentrated not on Austria-Hungary and the Balkans but on the Black Sea region. Here the consolidation in power of the Young Turk régime at Constantinople had brought with it also sustained efforts to augment and modernize the Ottoman armed forces, not surprising in light of the military background of most ministers at Constantinople. The projected growth of Ottoman naval

[42] N. Stone, *The Eastern Front, 1914–1917* (London, 1975), 24–36; D. Stevenson, *Armaments and the Coming of the War, 1904–1914* (Oxford, 1996), 315–23; J. W. Steinberg, *All the Tsar's Men: Russia's General Staff and the Fate of the Empire, 1898–1914* (Baltimore, MD, 2010), 184–9.

[43] See Stone, *Eastern Front*, 32, on this; D. G. Herrmann, *The Arming of Europe and the Making of the First World War* (Princeton, NJ, 1996), 195–8.

[44] Neilson, 'Russia', 105–6.

power was a particular source of concern for Russia. Two developments threatened to tilt the naval balance in the Black Sea against her. The first of these was the further fortification of the Turkish Straits, which would make the Ottoman capital more resilient to any attempts at coercive diplomacy backed by naval power. The second, more significant, development was the construction of two *Dreadnought*-class battleships of the latest type, laid down in 1913, and the planned purchase, in early 1914, of no fewer than five further such vessels, then under construction at British shipyards and originally intended for Brazil and Chile.[45]

The situation in the region that confronted Russian diplomats and ministers was nevertheless somewhat ambiguous. If the anticipated growth in Turkish naval power heralded the diminution of Russian influence at Constantinople, it also marked a shift in the regional balance after decades of gradual Ottoman decline. Even the eventuality of Turkey's collapse could not be ruled out altogether. The two recent conflicts in the Balkans, after all, had significantly reduced the Ottoman Empire; another crisis in the region might well complete the process of its destruction. In turn, this raised the question of the future control of the Turkish Straits. That maritime defile was a traditional object of Russian designs in the region. Whatever the sentimental attachment to the idea of Constantinople as the 'Second Rome' of Christian Orthodoxy, there were sound strategic reasons for ensuring that the Straits did not fall under the control of a foreign Power, as Sazonov reminded the Tsar at the end of 1913. Russia's own interests were focused on the further development of her own resources; and that required the preservation of peace. But any state in possession of the Straits would 'have in its hands not only the key to the Black Sea and the Mediterranean Seas … [but also] the key to forward movement into Asia Minor and for hegemony in the Balkans'.[46] If the Straits were ever closed to Russian trade, the principal source of Russian exchange – the grain trade – would be eliminated, with catastrophic consequences for the efforts to develop Russia's economy further.

The planned appointment of a German army officer, General Otto Liman von Sanders, as commander of the Ottoman forces at Constantinople lent greater urgency to Sazonov's arguments.[47] It also provided the

---

[45] For some of this see R. P. Bobroff, *Roads to Glory: Late Imperial Russia and the Turkish Straits* (London, 2006), 76–85; M. Aksakal, *The Ottoman Road to War in 1914: The Ottoman Empire and the First World War* (Cambridge, 2008), 42–7.

[46] Sazonov to Nicholas II, 23 Nov. 1913, *LN* II, 366; see also Bobroff, *Roads to Glory*, 84.

[47] U. Trumpener, 'Liman von Sanders and the German-Ottoman Alliance', *JCH* I, 4 (1966), 179–92; M. A. Reynolds, *Shattering Empires: The Clash and Collapse of the Ottoman and Russian Empires, 1908–1918* (Cambridge, 2011), 40–1.

background to a special ministerial conference at St Petersburg in early February 1914, convened at Sazonov's request to discuss recent regional developments. The foreign minister warned that, whilst there were no likely complications on the horizon, 'one could not guarantee, even for the near future, the maintenance of the current state of affairs in the Near East'. Should Turkey lose control over the Straits, no foreign Power was to be allowed to establish itself there, and this might entail Russian military operations against Constantinople. A whole range of military options was discussed, including amphibious landing operations in the vicinity of the Ottoman capital.[48]

It would be tempting to see in this evidence of aggressive designs on Russia's part. Yet in terms of practical politics, the conference pointed to two essential requirements for the foreseeable future: peace had to be preserved in Europe while Russia's modernization programme continued, and the strengthening of Ottoman naval power had to be countered by accelerating Russia's own construction programme for the Black Sea fleet. As Sazonov impressed on the Russian ambassador at London, Count Aleksandr Konstantinovich von Benckendorff, in May 1914: 'It is obvious what fateful consequences the loss of our controlling position in the Black Sea would have, and there we cannot simply watch the further and more-over swift build-up of Ottoman naval forces.' It was imperative then to avoid 'any cause for complications on account of the Oriental Question', given its potential for European tensions.[49]

As for the Liman von Sanders crisis, following a slow diplomatic shuffle it ended in minor German concessions that satisfied Russia's more immediate demands. But the affair had soured relations between St Petersburg and Berlin, and it kindled Sazonov's suspicions of ambitious German designs on the Balkans. It convinced him of the need to turn the existing arrangements with Britain and France into something more binding, cohesive and above all more visible. The 'consolidation and development of the so-called "Triple Entente" and, if possible, its conversion into a new Triple Alliance' had acquired greater urgency for Russian diplomacy, as Sazonov explained to Izvolsky, his predecessor and now ambassador at Paris: 'Such an alliance would completely secure the international position of Russia, France and England, and would not threaten anyone, since none of these Powers has expansionist designs, but be the best guarantee for preserving peace in Europe.'[50]

---

[48] Minutes of special conference, 8/21 Feb. 1914, *IBZI* I, no. 295.

[49] Sazonov to Benckendorff (confidential), 25 Apr./8 May 1914, *IBZI* II, no. 384. For an attempt at an aggressive interpretation see S. McMeekin, *The Russian Origins of the First World War* (Cambridge, MA, 2011), 31–5.

[50] Sazonov to Izvolsky (no. 23), 20 Mar./2 Apr. 1914, *IBZI* II, no. 137; see also S. D. Sazonov, *Fateful Years, 1909–1916* (London, 1928), 128–32.

Such considerations explain Sazonov's attempts in the spring of
1914 to entice Britain into talks on a naval agreement. These had no more
material substance than a mirage. But Sazonov pursued the option dog-
gedly, and, as was seen earlier, the secret intelligence on it caused a good
deal of headache at Berlin.

Calculations at the Choristers' Bridge

The attitude of Russian ministers on the eve of the Sarajevo crisis was
ambiguous, characterized by arrogance and anxiety in equal measure. The
recent deterioration in Russo-German relations did not prefigure a decision
to resort to armed force in any future crisis. But it certainly helped to create
a mindset which made the decision-makers at St Petersburg susceptible to
suggestions of a concerted effort by the two Germanic Powers to extend
their influence in the Balkans.

The initial Russian response to the events at Sarajevo was slow,
however.[51] It reflected the ongoing concerns with developments elsewhere
but it also established an interpretative framework which would help to
condition Russian decisions later in the month. It is true that there is
evidence of weeding in the Russian archives, all the more conspicuous for
the exceedingly liberal use of pre-1917 materials by the Soviet authorities in
their attempts to discredit the old régime.[52] Even so, there are no grounds
for suggesting that the government in St Petersburg had any knowledge of,
let alone any involvement in, the plot against the Archduke. Acts of
terrorism had left a long and bloody trail in Russian politics. Among its
victims was no less an exalted personage than Tsar Nicholas II's grandfather Alexander II. Regicide did not, as a rule, recommend itself as a sound
policy to Russia's autocrat and his ministers.

Strategic considerations that made it imperative to preserve peace
aside, there was a broad consensus amongst ministers at St Petersburg, as
the Austro-Hungarian chargé d'affaires observed at the end of 1913, that
'any external complication contained the greatest dangers because it would
automatically be succeeded by an internal one'.[53] The current government

---

[51] Shebeko, the ambassador at Vienna, reported on the assassination as soon as the
news broke: see tels. Shebeko to Sazonov (nos. 70, urgent, and 73), 15/28 June 1914,
IBZI iv, nos. 3–4; there was no immediate response from St Petersburg.
[52] For some reflections on this see McMeekin, *Russian Origins*, 257, n. 13.
[53] Otto Czernin to Berchtold (no. 43D), 8/21 Nov. 1913, HHStA, PA X/139; for a
discussion of domestic factors see D. Geyer, *Russian Imperialism: The Interaction of
Domestic and Foreign Policy, 1860–1914* (Leamington Spa, 1987), 293–317;

under the aged Ivan Loginovich Goremykin was no exception. An 'estimable functionary', he inclined towards '[u]nrestrained obscurantist reaction', as one Russian diplomat later reflected. Goremykin was, as the Habsburg representative at St Petersburg commented a little maliciously, 'an elderly gentleman devoted to quietism'[54] – and the absence of a firm hand at St Petersburg would present problems during the July crisis.

Goremykin's ineptitude was not the least of Russia's misfortunes. Another was that Sazonov presided over the foreign ministry at the *Pevcheski Most*, the Choristers' Bridge, across St Petersburg's Palace Square on the Moika river. Unassuming and modest, though of undoubted intelligence, he had strongly developed religious sensibilities – so much so that one wit observed that if Sazonov had fulfilled his youthful ambition of becoming a monk, the Orthodox church would have gained one more saint and Russia would have lost one more inadequate foreign minister.[55] Somewhat nervous and highly strung, he had slowly risen through the ranks of the Russian diplomatic service, spending no less than thirteen years at the Russian legation at the Holy See before being appointed foreign minister in 1910, having deputized for Izvolsky for the previous year. Although painstaking and diligent, he lacked the force of character and the robustness of personality that were necessary to succeed in the vicious politics at the imperial court. His greatest weakness was the Achilles' heel of many politicians – he was filled with good intentions. He was liable to change his mind, unable to follow an idea to its logical conclusion. As the British ambassador at Paris, Sir Francis Bertie, noted during the early stages of the war, 'he is dangerous and obstinate, without acumen and very shortsighted'.[56] A brother-in-law of Pyotr Arkadi'evich Stolypin, the former prime minister assassinated by a pan-Slav fanatic in 1911, Sazonov felt too insecure to advance his positions against stronger men. Mindful of the need to retain the Tsar's confidence and anxious not to offend the

---

D. M. Macdonald, 'A Lever without a Fulcrum: Domestic Factors and Russian Foreign Policy', Ragsdale (ed.), *Imperial Russian Foreign Policy*, 268–311.

[54] Quotes from R. R. Rosen, *Forty Years of Diplomacy* (2 vols., London, 1922) II, 149, and Otto Czernin to Berchtold (no. 8B), 31 Jan./13 Feb. 1914, HHStA, PA X/140; see also D. C. B. Lieven, *Russia's Rulers under the Old Regime* (New Haven, CT, 1989), 184–5.

[55] M. von Taube, *Der grossen Katastrophe entgegen. Die russische Politik der Vorkriegszeit und das Ende des Zarenreiches (1904–1914)* (Berlin, 1929), 225. Taube was a member of the Imperial Senate; see also B. Jelavich, *Russia's Balkan Entanglements, 1806–1914* (Cambridge, repr. 1993), 225–6.

[56] Bertie diary, 29 July 1915, Lady Gordon-Lennox (ed.), *The Diary of Lord Bertie of Thame, 1914–1918* (2 vols., London, 1924) I, 206.

vociferous pan-Slavs inside the Duma and without it,[57] he tended to yield rather than to press home his own views. Certainly, as will be seen, at the crucial stages of the July crisis Sazonov was inconsistent and showed an uncertain grasp of international realities.

M. Shebeko sends reassuring reports

On the eve of Sarajevo, Sazonov and his officials were preoccupied with the cooling in Russia's relations with Britain, largely on account of the two Powers' increasingly divergent interests in central Asia and in Persia especially.[58] True, Austro-Serb relations remained tense, and there was an ongoing Great Power struggle for influence over what remained of the Ottoman Empire. But neither the destruction of Austria-Hungary nor Russia's complete dominance in the Balkans were at this time aims of Russian policy. Russia's real interest lay in developing her own internal resources; and that required peace. Balkan troubles could not advance this immediate foreign policy goal. For that reason, Sazonov advised Belgrade to 'exercise extreme caution' in its relations with its Habsburg neighbour.[59]

Count Benckendorff at the London embassy reflected the revulsion that was felt by many on receiving the news of the 'terrible tragedy'. But he had a shrewd sense of the twin dangers that lay ahead: 'That racial hatred is at the bottom of it is undeniable. The misfortune however is that the persistent mistake will be repeated to hold the whole race responsible for the crimes of individuals. That is now the danger.'[60] His colleague at Vienna, Nikolai Nikola'evich Shebeko, offered a nuanced and not altogether unfair assessment of the slain heir to the Habsburg throne. He noted his pro-Slav sentiments and his preference for a 'trialist' reform of the constitution, but also pointed to his falling under the sway of such disparate influences as that of Kaiser Wilhelm II and the extreme clerical forces in Austria. Significantly, he hinted that Franz Ferdinand had been in favour of new taxes to be levied 'for war-like purposes'.[61]

---

[57] See also Szápáry to Berchtold (no. 58), 15 Feb. 1914, HHStA, PA X/140.
[58] See e.g. Benckendorff to Sazonov, 15/28 June 1914, IZBI iv, no. 2; M. Soroka, *Britain, Russia and the Road to the First World War: The Fateful Embassy of Count Aleksandr Benckendorff, 1903–1916* (Farnham and Burlington, VT, 2011), 243–5.
[59] Tel. Sazonov to Hartwig (no. 1351), 24 June/7 July 1914, IBZI iv, no. 112; also tel. Spalajković to Pašić, 21 June/4 July 1914, APS i, no. 405.
[60] Benckendorff to Sazonov, 17/30 June 1914, IBZI iv, no. 26.
[61] Shebeko to Sazonov (no. 38), 17/30 June 1914, IBZI iv, no. 32.

As was seen earlier, the Archduke was anything but a warmonger by the time of his murder, but an impression had gained ground that he was the leader of a war party at Vienna. As the Russian ambassador at Rome, Anatoli Nikola'evich Krupenski, reported, the Italian foreign minister, the Marchese di San Giuliano, had observed that the 'crime is detestable, but world peace will not complain'.[62] Here was at least the beginning of an argument that presented Austria-Hungary as bent on war, though ironically it was the killing of the Archduke that removed the brakes from the war party at Vienna.

There was an additional consideration that made Sazonov hesitate. Abhorrence at the Bosnian atrocity was no doubt genuine, and Russian diplomatic despatches were certainly couched in the appropriate, condemnatory language. But Sazonov was wary of Austro-Hungarian suggestions of an official Serb connection with the murder. This was not particularly rooted in a desire to deny the legitimacy of Austria-Hungary's case – though Russian officials had given at least tacit approval to the pan-Serb programme[63] – but rather reflected recent experience with Vienna's habit of deploying crude forgeries in pursuit of its anti-Serb policies, most notoriously during the Friedjung trial in 1909, a botched attempt by the Habsburg authorities to accuse Serbian leaders within the Empire of treason by using what soon turned out to be crudely forged documents. His reluctance to accept accusations directed at Belgrade now was at least understandable.[64]

At the beginning of July, ambassador Shebeko sent his second secretary, Prince Mikhail A. Gagarin, to assess the situation at Sarajevo and to verify some of the early claims of the assassins' Belgrade connections. Gagarin's report was the best evidence available to Sazonov. It derived much of the information it conveyed from open sources available at Sarajevo; and it was certainly not an unfair account, even if the lengthy section dealing with the ethnic violence in Sarajevo following the assassination bore traces of pro-Serb sentiments. Gagarin noted, rightly, that the two principal plotters, Prinčip and Čabrinović, were natives of Bosnia, and thus Habsburg subjects. He argued that

[62] Krupenski to Sazonov, 17/30 June 1914, *IBZI* IV, no. 29.
[63] B. Jelavich, 'Official Russia and the Balkan Slavic Communities', *Canadian Review of Studies in Nationalism* XVI, 1–2 (1989), 209–26; E. C. Thaden, *Russia and the Balkan Alliance of 1912* (University Park, PA, 1965), 86–92 *et passim*; and this author's 'Montenegro: Russia's Troublesome Ally, 1910–1912', in his *Interpreting History: Collective Essays on Russia's Relations with Europe* (Boulder, CO, 1990), 125–54.
[64] The trial and the revelation of official Austro-Hungarian forgeries had made a profound impression on Russian diplomats: see B. N. de Strandtmann, 'Vospominaniya', unpubl. TS, CUBA, Sviatopolk-Mirskii Collection, fo. 3.

suggestions of a vast conspiracy involving a larger number of terrorists ought to be treated with caution and considered as rumours generated after the bloody deed. Then there was the issue of the incompetent preparations for the Archduke's visit by the local military administration, which amounted to 'unforgiveable negligence'. Why indeed had the authorities not considered the likely effect the visit by a senior Habsburg royal on *vidovdan* would have on Serb national sentiment in the annexed provinces? The nationalist agitation there was a home-made Austro-Hungarian problem, and it suited the interests of the Habsburg authorities now to divert attention to Belgrade in order to be able to maintain the fiction of order and stability in Bosnia.

Gagarin also cast doubt on the suggestion that the assassins had been provided with their weapons by agents of the Serbian state. If that had been so, he speculated, they would have been better armed. That was an astonishing aside, one that is suggestive of a general awareness by Russian diplomats that some parts of the Serb security apparatus dabbled in terrorism. Even so, Gagarin's overall assessment was not overtly anti-Habsburg. The administration of Bosnia, he predicted, would gradually be taken over by pro-Habsburg Slavs. For now, however,

> [t]he Bosnia-Herzegovinian Question is not yet ripe [for a solution]. It is now an indivisible part of the Southern Slav Question, and its solution depends on whether Austria-Hungary knows how to turn the Southern Slav Question to its advantage, or whether that question will be decided against Austria-Hungary. On it will depend the fate of the Danube Empire.[65]

This was not an unreasonable conclusion. But Gagarin's report can only have reinforced Sazonov's suspicions of Austro-Hungarian assertions of Belgrade's complicity later on during the July crisis.

Also, Gagarin's chief at the Vienna embassy, Shebeko, reported on a demonstration outside the Serbian legation in the Habsburg capital, for which he held 'German elements in conjunction with the German embassy' responsible. Intriguingly in light of later developments, Shebeko suspected his German colleague, Tschirschky, of 'harnessing all his powers to exploit this sad event [the Archduke's murder]' to whip up anti-Serb and

---

[65] Memo. Gagarin, 25 June/8 July 1914, encl. in Shebeko to Sazonov (no. 44), 3/16 July 1914, *IBZI* IV, no. 248; Igelstroem [consul-general, Sarajevo] to Shebeko, (no. 5), 5 July 1914, *ibid.*, no. 120; see also D. C. B. Lieven, *Russia and the Origins of the First World War* (London, 1983), 140.

anti-Russian sentiments.[66] Whatever Shebeko's sources may have been, his suspicions were well-founded. For, as was seen earlier, behind the scenes, the German ambassador had indeed encouraged Austria-Hungary to opt for a military solution of the Serb problem.

If Shebeko harboured suspicions about his German colleague, his despatches tended to emphasize the pacific aspects of the official Habsburg reaction. He noted the calming intentions behind Franz Joseph's manifesto to his peoples in which the monarch had expressed his confidence that the 'madness of a small band of misguided individuals' would not shake the ties of loyalty that kept the Empire together. True, Shebeko did not fail to point out that the Emperor also had affirmed that the planned military and naval armaments programmes, pet projects of the slain Archduke, would go ahead. But this was for the future. It was no indication of an imminent military strike.[67]

His own conversations with Berchtold had alerted Shebeko to the fact that some Austro-Hungarian démarche had to be expected. During their interview on 8 July, the day after the ministerial council meeting, the foreign minister left the ambassador in no doubt as to the depth of official suspicions of Serbia. After all, Berchtold observed, leading members of the current government at Belgrade had been implicated in the bloody coup against their own monarch in 1903. At the same time, Berchtold's comments dispelled any apprehension the Russian diplomat may have had. Vienna, he reported, would make 'no demands on the Serbian government that would be irreconcilable with the dignity of the neighbouring state'.[68] There was an element of wishful thinking in Shebeko's reporting at this stage of the July crisis, but also later. The ambassador could not bring himself to believe, as he confessed to his British colleague, Sir Maurice de Bunsen, that the Habsburg Monarchy 'will allow itself to be rushed into war'. The economic effects of the mobilization against Serbia in 1913 would restrain Vienna. If they did not, any strike against Serbia would escalate, he thought: 'Of this there could be no question. A Servian war meant a general European war.' There was an undeniable lack of empathy with Austria-Hungary's predicament in Shebeko's attitude. Vienna had thwarted Serbia

---

[66] Shebeko to Sazonov (nos. 39 and 104), 30 June/13 July 1914, *IBZI* IV, no. 46 and V, no. 139.

[67] Shebeko to Sazonov (no. 41), 5/22 July 1914, *IBZI* IV, no. 90.

[68] Tel. Shebeko to Sazonov (no. 85), 25 June/8 July 1914, and private letter, 25 June/8 July 1914, *IBZI* IV, nos. 132 and 133; also Dumaine to Viviani (no. 94, very confidential), 8 July 1914, *DDF* (3) X, no. 484; and N. Shebeko, *Souvenirs. Essai historique sur les origines de la guerre de 1914* (Paris, 1936), 203–5 (though not entirely reliable on details, this gives a good impression of the atmosphere at Vienna).

at every possible occasion, he argued, and implied that the plot against the Archduke was self-inflicted. To make Serbia now responsible for the actions of ethnic Serb assassins 'was a new doctrine'.[69] And in that Shebeko was entirely correct, as Tisza had pointed out and as the Habsburg ministers had acknowledged when accepting the need for a diplomatic approach.

Nikolai Genrikovich Hartwig visits his Habsburg colleague

What Shebeko's comments and those of other Russian officials in the days immediately after Sarajevo indicate, however, is how narrow the path open to diplomacy had become. For his part, Sazonov contributed to this on 7 July. In response to a hint by the Austro-Hungarian chargé d'affaires, Count Otto Czernin, that his government might insist on an enquiry at Belgrade into any possible official involvement in the Sarajevo plot, Sazonov warned Vienna against 'entering on such a very dangerous path'.[70] All the same, aware of the risk of complications, the Russian foreign minister sought to moderate Belgrade's behaviour. In light of the hardened anti-Serb mood in Austria-Hungary, he counselled Pašić 'to exercise extreme caution with regard to any question that was apt to increase that mood and so lead to a dangerous situation'.[71]

The comments by Sazonov and Shebeko underscored the prevailing mistrust of Austria-Hungary in Russian circles. It was a reflection more of Russia's troubled recent experience with the Habsburg Empire rather than a deliberate attempt purposely to delegitimize any Austro-Hungarian case for redress. This also applied to those Russian diplomats usually associated with a fiercely anti-Habsburg orientation in Russian foreign policy. The Tsar's diplomatic agents frequently acted off their own bat, and were rarely subject to strict central control. The excessive indulgence St Petersburg showed towards the personal peculiarities and whims of its diplomats abroad owed something to the leisurely ways of the Russian gentry, but it also reflected the fact that the connections

---

[69] Bunsen to Grey (no. 137, confidential), 5 July 1914, TNA (PRO), FO 371/1899/30991.
[70] Tel. Carlotti to San Giuliano (no. 6025/418), 7 July 1914, *DDI* (4) XII, no. 109; also in *IBZI* IV, no. 128, but misdated. There seems to be no Russian report on the conversation; Czernin also did not touch upon it in his despatch: see tel. Czernin to Berchtold (no. 139), 7 July 1914, *ÖUA* VIII, no. 10106. Presumably Czernin told his Italian colleague, but not his superiors at Vienna.
[71] Tel. Sazonov to Hartwig (no. 1351), 7 July 1914, *IBZI* IV, no. 112.

these individuals had at St Petersburg made it advisable for any foreign minister to treat them leniently.[72]

The Russian minister at Belgrade was no exception to that rule. Despite his German name and ancestry, Nikolai Genrikovich Hartwig was no friend of the Habsburg Monarchy. If anything, he was one of the most ardent pan-Slav sympathizers amongst imperial Russian diplomats. Following his transfer to the Serbian capital in 1909, he had assiduously worked behind the scenes to facilitate the conclusion of the 1912 Balkan League. He had variously stated his belief that, ultimately, Bosnia and Herzegovina would fall to Serbia. 'After the question of Turkey, it is now the turn of Austria', he reportedly claimed at the end of 1913: 'The day approaches when … Serbia will re-acquire *her* Bosnia and *her* Herzegovina.'[73] At Belgrade itself he occupied a special position as 'a power behind the throne', very influential but not all-powerful as was often asserted at the time. He was particularly close to Pašić, the prime minister, and had in fact kept him in office during the recent 'May crisis' in Serbia.[74]

In his official reports, Hartwig certainly disguised the extent to which anti-Habsburg sentiments had been openly displayed in Belgrade and other Serbian towns. Indeed, he presented a highly colourful, if entirely misleading, picture of a court and a political élite plunged into deep mourning at the Archduke's demise.[75] And there were rumours that the imperial Russian flag above the legation building was not flown at half-mast after Sarajevo.[76] Yet, whatever Pašić himself may have known of a plot, there is no reason to suspect that Hartwig had any foreknowledge of the Sarajevo conspiracy. If anything, he impressed upon the Serbian government to do nothing to inflame the situation, just as he had encouraged Pašić previously to pursue a policy of consolidation at home and conciliation abroad.[77]

Whatever the final shape of south-eastern Europe, to Hartwig's mind the time was not yet ripe for Serbia's further expansion, nor was Russia ready for renewed convulsions in the Balkans. For that reason, he sought out Baron Giesl, his Habsburg colleague, who had returned to

---

[72] See Lieven, *Russia*, 60–4; T. G. Otte, '"Outdoor Relief for the Aristocracy"?: European Nobility and Diplomacy', M. Mösslang and T. Riotte (eds.), *The Diplomats' World: A Cultural History of Diplomacy, 1815–1914* (Oxford, 2008), 41–3 [23–58].

[73] Memo. de Margerie, 'Note pour le ministre. Relations de l'Autriche-Hongrie et de la Russie', 11 July 1914, *DDF* (3), no. 500; Jelavich, *Entanglements*, 228–9 and 252–4; E. C. Thaden, 'Public Opinion and Russian Foreign Policy', in his *Interpreting History*, 166–7 [155–71].

[74] M. Cornwall, 'Serbia', Wilson (ed.), *Decisions 1914*, 57–8.

[75] Hartwig to Sazonov (no. 40), 17/30 June 1914, *IBZI* IV, no. 35.

[76] Giesl, *Zwei Jahrzehnte*, 256–7.

[77] Tel. Hartwig to Sazonov (no. 187), 26 June/9 July 1914, *IBZI* IV, no. 148.

Belgrade on 10 July. Hartwig requested a meeting for 9 p.m. that same evening. After a few conciliatory words, the Russian envoy turned to the pressing question of the moment: what were Austria's intentions towards Serbia? Giesl's reply was carefully worded. An investigation was ongoing, and if it proved that the assassination was the deed of individuals, no blame would attach to the Belgrade government. But whatever the outcome of the investigation, he assured Hartwig that 'Serbia's sovereignty would not be touched, and that, with some good will on the part of the Serb government, a mutually satisfactory solution will be found.' His colleague was well-satisfied: 'Thank you, you have relieved me and now one more thing but also as a friend ... [*Merci, Vous m'avez soulagé et maintenant encore une chose mais aussi en ami ...*]', and with these words he slumped back, sighed and died of a massive heart attack on Giesl's sofa.[78]

It would be tempting to speculate whether his presence in the Serbian capital at the end of the crisis would have made a difference to the course of events. He had been 'a bitter and convinced enemy of Austria-Hungary',[79] but conflict now was neither in his country's nor in Serbia's interest, and he had so far urged restraint on Pašić. Whatever might have been, Hartwig's sudden demise soon gave rise to rumours that Giesl had poisoned him, or that he had brought with him from Vienna an electric chair on which the unsuspecting Hartwig had then duly expired – one of the many bizarre stories generated by the events of July 1914.[80]

Scandals and stability: the French perspective

As for Russia's ally, French diplomacy remained largely reactive during much of the July crisis. The reasons for this were rooted partly in French domestic affairs and partly in diplomatic and strategic calculations. It is one of the peculiarities of Europe on the eve of the First World War that few régimes were as stable as the French Republic. Its domestic enemies, the Bonapartists, royalists and assorted other anti-republicans, had long been in retreat, even if anti-parliamentary attitudes had not entirely faded away. But if the republic was secure and its foundations were solid, the same could not be said of French party politics.[81] They were as volatile as ever,

[78] Giesl, *Zwei Jahrzehnte*, 258–9.
[79] Giesl to Berchtold (no. 115), 11 July 1914, ÖUA VIII, no. 10193.
[80] Tel. Strandtmann to Sazonov (no. 189), 27 June/10 July 1914, *IBZI* IV, no. 164.
[81] J.-M. Mayeur, *La vie politique sous la Troisième République* (Paris, 1984), 220–4; Z. Sternhell, *La droite révolutionnaire. Les origines françaises du fascisme, 1885–1914* (Paris, 1978), 385–400.

subject to confused tensions and counter-currents. The three-year army law of July 1913 – partly a reaction to the 1912 German army bill, and partly dictated by the needs of the Russian alliance – had polarized French domestic politics, and the parliamentary elections of April/May 1914 had produced a left-wing majority in the chamber, the first for some time.[82]

In reality, the Radical-Socialist majority was not as strong as it appeared. Nor was it a cohesive force, over a whole host of ideological concerns and considerations of parliamentary tactics. Of the 238 radicals, for instance, some 100 regarded themselves as 'non-radical'; and among the socialists there were some 30 'non-socialists'. An added complication was the absence of a dominant personality capable of leading such disparate political forces. This was felt all the more acutely after Joseph Caillaux, the former premier and finance minister and a leading light on the left, had to renounce all ideas of a government position after his wife, Henriette Caillaux, had broken into the offices of the conservative-leaning newspaper *Le Figaro* and shot dead its editor, Gaston Calmette, on 16 March 1914. Calmette had pursued a campaign against Caillaux, orchestrated by a former prime minister, Aristide Briand, and condoned, it seems, by the current president, Raymond Poincaré. Motivated by politics and designed to discredit Caillaux as a serious politician by impugning his financial rectitude, Calmette had also stooped to low journalism and published compromising letters between the former minister and his then mistress, now his wife. The salacious tittle-tattle surrounding the forthcoming trial, which commenced on 20 July and culminated in the defendant's triumphant acquittal on 31 July, with its potent mixture of sex, money and politics, kept the French public and political élite enthralled, not least also because it threatened to reveal embarrassing details about the events during the Franco-German Agadir crisis in 1911.[83]

Indeed, until the end of July, the French papers gave greater prominence to the trial than to the events in a faraway corner of the Balkans. If the Parisian papers devoted any column inches to the events at Sarajevo at all, they tended to imply that Austria-Hungary was bent on exploiting the situation created by the Archduke's assassination.[84]

[82] For a detailed discussion see G. Krumeich, *Armaments and Politics in France on the Eve of the First World War: The Introduction of Three-Year Conscription, 1913–1914* (Leamington Spa, 1984), 103–17 and 181–93.

[83] J. Caillaux, *Mes Mémoires* (3 vols., Paris, 1942–7) III, 133–7; J. C. Allain, *Caillaux* (2 vols., Paris, 1981) II, 403–43; G. Krumeich, 'Raymond Poincaré et l'affaire du "Figaro"', *RH* 264, 3 (1980), 365–73.

[84] Tels. Szécsen to Berchtold (nos. 97 and 103), 1 and 9 July 1914, ÖUA VIII, nos. 9970 and 10159.

As for the current administration, in office since 14 June, like so many governments of the Third Republic it was not built on solid foundations and was always in danger of turning into yet another revolving-door cabinet. It was ostensibly more to the left than any of the recent governments. But the prime minister, the anti-clerical, republican-socialist René Viviani, was yoked together in an uneasy partnership with the right-wing president, Raymond Poincaré. Viviani, who also held his post in conjunction with that of foreign minister, was a flighty rhetorician, nervous and highly excitable, and – in so far as foreign affairs were concerned – profoundly ignorant. On reading telegrams from Vienna, as Poincaré recorded maliciously in his diary, Viviani was wont to refer to the Habsburg foreign ministry at the Ballhausplatz as 'the Boliplatz or the Baloplatz'.[85] His relations with his own officials at the Quai d'Orsay were characterized by mutual suspicions. The latter regarded their new chief as an ignorant interloper, one, moreover, whose inexperience might damage the alliance with Russia. His habit of losing papers and, more so, of loosening off torrents of abuse at his officials during his frequent fits of nervous rage, did little to endear him to the ministry.[86] As for the minister himself, he was sceptical of what he considered to be the pessimistic outlook of senior diplomats and their undue deference to the alliance with Russia. Indeed, as will be seen later, he harboured suspicions of Russia's Balkan policy, too.[87] Throughout the July crisis Viviani adopted a cautious and moderate stance. Yet, he faced the predicament that all French foreign ministers had faced since 1894. Whilst reluctant to encourage Russia to interfere in any Austro-Serbian dispute, he was at the same time anxious to do nothing that would strain France's vital relations with St Petersburg. For that reason, for instance, he went out of his way to assure Russia of the new government's desire to maintain France's armed strength.[88]

[85] Poincaré diary, 3 Aug. 1914, Papiers de Poincaré, BN, Bnfr 16027; also in M. B. Hayne, *The French Foreign Office and the First World War, 1898–1914* (Oxford, 1993), 274, but misdated. Viviani had his uses, however, as a popular linkman with parliament: see Paléologue diary, 13 June 1914, M. Paléologue, *Au Quai d'Orsay à la veille de la tourmente. Journal, 1913–1914* (Paris, 1947), 302.

[86] B. Auffray, *Pierre de Margerie (1861–1942) et la vie diplomatique de son temps* (Paris, 1976), 256–8.

[87] See Paléologue diary, 23 July 1914, M. Paléologue, *La Russie des Tsars pendant la grande guerre* (3 vols., Paris, 1921) I, 17.

[88] Tel. Viviani to Paléologue (no. 318, very confidential), 10 July 1914, DDF (3) x, no. 491; Herrmann, *Arming of Europe*, 191–5.

The 'man of Lorraine' and Russia

Personality mattered. By any standard, Viviani was no ideal foreign minister. 'I fear he is hesitant and pusillanimous', Poincaré observed at the end of July before assuming tighter control of foreign policy himself. He was also given to violent mood-swings, especially during the final stages of the crisis.[89] If Viviani lacked the force of character and personality to stamp his authority on French foreign policy, the reverse held true of Poincaré. An experienced politician, he had held both of Viviani's offices before becoming president. As a native of Lorraine, moreover, he was deeply imbued with suspicions of Germany. No doubt, Poincaré's youthful experiences of the 1870 war and his family's flight from their ancestral province were formative, and left him with an inveterate hatred of all things Prussian.[90]

Yet although his political outlook was formed in the 1870s and 1880s, he was no advocate of that type of *revanchisme* that so frequently dominated at least the tone of French politics in those decades. Even so, the effect of his foreign policy was somewhat ambiguous. Whilst he abjured war as a means of politics, in practice he advocated a hardline policy towards Germany. He viewed any attempts by Berlin at a rapprochement with either Britain or Russia as designed to isolate France. The nation's security was founded upon the rock of the Russian alliance. To his mind, it was 'the supreme guarantee of the European order'.[91] The principal task of French foreign policy was to cultivate the existing ties with Britain and Russia, ideally to turn them into a new triple alliance. In parallel with this, France's military striking power was to be enhanced further. The policy was later called 'Poincaristic', but it chimed in with French military thinking in the aftermath of the Agadir crisis and its emphasis on offensive warfighting doctrines.[92] For Poincaré French national security and the stability of Europe rested on the balance of power based on a clear and strict separation of two alliance blocs, without any softening along their edges, let alone interpenetration of any kind.[93]

[89] Poincaré diary, 29 and 31 July 1914, Papiers de Poincaré, Bnfr 16027 (quote from former); Poincaré's memoirs give no indication of this: *Au service de la France. Neuf années de souvenirs* (10 vols., Paris, repr. 1946) IV, 374.

[90] P. Miquel, *Poincaré* (Paris, 1984), 34.

[91] As quoted in *ibid.*, 333; see also M. B. Hayne, 'The Quai d'Orsay and Influences on the Formation of French Foreign Policy, 1898–1914', FH II, 4 (1988), 431–2.

[92] D. B. Ralston, *The Army of the Republic: The Place of the Military in the Political Evolution of France, 1871–1914* (Cambridge, MA, 1967), 319–71.

[93] See Poincaré's official announcements on assuming the seals of the foreign ministry: *Au Service* I, 23–5; for further discussions see Krumeich, *Armaments*, 27–9; J. F. V. Keiger, *France and the Origins of the First World War* (London, 1983), 55–6.

Poincaré's forceful character and the clarity of his views helped him to dominate policy-making. They were, however, accompanied by a certain inflexibility and intellectual rigidity that were the product of his legal training but made him ill-equipped to deal with the ambiguities and fluidities of diplomacy. He was no diplomat, observed Paul Cambon, the French ambassador in London; he was an administrator, with a strong sense of order and a lawyerly preference for neat solutions. 'With all his talents and his intelligence', mused Cambon, 'Poincaré is yet inconsistent.' He feared responsibility and was often uncertain about the correct policy response.[94]

In practice, Poincaré tended to defer decisions, satisfied to let matters drift. He did little to bring about war, yet he did even less to defuse the often tense relations with Germany. In one respect, however, Poincaré had helped to restrict the choices available to French diplomacy in 1914, and in so doing he also contributed to a considerable narrowing of the path along which European diplomacy could travel. On becoming prime minister in January 1912, he affirmed to Izvolsky, Russian ambassador at Paris, his ambition 'to maintain the most sincere relations with us [Russia] and to conduct France's foreign policy in fullest accord with her ally'.[95] Poincaré never deviated from this line of policy later. Indeed, he went further than previous French foreign ministers in supporting Russia. At the height of the Austro-Serb crisis in late 1912, Poincaré sought to stiffen Russian diplomacy, then seemingly disinclined to take a firm line against Vienna. In so far as France was concerned, he impressed on Izvolsky that there was nothing that might imply 'a lapse in the competition on her [France's] part'.[96] Advanced in Poincaré's peculiarly lawyerly fashion, the Russian ambassador rendered these words in equally characteristic and colourful terms: 'If Russia wages war, France also will wage war.'[97]

The exchanges of November 1912 were not a 'blank cheque' *avant la lettre*, nor did they necessarily constitute some form of 'Balkanization' of

---

[94] P. Cambon to J. Cambon, 28 Nov. 1912, PCC III, 29; also Hayne, *French Foreign Office*, 237–43, for a discussion of Poincaré's relations with senior diplomats.

[95] Tel. Izvolsky to Sazonov (no. 2, secret), 2/15 Jan. 1912, DSI II, no. 186; see also F. Stieve, *Isvolsky and the World War* (London, 1926), 54.

[96] Poincaré to Izvolsky, 16 Nov. 1912, DDF (3) IV, no. 468. Further evidence of Poincaré's hawkish stance can be found in his proposal of a pre-emptive triple intervention in the Balkans to thwart Austria-Hungary, which so startled St Petersburg: Izvolsky to Sazonov, 25 Oct./7 Nov. 1912, DSI IV, no. 554; see also J.-J. Becker, 'La guerre était-elle inévitable?', A. Prost (ed.), *14–18: Mourir pour la patrie* (Paris, 1992), 52.

[97] Izvolsky to Sazonov, 17 Nov. 1912, IBZI IV/I, no. 258. *Caveat lector*: Poincaré later suggested that Izvolsky was in the habit of turning his reports into 'picturesque account[s] and one[s] somewhat laden with colours': *Au service* II, 199.

the Franco-Russian alliance.[98] But undoubtedly Poincaré had narrowed the French definition of the *casus foederis*. What mattered now were not the specific circumstances of any future conflict; what mattered was whether or not Berlin chose to move and how St Petersburg reacted. From now on, French diplomacy was far less inclined to exert a restraining influence on Russia, much to the annoyance of British diplomats.[99]

M. Paléologue warns of German intrigues at St Petersburg

But that change in French policy was not merely the result of Poincaré's personal preferences. It also reflected the resurgence of Russia's power since 1912. The country's progress made a profound impression on French diplomats. Russia, noted Georges Louis, the republic's representative at St Petersburg until 1913, 'has an immense future. Her power is in full development.'[100] In a similar vein, his Russophile successor but one, Maurice Paléologue, never ceased to impress on Paris that the economic, financial and military programmes of the Russian government were 'prodigious manifestations of the vitality' of this vast empire, and were likely to herald a more active foreign policy.[101]

Certainly, Paléologue and Théophile Delcassé, the architect of the 1904 entente with Britain and ambassador at St Petersburg during the brief interval between Louis and Paléologue, went far in associating France with Russia's regional interests. During the Liman von Sanders crisis at the turn of 1913–14, for instance, Delcassé encouraged the Tsar in his belief that the affair 'made manifest the German threat to Russia's essential interests', and that Berlin should not be allowed 'to stomp on [Russia's] feet'.[102] Indeed, Russia's revival encouraged some at Paris to contemplate the prospect of war with the two Germanic Powers. Britain's ambassador to France had grasped this, and warned that '[t]here are many Frenchmen who think that war is inevitable within the next two years and that it might be better for France to have it soon. The arguments in favour of an early war are the improbability of Austria on account of Slavs being able to give much assistance to Germany and the hostile feeling against Austria in the

---

[98] W. von Schoen, *Erlebtes. Beiträge zur politischen Geschichte der neueren Zeit* (Stuttgart, 1921), 144–5; and C. Clark, *The Sleepwalkers: How Europe Went to War in 1914* (London, 2012), 293–301, for the Balkanization argument.

[99] See e.g. Cartwright to Nicolson, 11 Apr. 1913, Cartwright MSS, NRO, C(A)45.

[100] Louis diary, 12 Jan. 1914, in his *Les carnets de Georges Louis (1908–1917)* (2 vols., Paris, 1926) II, 94.

[101] Paléologue to Doumergue, 21 Mar. 1914, *DDF* (3) X, no. 52.

[102] Delcassé to Doumergue, 29 Jan. 1914, *DDF* (3) IX, no. 189.

Balkans.'[103] General Édouard de Castelnau of the French general staff made similar comments to his British colleague, Lieutenant-General Sir Henry Wilson: 'It was curious to find that Castelenau is in favour of a war now as being a good opportunity, France [and] Russia being ready, Austria in a state of confusion. Germany unwilling.'[104]

Paléologue's reports frequently focused on the activities of the conservative clique at the Tsar's court, with its leanings towards Germany, or the manoeuvres of the former finance minister, Sergei Yulevich Witte, who favoured a continental bloc of Russia, Germany and France. Although Sazonov assured him that no change of course was likely or indeed possible, French diplomats were by no means convinced that the Russian foreign minister would remain in office himself.[105] Such warnings made an impression on the Quai d'Orsay. Gaston Doumergue, the foreign minister until June 1914, warned his British colleague 'that Germany would make great efforts to detach Russia from the French alliance, and might possibly succeed'.[106]

Not the least effect of the growth of Russia's power in those years was that it heightened French fears of a reversal of Russian policy. A strengthened Russia was likely to be less dependent on the French alliance and more willing to strike out on its own. The relative balance of influence within the Franco-Russian alliance was expected to tilt in favour of St Petersburg at any rate. In the worst case, Russia might eventually gravitate towards its old ally Germany. Certainly, few at Paris assumed that the antagonism between the two eastern military monarchies was bound to continue. If Paléologue is to be believed, even Viviani, otherwise sceptical of predictions of gloom, was exercised by the spectre of a reconstituted Romanov-Hohenzollern alliance: 'We would lose our national independence! ... This would be not merely the end of the republic, it would be the end of France.'[107] The revival of Russian power thus encouraged both French arrogance and anxiety, the two mutually reinforcing elements of French policy, and made Paléologue even more reluctant to exercise a moderating influence on Russia.

---

[103] Bertie to Grey (private), 3 Mar. 1913, Bertie MSS, TNA (PRO), FO 800/166. Grey reacted swiftly, impressing on Bertie that '[i]f France is aggressive to Germany there will be no support from Great Britain': vice versa (private), 4 Mar. 1913, *ibid.*
[104] Wilson diary, 13 Feb. 1913, Wilson MSS, IWM, DS/MISC/80 (not in C. E. Callwell, *Field-Marshal Sir Henry Wilson: His Life and Diaries* (2 vols., London, 1927) I, 122.
[105] Tel. Paléologue to Doumergue (nos. 128–9, very secret, and unnumbered), 24 and 25 Mar. 1914, *DDF* (3) X, nos. 20 and 26.
[106] Grey to Bertie (no. 249, secret), 1 May 1914, TNA (PRO), FO 371/2092/19288; for Doumergue see Hayne, *French Foreign Office*, 249–52.
[107] Paléologue, *Au Quai d'Orsay*, 318.

In the immediate aftermath of Sarajevo, however, French diplomacy was quiescent. The demonstrations outside the Serbian legation in Vienna briefly raised the spectre of the Habsburg government being driven into a conflict by an enraged public. The 'abominable assassination of Sarajevo', suggested Alfred Dumaine, the French ambassador at Vienna, might usher in a new round in the 'relentless and absurd struggle of Austria against Serbia', which might imperil the 'general peace'. In early July, he warned that the slaying of the Archduke might furnish Vienna with the grievance necessary to justify a military strike against Serbia.[108]

But such fears were short-lived. When Paléologue wired from St Petersburg that the Habsburg chargé d'affaires, Count Otto Czernin, had intimated to Sazonov that his government might extend its investigation of the Sarajevo plot to Serbia proper,[109] Dumaine poured cold water on the suggestion. His Russian colleague at Vienna remained calm, and so were the officials at the Ballhausplatz. Baron Giesl's impending return to his post at Belgrade and the resumption of talks about various Balkan railway projects were 'symptoms of a calming down [*apaisement*]'.[110] There was perhaps a touch of complacency about Dumaine's despatches from Vienna, a reflection no doubt of the relative political and social isolation of this very bourgeois diplomat in the aristocratic Habsburg capital. Key to his analysis of the situation, however, was the personality of the aged Emperor. Franz Joseph's 'higher wisdom and farsightedness' were a guarantee of Austria-Hungary's moderation. The ambassador invested the Emperor's manifesto of 4 July with great significance in this respect in that it had stressed the fact that the 'odious deed of Sarajevo' had been the work of misguided individuals. Dumaine attached more importance to the reigning monarch's wisdom than to the 'grandiloquence of Viennese publicists'. Vienna would find a way to stage a '*grand* fracas' in order to satisfy Habsburg vanity and frighten Serbia, but no more.[111] Nothing could shake Dumaine's optimism

[108] Dumaine to Viviani (no. 171) and tel. (no. 91), 30 June and 2 July 1914, DDF (3) x, nos. 462 and 470 (quote from former). Dumaine's apprehensions in early July are confirmed by the British ambassador: see de Bunsen to Grey (no. 137, confidential), 5 July 1914, TNA (PRO), FO 371/1899/30991.

[109] Tel. Paléologue to Viviani (no. 244, confidential), 6 July 1914, DDF (3) x, no. 477; see also tel. Carlotti to San Giuliano (no. 6025/418), 7 July 1914, DDI (4) xii, no. 109.

[110] Tel. Dumaine to Viviani (no. 94, confidential), 8 July 1914, DDF (3) x, no. 484.

[111] Dumaine to Viviani (no. 177), 10 July 1914, DDF (3) x, no. 493; see also S. Schmidt, *Frankreichs Aussenpolitik in der Julikrise 1914. Ein Beitrag zur Geschichte des Ausbruchs des Ersten Weltkrieges* (Munich, 2009), 66–7. At the Ballhausplatz Dumaine was 'not appreciated' and his relations with Berchtold were 'very cool': see de Bunsen to Grey (no. 31, confidential), 13 Feb. 1914, TNA (PRO), FO 371/1899/6900.

throughout the first half of July. There was nothing in consequence to alert the Quai d'Orsay of the impending strike against Serbia.

In calmer waters: Britain in June 1914

The position of the British government was comparable to that of the French. 'The spring and summer of 1914 were marked in Europe by an exceptional tranquillity', Winston Churchill, then First Lord of the Admiralty, later reflected.[112] Even the Permanent Under-secretary at the Foreign Office, Sir Arthur Nicolson, not generally known for his sunny optimism, observed at the time that since assuming his current post in 1910, 'I have not seen such calm waters'.[113]

There was an exception, however. Domestic politics were profoundly disturbed; and this circumstance also constrained the Foreign Secretary's handling of the July crisis. The Liberal government under Herbert Henry Asquith was in office, but seemed scarcely to be in power. Without a functioning parliamentary majority ever since the two inconclusive general elections of 1910 had reversed the great landslide four years previously, the ministers were dependent on a motley crew of Irish Nationalists, the nascent Labour party and their own truculent and capricious Radical wing. It was Ireland and industrial relations that consumed much of the government's political energy in the spring and summer of 1914. For any Liberal administration, this was a toxic combination, one that threatened to dissolve the broad coalition that was the Edwardian Liberal party.

Worse, still, the near civil war in Ulster over the proposed 'Home Rule' devolution scheme, largely meant to appease the Irish Nationalists on whom the Asquith administration depended, threatened to deepen further the already gaping fissures that rent British politics. In March, the so-called 'Curragh Mutiny' had laid bare the government's only imperfect control of the Army. Offers of concessions could not reconcile the leaders of Ulster Protestantism to the Home Rule legislation wending its way through

[112] W. S. Churchill, *The World Crisis*, 1911–14 (2 vols., London, 1923) I, 178. For scholarly discussions of the disturbed state of British politics see e.g. P. Rowland, *The Last Liberal Governments: Unfinished Business, 1911–1914* (London, 1971), 277–345; G. L. Bernstein, *Liberalism and Liberal Politics in Edwardian England* (Boston, MA, 1986), 135–65; P. F. Clarke, *Liberals and Social Democrats* (Cambridge, 1978).

[113] Nicolson to Goschen, 5 May 1914, Nicolson MSS, TNA (PRO), FO 800/374; see also K. R. Robbins, 'Britain in the Summer of 1914', in his *Politicians, Diplomacy and War in Modern British History* (London, 1994), 175–88.

Parliament. Ministers in London were resigned to the fact that, whenever Irish devolution reached the statute book, 'the Carsonite [Ulster] leaders would find it very difficult . . . to postpone doing something'; they would be 'compelled to raise the flag somehow or another in Belfast'.[114] All the while, a significant section of the Conservatives, 'His Majesty's Loyal Opposition', condoned the actions of mutinous army officers and encouraged rebellious Ulstermen, and an even larger proportion of the party sympathized with the anti-Home Rule cause.[115] Planned strikes on the railways and other vital industries compounded the government's problems. If mass industrial disputes coincided with civil unrest over Ulster, warned the Chancellor of the Exchequer, David Lloyd George, whose political fortunes were bound up with the Radicals, 'the situation will be the gravest with which any Government in this country has had to deal for centuries'.[116] For once the mercurial Lloyd George did not exaggerate. With the government's stock devalued and still slumping further, '[t]he Liberal Party in the House . . . is at present engaged in trying to save its own skin', observed a sympathetic parliamentary correspondent towards the end of July.[117]

Apart from the malaise of the Liberal government and party, the early summer of 1914 was calm enough, and seemed to promise, as one future Prime Minister wistfully recalled in later years, nothing but 'cloudless atmosphere, with soft, voluptuous breezes and a Mediterranean sky'.[118] For its part, the Cabinet remained focused on Ireland and domestic matters, and did not concern itself with the events in the Balkans until the Austro-Hungarian ultimatum to Serbia on 24 July. This was hardly surprising, and should not be taken as an indication of general British apathy or complacency. Foreign policy was in the hands of Sir Edward Grey, the Foreign Secretary, who retained complete

[114] Memo. Birrell, 'Impressions of Ulster', 15 June 1914, TNA (PRO), CAB 37/120/70; for the background see L. O. Broin, *The Chief Secretary: Augustine Birrell in Ireland* (London, 1969), 99–102; N. Mansergh, *The Unresolved Question: The Anglo-Irish Settlement and its Undoing, 1912–1972* (New Haven, CT, 1991), 41–78.

[115] D. Dutton, *'His Majesty's Loyal Opposition': The Unionist Party in Opposition, 1905–1915* (Liverpool, 1992), 226–37; P. Jalland and J. Stubbs, 'The Irish Question after the Outbreak of War in 1914: Some Unfinished Party Business', *EHR* xcvi, 4 (1981), 778–80.

[116] Lloyd George speech at the Mansion House, 17 July 1914, *The Times*, 18 July 1914.

[117] Mair to Scott, 22 July 1914, as quoted in C. Hazlehurst, *Politicians at War, July 1914 to May 1915: A Prologue to the Triumph of Lloyd George* (London, 1971), 27. G. H. Mair was the lobby correspondent of the *Manchester Guardian*.

[118] A. Horne, *Macmillan I, 1894–1956* (London, 1988), 27. No doubt, memories of Flanders mud made the summer of 1914 appear even more halcyon.

control over it until the prospect of war drew nearer and Cabinet approval for possible intervention was required.

Grey and his officials were by no means unaware of the potential of Balkan crises to cause European complications. The 'Eastern Question', that hardy perennial of Great Power politics, and the two recent wars in the region were reminders of that fact, if such were needed. The principal problem, as Nicolson observed at the time, was 'the rivalry which exists in an acute form between Russia and Austria'. If the two rivals ever were to come to blows, it was beyond question that 'Germany would stand by the side of Austria'. This would trigger the Franco-Russian alliance, and any government in London would be faced with an awkward choice: 'I should not like to attempt any forecast in regard to this, though I have myself very little doubt as to what our policy should be.'[119]

Nicolson's concluding comment foreshadowed some of the internal tensions within the British foreign policy-making élite that were to break out into the open in July 1914. In the more immediate context of the disturbed situation in the Balkans, however, senior British diplomats clearly appreciated that the more robust anti-Austrian policy pursued by Serbia in recent years risked destabilizing international politics. In light of the waxing antagonism between Vienna and St Petersburg, the then ambassador to Austria-Hungary, Sir Fairfax Cartwright, warned that 'Servia will some day set Europe by the ears and bring about a universal war on the Continent ... the Servs may lose their heads and do something aggressive against the Dual Monarchy which will compel the latter to put the screws on Servia'.[120]

Eighteen months later, British officials reacted with genuine shock to 'the terrible event at Serajevo'.[121] Grey himself hastened to add a personal note to official expressions of condolence. The 'loss which has befallen Austria-Hungary' was deeply felt in London, he assured the Austro-Hungarian ambassador, Count Albert Mensdorff, and 'the cruel circumstances attending it add to the tragedy'. The assassination of the heir to the Habsburg throne was a blow to the aged Emperor, whose 'life is bound up with the peace of Europe that I dread anything that must try his

---

[119] Nicolson to Rodd, 30 Nov. 1912, Rennell of Rodd MSS, Bodl., box 14; see K. Neilson, '"My Beloved Russians": Sir Arthur Nicolson and Russia, 1906–1916', IHR IX, 4 (1987), 546–8.

[120] Cartwright to Nicolson, 31 Jan. 1913, Nicolson MSS, TNA (PRO), FO 800/363; see also T. G. Otte, The Foreign Office Mind: The Making of British Foreign Policy, 1865–1914 (Cambridge, 2011), 369–75.

[121] Tel. Grey to de Bunsen (no. 119), 29 June 1914, BD XI, no. 14.

strength'.[122] Leaving aside Grey's genuine personal sympathy, two points are worth noting here, the first being the perception of Franz Joseph as a guarantor of peace. Yet, at the same time, Grey also suggested, albeit very much *sub rosa*, as befitted the sad occasion, that Austria-Hungary's reaction to the murder of the Archduke had the potential to shake that peace.

In this Grey showed greater perspicacity than some of his diplomats. Charles Louis Des Graz, who was to take up his new post as envoy to Serbia later in the summer, reacted to the news of the Sarajevo murders by a 'Servian-race student' with dismay – 'complications?', he added to the entry in his diary, before setting off to lunch at the Travellers' Club.[123] Cartwright's successor at the Vienna embassy, Sir Maurice de Bunsen, appreciated the strength of Serbian hostility towards Austria-Hungary. Apprehensions at Vienna 'that Servia would march at the dictation of Russia' had made some impression on him, all the more so given the 'state of considerable tension with Russia' over St Petersburg's involvement in the Balkans.[124] After Sarajevo, de Bunsen readily conceded that the Habsburg leadership was likely now to react to 'this hideous crime' with a harder line against Belgrade. But he did not anticipate immediate European complications. He cast his glance farther into the future, and discerned Austria-Hungary gradually falling under German domination as a result of an uncompromisingly anti-Slav policy. This, he reasoned, was very much against Austria-Hungary's own interests. The Monarchy's 'only chance of resisting the downward pressure of Germany ... would lie in a broad policy of conciliation towards the Southern Slav elements by which a broad Austro-Slav barrier might be drawn across the Southward march of Germany towards Trieste'.[125]

Nicolson at the Foreign Office concurred with this assessment. Indeed, he proved to be remarkably sanguine throughout much of July. The murder of Franz Ferdinand was, of course, an extraordinary act of political terrorism, but 'it will have no serious consequences, in any case

---

[122] Grey to Mensdorff (private), 29 June 1914, Nachlass Mensdorff, HHStA, Karton 11.

[123] Des Graz diary, 29 June 1914, Des Graz MSS, CUL, Add. 8883/D/2.

[124] Quotes from de Bunsen to Nicolson, 27 Feb. 1914, Nicolson MSS, TNA (PRO), FO 800/372; and to Grey (no. 32), 13 Feb. 1914, FO 371/1899/6901; see also T. G. Otte, '"Knavery or Folly": The British "Official Mind" and the Habsburg Monarchy, 1856–1914', in T. G. Otte and L. Höbelt (eds.), *A Living Anachronism? European Diplomacy and the Habsburg Monarchy. Festschrift für F. R. Bridge zum 70. Geburtstag* (Vienna, 2010), 153–5.

[125] De Bunsen to Nicolson, 3 July 1914, Nicolson MSS, TNA (PRO), FO 800/375. There is a curious parallel between de Bunsen's analysis and that advanced by Prince Gagarin of the Russian embassy at Vienna, *vide supra*.

outside Austria-Hungary'.[126] Moreover he doubted whether Vienna would 'take any action of a serious character & I suggest the storm will blow over'.[127] Britain's representatives in various Balkan capitals took a similar view. For as long as the old Emperor lived, 'Austria will also keep quiet, although the feeling against the Servians will be at fever heat for some time', opined Sir Henry Bax-Ironside at Sofia.[128] As late as 20 July, indeed, Nicolson was still hopeful that the 'Servian imbroglio will not be pushed to extremes'.[129]

There was more than a touch of complacency about British diplomatic reporting in the days and weeks after Sarajevo. Most of the country's representatives abroad, it seemed, were looking forward to a quiet summer. At the same time, politicians at Westminster reflected on the sudden death of Joseph Chamberlain on 2 July. As so often in British politics, the demise of a once-dominant political figure from an earlier age produced a form of collective introspection. And the death of the man whose manoeuvres and posturings had divided first the Liberals and then split the Conservative party was no exception.[130]

Sir Edward Grey issues an early warning

One of the few to have realized the gravity of the situation, almost from the moment the first news of the assassination reached London, was the Foreign Secretary. Sir Edward Goschen, the ambassador at Berlin, then on home leave, found the Foreign Secretary 'rather nervous as regards Austria & Servia'. The ambassador himself, his mind firmly on the Oxford-Cambridge cricket match – 'the dullest I have ever seen' – thought that there was no cause for anxiety on account of the European situation.[131] Grey was by no means so complacent. His handling of the Sarajevo crisis, however, has attracted a great deal of criticism, much of it quite unjustified. In part, that criticism may reflect Grey's personality. There was something aloof, elusive and enigmatic about him, so much so

---

[126] Nicolson to de Bunsen, 6 July 1914, De Bunsen MSS, Bodl., box 15.
[127] Min. Nicolson, n.d. [9 July 1914] on de Bunsen to Grey (no. 137, confidential), 5 July 1914, TNA (PRO), FO 371/1899/30991.
[128] Bax-Ironside to Nicolson (private), 9 July 1914, Nicolson MSS, TNA (PRO), FO 800/375.
[129] Nicolson to de Bunsen, 20 July 1914, De Bunsen MSS, Bodl., box 15.
[130] See Margot Asquith diary, 2 July 1914, Asquith MSS, Bodl., Ms.Eng.d.3210.
[131] Goschen to Rumbold, 11 July 1914, Rumbold MSS, Bodl., Ms. Rumbold dep. 16; see also Goschen diary, 6 July 1914, C. H. D. Howard (ed.), *The Diary of Edward Goschen, 1900–1914* (London, 1980), 290.

that even his biographer had to concede that 'neither his admirers nor his critics know quite what they should say about him'.[132] Grey's public persona was that of a north-country gentleman, happiest when far away from the madding crowd at Westminster, breeding exotic wildfowl at Fallodon, his Northumbrian estate, or casting a fly over the chalk streams of Hampshire. And yet there was more to Edward Grey than country pursuits. He was a shrewd political operator, driven to politics by a sense of patrician duty and a healthy appetite for power. During the Liberals' long years in the wilderness of opposition, he established a reputation for competence and expertise in the field of foreign affairs. Once installed at the Foreign Office in December 1905, he remained there until he relinquished its seals eleven years later, nearly blind and ground down by the unrelenting demands of two years of war.

Grey represented the Whiggish element in the party, once its dominant force socially and politically, but now much diminished. He also stood for continuity in foreign policy. To some of his critics, both in his day and in later years, he was a priggish Wykehamist who obstinately stuck to the policy of the ententes, and so helped to make Great Power politics more rigid. Here, too, his posthumous reputation is undeserved. If anything the reverse holds true, and here his reflections on his favourite pastime offer some pertinent insight. 'An angler', Grey wrote,

> must never be flurried by the perverseness of the wind, by the untoward tricks which the fly or line will sometimes play, or by the peculiarities of the stream; he cannot overcome these by sheer strength, and he must learn to dodge them and defeat them unobtrusively. Quiet, steady, intelligent effort is needed ... His observation should add to his knowledge in a manner which has a direct bearing on his sport. He should make guesses founded upon something which he has noticed, and be ever on the watch for some further indications to turn the guess into a conclusion. ... But there is a third which seems to me important. It is self-control.[133]

These attributes also characterized Grey's foreign secretaryship. He proved a skilled and flexible diplomat, yet with a clear appreciation of British interests. Above all, he had kept a 'free hand', neither

---

[132] K. Robbins, *Sir Edward Grey: A Biography of Lord Grey of Fallodon* (London, 1971), 13.
[133] [E.] Viscount Grey of Fallodon, *Fly Fishing* (London, rev. edn repr. 1947 [1st edn 1899]), 18–20.

committing Britain to France, let alone Russia, nor compromising her with Germany.[134]

According to his critics, Grey failed to react swiftly to the unfolding events in the summer of 1914. More significantly, it is claimed that he did not issue a clear and timely warning to Berlin. There is little new in that latter assertion. It first emerged a few days into the war in opposition circles. It was then given a wider airing in Lloyd George's wartime memoirs – mendacious even by the low standards of that genre in general and of their author in particular – and it has never gone away since. And yet it is problematic.[135] The extant evidence and the context of events suggest a different interpretation. Grey's conversations with the German and Russian ambassadors on 6 and 8 July are crucial here.

On 6 July, the German ambassador, just returned from a brief visit home, called upon Grey. Prince Karl Max Lichnowsky, who had taken up his current post in 1912, was an Anglophile. This suave, Silesian *grand seigneur* was well-liked in London Society, and invitations to the parties he and his artistic wife gave at Prussia House, the German embassy at 9 Carlton House Terrace, conferred something of a social cachet. In London Society he was generally regarded as 'a jolly good fellow',[136] and his two years at the London embassy coincided with a marked improvement in Anglo-German relations. Lichnowsky had established a personal rapport with Grey, and he was in the habit of talking freely with the Foreign Secretary.[137]

[134] See K. Neilson, '"Control the Whirlwind": Sir Edward Grey as Foreign Secretary, 1906–1916', T. G. Otte (ed.), *The Makers of British Foreign Policy: From Pitt to Thatcher* (Basingstoke and New York, 2002), 128–49; and T. G. Otte, '"Almost a Law of Nature": Sir Edward Grey, the Foreign Office and the Balance of Power, 1905–1912', E. Goldstein and B. J. C. McKercher (eds.), *Power and Stability: British Foreign Policy, 1865–1965* (London, 2003), 77–118. Grey's most persistent scholarly critic is Keith Wilson: see his 'Policy of the Ententes' and 'Grey' in Keith Wilson (ed.), *British Foreign Secretaries and Foreign Policy: From Crimean War to First World War* (London, 1987), 172–97, and 'The Making and Putative Implementation of a British Foreign Policy of Gesture, December 1905 to August 1914: The Anglo-French Entente Revisited', *CJH* xxxi, 2 (1996), 227–55.
[135] Bridgeman to Caroline Bridgeman, 7 Aug. 1914, P. Williamson (ed.), *The Modernisation of Conservative Politics: The Diaries and Letters of William Bridgeman, 1904–1935* (London, 1988), 81. Lloyd George's memoirs were a patent and unscrupulous attempt to discredit Grey: see D. Lloyd George, *War Memoirs* (2 vols., London, 1938) i, 55–60.
[136] H. Philippi, 'Das deutsche Diplomatische Korps, 1871–1914', K. Schwabe (ed.), *Das Diplomatische Korps, 1871–1945* (Boppard, 1985), 62 [41–80]; [K. M.] Prince Lichnowsky, *Auf dem Weg zum Abgrund. Londoner Berichte, Erinnerungen und sonstige Schriften* (2 vols., Dresden, 1927) i, 121.
[137] H. F. Young, *Prince Lichnowsky and the Great War* (Athens, GA, 1977), 32–48; L. Cecil, *The German Diplomatic Service, 1871–1914* (Princeton, NJ, 1976), 35–8.

Their meeting of 6 July was no exception. Lichnowsky spoke warmly of the favourable impression the recent visit of a Royal Navy squadron to the Kiel regatta had made in Germany. But he then turned to Sarajevo. He had found at Berlin an atmosphere of 'anxiety and pessimism'. Anti-Serb sentiments had increased markedly in Austria-Hungary, and 'he knew for a fact, though he did not know details, that the Austrians intended to do something and it was not impossible that they would take military action against Servia'. Austria-Hungary was not likely to seek Serb territory, but aimed at extracting some humiliating compensation from Belgrade. Germany, he explained, now found herself in an awkward bind. If she restrained Vienna, her Habsburg ally, and with it the *Zweibund* alliance itself would be weakened. If, on the other hand, Berlin 'let events take their course there was the possibility of very serious trouble'. Lichnowsky also touched on Russo-German strains at the beginning of the year, and hinted that Grey's recent attempts to allay German concerns on account of the rumours of an Anglo-Russian naval agreement had not had the desired effect at Berlin. The import of Lichnowsky's candid explanations was clear: Britain and Germany had to cooperate to ensure the peaceful outcome of the crisis. Grey reciprocated these sentiments. Britain, he stated, remained wedded to her traditional balance of power principles, 'yet we did not wish to see the groups of Powers draw apart'. As for the post-Sarajevo situation in the Balkans, if any complications arose, he 'would use all the influence [he] could to mitigate difficulties . . . and if the clouds arose prevent the storm from breaking'.[138]

Lichnowksy's account of the meeting, which the ambassador described as having been in the 'customarily comfortable and friendly form', was couched in somewhat less forthright language. In substance, however, it did not differ from Grey's version. But two points are worth noting. Grey, the ambassador observed, was alert to the danger of European complications arising out of any Austro-Hungarian move against Serbia. But he also appeared to appreciate the difficulty for the Habsburg leadership 'permanently to refrain from all energetic measures', and promised 'to remain in touch with us also about this question'. Grey returned to this point at the end of the interview, and emphasized that he wished 'to bring the two groups [of the Powers] closer together so as to prevent European complications and to facilitate an understanding about all emerging questions'.[139]

---

[138] Grey to Rumbold (no. 214, secret), 6 July 1914, BD XI, no. 32. For the earlier conversation on the state of Anglo-French relations and the rumoured naval talks with Russia, see Grey to Goschen (no. 197), 24 June 1914, *ibid.*, no. 4.

[139] Lichnowsky to Bethmann Hollweg (secret), 6 July 1914, DD I, no. 20.

Two days later, on 8 July, Grey made similar observations to Benckendorff, the Russian ambassador, who was also Lichnowsky's first cousin. There was a danger that the strength of public opinion might force the Austro-Hungarian government to make some démarche against Belgrade. 'Spirits run high, higher than before', he noted. Berchtold was not a strong minister and, whatever the Emperor's pacific inclinations, the authorities in Vienna 'might be swept off their feet'. He speculated that Vienna had evidence of some official Serb connection, and impressed on the ambassador what his German cousin had said about Berlin's unease at Russia's reaching out to Romania and the rumoured Anglo-Russian naval convention. It was imperative, Grey urged Benckendorff, that the Russian government 'should do all in their power to reassure Germany, and convince her that no *coup* was being prepared against her'. Here lay the crux of the matter, as Grey well knew: 'I often thought ... that things would be better if the whole truth were known. The difficulty was to tell people the truth, and make them believe that they really knew the whole truth. They were apt to think that there was a great deal more than they had been told.'[140]

This consideration was important to Grey. He well understood that recent developments had shifted the military balance in Europe to Germany's disadvantage. The further the French and Russian armaments programmes progressed, he explained to Benckendorff during their hour-long conversation, the more the military balance would shift against Germany. In consequence, 'the more valuable will be the Austrian alliance for Germany, and the more leverage Austria will have over Germany'. Grey was clearly seized of the severity of the current situation. On Benckendorff's concluding enquiry as to whether the situation really was as serious as all that, Grey replied: 'The idea that this terrible crime might unexpectedly produce a general war with all its attendant catastrophes – after all the great efforts in recent years to avoid it, and after things on the whole got back onto an even keel again – "made his hair stand on edge"'.[141] Even before meeting Benckendorff, Grey had impressed upon Paul Cambon, the French ambassador, that in the event of an Austro-Serb crisis, Britain and France 'must do all we could to encourage patience in St Petersburg'.[142]

---

[140] Quotes from Benckendorff to Sazonov, 26 June/9 July 1914, *IBZI* IV, no. 146, and Grey to Buchanan (no. 264), 8 July 1914, *BD* XI, no. 39.

[141] Benckendorff to Sazonov (private), 26 June/9 July 1914, *IBZI* IV, no. 146. This part of the conversation, which Benckendorff described as 'ultra-confidential', was not included in Grey's despatch to Buchanan.

[142] Grey to Bertie (no. 451), 8 July 1914, *BD* XI, no. 38; see also tel. Cambon to Viviani (no. 122), 8 July 1914, *DDF* (3) X, no. 483.

On 9 July, Grey asked Lichnowsky to call on him at the Foreign Office for a private and confidential conversation. The ambassador's gloomy account three days earlier of the apprehensive mood prevailing at the Wilhelmstrasse had made some impression on Grey. He returned to the subject of the alleged naval talks with Russia. He hinted that France and Russia wished for such talks to proceed, but underlined that 'the hands of the [British] Government were quite free'. Britain would not enter any agreement against Germany, nor had there ever been 'anything in the nature of preparing an attack on Germany'. He freely admitted that during the two Moroccan crises of 1905–6 and 1911 there had been fears 'that Germany might send an ultimatum to France: but to contemplate that was a different thing from preparing an attack on Germany'. Following these assurances, Grey then informed Lichnowsky of his conversation with Benckendorff. He also suggested that, 'if Austrian action with regard to Servia kept within certain bounds, it would of course be comparatively easy to encourage patience at St Petersburg'. He himself – according to Lichnowsky – was prepared to encourage the authorities there to adopt 'a calm stance and a conciliatory attitude'. If, however, Vienna overstepped the mark, pan-Slav sentiments would force St Petersburg's hand so 'that they must send an ultimatum or something of that sort'. For his part, Grey would continue the policy he had pursued during the previous Balkan crises, 'and do my utmost to prevent the outbreak of war between the Great Powers ... [Lichnowsky] could assure his Government that I not only did not wish to disturb the peace, but would also do my utmost to preserve it'. If a general European war did break out, he concluded, 'it would mean the failure of the great object for which all of us, who had been in the London Conference [of December 1912 to May 1913] ... had worked'.[143]

Grey, then, appreciated the potential risks of the post-Sarajevo situation in the Balkans; and this he clearly signalled to Berlin, Paris and St Petersburg. He had also given a strong indication that, in the event of an escalation of the crisis, Britain could not be ignored. His suggestion to Benckendorff that it was incumbent upon Russia to allay German fears of Russian designs upon the two Central Powers was sensible enough; and so was his appeal to Paris for joint efforts to moderate any Russian response in the event of an Austro-Serb stand-off. Equally, his offer to Lichnowsky of some form of Anglo-German crisis management was good practical politics.

---

[143] Quotes from Grey to Rumbold (no. 223, secret), 9 July 1914, *BD* XI, no. 41; and Lichnowsky to Bethmann Hollweg (confidential), 9 July 1914, *DD* I, no. 30.

And yet there were problems with all three propositions. For one thing, Grey and his officials did not grasp the full extent of Vienna's determination to act. Indeed, over the past few years, an impression had gained ground in London that Austria-Hungary had become some sort of appendix of Germany, entirely unable to act on her own. As Grey's comments to Benckendorff indicated, he appreciated that Vienna's relative inferiority gave it a negative power over Germany. Even so, the assumption, implicit in his conversations between 6 and 9 July, that Austria-Hungary could be reined in by Berlin was, at best, overly optimistic. By the same token, Grey did not fathom the extent to which Berlin was already committed to its ally in Vienna. He can scarcely be faulted for this, for Lichnowsky himself did not know of the 'blank cheque' and his assurances of Berlin's pacific intentions were made entirely in good faith. Finally, Grey's hopes for French support in restraining Russia were misplaced. As was seen earlier, Poincaré's redefinition of the terms of the Franco-Russian alliance effectively ruled out French attempts to moderate Russian policy.

It is true that Grey had not issued an explicit warning to Berlin. But, then, this was neither necessary nor desirable at this stage. It is important here to judge Grey's diplomacy against previous crises, for they had established the framework within which he operated. Key to understanding his calculations throughout the July crisis was the palpable improvement in Anglo-German relations during the course of the previous year or so. Three days before the assassination of the Archduke, the Foreign Secretary explained his thinking to Sir Francis Bertie, Britain's ambassador to France: 'we are on good terms with Germany now and we desire to avoid a revival of friction with her, and we wish to discourage the French from provoking Germany'. Berlin reciprocated such sentiments: 'the German Gov[ernmen]t are in a peaceful mood and they are very anxious to be on good terms with England, a mood which he [Grey] wishes to encourage'. Grey, in fact, had assured Lichnowsky during the spring of 1914 that, in the event of another Balkan crisis, London would once more seek the cooperation of Germany. This did not mean that Grey was prepared to neglect the existing entente with France: 'he would continue the intimate conventions and consultations with France and to a lesser degree with Russia and consult with Germany so far as it might be expedient so as to be the connecting link between Germany and the Triple Entente and a restraint on the hastiness of Austria and Italy'.[144] The Foreign Secretary was by no means naïve about German policy. But he understood that under

[144] Memo. Bertie (on conversation with Grey), 25 June 1914, Bertie MSS, BL, Add. MSS. 63033. Bertie's well-known leanings towards France may well have coloured some of Grey's explanations.

the current circumstances, with the military balance shifting against Germany, it was important not to encourage Berlin's fear of isolation. It could only lead to a further escalation of armaments efforts by the continental Powers, or it might induce the German leadership to 'bring on a conflict with Russia at an early date before the increases in the Russian army have their full effect and before the completion of the Russian strategic railways'.[145]

Events seem to indicate an Anglo-German détente

Even so, however one looked at the international situation, relations between London and Berlin had improved. There was no shortage of indications. A fortnight before Sarajevo, the two sides had brought five years of initially fraught and often disrupted negotiations to a close by signing a convention on the Baghdad railway and other such enterprises in the Near East. As its preamble attested, the agreement was meant 'to prevent all causes of misunderstandings between Germany and Great Britain'.[146] The naval race that had soured the relations between the two countries for so long was over. Even if Berlin did not publicly admit it, the armaments competition with Britain had ended in what amounted to a unilateral declaration of defeat by Germany in 1913. Faced with now much accelerated French and Russian military expenditure on land, and having reached its own iron fiscal ceiling, the German government was forced to channel defence spending towards the army in two army bills in 1912 and 1913, with no further funding available for the navy. Grey and his officials appreciated the constraints under which Germany had to operate, and attributed to them Berlin's now evident desire for better relations with Britain.[147]

[145] Memo. Bertie (on conversation with Grey), 16 July 1914, *ibid.*

[146] 'German-British Convention', 15 June 1914, *BD* x/2, no. 249; for the background see G. Schöllgen, *Imperialismus und Gleichgewicht. Deutschland, England und die orientalische Frage, 1871–1914* (Munich, 1992), 404–9.

[147] Grey to Goschen (private), 5 Mar. 1913, and memo. Grey, 25 May 1914, *BD* x/2, nos. 465 and 512; see also T. G. Otte, 'Grey Ambassador: The *Dreadnought* and British Foreign Policy', R. J. Blyth, A. Lambert and J. Rüger (eds.), *The Dreadnought and the Edwardian Age* (Farnham and Burlington, VT, 2011), 73–6. The fiscal powers of the *Reich* government were limited, with tax-raising powers largely devolved to the state governments. Raising revenues was therefore always liable to cause political ructions in Germany; for detailed discussions see P. C. Witt, *Die Finanzpolitik des Deutschen Reiches, 1903–1913* (Lübeck, 1970), and his 'Reichsfinanzen und Rüstungspolitik', H. Schottelius and W. Deist (eds.), *Marine und Marinepolitik im kaiserlichen Deutschland, 1871–1914* (Düsseldorf, 1972), 146–77.

During the protracted Balkan turmoil in the aftermath of the two recent wars in that region, the German government had loyally acted with London to contain the crises. Even Nicolson, the Permanent Under-secretary, acknowledged that 'Germany has of late been making great efforts to be on the best possible terms with us and she has to a certain extent succeeded'.[148]

The friendly nature of Anglo-German relations was publicly affirmed by leading politicians in both countries. In a much-noted New Year's Day interview with the Radical-leaning *Daily News*, Lloyd George praised the now 'infinitely more friendly' relations between Downing Street and the Wilhelmstrasse, which he attributed to 'the wise and patient diplomacy' of Grey.[149] Jagow, Grey's German colleague, spoke of a '*détente* and a rapprochement' with Britain during a *Reichstag* session in early February 1914.[150] Foreign diplomats also commented on the Anglo-German rapprochement. Some three weeks before Sarajevo, Count Otto Czernin, the Austro-Hungarian chargé d'affaires at St Petersburg, observed that Great Power politics were now 'under the auspices of an Anglo-German détente'.[151] The broader implications of this were not lost on the Russian ambassador at Berlin, Sergei Nikola'evich Sverbe'ev. Having settled economic questions in Africa, he thought that Berlin and London would 'in time move on to more political questions'.[152] His French colleague, Jules Cambon, had no doubts that the friendlier atmosphere between the two governments 'seems to indicate a détente ... which here [at Berlin] they wish to make durable', a desire which he thought was reciprocated by Grey.[153]

Indeed, though Cambon could not have known it, Grey was prepared to go further to improve relations with Berlin by despatching his Private Secretary, Sir William Tyrrell, on a clandestine mission to Germany. The plan had been hatched by Tyrrell and his close friend, Prince Gebhard von Blücher, a direct descendant of the Prussian field marshal of Waterloo fame. Tyrrell occupied an increasingly important position at the

---

[148] Nicolson to Hardinge (private), 29 Oct. 1913, Hardinge MSS, CUL, Hardinge 93.
[149] 'Arms and the Nation', *Daily News*, 1 Jan. 1914, copy in Lloyd George MSS, PAL, C/36/2/1; see also the French comments in Fleuriau to Doumergue (no. 4), 2 Jan. 1914, *DDF* (3) IX, no. 5.
[150] Goschen to Grey (no. 48), 5 Feb. 1914, TNA (PRO), FO 371/1987/5608; see also J. Cambon to Doumergue (no. 51), 5 Feb. 1914, *DDF* (3) IX, no. 220; F. Kiessling, *Gegen den 'grossen Krieg'? Entspannung in den internationalen Beziehungen, 1911–1914* (Munich, 2002), 224–34.
[151] Czernin to Berchtold (no. 26E), 23 May/5 June 1914, HHStA, PA X/140.
[152] Sverbe'ev to Sazonov, 31 Jan./13 Feb. 1914, *BDS* III, no. 1036.
[153] J. Cambon to Doumergue (no. 332), 8 June 1914, *DDF* (3) X, no. 341.

Foreign Office in the last years before 1914.[154] There was something enigmatic about this official who was notoriously averse to putting pen to paper: 'Sir William Tyrrell was intuitive, conciliatory, elastic, and possessed a remarkable instinct for avoiding diplomatic difficulties'. His effectiveness as a diplomat stemmed from his skill in creating the right 'atmosphere', his conversations being 'intangible but suggestive'.[155] Of partly Anglo-Indian descent, the 'small and dark' Tyrrell was related by marriage to Prince Hugo Radolin, a distinguished German ambassador and courtier who had also taken care of Tyrrell's education in Germany before he went up to Oxford.[156] His friendship with Blücher went back to these Oxford days. Blücher himself later married an English lady and settled in London. As Blücher recorded in later years, both men were convinced 'that an exchange between two leading personalities from both countries was urgently required in order to attain the objective which we then pursued – a closer rapprochement between the two countries'.[157] To that end, Blücher approached Jagow, whom he counted amongst his friends, and suggested a meeting with Tyrrell. Jagow accepted with alacrity: 'For I believe that a confidential verbal discussion is more useful than the continued exchanges by means of notes and intermediaries.' He tentatively suggested a meeting for sometime in July – the forthcoming budget negotiations in the *Reichstag* and his own wedding and honeymoon made an earlier meeting impossible.[158] Tyrrell himself was no less enthusiastic about the prospect of meeting the German state secretary: 'nothing would give me greater pleasure and satisfaction than to have a talk with Jagow'. Significantly, he added that Grey 'approved very much of the idea'.[159]

It is not possible to corroborate Tyrrell's statement, but nor is it possible to disprove it. Grey had certainly welcomed Jagow's appointment

---

[154] Z. S. Steiner, *The Foreign Office and Foreign Policy, 1898–1914* (Cambridge, 1969), 14 and 51–2; E. T. Corp, 'Sir William Tyrrell: The *Eminence Grise* of the British Foreign Office, 1912–1915', *HJ* xxv, 4 (1982), 697–708.

[155] H. Nicolson, *Sir Arthur Nicolson, Bart., First Lord Carnock: A Study in the Old Diplomacy* (London, 1930), 327–8. Richard von Kühlmann of the German embassy offered a very similar vignette in his *Die Diplomaten* (Berlin, 1939), 68.

[156] H. Beaumont, 'Diplomatic Butterfly', unpub. TS memoirs, IWM, PP/MCR/113, fos. 39–40. Tyrrell apparently 'spoke English with a slight German accent' when he arrived at Oxford: *ibid.*, fo. 40.

[157] Memo. Blücher, 25 Jan. 1918, Nachlass Jagow, TNA (PRO), GFM 25/15; for full discussion of the planned mission and its origins see my 'Détente 1914: Sir William Tyrrell's Secret Mission to Germany', *HJ* lvi, 1 (2013), 175–204.

[158] Jagow to Blücher, 15 Apr. 1914 (TS copy), Nachlass Jagow, TNA (PRO), GFM 25/16.

[159] Tyrrell to Blücher (private), 18 Apr. 1914 (TS copy), *ibid.*

to the Wilhelmstrasse: 'If we could only have ten years of a man like Jagow to deal with, really controlling the policy of Germany, we should be on intimate terms with her at the end of the time, and on increasingly good terms through it.'[160]

Plans were made for an incognito meeting between Tyrrell and Jagow, disguised as senior bankers conducting sensitive financial negotiations, at Schloss Dyck near Düsseldorf, a chateau in the Lower Rhine region which belonged to one of Blücher's many friends. Its location close to the railway line that connected the Dutch ferry port of Flushing with the central European railways network made it a convenient meeting place. Various developments now conspired to cause delays. As Grey was increasingly preoccupied with the affairs of Ireland, Tyrrell carried a larger burden at the Foreign Office, and was 'over-worked and over-wrought'.[161] The original plan to meet around 8 July had to be postponed, when Tyrrell fell ill and was sent on sick leave from which he did not return until 20 July. Shortly after the assassination of the Archduke, Lady Tyrrell wrote again: 'Willie asked me to tell you he can fix no date yet – the minute he can you shall hear. I cannot explain in a letter – but the next few weeks will decide his movements. *C'est quelque chose qui tient à son chef* [This is something that is up to his chief].'[162]

For Jagow, returning from his honeymoon on 6 July, there was little for it but to accept that a meeting with Tyrrell would have to be delayed 'for the moment'. But Jagow remained wedded to the notion of a 'rapprochement with England or at least the extinction [*Ausmerzung*] of all differences' as 'the only sensible policy in the interests of *both* countries'. Intriguingly, the state secretary also commented on Franz Ferdinand's murder:

> The catastrophe of Sarajevo is terrible; this house of Habsburg-
> Lorraine truly is an Atridite dynasty, moving from catastrophe to
> catastrophe. The political impact is difficult to calculate, because
> one knows too little about what sort the new heir to the throne is
> and what he promises. The life of the old emperor is coming to an
> end ... and the successor is very young. In the meantime, the empire

---

[160] Grey to Rodd (private), 13 Jan. 1913, Rennell of Rodd MSS, Bodl., box 15; Robbins, *Grey*, 267–71.

[161] Chirol to Hardinge (private), 22 May 1914, Hardinge MSS, CUL, vol. 93.

[162] Lady Tyrrell to Blücher, n.d. [but before 2 July 1914], Nachlass Jagow, TNA (PRO), GFM 25/16. The date can be deduced from her opening reference to 'the ghastly time for [the] poor wonderful old emperor', and the fact that Blücher informed Jagow on 2 July; see Jagow's reply, 6 July 1914, *ibid.*; Otte, 'Détente 1914', 200

is disintegrating more and more and loses consistency and prestige.
It needs a strong hand to gather strength again; does the young
prince have that?[163]

It is not clear whether Jagow penned these lines to his old friend Blücher
before he was acquainted with the various meetings at Potsdam and Berlin
on 5 and 6 July. Unless he deliberately dissimulated, his musings about the
fall-out of Sarajevo are certainly suggestive of the great uncertainty at
Berlin as to the future. As for the meeting with Tyrrell, the gathering crisis
now overtook previous plans. Tantalizingly, Lady Tyrrell suggested to
Blücher that he should come to Prince Radolin's estate at Jarotschin 'beginning of September'.[164] In the end, Tyrrell and Jagow never met.

Tyrrell's planned mission to Germany was indicative of the very
real improvement in Anglo-German relations. It also underlined the essential flexibility of Grey's foreign policy. Indeed, given the advanced state of
the Tyrrell-Blücher scheme, Grey's own planned visit to Germany in
September 1914, ostensibly to visit the famous oculist Dr Hermann
Pagenstecher, an international authority on degenerative diseases of the
eye, raises the prospect of more far-reaching plans still.[165]

If there was a palpable improvement in Anglo-German relations,
the reverse held true for relations with Russia. The two developments, in
fact, were linked, as Grey's observations to Benckendorff on 8 July indicated. The revival of Russian power since 1912 had very nearly restored the
European equilibrium after the events of 1905 had disturbed it. Russia's
resurgence placed Germany in a more difficult position, and puts into
perspective Berlin's efforts to improve relations with Britain. But a re-
energized Russia posed an awkward challenge for Grey. Especially in Persia
and Central Asia, relations with Russia were strained. The 1907 Anglo-
Russian convention, itself a consequence of Russia's weakness after 1905,
was meant to place relations between these two Asiatic Powers on a more
stable footing. With Russia now much strengthened, the agreement could
scarcely contain the efforts of the Tsar's agents in the region to extend
Russian influence. There was a 'growing catalogue of our grievances
against Russia' in the Near East, an internal Foreign Office memorandum
warned.[166] Sir Eyre Crowe, Assistant Under-secretary and one of the
sharpest minds in the department, pointed to the 'real danger ... [in] our

---

[163] Jagow to Blücher, 6 July 1914 (TS copy), Nachlass Jagow, TNA (PRO), GFM 25/16.
[164] Lady Tyrrell to Blücher, n.d., Nachlass Jagow, *ibid.*
[165] See Oppenheimer diary, 8 Oct. 1914, Oppenheimer MSS, Bodl., box 5.
[166] Memo. Clerk, 'Anglo-Russian Relations in Persia' (confidential), 23 July 1914, TNA
(PRO), FO 371/2076/33484.

continuing to remain closely associated in one and the same region with the absolutely dishonest policy of the Russian authorities'. Indeed, the policy pursued since 1907 'of relying on Russia to carry out the spirit of the Anglo-Russian agreement concerning Persia is bankrupt'.[167]

Neither Grey nor his senior advisers contemplated throwing British foreign policy into reverse gear. Renegotiating the 1907 arrangement with Russia when it was up for renewal in 1915 was preferable to ditching Russia altogether. Even so, it was widely accepted in Whitehall that these talks would raise 'awkward questions'.[168] For his part, Grey accepted that the 'idea of a general discussion with the Russians is right'. But he was sceptical of its chances of success. The room for compromise was too narrow: 'all along the line we want something, and we have nothing to give. It is therefore difficult to see how a good bargain is to be made.' It was better, then, to delay formal talks and to keep various options open.[169] The uncertainties engendered by the cooler relations with Russia and the potential prospects opening up in consequence of the friendlier relations with Germany thus framed Grey's response to the unfolding July crisis.

Count Tisza performs a u-turn

At the end of the first week of July, the chancelleries in St Petersburg, Paris and London had adopted a largely passive stance, and so, in a manner, had the government in Berlin. The initiative, however, lay with Vienna. Much would depend now on how Austria-Hungary proceeded. The difficulties of reconciling the plans of the two halves of the Dual Monarchy meant that Habsburg decision-making remained excruciatingly slow. Tisza's reluctance to accept a military strike and his preference for a two-stage approach remained the principal obstacles to a swift solution. Count Forgách, one of the three hawkish section chiefs in Berchtold's entourage, summed up the situation after the ministerial council of 7 July in a private letter to the ambassador at Rome, Count Kajetan von Mérey: 'The minister [Berchtold]

---

[167] Quotes from mins. Crowe, [?] May 1914, on Townley to Grey (no. 123), 28 Apr. 1914, *ibid.*, FO 371/2073/22510, and 2 June 1914, on Townley to Grey (no. 143, confidential), 13 May 1914, FO 371/2059/24443; I. Klein, 'The Anglo-Russian Convention and the Problem of Central Asia, 1907–1914', *JBS* XI, 1 (1971), 142–5.

[168] Buchanan to Nicolson (private), 21 Jan. 1914, Nicolson MSS, TNA (PRO), FO 800/372; see also Mensdorff's perceptive comments, Mensdorff to Berchtold (no. 30P), 3 July 1914, HHStA, PA VIII/151.

[169] Grey to Buchanan (private), 18 Mar. 1914, *BD* X/2, no. 535. There were also strains in relations with France over various colonial matters: see memo. Bertie, 16 July 1914, Bertie MSS, BL, Add. MSS. 63033.

determined – in so far as this word applies to him – to use the ghastly misdeed of Sarajevo for a military cleansing [*Bereinigung*] of our impossible relations with Serbia.' Stürgkh and the Austrian (Cisleithanian) government supported a military strike, as did the military leadership and Biliński, 'who declared ruling Bosnia to be impossible without crushing pan-Serb illusions'. The Magyar prime minister, meanwhile, was 'rather against it'. Tisza favoured demands on Serbia 'that would humiliate her, but the acceptance of which was not impossible, possibly to issue an ultimatum, [and] only then to mobilize'. Crucially, Forgách noted that Germany would provide 'complete cover against Russia, even *en risque* of a not impossible world war'. Berlin, indeed, urged an early move without prior consultation of Italy and Romania.[170]

Forgách was close to Tisza, and his summary offered an accurate description of the premier's stance. But it was also suggestive of the interpretation that the hawks at the Ballhausplatz had begun to put on the German 'blank cheque'. As for the Hungarian prime minister, he sought and received the support of his cabinet immediately upon his return to Budapest on 9 July. The Magyar ministers asserted Hungary's right to a voice in foreign policy decision-making in accordance with the 1867 constitutional compromise.[171]

And yet, at some stage between 9 and 14 July Tisza performed a u-turn. On 10 July, Tschirschky, the German ambassador at Vienna, still complained of the Magyar magnate's misguided idea that 'one ought to proceed "*gentleman-like*"' against Serbia.[172] Four days later, Tisza, back in Vienna, fell into line. What had caused him to change his mind? Conrad's vague assurances of sufficient troop strength in Transylvania to deter a Romanian move against it had clearly made no impression on Tisza at the 7 July meeting. His thinking remained focused on the Romanian aspect of Austria-Hungary's Balkan problems. Information provided by Tschirschky on 12 July therefore acquired greater significance. The ambassador told the Ballhausplatz that Germany had begun to apply diplomatic pressure on Bucharest, that King Carol had asserted his indifference as to relations with Serbia, and that Berlin supported efforts to bring about Bulgaria's adhesion

---

[170] Forgách to Mérey, 8 July 1914, Nachlass Mérey, HHStA, Karton 10; also G. Kronenbitter, '*Krieg im Frieden*'. *Die Führung der k.u.k. Armee und die Grossmachtpolitik Österreich-Ungarns, 1906–1914* (Munich, 2003), 472.

[171] Mins. of Ministerial Conference, 9 July 1914, in Kronenbitter, *ibid.*, 471; for Forgách's connections with Tisza, see K. von Macchio, 'Momentbilder aus der Julikrise 1914', *BMH* XIV, 10 (1936), 771.

[172] Tel. Tschirschky to Auswärtiges Amt (no. 85, very secret), 10 July 1914, *DD* I, no. 29.

to the *Dreibund* alliance.[173] This suggested that Romania's neutrality, at least during the opening stages of any conflict, was assured, and that there was therefore no need to purchase Bucharest's benevolence.

On the same day, Szögyény reiterated his impression that the German government stood resolutely behind the Habsburg Monarchy. The ambassador had not been in communication with any of the officials at the Wilhelmstrasse since 6 July but he reasoned that, from a German perspective, the present moment was propitious for a move against Serbia. Berlin had formed the impression that the Russian armament programmes were meant to prepare Russia for an offensive war against Germany. At the same time, Russia was not yet ready for war, Szögyény emphasized, and St Petersburg would hesitate to support Serbia in the event of a war now. He also speculated that, in light of the recent Anglo-German rapprochement, Britain was unlikely to participate in a Balkan war. Finally, the heinous nature of the Sarajevo regicide, he suggested, would deter other Powers from taking Serbia's side.[174]

Szögyény's despatch addressed some of Tisza's concerns about possible foreign intervention in an Austro-Serb conflict. His emphasis on Russia's lack of war-readiness, moreover, undermined part of the Hungarian leader's assessment of 7 July. It is clear also that Tisza had begun to contemplate the prospect of war on his return to Budapest. On 10 July, he requested the *ban* of Croatia, Ivan Skerlecz von Lomnicza, to compile a dossier on anti-Austro-Hungarian machinations by pan-Serb agitators in order to frame an intellectual and moral case for a démarche against Serbia.[175] On the same day he instructed Burián, the Hungarian minister at the imperial court and his close confidant, to impress upon Berchtold the need to influence public opinion in Britain so that London 'would throw its weight into the scales in favour of localizing a possible war'.[176]

Burián's role was crucial in completing Tisza's change of mind. Over a decade later, Forgách reflected that Burián alone had persuaded his prime minister to change course and accept war as an option.[177] There was

---

[173] Daily report Forgách, 12 July 1914, and tel. Berchtold to Czernin (strictly secret), 12 July 1914, *ÖUA* VIII, nos. 10214 and 10216. For the German efforts at Bucharest, see tels. Jagow to Waldburg [Bucharest] (no. 34, secret), 9 July 1914, and vice versa (no. 37), 10 July 1914, *DD* I, nos. 21 and 28.
[174] Szögyény to Berchtold (no. 60), 12 July 1914, *ÖUA* VIII, no. 10215.
[175] Tisza to Skerlecz, 10 July 1914, E. von Wertheimer (ed.), *Graf Stefan Tisza. Briefe (1914–1918)* (2 vols., Berlin, 1928) I, 39; note Skerlecz, 11 July 1914, *ÖUA* VIII, no. 10210.
[176] Tisza to Burián, 10 July 1914, as quoted in Galántai, *Österreichisch-ungarische Monarchie*, 267.
[177] Forgách to Berchtold, 27 Nov. 1925, in Hantsch, *Berchtold* II, 585–6. In essence, Forgách blamed Burián for the war.

an element of posthumous mischief-making involved in Forgách's post-war ruminations. Even so, in early July 1914, the officials at Vienna clearly appreciated that the proverbial cigarette paper could be inserted between the positions of Tisza and the Hungarian representative at the court; and accordingly they set to work to drive in a wedge. In part, this was the reason why they sought to involve Burián in drafting the note to Belgrade. No doubt it was politic to do so, and reflected the realities of the dualist constitutional structure of the Monarchy, but it also opened another channel for the Ballhausplatz to influence the truculent Tisza. As seen, in their first meeting on 8 July Burián, Conrad and Berchtold's three section chiefs had plotted the general course to be pursued against Belgrade. At their next meeting, on 11 July, they made good progress in drafting the text of the planned note. Significantly, as Burián informed his prime minister, no-one now favoured Tisza's idea of a note making certain demands, to be followed by an ultimatum and mobilization only if Belgrade rejected these demands. There had been unanimity that only one diplomatic move should be made, and that the note should have the character of an ultimatum by stipulating a timeframe for Belgrade's reply.[178]

Tisza did not respond to Burián's wire. His preferred two-stage approach was thus off the table. As Berchtold confidently intimated to Tschirschky on the same day, an 'approximation had been arrived at since yesterday with the [Hungarian prime minister]' with regard to the planned note. Tisza had been summoned to Vienna for Tuesday, 14 July, and by then Berchtold hoped the final version of the note would be agreed.[179] Indeed, so confident was the foreign minister that he also informed Mérey at Rome that the 'action', outlined to him in Forgách's letter four days earlier, 'will probably take place at the end of this month'. Italy was not to be consulted, though San Giuliano might be informed 'one day or a few hours beforehand to avoid a *froissement*'.[180]

On 12 July, Burián was received by the Emperor at Ischl. The audience lasted for forty-five minutes. The monarch, Burián recorded in his diary, 'feels that accounts need to be settled, despite the difficult situation which will never be better than now'. Franz Joseph made no secret of his concerns about the period of mobilization. Serbia, he reasoned, was prepared and might move before the Habsburg armed forces were ready. The Emperor also touched on Russia: 'He considers a clash with Russia to

---

[178] Tel. Burián to Tisza, 11 July 1914, in *ibid.*, 268. Conrad was also present, but did not contribute to the discussions, see Conrad, *Aus meiner Dienstzeit* IV, 71.

[179] Tschirschky to Jagow (private), 11 July 1914, *DD* I, no. 34a.

[180] Tel. Berchtold to Mérey (no. 801, strictly secret), 12 July 1914, *ÖUA* VIII, no. 10221.

be likely and a very serious eventuality, because he knows that Russia's resources are in a way unlimited and he therefore approves Tisza's argument in his memorandum that we should not make Russia's neutrality impossible.'[181] The sole purpose of the audience was to appeal to Tisza to fall into line. Franz Joseph confirmed that there was no question of annexing Serb territory after the war, and expressed his desire for the swift conclusion of an agreement with Bulgaria. As Burián telegraphed to Budapest: 'His Majesty wishes a framing of our demands that will allow no excuses and that fixes guarantees. He understands that this is difficult and is hopeful that unanimity of all responsible actors in this regard will emerge soon.'[182]

None of these factors – Germany's seemingly irrevocable offer of support, Russia's lack of war preparations, a diplomatic offensive at Sofia and Bucharest, Franz Joseph's appeal to Tisza – was sufficient in itself to move the Magyar prime minister. But combined they were irresistible, and the usually unyielding Tisza yielded: 'The only one against war was Tisza, but we eventually dragged him along', commented Stürgkh.[183]

The final act of István Tisza's conversion came on 14 July, at a conference with Berchtold and Stürgkh at the Strudelhof, Berchtold's Viennese residence. Burián, who was also present, argued against an immediate declaration of war following mobilization, but this was something of a sideshow. The four men agreed that the note to be addressed to Belgrade would take the form of an ultimatum, and that it was to expire after forty-eight hours. Tisza retracted his earlier objections to a military solution, while Berchtold smoothed his passage into the war camp by assuring him that even after mobilization war might be averted, provided Belgrade still submitted to Vienna's demands and also paid compensation for the mobilization costs. Tisza extracted one small concession in that the conference agreed that there should be no annexation of Serbian territory, though the door was left open for small-scale border rectifications. The four men firmly expected war to ensue now:

> The text of the note to be addressed to Belgrade, agreed today, is such that we must reckon with the probability of a warlike confrontation. Should Serbia nevertheless yield and concede to our

[181] Burián diary, 12 July 1914, Diószegi, 'Tagebuch', 206.
[182] Tel. Burián to Tisza, 12 July 1914, as quoted in Galántai, Österreichisch-ungarische Monarchie, 268.
[183] In conversation with Rudolf Sieghart, the governor of the Boden-Credit-Anstalt; see Sieghart, Die letzten Jahrzehnte einer Grossmacht. Menschen, Völker, Probleme des Habsburger-Reichs (Berlin, 1932), 173.

demands, then such a move by the kingdom [of Serbia] would not only mean its profound humiliation and *pari passu* a diminution of Russian prestige in the Balkans, but would also imply certain guarantees for us in the direction of a restraining of pan-Serb infiltration [*Wühlarbeit*] on our soil.[184]

The path had thus been cleared for war, though the note itself had still not been finalized and was not expected to be in its final form until Sunday, 19 July. Even so, a delighted Berchtold informed the German ambassador that Tisza's contributions to the discussions had helped to produce a sharper edge to the planned communication to Belgrade.[185] Tisza himself paid a call on Tschirschky immediately after the conference: 'The Count said that he had always been the one who had counselled caution, but that every day had strengthened him in the conviction more and more *that the Monarchy would have to come to an energetic decision* in order to demonstrate its vitality and *put an end to the intolerable conditions in the South East.*' Tisza had long wrestled with the problem of peace and war, he confessed, 'but I am now *firmly convinced of its* [the war's] *necessity*'. Significantly, he also intimated to the German ambassador that mobilization would follow immediately upon the expiry of the ultimatum, and that the demands contained in it were such 'that the possibility of its acceptance is as good as *excluded*'. Assurances and promises were no longer sufficient; what mattered now were deeds. In composing the note, Tisza said, it was important to ensure that its terms were intelligible to a wider European public – 'especially in England – and that Serbia was clearly put in the dock'. On leaving, Tisza grasped Tschirschky's hand and said in a flight of pathos: 'Together we shall now face the future calmly and firmly.'[186]

Baron Conrad intervenes

Without Tisza falling into line there would have been no ultimatum to Belgrade. Whatever his ultimate reasons for supporting the démarche now, Tisza's initial opposition to a military strike was not rooted in some sort of

---

[184] Berchtold to Franz Joseph, 14 July 1914, ÖUA VIII, no. 10272; see also Tucher to Ludwig III (no. 254/XXI), 14 July 1914, BayD no. 11.
[185] Tschirschky to Bethmann Hollweg (very secret), 14 July 1914, DD I, no. 50; Galántai, *Österreichisch-ungarische Monarchie*, 275.
[186] Tschirschky to Bethmann Hollweg (no. 233, very secret), 14 July 1914, DD I, no. 49 (emphasis in the original). The Kaiser's marginal comment against this passage reads: 'Well, a real man after all!'

pacifism that was alien to his character. Rather it was based on tactical considerations. He accepted the need for a final reckoning with Serbia, but wished to ensure that the latter would be isolated both internationally and in the region. To that extent, Tisza was as responsible as the hawks at the Ballhausplatz for what was to follow now. But his slow conversion to the cause of war also meant delay when a swift strike might just have prevented escalation into a general war later.

For now, however, there was 'a rare, completely unanimous view and conviction' among the Habsburg leadership, as Forgách noted with satisfaction. Vienna and Budapest appreciated that 'without asserting power [*Machtwort*] against Serbia or some action there' the Monarchy's hold over Bosnia would slowly disintegrate:

> In consequence such demands will now be made of Serbia, that their acceptance would mean humiliation for Serbia and the pan-Serb ideas and a diminution of her prestige; rejection would be a relatively welcome pretext for war at an internationally not disadvantageous moment. It would be the, in the interests of the Monarchy, sooner or later inevitable conclusion of the more and more intense struggle with our deadly enemies at Belgrade.
>
> At any rate, our rulers are ready for the most far-reaching steps and their possible consequences.

Austria-Hungary, Forgách explained, wished to avoid a continental war, 'though Germany is perfectly ready'. To that end, Vienna was ready to give assurances to Russia that Serbia's territorial integrity would be respected. Italy's foreign minister was to receive less than twenty hours' warning, lest he sought to mediate – and to make Rome's meddling impossible Mérey was encouraged to delay making his communication until the evening hours or when San Giuliano had gone to the country. In the meantime, an approach would be made to Bulgaria to open talks for her accession to the Austro-German camp.[187]

Unanimity in Habsburg counsels made war possible. But it did nothing to accelerate the pace of developments. Further obstacles now emerged. Already on 7 July, Krobatin, the war minister, had argued against putting the armed forces on alert, as any such move might trigger surprise Serbian attacks on railway lines and other vital installations.[188]

---

[187] Forgách to Mérey, 16 July 1914, Nachlass Mérey, HHStA, Karton 10; see also Galántai, *Österreichisch-ungarische Monarchie*, 276.

[188] Krobatin to Berchtold, 7 July 1914, HHStA, PA I/810, Liasse XX.

Even if the decision to mobilize had been taken now, it is doubtful whether the troops could have been readied for any military eventualities in a meaningful way. There was no disagreement at Vienna about the need for close coordination of the planned diplomatic démarche and any necessary military measures, but Habsburg war planning acted as a further brake on proceedings. The existing railway network would slow mobilization against Serbia and Montenegro ('Plan B') to a leisurely sixteen days.[189] As seen earlier, moreover, Conrad, the chief of staff and the most vociferous advocate of a preventive war against Serbia, was anxious to mobilize only if war was a certainty. The crippling financial costs of the abortive mobilization of 1913 apart, Conrad feared the demoralizing effect on the armed forces of another such effort.[190]

The chief of staff was responsible for yet another delay. He had earlier introduced harvest leave for the army, largely in order to placate the powerful agrarian interests in the Dual Empire. Under this scheme, conscripts were temporarily released from active military service to help with the harvest, before returning to their units for the summer manoeuvres. Recalling the troops now on leave to the colours would delay bringing in the harvest, be financially costly and cause supply bottlenecks in a military campaign. Above all, it would alert the Powers to Vienna's plans to resort to force. Even as late as 24 July, the commanding officer of the VII Army Corps at Temesvár (now Timişoara), near the Serbian frontier, was under orders not to recall soldiers currently on leave.[191] Thus the Empire's dualist constitutional arrangements, the pre-industrial character of its economy and Conrad's organizational measures, combined, prevented the surprise attack on Serbia, previously advocated by Conrad himself and hinted at by Hoyos in Berlin.

Yet another problem arose, this time affecting the desired dovetailing of diplomatic and military steps. It emerged that the harvest leave was to end shortly before the long-planned state visit by Poincaré and Viviani to St Petersburg on 20–23 July.[192] Already at the meeting on 14 July, Berchtold and the other ministers had decided to delay delivering the ultimatum until after the French delegation had left St Petersburg. To do so during the

[189] For detailed discussions see Kronenbitter, 'Krieg im Frieden', 100–20; R. Kiszling, 'Kriegspläne und Aufmärsche der k.u.k. Armeen sowie der Feindheere im Sommer 1914', Institut für Österreichkunde (ed.), Österreich am Vorabend des ersten Weltkrieges (Graz, 1965), 83–96; G. A. Tunstall, Planning for War against Russia and Serbia: Austro-Hungarian and German Military Strategies, 1871–1914 (Boulder, CO, 1993), 159–88.
[190] Conrad, Aus meiner Dienstzeit IV, 61–3.
[191] Ibid., 61–2; S. R. Williamson, 'Confrontation with Serbia: The Consequences of Vienna's Failure to Achieve Surprise in July 1914', MÖStA XLIII (1993), 168–77.
[192] Czernin to Berchtold (no. 32 A-B), 25 June/8 July 1914, HHStA, PA X/140.

visit would have been regarded as an affront at St Petersburg, Berchtold observed. It was not the finer sensibilities of Russia's rulers, however, that weighed on Berchtold's mind. More important was the consideration that making the move while Poincaré was at St Petersburg would allow the French president and the Tsar to coordinate their policies, and this 'would heighten the possibility of a military intervention by Russia and France'.[193] It was important, Berchtold argued in justifying this further delay to Tschirschky, to deny the two governments the opportunity to consult with each other. He wished to avoid that, 'fuelled by champagne and under the influence of Messrs Poincaré, Isvolsky and the Grand Dukes, some fraternization would be celebrated, that might shape and indeed determine the position of the two empires. It were better if the toasts were over before the communication of the note [to Belgrade].' The ultimatum could not, then, be delivered any earlier than 23 July.[194]

There is a profound irony in this. Immediately after the assassination of the Archduke, the Ballhausplatz resolved swiftly to exploit the event in order to settle the Monarchy's most pressing strategic problem. Tactical, diplomatic considerations now demanded delay. In turn, this meant that the Powers had to be lulled into a false sense of tranquillity. And this Berchtold and Conrad accomplished with great aplomb. The chief of staff went on vacation, and so did Krobatin, the war minister. Meanwhile, preparations for the manoeuvres scheduled to take place in western Hungary in September carried on.[195]

Count Mensdorff tries to influence the fourth estate

It was at this stage that Berchtold began to take steps to influence the foreign press. The idea may well have originated with Jagow at Berlin, who suggested compiling a dossier on Serbian provocations in an attempt to encourage papers abroad to take a more hostile attitude towards Serbia. Berchtold needed no persuasion.[196] Mensdorff in London and his colleague

---

[193] Berchtold to Franz Joseph, 14 July 1914, ÖUA VIII, no. 10272. Otto Czernin, the chargé d'affaires at St Petersburg, was instructed to report immediately on Poincaré's departure: tel. Berchtold to Czernin (no no.), 14 July 1914, HHStA, PA X/140, Weisungen.

[194] Tschirschky to Bethmann Hollweg (very secret), 14 July 1914, DD I, no. 50.

[195] Conrad, Aus meiner Dienstzeit IV, 77–9; Kronenbitter, 'Frieden im Krieg', 478–9.

[196] Tel. Szögyény to Berchtold (no. 243), 8 July 1914, ÖUA VIII, no. 10127; tel. Jagow to Tschirschky (no. 117), 11 July 1914, DD I, no. 31; and vice versa (private), 11 July 1914, JK I, no. 72. Jagow gave similar instructions to Count Waldburg, the chargé d'affaires at Bucharest: tel. Jagow to Waldburg (no. 4, secret), 14 July 1914, DD I,

at the Paris embassy, Count Nikolaus Szécsen, were instructed to use their social influence and long-established ties with influential people in the two capitals 'to generate a mood in the English [and French] press that is friendly to us [and] negative to Serbia'.[197]

Szécsen, the seasoned Habsburg representative to the French republic, was pessimistic about his chances of persuading the Paris papers to develop 'a more objective attitude'. The French press, he noted, was strongly influenced by the French government, itself kowtowing to Russia and dependent on financial subsidies which flowed freely from Russian and Balkan sources.[198] But Mensdorff and his embassy staff set to work, trying to influence The Times and The Westminster Gazette through two former foreign secretaries, Lords Lansdowne and Rosebery, both of whom had been supplied with dossiers on the anti-Austrian agitation in the Serbian press. Mensdorff, or 'Royal Albert' as he was called at the Ballhausplatz on account of his familial connections with the British Royal family, was a courtier more than a diplomat, London's unofficial spokesman rather than the Austro-Hungarian representative in Britain and without much know-ledge of the press. Rarely was so much effort expended for so little achieve-ment. A leading article in The Times condemned the unrestrained language of some of the Serbian papers, but wound up by warning against resorting to force to solve the current crisis.[199] One of Mensdorff's counsellors, Baron Georg von Franckenstein, had a little more success with J. A. Spender, editor of the Liberal-leaning Westminster Gazette. Yet the paper's line, if couched in somewhat more pro-Austrian language, did not differ in substance from that of The Times. If anything, Franckenstein's insistence that the matter was 'urgent and dangerous' merely made Spender suspect that something more sinister was afoot. He himself could not regard the situation as dangerous: 'The matter was of no interest to Britain[;] and Russia, who was interested, was unlikely to object to measures taken to prevent the assassination of Archdukes.' Somewhat perturbed by the

no. 44; see also D. C. Watt, 'The British Reactions to the Assassination at Sarajevo', ESR I, 3 (1971), 241.

[197] Tels. Berchtold to Mensdorff and Szécsen (nos. 146 and 140), 9 July 1914, and reply tel. Mensdorff (no. 96), 10 July 1914, ÖUA VIII, nos. 10158 and 10180.

[198] Szécsen to Berchtold (private), 12 July 1914, ÖUA VIII, no. 10220; the Paris papers had close links with the Quai d'Orsay: see Hayne, 'Formulation of French Foreign Policy', 441–6.

[199] The Times, 16 July 1914; Mensdorff's despatches exaggerated the pro-Austrian tone of the leader: see Mensdorff to Berchtold (no. 34B), 17 July 1914, ÖUA VIII, no. 10336; for a further discussion see also P. Schuster, Henry Wickham Steed und die Habsbur-germonarchie (Vienna, 1970), 162–4; also E. U. Cormons [pseud. E. Urbas], Schicksale und Schatten. Eine österreichische Autobiographie (Salzburg, 1951), 124.

incident, Spender, who was well-connected in Liberal circles, called upon Grey at the Foreign Office to inform him of Franckenstein's communications.[200]

In the meantime, Mensdorff's German colleague, Lichnowsky, had received very similar instructions from his government. In contrast to the Habsburg ambassador, however, Lichnowsky took a pessimistic, and altogether more realistic, view of the undertaking. It would be difficult 'to brand the entire Serb nation as a people of scoundrels and murderers', he warned. It was more likely, indeed, that 'sympathies here would shift immediately and vigorously towards Serbdom as soon as Austria resorted to force'. Public opinion in Britain, he observed, had always tended to favour the 'nationality principle'.[201] For his part, Jagow pinned his hopes on the public revulsion in Britain at the assassination of the Serbian royal couple in 1903, which he hoped would be a precedent. The current situation, he impressed on Lichnowsky, was 'an eminently political question, possibly the last opportunity to deliver the coup de grâce to pan-Serbdom under relatively advantageous circumstances'.[202] As instructed, Lichnowsky extended a few feelers to various London journalists, but the whole enterprise struck him as utterly futile. In the 1850s, he noted, 'Austria succeeded as little in dealing the coup de grâce to the Italian movement as she will now succeed in arousing sympathy for herself'.[203]

Prince Lichnowsky intervenes

Lichnowsky's prognostication was as shrewd as Jagow's marginal comment on his telegram was revealing: 'Alas, it is all true.' To a large extent, the efforts to influence the London press were little more than diplomatic displacement activity. What mattered for Jagow was that Austria-Hungary moved with the utmost speed now. Tellingly (and characteristically), the Kaiser vented his frustration at the delays at Vienna in the margins of Tschirschky's telegrams and despatches. The ambassador's report of 10 July that the Habsburg leadership was close to coming to a decision elicited

---

[200] Memo. Spender, n.d. [Aug. 1914], Spender MSS, BL, Add. MSS. 46392; see also J. A. Spender, *Life, Journalism and Politics* (2 vols., London, 1927) II, 9–10; A. F. Pribram, *Austria-Hungary and Great Britain, 1908–1914* (London, 1951), 222.

[201] Tel. Lichnowsky to Jagow (no. 129, secret), 14 July 1914, *DD* I, no. 43; instructions in tel. vice versa (no. 155), 12 July 1914, *ibid.*, no. 36.

[202] Tel. Jagow to Lichnowsky (no. 159), 15 July 1914, *DD* I, no. 48.

[203] Tel. Lichnowsky to Jagow (no. 133, secret), 15 July 1914, *DD* I, no. 52; Watt, 'British Reactions', 241.

various caustic comments from his pen: 'as H[is] M[ajesty's] memorandum [handed over on 5 July] is now about 14 days old, this takes a long time' and 'they have had enough time'.[204] When Tschirschky announced that Vienna's note to Serbia would not be delivered until President Poincaré had left St Petersburg, Wilhelm commented 'alas! [*schade!*]'.[205]

If Berlin had ever expected a swift Austrian attack on Serbia, leading German diplomats did not react to Berchtold's explanations that Hoyos had gone a little too far in his assertion that Vienna would strike quickly and that some sixteen days would be required for mobilization against Serbia.[206] There was no change in German policy. Indeed, the exchanges between the two allied capitals suggest a mutual fear that the other might 'wobble'. While officially the Wilhelmstrasse declined to advise Vienna on the demands on Serbia, Tschirschky now constantly exhorted the Ballhausplatz to act soonest.[207] Indeed, one year into the war, in the summer of 1915, Josef Redlich reflected that Hoyos, Tschirschky and his embassy secretary, Dietrich von Bethmann Hollweg, a cousin of the German chancellor, had been the real instigators of the war – to which Dietrich Bethmann vigorously assented.[208]

On 11 July, that is before Tisza's final conversion to war, Tschirschky informed Jagow privately of the outlines of the Austro-Hungarian ultimatum. The principal demands were to be a Royal decree officially renouncing the Belgrade government's pan-Serb programme and the installing of Habsburg officials in Serbia to monitor Serbia's compliance. Tschirschky was under no illusions: the demands on Belgrade were supposed to be rejected, and Tschirschky was well satisfied with this.[209] The fact that this latest information was transmitted privately once more underlines the marginal role of the German chancellor at this stage.

Bethmann, as was seen earlier, was still on leave and took no active part in the discussions at Berlin. On 16 July, Lichnowsky alerted him to the potential breakers ahead. The German ambassador was one of the truly tragic characters in the events of July 1914. His diplomatic career was unusual, even by the standards of pre-1914 international diplomacy,

---

[204] Marginal comments Wilhelm II on tel. Tschirschky to Auswärtiges Amt (no. 85, very secret), 10 July 1914, *DD* I, no. 29; see also testimony Jagow, *OGD* I, 28.
[205] Marginal comment Wilhelm II, on Tschirschky to Jagow (very secret), 14 July 1914, *DD* I, no. 50.
[206] Tels. Tschirschky to Jagow (nos. 83 and 84, secret), 7 and 8 July 1914, *DD* I, nos. 18 and 19.
[207] Tel. Tschirschky to Jagow (no. 87), 13 July 1914, *DD* I, no. 40.
[208] Redlich diary, 13 June 1915, F. Fellner (ed.), *Schicksalsjahr Österreichs, 1908–1919. Das Politische Tagebuch Josef Redlichs* (2 vols., Graz and Cologne, 1953) II, 43.
[209] Tschirschky to Jagow (very secret), 11 July 1914, *JK* I, no. 72.

dominated as it was by an aristocratic fraternity that often placed greater value on pedigree than professionalism. He hailed from a very wealthy Silesian noble family with roots and property in Austrian Silesia and Bohemia; indeed, he was one of the richest men in Germany.[210] He came late to diplomacy and achieved no great distinction in the service. Having spent five years at the Vienna embassy in the late 1890s, he was recalled to Berlin to head the foreign ministry's personnel department. In 1904 he retired to his vast estates, occasionally to appear in the Prussian *Herren-haus* where he attracted attention with moderate and unprejudiced speeches, unusual fare for the hereditary members of the upper chamber of the Prussian parliament. He had published the odd pamphlet on foreign policy, in which he advocated an Anglo-German settlement without deny-ing the difficulties involved. His 'wilderness' years came to an end when he was appointed ambassador at London, a post for which his Anglophilia, wealth and social standing predestined him. It was to be his first ambas-sadorial posting – and his last.[211]

There was more to Lichnowsky than fabulous wealth and social graces, however. Few ambassadors in Europe matched his analytical powers, certainly none in the German service. He understood that Grey's policy was driven by balance of power calculations, not by the naval question. In sharp contrast to his colleagues, and despite his family's ancestral connections, he was also critical of the combination with Austria-Hungary and Germany's growing dependence on the Habsburg ally. Since his arrival at the London embassy in 1912, he had consistently worked for a rapprochement with Britain, and did so with some success. Yet for all his intelligence and all his realistic appreciation of the inter-national situation the ambassador was not without flaws. He lacked 'grit'. His analyses were not matched by an even temper. Of an extremely nervous disposition, he was given to bouts of blackest despair and he tended to avoid unpleasantnesses.[212] Although on very friendly terms with Grey, he perhaps did not explain sufficiently clearly to him that Vienna should not be manoeuvred into a position in the Balkans where reckless unilateral action might appear to be preferable to working in concert with the

---

[210] Otte, '"Outdoor Relief "', 43; R. Martin, *Jahrbuch des Vermögens und Einkommens der Millionäre in Preussen* (2 vols., Berlin, 1912) I, 15 and 38.

[211] Müller diary, 1 Oct. 1912, W. Görlitz (ed.), *Der Kaiser. Aufzeichnungen des Chefs des Marinekabinetts Admiral Georg von Müller über die Aera Wilhelms II* (Göttingen, 1965), 121; see also O. Graf zu Stolberg-Wernigerode, *Die unentschiedene Generation. Deutschlands konservative Führungsschicht am Vorabend des Ersten Weltkrieges* (Munich, 1968), 299–302.

[212] Young, *Lichnowsky*, 64; B. von Bülow, *Denkwürdigkeiten* (4 vols., Berlin, 1930) III, 124.

European Powers; nor did he make urgent representations at Berlin during the latter stages of the July crisis. He was, indeed, somewhat isolated in the German service and his advice did not carry sufficient weight, as he himself knew well enough. 'The Kaiser', he burst out in conversation with Margot Asquith shortly before his mission came to an end, 'is not a genius! he is ill informed – *impulsive* – *Mad*! Never listening or believing one word [of] what I say – never answering telegrams!!'[213]

In the past, however, Lichnowsky had enjoyed the support of the chancellor, and it was to Bethmann Hollweg that he turned on 16 July, quite possibly in reaction to the leading article in *The Times* that morning. Lichnowsky reiterated his earlier warning that, if Vienna resorted to force, public opinion in Britain would swing against Austria-Hungary.[214] Privately, he now warned Bethmann against encouraging Austria-Hungary to seek a military confrontation – he was in utter ignorance of the events of 5 and 6 July. The ambassador expressed some sympathy with Berchtold's Balkan predicament, especially the seemingly impending loss of Romania. As for the Southern Slav problem, he doubted that Serbia could be compelled 'by military deeds à la Prince Eugene [of Savoy] to renunciation and better mores'.[215] The Habsburg leadership, he argued, had no clear political programme for dealing with the national aspirations of the Balkan Slavs. The current position of the 'Serbo-Croat ethnic family', divided as it was between Austria, Hungary and the separate administrations in Bosnia, Dalmatia and Serbia, was untenable. But Austria-Hungary lacked the political will and imagination to implement a trialist reform of the Monarchy that also included Serbia. Vienna did only what was needed to meet the demands of the moment so that it could continue to 'muddle through [fortwursteln]'. Yet all attempts 'to maintain under all circumstances the sainted status quo for reasons of convenience have often and again during the latest Balkan crisis led to a collapse of the whole political house of cards built on such foundations'. A military strike against Serbia would therefore not lead to a durable new settlement. It might purchase moral satisfaction for Austria-Hungary, but at the price of opening up again the entire Eastern Question.

[213] M. Asquith diary, 2 Aug. 1914, Asquith MSS, Bodl., Ms.Eng.d.3210; for Asquith's views of Lichnowsky see H. H. Asquith, *The Genesis of the War* (London, 1923), 104–5. For some discussion of British perceptions of the Kaiser's mental state see T. G. Otte, '"The Winston of Germany": The British Foreign Policy Elite and the Last German Emperor', *CJH* XXXVI, 4 (2001), 471–504.

[214] Tel. Lichnowsky to Auswärtiges Amt (no. 134), 16 July 1914, *DD* I, no. 55; Lichnowsky, *Abgrund* II, 241–5.

[215] A caustic reference to Prince Eugene of Savoy (1663–1736), the Habsburg field marshal who commanded Austrian forces during two Austro-Turkish wars.

Lichnowsky reiterated Grey's and his cousin Benckendorff's assurances that Russia harboured no antagonistic designs on Germany, even if there were strongly anti-Austrian sentiments still present in Russia. He hinted that it would be unwise to expect Russia's 'passive assistance' to Austria-Hungary in a war with Serbia, and emphatically warned that the British public would take against Vienna in such an eventuality. Jagow's idea of playing up Serbia's bloody past would make no impression on a country in which even the better educated had less historical awareness of foreign countries 'than the average sixth-former at home [in Germany]'.

The prince did not advocate relinquishing the alliance with Austria-Hungary. The existing ties had endured for too long, and the current moment was scarcely ripe for a latter-day diplomatic revolution. Even so, Lichnowsky implied that Vienna needed to be restrained:

> I wonder whether it is recommendable for us to support our ally in a policy or rather to underwrite a policy that I regard as adventurous because it will lead neither to a radical solution of the problem nor to the destruction of the pan-Serb movement. If the Imperial and Royal [Austro-Hungarian] police and the Bosnian authorities led the heir to the throne through an 'avenue of bomb throwers', I can see no sufficient grounds in it to risk the proverbial Pomeranian grenadier for this Austrian *Pandurenpolitik*, just so that Austrian self-confidence may be strengthened.

Those at Berlin, who might expect Habsburg gratitude afterwards, ought to remember Austria's ingratitude to Russia for her help in suppressing the Hungarian revolution in 1848–9, one of the longer-term root causes of the Austro-Russian antagonism of the second half of the long nineteenth century.[216]

Herr von Jagow abdicates an independent German policy

By any standard, this was an explosive epistle. And yet, the German chancellor, it seems, was never shown Lichnowsky's letter. Instead it was answered by foreign minister Jagow.[217] This was further evidence that for

---

[216] Lichnowsky to Bethmann Hollweg, 16 July 1914, *DD* I, no. 62. *Pandurs* were irregular light infantry in the eighteenth-century Austrian army, recruited from among Croat noblemen. It may well be an ironic reference to Musulin, who hailed from a Croat military family: see Musulin, *Ballhausplatz*, 28.

[217] Fritz Fischer speculates that Jagow's response was written following consultation with Bethmann: see his *Juli 1914. Wir sind nicht hineingeschlittert. Das Staatsgeheimnis*

much of July 1914 Bethmann's role was marginal in German decision-making. As for Jagow, his attention was focused on containing any Austro-Serb conflict. Two Powers were important to achieving this, Italy and Britain. With that aim in view, Jagow, a former ambassador at Rome himself, informed his successor at the Villa Caffarelli, Hans von Flotow, in the broadest outlines of the events of 5 and 6 July. Energetic measures against the pan-Slav agitation against the Habsburg Monarchy were to be expected, but it was not for Berlin to stipulate what shape such measures should take. The Italian foreign minister, San Giuliano, suspected of harbouring pro-Serb sentiments, was not to be told in advance, however, though Flotow was to hint that 'it would be scarcely possible for Austria-Hungary calmly to tolerate such provocations'.[218]

Flotow's reports were encouraging. San Giuliano had urged restraint on the Belgrade authorities, and the Italian ambassador at Vienna, the long-serving Giuseppe Duke di Avarna, could discern no prospect of serious Austro-Serb complications.[219] There were nevertheless problems now. On 14 July, San Giuliano hinted that Italy would never act against the principle of nationality, conveniently ignoring Italy's own designs on Albania. It was obvious therefore that, in the event of a conflict, Austria-Hungary would not find Italy on her side.[220]

It was equally obvious now that Flotow's and Mérey's principal task at Rome was to keep San Giuliano in the dark about the planned démarche against Belgrade. Jagow was not slow to grasp the broader implications of Flotow's latest communications. If Italy openly sided with Serbia, he warned Tschirschky, 'it would unquestionably considerably encourage Russian activism [Aktionslust]. In St Petersburg they reckon not only that Italy would fail to fulfil her alliance duties towards Austria-Hungary, but that she might possibly turn openly against Austria-Hungary.' The collapse of the Habsburg Monarchy, after all, would open the prospect of redeeming the last remaining parts of *Italia irredenta*. It was imperative, therefore, for Vienna to come to some sort of an arrangement with Rome. This, he reasoned, would entail ceding the Trentino to Italy, rather than compensating her with parts of Albania: 'This morsel would be

---

um die Riezler-Tagebücher (Reinbek, 1983), 91. The fact that Jagow responded on the day of receipt, 18 July, would suggest otherwise.

[218] Tel. Jagow to Flotow (no. 1, very secret), 11 July 1914, *DD* I, no. 33.

[219] Tel. Flotow to Jagow (no. 2), 12 July 1914, *DD* I, no. 38; cf. tel. Avarna to San Giuliano (no. Gab. 730/58), 11 July 1914, *DDI* (4) XII, no. 154; Afflerbach, *Dreibund*, 835–6.

[220] Tel. Flotow to Auswärtiges Amt (no. 5), 14 July 1914, and to Bethmann Hollweg, 16 July 1914, *DD* I, nos. 42 and 64.

so fat that it would stuff the mouth of Austrophobe public opinion.' Jagow understood that this would be a painful concession for Vienna, but the Habsburg government had to judge what price it was willing to pay for Italian benevolence. The state secretary himself was in no doubt that 'Italy's attitude will be significant for Russia's attitude in the event of a Serbian conflict; if a general conflagration were to arise from the latter, then this would also be of great military importance for us'.[221]

This was quite an extraordinary statement to make. Jagow clearly appreciated the risk of escalation, and was anxious that Austria-Hungary ought to take whatever steps were necessary to ensure that any conflict with Serbia remained localized. And yet he was not prepared to restrain Vienna. There was to be no change in German policy. Too engrained was the fear that, after the perceived setbacks during the previous Balkan crises, Berlin would be blamed for yet another unsatisfactory outcome of the latest regional stand-off. It was tantamount to abdicating an independent German policy. Jagow merely confined himself to pressing Vienna to clarify its post-conflict plans for Serbia 'as this would have considerable influence on the attitude of Italy and the public opinion and the attitude of England'. Any existing plans, he suggested, were liable to change in light of the evolving international situation. Tschirschky was to probe Berchtold on the nature of the current plans. At the same time, he was to avoid giving the impression 'as if we wished to block the path for Austria's action or to prescribe for it certain limits or aims. Only it would be of value to us to know where that path might lead.'[222]

Jagow realized that Germany was being led by the nose down a path towards a very uncertain outcome. Yet he was not prepared to retract the Kaiser's commitment to Austria-Hungary. On the day he instructed Tschirschky to make the above communication to Berchtold, he also for-warded the Kaiser's formal reply to Franz Joseph's private letter that Hoyos had delivered personally on 5 July. Wilhelm II's letter was long in expres-sions of monarchical solidarity but, like Jagow's statements, refrained from expressing any views on the nature of Austria-Hungary's response to Sarajevo. Pan-Serb agitation threatened to undermine the 'state edifice' of the Danube Monarchy, and it was 'not just the moral duty of all civilized states, but also an imperative of their self-preservations, for them to stand up to the propaganda of terrorist deeds [*Propaganda der Tat*] ... with all means available'. This was the closest the Kaiser's letter came to touching on military conflict. The rest of the document dealt with the now agreed

---

[221] Jagow to Flotow (secret), 15 July 1914, *DD* I, no. 46.
[222] Jagow to Tschirschky (secret), 17 July 1914, *DD* I, no. 61.

diplomatic offensive in the Balkans with the aim of winning over Bulgaria to the *Dreibund* and preventing Romania's drifting into the Russian orbit.[223]

German policy had thus reached an important juncture, and the decision-makers at Berlin faced for the first time the prospect of a wider conflict. Around 18 July, Jagow began to rationalize Berlin's decisions so far, and he did so by replying to Lichnowsky's letter to the chancellor. The decline of the Habsburg Empire had to be reversed, not least also in order to stabilize the *Dreibund*, he explained to Lichnowsky. There was no alternative, as he explained with a touch of flippancy:

> But we have this alliance with Austria: *hic Rhodus, hic salta* [Here is Rhodes, jump here]. And we may certainly discuss whether with the alliance with the more and more decaying entity on the Danube we will achieve our aims, but I reply with the poet: '*Wenn Dir die Gesellschaft nicht mehr passt, such' Dir eine andere, wenn Du eine hast* [If you do not like this company, choose a different one, if you can find one].'

There, of course, lay the crux, for efforts to bring about a rapprochement with Britain had not made such progress as would allow Berlin to ditch Vienna. Jagow also asserted that '[w]e did not drive Austria into this decision [to make demands on Serbia]. We cannot and must not now stay her hand.' If Germany did so, she would help to expedite the 'process of [Austria-Hungary's] decay and internal collapse'. Under these circumstances, German diplomacy had to ensure that an Austro-Serb conflict remained localized. Success depended largely on Russia's attitude and, albeit to a lesser degree, on the moderating influence of Britain and France. Some 'rumblings' at St Petersburg were likely, but Russia was not yet ready to strike. Neither France nor Britain wished for foreign complications. Indeed, Britain was crucial to the success of all efforts to localize the conflict. Given Britain's traditional interest in a continental equilibrium, he reasoned, London could not possibly wish to see Austria-Hungary deserted by Germany and then smashed by Russia, and the balance thus destabilized by a world inferno ('*Weltenbrand*'). The firmer the line pursued by Vienna, the more likely it was that Russia would yield. If, however, Russia did interfere in an Austro-Serbian conflict militarily, Jagow confirmed that the *casus foederis* would arise. With a view to Russia's growing

---

[223] Wilhelm II to Franz Joseph, 14 July 1914, *DD* I, no. 26 and *ÖUA* VIII, no. 10262. The letter was transmitted to Vienna through Tschirschky on 17 July.

military strength, the foreign minister concluded: 'We would then find ourselves in what one could not call "proud" isolation. I do not want a preventive war, but if the opportunity offers itself, we must not shirk it.'[224]

Jagow's letter was an amalgam of delusion and recklessness, but it still offers the best insight into his rationale. He hoped to localize an Austro-Serbian war, in which case the *Zweibund* would have achieved a considerable diplomatic and military success. But he had also come to accept that the conflict could perhaps now no longer be localized. In that case, he was prepared to accept the risk of a continental war. A sense of honour and obligation towards the Austrian ally and a fear of isolation strengthened his resolve. But Germany would not disengage, nor would she restrain Austria-Hungary. All of this reinforced Berlin's fatal dependence on the Ballhausplatz.

[224] Jagow to Lichnowsky, 18 July 1914, *DD* I, no. 72. Jagow used the English word 'proud'. The poet in question was Wilhelm Busch, a cartoonist and author of popular ditties.

4 LOCALIZING THE CRISIS: 19 TO 23 JULY

> [S]uch moments of worry flew away like cobwebs in the wind.
> Although, every now and then, we thought of war, it was no different
> from contemplating death – as something that was possible but
> presumably far away.
>
> STEFAN ZWEIG (1944)[1]

Jagow's attempt to rationalize German decision-making up to this point of the crisis was tantamount to a declaration of political bankruptcy. Even though the head of the Wilhelmstrasse was acutely aware of the risks entailed in Berlin's self-imposed passivity, he was determined to stay on the sidelines. There was, it is true, some tactical advantage to be gained from being able to maintain ignorance of Vienna's intentions, if the crisis later escalated. But that in itself contained the risk – a not inconsiderable one as it turned out – of not being wholly credible. Above all, however, it meant abdicating all influence over the Habsburg leadership at the inception of Austria-Hungary's planned offensive against Serbia; and that would make it all the more difficult to re-establish any kind of influence later on. Apparent ignorance was thus purchased at the price of impotence. To some extent, Berlin was driven by the perceived weakness of the Austro-Hungarian ally; and that fear of the spiralling decline of the Habsburg Empire gave Vienna a form of negative power over Germany. It was a case of the strong submitting to being led by the weak.

Being led by Vienna also meant being misled. For, by the middle of July, Count Berchtold no longer consulted with the government at Berlin. Indeed he was reluctant to share any information with the Wilhelmstrasse,[2] and would not do so until he communicated, on 22 July, the full text of the ultimatum to be delivered to Belgrade. Berchtold did not wish to give Berlin the opportunity to change course and restrain Habsburg policy, as had

---

[1] S. Zweig, *Die Welt von Gestern. Erinnerungen eines Europäers* (Frankfurt, 1981 (pb) [1st edn 1944]), 246.

[2] In his memoirs Berchtold argued that 'at perhaps no other time had diplomacy in Vienna and Berlin worked so much in parallel and in harmony': Berchtold, 'Am Vorabend', H. Hantsch, *Leopold Graf Berchtold. Grandseigneur und Staatsmann* (2 vols., Graz and Vienna, 1963) II, 599, n. 15.

been the case during the Balkan turmoil in 1912–13. But his sudden reserve also stemmed from a fear of leaks. By now almost three weeks had passed since the murder of the Archduke and his wife. Any careless indiscretion, any mischievous rumour – the two banes of the diplomatic profession – might force open the whole issue and bring about the interference of the other Powers. Such fears were not groundless. As Forgách, one of the hawkish section chiefs, hinted to Kajetan Mérey at Rome, Vienna knew – 'from our secret sources' – that the Italian government was becoming nervous, and that it had made 'not warmly alliance-loyal [*bundeswarme*] suggestions' of mediation at Belgrade and St Petersburg'.[3]

The Marchese has a price

The Ballhausplatz was, in fact, reading Italian diplomatic traffic, and therefore knew that Jagow had outlined Vienna's aims to the German ambassador at Rome, Hans von Flotow. The ambassador had hinted at this in conversation with the Italian foreign minister, who duly informed various Italian missions abroad.[4] Since it was well-known that the *cabinet noir* at the Choristers' Bridge routinely read foreign diplomatic traffic, Berchtold was justified in assuming that the Russian foreign ministry was broadly aware of Vienna's intentions.[5]

As for Italy, her foreign minister, Marchese Antonino di San Giuliano, was well-versed in the arts of politics, having been in turn a journalist and parliamentarian, a minister and a diplomat. He had been foreign minister for a brief spell in 1905–6 before becoming ambassador at London and Paris. He returned in 1910 to the Consulta, the ochre-coloured palazzo on the Quirinale which houses the Italian foreign ministry. San Giuliano is often seen as a timid head of that department. In Albertini's magisterial assessment, his 'policy was one of utter, unreserved surrender to the Central Powers, inspired by sympathy and admiration for them ... by fear of their strength and the opposite feelings towards the *Entente* Powers whom he had not learnt either in London or Paris to know, to like and to judge at their true value'.[6]

---

[3] Forgách to Mérey (private), 16 July 1914, Nachlass Mérey, HHStA, Karton 10; tel. Berchtold to Mérey (no. 842, secret), 20 July 1914, ÖUA VIII, no. 10418; see also Hantsch, *Berchtold* II, 592–3.
[4] San Giuliano circular, 16 July 1914, DDI (4) XII, no. 272.
[5] The Ballhausplatz also knew from Rome that Flotow had adumbrated Austro-Hungarian intentions to San Giuliano: see tel. Mérey to Berchtold (very secret), 18 July 1914, ÖUA VIII, no. 10364.
[6] L. Albertini, *The Origins of the War of 1914* (3 vols., London, 1953) II, 245.

Yet he was a man of quick intelligence and many languages, well-trained and experienced in international diplomacy. He was 'a clever diplomat'[7] – if, that is, one defines diplomacy as an exercise in equivocation, manipulation and subterfuge to the point of cynicism.

If San Giuliano gave the impression of timidity, that was as much a reflection of Italy's precarious international position as of his character traits. As the least of the Great Powers, the crisis that was to unfold in the summer of 1914 posed a considerable challenge to Italy, one that threatened to reveal her foreign policy for the smoke-and-mirrors trick that it was. San Giuliano was in no doubt that in the other capitals of Europe Italy was seen as economically and militarily weak and unsteady in her political orientations. Italian foreign policy, he reflected shortly before relinquishing the London embassy at the end of 1909, ought to give the impression of strength, anchored in the *Dreibund* alliance with Germany and Austria-Hungary – despite the coolness of relations with the latter – but open to Britain, as the leading Mediterranean Power, and to a lesser extent also to France.[8] In this way it was possible for Italian diplomacy to peg away at Albania, Asia Minor and the Dodecanese in order to carve out a quasi-imperial niche in the eastern Mediterranean. A degree of tension between the Great Powers was thus conducive to enlarging Rome's room for manoeuvre and scope for territorial acquisitions. A general war, by contrast, would put a stop to its ability to pursue its diplomatic conjuring tricks by forcing it to choose between the belligerents.[9]

San Giuliano's initial assessment of the situation after Sarajevo was framed by the recent events in Albania where the Prince of Wied's régime was tottering towards total collapse and where Italy and Austria-Hungary had long been locked into some kind of 'cold war', surreptitiously competing for influence whilst trying to exclude the other from that country. It was not to be assumed, San Giuliano observed on 28 June, just after news of Franz Ferdinand's assassination had reached Rome, that Italy was not 'ready to act energetically to protect her own interests in the Adriatic

---

[7] R. J. B. Bosworth, *Italy, the Least of the Great Powers: Italian Foreign Policy before the First World War* (Cambridge, 1979), 69; for a good biographical portrait of San Giuliano see *ibid.* 68–94; on the cooling of Austro-Italian relations see F. R. Bridge, *The Habsburg Monarchy among the Great Powers, 1815–1914* (New York and Oxford, 1990), 332–4.

[8] See San Giuliano to Guicciardini, 15 Dec. 1909, as quoted in F. Tommasini, *L'Italia alla vigilia della guerra: la politica di Tommaso Tittoni* (5 vols., Bologna, 1934–41) V, 209–11.

[9] War, of course, offered its own opportunities; for further thoughts on this see W. A. Renzi, 'Italy's Neutrality and Entrance into the Great War: A Re-examination', *AHR* LXXIII, 5 (1968), 1414–32; and the same author's *In the Shadow of the Sword: Italy's Neutrality and Entrance into the Great War, 1914–1915* (Berne and New York, 1988).

should Austria-Hungary take the grave decision to proceed to a territorial occupation' in the region.[10] Whilst such statements of intent highlighted the delicate state of Italo-Habsburg relations, for the moment San Giuliano was confident that Italy's adherence to the combination with the two Germanic Powers would continue to work in her favour. Zimmermann's statement, on 30 June, that Berlin would exercise a restraining influence at Vienna, lest the Habsburg leadership adopt measures 'too rigorous and provocative for the neighbouring kingdom [Serbia]' – assurances he repeated on 4 July – could only suggest that the Wilhelmstrasse was working for a restoration of the triplice in the Balkans.[11]

As already seen, *pace* Zimmermann, following the 'blank cheque' Germany had relinquished all means of moderating Austro-Hungarian foreign policy and, in contrast to previous crises in south-eastern Europe, privileged Vienna over Rome. This and the decision of the Habsburg ministerial council of 7 July to confront Italy with a *coup de main* against Belgrade, rather than consult with her prior to any such action, undermined the rationale of San Giuliano's policy so far, though the foreign minister did not and could not know it at that moment.

There were some straws in the wind, however. On 9 July, Jagow, recently returned from his honeymoon, had reiterated his under-secretary's assurances that Berlin would continue to give moderating advice to Austria-Hungary. Speaking privately, however, Jagow added that if the Habsburg Empire did not wish to abdicate its position as a Great Power, it could not afford to be 'too meek in the face of Serbia supported and pushed forward by the provocative assistance of Russia'. Indeed, the state secretary added that 'a truly energetic and consistent action' by Austria-Hungary was not likely to lead to conflict – further evidence that the Wilhelmstrasse expected a swift strike and no further escalation.[12]

---

[10] Tel. San Giuliano to Bollati and Avarna (no. 3862), 28 June 1914, *DDI* (4) XII, no. 3; R. J. B. Bosworth, 'The Albanian Forests of Signor Giacomo Vismara: A Case Study of Italian Economic Imperialism during the Foreign Ministry of Antonino di San Giuliano', *HJ* XVIII, 3 (1975), 571–86; see also F. R. Bridge, 'Austria-Hungary and the Ottoman Empire in the Twentieth Century', *MÖSTA* XXXIV (1981), 263–4.

[11] Tels. Bollati to San Giuliano (nos. 5828/490 and 5967/501), 30 June and 5 July 1914, *DDI* (4) XII, nos. 25 and 78 (quote from former); for the importance of Zimmermann's statement in this respect see Bosworth, *Least of the Great Powers*, 380. Bollati's reports from Berlin suggested that the Wilhelmstrasse appreciated the potential dangers which the affairs of Albania posed to the internal cohesion of the *Dreibund*: see Bollati to San Giuliano (private), 8 July 1914, *DDI* (4) XII, no. 120.

[12] Tel. Bollati to San Giuliano (no. 6055/503), 9 July 1914, *DDI* (4) XII, no. 123; H. Afflerbach, *Der Dreibund. Europäische Grossmacht- und Allianzpolitik vor dem Ersten Weltkrieg* (Vienna, 2002), 836–41.

If Jagow had meant to calm any concerns the Consulta may have had, his words had the opposite effect. But there was further news, at once disturbing and enticing. Also on 9 July, in the seclusion of the spa town of Fiuggi-Fonte, to where San Giuliano had withdrawn on account of his heart weakness, Flotow spoke confidentially of the possibility of a surprise Austrian seizure of the strategically important Mount Lovćen on the Dalmatian-Montenegrin frontier as a pre-emptive measure to weaken the adverse effects for the Monarchy of a union between Serbia and the neighbouring mountain kingdom.[13] Predictably, San Giuliano expressed his opposition to any such move unless there were some countervailing advantages for Italy, possibly in the shape of 'Italian territories today belonging to Austria'. Although Flotow initially demurred, he left San Giuliano with 'the impression that the cession to Italy of a part of the Italian provinces subject to Austria would be a very difficult matter, but not altogether impossible in return for fitting and effective assistance, maybe even military, by Italy for Austria'. He even got Flotow to concur with his idea that Berlin should 'prepare the terrain at Vienna' and then mediate an Austro-Italian accord.[14] In Flotow's version of the conversation, the Italian foreign minister initially used somewhat intemperate language and even spoke of a war if Austria-Hungary seized Montenegrin territory, before he suggested the possibility of the Trentino as compensation. 'We must not close our eyes to the fact', Flotow concluded, 'that here [at Rome] they are facing a very serious question that could at least shake the *Dreibund*, possibly even lead to a European conflagration'.[15]

The German ambassador had grasped a vital point, one that would complicate the diplomatic moves of Berlin and Vienna. As if to underline the fragile state of the *Dreibund*, San Giuliano circulated his report of the conversation with Flotow to the Italian representatives at Belgrade, Cetinje and St Petersburg, impressing upon them that Serbia and Montenegro should pursue the project of a union of the two countries gradually 'in a slow and imperceptible manner' so that Vienna had no pretext for a pre-emptive strike.[16]

[13] M. B. Petrovich, *A History of Modern Serbia, 1804–1918* (2 vols., New York, 1976) II, 603–5; B. Jelavich, *Russia's Balkan Entanglements, 1806–1914* (Cambridge, 1993), 250.

[14] Tel. San Giuliano to Avarna, Bollati, Carlotti, Negrotti Cambioso and Squitti (Cabinet 702), 9 July 1914, *DDI* (4) XII, no. 124. The Serbian chargé d'affaires at Berlin had, in fact, speculated about a union between the two countries: see tel. Czernin to Berchtold (no. 137), 6 July 1914, HHStA, PA X/140.

[15] Flotow to Bethmann Hollweg (no. 4, very confidential), 10 July 1914, *GP* XXXVIII, no. 15555.

[16] *DDI* (4) XII, no. 124; also Bosworth, *Least of the Great Powers*, 383.

San Giuliano clearly sensed that some crisis was brewing, whether triggered by the imminent collapse of the Wied régime in Albania, the rumoured Serbo-Montenegrin union or the Sarajevo assassination. The Italian ambassador at Vienna, the pro-Habsburg Giuseppe, Duke of Avarna di Gualtieri, a dull and ponderous Neapolitan nobleman, warned that the prospect of the merger of the two Southern Slav kingdoms and the continued pan-Serb agitation in Bosnia-Herzegovina would force Vienna 'to teach Serbia a lesson and not allow itself to be intimidated by the armaments of Russia' or by the apparent Russo-Romanian rapprochement in the spring.[17] A private observation by Szögyény, the Austro-Hungarian ambassador at Berlin, that his government contemplated an approach to Rome in the Albanian question lent weight to this tentative conclusion. The current state of affairs was no longer sustainable, and as part of a settlement, Szögyény had speculated, Italy would be granted 'the "cession" of Valona and all the surrounding territory'. Such a move, probably necessitated by the occupation of Mount Lovćen, ambassador Bollati observed, would restore the equilibrium in the Adriatic and increase Italy's naval power.[18]

Recent reports and the uncertain state of Austro-Italian relations had made an impression on San Giuliano, and on 14 July he delivered himself of a lengthy analysis of Italy's foreign affairs problems. Relations with Vienna, he noted, had soured, and the interests of these two Adriatic Powers could not easily be reconciled. Without Berlin's intervention, relations with the northern neighbour could now no longer be maintained on a tolerable basis. The situation in Albania remained at the forefront of San Giuliano's concerns; here lay the principal cause of Italo-Austrian disunity. Whatever the final arrangements for that country and whatever the outcome of the Mount Lovćen and Sarajevo affairs, Italy would have to receive compensation for any Austrian gains: 'All our policy must aim to hinder again on this occasion Austrian territorial aggrandisement without receiving adequate territorial compensation in our favour.' Adequate compensation, he suggested, could be found in the 'Italian provinces of Austria or in southern Albania'. Given the many uncertainties surrounding these matters, the foreign minister nevertheless speculated that, at some future date, Italy might be forced to leave the *Dreibund* combination with the two Germanic Powers.

---

[17] Tel. Avarna to San Giuliano (Gab. 730/58), 11 July 1914, *DDI* (4) XII, no. 154. Riccardo Bollati at Berlin also warned of the 'dangers of the situation': Bollati to Avarna (private), 9 July 1914, *ibid.*, no. 133.

[18] Tel. Bollati to San Giuliano (Gab. 734/55), 12 July 1914, *DDI* (4) XII, no. 169.

That moment had not yet arrived. The military balance was still in favour of Italy's current allies – 'and the outcome of a war is decided on land'. France would treat Italy as a negligible factor, if Paris divined that she was about to abandon Germany and Austria-Hungary. At the same time, it was necessary to mend fences with Britain and France. Italy could wait, however; time was on her side. Russia was steadily gaining in strength, and was likely to be far stronger still in four or five years' time. Romania was gravitating into the latter's orbit, the other small Balkan states and Spain into that of the two Western Powers by virtue of 'economic interest ... geographical situation, [and] intellectual and cultural affinity'. At the same time, 'the process of [Austria-Hungary's] enfeeblement and disintegration' would continue. For the moment, then, the

> prognosis is reserved for the future, and I do not wholly exclude the probability of our exiting the Triple Alliance in some years, to join the other grouping or to remain neutral, but today I would consider it a grave and dangerous error to weaken without absolute necessity the reciprocal bonds between us and our allies, and I believe it therefore necessary and urgent that Germany works to bring into accord both the defence of our interests and our loyalty to the Triple Alliance.[19]

It was a typical statement of San Giuliano's political credo, one that, for all its shrewd appreciation of the likely shifts in international power, preferred the opaque to clarity without gaining much constructive leverage from such equivocation. He had grasped Austria-Hungary's capacity for international disruption in the immediate future, but seemed resigned to her ultimate demise. With a view to either, his idea of exploiting any of the current crises in south-eastern Europe in order to regain Italy's *terra irridenta*, the 'unredeemed' lands under Habsburg rule, was not altogether unrealistic. For, as was seen earlier, Flotow had raised the idea with the Wilhelmstrasse.

By the middle of July, however, the Italian foreign minister had begun to realize that the present situation was different, and that this was not just another Balkan crisis. On 16 July, still at Fiuggi, Flotow hinted that Vienna would take a series of measures against pan-Serb propaganda in Bosnia. In the event of Belgrade resisting, Austria-Hungary would resort to force in order to coerce Serbia into submission. The ambassador suggested that Vienna had no territorial ambitions of any kind, but urged Rome to

---

[19] San Giuliano to Bollati (private), 14 July 1914, *DDI* (4) XII, no. 225; for the importance of this document see also Bosworth, *Least of the Powers*, 384.

rein in the Italian press so that any conflict would remain localized.[20] On the following day, San Giuliano wired to Italy's representatives at Berlin, Bucharest, St Petersburg and Vienna information he had received 'from a most authoritative source' (this presumably meant Flotow). Austria-Hungary, 'supported by Germany ... and convinced that Russia will not move', was about to present Serbia with 'unacceptable conditions' and then use this as a pretext for a military strike. The Russian government, he suggested, should be encouraged to let it be known at Berlin and Vienna that Russia could not remain indifferent and neutral in such an eventuality. Romania, meanwhile, should declare that any Austro-Hungarian attack on Serbia was against her own vital interests.[21]

It is not clear whether San Giuliano hoped that such a joint Russo-Romanian move would deter Austria-Hungary and so prevent an escalation of the situation, or whether he hoped that any sign of opposition from those quarters would make Vienna pay any price for Italian support. Either way he hoped that Bucharest and St Petersburg would pull Italy's chestnuts out of the Balkan fires. Two things, indeed, are clear. San Giuliano was determined to insist on compensation for any Austro-Hungarian occupation, whether 'temporary or permanent', in the interior of the Balkans or along the littoral of the region.[22] And it is also clear that San Giuliano's telegrams alerted Russian officials to the brewing crisis.

Sazonov takes note

Even if Russian cryptographers had not deciphered the Italian diplomatic telegrams, the officials at the Choristers' Bridge could hardly be under any illusions about Austrian intentions. At a soirée at one of St Petersburg's grand houses on 16 July, alerted by San Giuliano's wires, the Italian ambassador at St Petersburg, Marchese Andrea Carlotti di Riparbello, raised the matter with Sazonov's director of chancellery and the foreign ministry's head of the First Department (Western Europe), the experienced Baron Moritz Fabianovich von Schilling. Carlotti hinted that

[20] Tel. San Giuliano to Avarna, Bollati, Carlotti and Squitti (no. 4121), 16 July 1914, *DDI* (4) XII, no. 272. San Giuliano merely reiterated that 'a territorial aggrandizement of Austria was against our interests'.
[21] Tel. San Giuliano to Bollati, Carlotti, Avarna and Fasciotti (Gab. RR 720), 17 July 1914, *DDI* (4) XII, no. 311.
[22] Art. VII of the *Dreibund* treaty entitled either Power to compensation for gains by the other '*dans les régions des Balcans ou des côtes et îles ottomanes*': San Giuliano to Bollati (private), 18 July 1914, *DDI* (4) XII, no. 334.

'Austria was capable of taking an irrevocable step against Serbia' and suggested, as instructed, that an indication of Russian opposition would deter Vienna from resorting to military force. In response, Schilling observed that Russia could not tolerate any infringement of Serbia's integrity and independence. At the same time, he argued that any overt warning addressed to Vienna by Russia would inevitably be interpreted there as an ultimatum and so exacerbate the situation. Only Austria-Hungary's allies at Berlin and Rome could offer acceptable advice of moderation.[23]

Two points are worth noting here. For one thing, Carlotti's revelation did not come as a surprise to Schilling; and further, Russian officials clearly appreciated the risk of escalation inherent in any Austro-Serb crisis or an early intervention on the part of Russia. As for the former, Shebeko, the Russian ambassador at Vienna, had wired earlier on 16 July, before Carlotti sipped champagne with Schilling, that the Habsburg government, counting on Russian non-interference, would make 'certain demands on Serbia by connecting the Sarajevo assassination with the pan-Serb agitation inside the [Austro-Hungarian] empire'. He suggested that St Petersburg should leave the Habsburg leadership in no doubt as to its likely reaction to such a démarche.[24]

As for the danger of escalation, this weighed heavily on the minds of the senior officials at the Choristers' Bridge. Shebeko's report and the Italian ambassador's observations had discomposed Schilling so much that he personally collected Sazonov from the capital's Warsaw train station when the minister returned to St Petersburg on 18 July after several days' absence at his country estate near Grodno. Sazonov agreed with his head of chancellery that some way had to be found of impressing upon the Austro-Hungarian leadership that Russia would oppose any move designed to undermine Serbia's independence.[25] In conversation with Sir George Buchanan, Britain's seasoned ambassador, Sazonov expressed his growing unease at Vienna's seemingly hardening attitude. Pan-Serb agitation in Bosnia and other Habsburg dominions was an internal Austro-Hungarian problem, he asserted, and 'anything in the shape of an Austrian ultimatum

---

[23] Schilling journal, 3/16 July 1914, *IBZI* IV, no. 245; also M. Schilling, *How the War Began* (London, 1925), 25. Carlotti did not transmit the final observation but noted that Schilling had stressed Pašić's 'conciliatory spirit' and the inflammatory effect Austro-Hungarian provocation would have on public opinion in Russia: tel. Carlotti to San Giuliano (no. 6393/4), 17 July 1914, *DDI* (4) XII, no. 312.

[24] Tel. Shebeko to Sazonov (no. 88), 16 July 1914, *IBZI* IV, no. 247. Schilling later confirmed that he had received Shebeko's report before meeting Carlotti: see N. Shebeko, *Souvenirs. Essai historique sur les origines de la guerre de 1914* (Paris, 1936), 213–14.

[25] Schilling journal, 18 July 1914, *IBZI* IV, no. 272; Schilling, *How the War Began*, 26–7.

at Belgrade could not leave Russia indifferent, and she might be forced to take some precautionary military measures'.[26]

Shortly before his interview with Buchanan, Sazonov had met with the German ambassador, Count Friedrich Pourtalès. Their conversation moved along very similar lines. The minister, however, was more forthright still. Certain elements were gaining the upper hand at Vienna that did 'not baulk at the idea of plunging Austria into a war, even at the risk of unleashing a general world inferno [*Weltenbrand*]'. The aged Emperor and his weak foreign minister were scarcely in a position to rein in the belligerent elements. He dismissed the ambassador's suggestion that the Sarajevo assassination originated in Serbia and that no Great Power could tolerate the sort of propaganda that emanated from Belgrade. The agitation among the Slav subjects of the Dual Monarchy, Sazonov averred, was primarily the result of Habsburg malgovernance. Indeed he responded with some warmth to Pourtalès's intimation that Vienna might aim at some form of 'clarification' of its relations with Serbia. If the Habsburg leadership was 'intent on disrupting peace, it had in that case *to reckon with Europe*'. Russia could not stand by if Austria-Hungary sought to humiliate Serbia. To some extent the form of the contemplated move was more important than the precise nature of any demands addressed to the Serbian government. '[A]t any rate there must be no talk of an ultimatum', he impressed upon the ambassador: 'Russia could not tolerate it if Austria *used threatening language* against Serbia or *took military measures*. "La politique de la Russie ... est pacifique, mais pas passive* [The policy of Russia is pacific but not passive].'"[27]

In contrast to his interviews with the British and German representatives, Sazonov was more reserved when the Austro-Hungarian ambassador, Count Szápáry, called upon him immediately upon his own return to the Russian capital. Sazonov did not touch upon the state of Austro-Serbian relations; nor did he demur when Szápáry pontificated on the dangers of 'terrorist revolutionary methods' for the peaceful coexistence of nations. Instead he confined himself to emphasizing his vague unease at reports received from Vienna. The Habsburg ambassador assured Sazonov

---

[26] Tel. Buchanan to Grey (no. 161), 18 July 1914, *BD* XI, no. 60.
[27] Pourtalès to Bethmann Hollweg, 21 July 1914, *DD* I, no. 120 (original emphasis). Buchanan's telegram (*vide supra*) confirms that the conversation took place before Sazonov spoke to the British ambassador. Why Pourtalès did not report the conversation until 21 July, and then in the form of a despatch rather than a telegram, is not clear. Sazonov spoke in much the same vein to Carlotti: tel. Carlotti to San Giuliano (no. 6421/5), 18 July 1914, *DDI* (4) XII, no. 342: Russia's policy was one of '*pacifismo*' but not of '*passività*'.

that Vienna was convinced that the Serbian response to any representations made at Belgrade would be conciliatory. At no point did Sazonov repeat the earlier warning to Pourtalès about the form of the demands on the Serbian government, of which the latter had already informed his Austro-Hungarian colleague.[28]

Sazonov's conversation with Szápáry had an air of unreality about it. Whilst the latter wondered at the Russian foreign minister's reserve, Sazonov decided that the ambassador's pacific assurances were such that he did not have to raise the possibility of Russia's intervention in a conflict between Vienna and Belgrade. Szápáry, he noted, had been 'doux comme un agneau [gentle like a lamb]'.[29] Even so, Sazonov's various interviews on 18 July had revealed the terrible truth that in the regional antagonism between the Romanov and Habsburg Empires their respective relations with Serbia had become the touchstone of their positions in the Balkans; and as such Serbia had acquired a disruptive potential. If there was any doubt on that score, Tsar Nicholas II removed it when he minuted on Shebeko's telegram of 16 July that no state could make any demands on another unless it was determined on war.[30] Such convictions dovetailed neatly with the prevailing perception at St Petersburg that Austria-Hungary's Southern Slav problem was a matter of governmental malpractice but not a case of foreign-sponsored terrorism. As was seen earlier, Franz Ferdinand's murder had been framed very much in these terms right from the beginning. Clearly, this would have limited Austria-Hungary's room for manoeuvre, even if Vienna had not already decided upon war. Whilst all of this was suggestive of a certain lack of sympathy with Vienna's Bosnian predicament, the interviews of 18 July also emphasized the extent to which Sazonov understood that any overt Russian interference would raise the stakes considerably, and possibly move the dispute beyond the reach of diplomacy.

The various reports in the middle of July had clearly alerted Sazonov to Austria-Hungary's impending move. But he may even have had a shrewd sense of its likely timing. For the *cabinet noir* at the Choristers' Bridge had at about the same time intercepted and decrypted several diplomatic telegrams from Vienna enquiring about the programme of President Poincaré's long-planned visit to Russia later in July, and

---

[28] Tel. Szápáry to Berchtold (no. 146), 18 July 1914, ÖUA VIII, no. 10365. It is ironic that Vienna thus knew of Sazonov's concerns about the form of Austria-Hungary's demands before Berlin.

[29] Schilling journal, 18 July 1914, IBZI IV, no. 272.

[30] Min. Nicholas II on tel. Shebeko to Sazonov (no. 88), 16 July 1914, IBZI IV, no. 247.

especially about the date of his departure.[31] It did not require a major intellectual effort to make a connection between the two. For the moment, however, possibly under the impression of Szápáry's pacific assurances, Sazonov remained hopeful that 'reason will gain the upper hand over the belligerent tendencies at Vienna'.[32]

Sir Maurice de Bunsen learns a secret

A strong sense of an impending crisis was not confined to the Choristers' Bridge and the Consulta. On 16 July, the day of Shebeko's first warning, his British colleague at Vienna, Sir Maurice de Bunsen, had received similar information from an unofficial source. The Austro-Hungarian government was on the brink of indicting Belgrade for complicity in the Sarajevo plot, he telegraphed to London. Serbia would be expected to adopt 'certain definite measures' to suppress 'nationalist and anarchist propaganda'. If she failed to do so, Austria-Hungary was 'in no mood to parley with Servia ... [and] force will be used'. Germany, de Bunsen reported, was said to be 'in complete agreement with this procedure'. Europe was expected to be sympathetic and Russia was not thought likely to move, 'but in any case Austria-Hungary would go ahead regardless of results'.[33]

There was an ironic twist to Shebeko's and de Bunsen's telegrams of 16 July. While Berchtold was worried about the risk of Rome compromising the planned move against Serbia through indiscretion, there had been a leak closer to home. In a way, it was Roman at one remove – the informant of the two ambassadors was none other than the former Habsburg representative in the Italian capital, Count Lützow. Circumstance may well have aided the anglophile retired diplomat in his indiscretion. De Bunsen had rented Stixenstein castle, which belonged to Alek Hoyos's uncle, for the summer months. It was close to Lützow's own home, and contact with the genial British ambassador was swiftly established. In contrast to the 'anxious secrecy' observed at the Ballhausplatz, Lützow decided that openness was the better policy. The Powers, he warned de Bunsen over breakfast on 15 July, should expect 'a sharply worded note

[31] Tel. Berchtold to Czernin (no. 157), 14 July 1914, *IBZI* IV, no. 218, and n. 1; the original telegram is in HHStA, PA X/140, Weisungen.
[32] Tel. Sazonov to Shebeko (no. 1475), 9/22 July 1914, *IBZI* IV, no. 322.
[33] Tel. Bunsen to Grey (no. 85, confidential), 16 July 1914, *BD* XI, no. 50. Ominously, during his official interview with Berchtold, on 17 July, the foreign minister 'never mentioned general politics or the Servians': Bunsen to Nicolson (private), 17 July 1914, Nicolson MSS, TNA (PRO), FO 800/375.

addressed to Belgrade' within the next week or so. This was openness with an *arrière pensée*, however. Concerned about Berchtold's risky strategy, Lützow hoped that, stirred by his indiscretion, the British government would seek to persuade Pašić and his government to yield to Austro-Hungarian pressure.[34] De Bunsen lost no time to inform the Foreign Office of Lützow's revelation, but it seems he also imparted the news to his Russian colleague – hence Shebeko's telegram of 16 July.[35]

Pašić is alarmed

The various indiscretions around the middle of July affected Berchtold's operational planning. He certainly acted on the assumption that the Russian government had some foreknowledge of the planned démarche, and Sazonov's statements on 18 July confirmed him in that assumption. It was also reasonable to conclude that the Belgrade authorities might have been alerted to what was coming. The Russian and Serbian documents do not, in fact, bear out this assumption, and some of the relevant information may well have come from Rome.[36] There is evidence, however, to suggest that Pašić had some sense that a crisis was about to erupt. Already on 7 July, Jovan Jovanović, the envoy at Vienna, perturbed by the strident anti-Serbian tone of the Vienna press, prognosticated a Habsburg offensive of some kind.[37] That Pašić either had some clear understanding of what demands the Austro-Hungarian note might contain or that he had made a shrewd and largely accurate guess as to its likely contents is evident also from a telegraphic report by Britain's chargé d'affaires at Belgrade, Dayrell

---

[34] H. von Lützow, *Im diplomatischen Dienste der k.u.k. Monarchie*, ed. P. Hohenbalken (Vienna, 1971), 223. Lützow's mother was Lady Henrietta Seymour, daughter of the Marquess of Hertford; Berta de Bunsen diary, 15 July 1914, C. H. D. Howard, 'The Vienna Diary of Berta de Bunsen, 28 June – 17 August 1914', *BIHR* LI, 2 (1978), 215. In 1919, de Bunsen was told that Berchtold had commissioned Lützow to make the statement, but this flies in the face of the extant evidence: E. T. S. Dugdale, *Maurice de Bunsen: Diplomat and Friend* (London, 1934), 293, n. 2; Hantsch, *Berchtold* II, 597, equivocates; see also T. G. Otte, '"The Pick of Ambassadors": Sir Maurice de Bunsen, Edwardian Diplomatist', in T. G. Otte (ed.), *Diplomacy and Power: Studies in Modern Diplomatic Practice* (Leiden, 2012), 78–9.

[35] Shebeko, *Souvenirs*, 213.

[36] Tel. San Giuliano to Avarna, Bollati, Carlotti, Negrotti Cambioso and Squitti (Cabinet 702), 9 July 1914, *DDI* (4) XII, no. 124.

[37] Jovan Jovanović to Pašić, 7 July 1914, *DSP* VII/2, no. 355. The despatch reached Belgrade on 10 July, so coinciding with San Giuliano's telegram to Squitti, though already on 7 July Pašić had expressed his unease to the Italian chargé d'affaires: see tel. Cora to San Giuliano (no. 6009/138), 7 July 1914, *DDI* (4), no. 101.

Montague Crackanthorpe. The Serbian government's attitude was 'prudent and conciliatory', he observed. The Pašić administration would comply without demur with a request for a police investigation but was adamant that whatever measures Vienna demanded, these had to be 'compatible with [the] dignity and independence of [the] State'. In particular, Crackanthorpe was told, a mixed Austro-Serb commission of enquiry, press censorship or the curbing of nationalist societies would be rejected as an unacceptable interference in Serbia's domestic affairs.[38] Pašić also spoke of evidence of Austro-Hungarian troop movements along Serbia's northern frontier around Semlin, though it is unclear whether this was a misreading of intelligence or a deliberate misleading of his Russian interlocutor. There had, after all, been no change in Habsburg military dispositions in the area.[39]

Whatever the precise reasons for Pašić's alarm, he had come to understand that the critical moment was approaching. In the early hours of 19 July he set out the government's position in a circular to all Serbian missions abroad, with the notable exception of the legation at Vienna. Belgrade had behaved with suitable decorum and moderation since Sarajevo, while Austria-Hungary appeared bent on exploiting the situation with likely 'unfortunate consequences for the good-neighbourly relations' of the two countries. Serbia would assist in arresting any of the accomplices indicted by the Habsburg authorities and bringing them to justice. She would not brook any demands, however, that infringed upon her sovereignty.[40] This consideration had acquired totemic significance for the Serbian prime minister. Any form of official Austro-Hungarian investigation on Serbian soil was unacceptable, he had let it be known in early July.[41] All of this was significant on a number of counts. Already prior to the ultimatum, Pašić had thus staked out an uncompromising position. Its basis – the insistence of Serbia's sovereign rights – reflected the stance adumbrated by Sazonov. Some scholars have seen in this circumstantial evidence of coordination between Belgrade and St Petersburg,[42] though Pašić's position was one that has suggested itself to the leaders of many a small state ever since the Melians rejected the advances of their Athenian neighbours in 416 BC. The domestic pressures on Pašić militated against an overly conciliatory stance, and judged against the backdrop of recent Austro-Serb

[38] Tel. Crackanthorpe to Grey (no. 44), 17 July 1914, *BD* XI, no. 53.
[39] Tel. Strandtmann to Sazonov (no. 205), 6/19 July 1914, *IBZI* IV, no. 286.
[40] Tel. Pašić to missions abroad (except Vienna), 18 July 1914, *DSP* VII/2, no. 462.
[41] See Cora to San Giuliano (no. R 767/136), 7 July 1914, *DDI* (4) XII, no. 112.
[42] S. R. Williamson, *Austria-Hungary and the Origins of the First World War* (London, 1991), 201–2.

stand-offs the attraction of a firm line at the opening of a fresh crisis is not difficult to discern. And yet those same previous crises had hardened Vienna's determination that the planned move against Serbia would follow a different script. To that extent, Pašić's preference for a rejectionist opening gambit further narrowed the room for diplomatic manoeuvre.

It is difficult to judge whether the government in Belgrade could have gone further to avert the Austro-Hungarian démarche.[43] There was no shortage of advice of that kind from foreign diplomats. On 14 July, San Giuliano had urged Belgrade to take steps to silence pan-Serb propaganda in Bosnia-Herzegovina, a suggestion that elicited a muted response in the Serbian capital.[44] Nor was Pašić prepared to dissolve *Narodna Odbrana* in order to pre-empt Austro-Hungarian demands for its suppression 'for fear of provoking a popular revolution'.[45] Crackanthorpe, the British chargé d'affaires, had similarly urged the Serbian authorities to institute their own investigation into the background to the Sarajevo plot so as to remove any pretext Vienna might seek for coercing Serbia. The suggestion met with short shrift by Slavko Gruić, secretary-general of the Serbian foreign ministry: 'the Servian Government had no material on which such an enquiry could be based'. Belgrade would comply with requests for further investigation, provided these were 'in accordance with international usage'.[46]

Without doubt, Pašić's reluctance to rein in any of the pan-Serb organizations was dictated by domestic calculations. The general election campaign, after all, was about to commence. But there was more to his attitude than the fear of an ultra-nationalist backlash. As Gruić impressed upon Crackanthorpe on 18 July, Belgrade was certain that Germany would restrain her Habsburg ally. This was also the sense of the reports by Serbia's chargé d'affaires at Berlin.[47] In London, *The Times*, invariably, if wrongly, seen as the official mouthpiece of the British government, had urged restraint on all sides in a leading article on 16 July, and San Giuliano's various communications were suggestive of Italian efforts to defuse the situation. More significantly still, on 18 July, after his interview with the seemingly lamb-like Szápáry, Sazonov had expressed his

---

[43] See Albertini, *Origins* II, 275–6, who claims that Pašić 'did little or nothing'.

[44] Tels. San Giuliano to Cora (no. 4080), 14 July 1914, and vice versa (no. 6298/143), 16 July 1914, *DDI* (4) XII, nos. 201 and 285.

[45] Tel. Cora to San Giuliano (no. 6462/146), 20 July 1914, *DDI* (4) XII, no. 363; Cornwall, 'Serbia', 70.

[46] Tel. Crackanthorpe to Grey (no. 46), 19 July 1914, *BD* XI, no. 61. The conversation took place on 18 July: see Crackanthorpe to Grey (no. 133), 18 July 1914, *ibid.*, no. 80.

[47] *Ibid.*; tel. Milutin Jovanović to Pašić, 18 July 1914, *DSP* VII/2, no. 457.

conviction to the Serbian envoy, Miroslav Spalajković, that Austria-Hungary would not push matters to extremes.[48]

On the same day, Belgrade received a Russian promise of fresh supplies of rifles and ammunition. This had little to do with the post-Sarajevo situation and much with Serbia's depleted arsenal after the Balkan wars. It had in fact been requested already earlier in the spring of that year.[49] But all of this helps to explain the confident expectation at Belgrade that any Austro-Hungarian démarche would remain within certain limits, and further that, in the last resort, 'Russia would not remain quiet were Servia wantonly attacked ... Under present conditions a war between a Great Power and a Balkan State must inevitably ... lead to a European conflagration', as Gruić stated emphatically to Crackanthorpe on 18 July.[50] And so Pašić set off for the campaign trail in the morning of 20 July. He had not been complacent about the likelihood of an Austro-Hungarian démarche, but he was certainly 'rather presumptuous' in assuming that the Powers would intervene to de-escalate any subsequent stand-off.[51]

The Strudelhof meeting

Although the various indiscretions around the middle of July affected the execution of the planned démarche, the Habsburg leadership continued along its clandestine and ponderous course. It was not until Sunday, 19 July that the final step towards a military confrontation with Serbia was taken at a meeting of the common ministerial council. As if to underline the Monarchy's stealthy policy so far, the ministers gathered in secret away from any government building at the Strudelhof, Berchtold's private residence in Vienna, where they arrived separately and in unmarked motor cars. As with the two previous council meetings, Berchtold chaired the proceedings, which were attended by the two prime ministers, Stürgkh and Tisza, and the other two imperial ministers, Biliński and Krobatin, who were joined for the occasion by Conrad and Vice-Admiral Kailer, the deputy chief of the naval staff. The planned 'diplomatic action against

---

[48] Tel. Spalajković to Pašić, 18 July 1914, DSP VII/2, no. 455; The Times, 16 July 1914; see also Cornwall, 'Serbia', 70–1.
[49] Tel. Strandtmann to Sazonov (no. 202), 5/18 July 1914, IBZI IV, no. 274; see also Sazonov to Yanushkevich (secret and confidential), 7/20 June 1914, IBZI III, no. 313, and Belyayev to Sazonov (no. 3244), 20 June/3 July 1914, IBZI IV, no. 74.
[50] Crackanthorpe to Grey (no. 133), 18 July 1914, BD XI, no. 80.
[51] See Cornwall, 'Serbia', 71; for Pašić's departure see tel. Cora to San Giuliano (no. 6462/146), 20 July 1914, DDI (4) XII, no. 363.

Serbia' was the only item on the agenda. Following a somewhat desultory discussion of the text of the draft note to be addressed to Belgrade, the council unanimously agreed that the ultimatum was to be delivered at 5 p.m. on Thursday, 23 July, and that the Serbian government be given forty-eight hours to respond. The reason for the renewed delay, Berchtold explained, was Poincaré's state visit to St Petersburg, scheduled to end earlier that same day. This he described as a '*courtoisie*-consideration'. The real reason for this, of course, was that Vienna was anxious to deny France and Russia the opportunity to coordinate their responses to the Habsburg move. Any further delay would be problematic, the foreign minister warned; Berlin was becoming nervous, and news of Austria-Hungary's intentions had leaked out at Rome.

The draft note opened with a reminder that, in the aftermath of the 1908–9 annexation crisis, the Serbian government had recognized Austria-Hungary's sovereign rights over Bosnia-Herzegovina; that since then a subversive movement had sprung up that aimed at detaching this and other Slav provinces from the Habsburg Empire; and that the movement had its roots in Serbia proper, where its activities were officially condoned. The document thus linked the authorities at Belgrade with the plot to assassinate the Archduke, which had finally exhausted the forbearance so far shown by Vienna. It then demanded that the Belgrade government publish, on the day following the expiry of the ultimatum, Sunday, 26 July, an official declaration denouncing any anti-Habsburg activities among Serbian officers and officials and re-affirming its recognition of Bosnia as part of the Habsburg Empire. Beyond this, the note made ten further demands which Belgrade was expected to implement without delay. They included curbing the pan-Serb press; dissolving *Narodna Odbrana* and affiliated societies; removing from school textbooks anything liable to foment propaganda against Austria-Hungary; suspending officers and officials known to have been involved in such activities; arresting Voja Tankošić and Milan Ciganović, the two now known operators in the background at Belgrade; suppressing the illegal arms smuggling across the Drina river; and reprimanding those functionaries who had expressed openly hostile sentiments after the Sarajevo murders.

This was a far-reaching set of demands, designed, on the surface of it, to extract from Belgrade a pledge of good conduct in the future. In reality, it was an attempt to pull the teeth of pan-Serbism and to coerce Belgrade back into the Habsburg orbit. But it was the fifth and sixth demands – admitting organs of the Austro-Hungarian state onto Serb territory to assist in the suppression of pan-Serb societies, and instituting a joint judicial inquiry into the assassination plot on Serbian soil – which were bound to be objectionable to the Serbian government. As seen earlier,

Pašić's circular of 18 July had ensured that these demands would be problematic. But of course the Ballhausplatz had always intended a document that could not be accepted by Belgrade.

Any doubts on that score were removed by the ministerial council on 19 July. The discussion of Berchtold's draft ultimatum took up very little time, and the ministers focused primarily on the necessary military preparations and on how Serbia was to be treated after the military campaign. Two points are of note in this context. The first is Conrad's insistence on the 'swiftest possible initiation of the operation'. In part, the chief of staff justified this with reference to recent intelligence reports that suggested the northwards transfer of three Serbian army divisions. But the unspoken premise, of course, was that international diplomacy should not be allowed any time and space to prevent a punitive military campaign. What is striking in Conrad's summary of the military situation and the subsequent discussion was the exclusive focus on mobilization measures against Serbia, Conrad's 'Plan B' (B for Balkans). The chief of staff addressed Magyar concerns about the Carpathian salient by assuring Tisza that the available *Landsturm* militia formations would be sufficient to maintain order in Transylvania. Yet he was forced to admit that they would be in no position to repel a Romanian invasion. The scenario of Russian interference, backed up by some display of force – not unlikely in light of Sazonov's statements on the previous day – was ignored. 'Plan R' (for Russia) was not discussed. Habsburg policy thus remained characterized by 'tunnel vision'.

The exclusive focus on the Serbian factor was underlined also by the second noteworthy aspect of the council meeting. Tisza reiterated his insistence on some form of self-denying ordinance. There was to be no annexation of Serbian territory, with the exception of minor strategic rectifications to the Austro-Serb frontier. The Magyar leader's opposition to including yet further Slav subjects in the Habsburg Empire was, of course, well known. He nevertheless used somewhat peremptory language and insisted on a unanimous declaration by the ministers as a precondition for Hungary's support for the démarche. To an extent, Tisza was flexing his constitutional muscles to underline Budapest's undiminished importance in the dualist structures of Austria-Hungary, but the problem of the Slav territories would be a bone of major contention in the Monarchy's internal affairs for the whole duration of the war.

Tisza carried his point without encountering any opposition. But this did not mean that the integrity, let alone the independence, of Serbia would be preserved. Krobatin, the war minister, speculated about the permanent occupation of a bridgehead on the Serbian side of the Sava river, possibly around Šabac. Berchtold went further and suggested 'the largest possible cession of Serbian territory' to Albania, Bulgaria, Greece and possibly Romania in order to neuter Serbia in the politics of the region. Stürgkh, the Austrian prime minister, meanwhile, mooted the idea of a military convention, the deposition of the ruling Karadjordjević dynasty and other measures designed to make Serbia dependent on the Habsburg Empire. The ministers took note of Tisza's protestations that anything indicative of a desire to secure the 'complete annihilation' of Serbia was bound to bring Russia into the war, and should therefore be avoided. But they remained unmoved by them. And with that Berchtold closed the meeting, though not without a final dig at the Magyar premier by emphasizing that, 'refreshingly, complete unanimity had been achieved on all questions'.[52]

Even by the standards of earlier ministerial council meetings, that of 19 July was quite remarkable. The degree to which Habsburg decision-making was afflicted by 'tunnel vision' has already been stressed. No doubt also, the ministers were actuated by a growing sense that an opportunity was slipping away; that the Habsburg Empire was now faced with the urgent necessity of having to defend itself against a seemingly growing pan-Serb peril; and that Belgrade's previous promises had been honoured solely in the breaches and never in the observance. And yet notwithstanding such considerations, the Habsburg leadership had formulated no clear strategic objective for the campaign. Serbia was to be punished for past transgressions, but beyond that nothing had been decided. How Serbia was to be treated after the military campaign had been concluded, and how the international fallout was to be managed, were left unresolved.

To no small degree this failure reflected the peculiarities of Habsburg politics. The dualist structures of the Empire not only made for protracted decision-making; they also made it difficult for ministers to develop a coherent, holistic understanding of the Empire's strategic requirements. Just as the Monarchy's success in dealing with its many different ethnic groupings rested on a fragile balance of mutual dissatisfaction, so its foreign policy sought to assimilate, but could not conciliate, opposing interests. The self-denying non-annexation pledge, accepted at Tisza's insistence, was a case in point. Placating Magyar concerns about a growing Slavic tide was necessary to ensure that war was now in sight. But it was by no means certain that Habsburg policy would remain wedded to it. As Conrad muttered to Krobatin on leaving Berchtold's palais: 'We shall see;

---

[52] Mins. of Common Ministerial Council, 19 July 1914, M. Komjáthy (ed.), *Protokolle des Gemeinsamen Ministerrates der Österreichisch-Ungarischen Monarchie, 1914–1918* (Budapest, 1966), no. 2; for the note see 'Instructions for Belgrade', 20 July 1914, ÖUA VIII, no. 10395. Williamson, *Austria-Hungary*, 202, claims that Burián was also present at the meeting, but this is not recorded in the minutes.

before the Balkan War the Powers spoke of the status quo – after the war no-one bothered about it.'[53] The ministers assumed that the war would be won, but they never probed into Conrad's campaign plans. Above all, it could not be assumed any longer that the Austro-Serb stand-off could be isolated against outside interference and that the war would remain localized. Russia was simply a problem for the ally in Berlin. It would be tempting to suggest that the ministers had decided upon a 'leap in the dark', were it not for the fact that Habsburg policy was incapable of such exertions. Instead it crawled along the track already laid down, and into the dark.

On 21 July, two days after the council meeting, Berchtold, accompanied by Hoyos, his hawkish aide, travelled to Ischl, the Emperor's retreat near Salzburg. Franz Joseph commented on the harsh nature of the demands to be made on Serbia, particularly the fifth and sixth points. He also took it for granted that 'Russia cannot possibly tolerate this note'. Yet he duly gave his assent to the ultimatum. As Berchtold recorded in his diary: 'The Emperor was fully alive to the profound seriousness, indeed tragedy of the current historical moment.'[54] But already on 20 July, that is before imperial approval for the final act had been obtained, Berchtold had instructed Baron Giesl to hand over the ultimatum to Pašić on 23 July and told the Habsburg ambassadors at Berlin, Rome, Paris, St Petersburg and Constantinople to inform the governments there of the démarche on the following morning. The demands contained in it, he explained to Giesl, 'represented the minimum of what we require so that our now completely untenable relations with Serbia will be clarified'. There was to be no discussion; full compliance with the demands was expected, and the envoy was given carte blanche to sever relations with Serbia, should he judge the official reply insufficient. The ambassadors meanwhile were instructed to stress the defensive nature of the démarche. Vienna merely desired 'to secure the territory of the Monarchy against penetration by the insurrectionary miasms from the neighbouring kingdom' and to force Belgrade to rein in the anti-Habsburg movements that operated from Serbia proper.[55]

---

[53] As quoted in Conrad, *Aus meiner Dienstzeit* IV, 92; S. R. Williamson, 'Leopold Count Berchtold: The Man who Could have Prevented the Great War', G. Bischof, F. Plasser and P. Berger (eds.), *From Empire to Republic: Post-World War I Austria* (New Orleans, 2010), 34–5.

[54] Quotes from R. A. Kann, *Kaiser Franz Joseph und der Ausbruch des Ersten Weltkrieges* (Vienna, 1971), 12, and Hantsch, *Berchtold* II, 603; see also tel. Berchtold to Macchio, 21 July 1914, *ÖUA* VIII, no. 10471; see also J.-P. Bled, *François-Joseph* (Paris, 1987), 671–2.

[55] Quotes from Berchtold to Giesl (private), and circular, all 20 July 1914, *ÖUA* VIII, nos. 10396 and 10400; Bridge, *Habsburg Monarchy*, 341–2.

It is worth pausing here to emphasize the role played by Count Berchtold in the decisions arrived at by this point. For someone who had the unenviable reputation of a weak minister among his own diplomats and foreign statesmen alike, and whom historians tend to dismiss as an effete *grand seigneur*, he had shown considerable toughness and resilience. He had formulated the new objective of Habsburg policy in the immediate aftermath of Sarajevo, and he subsequently steered the decision-making process in the desired direction. But this meant patiently plotting a course that allowed for a consensus in favour of war to emerge, the slow and ponderous mechanism inherent in the dualist constitutional framework of Austro-Hungarian politics. Yet even a for-once vigorous Berchtold could not force strategic coherence on the Empire's foreign policy where there was none.

As for Conrad and the military, in the immediate aftermath of Sarajevo, the chief of staff had pushed for a surprise military campaign without any of the usual diplomatic preliminaries. But he did not push very hard. Berchtold had ruled out such a strike for diplomatic reasons; the need to secure Tisza's support made it an impracticable proposition at any rate. A swift and decisive outcome of a war against Serbia, moreover, was unlikely without at least the partial mobilization of the Habsburg armed forces.[56] It was imperative therefore to coordinate the desired diplomatic moves and the necessary military preparations closely. By the earlier decision of fixing the forty-eight-hour time-frame for Serbian response to the ultimatum, and by separating mobilization and the declaration of war, the political leadership of the Monarchy had gone to some lengths to accommodate the demands of the military. By the time of the ministerial council meeting of 14 July, then, a consensus had been achieved at the political level between the authorities in Vienna and Tisza's administration at Budapest, and between the civilian leadership and the Habsburg military. Conrad and Krobatin were not forced to alter their war plans to suit the specific circumstances of post-Sarajevo relations with Serbia. The civilian ministers, for their part, were satisfied with the chief of staff's expositions on the slow timetable for mobilization against Serbia and the logistical problems that would arise if both war plans had to be implemented. Military influence, however, was not predominant. For, as will be seen, the commencement of military operations was postponed again at the end of July, after the expiry of the ultimatum, for political reasons.

---

[56] For this point see D. Stevenson, *Armaments and the Coming of the War: Europe, 1904–1914* (Oxford, 1996), 370–1; G. Kronenbitter, *'Krieg im Frieden'. Die Führung der k.u.k. Armee und die Grossmachtpolitik Österreich-Ungarns, 1906–1914* (Munich, 2003), 115–20.

Sir Edward offers to mediate

By 20 July, some Austro-Hungarian move was now widely expected in the European capitals. Until the middle of the month, the Quai d'Orsay expected Austria-Hungary, on conclusion of the ongoing investigations into the Sarajevo murder, to present Belgrade with a series of demands. But as Alfred Dumaine, the ambassador at Vienna, speculated, Austro-Hungarian efforts were likely to concentrate on obtaining certain guarantees from the Belgrade government such as a heightened police presence along the common frontiers and the dissolution of certain pan-Serb organizations.[57] On 20 July, Dumaine's long-serving colleague at Berlin, Jules Cambon, and the Russian chargé d'affaires there, Arkadi Nikola'evich Bronevski, alerted their respective governments that a démarche was now imminent, though its precise terms were not known to them. Germany, Cambon warned, would throw its authority behind the demands and had no intention of mediating between Belgrade and Vienna.[58] Quite clearly, then, contrary to his later assertions, the Austro-Hungarian démarche did not come as a surprise to Sazonov. But what information he had was vague, and was not sufficient to shake his conviction, expressed to Spalajković on 18 July, that any move by Vienna would remain well within the confines of normal diplomatic exchanges. He saw no reason to withdraw his earlier permission for the ambassador at Vienna, Shebeko, to go on leave on 21 July; as, indeed, Russia was represented by chargés d'affaires at Paris, Berlin and Belgrade during the July crisis.[59]

In London, meanwhile, alerted by de Bunsen's telegram of 16 July and the various snippets of information passed on by Spender of the *Westminster Gazette* following his conversations with junior members of the Austro-Hungarian embassy, and somewhat uneasy at the prolonged official silence at Vienna, Grey raised the state of Austro-Serb relations with Lichnowsky, the German ambassador, on 20 July. This was in line with his previous policy of seeking the closest accord possible with Germany, something that had proved so effective during the previous two years. However, this approach was based on the now erroneous assumption that

---

[57] Dumaine to Viviani (no. 184), 15 July 1914, *DDF* (3) X, no. 516. Strangely, Dumaine's chief source seems to have been the Serbian minister at Vienna, Jovan Jovanović.

[58] Tel. J. Cambon to Bienvenu-Martin (no. 178), 21 July 1914, *DDF* (3) X, no. 539; tel. Bronevski to Sazonov (no. 115), 7/20 July 1914, *IBZI* IV, no. 297.

[59] Tel. Shebeko to Sazonov, 21 July 1914, *IBZI* IV, no. 307. He left St Petersburg again to return to Vienna on 25 July: see Shebeko, *Souvenirs*, 218–19; see also D. C. B. Lieven, *Russia and the Origins of the First World War* (London, 1983), 140.

Austria-Hungary would not act independently of her ally at Berlin. Although the ambassador himself was without precise information, Lichnowsky hinted that Vienna would take some step in the matter of the Sarajevo murders. He confessed that 'he regarded the situation as very uncomfortable' and raised the possibility of Russia moderating Serbia's response to any démarche, which he suggested 'would be a very desirable thing'. In response, Grey made two observations, the first being that he expected Vienna to disclose its case to the European public before it took any further steps. He further noted that, if Vienna kept its demands 'within reasonable limits', and the stronger the evidence it presented to support its demands on Serbia, 'the more chance there would be of smoothing things over'. He added: 'I hate the idea of war between any of the Great Powers, and that any of them should be dragged into a war by Servia would be detestable.'[60]

Grey's interview with Lichnowsky was significant on a number of counts. Within the established parameters of his foreign policy – redefined during the recent Balkans wars – this was as direct a hint to Berlin to moderate Austria-Hungary's response to the murder of the Archduke as was politic. Any more unequivocal choice of words contained the risk of rekindling German suspicions of British policy, thereby forfeiting Berlin's cooperation in south-eastern Europe without which he considered it impossible to restrain Vienna. At the same time, the Foreign Secretary did not specify what might constitute 'reasonable limits' for any demands to be made on Serbia, but to do so would have narrowed yet further the room for diplomacy. Indeed, Grey did not seek to delegitimize Austria-Hungary's concerns, but made it incumbent upon her to act with moderation, to prove her case and to proceed in accordance with diplomatic custom. Just as Sazonov had argued two days previously, Vienna was not to spring a surprise on the Powers. If the Habsburg leadership acted in a peremptory manner, it would be difficult to prevent matters from escalating. It is also clear that Grey assumed that the Wilhelmstrasse would be inspired by similar sentiments.

Certainly, senior officials at the Foreign Office – and presumably Grey, too – were still hopeful on 20 July that the 'Servian imbroglio will not be pushed to extremes'. A punitive military expedition against Belgrade was not likely to put a lasting stop to pan-Serb agitation inside the Habsburg Empire or without, noted Nicolson, the Permanent Under-secretary, and any invasion of Serbian territory increased the likelihood of Russia's interference in the conflict.[61] For the moment, as Lichnowsky reported,

[60] Grey to Rumbold (no. 285), 20 July 1914, *BD* XI, no. 67.
[61] Nicolson to de Bunsen, 20 July 1914, De Bunsen MSS, box 15. He made similar comments to the Italian and Russian ambassadors, emphasizing the restraining influence

Grey was optimistic about a peaceful outcome of the crisis. What mattered, he impressed on Berlin, was the form in which Austria-Hungary's demands were presented. In this manner, he hoped that the Austro-Serbian quarrel could be limited and then settled.[62]

If Grey was hopeful that peace could be maintained, he was nevertheless not complacent. At 7 p.m. on 20 July, after his conversation with Lichnowsky, he wired to Buchanan, the ambassador at St Petersburg. It was possible, he observed, that there was a degree of culpability on Serbia's part, whether owing to negligence by Serbian authorities or because the plot had been hatched on Serb soil. As long as Vienna's demands remained moderate, and were supported by proof, there was every chance of settling the dispute. It would be desirable, Grey concluded, that Vienna and St Petersburg 'should discuss things together if they become difficult'.[63] In Grey's conception, an Austro-Russian agreement, facilitated by London and Berlin acting in parallel, would provide the necessary framework for settling the Austro-Serbian dispute and so stabilize relations between these two difficult neighbours.

Sazonov's response, on 22 July, was superficially encouraging, but at the same time deeply problematic. He had no objection to Belgrade being asked to set up a judicial enquiry into the Sarajevo murder, if Austria-Hungary was capable of producing proof of it having been plotted in Serbia proper. How this might be possible, and what standard of proof would be applied, he left open; nor did he address the issue of how any enquiry at Belgrade could be enforced to ensure that it did not result in a 'whitewash'. Given the rather lackadaisical attitude shown at Belgrade in such matters previously, this was no small problem. Even more problematic was his suggestion that Britain, France and Russia should 'counsel moderation at Vienna', albeit separately and 'in [the] friendliest manner'.[64] Another problem now emerged when, also in the afternoon of 22 July, Jagow insisted that the Austro-Serbian dispute was for those two countries alone to settle 'without interference from [the] outside'. He was therefore not ready, he explained to the British chargé d'affaires, Sir Horace Rumbold, to make any representations at Vienna. He had, however, impressed upon the Serbian chargé d'affaires, Milutin Jovanović, that Belgrade needed to put

of the Emperor Franz Joseph: see tel. Imperiali to San Giuliano (no. 6508/290, confidential), 21 July 1914, *DDI* (4) XII, no. 382; and Benckendorff to Sazonov (private), 3/16 July 1914, *BDS* III, no. 1068; also T. G. Otte, *The 'Foreign Office Mind': The Making of British Foreign Policy, 1865–1914* (Cambridge, 2011), 388–9.

[62] Tel. Lichnowsky to Auswärtiges Amt (no. 143), 20 July 1914, *DD* I, no. 92.

[63] Tel. Grey to Buchanan (no. 336), 20 July 1914, *BD* XI, no. 67.

[64] Tel. Buchanan to Grey (no. 163), 22 July 1914, *BD* XI, no. 76.

its relations with Austria-Hungary 'on a proper footing'. Jagow added 'that if a man had a neighbour who either could not or would not put a stop to a nuisance, he had a right to help himself as best he could'. If anything, he noted, Vienna had shown 'great forbearance' over the past few years.[65]

The reports from Russia and Germany on 22 July presented Grey and the Foreign Office with a challenge. Sazonov's idea of a loose form of triple intervention at Vienna was a transparent attempt to bind Britain more firmly to France and Russia, something that Paris and St Petersburg had attempted before and something that limited Britain's freedom of manoeuvre. Besides, as Nicolson noted, any representations by the three Powers at Vienna were bound to 'be resented and would do harm'. Jagow's statement was even more problematic, for it was an unexpected deviation from Berlin's policy during the previous Balkan crises. These had shown that if anyone could keep Vienna 'reasonably in check', it was the German government, argued Sir Eyre Crowe, the Assistant Under-secretary. Possibly, Berlin did not believe in the danger of war. But the Wilhelmstrasse appeared to rely on Britain to amplify and thus reinforce the Austrian and German threats to Belgrade. If London did intervene in the quarrel or unilaterally sought to restrain Russia, Crowe warned, 'the much desired breach between England and Russia would be brought one step nearer realisation'. Whether this was the avowed aim of the Wilhelmstrasse was difficult to establish, but Crowe was certain that Jagow and his officials understood the forthcoming démarche to escalate the dispute with Serbia, and 'that they have expressed approval of those demands and promised support, should dangerous complications ensue'.[66] That was also the conclusion Rumbold drew from his interview with Jagow. The state secretary, he thought, 'would approve prompt and vigorous action' by Vienna and Jagow was 'aware of the general character of the démarche to be made at Belgrade'.[67]

Thus, 22 July brought the first indications that Grey's hitherto successful policy of mediating between the Franco-Russian and Austro-German groupings, closely tied to the former yet cooperating with Berlin, was coming up against its limits. There were further indications of the

---

[65] Quotes from tel. Rumbold to Grey (no. 88, confidential), 22 July 1914, and despatch (no. 299), 22 July 1914, BD XI, nos. 77 and 158; M. Gilbert, *Sir Horace Rumbold: Portrait of a Diplomat, 1869–1941* (London, 1973), 108–9.

[66] Quotes from min. Nicolson, 22 July 1914, on tel. Buchanan to Grey (no. 163), 22 July 1914, and min. Crowe, 22 July 1914, on tel. Rumbold to Grey (no. 88, confidential), 22 July 1914, BD XI, nos. 76 and 77. Crowe also indicated that Lichnowsky's statements were at variance with the actions of his government.

[67] Rumbold to Grey (no. 299), 22 July 1914, BD XI, no. 158.

breakers ahead. From Rome, Britain's ambassador, Sir Rennell Rodd, who had friendly ties with the German embassy, warned that Austria-Hungary was about to address 'a very strong communication' to the Serbian government, and that 'Servia, having a very swelled head, and feeling confident in the support of Russia, will reply in a manner which Austria can only regard as provocative'. There was a danger now that the situation would escalate unless Russia gave 'counsels of prudence at Belgrade'. Rodd was strongly impressed by the suggestions of Flotow's juniors that the only hope now lay in Britain and Germany acting together 'to exercise a moderating influence on our respective friends', and to localize any Austro-Serbian conflict.[68]

M. Poincaré sails to St Petersburg

Whilst there was now mounting evidence that the path of diplomacy was considerably narrower than Grey might have thought even two days previously, it was also clear that nothing practical could be done until Vienna showed its hand.

Berchtold had one last opportunity to abort the planned démarche against Serbia during the visit of Poincaré and Viviani to St Petersburg. At a reception for foreign diplomats at the Winter Palace the French president had a long talk with Szápáry, the Habsburg ambassador. After the obligatory warm words of sympathy for Austria-Hungary on account of the murder of the archducal couple, Poincaré steered the conversation onto political questions, initially the unsettled future of Albania and then the state of Austro-Serbian relations. The extant sources leave no doubt that the French president tried to gain a clearer sense of Vienna's likely demands. For his part, the ambassador sought to deflect Poincaré's probings by implying that any demands Vienna might make on Serbia would be reasonable. His superiors at the Ballhausplatz, he suggested, were confident that Belgrade could not possibly reject what would be demanded of it. On the president further pressing him on the nature of Austria-Hungary's demands, Szápáry pleaded ignorance and referred to the ongoing police investigation into the assassination plot. The lawyer Poincaré then pontificated on the need for conclusive evidence, laced with veiled hints at the infamous Friedjung forgeries, and the problem of assuming some form of collective responsibility on the part of the Serbian nation for the Archduke's murder, before pointedly and 'with much rhetorical effort'

---

[68] Rodd to Grey (private), 20 July 1914, Rennell of Rodd MSS, box 15; Sir J. R. Rodd, *Social and Diplomatic Memories, 1884–1919* (3 vols., London, 1922–5) III, 203–4.

warning that 'Serbia had friends'. If Vienna merely sought a pretext for the use of force, it would endanger the European peace. The encounter certainly made an unpleasant impression on Szápáry, who thought the president's intervention 'tactless' and menacing, and noted it stood in sharp contrast to Sazonov's reserved and cautious stance.[69]

The interview with the Habsburg ambassador left Poincaré in a state of considerable alarm. Szápáry's equivocal replies to his enquiries convinced him that Vienna planned a more far-reaching step than Dumaine's previous reports had suggested. Whether inadvertently or not, the Magyar count ('with a haughty appearance'), Poincaré recorded in his diary, let slip that the Ballhausplatz considered official Serbia somehow implicated in the assassination of the Archduke. It now appeared 'that the Austrian g[overnmen]t wishes to place the responsibility for the crime on the Serb g[overnmen]t and seeks to humiliate, through a menacing démarche [une démarche comminatoire], the kingdom of Serbia'. And he certainly used the phrase attributed to him by Szápáry 'that Serbia has friends in Europe who would be surprised by an action of this sort'. Indeed, as the reception drew to a close, on being told by Spalajković, the Serbian envoy, that the latest news was bad, Poincaré replied in front of the assembled foreign representatives: 'I hope that it will improve and we will endeavour to help you'.[70]

By any standards of professional diplomatic exchanges, Poincaré's conversation with Szápáry was anything but ordinary. He went rather further with his pointed reference to Serbia's friends than was politically prudent; and the less than decorous reference to the Friedjung scandal bore more than a hint of menace. There was a strong suggestion in it that, whatever evidence Vienna might produce, it could never carry much credibility. Such comments were certainly not designed to encourage Vienna's belief in the efficacy of Great Power diplomacy to solve its Serbian problem, and Szápáry was well justified in his comment that Poincaré acted 'in anything but a calming manner'.[71]

---

[69] Tel. Szápáry to Berchtold (no. 148, secret), 21 July 1914, ÖUA VIII, no. 10461; see also M. Paléologue, *La Russie des Tsars pendant la grande guerre* (3 vols., Paris, 1921) I, 9–10. All other official sources ultimately rely on Szápáry's version of events: see tel. Carlotti to San Giuliano (no. 6589/453), 23 July 1914, DDI (4) XII, no. 447, and tel. Pourtalès to Auswärtiges Amt (no. 147), 23 July 1914, DD I, no. 134.
[70] Poincaré notes journalières, 21 July 1914, BN, Bnfr 16027, fos. 105 v. and 106 v.; cf. tel. Spalajković to Pašić, 22 July 1914, DSP VII/2, no. 484; the version in Poincaré's memoirs is less emphatic: *Au service de la France. Neuf Années de souvenirs* (7 vols., Paris, repr. 1946) IV, 253.
[71] Tel. Szápáry to Berchtold (no. 148), 21 July 1914, ÖUA VIII, no. 10461. C. Clark, *The Sleepwalkers: How Europe Went to War in 1914* (London, 2012), 445, goes too far

This raises the question of what had induced Poincaré to use such sharp language. Certainly, the encounter with the Austro-Hungarian ambassador had unsettled him, as he confided to the French ambassador, Maurice Paléologue: 'I do not have a good impression of this meeting. The ambassador [Szápáry] clearly had instructions to say nothing. Austria is preparing a *coup de théâtre* for us. Sazonov needs to be firm and we need to support him.'[72] In this respect, the events of 21 July marked a significant turning point in French policy as well as in the history of the July crisis in general.

The effect of the meeting with Szápáry was all the more pronounced because Poincaré and prime minister Viviani had not expected to have to deal with the Austro-Serb quarrel when they set off from Dunkirk for the Russian capital aboard the two recently launched dreadnoughts *France* and *Jean Bart* on 16 July. The talks scheduled for Poincaré's first state visit to Russia were to cover the whole breadth of Franco-Russian relations and current international affairs more widely, but the relations between the Dual Monarchy and the neighbouring kingdom were not considered the most pressing item on the programme of the Franco-Russian summit. A briefing paper on Austro-Russian relations had been prepared for Poincaré in mid-July, but on the original seventeen-point draft agenda for the talks by Pierre de Margerie, the director of political affairs at the French foreign ministry, the Sarajevo assassination and its likely aftermath came fourteenth.[73] Indeed, as the two French armoured cruisers ploughed through the North and Baltic Seas, attended by a retinue of smaller naval vessels, the conversations between president and prime minister did not touch on the fraught question of Serbo-Habsburg relations.[74]

with his argument that Poincaré deliberately sought to delegitimize Austria-Hungary's case; J. F. V. Keiger, *France and the Origins of the First World War* (London, 1991), 151, does not go far enough in suggesting that Szápáry was not justified in reading Poincaré's comments as a warning.

[72] Paléologue, *Russie des Tsars* I, 10. The ambassador's memoirs nevertheless need to be taken with the proverbial *cum grano salis*: see also S. Schmidt, *Frankreichs Aussenpolitik in der Julikrise 1914. Ein Beitrag zur Geschichte des Ausbruchs des Ersten Weltkrieges* (Munich, 2009), 71–2, n. 77.

[73] 'Note pour le Ministre: Relations de l'Autriche-Hongrie avec la Russie', 11 July, and note Margerie, n.d. [12 or 13 July 1914], *DDF* (4) x, nos. 500 and 502; for a list of the briefing papers see *ibid.*, no. 500, n. 1; also P. Renouvin, 'La politique française en juillet 1914 d'après les documents diplomatiques français', *Revue d'histoire de la guerre mondiale* xv, 1 (1937), 7.

[74] See Poincaré, notes journalières, 16–18 July 1914, BN, Bnfr 16027, fos. 98–99 v.

On the contrary, the usual questions of bilateral relations were to the fore of their thinking – commercial matters, contracts for railway rolling stock and the construction of an armoured cruiser for the Imperial Russian Navy in a French shipyard. But there were also significant international questions to be discussed, some of them relevant to the situation in the Balkans, especially Russia's desire to raise the status of the Turkish Straits at the third peace conference at The Hague, scheduled to take place in 1915, and a possible loan to Bulgaria. However greater significance was accorded to the state of Russo-Swedish relations and the current frictions between Russia and Great Britain in Persia and Central Asia. St Petersburg's somewhat frosty relations with the Scandinavian kingdom had been a source of concern for some time. Already in July 1912, the Russian general staff had factored the latter into its war plans as a potential enemy; and Poincaré's stopover in Stockholm after his visit to the Russian capital was meant to assure the Swedish government of the pacific intentions of the Franco-Russian combination so as to avert Sweden's drift into the German orbit.[75] The uncertain state of Anglo-Russian relations, meanwhile, had even more far-reaching ramifications for international politics. It was imperative for France to use her close ties with St Petersburg and London to smooth relations between the two Asian competitors, lest the Anglo-Russian convention of 1907 unravel and the two countries lapse into their traditional antagonism in the Middle East. In this context, the mooted Anglo-Russian naval convention, the pet project of Franco-Russian diplomacy in 1914, seemed a suitable tool to attain that end.

Reconstructing the actual course of the St Petersburg talks is fraught with difficulties. It is not clear whether Russian officials kept a record of them. Certainly, none seem to have survived, not surprisingly perhaps given the many upheavals in Russia after 1914. Searches in French archives have been similarly fruitless.[76] But pertinent evidence is not entirely absent. Poincaré's diary especially offers some glimpse into the discussions, even though it needs to be read in conjunction with other source material.

What is evident from this material is the degree to which the events of Sarajevo gradually encroached upon the preplanned agenda. In the morning of 20 July, the *France* and her accompanying naval escort steamed into the Gulf of Finland and headed towards the little port at the Peterhof, the imperial palace on the coast. Ambassador Paléologue had made the

---

[75] See 'Procès-verbal de l'entretien du 13 juillet 1912 entre les chefs d'état-major des armées françaises', *DDF* (3) III, no. 200; see also Schmidt, *Aussenpolitik*, 70–1.
[76] See also the explanations in 'Avant-Propos', *DDF* (3) X, vi–vii; also Albertini, *Origins* II, 189.

short journey from the capital to attend the president's arrival. As the French squadron approached, Tsar Nicholas II, attired in an admiral's white uniform, engaged the ambassador in conversation: 'We shall have to talk seriously, he said to me. I am sure we shall agree on all matters. But there is one question which preoccupies me particularly: our understanding with England. We must make her enter into our alliance. That would be such a pledge of peace!' Paléologue made suitably encouraging noises and threw out a hint at his own disquiet at Germany's international intentions. After a few puffs at his cigarette, the Tsar replied 'with a firm tone': 'It is important that we shall be able to count on the English in the event of a crisis.' As the *France*, easily recognizable by the irregular arrangement of her three funnels, hove into view above the turquoise and emerald waters of the Baltic, Paléologue reflected: 'The mighty cruiser [*sic*] ... eloquently justified her name: she was indeed France coming to Russia. I felt my heart beat.'[77]

Paléologue's purple prose aside, none of this was out of the ordinary. French and Russian diplomacy had long sought to bind Britain more firmly to the Franco-Russian alliance; and, as seen earlier, the need for such a triplice had been the constant refrain of French politicians and the Tsar's diplomats during King George V's recent visit to Paris in May 1914. As Poincaré was taken across the water on the Tsar's yacht *Alexandria*, the monarch and the president were deep in conversation. Their talk turned to the state of the alliance between the two countries. In Russia, Nicholas observed, the recent revelations in the French Senate of France's lack of military preparedness despite the Three-Year Law had created an unfavourable impression. The president, in turn, made reassuring noises and emphasized that the newly elected chamber and Viviani's government strongly supported the army and the alliance with Russia. The Tsar then turned to the more pro-German policy advocated by the former Russian finance minister, Count Witte. Nicholas and Poincaré agreed on the inherent danger to the Franco-Russian alliance of the alternative foreign policy orientation, of which Witte, along with Poincaré's domestic rival Caillaux and Britain's Chancellor of the Exchequer, David Lloyd George, were thought to be the chief proponents. However, both also agreed that any scheme of a rapprochement between Britain, France, Russia and Germany – and the 'very democratic programme' and the disarmament this entailed – was not practicable politics.[78]

---

[77] Paléologue, *Russie des Tsars* I, 3–4.
[78] Poincaré, notes journalières, 20 July 1914, BN, Bnfr 16027, fos. 100 r. and v. Paléologue noted the appearance of sincere agreement during the lively conversation between Poincaré and the Tsar: *Russie des Tsars* I, 4; for the revelations by Senator

Again, none of this was particularly remarkable. After the exchange of the usual summitry pleasantries, the two heads of state had merely affirmed their countries' commitment to the alliance. The first substantive talks between the two men took place on the following day, Wednesday, 21 July, in Poincaré's suite of rooms at the Peterhof. The conversation lasted for about an hour-and-a-half and it covered the whole range of questions on the previously agreed agenda – the uncertain future of the Wied régime in Albania, the situation in Bulgaria and the continued tensions between Greece and Turkey, and the geopolitical orientation of the Scandinavian states. But much of the conversation revolved around the current Anglo-Russian difficulties in Persia. Poincaré advocated a conciliatory approach and urged the Tsar that his government do nothing to endanger the 1907 accord with Britain. It is not clear from the extant sources how extensively the Tsar and his French guest discussed the mounting tensions between the Habsburg Empire and Serbia. That they touched on this question, however, is clear, and it seems that it was the Tsar who raised it: 'But his most vivid preoccupation is focused on Austria. He wonders what she contemplates [doing] in the aftermath of the Sarajevo assassination. He repeats to me that, under current circumstances, the complete accord between our two governments seems to him more necessary than ever.'[79]

In his memoirs Poincaré later suggested that the Tsar had at this stage not yet grasped the full extent of the démarche contemplated by Austria-Hungary. The Russian Emperor, he noted, had not uttered a single word that suggested serious anxiety on his part, 'not a word that let me suppose that he believed in the imminence of a European conflagration'.[80] However, either Poincaré's memory played him false or – more likely – his vanity got the better of his judgment. For, as was seen, on 19 July Nicholas II was shown Shebeko's telegram of 16 July in which he alerted the Choristers' Bridge to an imminent and sharply worded Austro-Hungarian note. It was not that the Tsar had not grasped what was about to unfold; it was rather that Poincaré changed his views completely on that day.[81]

Charles Humbert, see G. Krumeich, *Armaments and Politics in France on the Eve of the First World War* (Leamington Spa, 1984), 213–15.
[79] Poincaré, notes journalières, 21 July 1914, BN, Bnfr 16027, fos. 103 v.–104 (quote from latter); Paléologue refers to the 'arrogant and secretive attitude of Austria': *Russie des Tsars* I, 7.
[80] Poincaré, *Au service de la France* IV, 248. This is preceded by the above diary entry, but the subsequent qualification of the Tsar's statements is a later addition.
[81] For a different view see J. F. V. Keiger, *Raymond Poincaré* (Cambridge, 1997), 167, who argues that the French president failed to appreciate the nature of the impending Austro-Hungarian move; see also Poincaré, *Au service de la France* IV, 253–4.

With the impressions of the morning conversation at the Peterhof on his mind, Poincaré set off for the capital and the reception for the corps diplomatique in the marble halls of the Winter Palace later that same afternoon. Flanked by Viviani and Paléologue, he first received, as was the custom, the doyen of the foreign diplomatic body at St Petersburg, the German ambassador Pourtalès, followed by the Japanese envoy, Baron Motono. Neither conversation was of any great significance. The amiable Pourtalès confined himself to beautifully turned compliments and evasive phrases,[82] the staple diet of diplomatic receptions, and Motono spoke hopefully of a quadruple entente between Japan, Britain, France and Russia in East Asia.

The next ambassador to be received was Buchanan, 'a cold man, ponderous and extremely courteous'. They spoke at some length about the difficulties in revising and renewing the Anglo-Russian convention of 1907, and the president passed on the Tsar's assurances that he wished to remain on the closest terms with Britain in Persia and elsewhere in Asia. But their conversation also touched upon the situation in south-eastern Europe. Vienna's attitude towards Serbia, Poincaré recorded in his diary, appeared to the British ambassador 'disturbing [*inquiétante*]'. Buchanan himself later recalled that Poincaré spoke 'with considerable emotion'.[83] Just before he spoke to Poincaré, Buchanan had, in fact, spoken to Spalajković, the Serbian envoy, who had held forth with some warmth on the dangers of the present situation and on Vienna's evident desire for a pretext to fall upon Serbia. Buchanan repeated all this to the French president and suggested, as previously instructed by Grey, that Austria-Hungary and Russia ought to open direct talks about a possible settlement of the quarrel with Belgrade. In reply, Poincaré warned that direct Austro-Russian talks were 'very dangerous at [the] present moment', and instead mooted the idea of Franco-British representations at Vienna.[84]

---

[82] Poincaré described Pourtalès as 'courtois et médiocre': notes journalières, 21 July 1914, BN, Bnfr 16027, fo. 106. For a general account of the visit see P. Miquel, *Poincaré* (Paris, 1984), 336–40.

[83] Poincaré, notes journalières, 21 July 1914, BN, Bnfr 16027, fos. 105 r. and v.; Sir G. Buchanan, *My Mission to Russia and Other Diplomatic Memories* (2 vols., London, 1923) I, 188; see also tel. Buchanan to Grey (no. 162), 22 July 1914, *BD* XI, no. 75. For a more nuanced look at Buchanan see also B. Pares, 'Sir George Buchanan in Russia', *SR* III, 9 (1925), 576–86.

[84] Tel. Buchanan to Grey (no. 163), 22 July 1914, *BD* XI, no. 76; cf. tel. Benckendorff to Sazonov (no. 194), 10/23 July 1914, *BDS* III, no. 1070. The conversation with Carlotti, the Italian ambassador, was confined to Albanian affairs; Poincaré stressed the importance of maintaining the equilibrium in the Adriatic, a point he had also made to Szápáry: see tel. Carlotti to San Giuliano (no. 6541/448, confidential), 22 July 1914,

Given that Sazonov later that same evening developed much the same scheme of some loosely organized triple intervention in the Habsburg capital, it is of course possible that the Russian foreign minister and the visiting French politicians had coordinated their positions on 21 July.[85] On the other hand, it had long been the avowed aim of the Choristers' Bridge and the Quai d'Orsay to bind London more firmly to the Franco-Russian alliance, and the idea of joint diplomatic initiatives had been their preferred policy tool during previous Balkan crises. To that extent, then, none of this was unusual. What, however, is noticeable is that, under the impression of the talks on 21 July, Poincaré had begun to sense that a serious development was about to unfold in the Balkans. His conversation with the next ambassador to be introduced to him underscored this. This was Szápáry, the less than emollient exchanges with whom have already been discussed.

But it was not merely the conversations at St Petersburg that alarmed Poincaré. On 21 and 22 July further evidence reached him that supported what he had learnt since his arrival in Russia. Late on 21 July, Jules Cambon's warning of an imminent Austro-Hungarian démarche, supported by Germany, was circulated to St Petersburg.[86] On the following day, Poincaré received two further reports. The first was a follow-up to Cambon's telegram, and contained a brief summary of the ambassador's conversation with Jagow at the Wilhelmstrasse, in which the German state secretary had denied all knowledge of the contents of Vienna's note. The second report was from Rome, where the absence of any precise knowledge of the nature of the contemplated Austro-Hungarian move had generated a sense of unease. Subject to pressure from the press and the war party, San Giuliano had speculated in conversation with the French ambassador, Camille Barrère, that Vienna 'would seek to obtain the maximum from Serbia, through intimidation beforehand, direct and indirect'. The Italian foreign minister also suggested that Germany supported the planned action.[87] The information received since his arrival in St Petersburg, Poincaré noted succinctly in his diary, was 'highly disturbing [*fort inquiétant*]'.[88]

DDI (4) XII, no. 404; and tel. Szápáry to Berchtold (no. 149), 22 July 1914, ÖUA VIII, no. 10497.

[85] Certainly Pourtalès and Szápáry thought so: see tel. Szápáry to Berchtold (no. 152), 23 July 1914, ÖUA VIII, no. 10546.

[86] Tel. Jules Cambon to Bienvenu-Martin (no. 178), 21 July 1914, DDF (3) X, no. 539, n. 3.

[87] Tel. Bienvenu-Martin to Paléologue (no. 377), 22 July 1914, DDF (3) X, no. 555. For Barrère's conversation see his tel. to Bienvenu-Martin (no. 8), 21 July 1914, *ibid.*, no. 546.

[88] Poincaré, notes journalières, 21 July 1914, BN, Bnfr 16027, fos. 105 v.–106.

While there is conclusive evidence to suggest that the French president had begun to grasp the fact that a major international crisis was brewing, it is more difficult to judge Viviani's attitude. In his memoirs he recalled a certain unease following the encounter with Szápáry, but for the most part the prime minister seems to have spent the days in St Petersburg fretting about domestic politics, and the trial of Mme Caillaux in particular, much to Poincaré's intense irritation. The president noted Viviani's preoccupations with disgust: 'And we are in Russia, and we have great matters to deal with here.'[89]

In the morning of 22 July, news arrived of the latest twist in the Caillaux trial and, as Poincaré noted, the attention of the French delegation was diverted to the *Cour d'assises* in Paris rather than the imperial court at St Petersburg; the drama of Sarajevo was overshadowed again by the drama of what had happened at the offices of *Le Figaro*.[90] With the Damocles sword of awkward revelations during the court hearings hanging over him, Viviani was unsurprisingly sombre and preoccupied. But whatever unpleasantnesses awaited him back in Paris, he may simply have been overawed by the occasion. He had, after all, only been in office for a little over six weeks, and he was a complete neophyte when it came to international summitry. Perhaps Viviani had a nervous breakdown, as has been suggested. After all, he was a profoundly pacific bourgeois, and the military pomp and circumstance on display during the state visit, let alone the casino braggadocio so common among the officers in the imperial and presidential entourages, were little to his taste. Certainly, the prime minister's behaviour was erratic. He was making a spectacle of himself, and 'tout le monde' noticed it, a piqued Poincaré noted. In the afternoon, while the president and the Tsar were attending a promenade concert given by one of the Guards bands, Viviani was seen standing outside the imperial tent groaning and talking to himself. Ambassador Paléologue sought to calm him, but his efforts were in vain. In the end, it was put about that the prime minister suffered from a 'touch of liver [*crise de foie*]'. Dr Cresson, head of the French hospital at St Petersburg, was called to attend to him, and Viviani retired from the scene. 'Viviani is more and more sad and everyone is noticing it', Poincaré recorded in his diary.[91]

---

[89] Poincaré, notes journalières, 22 July 1914, *ibid.*, fo. 108 v.; Schmidt, *Aussenpolitik*, 77–8; see also R. Viviani, *Réponse au Kaiser* (Paris, 1923), 104.

[90] Poincaré, *Au service de la France* IV, 261; see also C. Andrew, 'Governments and Secret Services: A Historical Perspective', *International Journal* XXXIV, 2 (1979), 174.

[91] Poincaré, notes journalières, 22 July 1914, BN, Bnfr 16027, fos. 111 r. and v. In his memoirs Poincaré is more discreet on Viviani's odd behaviour: see *Au service de la France* IV, 268–9; see also Clark, *Sleepwalkers*, 446, for the notion of a nervous

Whatever may have ailed the prime minister, he missed the boisterous demonstration of Franco-Russian amity later that evening at a
military gala at Krasnoe Selo, presided over by the Tsar's cousin, Grand
Duke Nikolai Nikola'evich, a noted pan-Slavist and commander of all the
Guards regiments. The tensions in the Balkans were certainly talked about
freely, and possibly irresponsibly, during the festivities. During the dinner,
while the bands played *Marche Lorraine* – almost obligatory ever since the
'man of Lorraine' had become president – Poincaré noted that the Russian
foreign minister was being chided by two princesses for allegedly sacrificing
the interests of Serbia: 'The emperor [Nicholas II], for his part, without
getting so excited as the two grand duchesses, appears more determined
than Sazonoff to defend Serbia diplomatically.'[92]

Poincaré himself had found Sazonov 'preoccupied and little disposed towards firmness' when the two men discussed the international
situation at the end of 21 July: 'The moment is bad for us, he said to me,
our peasants are busy working the fields.'[93] Sazonov, in fact, was not only
reluctant to take a firm line in the Serbian crisis, he had also been somewhat
lukewarm towards the president's state visit. Much as the minister advocated a policy of deterrence towards the two Germanic Powers, the frictions
with Berlin at the turn of 1913/14 had been unwelcome, and he feared that
Poincaré's presence at St Petersburg and the loose talk that swirled around
the capital had the potential to rekindle tensions with Germany. The state
visit was something of an 'awkwardness', he let it be known at Berlin. He
wished for better relations with Germany; Russia's military programme
was the consequence of the armaments efforts of the other Powers and of
Russia's own much-improved finances; and Russian diplomats were giving
moderating advice at Belgrade.[94]

Sazonov's apparent vacillation in the matter of the Austro-Serbian
dispute ran against the grain of Poincaré's foreign policy ideas, predicated
as they were on an assumption of the need for clarity and firmness. Sazonov
and Viviani nevertheless found time to formulate a common approach to
the brewing Balkan quarrel. Russia and France, Shebeko was informed,
shared a certain unease at the rumoured intention of the Habsburg

---

breakdown. Viviani may simply have over-indulged at the luncheon table – 'The dinner
is excellent', as Poincaré noted, notes journalières, *ibid.*

[92] Poincaré, notes journalières, 22 July 1914, BN, Bnfr 16027, fo. 112 r. Poincaré
described the state of mind of the two princesses as *'exalté'*, which can also be translated
as 'hot-headed'. Paléologue gives a more colourful account of the antics of the two
exalted personages: see his *Russie des Tsars* I, 14–15.

[93] Poincaré, notes journalières, 21 July 1914, BN, Bnfr 16027, fo. 107 v.

[94] Tel. Lichnowsky to Jagow (no. 138), 20 July 1914, *DD* I, no. 85; for Sazonov and
deterrence see Lieven, *Russia*, 48–9.

government to make certain demands on Serbia. The ambassador was instructed to alert, 'in a friendly but energetic manner', the Ballhausplatz to the dangerous consequence of any such step, if the demands to be made proved irreconcilable with the 'dignity of Serbia'. Neither the Russian nor the French government could tolerate the 'unjustifiable humiliation' of that country. Shebeko was instructed to coordinate his representations with his French colleague and, if possible, with the British ambassador as well.[95]

This was a démarche designed to pre-empt the anticipated Habsburg démarche on Serbia. It was not without risk, however, and could very easily have led to an early escalation. If Sazonov struck Poincaré as not sufficiently tough in his attitude towards the mounting crisis, Viviani was even less enthusiastic about any kind of representations at Vienna. The president found him 'somewhat exasperated', and he fell into line 'with little eagerness'. Indeed, he delayed issuing the agreed instructions until after the departure of the French delegation.[96] There was a further semipublic spat between Viviani and Poincaré on the evening of 23 July. Somewhat ominously, it took place underneath the four twelve-inch guns at the stern of the *France* during the farewell banquet for the Tsar. The French delegation was due to leave later that evening, and a communiqué was to be issued for the press. Paléologue's draft document, scribbled on the back of his menu, affirmed 'the perfect accord' of French and Russian 'views and intentions' with regard to the maintenance of the European equilibrium, 'notably in the Balkan peninsula'. Viviani signalled his disapproval across the dining table. At the end of the banquet, he suggested that the final phrase of Paléologue's draft 'seemed ... to entangle us a little too much in Russia's Balkan policy'. In the final version, the communiqué was less strident in tone, but its meaning was no less clear. It confirmed 'the perfect community of their views on the diverse problems relating to the general peace and the European equilibrium between the Powers, notably in the Orient'.[97]

The French president was well satisfied with his visit to Russia. The thunderous downpour in the afternoon of the final day had dampened spirits somewhat, and the presidential chef 'did not distinguish himself'

---

[95] Tel. Sazonov to Shebeko (no. 1475), 9/22 July 1914, *IBZI* IV, no. 322. The telegram was despatched at 4 a.m., so the conversation with Viviani must have taken place earlier on 21 July: see *ibid.*, 353, n. 292a. Poincaré described the planned move as an 'amicable demand': notes journalières, 23 July 1914, BN, Bnfr 16027, fo. 113 v.

[96] Poincaré, notes journalières, 23 July 1914, BN, Bnfr 16027, fo. 113 v.; see tel. Viviani to Bienvenu-Martin (no no.), 24 July 1914, *DDF* (3) XI, no. 1.

[97] Paléologue, *Russie des Tsars* I, 19; for the menu, see Schmidt, *Frankreichs Aussenpolitik*, 95.

with the spread laid on for the imperial visitors.[98] Politically, however, the visit had been an undoubted success. It had been intended as a gesture of goodwill, a personal assurance of France's loyalty to the Franco-Russian alliance, and the summit had certainly underscored the political solidarity between the two countries.

The visit was significant also because, his later protestations notwithstanding, Poincaré had begun to sense an imminent international crisis by 21 July. The summit had laid the foundations for a common Franco-Russian approach to the crisis, though in essence it was little more than an extension of the crisis diplomacy pursued during the Balkan turmoil in recent years. The démarche to pre-empt Vienna's démarche, to which Viviani had agreed with such reluctance, was predicated on the assumption that joint pressure would be sufficient to deter the Habsburg government from forcing the issue with Serbia. It was a tactic that had been tried, and had to an extent succeeded, during the recent crises in south-eastern Europe. Then it had depended on Anglo-German suasion to restrain Vienna and St Petersburg alike. Whether this could be replicated in July 1914 had not been discussed during the French state visit to Russia. Indeed, little thought seems to have been given to what further steps might become necessary should Vienna ignore the Franco-Russian warning. And no thought was given to whether military posturing was needed to amplify diplomatic pressure.

The Franco-Russian summit was important also in two other respects, both of them connected with the dynamics of the crisis that was about to unfold. In the first instance, French decision-making would be severely hampered for the next few days, until 29 July, while the president and prime minister travelled back to France, out of the telegraphic reach of Paris and reliant now on wireless telegraphy, which was not secure and therefore used only infrequently. The communication difficulties were further exacerbated by the overt policy divisions between Viviani and the president. In consequence of these divisions, ambassador Paléologue was to play a very significant role in the crisis.

Count Benckendorff issues a warning

While Poincaré and Viviani sailed back to France, news arrived at St Petersburg that the anticipated Austro-Hungarian move was now imminent. Already on 22 July, Spalajković had submitted a lengthy

---

[98] Poincaré, notes journalières, 23 July 1914, BN, Bnfr 16027, fo. 113 v. Pourtalès reported on the unenthusiastic response of the local population to the state visit: see tel. Pourtalès to Auswärtiges Amt (no. 146), 23 July 1914, *DD* I, no. 130.

communication in which he pointed to the anti-Serbian campaign by Viennese and Budapest papers. This, he asserted, could have no other purpose than to fan belligerent sentiments in the Habsburg Empire, and to prepare the ground for the expected démarche. The Serbian envoy was generally known to be a 'noted Austrophobe', however, and his *aide-mémoire* contained little concrete evidence.[99] At any rate, Sazonov was too preoccupied with the French visitors to offer the assurances of Russian support and protection that Spalajković had sought.[100]

Far more significant was a private letter from Benckendorff in London, reporting a confidential conversation with his cousin, Prince Lichnowsky, the German ambassador. As was seen earlier, the latter's recent visit to Berlin had left him in a state of considerable anxiety, and he did not hide his concerns from Benckendorff. He feared 'Austrian stupidities, which would be unacceptable at Belgrade', and suggested that the Wilhelmstrasse was not likely to restrain Austria-Hungary, much to his dismay: 'Zimmermann was the one at Berlin who best understood the situation, but he was too little a man to exercise any great influence.' Lichnowsky suggested a Russian hint, 'without it being a direct threat', addressed to Vienna, possibly in the form of a letter from the Tsar to the Emperor Franz Joseph. But he made little headway. Benckendorff raised the usual objections: 'Relations with Austria, political and moral situation in Russia, public opinion, impossibility of our facilitating the strengthening of Austrian influence in Serbia, absence of clear case.' Lichnowsky's reply was prescient. It was imperative to avert a démarche or to modify it. Once direct talks had commenced, 'we [Russia] would remain masters of the situation because we were masters at Belgrade'. Every day gained made war more unlikely. If the Austrians willed war, he conceded, nothing could be done; but he feared that 'they might stumble into war through clumsiness and weakness'. For his part, Benckendorff accepted that the situation was critical, but thought his cousin's worries exaggerated. Even so, he impressed on Sazonov that were war to ensue, Russia's position would be all the better 'the more ostentatiously, the more manifestly and the more effectively we had worked towards avoiding it'. Ultimately, he reminded the foreign minister, this would weigh heavily with the British government.[101]

---

[99] Serbian aide mémoire (confidential), 9/22 July 1914, *IBZI* IV, no. 319 (also in *DSP* VII/2, no. 474, but dated 21 July); for the description of Spalajković see Cora to San Giuliano (no. R. 767/136), 7 July 1914, *DDI* (4), no. 112. The Serbian minister at London made a similar communication: see note, 23 July 1914, *BD* XI, no. 87; Cornwall, 'Serbia', 72.

[100] Tel. Spalajković to Pašić, 22 July 1914, *DSP* VII/2, no. 477.

[101] Benckendorff to Sazonov (strictly private), 22 July 1914, *IBZI* IV, no. 328; for general comments see M. E. Soroka, *Britain, Russia and the Road to the First World*

The ambassador's private communication was significant because it furnished further evidence that, at least for now, Berlin would not rein in the Habsburg ally. Any attempt to pre-empt the Austro-Hungarian démarche, then, would have to be made by Russia and the other Powers. Benckendorff's concluding observation, on the other hand, underlined the extent to which considerations of the British factor featured in Russian calculations. At the beginning of 1914, Sazonov had complained, not for the first time, of Britain's relative aloofness and 'the vacillating and opaque policy of the English Cabinet', which he considered a hindrance in his attempts to settle south-eastern Europe.[102] Now faced once more with the irruption of Balkan problems into Great Power politics, Russian diplomacy would strive to force Britain to range herself alongside the Franco-Russian combination.

In the late afternoon of 23 July, Prince Nikolai Aleksandrovich Kudashev, in charge of the Vienna embassy during Shebeko's absence, telegraphed that the Austro-Hungarian note would be presented at Belgrade that same day: 'Sharp in its form, it is, as the Austrians assure me, perfectly acceptable.'[103] It seems that during the day, Kudashev had in vain sought an interview with Berchtold, possibly to intercede with him as instructed by Sazonov. The minister was busy, he was told by Macchio and Forgách, who then assured him that the note to Serbia would be acceptable.[104] Later in the evening, at St Petersburg, while Poincaré and the imperial party toasted the Franco-Russian alliance on board the *France*, the head of the Second Department of the Choristers' Bridge, Konstantin Yevgeni'evich von Bützow, learnt from an Italian source that the note amounted to 'a completely unacceptable ultimatum'. At the same time, Szápáry telephoned to request an urgent meeting with Sazonov early the next day.[105]

There was little now that Sazonov could do until Szápáry communicated the Habsburg note addressed to Belgrade. But the foreign ministers in London and Berlin were not so passive. The imminent Austro-Hungarian move affected them in quite different ways. In an effort to head off

War: The Fateful Embassy of Count Aleksandr Benckendorff, 1903–1916 (Farnham and Burlington, VT, 2011), 250–1.

[102] Sazonov to Benckendorff (private), 6/19 Feb. 1914, *IBZI* I, no. 289.

[103] Tel. Kudashev to Sazonov (no. 89), 10/23 July 1914, *IBZI* v, no. 6.

[104] See Shebeko, *Souvenirs*, 219; for the instructions see tel. Sazonov to Shebeko (no. 1475), 9/22 July 1914, *IBZI* IV, no. 322; also K. von Macchio, 'Momentbilder aus der Julikrise 1914', *BMH* XI, 10 (1936), 784.

[105] Foreign Ministry daily journal, 10/23 July 1914, *IBZI* v, no. 5. The Italian ministers at Belgrade and Bucharest made similar statements there, see tel. Crackanthorpe to Grey (no. 47), 23 July 1914, *BD* XI, no. 89, and tel. Walburg to Auswärtiges Amt (no. 41, secret), 23 July 1914, *DD* I, no. 135.

Sazonov's suggestion of some form of pre-emptive triple intervention at Vienna, Grey sought out Benckendorff on 21 and 22 July to impress upon him the need for direct talks between Russia and Austria-Hungary. They were 'the surest means' of de-escalating the situation.[106] If the two Powers 'kept each other at arm's length meanwhile, it would be a very difficult situation'. If, on the other hand, St Petersburg initiated direct Austro-Russian talks as a means of crisis management, it might be possible to keep Vienna's demands 'within reasonable limits'. As for Britain's own position, Grey left Benckendorff in no doubt that 'it was not our business to take violent sides in this matter'. Much would depend on the case presented by Vienna. If the plot to kill Franz Ferdinand was shown to have originated on Serbian soil, Grey signalled his willingness to urge Belgrade to give Austria-Hungary 'the utmost assurances ... for the prevention of such plots ... being carried on in Servia in the future'.[107]

Grey's initiative was in line with the stance he had taken so far. Any suggestion of Britain aligning herself with France and Russia against Austria-Hungary would have made impossible the sort of diplomatic cooperation with Germany that had proved so successful during the recent crises in the Balkans; and it might also have smothered the tender plant of an Anglo-German rapprochement to which he had come to attach such importance. By contrast, given Sazonov's repeated protestations of his desire for closer Anglo-Russian relations, London's reluctance to fall into line with the idea of a triple intervention might make the Russian foreign minister more amenable to Grey's scheme of direct talks between St Petersburg and Vienna. Once a channel of communication had been established, and international diplomacy had thus begun to gather momentum, Anglo-German crisis management could swing into action, as before, and mediate a settlement. It should also be noted that Grey's concluding comments offered a clear indication that, at least at this point of the crisis, he was generally sympathetic to Austria-Hungary's predicament. Whatever might be said about Franco-Russian subliminal attempts to delegitimize Vienna's case against Serbia, the same cannot be said of Grey. Even Nicolson, who tended to view Balkan problems through Russian eyes, impressed on the new Serbian minister, Mateja Bošković, that London would expect Serbia 'to meet the Austrian requests in a conciliatory and moderate spirit'.[108]

---

[106] Tel. Benckendorff to Sazonov (no. 192), 9/21 July 1914, *BDS* III, no. 1069.
[107] Grey to Buchanan (no. 289), 22 July 1914, *BD* XI, no. 79; cf. tel. Benckendorff to Sazonov (no. 192), 9/22 July 1914, *IBZI* IV, no. 323; and tel. Lichnowsky to Jagow (no. 143), 20 July 1914, *DD* I, no. 92.
[108] Min. Nicolson, 23 July 1914, *BD* XI, no. 87. Serbia's representatives abroad were slow to act on Pašić's circular of 18 July: see Cornwall, 'Serbia', 74–5. Bošković,

Grey's sympathetic attitude was to be severely tested by the nature of Austria-Hungary's démarche. On 22 July, the Foreign Secretary had requested a meeting with the Habsburg ambassador, Count Mensdorff, but this did not take place until the following evening. Mensdorff explained that the investigations at Sarajevo had established a connection between the assassins and 'official Serbia', and that certain unspecified demands would be made. He also intimated that 'there would be something in the nature of a time limit, which was in effect akin to an ultimatum'. This revelation was something of a bombshell. It threatened to unravel Grey's crisis management; the delicate balancing act he had to perform was in danger of being upended. Anything in the nature of an ultimatum would inflame opinion in Russia, so limiting the Russian government's room for manoeuvre and thus narrowing the wiggle-room for international diplomacy. If there was no ultimatum, and if Austria-Hungary's case proved convincing, Russia could be won over. Grey repeatedly warned of the 'awful consequences' and urged 'patience and moderation' in Vienna and St Petersburg. The potential risks inherent in the situation created by Vienna's impending démarche were

> terrible. If as many as four Great Powers of Europe ... were engaged in war, it seemed to me that it must involve the expenditure of so vast a sum of money and such an interference with trade, that a war would be accompanied or followed by a complete collapse of European credit and industry. In these days, in great industrial States, this would mean a state of things worse than that of 1848, and, irrespective of who were victors in the war, many things might be completely swept away.[109]

According to Mensdorff's account of the interview, Grey argued for a 'direct exchange of ideas' between the two eastern empires. Ordinary diplomatic representations at St Petersburg, he observed, would have no effect this time. Russia needed to be convinced that Austria-Hungary's grievances were well-justified and that her demands were acceptable. Mensdorff found Grey 'cool and objective, friendly as always and not without sympathy for us. He is undoubtedly very worried about the possible consequences. I fear he will criticise the character of an ultimatum and the short time limit of our démarche.'[110]

moreover, was slow and inaccurate in reporting Nicolson's statement: see tel. Bošković to Pašić, 24 July 1914 (received 25 July), DSP vii/2, no. 536.

[109] Grey to de Bunsen (no. 121), 23 July 1914, BD xi, no. 86.

[110] Tel. Mensdorff to Berchtold (no. 107), 23 July 1914, ÖUA viii, no. 10537. Mensdorff reported Grey as warning that 'many an existing institution would be swept away', a clear hint at war as threat to the monarchical order in Austria-Hungary and Russia.

The interview with Mensdorff brought home to Grey for the first time how narrow the path left for diplomacy had become. It was clear by now that the démarche could not be averted. His warning of a general European war was a last-minute attempt to moderate it by persuading Vienna to remove the time limit. Neither this warning, nor his suggestion that Russia might be biddable if Vienna's case were strong, was sufficient either to deter or to persuade the Habsburg leadership.

Zimmermann and Jagow contemplate the situation

If Grey sought to gain time for diplomacy to work, the decision-makers at Berlin were driven by rather different calculations. Here, as the Bavarian chargé d'affaires reported, it was accepted that Vienna's demands would be irreconcilable with Serbia's sovereignty and independence, and that the Habsburg move was likely to result in war. The Sarajevo assassination nevertheless furnished a suitable pretext for the Dual Monarchy to deal with its Serb problem and clear out the 'Belgrade nest of anarchists', explained Zimmermann, the under-secretary, though he confessed to doubts, widely held at Berlin, as to whether Vienna 'would muster sufficient energy' to act. Settling the matter had become vital to the survival of the Habsburg Empire. Owing to its 'indecisiveness and incoherence it had become the true sick man in Europe, just as Turkey had been, for whose partition Russians, Italians, Romanians, Serbs and Montenegrins were waiting'.

In a wide-ranging *tour d'horizon*, Zimmermann examined the current state of affairs and developed a series of different scenarios. What is striking about the under-secretary's statement is its curious mixture of deeply intelligent analysis and delusion. Intriguingly, he characterized the unconditional support offered to Vienna on 5 July as a 'blank cheque' ('*Blankovollmacht*'), the first instance of a German diplomat using this phrase. Equally intriguingly, he placed greater emphasis on the fact that this meant full powers for Vienna to secure Bulgaria's adhesion to the *Dreibund* alliance. There was a risk, he conceded, that the contemplated démarche might embroil Austria-Hungary, and therefore also Germany, in a war with Russia. For that reason, it would have been preferable if Vienna had struck immediately rather than waiting for so long. Whether an Austro-Serbian conflict would escalate now, he reasoned, depended largely on the nature of the démarche. If it aimed at punishing Belgrade for past misdemeanours, the conflict could be localized; if, however, Austria-Hungary sought to secure territorial compensation for herself, 'larger complications would be inevitable'.

Once the note had been communicated to Belgrade, Zimmermann explained, the Wilhelmstrasse would launch a diplomatic initiative to ensure the localization of any Austro-Serb war. There would be no mobilization of the German army, and Berlin would seek to persuade the Habsburg leadership not to place the Austro-Hungarian forces along the Russian frontier on alert so as to avoid counter-measures by Russia. Key to the success or failure of the initiative would be Russia's stance. If Russia wished to avoid a war with the two Germanic Powers, it could remain passive, since 'throwing bombs and firing revolvers' was as unacceptable to the Russian government as to 'the other civilized states'. Zimmermann assumed that both Britain and France would act in a moderating sense at St Petersburg as neither could wish for war under present circumstances. Finally, the chargé noted, Zimmermann banked on the fact 'that "bluff" is the preferred tool of Russian policy, and that the Russian likes to threaten with his sword, but in the last moment he will not draw it on behalf of others'.

As for Britain, she would remain aloof for as long as Austria-Hungary did not aim to destroy Serbia. If the crisis nevertheless escalated to a full-scale war between the two alliance groups, 'then we would find ... our English cousins on the side of our enemies'. No British government could accept the renewed defeat of France, and her subsequent relegation to the second flight of Powers, which would unsettle the European balance of power. But Zimmermann was more concerned about Italy, and indicated that Berlin would continue in its efforts to persuade the Habsburg leadership to secure Rome's support by offering territorial compensation – he suggested either central Albania, which would be 'a new Achilles heel for Italy', or the cession of the southern districts of the Trentino.[111]

Zimmermann's analysis was clear-sighted and intelligent. But it is remarkable for a number of other reasons. In the first instance, it shows close parallels with the arguments Jagow deployed in his letter to Lichnowsky on the same day, and is suggestive of a collective effort at the Wilhelmstrasse to take stock of the developments since 5 July. For his part, Zimmermann, who had advocated a cautious policy in the immediate aftermath of the Sarajevo assassination, showed a greater awareness of the extent to which German policy had been made dependent on Austria-Hungary by the events of that day. Here, the admission that Berlin had preferred – indeed had expected – a swift strike against Serbia immediately after Sarajevo is significant, as are the assumptions that Russian policy

---

[111] Schoen to Hertling (no. 386), 18 July 1914, *DD* IV, app. IV, no. 2. Zimmermann also spoke at length about relations with Bulgaria and Romania.

relied on 'bluff' and that French diplomacy would act to restrain
St Petersburg. But Zimmermann's reference to the alliance and mobilization mechanisms, potentially set in motion by the Austro-Hungarian
démarche, also underscored that the Wilhelmstrasse was fully alive now
to the increased risk of escalation. There could be little doubt as to
how narrow the dividing line between localized war and a general war
had become.

While Sazonov had decided to await the Austrian démarche, and
Grey sought to create some space for international mediation, Jagow
aimed at shielding the planned move against any pre-emptive diplomatic
measures. He parried a Serbian move to enlist German support in an
attempt to mollify Austria-Hungary by pretending ignorance of the
demands Vienna was likely to make, though not without impressing
upon the Serbian chargé d'affaires that so far Vienna had shown remarkable patience in the face of persistent pan-Slav provocations. On no
account was the démarche to be aborted by pre-emptive, and very likely
only partial, concessions by Serbia.[112] Ambassador Tschirschky meanwhile was set to work to sensitize the Ballhausplatz to the necessity of
keeping Italy within the fold of the *Dreibund*. For once, however, his
forthright representations made little impression on Berchtold. Irked by
Germany's willingness to appease Italy by means of judicious cessions of
Habsburg territory, he asserted that there was no case for compensating
Italy. Austria-Hungary would not seize Serbian soil, and even the subjugation of Serbia would further Italian interests, because 'Italy needed a
strong Austria, not least as a protective wall against the Slavic tide.'
Berchtold promised to assuage Italian sensitivities as much as possible,
and undertook to inform San Giuliano of the contents of the note as it
was delivered at Belgrade, 'which appeared to me [Berchtold] entirely
sufficient as an act of courtesy towards an unreliable ally'.[113] Inducing
the Italian press into taking a favourable line through the liberal dispen-
sation of Habsburg reptile funds seemed a better course of action to the
Austro-Hungarian foreign minister.[114] In substance Berchtold had not
yielded in inch. This response underlined the role-reversal within the
Austro-German *Zweibund* following the 'blank cheque' in early July.
Indeed during his conversation with Berchtold, Tschirschky had repeatedly angled for further information about Vienna's plans. Jagow, too,

[112] Tel. Jagow to Tschirschky (no. 127), 20 July 1914, *DD* I, no. 91.
[113] Quotes from Tschirschky to Bethmann Hollweg (no. 242, secret), 20 July 1914, *DD*
I, no. 94; and daily report Berchtold, 20 July 1914, *ÖUA* VIII, no. 10398; see also tel.
Szögyény to Berchtold (no. 273), 21 July 1914, *ibid.* no. 10447.
[114] See Tschirschky to Bethmann Hollweg (secret), 22 July 1914, *DD* I, no. 128.

found himself in the position of a mendicant in his conversations with Szögyény. Having reiterated his concerns about the need to carry Italy along with the planned action against Serbia, he assured the ambassador of Germany's loyal support, but underlined that 'it was therefore a vital interest of the German government to be informed in a timely manner "where our path leads"'.[115] Hoyos's loose talk of a Serbian partition had cast a long shadow, indeed. But for as long as the crisis lasted, Vienna remained in the driving seat, while Berlin had to make do with the role of an anxious passenger.

Count Berchtold contemplates the past and the future

In the meantime, the Wilhelmstrasse prepared the ground for a diplomatic initiative to prevent any escalation of the situation after the Austro-Hungarian démarche. The ambassadors in London, Paris and St Petersburg were instructed to impress upon the governments there the strength and justice of Austria-Hungary's case. The investigations into the Sarajevo plot had established beyond doubt strong connections between the murderers and 'official' Serbia. For several years, Greater Serbian chauvinist agitation, which had inspired the assassin, had sought to destabilize and undermine the Habsburg Empire; and previous promises of proper conduct on the part of the Belgrade government had never been kept. The activities that originated in Belgrade threatened the 'security and integrity' of Austria-Hungary's territories. To protect them, Vienna had to act. In light of Serbia's provocative behaviour in recent years, there was the strong risk, however, that the Belgrade government would reject the justified demands made upon it. Under these circumstances, 'if she did not wish to forgo her position as a Great Power', Austria-Hungary had to use 'strong pressure and, if necessary, the deployment of military measures'. The matter was nevertheless solely for Austria-Hungary and Serbia to settle. The ambassadors were to explain that '[w]e [Germany] urgently desire the localization of the conflict because any interference by another Power, given the various alliance obligations, would have incalculable consequences'. Pourtalès at St Petersburg, moreover, was instructed to appeal to Russia's sense of monarchical solidarity and her conservative ideological affinities with Germany. The two empires had a common interest in administering a

---

[115] Szögyény to Berchtold (strictly secret), 21 July 1914, ÖUA VIII, no. 10448. Baron Julius Adolf von Griesinger, the German envoy at Belgrade, also sought to elicit details of the note from Giesl: see W. Baron Giesl, *Zwei Jahrzehnte im Nahen Orient. Aufzeich-nungen*, ed. [E.] von Steinitz (Berlin, 1927), 266.

crushing blow to 'political radicalism [in Serbia] that does not shy away from crimes against members of its own dynasty'.[116]

The instructions to Pourtalès were an attempt to rekindle memories of the *Dreikaiserbund* of the 1880s, the conservative alliance of Germany, Russia and Austria-Hungary, which was calculated to resonate with the still-influential conservative, broadly pro-German cliques at the St Petersburg court.[117] More importantly, the implicit threat of a wider conflict marked a significant further escalation of the crisis. The aim of German policy, however, remained the localization of any Austro-Serbian war. To that extent, then, the implied escalation served a limited and largely defensive objective. The spectre of a general war in Europe was to ensure that the conflict in the Balkans did not spill over. It was not unlike the tactics employed by German diplomacy during the days of Bismarck or towards the end of the Bosnian annexation crisis of 1908–9.

While German diplomacy was thus prepared for the escalation of the Austro-Serbian quarrel, Pourtalès reported on the unenthusiastic reception of Poincaré and the French delegation among the local population in the Russian capital. Pointing to the industrial strikes in the Putilov and other works in St Petersburg, he observed that '*[i]n the event of external complications these could certainly create a difficult situation for the [Russian] government*'.[118] Such information could only encourage the already firmly entrenched conviction at Berlin that Russia's fragile domestic politics would counsel against a firm foreign policy and that any sabre-rattling by the government at St Petersburg was just that. Conflicting signals by French and Russian diplomats, moreover, helped to confirm this impression. Dumaine, the French ambassador at Vienna, for instance, whilst urging moderation on the Ballhausplatz, explained that Russia was not ready to offer more than moral support to Serbia: 'In the event of an armed conflict between us [Austria-Hungary] and Serbia Russia would ... not actively intervene, but rather seek to ensure that the war remains localized.'[119]

---

[116] Bethmann Hollweg circular, 21 July 1914, *DD* I, no. 100. The instructions were drafted by Stumm, but bear minor amendments in the chancellor's hand. Bethmann remained at Hohenfinow, and remained in ignorance of the terms of the Austrian démarche: see tel. Bethmann Hollweg to Jagow (no. 3), 22 July 1914, *ibid.*, no. 116.

[117] For this see D. C. B. Lieven, 'Pro-Germans and Russian Foreign Policy', *IHR* II, 1 (1980), 34–54.

[118] Tel. Pourtalès to Auswärtiges Amt (no. 146), 23 July 1914, *DD* I, no. 130 (original emphasis); see also tel. Szápáry to Berchtold (no. 153), 10/23 July 1914, *ÖUA* VIII, no. 10548 (also intercepted by the Russian *cabinet noir*: see *IBZI* v, no. 4).

[119] Daily report Macchio, 22 July 1914, *ÖUA* VIII, no. 10491; also transmitted to Berlin: see tel. Tschirschky to Auswärtiges Amt (no. 97), 23 July 1914, *DD* I, no. 131.

As for the Ballhausplatz, neither Poincaré's sharp exchange with Szápáry nor Grey's counsel of moderation had much effect. Giesl was instructed to inform the foreign ministry at Belgrade that he had an important communication to make to Pašić at 5 p.m. on Thursday, 23 July. As the prime minister had left the capital for election rallies in the south, Giesl was to hand the note to the most senior Serbian minister available at Belgrade; as seen already, he had full powers to break off relations forty-eight hours hence, should the Serbian reply be insufficient, which it was expected to be, of course.[120] Such was the secrecy surrounding the planned move against Belgrade that the note itself was only transmitted to Giesl late at night on 21 July, Baron Storck, his legation counsellor, having been called to Vienna to act as a personal courier.[121]

The extraordinary lengths to which Habsburg officials went to camouflage the démarche aimed at shielding it against foreign interference. If the quarrel had been made a matter for the Great Powers, the desired neutering of Serbia would move beyond Austria-Hungary's grasp, and the desired 'clarification' of relations with the difficult neighbouring kingdom would remain elusive. Berchtold was remarkably open about the calculations behind 'the planned forceful move'. As he explained to Mérey at Rome in a lengthy private letter, 'domestic and foreign policy motives' had been decisive. The growing pan-Serb 'sabotage work [*Minirarbeit*] on Bosnia-Herzegovinian soil, with ramifications for Dalmatia, Croatia, Slavonia and Hungary', could only be halted by means of an 'energetic intervention at Belgrade, where the threads run together'. In addition, with the connivance of Russia and now Romania, Balkan politics were in the process of a reorientation whose 'ultimate aim was the smashing of the Monarchy'.

Berchtold admitted that the planned move entailed the risk of escalation, 'given the unreliability and envy of our Italian ally, the hostility of Romanian public opinion and the weight of Slavophile counsellors at the court of the Tsar'. Yet, he asserted that it was better to face that danger now than to remain passive and to wait 'until the flood tides come crashing over our heads'. It was therefore necessary to force Belgrade to declare itself '*pro praeterito* and *pro futuro* [for the past and for the future]', as Berchtold put it, against anti-Habsburg propaganda, effectively coercing Serbia into Austria-Hungary's orbit. A merely diplomatic triumph, as envisaged by Tisza, was no longer enough; the successful coercion of Serbia in

---

[120] Berchtold to Giesl (private), 20 July 1914, *ÖUA* VIII, no. 10396; tel. Tschirschky to Jagow (no. 94, secret), 22 July 1914, *DD* I, no. 110.
[121] Tel. Giesl to Berchtold (no. 168), 22 July 1914, *ÖUA* VIII, no. 10474. Storck arrived at the legation at 11 p.m. on 21 July.

1909 and 1912 had shown that such triumphs were fleeting achievements only. There were other problems. In particular Italy would be difficult to keep on side. But Austria-Hungary had been supportive during the recent Italo-Turkish war, and this should strengthen Vienna's hand in any diplomatic tussle with Rome. Any compensation for Italy in Albania threatened to unravel the arrangements come to at the London ambassadorial conference in 1913, which had established the framework for a new Balkans settlement; and such a move would therefore run into the opposition of the Powers.

Berchtold's ruminations were a curious mixture of levity and Latinicity. There was also a whiff of unreality about them. Italy, for instance, was to be deterred from demanding compensation in Albania because it would undermine the recent Great Power settlement for the Balkans, while at the same time Vienna's own plans for the post-war partition of Serbia aimed at nothing less than the unilateral re-ordering of south-eastern Europe in the Habsburg image. But whatever the inconsistencies in Berchtold's reasoning, clearly, the Habsburg foreign minister, who had so often equivocated and procrastinated in the past, was determined not to be dissuaded now. As he explained to Mérey, 'I have the sense of having been chosen by providence to join the ranks of those ministers who desired to pursue a policy of peace but had to make war – from Cardinal Fleury to [Count] Lambsdorff – hopefully with more success as the last representative of this tendency.'[122]

The recourse to history and to providence when explicating problematic decisions is the politican's form of 'Dutch courage'. Yet, however he justified the decisions made, Berchtold was not for turning. Even the Emperor Franz Joseph concurred with him: 'We cannot back off now.'[123] Berchtold would not threaten military action only to settle for a compromise as before; and Belgrade was not to be allowed, as before, to deny any official involvement before offering recompense later, only afterwards to break any promises made. And yet, the back door had by no means been bolted for a last-minute change. In the late morning of 23 July, when the letter to Mérey was despatched, and some six hours before Baron Giesl, the minister at Belgrade, was to deliver the note, the foreign minister met with Conrad, the chief of staff, to discuss the military aspects of the crisis. If Serbia yielded to Austro-Hungarian pressure after mobilization, Conrad

---

[122] Berchtold to Mérey, 21 July 1914 (despatched 23 July), ÖUA VIII, no. 10459; Hantsch, *Berchtold* II, 606–7. Cardinal André-Hercule de Fleury (1653–1743) was Louis XV's chief minister; Count Vladimir Nikola'evich Lamsdorf (1845–1907) was Russian foreign minister, 1900–6.

[123] On 9 July, as quoted in Hantsch, *Berchtold* II, 608.

insisted, Belgrade would have to pay the costs of mobilizing the Habsburg armed forces in addition to accepting the demands made of it in the note. When Berchtold then raised the uncertain attitude of the Italian ally, the chief of staff replied: 'If we also have to fear Italy, then we shall not mobilize.' Austria-Hungary could not fight a war on three fronts.[124]

In equal measure, Berchtold's enquiry and Hötzendorf's reply were an admission of the constraints placed on Austria-Hungary's power to act. Above all, they were an acknowledgement of strategic failure. If both men regarded the double murder at Sarajevo as a welcome pretext to clarify relations with Serbia on Habsburg terms, neither the foreign minister nor the chief of staff had made the necessary preparations for any recourse to military force. International diplomacy and the weight of military factors were ranged against such a move. With neither a political nor a military strategy for a limited war against the troublesome southern neighbour in place, in six hours' time the Habsburg envoy was to present the Belgrade government with demands that would escalate the situation and throw into sharper relief the flaws in Vienna's policy.

[124] Conrad, *Aus meiner Dienstzeit* IV, 108.

5 THE ULTIMATUM: 23 TO 26 JULY

Count Leopold Franz Rudolf Ernest Vinzenz Innocenz Maria: 'The ultimatum was first-rate! At last, at last!'

Baron Eduard Alois Josef Ottokar Ignazius Eusebius Maria: '*Foudroyant*! They nearly accepted it!'

The Count: 'That would have infuriated me. Fortunately, we had the two little points in it, our investigations on Serbian soil and all that – well, they didn't take that. They only have themselves to blame, the Serbs.'

The Baron: 'If one thinks about it – because of two little points – and so because of a *bagatelle* a world war broke out! It is just too comical.'

KARL KRAUS[1]

In the three weeks since Sarajevo, the Habsburg leadership had kept the other Powers guessing as to how Austria-Hungary was likely to react to the assassination of the Archduke. In their different ways Jagow, Grey, Poincaré and Sazonov had indicated their respective positions in anticipation of international complications. Jagow had affirmed the 'blank cheque', committing Berlin to unconditional support of its Austro-Hungarian ally without retaining any means of controlling, let alone restraining, its actions. Grey had correctly identified Germany and Russia as key to preventing the further escalation of the Austro-Serbian crisis, but had – again correctly – confined himself to encouraging Berlin and St Petersburg to exchange views on the situation in the Balkans. As for the Franco-Russian allies, the French president had sought to stiffen what he considered to be Russia's flaccid stance in the face of a likely Austro-Hungarian move against Serbia. Sazonov, meanwhile, plagued as much by doubts about the correct policy response to the crisis as by his suspicions of Habsburg policy, had failed to communicate a consistent line to the other Powers, most significantly Austria-Hungary and Germany. Until Vienna revealed its hand, however, there was little more that any of the other chancelleries of Europe could do.

---

[1] K. Kraus, *Die letzten Tage der Menschheit* (Vienna and Leipzig, 1922), act I, scene v, 49–50.

Baron Giesl calls on the Belgrade government

And so 23 July arrived. Earlier in the day, Giesl had received his final instructions. They included an order now to communicate the note at 6 p.m., an hour later than originally intended. Once again, the reason for this latest delay was tactical. Szápáry had earlier wired that the *France*, with Poincaré and Viviani on board, was to weigh anchor at 11 p.m. St Petersburg time, or 9.30 p.m. central European time. Three-and-a-half hours were not likely to be sufficient for full and reliable information concerning the démarche to be transmitted to St Petersburg. In practice, then, it would be impossible, at this late stage, for the Russian and French governments to coordinate their positions. In the event of the Pašić administration resigning rather than assuming responsibility for accepting the note, Giesl was to explain that such a step would not remove the forty-eight-hour time limit, and that any caretaker government at Belgrade would be held responsible for submitting Serbia's official response to the démarche.[2]

Clearly, the latest instructions were something of an afterthought. All eventualities, however, were now covered, and at 6 p.m. Giesl delivered his note to Lazar Paču, the finance minister who acted in Pašić's place while the prime minister was on the hustings at Radujevac and Niš. There was some further delay, this time unexpected. For the corpulent and chain-smoking Paču spoke no French, and Slavko Gruić, the secretary-general of the foreign ministry, had to be called to act as translator. When Paču realized that Giesl had delivered an ultimatum into his hands, he sought to gain time – he himself was not competent to transact diplomatic business and Pašić was out of town. But Giesl, as instructed, remained unyielding. There could be no change to the forty-eight-hour time limit; given modern transport facilities, it should be possible to bring Pašić back to Belgrade in a matter of a few hours. If the demands set out in the note were not met, he had orders to sever diplomatic relations and to leave Belgrade immediately. With that he bowed and left Paču.[3]

The episode had a curious postscript. In informing the Ballhaus-platz of the delivery of the note, Giesl had used the term 'ultimatum'. This

[2] Tels. Berchtold to Giesl (nos. 80 and 81), 23 July 1914, *ÖUA* VIII, nos. 10518–9.
[3] Tel. Giesl to Berchtold (no. 173), 23 July 1914, *ÖUA* VIII, no. 10524; W. Baron Giesl, *Zwei Jahrzehnte im Nahen Orient. Aufzeichnungen*, ed. [E.] von Steinitz (Berlin, 1927), 266–7. Griesinger, Giesl's German colleague, claimed that Paču did not read the note: see tel. Griesinger to Auswärtiges Amt (no. 30), 24 July 1914, *DD* I, no. 139. According to L. Albertini, *The Origins of the War of 1914* (3 vols., London, 1953) II, 285, Paču hesitated to receive the document into his hands, whereupon Giesl left it on the table. There is no evidence of this.

earned him an immediate rebuke from the Ballhausplatz. Austria-Hungary's step was a démarche, and the term 'ultimatum' was wholly inappropriate, he was told. If, on expiry of the deadline, the Serbian government did not accept Vienna's demands, relations between the two states would be broken off, but a state of war would only exist after a formal declaration of war, or following a Serbian attack on Austro-Hungarian territory.[4] It is difficult to establish with certainty whether this was merely legal sophistry to maintain the pretence of pacific intentions, or whether Berchtold somehow hoped, at this late hour, that a military conflict could still be averted. If so, it stood in sharp contrast to his previous statements; and it was certainly not a view shared by others in Vienna.

Count Hoyos thinks of Alexander the Great

With the note delivered at Belgrade, the reaction of the other Powers would now decide the course of the next events. While German diplomacy moved to localize any Austro-Serbian conflict, Berchtold's contribution was yet another attempt to influence particularly British official and public opinion. On his suggestion, Hoyos contacted Viscount Haldane, Britain's Lord Chancellor, whom he knew from his days at the London embassy. The product partly of Göttingen and partly of Balliol, the lawyer-philosopher Haldane was widely thought to be sympathetic towards the two Germanic Powers.[5]

Hoyos's fifteen-page letter was dated 20 July, though he had composed it a good five days earlier, and the extant evidence would suggest that it was delivered to Haldane just at the moment when ambassador Mensdorff informed the Foreign Office of the impending démarche on 23 July. Hoyos had lost none of his hawkishness. Vienna was resolved to have its war, he explained to his confidant, the constitutional lawyer and historian Josef Redlich. And, he added, '[i]f it leads to world war, then it is all the same to us.' Germany supported the move; and, said with a touch of flippancy: 'If our army fails, then the Monarchy cannot be preserved, because it is the only unifying element of the empire.'[6]

[4] Tel. Berchtold to Giesl (no. 83), 23 July 1914, ÖUA VIII, no. 10521.

[5] Haldane's innocent comment that Germany was his 'intellectual home' later made him the target of Britain's 'super-patriots': see S. E. Koss, *Lord Haldane: Scapegoat for Liberalism* (New York and London, 1969), 133–4.

[6] Redlich diary, 15 July 1914, F. Fellner (ed.), *Schicksalsjahre Österreichs. Das politische Tagebuch Josef Redlichs, 1908–1919* (2 vols., Graz and Cologne, 1953) I, 237.

None of this, of course, made it into the letter to Britain's Lord Chancellor. Hoyos prefaced his letter with the observation that in light of the now proven Serb connections of the Sarajevo assassins, 'no other way was open to us but to try and force Servia to renounce her ambitions on our territory and to suppress the [anti-Habsburg] agitation'. The letter conveyed a carefully and cleverly constructed argument that was meant to appeal to Haldane's – and the British Cabinet's – liberal instincts and appreciation of Britain's wider international interests, and to engender sympathy for Austria-Hungary's predicament. Berchtold's *chef de cabinet* sought to anchor his government's position firmly in international law. The Powers had recognized at the Berlin congress in 1878 that only the Habsburg Empire was capable of dealing with the administrative and political problems of Bosnia-Herzegovina. There was no officially sanctioned racial or religious discrimination in the two provinces, in sharp contrast to most other Balkan states, where Christian majority rule was usually accompanied by official or at any rate government-sponsored suppression of religious and ethnic minorities. Vienna had given Bosnia-Herzegovina 'a very liberal constitution', Hoyos asserted, and a clear majority of Serbs, Croats and Bosniaks in the provincial diet loyally supported Habsburg rule.

Since the coup in Serbia in 1903, however, Belgrade had sponsored an anti-Austro-Hungarian agitation which aimed at bringing about 'a revolution in Bosnia-Herzegovina and our other Southern Slav provinces' at a moment advantageous to Serbia. The recent wars in the region had fuelled pan-Serb nationalism at all levels of Serbian society and had given rise to an impression 'that Austria is too weak to interfere in the Balkan struggle and that she will fall to pieces as soon as the great day dawns when Russia decides to plant her flag on the Carpathian mountains'. The Sarajevo assassins, Hoyos explained, belonged to *Narodna Odbrana* (the connection with Apis and the 'Black Hand', of course, had not yet been uncovered by Austro-Hungarian investigators); they had been equipped and trained by Serbian officers and smuggled across the frontier by customs officials: 'About 40 people were in the plot and our poor Archduke had 6 more bomb throwers and Assassins waiting for him in case he escaped the first two' (he had, of course, already passed the six would-be assassins when he was shot).

Behind 'all these deadly intrigues', Hoyos asserted, loomed Russia. The latter was not only the self-appointed protector of the Southern Slavs but also a disturbing force 'as the missionary of militant orthodoxy in Galicia and Hungary'. It was Russia's ambition 'to destroy Austria-Hungary to bar any interference in the future when Russia decides to go to Constantinople and further'. Under these circumstances Austria-Hungary could no longer remain passive but had to act 'to break through the chain of iron that is being forged to bind and destroy us'. Vienna had to act 'even at the risk of a general European war breaking out', for the Monarchy's existence was now in danger. Remaining passive in the face of such deadly challenges meant 'signing her [Austria-Hungary's] own death-warrant'. The British, however, Hoyos concluded with a flourish, also had to understand the wider consequences of Russia's supremacy in the Balkans and Near East. Thus secure in her back and flanks, she would follow 'the example of Alexander the Great and turn ... her eyes towards India'. The problems faced by Austria-Hungary were thus 'world wide problems and I cant [sic] help hoping that their vital importance for Europe, for our culture and western tradition will be realized in England'.[7] Ambassador Mensdorff and his staff, meanwhile, resumed working on liberal-leaning journalists such as Spender of the *Westminster Gazette* by supplying him with further information on Serbian misdemeanours and by underlining Austria-Hungary's hitherto patient and reasonable attitude.[8]

Pašić contemplates a trip to the sea and returns home

Despite Paču's protestations during the meeting with Giesl, neither the note nor its sharply worded contents came as a complete surprise to the Belgrade government, even though Pašić himself may have expected the Powers to intervene to defuse the crisis. From the beginning, moreover, it was clear that Serbia was determined to resist the Austro-Hungarian demands.[9] Undoubtedly, reported Vasili'i Nikola'evich von Strandtmann, in charge of the Russian legation at Belgrade since Hartwig had met with his unfortunate end at Giesl's residence on 10 July, a quarrel with the Habsburg Empire was not desirable for Serbia at the present juncture. The kingdom

---

[7] Hoyos to Haldane, 20 July 1914, Haldane MSS, NLS, MS 5910. Mensdorff officially informed Grey that a note would be submitted on 23 July: see Grey to de Bunsen (no. 121), 23 July 1914, BD XI, no. 66. There is an interesting parallel here between the perception of a Russian threat in the Matscheko-Hoyos memorandum of 5 July and Hoyos's letter to Haldane.

[8] See memo. Spender, n.d. [Aug. 1914], Spender MSS, BL, Add. MSS. 46392, fos. 168–9.

[9] Since the publication of Albertini's work it has usually been asserted that, on the contrary, Belgrade was ready to submit to the demands: see esp. Albertini, *Origins* II, 351–3. But Albertini's argument is based on the writings of the not altogether reliable Italian journalist, Luciano Magrini, who had pronounced pro-Serb proclivities: see L. Magrini, *Il dramma di Sarajevo. Origine e responsabilità della guerra europea* (Milan, 1929), 203–4.

was in the process of consolidating the gains made during the two Balkans wars. Only after this had been accomplished would Belgrade embark upon the next phase of its national mission, the unification of all Serbs under the roof of the Karadjordjević monarchy and with secure access to the Adriatic. Strandtmann nevertheless detected a certain unease in Belgrade court and government circles. From a Habsburg perspective, he had been told by the Regent, Crown Prince Aleksandar, it would be foolish if Vienna exploited the Sarajevo affair 'to make unacceptable demands [on Serbia] and so start a military conflict'. Even so, Strandtmann was certain that Belgrade would accept all demands, 'provided they can somehow be reconciled with the dignity of a sovereign state'.[10]

The chargé's confident prognostication had been made a few hours before Giesl communicated his government's demands. However, he soon had reason to change his mind. Immediately after Giesl had left him, Paču contacted Strandtmann: '[Paču] requests Russia's protection and declares that no Serbian government could comply with the demands made of it'.[11] The remaining members of the government still in Belgrade then assembled to discuss the note and Serbia's response. It was a heated and emotionally charged meeting. Like Pašić, Paču seems to have expected Germany to exercise a moderating influence on her ally. There was, as Gruić later recalled, 'a deathly silence' in the room. Too weighty was the responsibility for prejudging the response to the démarche. In the end it was Ljuba Jovanović, the minister of education, who first broke the silence: 'After several times pacing the length of the spacious room, he stopped and said: "We have no other choice but to fight it out."'[12] He was certain, he reflected a decade later, that even the complete and unreserved acceptance of the demands would not have settled the matter. Fulfilling the obligations thus undertaken, he reasoned, would have given rise later on to innumerable complications 'which would in the end have had to be settled by war'.[13]

Indeed, military preparations were taken that same night. They fell well short of full mobilization, but were certainly preliminary steps

---

[10] Strandtmann to Sazonov (no. 41), 10/23 July 1914, *IBZI* v, no. 9. On the sense of nervousness at Belgrade see also Griesinger to Bethmann Hollweg, 21 July 1914, *DD* I, no. 137.

[11] Tel. Strandtmann to Sazonov (no. 207), 10/23 July 1914, *IBZI* v, no. 10; see also Mark Cornwall's magisterial account of decision-making at Belgrade, 'Serbia', in K. M. Wilson (ed.), *Decisions for War, 1914* (London, 1995), 72–84.

[12] As quoted in Albertini, *Origins* II, 346. Gruić's memoirs were first published in *Politika*, 22–26 July 1934; they are not entirely reliable in all details: see Cornwall, 'Serbia', 92, n. 113.

[13] As quoted in Albertini, *Origins* II, 347.

towards it. The country's underdeveloped railway network certainly made such measures necessary, as did the fact that some four-fifths of the entire Serbian army, around 65,000 men, were deployed on policing duties in the newly acquired territories in the south, populated primarily by ethnic Albanians and Bulgar-speaking Macedonians who were generally considered to be unreliable. At the same time, recruits from those same areas formed the bulk of the regiments currently garrisoned in pre-1912 'old Serbia'. Given that almost all regiments were at that moment deployed outside their home districts, full mobilization and the call-up of reserves presented significant organizational and logistical difficulties. Already on 3 July, anticipating an escalation with Austria, the war minister, General Dušan Stefanović, had ordered half the regimental officers in the south to return to their divisional bases in the north. Now regimental commanders were instructed to set up assembly points in preparation for full mobilization; railway officials were put on alert; divisional staff officers were recalled to duty; and the Chief of the General Staff, *voivode* (or Field Marshal) Radomir Putnik, who was taking the waters in the Styrian spa town of Bad Gleichenberg, was ordered to return to Belgrade.[14]

Given Serbia's precarious military position, these measures were sensible precautions. Any surprise strike by the Austro-Hungarian army across the Sava and the Danube rivers, as Alexandar stressed in conversation with Strandtmann, would have disrupted the later mobilization of four divisions, around a third of Serbia's armed forces.[15] There was the risk, however, that the preliminary measures might be judged to be provocative in Vienna and elsewhere in Europe. Whatever the risks these steps contained, the preparations underlined the extent to which Belgrade was prepared to resist Austro-Hungarian pressure. A circular telegram to Serbia's representatives abroad, issued by Paču that same night, reinforced this line of resistance. The demands contained in the Austro-Hungarian note were 'such that no Serbian government could accept them in full'.[16] The last two words were an important qualification that was to establish the parameters of Serbia's strategy for dealing with the altered situation.

The most pressing concern for Paču and the other ministers, however, was to persuade Pašić to return to Belgrade. Just as the delivery of the

---

[14] For full details see R. Kiszling, 'Die serbische Mobilmachung im Juli 1914', *BMH* x, 7 (1932), 674–86. Kiszling had served as a general staff officer during the war, and later became one of the most distinguished Austrian military historians.

[15] Strandtmann to Sazonov (no. 42), 24 July/6 Aug. 1914, *IBZI* v, app. 5. The despatch was sent from Niš where the Serbian government had retreated on 26 July.

[16] Tel. Paču to all Serbian missions, 24 July 1914, *DSP* vii/2, no. 498. This line was prefigured by Pašić: see tel. Pašić to missions abroad, 6/19 July 1914, *APS* i, no. 408.

note had a curious epilogue for Giesl, so it had for the Serbian government. For the prime minister had no intention of heading back to Belgrade. His decision to leave the capital in the morning of 23 July shortly before the expected communication by Giesl had been odd to begin with, however pressing the prime minister's electioneering commitments might have been. There were three campaign stops before Pašić reached Niš in central Serbia for the main rally that day. Afterwards he turned to his entourage and suggested that they should have a break from the strenuous campaigning routine by taking themselves off to Salonika (now Thessaloniki) where they could remain incognito for a few days. Instructions were duly issued for Pašić's carriage to be coupled onto the express train bound for the Greek port city. While the prime minister was waiting for the train to arrive, he was called to the stationmaster's office to take an important telephone call. It was Paču, who informed him of Giesl's request to make his communication at 6 p.m., and begged him to return to Belgrade. But Pašić was not to be swayed. The matter could wait, he decided, and he would not listen to Paču's warning that 'the note was not to be an ordinary note'. And with that the Salonika express pulled out of Niš station, and Pašić and his entourage set off on their journey. At the next stop, at Leskovac, some twenty-five miles south of Niš, the stationmaster there hurried along the train to hand over a personal telegram from the Regent requesting Pašić's immediate return. Thus a reluctant prime minister headed back to the capital. Attempts by the foreign ministry to make contact with him at various intermediate stations all failed.[17]

The decision to abandon campaigning and head to the Aegean had clearly not been taken on the spur of the moment. His motivation, however, is less clear. He may, as Albertini suggested, have hoped that his absence would gain Serbia some time before replying to the Austro-Hungarian note, thus opening up the possibility of foreign intervention in the quarrel. Since Pašić's initial efforts following his eventual return to Belgrade were aimed at lifting the time limit of the démarche, it may well be that his planned Salonikan sojourn was part of this strategy. On the other hand, the wily survivor of internecine Serbian politics may have sought to evade being tarnished with receiving the ultimatum and any decisions the government would take. Plausible deniability with the ultra-nationalists in the military and their supporters in press and parliament was a valuable political commodity at Belgrade.

Pašić returned to the capital in the early hours of 24 July, looking 'very anxious and dejected',[18] to preside over two cabinet meetings that

[17] Gruić memoirs, as quoted in Albertini, *Origins* II, 347.
[18] Tel. Crackanthorpe to Grey (no. 49, urgent), 24 July 1914, *BD* XI, no. 92.

day, at 10 a.m. and again in the afternoon. The most pressing issue to be addressed was the time limit attached to the Austro-Hungarian démarche. Pašić and the ministers realized that the deadline could only be extended, if not altogether lifted, with the support of other Powers. Serbia's predicament was serious, as Pašić explained to Strandtmann after the first ministerial meeting. The note could neither be accepted nor rejected: 'they had to gain time at all costs'. In the meantime, he would seek the approval of the Skupština (the parliament) to suspend the general election so that his hands would be free to deal with the external crisis; the government meanwhile might be evacuated to Kruševac in central Serbia.[19]

While Pašić and his ministers wrestled with the difficult decisions before them, the Regent, Prince Alexandar, played a significant role in the background. From the outset he took a defiant stance, albeit one tempered by his knowledge of the poor state of the Serbian army. It was at the prince's suggestion that the ministers agreed, at the afternoon cabinet meeting, to appeal to King Victor Emmanuel III of Italy, the Regent's uncle, to mediate between Vienna and Belgrade with a view to securing an extension of the ultimatum. The terms of the note were 'unnecessarily humiliating', and the Regent hoped that 'the harshest conditions be mitigated'.[20] Alexandar had also issued an appeal to Tsar Nicholas earlier that same day. In tone and composition the two texts are very similar. But the appeal to the ruler of all the Russias contained a separate concluding paragraph. In it Alexandar laid on flattery with an imperial-sized trowel and in elaborate language calculated to resonate with feelings of Slav solidarity: 'Your Majesty has given us ample proof of your valuable benevolence, and we are hopeful that this appeal will echo in your Slavic and generous heart. I make myself the translator of the sentiments of the Serbian people who, at this fateful moment, beseech Your Majesty gracefully to engage yourself in the affairs of Serbia.'[21]

After these first diplomatic and military steps, there was little that Belgrade could do now but to wait. Pašić was by no means confident that Russia more especially would aid Serbia in a quarrel with Austria-Hungary. Izvolsky's ignominious retreat in March 1909 and Sazonov's

---

[19] Tels. Strandtmann to Sazonov (nos. 213 and 214), 11/24 July 1914, *IBZI* v, nos. 35–6.
[20] Tel. Cora to San Giuliano (no. 794/153), 24 July 1914, *DDI* (4) XII, no. 473. The appeal to Italy had already been discussed at the morning cabinet: see *IBZI* v, no. 36. Pašić addressed a similar appeal to the British government after the morning's cabinet meeting: tel. Crackanthorpe to Grey (no. 49, urgent), 24 July 1914, *BD* XI, no. 92; and more emphatic in tel. Pašić to Bošković, 24 July 1914, *DSP* VII/2, no. 502.
[21] As transmitted in tel. Strandtmann to Sazonov (no. 215), 11/24 July 1914, *IBZI* v, no. 37 (also in *DSP* VII/2, no. 505).

lukewarm support during the last Austro-Serbian stand-off in 1913 had evidently not been forgotten. Pašić and his ministerial colleagues, hinted the envoy at Vienna, Jovan Jovanović, were plagued by doubts that Russian diplomacy would remain firm.[22] Lack of confidence in Russia's firmness also explains the almost submissive language used by Pašić, but also by Alexandar, in their conversations with Strandtmann. Calling on the Russian chargé d'affaires before the first cabinet council on 24 July, Pašić explained that his own 'fidelity to Russia unmistakably made him conclude that only Russia could save Serbia'.[23] Doubts about Russia's willingness to aid Serbia against Austria-Hungary were by no means without foundation. Certainly, Sazonov's initial advice, transmitted by Strandtmann and Spalajković on 24 July, did not appear especially encouraging. Given Serbia's military inferiority, Belgrade ought not to resist but withdraw southwards, permit the occupation of the country by Austria-Hungary and then appeal to the Powers for assistance.[24]

Sazonov makes two telephone calls

Sazonov was, in fact, far from advising Belgrade to yield to Austro-Hungarian pressure. If anything, he may have been misled by an oblique observation by Spalajković into believing that the Serbian government had already decided upon evacuating much of the country before the advancing Habsburg army.[25] And his advice was certainly no indication of Russia's likely response to the escalation of the Austro-Serbian quarrel. According to Baron Schilling, the director of chancellery, Strandtmann's telegram informing the Choristers' Bridge of the ultimatum arrived at St Petersburg in the early hours of 24 July. Schilling himself then telephoned the ambassadors Izvolsky and Shebeko, currently on leave and in the capital, to return to their posts without delay. The foreign minister himself arrived at 10 a.m. from Tsarskoe Selo. The overnight news from Belgrade made a strong impression on him, 'and he said spontaneously: "*C'est la guerre européenne.*"' He then put through a telephone call to the palace – the first

[22] In conversation with the French ambassador there: see tel. Dumaine to Bienvenu-Martin (no. 109), 25 July 1914, *DDF* (3) XI, no. 55.

[23] Strandtmann to Sazonov (no. 42), 24 July/6 Aug. 1914, *IBZI* V, app. 5; see also Cornwall, 'Serbia', 75.

[24] Tel. Sazonov to Strandtmann (no. 1487, personal), 11/24 July 1914, *IBZI* V, no. 22; tel. Spalajković to Pašić, 25 July 1914, *DSP* VII/2, no. 503.

[25] See Sazonov's explanations to Buchanan, tel. Buchanan to Grey (no. 169, very confidential), 25 July 1914, *BD* XI, no. 125.

time he had used the instrument – to report personally to the Tsar. The monarch's response was a little more placid than his foreign minister's outburst, but there was no mistaking that he, too, was disturbed: '"This is outrageous!", and ordered to be kept informed.'[26] According to Pyotr Lvovich Bark, the finance minister who was with the Tsar at that moment, Sazonov used rather more emphatic language than Schilling's journal suggests. Sazonov suspected German connivance in the Austro-Hungarian move, and suggested that the two Germanic Powers were intent upon war now while they enjoyed a degree of military superiority over France and Russia.[27]

While Sazonov was reporting to his imperial master, Schilling arranged for a ministerial council meeting to take place that same afternoon; senior foreign ministry officials were recalled from leave, and he impressed upon Bark, who had just returned from the palace, to withdraw any state funds currently deposited in German banks.[28] Then Szápáry called at the Choristers' Bridge to submit a copy of the note addressed to Belgrade. This gave rise to a heated conversation with the minister that lasted for an hour-and-a-half. Sazonov declined to comment on the démarche lest he prejudice Russia's official response, but he did not hide what he really thought: 'I know what it is. You want to make war on Serbia! I see what is going on – the German papers encourage you. *Vous mettez le feu à l'Europe* [You are setting Europe on fire].' He criticized Vienna for having issued its demands in the form of an ultimatum, and described the demands made as unacceptable. As for the evidence produced by the official Austro-Hungarian investigation, he dismissed this as 'the policy of Count Forgách' – shades of the Friedjung trial again. If Sazonov used language that was not particularly well-tempered, the impression he left on the Habsburg ambassador was nevertheless 'more one of depression than of violent excitement'.[29]

Given his earlier warnings it was scarcely surprising that much of Sazonov's ire appeared reserved for the form of the démarche. Serbia was not given an opportunity to disprove the allegations made against her by the Habsburg government. This, in turn, suggested that Vienna was not interested in establishing the facts, with the clear implication that

---

[26] Schilling daily journal, 11/24 July 1914, *IBZI* v, no. 25.
[27] Bark memoirs, as quoted in D. C. B. Lieven, *Russia and the Origins of the First World War* (London, 1983), 141.
[28] Schilling daily journal, 11/24 July 1914, *IBZI* v, no. 25.
[29] Tel. Szápáry to Berchtold (no. 156), 24 July 1914 (D 3.35 p.m., R 11 p.m.), *ÖUA* VIII, no. 10616; also tel. Carlotti to San Giuliano (no. 818/8), 25 July 1914 (D 3.45 p.m., R 6.45 p.m.), *DDI* (4) XII, no. 519.

Austria-Hungary was bent on war: 'It means that you want war and you have burnt your bridges.' As instructed, Szápáry sought to appeal to a sense of conservative, monarchical solidarity, but this was given short shrift by Sazonov: 'The monarchical idea has nothing to do with this.' Indeed, Szápáry noted that the foreign minister did not once mention Russia, Slavdom and Orthodox Christianity – the holy trinity of pan-Slavism – but continually emphasized the bad impression the Austro-Hungarian move would make on Britain, France and Europe at large.[30]

If the Habsburg ambassador found Sazonov hostile, the Russian foreign minister's firm response had no effect on Vienna. The Ballhausplatz continued to conduct diplomacy by dissimulation. When Kudashev, acting on his pre-ultimatum instructions, called on Berchtold in the morning of 24 July, the foreign minister did his mellifluous best repeatedly to assure the chargé d'affaires that the note was not meant to humiliate Belgrade: 'Nothing could be further from our minds than to wish to humiliate Serbia; we have not the slightest interest in this.' Indeed, Berchtold suggested that he had personally eliminated from earlier drafts of the note any passages that could have given rise to the impression that this was Austria-Hungary's objective. Kudashev was clearly worried about the wider ramifications of the note. How would Vienna respond if the Serbian answer failed to satisfy its expectations? On Berchtold's reply that Giesl and his legation staff would then leave the Serbian capital, Kudashev replied: '*Alors c'est la guerre.*'[31]

In St Petersburg, meanwhile, Paléologue, the French ambassador, exhausted after the previous night's farewell banquet for Poincaré, had given instructions to be left undisturbed the next morning. It was not to be. At 7 a.m. his valet woke him with the news of the ultimatum. At first, he later recalled, in his half-awake state the news 'produced a strange sensation of surprise and authenticity; the event appeared to me at one and the same time unreal and certain, imaginary and authentic'.[32] The ambassador soon rallied, cancelled his other engagements that morning, and invited Sazonov to luncheon with him at the embassy at 12.30 p.m. to confer about the situation. The foreign minister meanwhile decided

---

[30] Tels. Szápáry to Berchtold (nos. 157 and 159), 24 July 1914 (D 7.20 p.m. and 8 p.m., R 12.50 a.m. and 7 a.m.), *ÖUA* VIII, nos. 10617 and 10619. It is not entirely clear why the ambassador reported the interview in three separate telegrams.

[31] Berchtold daily report, 24 July 1914, *ÖUA* VIII, no. 10615; cf. tels. Kudashev to Sazonov (nos. 90 and 91), 11/24 July 1914, *IBZI* V, nos. 31–2. Kudashev stuck closely to his earlier instructions: see tel. Sazonov to Shebeko (no. 1475), 9/22 July 1914, *ibid.* IV, no. 322.

[32] Paléologue diary, 24 July 1914, M. Paléologue, *La Russie des Tsars pendant la grande guerre* (3 vols., Paris, 1921) I, 22–3.

that someone else ought to be present as well. As Buchanan, the British ambassador, later recalled:

> [I was] sitting in my study the next morning (the 24th) musing on all that I was going to do during my approaching holiday, [when] I was roused by the ringing of the telephone. 'Who's there?' I asked. 'I, Sazonoff', was the reply. 'Austria has presented an ultimatum at Belgrade couched in terms which mean war. Please meet me at the French embassy in an hour's time as I must discuss matters with you and Paléologue.'[33]

Since Poincaré and Viviani were now out of telegraphic reach, a great burden rested on the French ambassador's shoulders. But the situation also gave him greater opportunity to act as he saw fit. According to his memoirs, Paléologue led the discussions. Taking his stand on the toasts exchanged between the Tsar and his president only a little over twelve hours earlier, and emphasizing the identity of French and Russian views, he urged a policy of firmness. On Sazonov's observation that such a policy might lead to war, the ambassador replied that conflict would ensue only if Berlin and Vienna were resolved to use force to secure 'hegemony in the East. Firmness does not exclude conciliation. But it is essential that the other side is prepared to negotiate and to compromise.' The Austro-Hungarian ultimatum had, however, created a dangerous crisis, and war was now a distinct possibility: 'And that perspective must dominate all our diplomatic moves.'[34]

In his official report Paléologue gave a characteristically bland and tame account of the conversation. Little of what he recorded in his diary comes as a surprise; much of it, in fact, reflected the views he and Poincaré had held for some time. That he advocated a hard line against the two Germanic powers is beyond doubt. Indeed, he impressed on Buchanan that France 'would not only give Russia strong diplomatic support but would, if necessary fulfil all the obligations imposed on her by the alliance'. It may, however, be doubted whether the Russian foreign minister was quite as hesitant and indecisive as Paléologue made him appear in his diary. According to Buchanan, Sazonov took a more hawkish line from the outset. The Austro-Serbian dispute was part of a wider problem, he asserted, and he 'personally thought that Russia would at any rate have to mobilise'. Sazonov, forcefully assisted by their host Paléologue, pressed

---

[33] Sir G. Buchanan, *My Mission to Russia and Other Diplomatic Memories* (2 vols., London, 1923) I, 189.
[34] Paléologue diary, 24 July 1914, in his *Russie des Tsars* I, 23.

the British ambassador, who took a more non-committal stance, to declare London's solidarity with France and Russia: 'If war did break out, we [Britain] would sooner or later be dragged into it, but if we did not make common cause with France and Russia from the outset we should have rendered war more likely, and we should not have played a "beau rôle".' This, of course, was the familiar refrain of Franco-Russian diplomacy during recent years, and can have come as no surprise to Buchanan or the Foreign Office. Significantly, the ambassador added that his French colleague's language 'almost looked as if France and Russia were determined to make a strong stand even if we declined to join them. Language of Minister for Foreign Affairs, however, was not so (? decided) on this subject.'[35]

It is impossible to reconstruct with absolute certainty who said what and in what order. What matters in the wider context of the July crisis is that Paléologue, unfettered for now by instructions from Paris, urged Russia to take a hard line from the outset, and that Sazonov inclined to that view himself. Their hawkish stance thus contributed to the further escalation of the crisis. Buchanan's concluding reflections, meanwhile, indicated the constraints placed on British diplomacy by this latest turn of events, but they also suggested opportunities. French support for restraining Russia might not be had any more, but Buchanan had clearly detected some uncertainty on Sazonov's part, and that gave British policy something with which to work towards a peaceful outcome of the crisis.

Sazonov demands mobilization and confusion ensues

Whatever impression he had made on the British ambassador, that Sazonov supported an energetic response is beyond doubt. Already before the meeting at the French embassy, the foreign minister had contacted General Nikolai Nikola'evich Yanushkevich, the Chief of the General Staff. The Serbian crisis, he explained, might force Russia to take a more robust stance, and Yanushkevich was asked to prepare plans for a partial mobilization against Austria-Hungary alone.[36] Sazonov developed this line more

---

[35] Tel. Buchanan to Grey (no. 166, urgent), 24 July 1914 (D 5.40 p.m., R 8 p.m.), *BD* XI, no. 101; Paléologue's report is devoid of all content: tel. Paléologue to Bienvenu-Martin (no. 281), 24 July 1914 (D 2.45 p.m., R 6.55 p.m.), *DDF* (3) XI, no. 19.

[36] Yanushkevich related the conversation with Sazonov to General Sergei K. Dobrorolski, head of the mobilization department of the General Staff: S. Dobrorolski, *Die Mobilmachung der russischen Armee* (Berlin, 1922), 17–18. The oral nature of the evidence may explain the confusion about the precise timing of the conversation,

fully at the ministerial council, which commenced at three o'clock that same afternoon and was opened by the foreign minister with a lengthy exposition on the situation created by Austria-Hungary's démarche. He laid particular stress on its form as an ultimatum, and on the fact that the demands contained in the note were unacceptable for any sovereign state. As Belgrade had appealed to Russia for assistance, it was now for the government to fashion a response to the crisis.[37] Sazonov, however, left his fellow ministers in no doubt that the Austro-Serbian quarrel was part of a wider international problem. He underlined Germany's 'systematic preparations' in recent years, which were aimed at strengthening her position and allowing her to project her power 'in all international questions'.[38] In essence this was a more elaborate version of the arguments he had deployed in conversation with Buchanan and Paléologue at lunchtime. It was almost as though this had been a dress-rehearsal for the council meeting afterwards.

Russia had shown great moderation in her dealings with Berlin, Sazonov pointed out, but this had been interpreted there as a sign of weakness 'and far from having prevented our neighbours from using aggressive methods, we had encouraged them'. Behind the Austro-Hungarian démarche stood Germany. If Serbia were coerced into compliance, it would turn the kingdom into a satellite of the two Germanic Powers, thus further increasing Berlin's ability to throw its weight about. Russia therefore had to take a firm line now. If she failed to aid Serbia, her prestige and influence in the Balkans would be lost and her standing among the Powers much reduced. Acquiescing in the Austro-German move would do little to preserve peace but merely encourage Germany to challenge Russian interests again in the near future. There was no alternative now but to take a firm line, even though such a stance entailed the risk of war, itself incalculable in its consequences 'since it was not known what attitude Great Britain would take in the matter'.

The agriculture minister, Aleksandar Vasilevich Krivoshein, spoke next. His, to modern eyes, lowly ministerial position was, in fact, anything but that. Given the importance of the agricultural sector for Russia's economic development and her social stability, his portfolio was one of the most important in the government; and given Krivoshein's undoubted successes in implementing the various agrarian reform schemes, his

which Dobrorolski gives as 11 a.m. According to Szápáry's reports, by contrast, Sazonov was then still locked into his heated interview with himself.

[37] Minutes of Ministerial Council, 11/24 July 1914, *IBZI* v, no. 19.

[38] This and what follows is based on Bark's unpublished memoirs, as quoted in Lieven, *Russia*, 141–3.

influence extended well beyond his ministerial remit. A skilled political operator, he was one of the most powerful figures at St Petersburg, a position which was further enhanced by his close ties with the Tsar himself and some of the nationalist circles in the Duma.[39] Krivoshein's statement, judiciously balancing the various aspects of the current situation, 'made a profound impression' on the other ministers, as Bark later recalled. Indeed, it was Krivoshein's speech that 'was the most instrumental in influencing our decisions'. He was by no means blind to the risks. Despite Russia's recent military advances and her greater financial stability, he doubted that the Russian armed forces would ever match those of the two Germanic Powers – in terms of cultural and industrial development the country lagged too far behind the rest of Europe. Even so, vital Russian interests were at stake in the present quarrel, and the public and political forces in the Duma would not tolerate a passive attitude by the government. 'No one in Russia desired war', he said. The events of 1904–5 had underlined the grave risks of external complications for Russia. Russia's response to the unfolding crisis should therefore 'aim at reducing the possibility of a European war', and he hinted at the need for conciliation. At the same time, remaining passive would not help to secure Russia's interests, and therefore he favoured a strongly worded response: 'All factors tended to prove that the most judicious policy Russia could follow in present circumstances was a return to a firmer and more energetic attitude towards the unreasonable claims of the Central European powers.'

After Krivoshein, the two service ministers, General Vladimir Aleksandrovich Sukhomlinov and Rear-Admiral Ivan Konstantinovich Grigorovich, were called upon to give their views. Both concurred that, whilst the respective army and navy armaments programmes had not yet been completed, there were no obstacles 'to a display of greater firmness in our diplomatic negotiations'. Then Bark spoke. He was close to Krivoshein, and although he had some doubts about the country's economic and financial ability to sustain a major war effort, he too agreed with the need for a firm line.

When the meeting broke up at around 6 p.m., the ministers had decided on a programme of action. In the first place, Sazonov was to seek the cooperation of the other Powers to secure an extension of the Austro-Hungarian ultimatum to Serbia so that the Powers could then examine the evidence produced by the official investigation into the Sarajevo murders.

---

[39] K. A. Krivoshein, *Aleksandr Vasil'evich Krivoshein: sud'ba rossi'iskogo reformatora* (Moscow, 1993) and K. A. Krivoshein, *A. V. Krivoshein 1857–1921 g[od]: ego znachenie v istorii Rossii nachala XX veka* (Paris, 1973); also R. Pearson, *The Russian Moderates and the Crisis of Tsarism, 1914–1917* (London, 1977), 13–14.

Sazonov was further to advise Belgrade not to resist any invasion of Serbia but to 'entrust her fate to the decision of the Great Powers'. These diplomatic moves were to be underpinned by military preparations, and the war and navy ministers were instructed to obtain the Tsar's approval for the mobilization of the military districts of Kiev, Odessa, Moscow and Kazan as well as the Baltic and Black Sea squadrons 'in accordance with the further course of events'. Finally, Sukhomlinov was ordered to stock up the army's stores of provisions, and Bark – as already suggested by Schilling earlier in the day – was to withdraw state funds deposited in German and Austrian banks.[40]

Immediately after the council meeting Sazonov met with Spalajković, the Serbian envoy, who had hastened back to St Petersburg from his summer retreat on the northern shores of the Gulf of Finland. The interview is highly instructive, both in terms of Russian calculations and, as will be seen, Serbia's eventual response to the Austro-Hungarian ultimatum. According to the envoy's report, Sazonov left him in no doubt that no sovereign state could accept the démarche, and he condemned the note in the strongest terms. Russia would take 'energetic steps' and Belgrade could rely on her support. What precisely these steps were, Sazonov did not specify; nor did he give a clear indication of how far Russia would go in her support for Serbia. According to Schilling's daily journal, moreover, the foreign minister counselled the Belgrade government to show 'extreme moderation' in its response to the Austro-Hungarian note.[41] He further advised the Serbs, as agreed by the ministerial council, not to offer any military resistance, and instead to appeal to the Powers for assistance.[42] Altogether Sazonov's comments to Spalajković were vague and not entirely consistent. Whilst he acknowledged that Vienna's demands were unacceptable, his advice appeared anything but hardline. Far from urging the Serbs to resist Habsburg pressure, he seemed to suggest that they ought to yield and then appeal to the Powers. Alternatively, he suggested that, 'with a view to England's special position', the Pašić government should turn to London for mediation in the dispute with Austria-Hungary.[43] It is true that in a later telegram, received at Belgrade in the late morning of 25 July, Spalajković indicated that Russia might mobilize and that an official pro-Serbian

---

[40] Minutes of the Ministerial Council, 11/24 July 1914, *IBZI* v, no. 19.
[41] Tel. Spalajković to Pašić, 24 July 1914, *DSP* vii/2, no. 527; Schilling daily journal, 11/24 July 1914, *IBZI* v, no. 25; also M. Spalajković, 'Une journée du ministre de Serbie à Petrograd. Le 24 juillet 1914', *RHD* xlviii, 1 (1934), 143.
[42] Tel. Sazonov to Strandtmann (no. 1487, personal), 11/24 July 1914, *IBZI* v, no. 22.
[43] Tel. Sazonov to Strandtmann (no. 1494), 12/25 July 1914, *ibid.*, no. 49.

declaration might be issued at St Petersburg.[44] Even so, it was clear that Sazonov did not wish Serbia to complicate matters by taking a provocative stance. 'Energetic steps' were the prerogative of the Great Powers.

Sazonov underlined this during his second interview that evening, with Pourtalès, the German ambassador, at 7 p.m. The foreign minister, whom Pourtalès described as *'very excited'*, explained that Russia could not accept that the current quarrel between Vienna and Belgrade was solely for the governments there to settle. The obligations which Serbia had undertaken in 1909, and to which the Viennese note attached such importance, were obligations towards Europe, and it was therefore for the Powers to determine whether Belgrade had fulfilled them or not: 'Austria could not be judge and prosecutor in her own cause.' Sazonov, indeed, cast doubt on the reliability of the Sarajevo investigations without, however, making any overt reference to the notorious Friedjung forgeries. As with Szápáry, and in the face of Pourtalès's best efforts to appeal to Sazonov not to make common cause with regicides, the minister dismissed the suggestion that the archducal assassination was an attack on the monarchical principle. In the course of the interview he exclaimed: 'If Austria-Hungary swallows Serbia, we shall wage war against her.'[45]

There had been no hint at any military measures on Russia's part. Indeed, Pourtalès concluded that Russia would only intervene militarily in the event of Austria-Hungary annexing Serbian territory. And further, he took Sazonov's expressed desire to internationalize the Austro-Serb dispute as an indication 'that an immediate intervention by Russia is not to be expected'. The ambassador's assessment was to influence the calculations of the Wilhelmstrasse over the next few days. But in the context of the evolving Russian position, Sazonov's conversations with Spalajković and Pourtalès are very instructive. The moderating advice imparted on the former was clearly meant to defuse and insulate the Austro-Serbian quarrel as much as possible. At the same time, the firm, but not yet openly threatening language used with the German ambassador was meant to increase pressure on Berlin and, by implication, on Vienna so that a diplomatic solution – presumably on Russia's terms – could be found. It was a high-risk strategy. For its success it relied on Serbian moderation and on a precisely calibrated deterrence signal to

---

[44] Tel. Spalajković to Pašić, 25 July 1914, *DSP* VII/2, no. 503; see also Cornwall, 'Serbia', 80.

[45] Tel. Pourtalès to Auswärtiges Amt (no. 149), 25 July 1914 (D 1.08 a.m., R 3.45 a.m.), *DD* I, no. 160 (original emphasis); see also tel. Carlotti to San Giuliano (no. 818/8), 25 July 1914 (D 3.40 p.m., R 6.45 p.m.), *DDI* (4) XII, no. 519.

Germany. In the end, the former was not to be had, and the latter proved elusive – with disastrous consequences.

Sazonov had one more visitor that evening. At around 8 p.m., Paléologue called on the Choristers' Bridge. Finding that the minister was still engaged with Pourtalès, he went to see Schilling in his office as he had no wish to encounter his German colleague. Paléologue then suggested that his president's naval convoy should call, as planned, at Stockholm and Copenhagen so as to avoid any impression of panic. The argument was not without merit – though, as will be seen, Poincaré's sea voyage meant that France's ambassador at St Petersburg was to have greater influence. As for the crisis itself, Paléologue professed himself to be optimistic. Germany would not now support Austria-Hungary, he suggested. The recent speeches at Peterhof and the final communiqué issued on board the *France* the night before would act as a deterrent upon Berlin, and the German leadership now appreciated the 'serious consequences' of its support for Austria-Hungary.[46]

The deterrence aspect, then, was quite clearly well developed in Franco-Russian thinking. Sazonov reaffirmed this in his own conversation with Paléologue after Pourtalès had left the Choristers' Bridge. The German ambassador's evasions and recriminations had made an unfavourable impression on him, he told Paléologue. He had impressed upon Pourtalès the danger of the current situation without, however, alluding to the measures Russia would take 'if Serbia were threatened in her national independence or territorial integrity'. He himself would act in a moderating sense: 'Everything must be avoided ... that could precipitate the crisis. We have to let the Vienna cabinet put itself in the wrong. I think, indeed, that, should the Austro-Hungarian government take action, Serbia should withdraw without a fight and denounce Austria's infamy to the whole world.' But in the meantime, he would seek to obtain an extension of the deadline in the Austro-Hungarian ultimatum so that diplomacy could search for a solution to the crisis.[47]

In all of this, the precise nature of the deterrence element was left unspecified. An official communiqué, issued on Saturday, 25 July, sent a clear signal to Vienna and Berlin that Russia could not be ignored. The

---

[46] Schilling daily journal, 25 July 1914, *IBZI* v, no. 25. The fact that Schilling recorded the conversation as taking place in his office, out of sight of the minister's ante-chamber, puts into perspective Paléologue's own colourful references to Pourtalès parting from Sazonov, 'face flushed, eyes blazing': Paléologue diary, 24 July 1914, in his *Russie des Tsars* I, 24.

[47] Tel. Paléologue to Bienvenu-Martin (no. 283), 25 July 1914 (D 0.45 a.m., R 3.45 a.m.), *DDF* (3) XI, no. 34; Paléologue diary, 24 July 1914, in his *Russie des Tsars* I, 25–6.

imperial Russian government, it stated, 'follows attentively the development of the Serbo-Austrian conflict, with respect to which Russia cannot remain indifferent'.[48] This was clear enough. But the secretive manner in which Russian ministers implemented the military measures discussed at the ministerial council meeting in the afternoon of 24 July ensured that the intended deterrence element would remain deeply problematic. On the following day, Nicholas II accepted his ministers' proposals at an extraordinary session of the council at Krasnoe Selo. The Tsar, attired in the white summer uniform of the Guard hussars, presided over the meeting, whose setting – the dining room with french windows leading out to the park – seemed singularly inappropriate to the serious purpose of the meeting. Sazonov opened proceedings with another lengthy exposition of the situation, leaving no one in doubt that the Austro-Hungarian move was a carefully planned challenge to Russia. In contrast to the previous day's council meeting, the minister laid greater stress on Slav solidarity. Vienna's provocative step 'could only be met by means of a military demonstration, if once all diplomatic means of conciliation had failed'. According to Sukhomlinov's later recollections, Sazonov concluded by stressing that 'Russian diplomacy could now, by means of a partial mobilization against Austria, call the latter's diplomacy to order.' There was no mention, Sukhomlinov noted, of any declaration of war.[49] The Tsar, who had remained very calm throughout the meeting, then approved the mobilization of the four south-western and central military districts, and to that end, during the night of 25–26 July, an order was to be issued commencing the 'Period Preparatory to War', in practice a complex sequence of measures intended to prepare the armed forces for full-scale mobilization fixed in law in February/March 1913. Significantly, the order, and therefore the arrangements to be made subsequently, applied across the whole of European Russia, and not just the four districts specified.[50]

At a subsequent meeting of the general staff mobilization committee, General Yanushkevich, the chief of staff, impressed upon the assembled officers the need for swift action. If need be, he pointed out, it would be permissible to transgress the limitations imposed upon them by the mobilization law. Thus the pre-mobilization period for the four districts came into force. The other districts, Yanushkevich emphasized, would mobilize

---

[48] Russian communiqué, 12/25 July 1914, *IBZI* v, no. 43; see also tel. Buchanan to Grey (no. 167), 25 July 1914, *BD* xi, no. 109.

[49] V. A. Sukhomlinov, *Erinnerungen* (Berlin, 1924), 357–8.

[50] Minutes of Extraordinary Ministerial Council, 12/25 July 1914, *IBZI* v, no. 42; see also G. Frantz, *Russlands Eintritt in den Weltkrieg. Der Ausbau der russischen Wehrmacht und ihr Einsatz bei Kriegsausbruch* (Berlin, 1924), 55–6.

only if Germany 'sided with Austria, not sooner so that even greater diplomatic complications could be avoided'. Full mobilization of the four districts would commence only after an Austro-Hungarian invasion of Serbia, but no sooner than twenty-four hours after the pre-mobilization order had been issued, i.e. by 27–28 July at the earliest. As additional precautions, the maritime approaches to the Baltic fortresses of Kronstadt, Reval (now Tallin) and Sveaborg (now Suomenlinna) were to be mined and their stockpiles of artillery shells augmented. A state of siege was declared for Kronstadt, though no reserves were called up; and the frontier fortresses in the west and the fortress of Mikhailovsk, near Batum on the Black Sea, were placed on alert.[51] With the order a whole raft of dispositions came into force. All leave, for instance, was cancelled; reservists had to report to training camps rather than to their designated barracks; additional train horses were requisitioned; assembly points and depots were set up and made ready; the railways were put on alert and liaison officers despatched to key railway junctions.[52]

It would be tempting to see in these measures a deliberate escalation of the crisis.[53] The chief problem for now, however, lay in the fact that the senior military officers had failed to alert ministers to the logistical and other difficulties that any partial mobilization would create if a general mobilization became necessary at a later stage – the so-called Schedule 19 (A). As with the other continental Powers, Russia's mobilization schemes relied on the country's railways. But, in sharp contrast to the other Powers, the Russian strategic railway network was underdeveloped. The army could draw on only a handful of lines to the deployment theatres in the west and south-west. Redeploying against the German frontier some of the army groups that had already taken up position against Austria-Hungary, whilst moving the units not yet mobilized in the same direction, would overstrain Russia's railway capacity. Transport gridlock would bring general mobilization, if ordered after partial mobilization, to a grinding halt. In essence, it meant that Russia could opt for either partial or general mobilization, but she could not move from one to the other. The root cause of St Petersburg's failure to appreciate this fact was lack of professionalism. Yanushkevich, the chief of staff, and Sukhomlinov, the war minister, have

[51] Minutes of the General Staff Committee, 12/25 July 1914, *IBZI* v, no. 79.
[52] See 'Order for the Period Preparatory to War', 17 Feb./2 Mar. 1913, *ibid.*, no. 80, app.; see also Frantz, *Russlands Eintritt*, 57–60.
[53] Thus, for instance, S. McMeekin, *The Russian Origins of the First World War* (Cambridge, MA, 2011), 59–62; C. Clark, *The Sleepwalkers: How Europe Went to War in 1914* (London, 2012), 475.

rightly been singled out for blame.[54] The former, installed in his post only in March 1914, lacked the strength of character and sufficient technical knowledge to advance a coherent argument against the kind of partial mobilization pressed for by Sazonov. The war minister, meanwhile, though a former chief of staff himself, was not known for his attention to detail. A cavalryman by training and a favourite with the Tsar, he had been, as seen, a successful military reformer, but his grasp of the operational problems of mobilization was limited, and so was his advice to the ministerial council. Indeed, Dobrorolski later recalled Sukhomlinov as 'very reserved', leaving pride of place to the chief of staff.[55]

It was only later on 26 July that the problems inherent in any partial mobilization became apparent, when Yuri Nikoforovich Danilov, the Quartermaster-General in charge of the mobilization planning, returned to St Petersburg. Their practical impact on Russian policy, however, was not immediately apparent, and Sazonov himself was to veer between optimism and resignation over the next few days. The foreign minister was not noted for his steady nerves. During earlier crises he had often been irresolute, prone to yielding to external pressures at the last moment. Unsurprisingly, like Berchtold at Vienna, the more hawkish elements at home reserved their ire for him. And like Berchtold, Sazonov was not prepared to succumb again. It is also true that, as a civilian operating in an environment in which the military elements were hermetically sealed from the rest of the governmental apparatus, the foreign minister was largely ignorant of military planning.

Past irresolution and current ignorance, however, did not mean that Sazonov lacked a 'road map' for Russia's crisis diplomacy. In this context, his report to the Tsar before the extraordinary council meeting is instructive. In it he rehearsed the familiar arguments about the excessive and unacceptable nature of the Austro-Hungarian démarche, which aimed at the destruction of Serbia and the disruption of the political balance in the Balkans. Russia could therefore not remain indifferent, and complications had to be expected. But Sazonov placed the current crisis in a broader, international context. Russia, he argued, pursued an 'unselfish policy, the sole aim of which is to prevent the creation of Austrian hegemony in the Balkans'. But Habsburg dominance in south-eastern Europe would destabilize the European equilibrium. This prospect, in turn, furnished a strong basis for common action with Britain. He was hopeful London would

---

[54] Lieven, *Russia*, 145.
[55] Dobrorolski, *Mobilmachung*, 24–5. Sukhomlinov was nevertheless a talented commander, see J. W. Steinberg, *All the Tsar's Men: Russia's General Staff and the Fate of the Empire, 1898–1914* (Baltimore, MD, 2010), 100–1.

adhere to its 'centuries-old policy' of preserving the balance of power. Indeed, what is striking is the prominence Sazonov gave to Britain and his desire for closer Anglo-Russian relations.[56]

Sazonov's report to the Tsar makes it possible to trace the outlines of his diplomatic crisis strategy. He and the Tsar's other ministers had decided that a firm line offered the best guarantee of maintaining peace. Russia's crisis strategy was broadly and predictably pro-Serb; and it was based on a twin-track approach. The principal track was the diplomatic one. Vienna was to be coerced by a display of firmness into conceding an extension of the ultimatum (tellingly, Paléologue commented on the official communiqué of 25 July as the beginning of the 'process of intimidation').[57] This was to be reinforced by a parallel move aimed at Berlin. At the same time, Belgrade was to be encouraged to give a conciliatory reply to the demands. Once the time limit was removed, and the démarche thus no longer an ultimatum, the Powers could hammer out a solution. There was certainly a general sense at St Petersburg, as Tsar Nicholas II recorded in his diary, that '8 [of the Austrian demands] are unacceptable for an independent state'.[58] Taking a firm line, moreover, was also meant to force Britain to relinquish her hitherto seemingly equivocating stance and side with Russia, thus strengthening the ties with London and laying the foundations for a renewal and tightening of the 1907 accord in the near future.

There will, of course, always be an element of uncertainty in all reconstructions of Sazonov's moves. The Russian foreign minister was not particularly straightforward, and in the end perhaps only he knew what he was doing, if indeed he did know. But this interpretation fits the extant evidence, and it fits also the pattern of Russian policy in recent years. Sazonov's strategy was nevertheless deeply problematic. His protestations of Russian disinterestedness, for one thing, were somewhat disingenuous. Preventing the consolidation, let alone a strengthening, of Austria-Hungary's position in the Balkan region had greater strategic priority than finding a lasting settlement to the Austro-Serb quarrel. Here it is important to see the Sarajevo crisis in the context of the Russian leadership's ongoing concerns about the future of Turkey and the Straits of Constantinople, which had deepened significantly since the Ottomans had been swept from the Balkans in the two Balkan wars. Any strengthening of Habsburg regional influence had the potential of complicating matters in the event

---

[56] Sazonov report for the Tsar, 12/25 July 1914, *IBZI* v, no. 47.

[57] Paléologue diary, 25 July 1914, in his *Russie des Tsars* I, 26.

[58] Nicholas II diary, 12/25 July 1914, 'Nikolai Romanov v pervikh dniakh voyni', *KA* LXIV (1934), 133; tel. Nicholas II to Crown Prince Alexander of Serbia, 11/24 July 1914, *APS* I, no. 411.

of Turkey's complete collapse. Until that eventuality arose, nothing was to be done that would allow the Danubian Monarchy to recover its influence over the smaller states in the region. Certainly that the settlement Sazonov envisaged would do little to address Austria-Hungary's grievances, but preserve Serbia intact, and thus presumably also her Yugoslav aspirations, is obvious from his subsequent interview with Szápáry on 27 July.[59] As for coaxing Britain into Russia's warm embrace, Sazonov's assumptions about London's likely attitude were based on a profound misunderstanding of British policy.

This still leaves the problem of the partial mobilization, the second track of Sazonov's crisis strategy. If he had already decided in favour of war, and subsequently dissimulated in his conversations with Pourtalès and Szápáry, it made little sense to impress upon the belligerent Paléologue the need to avoid anything 'that could precipitate the crisis'.[60] The 'energetic steps' he had promised, then, were strictly diplomatic; the military preparations were a form of reinsurance for the event, not unlikely now, that Vienna could not be deterred any more at this stage. Partial mobilization would thus be the second phase of Russian crisis diplomacy, following the opening of Austro-Serbian hostilities. As the relevant 1913 order explained, the 'Period Preparatory to War' was 'a period of diplomatic complications, which precede the opening of military operations, and during which all departments must take the necessary measures for preparing and ensuring the success of the mobilization of the army, navy and fortresses and the deployment of the army along the threatened frontier'. The bundle of dispositions and measures to be implemented, moreover, was dependent on the 'course of the diplomatic talks'.[61] And mobilizing the Odessa district had the beneficial side-effect of securing Romania's leaning towards Russia and signalling Russian intent towards Bulgaria lest the latter and her mercurial ruler, King Ferdinand ('Foxy Ferdy'), join Austria-Hungary in a war against Serbia. To that extent Russian concerns were the mirror image of Habsburg foreign policy planning.[62]

The military preparations, then, ought to be seen as part of Russia's diplomatic moves rather than a deliberate move towards war,

[59] Tel. Szápáry to Berchtold (no. 165, secret), 27 July 1914 (D 2.15 p.m., R 4.30 p.m.), ÖUA VIII, no. 10835; for the concerns about Turkey, see M. A. Reynolds, *Shattering Empires: The Clash and Collapse of the Ottoman and Russian Empires, 1908–1918* (Cambridge, 2011), 82–106.

[60] Tel. Paléologue to Bienvenu-Martin (no. 283), 25 July 1914 (D 0.45 a.m., R 3.45 a.m.), *DDF* (3) XI, no. 34; Paléologue diary, 24 July 1914, in his *Russie des Tsars* I, 25–6.

[61] 'Order on the Period Preparatory to War', 17 Feb./2 Mar. 1913, *IBZI* V, no. 80, app.

[62] For a different suggestion, that mobilizing Odessa was meant to prepare an amphibious onslaught on Constantinople, see McMeekin, *Russian Origins*, 59.

itself an incalculable risk for the Russian Empire especially, as the statements by Krivoshein and Bark made clear. The implementation of the 'great programme' had scarcely begun, and would not be completed until 1917. Its main emphasis, moreover, was on defensive weapons systems such as fortresses and fortress artillery. To commence an offensive war, then, made little sense. Yet this second track of Sazonov's crisis strategy was also fraught with difficulties and risks. No doubt, any crisis strategy would be thus encumbered, but the inherent problems of partial mobilization and the reality of Russia's 'mobilization gap' would soon force Tsar Nicholas to order a general mobilization.

The official communiqué of 25 July warning against any violation of Serbia's independence and integrity implied a resolve to interfere in the conflict. In hindsight, there might have been advantages in underlining the implied threat of intervention with an overt threat to mobilize.[63] The responsibility for any further escalation of the Austro-Serbian dispute would thus have been devolved onto Vienna. It might also have been a shrewd military move. For either the Austro-Hungarian military campaign would have concentrated on the Balkan theatre of war – in which case the Galician salient would have remained vulnerable to a Russian attack – or a significant proportion of the Habsburg forces would have had to be committed to Galicia, so complicating the conflict with Serbia. Whatever its superficial attractions for the later observer, there were problems with this course of action, too. Any threat to mobilize, even if ostensibly only against Austria-Hungary, entailed the risk of forcing Germany to give up her seemingly passive current stance; and in that case there was the very real danger of the two alliances swinging into operation. Further, any threat to mobilize made British support more unlikely. This had been the constant refrain of British diplomacy since 1908–9, and Grey had emphasized the point again in his conversations with Benckendorff in early July.[64] This last consideration alone was a sufficiently strong incentive for Sazonov to avoid any measures that were calculated to escalate the crisis at that moment.

There was, however, yet another problem. The furtive nature of Russia's military preparations after 25 July meant that the perceptions of the other Powers were now more important than official pronouncements at St Petersburg. What mattered was not so much what measures the Russian authorities were implementing, but rather what the other Powers thought these measures to be. Paléologue's impressions are a case in point. At around 7 p.m. on 25 July, he went to St Petersburg's Warsaw station to

---

[63] For this argument see L. C. F. Turner, 'The Russian Mobilization of 1914', *JCH* III, 1 (1966), 65–88.

[64] Grey to Buchanan (no. 264), 8 July 1914, *BD* XI, no. 39.

bid farewell to Izvolsky, who was hastening back to his post at Paris. 'There was brisk excitement on the platforms', he recorded in his diary: 'the trains are packed with officers and soldiers. This looks like mobilization. We quickly exchanged our impressions and our conclusions were the same: "This time it is war."'[65] And that, more importantly, was a view increasingly shared elsewhere.

Each of the different strands of Sazonov's policy, then, was deeply problematic; and their combined effect was to escalate the crisis. But this was not an indication of the foreign minister's aggressive intent. Rather it reflected the shortcomings of the Russian governmental system. There was no formal, integrated decision-making process that allowed for the framing and executing of a coherent policy. Sazonov and the military leadership were dangerously divorced from one another;[66] and these systemic flaws magnified the individual shortcomings of the members of Russia's official élite.

Poincaré and Viviani are at sea

While St Petersburg was a hive of activity on 25 July, President Poincaré and prime minister Viviani were at sea, and that in more senses than one. In the early hours of 24 July, somewhat belatedly – further illustration of his own reservations – Viviani despatched a telegram to the Quai d'Orsay for onward transmission to the Vienna embassy. Ambassador Dumaine was to urge Berchtold, 'in a friendly conversation', to act with moderation and restraint in making any demands upon the Serbian government.[67] The instructions reflected Viviani's discussions with Sazonov earlier on 23 July. But by the time the prime minister's telegram arrived at Paris, the French ambassador at St Petersburg had already woken to the news of Austria-Hungary's ultimatum, and Viviani's instructions had become redundant.

As seen earlier, Poincaré's conversations at St Petersburg over the previous days had aimed at fashioning a joint Franco-Russian approach to the crisis that threatened to erupt in the Balkans, one that was predicated on the assumption that firm language at Vienna would deter the Habsburg leadership from resorting to force. Unsurprisingly, once news of the

---

[65] Paléologue, 25 July 1914, in his *Russie des Tsars* I, 27–8.
[66] See the perceptive comments by B. Menning, 'Mukden to Tannenberg: Defeat to Defeat, 1905–1915', F. W. Kagan and R. Higham (eds.), *The Military History of Tsarist Russia* (Basingstoke and New York, 2002), 213 [203–26].
[67] Tel. Viviani to Bienvenu-Martin (no no.), 24 July 1914, *DDF* (3) XI, no. 1; cf. tel. Bienvenu-Martin to Paléologue (no. 381), 24 July 1914 (D 1.30 p.m.), *ibid.*, no. 8.

démarche reached the *France* at around 3 p.m. on 24 July, the president's immediate response to the 'crude and for Serbia unacceptable' note was to ask: 'What will Russia do? What will Europe do?'[68] The question itself, and how Poincaré phrased it, was an indication of his foreign policy priorities. Russia and the Russian alliance came first. If the banquet of the previous night had buoyed him – despite his underperforming presidential *chef* – he had nevertheless not shaken off his doubts about Sazonov's steadfastness. Indeed, when on the following day, news arrived of the Russian foreign minister's advice to Belgrade not to resist an Austro-Hungarian onslaught and to appeal to the Powers for assistance, the president was dismayed. More than that, he was plunged into deepest gloom: 'During this sinister day we move from feast to feast [at Stockholm] putting on a brave face when confronting ill fortune.' Paléologue's wires left him with the impression that Sazonov was 'very pacific'; and his counsel of withdrawal was tantamount to 'surrender'. But what could France do? 'We surely cannot show ourselves to be more Slav than the Russians. Poor Serbia has therefore a good chance of being humiliated.'[69]

To Poincaré's mind there were ominous parallels with the events of late 1912, when Sazonov appeared weak and vacillating during the opening phase of the First Balkan War. Yet, as seen, the Russian foreign minister was anything but prepared to surrender to Austro-Hungarian bullying. But Poincaré was not to know this. He and Viviani, in fact, were misled by Paléologue about events at St Petersburg. The ambassador's reports contained carefully calibrated doses of selective information, calculated half-truths and positive untruths. It proved a toxic mixture. In what he told his political masters as much as in what he omitted to tell them, Paléologue misled them. It was the ambassador, not Poincaré's and Viviani's preferred mode of transport, who ensured that they were all at sea until the end of July. And it was Paléologue who determined France's policy towards Russia, the alliance with whom remained the principal concern of French diplomacy.

Repeated bouts of political instability for much of the Third Republic, accompanied by 'revolving door' ministries, had allowed French ambassadors to carve out niches for themselves. In general, they enjoyed a good deal of freedom to act on their own initiative. If in the past this had

---

[68] Poincaré, notes journalières, 24 July 1914, BN, Bnfr 16027, fo. 115 r.

[69] Poincaré, notes journalières, 25 July 1914, *ibid.*, fos. 116 r. and v. As so often Poincaré's handwriting is difficult to decipher here, and the relevant passage may read 'plus slaves que les Russes' or 'plus braves [i.e. committed] que les Russes'; the difference is nevertheless small. For Sazonov's advice see tel. Paléologue to Bienvenu-Martin (no. 283), 25 July 1914 (D 0.45 a.m., R 3.28 a.m.), *DDF* (3) XI, no. 34.

helped to lend greater stability to French policy, Paléologue's determination to do likewise contributed to the international complications in July 1914. A man of certain literary ambitions, he was not a war-monger as such, but he was easily impressed by displays of military might. He also believed that history was forged by 'great men', men such as the Piedmontese Cavour, whose exploits and steely determination to utilize the crises of the late 1850s to unite Italy he so admired.[70]

No doubt Paléologue was genuinely imbued with a sense that the Viviani administration's fragility placed upon him the responsibility to advance France's true interests; and he believed those to be best safe-guarded by a policy of firmness, as advocated by Poincaré, to whom he was close. At the same time, as the Quai's former political director, he was also convinced that a future conflict with Germany could not be avoided. At the luncheon with Sazonov and Buchanan, he talked at length about 'my personal ideas about the designs of Germany. The Austrian ultimatum seemed to me to open the dangerous crisis that I had forecast for some time.'[71] From the moment of his arrival in the Russian capital in early 1914, he sought to convince Sazonov and anyone else prepared to listen that France's support for Russia was absolute and unconditional. Certainly, from the outset of the July crisis he assured Sazonov that France would offer the strongest diplomatic support; more than that, she would 'if necessary fulfil all the obligations imposed on her by the alliance'. Following the pre-mobilization decision of 25 July, he was more emphatic still. He had received a number of telegrams from Paris, he explained: 'not one of them displayed [the] slightest sign of hesitation, and ... he was in [a] position to give his Excellency [Sazonov] [the] formal assurance that France placed herself unreservedly on Russia's side'.[72]

Paléologue had, in fact, received no instructions to that effect. His own reports also conveyed a rather different picture of his conversations at St Petersburg. Although he reported that he and Sazonov had re-emphasized their commitment to the alliance, the actual phrasing was identical with sections of the Franco-Russian end-of-summit communiqué and the presidential toast of 23 July, to which he had attached such importance. There was not a scintilla of a hint of his rather more

---

[70] See Schmidt, *Frankreichs Aussenpolitik*, 81–3; M. B. Hayne, *The French Foreign Office and the Origins of the First World War, 1898–1914* (Oxford, 1993), 294–5; for Paléologue's hero-worship of Cavour see his *Cavour. Un grand réaliste* (Paris, 1926).

[71] Paléologue diary, 24 July 1914, in his *Russie des Tsars* I, 23.

[72] Quotes from tels. Buchanan to Grey (nos. 166, urgent, and 169, very confidential), 24 July 1914 (D 5.40 p.m., R 8 p.m.) and 25 July 1914 (D 8 p.m., R 10.30 p.m.), *BD* XI, nos. 101 and 125.

far-reaching assurances.[73] At the same time, he withheld Buchanan's moderating advice and call for prudence during their meetings on 24 and 25 July. Instead he implied that the British ambassador concurred with his and Sazonov's assessment of the situation, and especially that '[t]he solidarity of the Triple Entente must be resolutely affirmed. Any lapse would encourage the Germanic Powers to accentuate their provocative attitude and would precipitate events ... The Triple Entente has indeed sufficient force to preserve peace. It must not hesitate to show that force.'[74]

In the days after the Austro-Hungarian ultimatum, Paléologue also consistently portrayed his German colleague as menacing, and omitted to inform the Quai d'Orsay of Pourtalès's attempts to persuade Sazonov to seek direct talks with Vienna.[75] At the same time, Sazonov and the Russian government were described as 'most pacific' and 'conciliatory', though increasingly disturbed by the harshness of the Austro-Hungarian move against Belgrade.[76] More importantly, while he assured Sazonov of France's unequivocal support, Paléologue failed to report to the Quai the full extent of the military measures that the Russian council of ministers had decided upon on 24 and 25 July. In a telegram, despatched at 6.22 p.m. on 25 July – a good six hours after the meeting at Krasnoe Selo – he wired to Paris that the Russian government had 'decided *in principle* to mobilize thirteen army corps which, if necessary, are meant to operate against Austria'. Indeed, the ambassador laid particular stress on the conditional nature of the measures. Mobilization would only become 'effective and public' if Austria-Hungary invaded Serbia; and the troops mobilized would be concentrated along the Galician frontier but would not commence operations unless Germany decided to declare the *casus foederis* and began to mobilize herself. This may well have been true, but Paléologue did not explain that the pre-mobilization measures had already begun. His telegram indicated that 'clandestine preparations are nevertheless commencing', but gave no specific details.[77]

---

[73] Tel. Paléologue to Bienvenu-Martin (no. 281), 24 July 1914 (D 2.45 p.m., R 6.55 p.m.), *DDF* (3) XI, no. 19.

[74] Tel. Paléologue to Bienvenu-Martin (no. 282), 24 July 1914 (D 9.12 p.m., R 3.10 a.m.), *DDF* (3) XI, no. 21. For his failure to report Buchanan's warnings see tel. (no. 281), 24 July 1914 (D 2.45 p.m., R 6.55 p.m.), *ibid.*, no. 19; also Buchanan, *Mission to Russia*, 190.

[75] See tel. Pourtalès to Jagow (no. 177), 28 July 1914 (D 8.12 p.m., R 6.15 a.m.), *DD* no. 338; see also Hayne, *French Foreign Office*, 299.

[76] See e.g. tels. Paléologue to Bienvenu-Martin (nos. 283 and 292), 25 July 1914 (D 0.45 a.m., R 3.28 a.m.) and 27 July 1914 (D 5.24 p.m., R 5.30 p.m.), *DDF* (3) XI, nos. 34 and 141.

[77] Tel. Paléologue to Bienvenu-Martin (no. 284, secret), 25 July 1914 (D 6.22 p.m., R 7.35 p.m.), *DDF* (3) XI, no. 50.

It is true that, in a follow-up telegram, sent in the afternoon of the following day, Sunday, 26 July, the French military attaché, General Marquis de Laguiche, sent confirmation of the mobilization in the districts of Kazan, Kiev, Moscow and Odessa, and of secret dispositions being made in the districts of Vilnius and Warsaw.[78] But this information did not reach Paris until much later in the day. In fact, the French foreign ministry informed its missions abroad in the late afternoon of that Sunday that Russia had decided '*in principle*' to mobilize and that St Petersburg was not prepared 'to let Serbia be crushed'.[79] This news reached the *France* on the morning of Monday, 27 July. By now Poincaré and Viviani had also been informed of the *note verbale* which the German ambassador at Paris, Baron Wilhelm von Schoen, had left at the Quai d'Orsay on the 24th, and in which, as instructed and with a view to the various alliances, he warned of the 'incalculable consequences' of any foreign intervention in the Austro-Serbian dispute.[80]

The information thus received shaped Poincaré's assessment of the situation. The German note struck him as 'a barely concealed menace'.[81] The president took note of the Russian decision in favour of mobilization, but misled by Paléologue's selective reporting, judged that 'that decision remains theoretical'.[82] For the moment, then, to Poincaré's mind, there was no reason to rein in Russia. On the contrary, he wished to strengthen the resolve of the Russian government in the face of Austro-German pressure. This was in line with his previous policy. He was convinced, moreover, that Austria-Hungary and Germany would yield to Franco-Russian pressure. As he noted in his diary on the day after his arrival at St Petersburg when confronted with the first indications of Vienna's impending démarche: 'Still evidently a bluff, on the plan of intimidating the other Powers and humiliating Serbia, out of friendship for Austria.'[83]

Poincaré's assessment of Berlin's policy was not entirely erroneous, as seen earlier, though he underestimated Germany's commitment to Austria-Hungary. But it was also the source of profound divisions with Viviani, who was sceptical about the wisdom of a policy of confronting the

---

[78] Tel Paléologue to Bienvenu-Martin (no. 288), 26 July 1914 (D 1.55 p.m., R 4 p.m.), *DDF* (3) XI, no. 89.

[79] Bienvenu-Martin circular tel., 26 July 1914 (D 4.30 p.m.), *DDF* (3) XI, no. 90 (original emphasis).

[80] Bienvenu-Martin circular tel., 24 July 1914 (D 9 p.m.), *DDF* (3) XI, no. 20; for the instructions see Bethmann Hollweg to Pourtalès, Schoen and Lichnowsky, 21 July 1914, *DD* I, no. 100.

[81] Poincaré, notes journalières, 25 July 1914, BN, Bnfr 16027, fo. 115 r.

[82] *Ibid.*, 27 July 1914, fo. 121 r.; also Schmidt, *Frankreichs Aussenpolitik*, 94.

[83] Poincaré, notes journalières, 21 July 1914, BN, Bnfr 16027, fo. 196 r.

Austro-German combination. Indeed, the policy arguments between the two men on the fringes of the state visit to St Petersburg carried on in the confined space of the *France* as the warship made its stately progress through the Baltic and North Seas. In the face of the president's persistent pressing for firmness, Viviani appeared 'more and more troubled and disturbed, and ... turned over most contradictory ideas'. For his part, Poincaré took to lecturing the prime minister on the basics of foreign policy. Viviani had to understand 'that weakness in the face of Germany will always be the mother of complications and that the only way to ward off the danger is to show unflinching firmness and impassive *sangfroid*'. He found the premier wanting: 'But he is nervous, agitated' and his pronouncements showed 'an ignorance of matters of external policy'.[84]

What exactly those pronouncements were is not known. Poincaré did not record them – perhaps he regarded them as too trivial and Viviani as too insignificant – but Viviani also left no record. His instructions to Paléologue, issued at noon on 27 July, however, are suggestive of a more cautious approach. They affirmed the importance of demonstrating to the other Powers 'the perfect understanding' between France and Russia. The ambassador was to assure Sazonov that his government would not fail to undertake 'any effort with a view to a solution of the conflict, and was ready fully to support, *in the interest of general peace*, the action of the Imperial government'.[85] The reference to the preservation of peace between the Powers is instructive. Whatever his shortcomings as a politician in general and as a foreign minister in particular, Viviani appreciated that Poincaré's 'policy of firmness' was inherently risky. Once France had committed to confronting Berlin and Vienna it would be difficult to row back. Unless the two Germanic Powers decided to disengage in the face of Franco-Russian 'unflinching firmness', the only possible outcome would be a diplomatic defeat for the Franco-Russian grouping or war. Neither was palatable to the thoroughly bourgeois and pacific Viviani.

Viviani's concerns about the binary nature of Poincaré's policy were the exact mirror-image of the views of Jean-Baptiste Bienvenu-Martin, the minister of justice who took charge of the day-to-day running of the Quai d'Orsay during the president's and Viviani's absence from France. A cultured lawyer-politician of no great distinction and with no foreign policy experience, Bienvenu-Martin nevertheless was a competent

---

[84] Poincaré, notes journalières, 27 July 1914, *ibid.*, fos. 121 r. and 122 r.

[85] Tel. Viviani to Paléologue (no no.), 27 July 1914 (D 12 p.m.), *DDF* (3) XI, no. 138 (my emphasis). For a different interpretation see Schmidt, *Frankreichs Aussenpolitik*, 95, who argues that the reference to the general peace was inserted by Poincaré to appease Viviani; if so, it does not weaken the argument made here.

administrator. Indeed, he showed a considerable calmness during the crisis. He remained confident throughout that a solution could be found, though whether this was a reflection of his innate optimism, or the fact that Viviani had left him no particular instructions, or the support he received from the Quai's political director Philippe Berthelot, it is difficult to judge.[86]

The acting foreign minister used conciliatory language during his interviews with the German and Austro-Hungarian ambassadors. When the latter, Count Nikolaus Szécsen, communicated a copy of the note addressed to Belgrade, Bienvenu-Martin evinced some sympathy for Austria-Hungary's Serbian predicament. Although he intimated that he thought the fifth demand – the admission of Habsburg police onto Serbian soil – problematic, he did not comment on the note, and confined himself to expressing his hope for a peaceful solution of the dispute. Szécsen did not fail to note that the minister 'refrained from any attempt to justify or put a gloss on the attitude of Serbia'.[87]

In his subsequent interview with Baron Schoen, Bienvenu-Martin was more forthright, warning of the dangers of a nationalist-revolutionary backlash in Serbia in the event of the Pašić administration being humiliated. Significantly, however, he criticized the approach chosen by Vienna for being based on only two possible hypotheses, either rejection of the note by Belgrade or Serbia's complete submission. A third option which would allow for some accommodation should not be lost sight of, he emphasized. If Serbia promised to punish those officials implicated in the plot and gave guarantees of good-neighbourly conduct in the future, concessions which were reconcilable with her independence and dignity, then Vienna ought to be prepared to negotiate on the modalities of its demands. Under such circumstances, those Powers inclined to side with Serbia should be able to accept the localization of the conflict as desired by Germany.[88] This was good, lawyerly advice. In essence, it was an attempt to remove the time limit of the Austro-Hungarian note so that international diplomacy could swing into action. According to Schoen's report, Bienvenu-Martin, who was assisted by Berthelot on this occasion, hinted that the strength of pan-Slavism would make it difficult for the Russian government to accept any demands that infringed upon Serbia's sovereignty. The French government

---

[86] J. B. Bienvenu-Martin, 'Mon intérim de chef du gouvernement, 15–29 juillet 1914', *La Revue de France*, 15 Aug. 1933, 639–52; for Berthelot's role see Hayne, *French Foreign Office*, 279–84.

[87] Tel. Szécsen to Berchtold (no. 119), 24 July 1914 (D 4.55 p.m., R 9 a.m.), *ÖUA* VIII, no. 10606; cf. tel. Bienvenu-Martin to Viviani (no. 13, very urgent), 24 July 1914 (D 1 p.m.), *DDF* (3) XI, no. 7.

[88] Bienvenu-Martin circular tel., 24 July 1914 (D 9 p.m.), *DDF* (3) XI, 20.

would counsel Belgrade to yield as far as possible. At the same time, Austria-Hungary had to show willingness 'to discuss individual points'.[89]

At one level Bienvenu-Martin's suggestions, his casting about for a peaceful solution to the Austro-Serb dispute, did not matter. For ultimately he carried no real weight in French decision-making. But at another level they did matter because they illustrated the divisions within the current government. The differences between the hardliner Poincaré and the altogether more reluctant Viviani and Bienvenu-Martin increased Paléologue's already significant latitude at St Petersburg. Of course, his firm commitment to the Russian alliance and his offer of full support for Russia were in line with Poincaré's own views. As seen earlier, the president advocated a policy of firmness in the current crisis. But this stance was based on the distorted picture transmitted by Paléologue; the president wished Russia to be firm because he did not know that Russia had already committed to some form of mobilization. Had he known this, he might very well have couched French support in less emphatic terms; he might even have decided to hurry back to Paris. As it was, he decided otherwise,[90] and it was not until the *France* reached Dunkirk on 29 July that Poincaré and Viviani realized that the situation was far more serious.

Grey receives the most formidable declaration

The events at St Petersburg and Paléologue's hijacking of French policy decisions also affected British diplomacy, though the full extent of this was only gradually becoming apparent to Sir Edward Grey and his officials. That the Austro-Hungarian démarche marked a significant escalation was beyond doubt. Vienna's note, reflected Charles Louis Des Graz, the envoy-designate at Belgrade, was 'so stiff as to be read as an ultimatum'.[91] When Mensdorff communicated the text to Grey on the morning of Friday, 24 July, the Foreign Secretary commented that it was 'the most formidable a declaration I had ever seen addressed by one State to another that was independent'. The nature of the ultimatum, more especially, caused him

---

[89] Tel. Schoen to Auswärtiges Amt (no. 210), 24 July 1914 (D 8.05 p.m., R 10.35 p.m.), *DD* I, no. 154; and Schoen to Bethmann Hollweg, 24 July 1914 (D 26 July, R 28 July p.m.), *DD* II, no. 292: Schoen emphasized, as instructed, the risks of the 'jeu des alliances'.

[90] Poincaré, notes journalières, 26 July 1914, BN, Bnfr 16027, fos. 119 v.–120 r.; for the Russian alliance as the pivot of French policy see also Krumeich, *Armaments and Politics*, 224.

[91] Des Graz diary, 24 July 1914, Des Graz MSS, CUL, Add. 8883/D/2.

concern. A time limit could have been introduced at a later stage if Belgrade had procrastinated. As matters now stood, Vienna had demanded a reply within forty-eight hours, and it had also 'dictated the terms of the reply'. Although Grey evinced some sympathy with Austria-Hungary, he would not be drawn into discussing the merits of her case: 'that was not our concern. It was solely from the point of view of the peace of Europe that I should concern myself with the matter, and I felt great apprehension.'[92] According to Mensdorff, the fifth demand in Vienna's note – Austro-Hungarian police being placed in Serbia – struck Grey as especially prob-lematic as it would effectively put an end to Serbia as an independent state. The Foreign Secretary, Mensdorff noted, 'repeated several times in the course of the conversation that he was very anxious about preserving peace between the Great Powers'. In the first instance, Grey would seek to consult with 'the allies of Austria-Hungary and Russia, who have no interests of their own in Serbia'.[93]

Clearly, Grey still thought it possible to find an Austro-Russian solution to the brewing Balkan crisis, and to facilitate this remained his principal concern until 29 July. Even so, he appreciated the risk of escal-ation. That he judged the situation created by the ultimatum to be serious is underlined by the fact that he brought the matter before the Cabinet on Friday, 24 July. It was the first time that the ministers were confronted with the events in the Balkans. Until then they had been preoccupied with the all-absorbing situation in Ulster. The crisis in the Balkans was 'the gravest of many years past in European politics', Prime Minister Asquith afterwards informed the King; there was the real risk of four of the Great Powers being embroiled in a war.[94] With the approval of the Cabinet, Grey moved along the lines established during the previous Balkan crises, seeking the

---

[92] Tel. Grey to de Bunsen (no. 148), 24 July (D 1.30 p.m.), *BD* XI, no. 91. Later that evening Mensdorff informed the Foreign Office that the note addressed to Belgrade was not an ultimatum, but a 'démarche with a time-limit', upon whose expiry relations would be severed and military preparations (but not operations) commence: min. Montgomery, 24 July 1914, *ibid.*, no. 104; cf. tel. Berchtold to Mensdorff (no. 161), 24 July 1914 (D 3.30 p.m.), *ÖUA* VIII, no. 10599.
[93] Tel. Mensdorff to Berchtold (no. 108), 24 July 1914 (D 2.50 p.m., R 9 a.m.), *ÖUA* VIII, no. 10600. Mensdorff privately conceded that the demands on Belgrade were such that they could not be accepted: see Mensdorff diary, 26 July 1914, Nachlass Mensdorff, HHStA, Karton 4.
[94] Asquith to George V, 24 July 1914, TNA (PRO), CAB 41/35/19; for a penetrating discussion of the crisis see M. G. Ekstein and Z. S. Steiner, 'The Sarajevo Crisis', F. H. Hinsley (ed.), *British Foreign Policy under Sir Edward Grey* (Cambridge, 1977), 397–410.

cooperation of Paris and Berlin in an effort to restrain Austria-Hungary and Russia.

After the Cabinet meeting, Grey saw the French ambassador, Paul Cambon. There were good tactical reasons for seeking him out first. Since the news of Sarajevo had reached London, the Foreign Secretary had acted on the assumption that the attitudes of the Russian and German governments were key to any solution of the Austro-Serbian quarrel; and this was a view he had impressed upon ambassadors Benckendorff and Lichnowsky in early July. Now, following the ultimatum, moderating advice to St Petersburg was more likely to be effective if it were supported by Russia's ally France, while parallel representations by Grey would have to be addressed to the German leadership. To a degree this was also Cambon's view. Having received Grey's request to call on him at the Foreign Office after that morning's Cabinet meeting, the ambassador conferred with his Russian colleague. Benckendorff thought it difficult for his government to remain aloof in the event of a military conflict between Austria-Hungary and Serbia. Both diplomats agreed that a British intercession at Berlin, requesting what Cambon described as a 'semi-official' mediation effort by Germany at Vienna, would prevent a sudden strike against Serbia; and this was central to any solution of the crisis. For if Russia sided with Belgrade, there was the risk of offensive Russian operations against Austria-Hungary. In such an event, Cambon concluded, 'Germany would have to support that latter Power. This would be the general war.' Berlin, therefore, had to be persuaded to press for a conference and for postponing the ultimatum.[95]

Cambon's views coincided with those of the Foreign Secretary, but only up to a certain point, as their conversation that afternoon showed. Grey advanced the idea of some form of collective intervention by the four Powers not directly interested in the Balkans – Britain, France, Italy and Germany – acting simultaneously in Vienna and St Petersburg. In essence, this scheme still kept in view an Austro-Russian arrangement that would provide the framework for settling the dispute between Vienna and Belgrade. But this is where the problem lay. In light of recent experience, Grey understood that without pressure on Berlin to restrain Austria-Hungary, France would be reluctant to moderate her ally. What Grey underestimated was the degree to which Paris would reject any suggestion of reining in the Russian government. Indeed, although he did not openly refuse French cooperation, Cambon insisted that only restraint on Austria-Hungary's

[95] Tel. P. Cambon to Bienvenu-Martin (nos. 132–3), 24 July 1914 (D 1.54 p.m., R 4.25 p.m.), DDF (3) XI, no. 12.

part could prevent the further escalation of the crisis. In two days, after the expiry of the ultimatum, he argued, Habsburg forces would march into Serbia, and Russia would be compelled to resort to force in response: 'once the Austrians had attacked Servia, it would be too late for any mediation'.

Grey took a less pessimistic view of the matter. Even if Austria-Hungary invaded and Russia mobilized, the four Powers would still be able to persuade Vienna to halt the advance and St Petersburg to suspend its military preparations. This would then give international diplomacy the space and time it needed to mediate. There was no agreement between Grey and Cambon on the subject, and the ambassador continued to insist that the 'important thing was to gain time by mediation in Vienna'.[96] This was a first indication, albeit ameliorated by Cambon's polished politeness, that French diplomacy was unlikely to restrain Russia. As for Grey, the notion that four-Power intervention remained a viable option even after Austro-Hungarian military operations against Serbia had commenced prefigured a strand of his policy for the last week of that month. There was another problem, however. Cambon left the meeting with the impression that Grey had given up on his project of mediating between Russia and Austria-Hungary, that he had, in fact, accepted the ambassador's advice that Berlin had to be made to restrain Vienna.[97]

This was not at all the case, as Grey's subsequent interview with Lichnowsky made clear. The Foreign Secretary rehearsed much the same arguments as he had with Cambon, with one difference, however. Whilst he had urged the need for French cooperation on Cambon, with Lichnowsky he laid particular stress on Germany's central role in settling the crisis. The stiff character of Vienna's démarche and its presentation in the form of an ultimatum had increased the stakes; it would be difficult to exercise moderating influence on Russia alone. Four-Power mediation was the only way forward, but for it to have any chance of success Vienna had to be induced 'not to precipitate military action and so to gain time'. Only Germany could persuade the Habsburg leadership to do so.[98] The key to containing the dispute then lay in Berlin; and Grey applied considerable pressure on Lichnowsky, whom he sought to leave with the impression 'that a war between Austria and Servia cannot be localised'.[99] Vienna's

---

[96] Grey to Bertie (no. 491), 24 July 1914, *BD* XI, no. 98.

[97] Tel. P. Cambon to Bienvenu-Martin (nos. 14–15), 24 July 1914 (D 5.53 p.m., R 8.45 p.m.), *DDF* (3) XI, no. 23.

[98] Tel. Grey to Rumbold (no. 196), 24 July 1914 (D 7.45 p.m.), *BD* XI, no. 99; see also tel. Imperiali to San Giuliano (no. 786/208), 24 July 1914 (D 5.25 p.m., R 10 p.m.), *DDI* (4) XII, no. 474.

[99] Min. Grey, n.d. [25 July 1914], on German note, 24 July 1914, *BD* XI, no. 100.

démarche was of such a character, Lichnowsky reported on his interview with Grey, that '[a]ny state that accepted something of this kind would cease to exist as an independent state'. Grey could only hope that 'a mild and calm view' would ultimately prevail at St Petersburg, but this would depend on what Austria-Hungary did next. An invasion of Serbian soil would bring with it the danger of a European war, the consequences of which were incalculable. Whatever its outcome, he argued, as he had already done during the interview with Mensdorff prior to the delivery of the ultimatum, Europe would be left exhausted and impoverished; 'industry and commerce would be destroyed and capital ruined', and the consequence would be social and political collapse as in 1848. Indeed, unnamed Foreign Office officials warned Lichnowsky that Vienna underestimated Serbia's powers of resistance; that any military campaign would be protracted and bloody; and that the Habsburg Empire would 'bleed to death' as a result.[100]

Grey's interviews with the French and German ambassadors conformed to the pattern established during earlier international crises, albeit slightly altered to fit the specific circumstances of the current situation. Since 1906, Grey had sought to manage international complications in the east by encouraging Paris to act as a check on Russia and by placing the onus of restraining Austria-Hungary on Berlin, with Grey himself occupying a mediating position. With this strategy Grey had been remarkably successful so far. Given the recent experience of mutually supportive Anglo-German crisis diplomacy in south-eastern Europe, and on the basis of the information at Grey's disposal before the interviews with Cambon and Lichnowsky, his mediation scheme was sensible enough. But the two interviews of 24 July produced the first, tentative evidence that this approach could not easily be replicated now. Cambon's less than enthusiastic reaction to Grey's scheme of some form of collective intervention was suggestive of French reluctance to restrain Russia.

It was also not clear whether Austria-Hungary could be at all dissuaded from resorting to military force. Certainly, on taking leave from Grey, Lichnowsky had hinted that Vienna was likely to move unless the Serbian government accepted unconditionally all of the demands made of it. As a personal suggestion, he urged Grey to impress upon Belgrade the need for 'a reply that was favourable on some points, sufficient to give Austria an excuse for not taking action immediately'.[101] The implication was obvious: Lichnowsky did not believe that Berlin would rein in Vienna

---

[100] Tel. Lichnowsky to Auswärtiges Amt (no. 151), 24 July 1914 (D 9.12 p.m., R 1.16 a.m.), DD I, no. 157.
[101] Tel. Grey to Rumbold (no. 196), 24 July 1914 (D 7.45 p.m.), BD XI, no. 99.

for the moment. Doubts about the German attitude were also fuelled by the tone of the German note, which the ambassador, as instructed, had left with Grey. It offered '[v]ery strong support' for Austria-Hungary, the head of the Foreign Office's Eastern department noted. Moreoever, the terms of the Austrian démarche appeared to be 'design[ed] to provoke war', observed Sir Eyre Crowe, the Assistant Under-secretary. Vienna had as yet presented no evidence to support its case against the Serbian government, and the notes delivered by Mensdorff and Lichnowsky suggested a concerted effort by the Austro-German group to induce the Powers to acquiesce in the subjugation of Serbia.[102]

Whatever the recent complications, at the close of 24 July Grey was still hopeful of a peaceful outcome. That evening he dined at Haldane's London house at 28 Queen Anne's Gate, a short distance from the government buildings in Whitehall. The other guests were Lord Morley, the elder statesman of the Liberal administration, Winston Churchill, the First Lord of the Admiralty, and Albert Ballin, the German-Jewish shipping magnate and head of the Hamburg-America Line.[103] Ballin had excellent contacts with various government officials at Berlin and was something of a 'shipping diplomat' who had been used in the past for semi-official missions on behalf of the German government. He was in London now chiefly on private business, but he had also been asked to sound out British ministers about the rumoured Anglo-Russian naval convention. Much of his post-prandial conversation with Grey and Haldane that evening seems to have revolved around this topic, and the Foreign Secretary gave the usual – and entirely accurate – explanation that no such arrangement existed with Russia and that Britain had no intention to enter into talks about one. Significantly, Grey spoke warmly of the much improved relations with Germany, which he attributed to the cooperation between London and Berlin 'during the Balkan troubles'. After the Foreign Secretary had left for his own house, 33 Eccleston Square (rented from Churchill), Haldane, a close personal friend of Grey, observed that the current 'distribution of forces' between the German-led Triple Alliance and the Franco-Russian group was the best guarantee of peace in Europe.[104] According to

---

[102] Mins. Clerk and Crowe, 25 July 1914, on German note, 24 July 1914, *BD* XI, no. 100.

[103] Haldane to mother, 24 July 1914, Haldane MSS, NLS, MS 5991.

[104] Ballin to Jagow, 24 July 1914 (R 27 July p.m.), *DD* I, no. 254; L. Cecil, *Albert Ballin: Business and Politics in Imperial Germany, 1888–1918* (Princeton, NJ, 1967), 206–9; W. E. Mosse (ed.), 'Drei Juden in der Wirtschaft Hamburgs. Heine, Ballin, Warburg', A. Herzig (ed.), *Die Juden in Hamburg, 1590–1990* (Hamburg, 1991), 435–9; and for further thoughts P. Pulzer, 'Die jüdische Beteiligung an der Politik',

Haldane's later recollections, Ballin also touched on the Serbian crisis and the risk of escalation. Both ministers told the German visitor that the friendly relations between their two countries were dependent on Germany not attacking France.[105] Even so, Ballin formed the impression that 'the Austrian note is judged here [at London] very calmly'.[106]

This was not entirely accurate. Grey's expressions of concern in the earlier conversations with Mensdorff and Lichnowsky had not been simulated to generate pressure on Vienna and Berlin. They were genuine enough. The German ambassador's parting private observation, more-over, had made some impression on him. Crackanthorpe, the chargé at Belgrade, was instructed to urge the Serbian government to offer some form of apology for any involvement of Serbian officials in the Sarajevo murder, and, if this were proved to have been the case, to 'give fullest satisfaction'. The only chance to avert conflict lay in 'a favourable reply to as many points as possible within the limit of time, and not to meet [the] Austrian demand with a blank negative'.[107] This bore a close resemblance to Lichnowsky's suggestions, though Grey seems to have arrived at this position already earlier in the afternoon of that day; he certainly indicated this kind of advice in his interview with the Italian ambassador, Marchese Guglielmo Imperiali di Francavilla, which took place before Lichnowsky saw Grey.[108] At any rate, it made practical sense to defuse as much as was possible the Austro-Serbian dispute as the core of the current crisis.

How difficult it would be, however, to implement Grey's medi-ation scheme became apparent later that night when Buchanan's urgent cable arrived from St Petersburg, informing the Foreign Office of Paléolo-gue's affirmation that France would 'fulfil all obligations imposed upon her by the [Franco-Russian] alliance'. This was a good deal stronger than Cambon's statement earlier in the day, but the latter's more nuanced arguments were nevertheless open to be interpreted in the same sense. It was no longer possible, noted Crowe, 'to enlist French support in an effort to hold back Russia'. Whatever view Britain might take of the Austro-Serbian dispute, France and Russia had decided that the charges brought

W. E. Mosse and A. Paucker (eds.), *Juden im Wilhelminischen Deutschland, 1890–1914* (Tübingen, 1976), 225–30.

[105] R. B. Haldane, *An Autobiography* (London, 1929), 271–2; B. Huldermann, *Albert Ballin* (Berlin, 1922), 301–2. Ballin made no mention of this in his letter to Jagow.

[106] Ballin to Jagow, 24 July 1914, *DD* I, no. 254.

[107] Tel. Grey to Crackanthorpe (no. 17), 24 July 1914 (D 9.30 p.m.), *BD* XI, no. 102.

[108] Tel. Imperiali to San Giuliano (no. 786/208), 24 July 1914 (D 5.25 p.m., R 10 p.m.), *DDI* (4) XII, no. 474.

against Belgrade were pretexts, 'and that the bigger cause of Triple Alliance versus Triple *Entente* is definitely engaged'. Although the notion of a triple entente had never been accepted in London, Crowe nevertheless counselled against making any representations in Paris or St Petersburg as counterproductive: 'The point that matters is whether Germany is or is not absolutely determined to have this war now.' War could only be averted if Berlin could be persuaded that, in the event of a continental war, Britain would join on the side of France and Russia. To that end Crowe suggested that the Royal Navy be put on an immediate war footing the moment either Austria-Hungary or Russia began to mobilize. It would be a clear signal of intent, but would not commit Britain to a definite course of action at this stage. If war broke out, Crowe argued, Britain would sooner or later be dragged into the conflict. If she decided to remain neutral, one of two things must happen:

(a.) Either Germany and Austria win, crush France, and humiliate Russia. With the French fleet gone, Germany in occupation of the Channel, with the willing or unwilling cooperation of Holland and Belgium, what will be the position of a friendless England?

(b.) Or France and Russia win. What would then be their attitude towards England? What about India and the Mediterranean?

If war now broke out, it would be because Germany wished it; and this would be confirmation that Berlin, irrespective of all recent talk of rapprochements and détente, was determined after all to establish 'a political dictatorship in Europe'.[109]

Crowe's analysis was characteristically blunt and incisive, ruthlessly logical in its argument and remorselessly practical in its conclusion. And yet it was flawed. The fault, however, did not lie with Crowe's powers of reasoning but with Paléologue's distortions. For, as seen earlier, the French government had not committed to supporting Russia; only its ambassador in St Petersburg had done so. The effect was to narrow the path of diplomacy yet further. The extent to which Paléologue acted outside the control of the Quai d'Orsay was not appreciated by British officials. But in London this apparent hardening of the French position opened up divisions within the upper echelons of the Foreign Office. Under the altered circumstances, Crowe advocated increasing pressure on Berlin to deter the German leadership from letting the crisis

---

[109] Tel. Buchanan to Grey (no. 166, urgent), 24 July 1914 (D 5.40 p.m., R 8 p.m.), and min. Crowe, 25 July 1914, *BD* XI, no. 101.

in the Balkans escalate; and this was supported by Grey's Private Secretary, Sir William Tyrrell. Nicolson, the Permanent Under-secretary and one of the few truly Russophile diplomats in Britain, was anxious to avoid anything that might alienate St Petersburg.[110] Grey, by contrast, was wary of such a sudden gear-shift. The navy, he had been informed, could be mobilized in twenty-four hours if necessary, but for now it was 'premature to make any statement to France and Russia'.[111] To do so would only harden their attitude further, and force Germany into choosing between a humiliating climb-down or war.

Grey and Sazonov seek to gain time, and Horace Rumbold fears a general bust-up

The events of the following day, Saturday, 25 July, were characterized by two separate developments – the efforts of Grey and Sazonov to secure an extension of the ultimatum and the delivery of Belgrade's reply to the Austro-Hungarian note at 6 p.m. that evening. Both of these had the potential to affect Austria-Hungary's next move. At Vienna, the only fear was that the Serbian government would cave in completely, as Dumaine reported.[112] The eminently bourgeois French ambassador was a somewhat marginal figure in the aristocratic capital of the Habsburg Monarchy, and he was not always well-informed. This time, however, he had sensed something of the truth. When in the course of 25 July a rumour began to circulate in the Habsburg capital that Serbia would accept all demands made of it, Conrad, the chief of staff, was dismayed, as the German military attaché recorded in his diary: 'now everything is all over again'.[113]

A more serious threat to Austria-Hungary's determination to have the war with Serbia, however, were the attempts by the Powers to force Vienna to lift the time limit on its démarche. Already in his interview with Lichnowsky on 24 July Grey had voiced his 'strong regret at the provocative tone of the Austrian note and its brief time limit'.[114] If one of the

[110] See min. Nicolson, n.d. [25 July 1914], *ibid.*; see also Neilson, 'My beloved Russians', 548–9. For Tyrrell's support for putting the fleet on alert, see W. S. Churchill, *The World Crisis, 1911–1914* (2 vols., London, 1923) I, 198.

[111] Min. Grey, n.d. [25 July 1914], *BD* XI, no. 100.

[112] Tel. Dumaine to Bienvenu-Martin (no. 105), 24 July 1914 (D 4.45 p.m., R 6.15 p.m.), *DDF* (3) XI, no. 16.

[113] Kageneck diary, 25 July 1914, as quoted in G. Ritter, *Staatskunst und Kriegshandwerk. Das Problem des Militarismus in Deutschland* (4 vols., Munich, 1954–68) II, 381, n. 13. For the false rumour see also Redlich diary, 26 July 1914, *Politische Tagebuch* I, 239.

[114] Tel. Lichnowsky to Auswärtiges Amt (no. 151), 24 July 1914 (D 9.12 p.m., R 1.16 a.m.), *DD* I, no. 157.

axioms of pressure was the denial of time, then conversely lifting the time limit would take much of the heat out of the current situation. For that reason, shortly after midnight on 25 July, Grey circulated Mensdorff's recent note to the embassies at St Petersburg and Paris. The démarche was not an ultimatum but a *note à terme*; relations would be broken off following its rejection, but military operations would not automatically commence.[115] That should create the space needed for Great Power diplomacy to work out a solution. There is no doubt, Mensdorff's 'clarifying' statement and Grey's circular had a calming effect. A more optimistic view gained hold among officials at the Choristers' Bridge and the foreign diplomats at St Petersburg, Schilling recorded in his journal.[116]

Grey pursued this line further and made it part of his Four-Power mediation scheme. Following Austro-Hungarian and Russian mobilization, the four would refrain from mobilizing and offer their good offices to the two eastern monarchies. An eventual direct Austro-Russian settlement was thus still very much to the fore of Grey's diplomatic effort. He understood, however, that the scheme could work only if Berlin supported it and pledged not to mobilize; and it was therefore of paramount importance to sound out Germany first. Russia, he urged Benckendorff in the morning of 25 July, had to counsel the Serbian government against rejecting the note: 'much would be gained, if German mobilization were postponed, and a last effort to prevent a general war was absolutely necessary'. Berlin, not Vienna, was the centre of action, and all de-escalation efforts had to go through Berlin. Grey would not, Benckendorff was certain, declare his hand while the crisis lasted, but 'preserve the position that ... conforms to the role of peacemaker'. All attempts to force Grey to side with France and Russia would make no impression, he concluded.[117]

While Benckendorff was with him, Grey received a telegram from Crackanthorpe at Belgrade – and this did make an impression. The Serbian government, the chargé wired, would meet Vienna's demands 'in as large [a] measure as possible'.[118] If Belgrade's reply was as conciliatory as reported, then it should be possible to induce the Habsburg leadership to reciprocate; and, again, time would be won. At the root of Grey's

---

[115] Tel. Grey to Buchanan (no. 352), 25 July 1914 (D 12.10 a.m.), *BD* XI, no. 105; see tel. Berchtold to Mensdorff (no. 161), 24 July 1914 (D 3.30 p.m.), *ÖUA* VIII, no. 10599; and aide mémoire Buchanan (urgent), 12/25 July 1914, *IBZI* V, no. 45.

[116] Schilling journal, 12/25 July 1914, *IBZI* V, no. 51.

[117] Tels. Benckendorff to Sazonov (nos. 200 and 201), 12/25 July 1914, *IBZI* V, nos. 54–5.

[118] Tel. Crackanthorpe to Grey (no. 52), 25 July 1914 (D 12.30 p.m., R 3 p.m.), *BD* XI, no. 114. Benckendorff's telegram (no. 201) confirms the good impression the news from Belgrade made on Grey.

calculations, as Benckendorff rightly surmised, was an assumption that the hard line taken by the two Germanic Powers contained 'a certain dose of bluff'. Suspending all military preparations by the four mediating Powers would thus allow for 'feeling Germany's pulse', as Benckendorff put it, to test how real 'the will to war in Berlin' was. Grey would wish to preserve his 'complete freedom of action' so that he could push his efforts to preserve peace to the utmost. Benckendorff's analysis offered a shrewd insight into Grey's thinking, shrewder and more perceptive than many later attempts by historians to reconstruct the Foreign Secretary's diplomatic strategy. Whether Grey was sceptical of his own chances of success, as the Russian ambassador intimated, however, may be doubted. But for the moment, Grey was certainly right: 'if it were possible that Germany at least temporarily loosened her ties with Austria, there would be a chance for peace again'.[119]

Grey felt obliged to explore this option to the end, and accordingly he tackled Lichnowsky again in the early afternoon of 25 July. The Foreign Secretary based his latest initiative on Mensdorff's explanations of the previous evening. If the rupture of relations led to military preparations but did not immediately initiate operations, then this 'interposed a stage of mobilisation before [the] actual crossing of [the] frontier, which I had urged yesterday to delay'. If Austria-Hungary and subsequently also Russia mobilized, then the four Powers had 'to keep together' and press Vienna and St Petersburg 'not to cross the frontier till there had been time for us to endeavour to arrange matters between them'. Grey repeatedly stressed that Germany's participation was essential, and that German mobilization would scupper the initiative. Lichnowsky argued, as instructed, that Vienna could not now draw back, but he at once appreciated what Grey was offering: 'mediation between Russia and Austria; this was a different question, and he thought Austria might with dignity accept'.[120]

Lichnowsky was receptive to Grey's scheme. Events in recent days had done nothing to dissipate his dismay at the Wilhelmstrasse's wilful negligence of Germany's strategic interests. Privately, he returned to the charge just before the ultimatum in what amounted to a neo-Bismarckian critique of Berlin's current policy. For all the criticism he had previously expressed of Austria-Hungary, he did not advocate abandoning the *Zweibund* alliance with the Monarchy. But the circumstances which had led to the combination with Vienna had changed beyond

---

[119] Benckendorff to Sazonov (private), 12/25 July 1914, *IBZI* v, no. 56.
[120] Tel. Grey to Rumbold (no. 197), 25 July 1914 (D 3 p.m.), *BD* xi, no. 116.

all recognition. Bismarck had sought the alliance to remove the option of a war of revenge, aided by Russia, from Vienna's political toolkit. Russia had no interest in a military confrontation with Germany. For the past thirty years, he observed, the leading lights in the general staff at Berlin had periodically predicted Russia's readiness for war 'in a few years'; and yet war never came. Nor would it come, for Russia's 'sphere of interest has shifted eastwards, where ever new territories are opened up to Russia's unfolding power'. This process fully occupied the attention of the Tsar's ministers, not least because it contained the seeds of future complications with Britain in Asia. For her part, Germany had little to gain from a 'prophylactic war … except turning a second neighbour into an irreconcilable enemy'.

This still left the problem of the Austro-German alliance. For all his Anglophilia and his relaxed view of relations with Russia, Lichnowsky did not advocate replacing the Habsburg alliance with an arrangement with either of these two Powers. But it was important to ensure that Germany was the 'leading, but not the suffering party [leitende, nicht aber der leidende Teil]'. This, of course, was precisely what between them the Kaiser and the Wilhelmstrasse had contrived to achieve. Originally intended as a form of 'insurance against political storm damage', the alliance was now in danger of merging the two countries into a 'joint political company'. The Great Power status of the Habsburg Empire needed to be preserved. It was not in Germany's strategic interest, however, to facilitate the spread of Austro-Hungarian influence in south-eastern Europe. On the contrary, in political terms, a beleaguered, but not enfeebled, Monarchy was a 'more congenial alliance partner', while commercially the waning of Habsburg influence was beneficial for Germany's growing trade presence in the Balkans: 'Whether they accuse us of going soft [Flaumacherei] there, is really completely immaterial; they will always complain about us there, and they only laugh about us and our much-vaunted Nibelungen fidelity'. The Habsburg Empire was no more going to disintegrate than a firm foreign policy was going to re-energize it. A Balkan war could not arrest the further growth of Southern Slav nationalism but fuel it and drive the smaller regional states into Russia's warm embrace. Austria-Hungary's alliance-worthiness lay in her military capabilities, not in her regional prestige; and at any rate, Germany's position was strong enough to maintain the influence of the Dreibund combination 'despite Count Berchtold's diplomatic defeats'.

All of this was a stinging indictment of Berlin's strategic myopia. But there was one more sting in the tail. In so far as localizing the Austro-Serbian quarrel was concerned, Lichnowsky observed, this belonged to the 'realm of pious hopes' as soon as Austria-Hungary resorted to force.

Vienna's démarche ought to be toned down so that Belgrade, under pressure from St Petersburg and London, could accept it, and not lead to a war 'ad majorem illustrissimi comitis de Berchtold gloriam [to the greater glory of the illustrious Count von Berchtold]'.[121]

The ambassador's warning of the need to frame the démarche in moderate terms, of course, came far too late; and he invoked the 'iron chancellor's' name and spirit in vain. Lichnowsky understood well enough that there was no Bismarck at the Wilhelmstrasse. If Berlin proved impervious to a reasoned strategic exposition then a more emphatic warning might have more success. Before his interview with the Foreign Secretary, and reflecting on the discussions of the previous evening, the ambassador, therefore, alerted the Wilhelmstrasse to the 'well-nigh devastating' impression created in London by Germany's strong support for Vienna's démarche. Unless Berlin joined Grey's initiative, 'confidence in us and our pacific intentions will be finally shaken here'.[122] The ambassador's insistence reflected his mounting desperation at the escalating Balkan crisis as much as it reflected his own isolated position in the German diplomatic service. It was indicative of his sense of urgency that he reported his interview with Grey twice. Significantly, the Foreign Secretary did not have to belabour the point he wished to drive home to the German ambassador. Lichnowsky understood, and Grey could rely on him to understand. In his first, shorter telegram the Prince enjoined Jagow to support Grey's proposal: 'I see in it the only means of averting a world war, in which for us there would be much at risk and nothing to gain'.[123]

Grey, he reported in the second telegram, had been very calm in his exposition of the risks of escalation. Without German support, mediation would have no chance of success. Grey made a sharp distinction between the Austro-Serbian dispute and the threatening Austro-Russian crisis. The former, Lichnowsky reported to the Wilhelmstrasse, was of no concern to Britain; indeed, Grey acknowledged Vienna's right to demand satisfaction for the assassination of the Archduke. The latter, however, had the potential to lead to world war, and London could not be indifferent to European complications. Anglo-German cooperation had helped to bring stability to the Balkans and Europe in 1912 and 1913, and Grey wished 'as before, so

---

[121] Lichnowsky to Jagow (private), 23 July 1914, *DD* I, no. 161; H. F. Young, *Prince Lichnowsky and the Great War* (Athens, GA, 1977), 105.

[122] Tel. Lichnowsky to Auswärtiges Amt (no. 152), 25 July 1914 (D 10.49 a.m., R 12.48 p.m.), *DD* I, no. 163; F. Fischer, *Der Griff nach der Weltmacht. Die Kriegszielpolitik des kaiserlichen Deutschland, 1914–1918* (Düsseldorf, 3rd rev. edn, 1964), 78–9.

[123] Tel. Lichnowsky to Auswärtiges Amt (no. 155), 25 July 1914 (D 2 p.m., R 5.21 p.m.), *DD* I, no. 179.

now, to proceed hand-in-hand with us [Germany] in the interest of preserving European peace'. Lichnowsky undoubtedly amplified Grey's statement. Berlin, he urged Jagow, ought to adopt 'a friendly and largely neutral position' and 'participate hand-in-hand with England in averting the threatening European thunderstorm'. Rejecting the initiative would drive Britain into the Franco-Russian camp.[124]

Grey was not alone in urging Vienna to agree to an extension of the deadline. Sazonov instructed Prince Kudashev, the chargé d'affaires at Vienna, to impress upon Berchtold the urgent need for lifting the time limit so that the Powers could put forward their good offices.[125] Grey was prepared to support the Russian move in general terms. From his perspective, however, matters had moved on since Mensdorff's explanations of the nature of his government's note to Serbia. What mattered now was not so much the time limit contained in the démarche; what was more important was that Vienna 'will ... give time in the sense and for the reasons desired by Russia before taking any irrevocable steps'.[126] But the Ballhausplatz was not inclined to heed the advice proffered, even though military operations would still be delayed for some time. Neither Grey nor any of the other foreign ministers, however, could know this.

In the morning of 24 July, Berchtold received Kudashev and was at pains to demonstrate his 'good dispositions' towards Russia. No territorial annexations were planned, he assured the chargé d'affaires; nor did he wish to bring about 'a shift in the power relations in the Balkans and in Europe'. On the contrary, it would be conducive to international calm if Serbia's subversive agitation were stopped, and – here again the appeal to monarchical solidarity – the European monarchies should join forces 'in rejecting the Serbian policy conducted with revolvers and bombs'.[127] Austria-Hungary could not possibly withdraw now for reasons of state, Berchtold informed Szápáry. To do so would amount to a form of 'Russian licence' for Serbia to continue her subversive agitation in the Habsburg dominions. The next few days would show whether Russia was really as ready for war as the belligerent articles in *Novoe Vremya* or *Birshevi'a Vedomosti* had been at pains to suggest. If St Petersburg

[124] Tel. Lichnowsky to Auswärtiges Amt (no. 154), 25 July 1914 (D 2.02 p.m., R 5.52 p.m.), *DD* I, no. 180. Telegram no. 155 thus preceded this report.

[125] Tel. Kudashev to Sazonov (no. 95), 12/25 July 1914, *IBZI* V, no. 66; Benckendorff note, 25 July 1914, *BD* XI, no. 117. Bronevski, the chargé d'affaires at Berlin, submitted a similar note at the Wilhelmstrasse: see *DD* I, no. 172.

[126] Tel. Grey to de Bunsen (no. 153), 25 July 1914 (D 3.15 p.m.), *BD* XI, no. 118.

[127] Tel. Tschirschky to Auswärtiges Amt (no. 101), 24 July 1914 (D 8.50 p.m., R 11.23 p.m.), *DD* I, no. 155.

showed willingness to resort to force, the ambassador was instructed to wave the big German stick. But otherwise Sazonov was to be assured that Austria-Hungary pursued no selfish interests in the Balkans but in self-defence and for self-preservation. The Monarchy had never sought to block the development of the Balkan nations, but, since the demise of the Ottoman Empire, Serbian nationalism had developed a strong poise against Austria-Hungary. Berchtold singled out the friendly relations with Montenegro, Southern Slav and Orthodox, to underline the non-religious nature of Habsburg foreign policy. Austria-Hungary would deprecate anything liable to disrupt the European peace. Her policy was a policy of peace. Indeed, over the past forty years, 'our Most Gracious Lord [the Emperor] had won for himself the title of the Defender of Peace'; and he hoped that the 'common conservative, monarchical and dynastic interests of the three empires' would ultimately lead to a restoration of closer ties between them: 'Our action against Serbia, whatever form it may take, is a thoroughly conservative one and its purpose is the necessary maintenance of our European position.'[128]

There was an element of truth in Berchtold's observations, but for the most part it was window-dressing. Indeed, when Kudashev returned with Sazonov's request for an extension of the ultimatum, he was met by Baron Macchio, the foreign minister having left for the Emperor's summer residence at Ischl shortly after the first meeting. Macchio reiterated the familiar line that the ultimatum was no such thing, but also stressed that Vienna would not consent to a line-by-line exegesis of its demands and its accompanying note to the Powers. The Monarchy had shown considerable patience with past Serbian provocations, and it now expected that its demands were accepted without reservations and without delay. On Berchtold's instructions, Macchio reaffirmed this line later in the day, adding that Belgrade's acceptance of the demands after the expiry of the time limit in the démarche could still avert military conflict, though Serbia would have to pay material compensation for the costs of Austria-Hungary's mobilization.[129] As Berchtold had left the capital for Ischl earlier that morning, Kudashev took the precaution of telegraphing his request directly to the foreign minister travelling on the express train 109 to Linz and on to the Emperor's

---

[128] Berchtold instructions for St Petersburg (no. 3530), 25 July 1914, ÖUA VIII, no. 10685.

[129] Tel. Macchio to Berchtold, and reply, both 25 July 1914 (D 1.45 p.m. and D 2 p.m., R 4 p.m.), ÖUA VIII, nos. 10703–4. The notion of additional compensation, of course, had been agreed between Berchtold and Conrad, *vide supra*.

summer residence. It was to no avail; Berchtold, Macchio informed the Prince, could not be contacted.[130]

Macchio's excuse was something of a terminological inexactitude, but it was one that also appealed to Jagow at the Wilhelmstrasse. There the British and Russian suggestions for an extension of the ultimatum were most unwelcome; and so was the Foreign Secretary's last-minute request, transmitted through Lichnowsky, that Berlin urge the Ballhausplatz to take a favourable view of Belgrade's anticipated conciliatory reply.[131] Grey's idea of 24 July of lifting the time limit elicited one of the Kaiser's characteristic outbursts. 'Useless', 'superfluous' and 'nonsense' he wrote in the margins of Lichnowsky's telegram along with the usual array of exclamation and question marks: 'I will not take part, except if Austria expressly begs me, which is not likely. In questions of honour and *vital* questions one does not consult others.'[132] As always when confronted with the Kaiser's marginalia, it is tempting to dismiss them as nothing more than the manifestation of a form of pen-and-paper violence. Eventually, once he had thrown his inky thunderbolts, the Kaiser's anger tended to dissipate. But his comments on the London telegram nevertheless touched on a key German consideration. Whereas ambassador Lichnowsky wished to relegate Austria-Hungary to the position of Germany's junior partner, at Berlin fears of the Habsburg Empire's further enfeeblement and ultimate collapse were never far from the surface. Reining in the ally at Vienna before Serbia had been cowed held few attractions for the Wilhelmstrasse.

Jagow and Stumm, the political director at the Auswärtiges Amt, reaffirmed this in conversations with Theodor Wolff, editor of the *Berliner Tageblatt*, in the morning of 25 July. The state secretary dismissed the distinguished journalist's warning that Russia might not yield, and that a European war would ensue: 'Neither Russia nor France nor England want war', he asserted. But if the situation escalated, he added with a smile, 'one day war will come, if we let things go on. And in two years Russia will be stronger than now.' This, of course, was the line Jagow had started to develop since the middle of July, when he had begun to rationalize the developments since 5 July. Even so, as Wolff left, Jagow called after him:

[130] Tel. Kudashev to Berchtold, 25 July 1914 (D 10.50 a.m., R 12.10 p.m.), ÖUA VIII, no. 10686; tel. Kudashev to Sazonov (no. 96), 12/25 July 1914, *IBZI* V, no. 67.

[131] Tel. Lichnowsky to Auswärtiges Amt (no. 156), 25 July 1914 (D 6.09 p.m., R 9.25 p.m.), *DD* I, no. 186; enclosed with this telegram was tel. Crackanthorpe to Grey (no. 52), 25 July 1914, *BD* XI, no. 114.

[132] Marginalia Wilhelm II, on tel. Lichnowsky to Auswärtiges Amt (151), 24 July 1914, *DD* I, no. 157. The telegram was seen by the Kaiser sometime after 3.45 p.m. on 26 July, and returned later that same day.

'I do not take the situation to be critical.' Stumm, whom Wolff saw immediately afterwards, offered an even more optimistic assessment of the situation. Berlin was determined 'to establish whether Austria was still worth anything as an ally. It must not yield.' The Russians, he predicted, 'would shout loudly and some hot days might follow'. Russia might even mobilize, in which case it would be important to restrain the military leadership at Berlin. But Russia would be reluctant to move any further. In the event of a war, there would be revolutions in Russia's Finnish and Polish provinces – 'and you will see that everything has been stolen (from Russian depots), even rifle locks, and that there is no ammunition'. In the worst case, Stumm assured his visitor, Berlin had a line of retreat in view. But Russia was simply paralyzed, and the situation would not escalate.[133]

Stumm was well-known at Berlin for his bouts of flippancy. Yet this was one of the most egregious cases of political leaders whistling in the dark, matched only by their recklessness. No line of possible retreat had been plotted beforehand, and no thought had been given to a possible 'endgame'. The notion, moreover, that Russia was somehow incapable of intervening was widely held amongst German diplomats. After his somewhat heated exchanges with Sazonov on the previous day, Pourtalès had concluded that Russia would resort to military force only if Austria-Hungary 'intended to make territorial acquisitions at the expense of Serbia'. If anything, the ambassador observed, Sazonov's insistence on some form of internationalization of the Austro-Serbian crisis further underlined that Russia would not intervene unilaterally.[134] In a similar vein, the ambassador at Constantinople, Baron Hans Wilhelm von Wangenheim, reported a conversation with his Russian colleague, Mikhail Nikola'evich de Giers. Vienna's demands were understandable, Giers suggested, but the demand for what he called 'Austrian control officials' operating in Serbia meant an infringement of her sovereignty. The situation was therefore serious. Even so, as Wangenheim observed, the ambassador's language was 'calm and contains no threats'.[135] Such information was not

[133] Wolff diary, 25 July 1914, B. Sösemann (ed.), *Theodor Wolff. Tagebücher, 1914–1919* (Boppard, 1984), no. 3; also T. Wolff, *Der Krieg des Pontius Pilatus* (Zürich, 1934), 324; F. Fischer, 'The Miscalculation of English Neutrality: An Aspect of German Foreign Policy on the Eve of World War I', S. Wank et al. (eds.), *The Mirror of History: Essays in Honor of Fritz Fellner* (Santa Barbara, CA, 1987), 380.

[134] Tel. Pourtalès to Auswärtiges Amt (no. 149), 25 July 1914 (D 1.08 a.m., R 3.45 a.m.), DD I, no. 160.

[135] Tel. Wangenheim to Auswärtiges Amt (no. 367), 25 July 1914 (D 6.35 p.m., R 9.03 p.m.), DD I, no. 184; see also tel. Pallavicini to Berchtold (no. 346), 25 July 1914 (D 5.20 p.m., R 9 a.m.), ÖUA VIII, no. 10672.

at all conclusive, of course, but it was sufficient to reinforce the 'group-think' at the Wilhelmstrasse.

Pourtalès was not prone to making racialist assumptions about Slavs, but others at Berlin were. In turn, this reinforced the line of argument developed by Stumm about the need to test Austria-Hungary's alliance-worthiness. As a Slavic entity, Serbia was expected to be unable to withstand the pressure of the neighbouring Great Power. Once again, the Kaiser's marginalia illustrate the point. When Griesinger, the German envoy to Serbia, reported on the crisis mood at Belgrade, the monarch scrawled on it: 'How hollow this so-called Greater Serbian state shows itself to be, and so it is with all Slav states! Always firmly step on the feet of these rascals!'[136]

With such arguments and delusions swirling around Berlin, Jagow decided to follow Macchio's example. He passed on Grey's request for an extension of the ultimatum to the Vienna embassy with the observation that since Berchtold was now at Ischl, it would be impossible to act on the British initiative.[137] As for Grey's idea of Four-Power mediation, Jagow sought to sidestep it. He shared the Foreign Secretary's desire to separate the Austro-Serbian and any putative Austro-Russian disputes. It was therefore incumbent on all Powers, he asserted, to ensure that the Serbian conflict remained localized; and this meant above all that Russia had to 'refrain from any active interference'. Were an Austro-Russian dispute to develop, then, Berlin would support international mediation, subject, however, to 'our known alliance obligations'.[138] He had no prior knowledge of Vienna's démarche, Jagow affirmed to Rumbold, the British chargé d'affaires. To an extent, of course, that was true, though Jagow knew, as seen earlier, that stiff demands were planned and that they were meant to be unacceptable. Rumbold nevertheless believed Jagow's assurances:

> As a rule, when I had my interviews with him, I used to sit facing him at a very large table. He generally spent his time drawing heads of men and women on bits of paper, which was one way of collecting his thoughts. When, however, he stated he had not known beforehand of the contents of the Austrian ultimatum, he

---

[136] Marginalia Wilhelm II, n.d. [25 July 1914], on tel. Griesinger to Auswärtiges Amt (no. 31), 24 July 1914 (D 9.45 p.m., R 2.33 a.m.), *DD* I, no. 159. The telegram was forwarded to the Kaiser's entourage at 2.10 p.m. (R 3.45 p.m.).

[137] Tel. Jagow to Tschirschky (no. 140), 25 July 1914 (D 4 p.m.), *DD* I, no. 171; cf. tel. Rumbold to Grey (no. 90), 25 July 1914 (D 3.16 p.m., R 6 p.m.), *BD* XI, no. 122.

[138] Tel. Jagow to Lichnowsky (no. 176), 25 July 1914 (D 11.05 p.m.), *DD* I, no. 192.

looked me straight in the fact [*sic, recte* face] and I certainly had the impression that he was telling the truth.[139]

Jagow further explained that he did not know 'what Austria-Hungary had ready on the spot, but he admitted quite freely that [the] Austro-Hungarian Government wished to give the Servians a lesson, and that they meant to take military action'.[140] This was a very risky line to take. In effect, it placed the burden of averting war on Grey and Sazonov. At the same time, it was clear that any settlement would have to be on Austro-German terms. 'It amounts to this', Rumbold retorted, 'you have given Austria a blank cheque'.[141] In the late afternoon, two hours before the expiry of the ultimatum, Rumbold wrote to his wife: 'The Lord only knows what will happen then [after the expiry] and I tell you … that we shall be lucky if we get out of this without the long-dreaded European war, a general bust-up in fact.'[142]

Count Mérey takes to his bed

There was, however, one problem for Jagow. Neither he nor anyone else at the Wilhelmstrasse knew precisely what the Austrians intended to do once their note had been rejected by Belgrade. As was seen earlier, there had been an expectation at Berlin that Austria-Hungary would strike soon after the 'blank cheque' had been issued. The prolonged delay since then had increased the risk of interference by the Powers. Any further delay in opening military operations after the expiry of the ultimatum would increase that risk exponentially. With that in mind, Jagow impressed upon Szögyény the imperative importance of swift action. 'They urgently counsel us to move at once and to confront the world with a *fait accompli*.'[143] The advice neatly dovetailed with the Wilhelmstrasse line so far. Following the 'blank cheque', however, short of cancelling it altogether, Berlin had no

---

[139] Rumbold to Drummond, 1 Aug. 1917, Rumbold MSS, Bodl., Ms. Rumbold dep. 22. In light of the post-war publication of documents, Rumbold later changed his mind. Jagow's 'denial merely referred to the form in which the note was couched and not its substance', Rumbold to Lindsay (private), 27 Feb. 1929, *ibid.*, Ms. Rumbold dep. 36.
[140] Tel. Rumbold to Grey (no. 90), 25 July 1914 (D 3.16 p.m., R 6 p.m.), *BD* XI, no. 122.
[141] Rumbold to Drummond, 1 Aug. 1917, Rumbold MSS, Bodl., Ms. Rumbold dep. 22.
[142] Rumbold to Louisa Rumbold, 25 July 1914, *ibid.*, Ms. Rumbold dep. 16; Gilbert, *Rumbold*, 111.
[143] Tel. Szögyény to Berchtold (no. 285), 25 July 1914 (D 2.15 p.m., R 8 p.m.), *ÖUA* VIII, no. 10656.

means of forcing the Habsburg leadership to heed its advice. And the German leadership was not yet ready to contemplate such a drastic step.

A swift strike against Serbia, however, was also considered necessary with a view to Italy. At Rome, the tardiness of Habsburg diplomacy and the delay in informing the Consulta of the impending démarche at Belgrade had made an unfavourable impression. Matters were not helped by the Austro-Hungarian ambassador. In his previous post at the Ballhausplatz, Kajetan von Mérey had proved to be an intelligent and effective official, albeit with a propensity to run the department on somewhat dictatorial lines. But at the Palazzo Chigi in Rome he was singularly misplaced. Irritable and highly strung, he was overtly suspicious of all things Italian and brusque in his personal conduct; and there was a hard edge to his character. He was a diplomat 'who said No more often than Yes', as the journalist and Berchtold-intimate Berthold Molden later recalled.[144] This might not have mattered if Mérey had been able to say 'No' in a manner that might have sounded more like 'Yes'. But this was beyond him. Scarcely able to suppress his distaste for most things Italian, he epitomized the many tensions in the relations between Rome and Vienna. Indeed, at Berlin it was observed with some dismay that Mérey and his superiors at the Ballhausplatz could not shake off their '*k.u.k. Katzelmacher*-point of view'.[145] It was almost symptomatic of the cold nature of these relations that Mérey, apparently ill in bed, left it to his embassy counsellor, Baron Ludwig Ambrózy von Séden, to inform the Italian foreign ministry of the note addressed to the Belgrade government, and that San Giuliano, still convalescing at Fiuggi Fonte, was represented by the department's secretary-general, Giacomo de Martino.[146]

---

[144] B. Molden, 'Botschafter von Mérey', *BMH* x, 5 (1932), 460 [460–1]; also E. Cormons [pseudo. E. Urbas], *Schicksale und Schatten. Eine österreichische Autobiographie* (Salzburg, 1951), 125. The palazzo is today the official seat of the Italian prime minister.

[145] M. Claas, 'Die römische Mission des österreichisch-ungarischen Botschafters von Mérey', *BMH* x, 3 (1932), 246; see also H. von Flotow, 'Um Bülows römische Mission', F. Thimme (ed.), *Front wider Bülow. Staatsmänner, Diplomaten und Forscher zu seinen Denkwürdigkeiten* (Munich, 1931), 240. 'Katzelmacher' was a pejorative Viennese term for southern Europeans, and especially Italians, indicating showy behaviour and untruthfulness.

[146] Tel. Mérey to Berchtold (no. 535), 24 July 1914 (D 4.30 p.m., R 9 a.m.), *ÖUA* VIII, no. 10611; tel. Flotow to Auswärtiges Amt (no. 19), 24 July 1914 (D 7.30 a.m., R 10.50 a.m.), *DD* I, no. 136. The lateness of Austria-Hungary's information was little more than a pretext for Italian grievance-mongering. Italy had not informed Berlin or Vienna of her own twenty-four-hour ultimatum to Turkey in September 1911: see tel. Szögyény to Berchtold (no. 283), 25 July 1914, *ÖUA* VIII, no. 10655. Macchio, by contrast, regretted

On perusing the Austro-Hungarian note, the Italian official noted its stiff terms and commented that 'we appeared to have arrived at a turning point of history'. This was also the foreign minister's impression. Already in the early morning of 24 July, in anticipation of the Austro-Hungarian démarche, he instructed the Italian ambassadors at Berlin and Vienna, but also at St Petersburg, to explain to the governments there that Italy had no formal obligation towards the two Germanic Powers in the event of a Balkan war. At the same time, he brought the recent developments to the attention of the prime minister, Antonio Salandra, and laid particular stress on the fact that any Austro-Hungarian occupation of Balkan territory without prior consultation with Italy, and even if it was meant as a temporary measure only, was in breach of article VII of the Triple Alliance treaty.[147]

Following Ambrózy's communication of the note, San Giuliano returned to the capital later on 24 July to meet Flotow, the German ambassador. That he sought him out rather than Mérey was no doubt a reflection of the friendly ties between the foreign minister and Germany's representative, and of San Giuliano's instinctive preference for some form of Italo-German combination. More importantly, just as Grey had been, San Giuliano was convinced that representations addressed at the Austro-Hungarian government would not be listened to at Vienna unless they were amplified through the Berlin loudhailer. The meeting with Flotow lasted several hours and was also attended by prime minister Salandra. By all accounts, it was a heated encounter. Austro-Hungarian aggression had violated the defensive and conservative spirit of the triplice, San Giuliano argued, and Italy was not, in consequence, bound to support the other two Powers in the event of further complications. Flotow's insistence that only the appearance of *Dreibund* unity could prevent attempts by the other Powers to intervene, and thus avert the further escalation of the crisis, was rebuffed by the foreign minister. Italy would keep her options open. According to his own account, San Giuliano developed this into the familiar theme of the need for some tangible compensation for Italy. The country's political system, he explained, made it necessary for the government 'to give the country the certainty of some advantage corresponding to the risks and such as

the manner in which Italy was informed: see tel. Tschirschky to Auswärtiges Amt (no. 103), 25 July 1914, *DD* I, no. 187.

[147] All of this went through de Martino at the Consulta: see tels. San Giuliano to de Martino, 23 July 1914 (D 10 p.m.), *DDI* (4) XII, nos. 449–50; see also R. J. B. Bosworth, *Italy, the Least of the Great Powers: Italian Foreign Policy before the First World War* (Cambridge, 1979), 388.

to overcome the resistance of public opinion to a war fought for the interests of Austria'.[148]

For his part, San Giuliano was positioning himself to extract some advantage from the unfolding crisis. A diplomatic solution was still possible at this stage, and by adhering to the *Dreibund* alliance, albeit with a strong display of reluctance, Italy might receive territorial compensation, facilitated by German pressure on Vienna.[149] If, on the other hand, the Austro-Serbian dispute could not be settled, then San Giuliano had taken the first steps towards reorientating Italian foreign policy towards neutrality. For now, no further decisions were necessary, he wrote to Salandra, safely ensconced again at his Fiuggi refuge. It was imperative 'to leave everyone … in uncertainty about our attitude and about our decisions so as to obtain some positive advantages. For the first time, since the kingdom of Italy has existed, has a German foreign minister said that the moment is favourable to have the Trentino.' The best course now was: 'work in silence, say little, do not be in a hurry, and be as far from Rome as possible'.[150] And yet, whilst he pretended to have avoided any premature decisions and to have different options still open to him, San Giuliano had in fact prepared the ground for Italy's drift away from the two Germanic Powers towards the entente after an initial period of neutrality.[151]

The Kaiser, on receiving Flotow's telegraphic report on the conversation with the two Italian ministers, might well fulminate that 'the little thief just has to have something to swallow as well',[152] but Flotow had clearly understood the full import of San Giuliano's hints. Three factors determined the minister's policy, he reasoned: a fear of Italian public opinion, his consciousness of Italy's military weakness, and the wish 'to extract something for Italy, if possible the Trentino'. Naturally, Flotow essayed not to encourage any such irredentist ambitions, though San Giuliano clearly was under quite a different impression. Even so, the ambassador pressed Berlin to accept that if Austria-Hungary acquired

---

[148] Quotes from tel. Flotow to Auswärtiges Amt (no. 20), 24 July 1914 (D 8.10 p.m., R 12.10 a.m.), *DD* I, no. 156; and tel. San Giuliano to Avarna and Bollati (no. 759), 24 July 1914 (D 10.40 p.m.), *DDI* (4) XII, no. 488; see also A. Salandra, *La neutralità Italiana (1914)* (Milan, 1927), 76–8.

[149] See tel. Flotow to Auswärtiges Amt (no. 24), 26 July 1914 (D 3.40 p.m., R 5.10 p.m.), *DD* I, no. 211; Flotow, 'Römische Mission', 239.

[150] San Giuliano to Salandra (private), 26 July 1914, *DDI* (4) XII, no. 560.

[151] Richard Bosworth goes further still, and argues that San Giuliano anticipated a prolonged conflict, which in turn would have offered Rome many 'exploitable complications': see *Least of the Powers*, 390.

[152] Marginal note Wilhelm II on tel. Jagow to Wilhelm II (incorporating tel. Flotow to Auswärtiges Amt (no. 134), 24 July 1914), 25 July 1914 (D 3 p.m.), *DD* I, no. 168.

territory in the Balkans – he mentioned again Mount Lovćen – Vienna would have to offer compensation beforehand. Given San Giuliano's repeated reference to the aggressive nature of the Austro-Hungarian move, Flotow warned, Italy would endeavour 'to slip away' from the *Dreibund* combination: 'The total result thus is: one can hardly count on the active assistance of Italy in any ensuing European conflict. An openly hostile attitude of Italy could, as far as can be seen today, be prevented by the prudent behaviour of Austria.'[153]

Therein of course lay the problem. What was deemed prudent by Berlin – the maintenance of the *Dreibund* alliance – could be achieved only by ceding Habsburg territory. A swift fait accompli now would reduce Italy's room for making mischief. Hence Jagow's urgent advice to Vienna to declare war immediately on rejecting the Serbian response to the note later that evening and to commence 'warlike operations' at once.[154] But this implied the need to resist all attempts by the other Powers to mediate until the moment Vienna proved incapable of subjugating Belgrade. And until then, Jagow could do no more than instruct Tschirschky at Vienna to impress upon the Ballhausplatz that it was imperative 'to find a practicable way forward'. Berchtold's reply – that the Italian acquisitions in the Aegean in 1911–12 had not triggered Austro-Hungarian counterclaims and that therefore Rome could not now demand compensation, and that any military operations against Serbia could not be classed as an occupation – was difficult to refute.[155] But it illustrated just how difficult it would be for German diplomacy to assert control over the *Dreibund* and to conciliate the other two partners in that combination.

Baron Giesl leaves Belgrade

While the chancelleries of Europe moved in anticipation of Belgrade's reply to the Habsburg démarche, the Serbian capital itself resembled a 'beehive', as Baron Giesl, the Austro-Hungarian minister there, later recalled. According to the recollections of his German colleague,

[153] Flotow to Bethmann Hollweg, 25 July 1914 (R 27 July), *DD* I, no. 244. The letter was reported to the Kaiser by the Chancellor; both Wilhelm and Bethmann agreed that Vienna had to reach a timely understanding with Italy on the question of compensation: min. Bethmann Hollweg, 27 July 1914, *ibid.*

[154] Tel. Szögyény to Berchtold (no. 285), 25 July 1914, ÖUA VIII, no. 10656.

[155] Tel. Tschirschky to Auswärtiges Amt (no. 106), 26 July 1914 (D 4.50 p.m., R 6.15 p.m.), *DD* I, no. 212; daily report Berchtold, 26 July 1914, ÖUA VIII, no. 10715.

Griesinger, the mood in the streets of Belgrade was 'uneasy, and yet unquestionably depressed'.[156]

Following the presentation of Vienna's démarche and in Pašić's absence from the capital, during the night of 23–4 July Dušan Stefanović, the war minister, ordered the first tentative military measures in preparation for full mobilization. The military flour mill and provisions were dispatched to Niš; the railways were placed under military control, and military trains left Belgrade station; explosive devices were fitted underneath the Sava bridge to blow it up on the outbreak of conflict; medical columns were heading out of Belgrade towards the south; secret government files and the gold reserves of Serbia's National Bank were transported to a secure location near Stalać, some thirty-eight miles north-west of Niš. Further preparations were made to evacuate the government to Niš. Later on 24 July, Field Marshal Putnik arrived at Orsova (now Orşova) from his sojourn at the Gleichenberg spa. He had been briefly detained by Austro-Hungarian police, but was then released on the orders of the Emperor himself.[157]

These were sensible military precautions, and were not in themselves an indication that the civilian authorities at Belgrade were coming under the influence of the military. They underlined the acute concerns about Serbia's lack of military preparedness, fuelled by rumours of Habsburg forces massing around Semlin (now Zemun) in readiness for a strike immediately on the expiry of the ultimatum. Certainly, however, the influence of the military party had been strengthened. Drum rolls in the squares of the capital and outside its many cafés called up reservists. It was this, presumably, that persuaded the Austro-Hungarian and German ministers that mobilization was already in full swing.[158] Having twice met on 24 July to discuss Vienna's note, on the following day the Serbian cabinet was sitting almost without interruption, its meetings presided over by the Regent, Prince Alexandar. By mid-afternoon, Serbia's official response to the Habsburg démarche was complete.[159]

---

[156] Quotes from W. von Giesl, 'Konnte die Annahme der serbischen Antwortnote den Ausbruch des Weltkrieges verhindern?', *BMH* XI, 5 (1933), 464; and [J. A.] von Griesinger, 'Die kritischen Tage in Serbien', *ibid.*, VIII, 9 (1930), 839.

[157] Strandtmann to Sazonov (no. 42), 24 July/6 Aug. 1914, *IBZI* V, app. 8; tel. Giesl to Berchtold (no. 182), 25 July 1914 (D 1 p.m., R 5.30 p.m.), *ÖUA* VIII, no. 10645; see also R. Kiszling, 'Die serbische Mobilmachung im Juli 1914', *BMH* X, 7 (1932), 680–1, who argues that the military asserted its control over the government.

[158] Tel. Griesinger to Auswärtiges Amt (no. 32), 24 July 1914 (D 11.50 p.m., R 25 July a.m.), *DD* I, no. 158; see Cornwall, 'Serbia', 82. On the rumoured massing of the Austro-Hungarian army see also tel. Strandtmann to Sazonov (no. 214), 11/24 July 1914, *IBZI* V, no. 36.

[159] Strandtmann to Sazonov (no. 42), 24 July/6 Aug. 1914, *IBZI* V, app. 8; also tel. Crackanthorpe to Grey (no. 52), 25 July 1914 (D 12.30 p.m., R 3 p.m.), *BD* XI, no. 114;

Belgrade's reaction to the note was, in part, conditioned by the attitude of the Powers. There was little direct support for Serbia – too objectionable had been the assassination of the Archduke, and too great appeared the risks of escalation. Even R. W. Seton-Watson, the historian and political commentator who as 'Scotus Viator' had acquired a reputation as a Balkans expert, was appalled by the murder of the Archduke. Although no supporter of Greater Serbian ideas, he was nevertheless sympathetic to the ambitions of the Balkan nations. Even so, he advised high-powered friends at Belgrade that 'Servia's duty today is to say as little as possible, to offer what little reparation it is possible to offer, without waiting to be asked to do so, and to do everything in her power to prove to the outside world that nobody in responsible positions had anything to do with the conspiracy.'[160] Isolating the Austro-Serbian dispute from the Habsburg-Romanov antagonism in the Balkans, by contrast, seemed the safer option, one that could conceivably be controlled by the Powers. This was Grey's position, and for that reason he had instructed Crackanthorpe to advise the Serbian government 'to give a favourable reply on as many points as possible within the limit of time'.[161] From that perspective, it made little sense to aid Serbia, and Mateja Bošković, the Serbian minister at London, made little headway with such demands at the Foreign Office.[162] Any such support would have made it more difficult to enlist German support for a diplomatic settlement of the dispute between Vienna and Belgrade. Sensing that the Serbian ministers were minded to satisfy Austria-Hungary's demands as much as possible, Crackanthorpe at any rate refrained from offering advice.[163]

Very likely Pašić never expected much support from this quarter. More disheartening, perhaps, was the cool response from Italy. The Regent's appeal to his uncle, the King, had produced no effect. Indeed, the Serbian chargé d'affaires at Rome was clearly given to understand that

tel. Squitti to San Giuliano (no. 810/154), 25 July 1914 (D 4.30 p.m., R 11 p.m.), *DDI* (4) XII, no. 520. Gruić later recalled that the document was already complete in the morning: see Cornwall, 'Serbia', 77.

[160] Seton-Watson to Mme Gruić, 21 July 1914 (copy), Seton-Watson MSS, SSEES, SEW/17/9/1. The addressee was the wife of Dr Slavko Gruić, secretary-general of the Serbian foreign ministry. Seton-Watson had pinned his hopes to Franz Ferdinand's 'trialist' reform schemes: see H. and C. Seton-Watson, *The Making of the New Europe: R. W. Seton-Watson and the Last Years of Austria-Hungary* (London, 1981), 95–8.

[161] Tel. Grey to Crackanthorpe (no. 17), 24 July 1914 (D 9.30 p.m.), *BD* XI, no. 102.

[162] See min. Nicolson [on meeting with Boskovic], 25 July 1914, *BD* XI, no. 119.

[163] Tels. Crackanthorpe to Grey (nos. 53 and 52), 25 July 1914 (D 12.30 p.m., R 2.10 and 3 p.m.), *BD* XI, nos. 111 and 114 (no. 53 was received first).

Belgrade should not expect Italy's assistance and that Russia's role would be central to the eventual outcome of the crisis. Pašić himself, reported the Italian minister at Belgrade, Baron Nicola Squitti of Palermiti and Guarna, had come to accept that only an appeal to the International Court at The Hague or an open appeal to the Great Powers could protect Serbia.[164] No doubt, Pašić's display of pessimism was calculated to present Serbia as the victim of a bullying Great Power neighbour and so deserving of support; some indication of willingness on Rome's part to mediate, moreover, might have helped to limit the extent of any Austro-Hungarian military response to any conditional Serbian reply to the démarche. The attitude of the Powers likely to favour Belgrade was nevertheless not encouraging. Even France remained passive, and Bienvenu-Martin was 'content to offer counsels of prudence to Serbia' but no more.[165]

Russia's attitude was always more significant for Pašić and his government. There was at any rate a widespread assumption at Belgrade, as the Regent explained to Strandtmann, that only Russia asserting her influence could save Serbia now.[166] And yet Sazonov's communications did not suggest energetic support for Serbia. News from St Petersburg certainly did not stiffen Pašić's resolve to resist Austro-Hungarian pressure. As seen already, the Pašić government was not minded to concede all of the demands made by Vienna. Around noon on 25 July, Gruić, the secretary-general of the Serbian foreign ministry, suggested as much in conversation with Crackanthorpe. The government's official reply would be couched in 'most conciliatory terms and will meet [the] Austrian demands in as large [a] measure as possible' – a clear indication that certain demands would not be met.[167] Nevertheless, it seems likely, as Mark Cornwall has suggested, that the lukewarm responses by Paris, Rome and St Petersburg lessened Serbian resolve in the course of 25 July. Certainly, on the following day, the Italian chargé d'affaires at Belgrade noted that the Serbian government was 'fearful at the last moment of remaining isolated'.[168] Two days later, following the evacuation of the government to Niš, Pašić himself asserted that had his government known in advance of the support Serbia would

[164] Tel. Squitti to San Giuliano (no. 810/154), 25 July 1914 (D 4.30 p.m., R 11 p.m.), *DDI* (4) XII, no. 520; for the Italian reaction see also Cornwall, 'Serbia', 78–9.
[165] Bienvenu-Martin circular, 25 July 1914 (D 11.55 a.m.), *DDF* (3) XI, no. 38.
[166] Tel. Strandtmann to Sazonov (no. 212), 12/25 July 1914, *IBZI* V, no. 75 (the conversation took place during the night of 24–5 July).
[167] Tel. Crackanthorpe to Grey (no. 52), 25 July 1914 (D 12.30 p.m., R 3 p.m.), *BD* XI, no. 114.
[168] Tel. Cora to San Giuliano (no. 6684/158), 26 July 1914 (D 2.15 p.m., R 7.18 p.m.), *DDI* (4) XII, no. 548.

receive later, 'it would not even have consented to the concessions made'.[169] It was just as well that Sazonov had not given Belgrade a 'blank cheque'.

Two points are worth bearing in mind when assessing Belgrade's response. In the first instance, the Serbian government was determined not to submit completely to the powerful northern neighbour, though the absence of clear indications of assistance by any of the Great Powers weakened that resolve to some degree on 25 July. As Velizar Janković, the trade minister and one of the chief authors of Belgrade's note, later testified, all members of the government, including the Regent, had been in favour of 'the utmost conciliation on all points, except those which directly and ostensibly violated the dignity of country and people and the sovereignty of king and state'.[170]

But equally important, however conciliatory the official reply to the Austro-Hungarian note, it was never likely to be sufficient. Vienna wanted war. Janković himself may well have caught an early glimpse of this. The education minister was in an awkward position personally. His wife and family were currently on holiday on Austria-Hungary's Adriatic coast, and might find themselves unable to return home on the severing of relations, possibly even interned in the event of hostilities. At the suggestion of Pašić, he decided to see Griesinger, the German envoy, to ask for his assistance in securing safe passage for his family. According to Janković's memoirs, his coachman misunderstood his instructions – a familiar theme in the events of the Sarajevo crisis – and deposited him outside the Austro-Hungarian legation. As his four-wheeler came to a halt at around 5 p.m., the door was opened and the envoy himself stepped out, seemingly expecting Pašić with the official Serbian note. After an embarrassing pause, Giesl bade Janković enter the legation. There he confirmed that the reply would be delivered, as requested, at 6 p.m. He then explained his personal business and Giesl undertook it 'as a gentleman's service' to see to it that Janković's wife and family would receive passports for the onward journey to Venice and a certain sum of money (ten gold *Napoléons*). While the envoy behaved in a perfectly friendly and correct manner, Janković could not help but notice that Giesl wore plus-fours and travel clothes rather than more formal attire and that the

---

[169] Chaprashikov to Bulgarian Foreign Ministry, 14/27 July 1914, 'Die bulgarischen Dokumente zum Kriegsausbruch 1914', *BMH* VI, 3 (1928), 245; Cornwall, 'Serbia', 81.
[170] A. von Wegerer, 'Die Erinnerungen des Dr Velizar Janković', *BMH* IX, 9 (1931), 861. According to Gruić, Pašić, Protić (minister of the interior) and Janković were the principal authors of the official Serbian reply: see Albertini, *Origins* II, 363.

corridors of the legation building were piled high with boxes, packing cases and portmanteaux.[171]

The meeting certainly took place, though Janković may possibly have embroidered on it – Giesl later denied the packed luggage and travel clothes – but there can be little doubt that Vienna was determined to break off relations. Giesl's last day at Belgrade wore on 'with leaden slowness'.[172] Eventually, at 5.45 p.m., Pašić's carriage set off down King Milan and Studenička streets towards the Austro-Hungarian legation, where it drew up five minutes to the appointed hour. The prime minister, wearing a black cutaway, delivered Belgrade's note personally. On arrival he was ushered into Giesl's study where he stood in front of the sofa on which the unfortunate Hartwig had suffered his fatal heart attack. The two men bowed and exchanged a few words, Giesl enquiring as to the substance of Serbia's reply and Pašić switching to broken German (he knew no French): 'Part of your demands we have accepted … for the rest we place our hope in the loyalty and chivalry of an Austrian general [Giesl]. We were always very satisfied with you.' Pašić then handed the note to Giesl. The envoy asked to be excused now as he wished to study the document. They bowed again, and Pašić slowly left the legation.[173]

Pašić's calm and dignified exit belied the hectic pace of events in the prime minister's office over the previous twenty-four hours. Indeed, the timely preparation of the note was a close-run thing, and Belgrade very nearly missed the deadline set for its reply. The final version had been settled only at around 4 p.m., as Slavko Gruić later recounted to Luigi Albertini. Over the previous twenty-four hours the text had been revised, amended and worked over again, so that in places it 'was almost illegible, [with] many sentences crossed out and many added'. It resembled a mediaeval palimpsest more than a diplomatic note, and it still had to be cast in its proper form. To that end a typist was called in. But he was inexperienced and nervous, and after a few lines the typewriter jammed 'with the result that the reply had to be written out by hand in hectographic ink, copies being jellied off'. Around 5 p.m., the moment Janković was at the Austro-Hungarian legation, further changes were decided upon, but Gruić refused, pointing to the now ominously close deadline: 'The last half-hour was one of feverish work. The reply was corrected by pen here and there. One whole

[171] Wegerer, 'Erinnerungen des Dr Velizar Janković', 863–4.
[172] Giesl, *Zwei Jahrzehnte*, 267; for his refutation see 268–9.
[173] See the eyewitness account by Dušan A. Lončarević, a journalist working for a Vienna telegraphic news bureau and with good contacts to the legation: *Jugoslawiens Entstehung* (Zürich,1929), 599–600. Pašić's words as recounted in Giesl, *Zwei Jahrzehnte*, 269; also Giesl, 'Antwortnote', 467.

phrase placed in parenthesis [i.e. thirteen words] was crossed out in ink and made illegible.' It was not until 5.45 p.m., with Pašić's carriage already waiting, that Gruić placed this oddly presented note in an envelope, sealed it and handed it to the prime minister.[174]

If in its form Belgrade's response was nowhere near conforming to the expected standards of diplomatic exchanges of the day, in its substance it was little short of masterly. It was 'the most brilliant example of diplomatic adroitness'.[175] This was praise indeed, for its author was none other than Baron Musulin, who had devised the first draft of Austria-Hungary's ultimatum. Giesl, too, acknowledged that it was 'quite a masterpiece', designed to suggest acceptance whilst aiming to achieve the opposite.[176] Belgrade's note was apologetic on past pan-Serb propaganda, conciliatory in its tone and in its offer of 'a peaceful understanding [*une entente pacifique*]'. It was not, however, the unreserved acceptance Vienna had demanded – far from it, in fact. In its reply to the ten points of the Austro-Hungarian démarche, the note was a clever concoction of acceptance and equivocation, evasion and rejection, and all dressed up in accommodating language. Of Vienna's ten demands, the first six had been political in character, the remaining four being of a juridical or administrative nature. Of the political demands, Belgrade accepted none in full. Of the others only two were accepted without reservation, i.e. the prevention of the illicit traffic in arms and explosives across the Drina frontier and the punishing of customs and border officials who had connived in such activities (point 8), and a pledge to inform Vienna as soon as any of the promised measures had been carried out (point 10).

As regarded the political demands, the first three were partially accepted, but in each case with expressions of conditionality and reservation. The demanded suppression of anti-Habsburg publications was promised, but subject to the Skupština amending the constitution after the forthcoming general election (point 1). The government agreed to dissolve *Narodna Odbrana*, but denied that this or any other similar organization had been involved in terrorist activities against the Habsburg Empire (point 2). On the third point – the elimination of anti-Habsburg materials from school textbooks – Belgrade promised to do so, subject to Vienna furnishing it with further proof. In a similar manner, in reply to the fourth demand – removal of government officials guilty of acts directed against

---

[174] Gruić interview as quoted in Albertini, *Origins* II, 363–4. There is photographic reproduction of the page in ÖUA VIII, no. 10648, encl.

[175] [A. von] Musulin, *Das Haus am Ballplatz. Erinnerungen eines österreich-ungarischen Diplomaten* (Munich, 1924), 241.

[176] Giesl, *Zwei Jahrzehnte*, 269.

the territorial integrity of Austria-Hungary – Belgrade promised compliance, but that was conditional on the Habsburg government communicating further evidence. The reply to the ninth demand was equally evasive, offering explanations of any hostile comments made by Serbian officials as soon as the Austro-Hungarian government submitted precise details of the alleged speeches. As for the seventh point of Vienna's démarche, the arrest of Tankošić and Ciganović, here the reply was mendacious, because the latter had been spirited away by Serbian officials.[177]

As seen earlier, points 5 and 6 of the Austro-Hungarian ultimatum were always going to be the most problematic. On the fifth demand, which called for a mixed Austro-Serbian commission of enquiry, Belgrade equivocated. The Serbian government 'do not clearly grasp the meaning or the scope of the demand made', but would collaborate in so far as it agreed 'with the principle of international law, with criminal procedure, and with good neighbourly relations'. This was more the prospect of a lawyers' feast than a firm commitment. On the sixth point, Belgrade's response was wholly negative, as no doubt the Ballhausplatz had expected it to be. Habsburg officials could not be admitted to take part in criminal investigations of the Sarajevo plot on Serbian soil, as any such involvement of foreign agencies would have violated Serbia's constitution and her sovereignty.[178] This was a somewhat wilful interpretation of the original demand. The real danger, of course, was that the foreign detectives might point their torchlights on the activities of the 'Black Hand' and its wire-puller in the background, Apis, both as yet unknown to Austro-Hungarian investigators.

However brilliant in its display of diplomatic and legal sophistry, what the note was not was an acceptance of Austria-Hungary's demands. It created no difficulties for its recipient. As instructed, Giesl studied the note. But even the most superficial glance told him what he needed to know and what the Ballhausplatz had expected: 'Certainly I found several intimations of a conciliatory acceptance – probably the remnants of the original version ... but ultimately nearly all our demands were twisted, robbed of their meaning and purpose, and their fulfilment, if not directly refused, was so hedged in reservations [*verklausuliert*] that it was *in praxi* useless. The matter was absolutely clear; I had nothing to weigh, nothing to decide, only to state the facts and then, as ordered, to depart.'[179] And so he did what

---

[177] For this see J. Remak, *Sarajevo: Story of a Political Murder* (London, 1959), 207.
[178] Pašić to Giesl, 12/25 July 1914, encl. note, ÖUA viii, no. 10648; M. Rauchensteiner, *Der Tod des Doppeladlers. Österreich-Ungarn und der Erste Weltkrieg* (Graz and Vienna, 1993), 85.
[179] Giesl, 'Antwortnote', 467.

Berchtold and the Ballhausplatz expected of him. He declared the note to be unsatisfactory, and severed diplomatic relations.[180] He then burned the cipher books and piles of decrypted telegrams in the legations garden, entrusted the legation building to the care of the German envoy, and set off for the railway station, the train for Budapest having been ordered already. A large, noisy crowd had gathered outside the legation and was thronging the streets now. The foreign diplomats appeared at the station to bid farewell to their Habsburg colleague, all except the Russian, French and Romanian representatives. Small groups of Serbian officers had also begun to congregate on the platform, and as Giesl, his family and the legation personnel boarded the train, a shout rang out: 'Au revoir à Budapest.'[181]

As it turned out, this was somewhat premature. When Pašić communicated Serbia's official response, he knew that it did not meet Vienna's demands, that, in fact, it was nowhere near doing so; and as the military preparations indicated, he knew that war might be the consequence. This raises the question whether Belgrade's note was intended to be rejected, whether it was composed already with a view to a conflict with Austria-Hungary in an effort to win international support.[182]

It will perhaps never be possible to have certainty on this point. Clearly, Pašić could not have had any interest in any investigation into the Sarajevo murders over whose findings he himself had no control, not least because there was the very real danger that it might establish the connection between the assassins and 'official Serbia', which he knew, or suspected, existed. Similarly, he could not really make a serious attempt to break with pan-Serb nationalism. In demanding it, Musulin and Forgách very well knew that this was near impossible. Irredentism, after all, was part of the political DNA of the Karadjordjević state and its political élite. As the official Austro-Hungarian dossier, circulated to the other European governments on 25 July, did not fail to note, outside the main reception hall of the Serbian ministry of war there were four allegorical paintings, three of which depicted past Serbian military successes. The fourth, however, showed an armed female figure at dawn ('the dawn of Serbia's hopes'); on her shield were listed the names of the '"still to be liberated provinces": Bosnia, Herzegovina, Vojvodina, Syrmia, Dalmatia etc'.[183]

And yet it was only when Giesl notified him, at 6.30 p.m., that relations were now severed that Pašić grasped the full reality of what had

[180] Telephone despatch Giesl to Budapest, 25 July 1914 (D 7.45 p.m., from Semlin), ÖUA VIII, no. 10646; Giesl, *Zwei Jahrzehnte*, 269–70.

[181] Giesl, 'Antwortnote', 468, and *Zwei Jahrzehnte*, 270.

[182] For this view see Clark, *Sleepwalkers*, 466.

[183] Berchtold circular, encl. mémoire, ÖUA VIII, no. 10654, here at p. 704.

happened. According to Strandtmann, the Russian chargé d'affaires who was with Pašić in his office when Giesl's note arrived, the prime minister was genuinely 'deeply shocked' by the news.[184]

Conrad postpones war

While Pašić left Belgrade for the fortified town of Niš immediately on receiving Giesl's note, war was still not imminent. Irrespective of Berlin's insistence on the need for an immediate opening of the military campaign against Serbia, energetically supported at Vienna by ambassador Tschirschky, the Habsburg leadership was reluctant to do so. Once again, the disjuncture between diplomatic and military preparations in Austria-Hungary is remarkable. When Tschirschky called on the Ballhausplatz at 12.30 p.m. on 26 July, he was met by Berchtold and Conrad, the chief of staff. It was important, the latter argued, not to commence the campaign with 'insufficient forces'. The Hungarian corps could be deployed along Serbia's northern frontier shortly, but the concentration of forces along the Drina frontier would require more time 'because of a lack of sufficient means of communication'. Austria-Hungary, Conrad observed, would not be ready to move before 12 August; and a declaration of war would probably not be necessary as Serbian irregulars could be relied upon to launch incursions into Habsburg territory. For now, it was not necessary to mobilize.[185]

This was a remarkable declaration. The swift, lightning strike against Serbia that Berlin had somehow persuaded itself would now follow had thus been postponed again. It was questionable, as Berchtold observed, that 'the diplomatic situation' could be maintained.[186] Conrad's reference to Serbia's western frontier, moreover, presaged an additional problem that was to complicate the moves and counter-moves of the Powers, though neither Berchtold nor Tschirschky grasped this at the time.

For the moment, war had been postponed. Mediation appeared to have been given another chance.

---

[184] Strandtmann to Sazonov (no. 42), 24 July/6 Aug. 1914, *IBZI* v, app. 5; for the time of Giesl's note see tel. Strandtmann to Sazonov (no. 217), 12/25 July 1914, *ibid.*, no. 76.
[185] Tel. Tschirschky to Auswärtiges Amt (no. 105), 26 July 1914 (D 4.50 p.m., R 6.20 p.m.), *DD* I, no. 213; for Jagow's pressure to open the campaign on expiry of the ultimatum, see tel. Szögyény to Berchtold (no. 285), 25 July 1914 (D 2.15 p.m., R 8 p.m.), *ÖUA* VIII, no. 10656.
[186] Conrad, *Aus meiner Dienstzeit* IV, 132.

6 LOCALIZING THE WAR: 26 TO 28 JULY

The initial fright at this war that no-one had wanted, not the peoples, not the government – this war, which had slipped out of the clumsy hands of the diplomats, who had played and bluffed with it – had turned into sudden enthusiasm.

STEFAN ZWEIG (1944)[1]

Giesl's departure from Belgrade and the severing of diplomatic relations between the Monarchy and Serbia created a new situation in Europe. From the beginning of the Sarajevo crisis, Berchtold later argued, Vienna's aim had been to coerce the Serbian government into giving both a guarantee that the assassination plot would be thoroughly investigated, and, to reinforce it, a pledge to refrain in future from any anti-Habsburg activities. Belgrade's reply to the démarche offered nothing of the kind, as Giesl confirmed personally when he called on Berchtold and his senior officials at the Ballhausplatz at 4 p.m. on 26 July. The envoy's declaration, Berchtold recalled, was decisive: 'practically nothing had been achieved with the Serbian move and that everything would remain unchanged ... It would have meant deceiving ourselves had we accepted an apparent but *in concreto* useless success.'[2]

It must be doubted whether Giesl's pronouncement was indeed key to decision-making at Vienna. Austria-Hungary's last envoy to Serbia had merely done what he had been told to do. But Berchtold was satisfied that the breach with Belgrade bore Giesl's imprimatur. 'None of us', one of the officials at the Ballhausplatz explained, 'could have done it; only a soldier could do it'.[3] Giesl's profound knowledge of the Balkans and the Southern Slav peoples – he was married to a Serbian lady – also offered a convenient

---

[1] S. Zweig, *Die Welt von Gestern. Erinnerungen eines Europäers* (Frankfurt, 1981 (pb) [1st edn 1944]), 257–8.
[2] Berchtold, 'Am Vorabend', H. Hantsch, *Leopold Graf Berchtold. Grandseigneur und Staatsmann* (2 vols., Graz and Vienna, 1963) II, 615–16; see also W. von Giesl, *Zwei Jahrzehnte im Nahen Orient. Aufzeichnungen*, ed. E. von Steinitz (Berlin, 1927), 272.
[3] As quoted in J. von Szilássy, *Der Untergang der Donaumonarchie. Diplomatische Erinnerungen* (Berlin, 1921), 266. Giesl, of course, was a General of Cavalry. Szilássy was the envoy at Athens.

umbrella for protection against current and later criticism. Berchtold himself had worked purposefully towards conflict with Serbia, a third Balkan war that would roll back the recent expansion of the neighbouring kingdom and reassert Austria-Hungary's beleaguered position and waning influence in the region. The 'tunnel vision' of the Habsburg leadership was exclusivly focused on this single object, the diminution, if not outright destruction, of Serbia. That such a conflict might trigger a wider war was accepted, but it was rarely articulated by Berchtold and the hawkish section chiefs at the Ballhausplatz. No doubt, they preferred a small war, a punitive expedition against the obstreperous neighbour. After Sazonov's outburst on 24 July at the latest, however, they could not pretend that there was no risk of escalation. But they were ready to accept a great war, or rather, as the liberal Viennese journalist Heinrich Kanner noted pointedly in 1921, they shifted the responsibility for it 'onto the broader shoulders of the ally' at Berlin.[4] The mood among the political élite at Vienna, wrote a leading financier, was: 'Better an end in horror than a horror without end.'[5]

The disjuncture between Berchtold's political strategy and the military preparations for a Balkan war is nevertheless remarkable. No doubt, Vienna's decision to refrain from any military measures to underline its resolve prior to the expiry of the ultimatum on 25 July helped to keep the dispute with Serbia on the diplomatic track. It certainly allowed the Habsburg leadership to maintain the pretence of pacific intentions. But if it had helped to contain the risk of escalation until then, it greatly increased it after the time limit had expired, especially so if any of the other Powers decided to reinforce diplomatic signals with military postures. Any further delay in opening operations against Serbia could only exacerbate the situation. That the campaign would be no Sunday outing with weapons was never in any doubt. Conrad's staff, for instance, reckoned with an enemy force of some 400,000 men after Serbian mobilization was completed, most of them battle-hardened veterans of the two recent Balkan conflicts and fired up by pan-Serb irredentist nationalism, something that Austro-Hungarian commanders could not hope to match with their troops.[6] Orders for the mobilization against Serbia, that is partial

---

[4] H. Kanner, *Kaiserliche Katastrophenpolitik. Ein Stück Zeitgeschichte* (Leipzig, 1922), 371. Kanner was the editor of the liberal Viennese paper *Die Zeit*.
[5] R. Sieghart, *Die letzten Jahrzehnte einer Grossmacht. Menschen, Völker, Probleme des Habsburger-Reichs* (Berlin, 1932), 169; for similar comments see Szilássy, *Untergang*, 265.
[6] For Austro-Hungarian assessments see G. Rothenberg, 'The Austro-Hungarian Campaign against Serbia in 1914', *JMilH* LIII, 2 (1989), 127–46; G. Kronenbitter, *'Krieg im Frieden'. Die Führung der k.u.k. Armee und die Grossmachtpolitik Österreich-Ungarns, 1906–1914* (Munich, 2003), 488–91.

mobilization, were issued late on 25 July. But as the following day was a Sunday, 27 July was fixed as the day on which the measure would be proclaimed, and Tuesday, 28 July as the first day of mobilization.[7] The slowness of the Austro-Hungarian military response, and Conrad's reluctance to commence active preparations, are thus all the more remarkable.

Sazonov and Count Pourtalès take the same train

There was indeed a certain unreality about the situation in Europe on 26 July. In Vienna, vast crowds had already been parading in the streets outside the Russian embassy the previous evening, and mounted troops had to be deployed to keep them away from the building. In the German capital, people gathered outside the Habsburg embassy singing patriotic songs; and, at the changing of the guards outside the Berlin Schloss, the marching band struck up the Austro-Hungarian anthem.[8] News of Giesl's departure from Belgrade had spread like a wildfire across the Habsburg and German Empires. For the envoy himself, the journey to Budapest and then on to Vienna had become something of an involuntary triumphal procession. The heat of the previous day had given way to thunderous downpours during the night. Yet all along the railway line large crowds had gathered in the rain to cheer the passing train. At Szabadka (now Subotica), where the train arrived at 3 a.m., Giesl was taken out of his carriage and treated to long, patriotic speeches by the assembled local notables, much to the envoy's private dismay, for he himself felt rather more ambiguous about the pending conflict than those who welcomed him so enthusiastically.[9]

At the same time an eery calm seemed to have descended on the chancelleries of Europe on 25 and 26 July. The news that Serbia had apparently accepted most of Vienna's demands was received with a sense of relief in most capitals. In London, a junior Foreign Office clerk later

---

[7] J. Galántai, *Die österreichisch-ungarische Monarchie und der Weltkrieg* (Budapest, 1979), 346–8; S. R. Williamson, *Austria-Hungary and the Origins of the First World War* (London, 1991), 205.

[8] Tels. de Bunsen to Grey (no. 103), 25 July 1914 (D 11.20 p.m., R 8 a.m.), and Rumbold to Grey (no. 92), 26 July 1914 (D 2.20 p.m., R 4.30 p.m.), *BD* XI, nos. 135 and 147; also tel. Bronevski to Sazonov (no. 127), 13/26 July 1914, *IBZI* v, no. 96. For an eyewitness impression see also T. Wolff, *Der Krieg des Pontius Pilatus* (Zürich, 1934), 331. The Austrian *Kaiserhymne*, of course, was based on the same Haydn tune as the *Deutschlandlied*: see T. Leibnitz, '"Gott erhalte…".. Joseph Haydns Kaiserlied und die Hymnen Österreichs', in T. Leibnitz (ed.), *Joseph Haydn Gott erhalte. Schicksal einer Hymne* (Vienna, 2008), 8–69.

[9] See Giesl, *Zwei Jahrzehnte*, 272.

recalled, there was a strong belief that 'another crisis had been surmounted'.[10] In St Petersburg, too, the mood seemed calm. After the somewhat heated interview with Pourtalès two days previously, Sazonov, especially, appeared more relaxed about the international situation. Like Sazonov, during the stifling summer months the ambassador lived in one of the villas in leafy Tsarskoe Selo rather than in the capital, and on that Sunday morning the two travelled together on the train to St Petersburg. As other passengers shared the compartment, their conversation was confined to meaningless pleasantries. On arrival at the Vitebski station, however, Sazonov turned to political matters. To Pourtalès's surprise, the minister was in a 'much calmer and more conciliatory' frame of mind on that Sunday morning. Russia would use all means, Sazonov emphasized, to avoid war. He acknowledged Vienna's demands as legitimate in so far as they related to the prosecution of the instigators of the Sarajevo murders. He pleaded for Berlin to assist 'in finding a bridge' so that the Balkan dispute might be settled. Some of Vienna's original demands, he warned, violated Serbia's sovereignty and therefore had to be ameliorated, and to achieve this German support was necessary. Russia's policy was not guided by Slav sympathies, he explained, but by a clear appreciation of the country's national interests: 'For Russia, however, the equilibrium in the Balkans is a vital question, and she could not possibly tolerate the reduction of Serbia to a vassal state of Austria.' According to Pourtalès, Sazonov envisaged some form of international mediation in which Germany and Italy would play significant roles.[11]

Sazonov's subsequent conversation with Szápáry left both with 'a satisfactory impression', as Pourtalès reported to Berlin.[12] The Russian foreign minister, too, emphasized the 'very friendly tone' of his interview with Vienna's ambassador. Sazonov admitted the clumsy and inelegant form of the Serbian reply, but suggested that some of the original demands had been accepted in full. Others, such as the suppression of anti-Habsburg sentiments in the Serbian press, required a change in the law, and so could not be implemented immediately – the line Belgrade itself had taken. Fulfilling the notorious points 5 and 6, Sazonov warned, would lead to a revolutionary backlash in Serbia and 'acts of terror' which could hardly be

[10] R. Vansittart, *Mist Procession* (London, 1958), 124.
[11] Tel. Pourtalès to Auswärtiges Amt (no. 157), 26 July 1914 (D 3.15 p.m., R 7.01 p.m.), *DD* I, no. 217; see also F. Pourtalès, *Meine letzten Verhandlungen in St Petersburg Ende Juli 1914. Tagesaufzeichnungen und Dokumente* (Berlin, 1927), 22–4. Pourtalès's assessment was accurate: see tel. Sazonov to Krupenski (no. 1505), 13/26 July 1914, *IBZI* v, no. 84.
[12] Tel. Pourtalès to Auswärtiges Amt (no. 163), 26 July 1914 (D 10.10 p.m., R 12.45 a.m.), *DD* I, no. 238.

in Vienna's interest. As to the other demands, with some modification of details, an arrangement could be found, provided sufficient evidence was produced by the Austro-Hungarian authorities. The minister then moved on to the bigger question. In the interest of European peace, the 'current tense situation' ought to be brought to an end as soon as possible. To that end he suggested that Szápáry be empowered to open direct talks with him at St Petersburg with the aim of jointly modifying some articles of the original démarche. 'In this way', he thought, 'it might be possible to find a formula that would be acceptable for Serbia and would satisfy the demands of Austria in principle'.[13]

The idea of direct talks between Sazonov and Szápáry, it seems, originated with the German ambassador, but his Austro-Hungarian colleague accepted the notion with alacrity. According to his own account, he certainly went to some lengths during the interview to signal his willingness to explore this route. Austria-Hungary's action against Serbia was motivated entirely by self-defence, he explained. Various schemes, attributed to Vienna by certain circles in Russia, for a major push towards Salonika were entirely fictitious; and the same applied to the idea that the démarche against Serbia was the opening move of a German preventive war against Russia. If it nevertheless came to a European conflict, Szápáry warned, elaborating on the theme of Sir Edward Grey's recent conversations with various ambassadors, 'this would have terrible consequences and the religious, moral and social order would then be at risk'. This was a theme that Sazonov himself picked up. Vienna had to bear in mind that the Karadjordjević dynasty 'would be the last Serbian dynasty and we [Austria-Hungary] would surely not want to produce an anarchist witches' cauldron on our borders'. Like most responsible politicians and officials in 1914, the two men harboured no illusions about the disruptive social consequences of a general war. On discussing the various points of the original démarche and Serbia's replies to them, Sazonov then specifically raised the possibility of either Italian or British mediation. Szápáry was too skilled and experienced a diplomat to commit himself on this point. Even so, he concluded that Russian policy had moved some distance over the past two days. Sazonov no longer queried the legitimacy of Austria-Hungary's action at Belgrade; there was no more talk of internationalizing the Austro-Serb dispute; and Sazonov now appeared anxious to find suitable mediators.[14]

---

[13] Tel. Sazonov to Shebeko (no. 1508), 26 July 1914, *IBZI* v, no. 86.
[14] Tel. Szápáry to Berchtold (no. 165), 27 [*recte* 26] July 1914 (D 2.15 p.m., R 4.30 p.m.), *ÖUA* VIII, no. 10835. Both the telegram's contents and serial number would suggest that the correct date was 26 July: see also *JK* II, no. 397, n. 1.

Indeed, Sazonov instructed Russia's representatives in London, Paris and Berlin to support the idea of direct Austro-Russian talks, with Britain and Italy waiting in the wings should further mediation be necessary.[15] All of this complemented the British Foreign Secretary's preference for a settlement between Vienna and St Petersburg, and was no doubt also calculated to curry favour with London. There is no reason to doubt Sazonov's sincerity in urging mediation. But he had not shifted his position quite as much as Szápáry thought. His insistence on the need for Vienna to produce further evidence was certainly meant to help Serbia; and his repeated references to the desirability of compromise implied that the Habsburg government could not expect full compliance with all of its demands, especially on the fifth and sixth points of the original démarche. Finally, the suggestion of future acts of Serb nationalist terrorism against Austria-Hungary, if somewhat speculative and certainly not a direct threat, was nevertheless meant to ensure that pressure would not be lifted from Vienna entirely.

After the interviews, Pourtalès formed the view that prior to the ultimatum Sazonov 'had somewhat lost his nerve and now [after it] seeks ways out' of the crisis.[16] This, of course, chimed in with his own previous predictions of Russia's reluctance to intervene in the Austro-Serbian stand-off. His assessment of Sazonov's position on that Sunday was perceptive enough. But there was one element that he had failed to appreciate. For the Russian foreign minister mediation and conciliation still had to be paired with firm pressure on Vienna. Some of it was to be applied by Italy. This was the function which he intended the least reliable member of the Dreibund alliance to fulfil in the crisis talks. Rome, he wired to the ambassador there, Anatoli Nikola'evich Krupenski, could 'play a prominent role in preserving peace' by distancing itself from Austria-Hungary. In this way, Vienna could be made to understand that 'the conflict … cannot remain localized' because it was impossible for Russia not to support Serbia.[17] If Sazonov showed himself more conciliatory on the Sunday after Austria-Hungary broke off relations with Serbia, in essence, then, his policy remained unaltered. The pressure to be applied on Vienna via Rome and the hints at insurrection in Serbia demonstrate how central the notion of deterrence was to his crisis diplomacy. Seen in connection with the military

[15] Tels. Sazonov to Shebeko and Bronevski (nos. 1508/9), 13/25 July 1914, IBZI v, nos. 86–7.
[16] Tel. Pourtalès to Auswärtiges Amt (no. 163), 26 July 1914 (D 10.10 p.m., R 12.45 a.m.), DD i, no. 238.
[17] Tel. Sazonov to Krupenski (no. 1505, urgent), 13/26 July 1914, IBZI v, no. 84 (this was also transmitted to Paris and London).

preparations ordered on 25 July a clearer picture of some form of graduated deterrence emerges; and here the early indications of military measures
at St Petersburg and elsewhere could only help to keep pressure on Austria-
Hungary, with later mobilization as a form of reinsurance.

In his conversations with the German and Austro-Hungarian
ambassadors Sazonov did not deny that certain preparations had been
ordered, but assured Pourtalès that mobilization was conditional on
Austria-Hungary assuming 'a hostile attitude against Russia'.[18] Habsburg
diplomats, meanwhile, felt that pressure. After his friendly interview with
Sazonov on 26 July, Szápáry warned that whilst Russian diplomacy was
rowing back, 'energetic military activity' carried on 'through which
Russia's military and thus also her diplomatic position daily threatens to
shift to our disadvantage'.[19] That Sazonov had no intention of easing the
pressure on Vienna was also the conclusion at which Paléologue arrived in
the evening of 26 July. The minister remained determined, he cabled to
Paris, to find a peaceful solution, but Paléologue attributed to him a firmer
tone than either Szápáry's account or Sazonov's own did. There had been a
'frank and loyal exchange' with the ambassador, in the course of which
Sazonov acknowledged the legitimate nature of the action against Belgrade
if it aimed at nothing else but to protect Habsburg territory against 'the
intrigues of Serbian anarchists'. Its form, however, was indefensible, and
Sazonov concluded with the words: 'Take back your ultimatum, modify its
form and I guarantee the result.' As for Paléologue, he concurred with
Sazonov's idea that direct talks between Russia and Austria-Hungary
offered the best way forward, especially now, 'because military preparations do not leave much time for diplomatic action'.[20] The ambassador's
reference to military preparations was somewhat misleading. For, as seen
earlier, he had not informed the Quai d'Orsay properly of the Russian
decisions of the previous day, and his hint was therefore open to be
interpreted as a reference to any measures Austria-Hungary might adopt.[21]

---

[18] Tel. Pourtalès to Auswärtiges Amt (no. 164), 26 July 1914 (D 9.30 p.m., R 10.05
p.m.), DD I, no. 230.
[19] Tel. Szápáry to Berchtold (no. 165), 27 [recte 26] July 1914 (D 2.15 p.m., R 4.30
p.m.), ÖUA VIII, no. 10835.
[20] Tel. Paléologue to Bienvenu-Martin (no. 290), 26 July 1914 (D 8.58 p.m., R 3.40
a.m.), DDF (3) XI, no. 103.
[21] Dumaine at Vienna had reported earlier that the partial mobilization of eight army
corps, the Landsturm reserves and the Danube flotilla had been ordered: see tels.
Dumaine to Bienvenu-Martin (nos. 110 and 111), 26 July 1914 (D 11 a.m. and 7.30
p.m., R 1.25 p.m. and 9.30 p.m.), DDF (3) XI, nos. 77 and 99. Paléologue himself
reported that Romania was mobilizing the Bucharest army corps which was to be

At Paris, Bienvenu-Martin, the acting foreign minister, remained optimistic about a settlement of the Austro-Serbian crisis. Jagow's earlier reluctance to support an initiative aimed at extending the ultimatum had made a poor impression on him. Yet he concurred with ambassador Dumaine at Vienna that Austria-Hungary, 'after having humiliated and delivered a blow to Serbia might be disposed to accept mediation to avoid the grave risks of a long war and internal disorganization'.[22] For his own part, Bienvenu-Martin leant towards Grey's suggestion of Four-Power mediation in the conflict, as he explained to the German ambassador, Baron Wilhelm von Schoen, when the latter called in on the Quai at 5 p.m. on 26 July. Schoen had sought to convince the acting foreign minister that Russia's attitude was key to preservation of peace; and only France was in a position to exercise a restraining influence over St Petersburg. According to Schoen, Bienvenu-Martin proved receptive to the idea, but insisted that this could only be done on the basis of firm understanding that there would be no annexation of Serbian territory. Schoen, however, was not prepared to accept the suggestion that a parallel effort by Germany at Vienna would help to secure an arrangement. In consequence, Bienvenu-Martin proposed that the not directly interested governments – Grey's quartet – ought to mediate at Vienna and St Petersburg.[23]

Schoen's interview had an instructive sequel. On leaving the acting foreign minister, the ambassador called on Philippe Berthelot, the political director at the Quai d'Orsay, to discuss certain misleading reports that had appeared in various Paris papers. At the end of the meeting Berthelot requested permission to speak privately and confidentially about the situation in the Balkans. Germany's attitude was incomprehensible, he explained, unless she was determined to have war. Berlin's self-confessed ignorance of the terms of the Austro-Hungarian note could not be doubted given the Wilhelmstrasse's repeated assurances to that effect. But 'was it likely that Germany should have ranged herself alongside Austria in such an adventure with her eyes shut?' Was it likely, in light of what Berthelot called the 'psychology of all past Austro-German relations', that Vienna should have embarked on such a risky course without having weighed the possible consequences together with its ally? Germany's refusal to counsel moderation at Vienna was thus all the more surprising, 'now that she knew

deployed towards the Carpathian frontier: see tel. Paléologue to Bienvenu-Martin (no. 289), 26 July 1914 (D 1.50 p.m., R 2.15 p.m.), *ibid.*, no. 85.

[22] Bienvenu-Martin circular tel., 26 July 1914 (D 8.20 p.m.), *DDF* (3) XI, no. 98.

[23] Bienvenu-Martin circular tel., 26 July 1914 (D 8.20 p.m.), *DDF* (3) XI, no. 98; tel. Schoen to Auswärtiges Amt (no. 220), 26 July 1914 (D 7.40 p.m., R 12.07 a.m.), *DD* I, no. 235.

the extraordinary text of the Austrian note'. Germany was assuming a grave responsibility if she placed herself between Austria-Hungary and the Powers 'after Serbia's as it were absolute submission'. The slightest pressure from Germany on her ally would 'end the nightmare that lay on Europe'. Austria-Hungary's decision to sever relations with Serbia, her threat of war and her mobilization measures lent great urgency to a 'peacemaking action' on Germany's part. These were pertinent observations, indeed; and Schoen, who had smiled throughout Berthelot's monologue, could do little more than assert that Serbia needed to be taught a lesson. Austria-Hungary was not intransigent, he suggested, 'but what she rejected was formal mediation, the spectre of a conference'.[24]

Sir Edward goes fishing

Berthelot's impressions were shared to some extent by senior officials at the Foreign Office in London, but there was not as yet an immediate sense of impending conflict. Grey himself had left late on Saturday for a weekend away from the hurly-burly of the capital in the seclusion of his country cottage at Itchen Abbas on the River Test in Hampshire. More tellingly, that Sunday morning, the department's legal adviser, Sir W. Edward Davidson, had left London's Victoria Station on the Dover boat train, bound for Switzerland. He reached his destination without much difficulty, as, indeed, he had done nearly every summer over the past two decades. Given that, in the event of war, formal declarations of war, questions of belligerent rights, of neutral shipping and similar such matters of international law would require a great deal of attention at the Foreign Office, and given that Davidson's Swiss destination was the Riffelalp, a mountain he had ascended 252 times before, his leaving London throws a revealing light on the relative calm at the Foreign Office at that moment.[25]

Calm did not mean complacency, however. That Sunday the department was in the care of Sir Arthur Nicolson, the Permanent Under-secretary. As seen earlier, by the afternoon of 24 July, Nicolson and Sir Eyre Crowe, the man then widely tipped to succeed him at the top of the Foreign Office, had grown alarmed at the harder line adopted by Paris and

---

[24] Min. Berthelot, 26 July 1914 (after 7 p.m.), *DDF* (3) XI, no. 109.
[25] Davidson diary, 26 July 1914, Davidson MSS, Alpine Club, London, C. 37; see also memo. Ottley, 'Coordination of Departmental Action on the Outbreak of War', 4 Nov. 1910, TNA (PRO), CAB 4/3/121B. For Davidson's mountaineering see J. W. Hartley, G. Fitzgerald and J. P. Farrar, 'In Memoriam: William Edward Davidson', *Alpine Journal* XXXV, 227 (Nov. 1923), 259–67.

St Petersburg. What alarmed them further was Berlin's obvious reluctance to support Grey's initiative of the previous day to induce the Austro-Hungarian government to take a more lenient view of Serbia's official reply. Jagow's decision merely to pass on the Foreign Secretary's suggestion, without associating himself with it, had made a poor impression on the Foreign Office. It was 'a somewhat peculiar way of treating our suggestion', Crowe noted. Jagow's behaviour, in fact, suggested anything but straightforwardness and was sufficient to rekindle suspicions of the Wilhelmstrasse, buried for the past eighteen months or so by the recent détente in Anglo-German relations.[26] Similarly, Tschirschky's reported confidence that Russia, having received assurances by Vienna that there would be no annexation of Serbian territory, would not now intervene in Austria-Hungary's punitive campaign, was received with incredulity at the Foreign Office. The German ambassador at Vienna, Nicolson minuted, was 'spreading the belief that Russia will keep quiet if no annexations occur! How little can he grasp the real situation.'[27] Nicolson, moreover, was gravely concerned that the two Germanic Powers were inclined to believe that, in the current situation, there could be a re-run of the Bosnian crisis of 1908–9, which ended in Russia's ignominious diplomatic defeat, a belief he himself did not share.[28]

The Permanent Under-secretary himself was far less sanguine than de Bunsen's German colleague in the Habsburg capital. Late on Saturday night Buchanan's telegram had arrived informing the Foreign Office of the Russian government's decision to begin pre-mobilization preparations. Sazonov's assurances that St Petersburg would take no further action unless forced to do so were not very reassuring. When in the course of the following morning the Director of Military Operations, General Sir Henry Wilson, called on the Foreign Office, he found Nicolson impressed by the 'warlike' telegrams that had come in over night: 'Austria, Russia, and Serbia seem to be going to mobilize, but, so far, no news of Germany moving. Until she moves there is no certainty of war'. Significantly, Wilson

[26] Min. Crowe, 27 July 1914, on tel. Rumbold to Grey (no. 94), 26 July 1914 (D 7.35 p.m., R 8.15 p.m.), *BD* XI, no. 149; see also min. Crowe, 29 July 1914, on Rumbold to Grey (no. 299), 22 July 1914 (R 27 July), *ibid.*, no. 158. Jagow, in fact, had left Vienna in no doubt that he did not associate German diplomacy with Grey's suggestion: see tel. Jagow to Tschirschky (no. 140), 25 July 1914 (D 4 p.m.), *DD* I, no. 171.

[27] Min. Nicolson, n.d. [27 July 1914], on tel. de Bunsen to Grey (no. 106, confidential), 26 July 1914 (D 7 p.m., R 10 p.m.), *BD* XI, no. 150; K. Neilson and T. G. Otte, *The Permanent Under-Secretary of State for Foreign Affairs, 1854–1946* (New York and London, 2009), 149.

[28] See tel. Imperiali to San Giuliano (no. 821/212), 25 July 1914 (D 9.37 a.m., R 12 p.m.), *DDI* (4) XII, no. 503.

concluded, presumably following Nicolson's explanations, that Serbia had agreed 'to almost all the Austrian demands'. This, he thought, made it 'difficult for Austria and Germany to have a European war. My own opinion is that if Germany does not mobilize to-day there will be no war.'[29]

Buchanan's telegram no. 169 of 25 July played a significant role in shaping British diplomacy during the next few days. It communicated several items of importance. Sazonov's powers now to order mobilization aside, Buchanan also told London that Serbia would offer no military resistance to an Austro-Hungarian onslaught but would withdraw and might then appeal to the Powers. In that eventuality, Sazonov had explained, 'Russia would be quite ready to stand aside and leave [the] question in [the] hands of England, France, Italy and Germany'. In other words, Sazonov appeared to back Grey's quadruple mediation scheme. Buchanan also reported that Paléologue had sought to put pressure on him by raising the question of British naval assistance to France. This was Paléologue's own doing. Paris had not instructed him to raise the matter of the Anglo-French notes of November 1912, and this latest initiative was very much part of Paléologue's private diplomacy at St Petersburg. He could not believe, he suggested to Buchanan, 'that England would not stand by her two friends, who were acting as one in this matter'.

As instructed, Buchanan confined himself to repeated calls for 'prudence', and he warned Sazonov that, 'if Russia mobilised, Germany would not be content with mere mobilisation, or give Russia time to carry out hers, but would probably declare war at once'. Sazonov did not wish to precipitate a conflict, but he made it plain to Buchanan that, unless Berlin restrained its ally, the situation was serious: 'Russia cannot allow Austria to crush Servia and become [the] predominant Power in [the] Balkans, and, secure of [the] support of France, she will face all the risks of war.' Given this, to the ambassador's mind, the current situation was thus no longer of purely academic interest. It had profound implications for British policy now and in the future: 'For ourselves [the situation] is a most perilous one, and we shall have to choose between giving Russia our active support or renouncing her friendship. If we fail her now we cannot hope to maintain that friendly cooperation with her in Asia that is of such vital importance to us.'[30]

---

[29] Wilson diary, 26 July 1914, in C. E. Callwell, *Field-Marshal Sir Henry Wilson, Bart., GCB, DSO: His Life and Diaries* (2 vols., London, 1927) I, 151–2.

[30] Tel. Buchanan to Grey (no.169), 25 July 1914 (D 8 p.m., R 10.30 p.m.), *BD* XI, no. 125. Buchanan had taken this line since the turn of 1913/14: see Buchanan to Grey (no. 60), 4 Mar. 1914, TNA (PRO), FO 371/2092/10333; K. Neilson, *Britain and the Last Tsar: British Policy Towards Russia, 1894–1917* (Oxford, 1995), 334–9.

1 Franz Ferdinand and his wife Sophie being welcomed by Potiorek at the spa hotel of Ilidže

2 Franz Ferdinand and the Duchess of Hohenberg arriving at Sarajevo town hall

3 The archducal car returning along Appel Quay shortly before the assassination

4 The original Austro-Hungarian memorial at the Lateiner Bridge to the first two victims of the First World War

5 Count Albert Mensdorff, 'Royal Albert', the perfect courtier-ambassador

6 General Oskar Potiorek, the Bosnian Bungler

7 Count Ladislaus Szögyény, the faux Gypsy ambassador, who secured the 'blank cheque'

8 Baron Wladimir Giesl von Gieslingen, the cavalry general who delivered the ultimatum to Serbia

9 Count Friedrich Szápáry von Szápár, the ambassador who had nothing to say

10 Count Leopold Berchtold von und zu Ungarschitz, dancing on egg shells towards war. Cartoon in *Die Zeit*, Nov. 1912.

11 René Viviani, the prime minister who made a spectacle of himself

12 Maurice Paléologue, the ambassador who misled his own government

13 Paul Cambon, the ambassador who despaired of Britain's commitment

14 Prince Karl Max Lichnowsky, a truly tragic figure (here in happier days in Oxford doctoral robes)

15 Theobald von Bethmann Hollweg, 'The Philosopher of Hohenfinow' or 'Hamlet of Berlin'?

16 Baron Heinrich von Tschirschky und Bögendorff, the warmonger at Vienna

17 Arthur Zimmermann, the jovial under-secretary at the Wilhelmstrasse

18 Gottlieb von Jagow, the 'little misunderstanding', a reckless foreign minister

19 Sir Edward Grey, 'Man of Action' whose creative ambiguity no longer worked

20 Sir William Tyrrell, Grey's secretive Private Secretary

21 Herbert Henry Asquith, the prime minister who waited and saw

22 Sir George Buchanan, cold and courteous at St Petersburg

23 Aleksandar Konstantinovich von Benckendorff, who personified Anglo-Russian relations

24 Sergei Dmitrievich Sazonov, 'Holy Fool' masquerading as foreign minister

25 Nikolai Nikola'evich Shebeko, who wished to hear good news at Vienna

26 Nikolai Genrikovich Hartwig, Habsburg's foe who wished for peace in July 1914

27 Sergei Nikola'evich Sverbe'ev, who believed the Berlin papers

28 General Vladimir Aleksandrovich Sukhomlinov, the fatalistic war minister (here laying the foundation stone of the Russian memorial church near the battlefield of Leipzig (1813) in 1913)

29 Marchese Antonio Paterno-Castelli di San Guiliano, pondering Italy's advantage

Jovan M. Jovanović

30 Jovan Jovanović, 'shots will go off by themselves'?

31 Clash of two Balkan visions: Prince Aleksandr Karadjordjević (left) with
Wilhelm Ritter von Storck, Austro-Hungarian legation counsellor, in August 1913

32 Nikola Pašić, wily survivor of Serbian politics

Buchanan's telegram was significant on a number of counts. In the first instance, it foreshadowed the line the French would take a few days later as the prospect of war grew closer, Paléologue's appeal to Britain's friendship containing the nucleus of the suggestion of a 'moral commitment' to France on Britain's part.[31] Buchanan's telegram also introduced another factor – Britain's relations with Russia as a past and likely future competitor for influence in Asia. This was not, of course, a new consideration for the British foreign policy élite. As seen earlier, Grey himself had grown sceptical of the chances of renewing the arrangement with Russia in 1915, and he had begun to contemplate the alternatives. Buchanan's observations did not force him now to change course and submit to the diktat of Russia.[32] But they sharpened the focus on the potential, broader ramifications of the crisis looming in south-eastern Europe for Britain's global interests.

Sazonov's much harder line in conversation with Buchanan than in his interviews with Pourtalès and Szápáry the following morning was, no doubt, calculated to force London to abandon its aloofness and to side with France and Russia. It is a further indication of the extent to which Sazonov was wedded to a deterrence strategy. From the Russian perspective it certainly made sense to generate an impression in London that it held the key to the situation. Hence Benckendorff's suggestion to Nicolson, on that Sunday, that his cousin Lichnowsky was convinced that Britain would stand aside in a conflict – 'an unfortunate conviction', he added, as 'a restraining influence would be exercised on Berlin' if the decision-makers there came to realize that Britain could not remain indifferent 'when all Europe was in flames'.[33] Of course, Lichnowsky's advice to Berlin was precisely that Britain would not remain neutral, and, as seen before, Stumm and Zimmermann understood this. To that extent – whether deliberately or not – Benckendorff's suggestions were misleading. But that is almost beside the point. What matters here is the deliberate attempt by Russian diplomacy to inveigle Grey into committing Britain openly to the Franco-Russian combination.

If the latest news from St Petersburg was somewhat ominous, there was, however, one positive aspect to Buchanan's telegram. Sazonov had

[31] See T. Wilson, 'Britain's "Moral Commitment" to France 1914', *History* LXIV, 212 (1979), 380–90.
[32] For this argument see K. M. Wilson, *The Policy of the Ententes: Essays on the Determinants of British Foreign Policy, 1904–1914* (Cambridge, 1985), 81–2; for a corrective see my '"Détente 1914": Sir William Tyrrell's Secret Mission to Germany', *HJ* LVI, 1 (2013), 175–204.
[33] Tel. Nicolson to Grey, 26 July 1914, *BD* XI, no. 144.

clearly indicated his willingness to stand aside for Four-Power mediation. Nicolson at once saw the importance of this, and an idea occurred to him of a possible scheme for settling the Austro-Serbian dispute. The governments in Berlin, Paris and Rome, he wired to Grey in Hampshire, should be approached to authorize their ambassadors in London to attend a conference there to explore a diplomatic solution to the crisis. In the meantime, Austria-Hungary, Russia and Serbia were to be asked to refrain 'from active military operations ... pending the results of [the] conference'.[34] There was perhaps a little studied ambiguity about what precisely constituted 'active military operations', but it was sufficiently elastic to allow for diplomatic flexibility. In essence, however, Nicolson suggested using again the diplomatic tool that had been employed so successfully in the aftermath of the First Balkan War. At that time, the London ambassadorial conference had helped to defuse the tensions in the region to a considerable extent and to bring a degree of stability to it. Its success then had been guaranteed by Germany's willingness to cooperate with Grey; its renewed success now would again depend on Berlin. And on this point Nicolson himself was doubtful. The conference proposal, he explained to Grey, 'seems to me the only chance of avoiding a conflict – it is I admit a poor chance – but in any case we shall have done our utmost'. Jagow was merely 'playing with us', having passed on Grey's moderating advice to Vienna without backing it: 'This is not what was intended or desired.'[35]

If the Permanent Under-secretary was an avowed sceptic on the subject of working with Germany, Grey had by no means written off German cooperation; nor did he concur with Nicolson's gloomy prognostications. Without German cooperation, at any rate, neither Four-Power mediation nor an ambassadorial conference, whether separately or as a combination of the two, could work. Grey therefore endorsed Nicolson's proposal.[36] At the very least, it offered the chance to gain time, and that had always been the principal objective of Grey's diplomacy so far. Any day gained would make conflict between the Powers more unlikely.

Grey was by no means complacent, however. Rather, he interpreted the available evidence differently. That Sazonov and Benckendorff

[34] Tel. Nicolson to Grey, n.d. [26 July 1914], *BD* XI, no. 139 a.
[35] Tel. Nicolson to Grey, 26 July 1914, *BD* XI, no. 144. The precise timing of the telegram is not clear. Contextual evidence would suggest that it was sent sometime around 3 p.m.; Grey himself returned to London in the evening; for the ambassadorial conference see R. J. Crampton, *The Hollow Détente: Anglo-German Relations in the Balkans, 1911–1914* (London, s.a. [1979]), 75–138, and his 'The Balkans, 1909–1914', F. H. Hinsley (ed.), *British Foreign Policy under Sir Edward Grey* (Cambridge, 1977), 256–70.
[36] Tel. Grey to Resident Clerk, 26 July 1914 (D 2.20 p.m.), *BD* XI, no. 139 b.

would seek to put pressure on London to force it to side with Russia was only to be expected. More significant for Grey was the advice of Britain's long-serving ambassador at Paris. Sir Francis Bertie was the most senior British representative abroad, and Grey had come to value his advice more especially in recent years. Although an early advocate of the entente with France, Bertie supported Grey's policy of the 'free hand'. He was, more-over, instinctively wary of Russia and had tended to oppose closer ties with her. In the current crisis he suggested that French public opinion was not likely to back Russia 'in so bad a cause' if St Petersburg decided to make the Austro-Serbian dispute a pretext for a conflict with Austria-Hungary. In consequence, he was certain that Paris would advise the Russian government 'to moderate any excessive zeal that they may be inclined to display to protect their Servian client'.[37]

Bertie's assessment of French attitudes reflected both Bienvenu-Martin's own statements in recent days and what was known of Viviani's altogether more pacific inclinations. That at St Petersburg Paléologue had already committed French policy in the opposite direction Bertie could not, of course, know, any more than Bienvenu-Martin could. But from Grey's perspective, if Bertie's assessment were correct, then another piece of the diplomatic jigsaw was in place, and either conference diplomacy or Four-Power mediation offered a realistic option to avoid a wider military conflict. Grey's subsequent instructions to Bertie to encourage the French government to attach ambassador Cambon to the proposed London conference, then, was influenced as much by Nicolson's scheme as by Bertie's assessment of the moderating influence Paris was prepared to bring to bear on its Russian ally.[38] As an additional precaution, Grey had agreed to Churchill's idea not to disperse the fleet currently concentrated at Spithead for the naval review which had just ended. A note to that effect appeared in all the papers on Sunday, 26 July.[39] The navy, of course, was the arm of British diplomacy; and in making such dispositions, Grey signalled to the other Powers that Britain was not indifferent to the unfolding crisis.

As for mediation, Nicolson reiterated his proposal to Lichnowsky. The ambassador had walked the short distance from Prussia House across

---

[37] Bertie to Grey (private), 25 July 1914, Bertie MSS, BL, Add. MSS. 63033; K. A. Hamilton, *Bertie of Thame: Edwardian Ambassador* (Woodbridge, 1991), 321–2; T. G. Otte, *The Foreign Office Mind: The Making of British Foreign Policy, 1865–1914* (Cambridge, 2011), 389.

[38] Tels. Grey to Bertie (no. 232) and to de Bunsen (no. 160), both 26 July 1914 (both D 3 p.m.), *BD* XI, nos. 140–1. The telegrams were despatched in Grey's name; he was still at Itchen Abbas. Rodd at Rome duly submitted the proposal: see note Rodd, 26 July 1914, *DDI* (4) XII, no. 553.

[39] W. S. Churchill, *The World Crisis, 1911–14* (London, 1923), 198–9.

St James's Park to call on the Foreign Office in the afternoon of 26 July with information that St Petersburg had called up reserves. This might mean mobilization, he warned, and Germany would be compelled to react in kind, which in turn would lead to French mobilization. Lichnowsky added: 'The Germans would not mind a partial mobilisation say at Odessa or Kieff – but could not view indifferently a mobilisation on the German frontier.' In reply, Nicolson argued that pressure on St Petersburg not to mobilize would be fruitless – 'we should not be listened to. The main thing was to prevent, if possible, active military operations.' He then developed his scheme of 'a meeting à quatre' in London on the condition that Austria, Russia, and Serbia suspended 'active military *operations*' during the conference. 'Prince Lichnowsky liked the proposal. (He was very excited.)'[40]

Lichnowsky was indeed in an agitated frame of mind. Before his meeting with Nicolson he had already warned the Wilhelmstrasse that localization was now doubtful, and that Austria-Hungary's move might trigger a 'world war'. He considered the moment ripe to endorse Grey's mediation proposals; the precondition for this, of course, was that Vienna would have to 'forgo further laurels'.[41] Following his meeting with Nicolson and also with Grey's Private Secretary, Sir William Tyrrell, Lichnowsky urgently reiterated his earlier advice. So far, Russia contemplated only partial mobilization 'far from our borders'. Both senior officials had impressed upon him that the proposed Four-Power conference was the last chance of securing peace. In this way Austria-Hungary would receive 'full satisfaction' because Serbia would yield to the united will of the Powers rather than Vienna's threats. Such a conference proposal, however, was only viable if all 'military movements' were suspended. Once Austrian troops entered Serb territory, as Lichnowsky had been told, the dispute could no longer be localized: 'all would be lost, since no Russian government could tolerate this and would be forced to attack Austria, lest it loses its position with the Balkan states for ever'. The partly German-educated Tyrrell, a warm advocate of Anglo-German détente in recent months, was noticeably serious on this point. He had been with Grey the previous evening and usually shared the Foreign Secretary's views, and he 'repeatedly and emphatically' underscored the 'tremendous importance' of the armed forces being kept in check until the conference option had been explored. Otherwise, Tyrrell observed, 'all efforts would be in vain and world war inevitable'. Localization as advocated by Berlin was no longer practicable politics. If the two governments, he observed in conclusion,

---

[40] Min. Nicolson, 26 July 1914, *BD* xi, no. 146 (original emphasis).
[41] Tel. Lichnowsky to Auswärtiges Amt (no. 160), 26 July 1914 (D 4.25 p.m., R 7.01 p.m.), *DD* i, no. 218.

succeeded 'in preserving the European peace, then Anglo-German relations would be placed on a secure footing for all times. If they failed, everything would be called into question.' This, of course, was very much Lichnowsky's position, too. Berlin, he warned, should no longer pursue the idea of localization, but support Grey's mediation scheme and be guided solely 'by the necessity of saving the German people a fight from which it has nothing to gain and everything to lose'.[42]

During his Sunday afternoon call on the Foreign Office Lichnowsky had gleaned one further piece of diplomatic intelligence, one that should have been of the greatest interest to the Wilhelmstrasse. Information received at the Foreign Office indicated clearly that Italy would not join a war on the side of her *Dreibund* allies, he reported to Berlin; all suggestions of 'loyal assurances' by the Consulta, as put out at Vienna, were wrong.[43] The information Lichnowsky was given was, indeed, accurate. London had been told as much during the previous twenty-four hours. On 25 July, ambassador Imperiali warmly endorsed Grey's Four-Power talks; and on Sunday afternoon Sir Rennell Rodd wired from Rome that Italy would remain neutral in the event of Russian intervention. Austria-Hungary had not consulted with Rome, and her heavy-handed move against Serbia amounted to a deliberate provocation of Russia. Under such circumstances, the Consulta contended, the *casus foederis* would not arise – Italy would not be obligated to support Austria-Hungary.[44]

From Britain's perspective the latest news from Rome was significant. For one thing, Italy's assistance as part of Grey's international mediation scheme could now be counted upon. Beyond that, the Italian position was expected to affect German calculations. Italy's function as a sort of 'drag-weight' on the *Dreibund* alliance had long been appreciated at London.[45] Rome's obvious reluctance to fulfil her obligations towards her two northern allies – practically a renunciation of the alliance – might

---

[42] Tel. Lichnowsky to Auswärtiges Amt (no. 161), 26 July 1914 (D 8.25 p.m., R 12.07 a.m.), *DD* I, no. 236.

[43] Tel. Lichnowsky to Auswärtiges Amt (no. 162), 26 July 1914 (D 8.48 p.m., R 12.45 a.m.), *DD* I, no. 237.

[44] Grey to Rodd (no. 217, confidential), 25 July 1914, and tel. vice versa (no. 122), 26 July 1914 (D 3.45 p.m., R 5.30 p.m.), *BD* XI, nos. 133 and 148; see also tel. Imperiali to San Giuliano (no. 6654/215), 25 July 1914 (D 8.25 p.m., R 12.40 a.m.), *DDI* (4) XII, no. 528. San Giuliano was less emphatic with Flotow, but advised not to reject Grey's proposal: tel. Flotow to Auswärtiges Amt (no. 25), 26 July 1914 (D 4.50 p.m., R 9. 30 p.m.), *DD* I, no. 225.

[45] This had been a consistent theme in Foreign Office analyses: see T. G. Otte, '"Makeweight in the Balance": Italian Diplomatic Documents, 1893–5', *D&S* XI, 3 (2001), 272–7.

act as a further restraining factor on Germany, and so convince Berlin to back mediation. As even the expected Austro-Hungarian campaign against Serbia could not commence for another fortnight, the Grey-Nicolson proposal was a realistic scheme. Everything then pointed to Germany.

Bethmann Hollweg takes charge

At the Wilhelmstrasse, Lichnowsky's advice was anything but welcome. 'What concern is Italy to the ambassador!', minuted Zimmermann.[46] The under-secretary's outburst was extraordinary, and it cannot simply be explained away as the Wilhelmstrasse's suspicions of the ambassador in London, where he was thought to have 'gone native'. It underlines the recklessness of decision-making at Berlin. But it is also suggestive of the growing mental and psychological stress under which the key officials there operated, now that it was becoming increasingly apparent that the crisis would not unfold as originally hoped.

There was, however, also an element of self-delusion at Berlin. Chancellor Bethmann Hollweg had returned to the capital on 24 July. On the following day he telegraphed to the Kaiser, still at sea in northern waters, that Britain's 'direct participation in a possible European war' did not appear likely. Later that same evening he reported that at London and Paris 'they are working energetically towards a localization of the conflict'.[47] While he had been away from the bustle of Berlin at his Hohenfinow country estate, the chancellor had been kept abreast of the principal international developments since 5 July, but had played no part in the day-to-day management of foreign policy. He remained wedded to the idea of localization, and even took the Kaiser to task when the Prussian Crown Prince, the notoriously brash and indiscreet Prince Wilhelm, was reported to have ventilated unguarded comments on Germany's international position. The Kaiser's son, he insisted, had to refrain from any public displays that might be construed as warmongering. Such indiscretions were liable to complicate the task of German diplomacy to localize any conflict between Austria-Hungary and Serbia: 'The solution of this problem is already difficult in itself, so that even minor incidents can tip the scales.'[48]

---

[46] Min. Zimmermann, n.d., on tel. Lichnowsky to Auswärtiges Amt (no. 162), 26 July 1914, *DD* I, no. 237.

[47] Tels. Bethmann Hollweg to Kaiser (nos. 139–40), 25 July 1914 (D 8.35 p.m. and 10.45 p.m., R 7 a.m. and 11.50 a.m.), *DD* I, nos. 182 and 191.

[48] Bethmann Hollweg to Wilhelm II, 20 July 1914 (D 12.15 p.m.), *DD* I, no. 84. The Kaiser acted accordingly: see tel. Wilhelm II to Crown Prince, 21 July 1914,

The chancellor was, however, by no means sanguine about the chances of confining the conflict to the Balkans. Even on the eve of the Austro-Hungarian ultimatum, as was seen, Bethmann was ignorant of its wording.[49] But through this wilful ignorance Berlin had effectively associated itself with the move against Serbia, and so lost much of its ability to moderate Habsburg policy. 'Did it have to go this far?', Bethmann wondered during one of his bouts of introspection. Russia in particular preoccupied him, according to his Boswell, Kurt Riezler. The incessant growth of her power would make her more difficult to deal with in a few years. For the moment, St Petersburg's policy had to bend to the gust of pan-Slavism that swept through Russian internal politics. But Vienna's self-denying ordnance with regard to Serbian territory, Bethmann hoped, was sufficient to prevent Russian mobilization, and so opened the possibility of negotiations. Germany could not sacrifice the Austro-Hungarian ally, but if 'the Serbian quarrel passes without Russian mobilization and consequently without war, we might safely come to an understanding with St Petersburg, disappointed in the Western powers, since Austria would already be satisfied'.[50] On the train journey back to Berlin, the chancellor had studied the latest telegrams. The reaction to Vienna's breaking off relations with Serbia, he decided, was not altogether unfavourable. For all his excitement, Sazonov had not committed himself to any particular course of action: 'an Austro-Serbian conflict does not concern me; Italy blackmails.' But everything depended on St Petersburg. If Sazonov could be persuaded not to mobilize, some sort of settlement could be found.[51]

The terrible 'ifs' had thus begun to accumulate in terrifying numbers in Bethmann's calculations. The Russian factor, meanwhile, was important to Bethmann also for domestic reasons. For in the event of further escalations, the chancellor was by no means confident of the support of large sections of the German people. In the *Reichstag* elections two years previously, the Social Democratic Party (SPD) had emerged as by far the largest political party; and, although not responsible to the parliament, Bethmann Hollweg had been forced to cobble together shifting alliances

---

ibid., no. 105; see also K. H. Jarausch, *The Enigmatic Chancellor: Bethmann Hollweg and the Hubris of Imperial Germany* (New Haven, CT, 1973), 161.

[49] Tel. Bethmann to Jagow (no. 3), 22 July 1914 (D 11.40 p.m., R 1.25 a.m.), *DD* I, no. 116; Jarausch, 'Statesmen versus Structures: Germany's Role in the Outbreak of World War One Re-examined', *LUR* v, 3 (1973), 141–2.

[50] Riezler diary, 20 and 23 July 1914, K. D. Erdmann, *Kurt Riezler. Tagebücher, Aufsätze, Dokumente* (Göttingen, 1972), 188–90.

[51] Riezler diary, 27 July 1914, *ibid.*, 193; F. Stern, 'Bethmann Hollweg and the War: The Limits of Responsibility', F. Stern and L. Krieger (eds.), *The Responsibility of Power: International Essays in Honor of Hajo Holborn* (New York, 1967), 261–2.

with different parties to secure the votes necessary in the *Reichstag*. In consequence, he had lost what little influence he had enjoyed among the Conservatives, the political arm of the Prussian *Junker* class and the most loyal supporters of the imperial régime. In their eyes the chancellor was not conservative enough, not patriotic enough, not Prussian enough. There were those on the extreme right who even favoured the idea of a form of more or less permanent coup d'état to establish some kind of emergency régime after a war.[52] Bethmann knew better. But he also understood that, if war came about after all, he had to reach out to the SPD lest the country divide over the issue. But to achieve unity in the event of war, it was important to convince the leading Social Democrats that German policy was defensive and pacific. To that end, Russia had to be put 'ruthlessly and under all circumstances in the wrong', thus playing on the innate suspicions of Tsarist autocracy amongst German socialists.[53] With this consideration in mind, Bethmann and the vice-chancellor, Clemens von Delbrück, arranged for a secret meeting with the SPD leadership, held on 26 July far from prying eyes at the ministry of the interior, at 74 Wilhelmstrasse. The chancellor, it seems, succeeded in convincing the SPD leader, Hugo Haase, and one of his deputies, Otto Braun, that Berlin wished to preserve peace and had taken steps to mediate between Vienna and St Petersburg.[54]

By supplying that information, the chancellor had practised a deliberate deception on the SPD leadership. A lie thus inaugurated tactical efforts to coax Germany's Social Democracy into the patriotic camp if conflict erupted later on. Much ink has been spilled by historians on the domestic constraints and difficulties of the *Reich* leadership before 1914.[55]

---

[52] In 1910, one of the leading East Elbian *Junkers* of the day, Elard von Oldenburg-Januschau, famously declared that the Kaiser, as King of Prussia, ought to be able to order 'a lieutenant and ten men' to close down the *Reichstag*: see von Oldenburg-Januschau, *Erinnerungen* (Leipzig, 1936), 109–10; for the background to some of this see H. Pogge-von Strandmann, 'Staatsstreichpläne, Alldeutsche und Bethmann Hollweg', in H. Pogge-von Strandmann and I. Geiss, *Die Erforderlichkeit des Unmöglichen. Deutschland am Vorabend des ersten Weltkrieges* (Frankfurt, 1965), 7–45.
[53] Tel. Bethmann Hollweg to Wilhelm II, 26 July 1914 (D 3.30 p.m.), in E. Zechlin, 'Motive und Taktik der Reichsleitung 1914', *Der Monat* XIII, 209 (1966), 91–5.
[54] For details of the meeting see D. Groh, *Negative Integration und revolutionärer Attentismus. Die deutsche Sozialdemokratie am Vorabend des Ersten Weltkrieges* (Frankfurt, 1973), 632–4; E. Zechlin, 'Bethmann Hollweg, Kriegsrisiko und die SPD 1914', in his *Krieg und Kriegsrisiko. Zur deutschen Politik im Ersten Weltkrieg* (Düsseldorf, 1979), 75–8.
[55] See *inter alios* L. Farrar, *The Short-War Illusion: German Policy, Strategy and Domestic Affairs, August–December 1914* (Santa Barbara, CA, 1973), 38–47, and his *Arrogance and Anxiety: The Ambivalence of German Power, 1848–1914* (Iowa City, 1981), 89–122; V. R. Berghahn, *Germany and the Approach of War in 1914*

Yet, neither Bethmann nor any of the other senior officials bowed to the diktat of domestic political considerations. Their decisions were not driven by some 'primacy of domestic politics'. But certainly Germany, as currently constituted, had possibly reached the limits of governability, and the chancellor thus had to keep in view the country's internal state of affairs when pursuing his foreign policy goals. For the moment, Bethmann Hollweg was impressed with the sympathetic and pro-Habsburg attitude of the large crowds that had gathered *Unter den Linden* and on the other thoroughfares of the capital following his return there.[56] But this made it all the more important to keep the SPD on board and Russia in the wrong.

Since Bethmann Hollweg's return to Berlin, the pace of events at the Wilhelmstrasse had accelerated. The chancellor, noted Riezler, 'has almost always been on the phone', making dispositions and issuing orders to prepare for all eventualities. The merchant marine was put on alert, and the *Reichsbank* was instructed to make the financial arrangements necessary in the event of a war.[57] These were sensible precautions. They did not prefigure a decision in favour of war. But war was certainly now factored into Berlin's planning. Indeed, it seems as if, after three weeks of drifting at Berlin, Bethmann Hollweg took hold of the wheel. The Kaiser, who had returned from his Nordic cruise and arrived at Kiel early that Sunday morning, was requested not to return to the capital, but instead to go to Potsdam.[58] The chancellor was determined to avoid any kind of patriotic demonstration that might give Russia even the slightest pretext to mobilize. Besides, keeping the Emperor away from Berlin limited the monarch's capacity for meddling in official business. It was not, of course, the first time that the chancellor had imposed his will on the mercurial monarch. In early July, he had prevented Wilhelm from attending the murdered Archduke's funeral, and on 5 July he had made sure that the Kaiser left for the Norwegian fjords, though not, of course, until after his fateful déjeuner with ambassador Szögyény.

(London, 1973), 145–85; for a balanced assessment of Bethmann's limited room for manoeuvre see H.-G. Zmarzlik, *Bethmann Hollweg als Reichskanzler, 1909–1914. Studien zu Möglichkeiten und Grenzen seiner innenpolitischen Machtstellung* (Düsseldorf, 1957), 75–83 and 130–9, and (with a view to the 1913 army finance bill), S. Förster, *Der doppelte Militarismus. Die deutsche Heeresrüstungspolitik zwischen Status-Quo-Sicherung und Aggression, 1890–1913* (Stuttgart, 1985), 247–96.

[56] See Jarausch, *Enigmatic Chancellor*, 165–6; Wolff, *Krieg*, 330–1.

[57] See Riezler diary, 23 and 25 July 1914, Erdmann (ed.), *Riezler*, 190; also Jarausch, *Enigmatic Chancellor*, 165.

[58] Tel. Bethmann Hollweg to Wilhelm II, 26 July 1914 (D 3.30 p.m.), Zechlin, 'Bethmann Hollweg', 93–4.

The chancellor had undergone a remarkable transformation since he had returned to the capital. Bethmann Hollweg was no longer the 'Hamlet of Berlin', unable to decide whether to be or not to be a leader. Gone was the 'philosopher of Hohenfinow', and in its place emerged a man of action. 'He is quite changed', observed Riezler, '[he] has not a minute to introspect and is fresh, active and lively and without any anxiety'.[59] One can only speculate as to what might have brought about this change. Possibly, it was the electrifying effect of a major political crisis, possibly the sense that for the first time in a long while Bethmann himself was making decisions.

There was certainly something more hawkish and resolute about the chancellor during the days after his return from the country. In the absence of any clear indications about Russia's likely attitude, he impressed on the Kaiser, in the early afternoon of 26 July, that it was important 'that our position, aiming at *localization*, has to be to *remain calm*'. If Russia showed a readiness to resort to force against Austria-Hungary, Britain was ready to offer mediation, assisted, it was hoped in London, by France.[60] To some extent the chancellor put a more positive gloss on Lichnowsky's recent communications, though of course the latter's three alarming telegrams of 26 July were yet to be despatched. There was, however, one piece of encouraging news that offered a correction to the ambassador's earlier prognostications of British intervention. At 9.30 a.m. on 26 July, the Kaiser's younger brother, Prince Heinrich of Prussia, who was then on a brief visit to Britain, called on his cousin, King George V, before heading south to Eastbourne to see his sister Sophie, the Queen of the Hellenes. The meeting was very cordial, but lasted no more than eight minutes, as the meticulous monarch recorded. The two men touched on the current situation. The news 'was very bad & it looked like a European war', said the King: 'I said "I don't know what we shall do, we have no quarrel with anyone & I hope we shall remain neutral. But if Germany declared war on Russia, & France joins Russia, then I am afraid we shall be dragged into it. But you can be sure that I and my Government will do all we can to prevent a European war!"'[61] Prince Heinrich's version of events in essence confirms

[59] Riezler diary, 27 July 1914, Erdmann, *Riezler*, 193; see also the observations – partly perceptive, partly tendentious – by W. Gutsche, *Aufstieg und Fall eines kaiserlichen Reichskanzlers. Theobald von Bethmann Hollweg, 1856–1921. Ein politisches Lebensbild* (East Berlin, 1973), 124–5.
[60] Wireless tel. Bethmann Hollweg to Wilhelm II (no. 146), 26 July 1914 (D 1 p.m., R 4 p.m.), *DD* I, no. 197 (original emphasis).
[61] George V journal, 26 July 1914, as quoted in H. Nicolson, *King George V* (London, 1964), 327; see also tel. Lichnowsky to Auswärtiges Amt (no. 159), 26 July 1914, *DD* I, no. 201.

that of his cousin. 'Georgie', he informed the Kaiser, fully appreciated the seriousness of the situation. The British government wished to localize the Austro-Serbian quarrel, and to that end had suggested mediation by the four Powers 'to rein in Russia'. Europe was closer to a conflict than ever before, the King had said, and then continued: 'we shall try all we can to keep out of this and shall remain neutral'. The Prince was in no doubt that his Coburg cousin was sincere in his professions, but he warned his brother that Britain would eventually join a continental war 'because of the relations with France'. Otherwise, he had detected no trace of anxiety in Britain, though this may have had more to do with the fact that his visit occurred over the weekend, which played such a prominent role in a country 'which was geographically so advantageously situated as England'.[62]

Prince Heinrich's account was only sent once he made landfall at Kiel on 28 July. But, already during the afternoon of 26 July, Bethmann Hollweg had learnt through naval channels – the Prince was an admiral in the Imperial German Navy – that 'England would remain neutral if [a] war broke out between [the] continental Powers'.[63] Against this backdrop, Bethmann Hollweg issued instructions to the ambassadors at London, Paris and St Petersburg, which were remarkable for their resolute tone and adherence to the idea of localizing any conflict between Austria-Hungary and Serbia. Lichnowsky was to hint that the call-up of reservists in Russia amounted to a form of mobilization against Germany; if confirmed, then Berlin would have to take countermeasures. Germany wished to localize the Balkan quarrel 'and to preserve European peace'. The chancellor therefore requested Grey 'to work in this sense at [St] Petersburg'.[64] Schoen at Paris, meanwhile, was to impress upon the Quai d'Orsay that the question of war or peace in Europe now rested on Russia, and that Berlin trusted that French diplomacy would exercise a calming influence on the Russian government. Pourtalès received instructions along similar lines, but was to emphasize 'our old-established good relations' and to explain that Berlin was confident that the Tsar's ministers would not make a move 'which would seriously imperil European peace'.[65]

---

[62] Heinrich of Prussia to Kaiser Wilhelm, 28 July 1914, DD II, no. 374.
[63] Tel. Wiedemann to Imperial Navy Office, and min. Zimmermann, 26 July 1914, DD I, no. 207.
[64] Tel. Bethmann Hollweg to Lichnowsky (no. 178, urgent), 26 July 1914 (D 1.35 p.m.), DD I, no. 199.
[65] Tels. Bethmann Hollweg to Schoen and to Pourtalès (nos. 167 and 126), both 26 July 1914 (D 1.35 p.m.), DD I, nos. 200 and 198 (quote from latter).

The focus of German diplomatic activities thus remained firmly fixed on Russia. The international situation remained uncertain, Jagow told General Helmuth von Moltke, the Chief of the General Staff. The course of events would depend on Russia's attitude: 'were she not to take hostile action against Austria, then the war will remain localized'.[66] Using the spectre of successive Russian and German mobilizations, especially London but also Paris were to be encouraged to restrain Russia. At the same time, the conciliatory tone to be adopted by Pourtalès at St Petersburg was to signal that, in the absence of firm Franco-British support, talks with Germany were the only sensible option for Russia.[67] Focusing attention on St Petersburg thus served diplomatic purposes, but it was also calculated to win over the Social Democrats at home in the event of a further escalation later on.

The chancellor was nevertheless confident enough on 26 July to take a harder line. When Pourtalès reported later that evening news of the possible mobilization of the Kiev and Odessa military districts, Bethmann Hollweg sharpened the tone of his instructions for the ambassador. Germany would have to respond to Russia's military measures by mobilizing her armed forces. Mobilization meant war against Russia and France on account of the Franco-Russian alliance: 'We cannot assume that Russia should wish to unleash such a European war.' Austria-Hungary had declared her intention not to annex Serbian territory. With the Kingdom's integrity not called into question, there was thus the 'basis of an arrangement'.[68] The more hawkish stance was also apparent in draft instructions of the same day for the London, Paris and St Petersburg embassies in Bethmann's own hand. In this document, the chancellor reiterated the argument that Austria-Hungary acted in self-defence and out of self-preservation. If Russia intervened on the side of Serbia, then she aimed at undermining the existence of another Great Power – one of the cornerstones of the international system – and in that case she would bear sole responsibility 'if out of the Austro-Serbian quarrel, which the other Great Powers wish to localize, a European war arose'. This responsibility was all

---

[66] Moltke to Eliza von Moltke, 26 July 1914, E. von Moltke (ed.), *Generaloberst Helmuth von Moltke. Erinnerungen, Briefe, Dokumente, 1877–1916* (Stuttgart, 1922), 381; see also Riezler diary, 25 July 1914, Erdmann (ed.), *Riezler*, 190–1.

[67] See Bethmann Hollweg's musings about a future Russo-German agreement, Riezler diary, 20 and 23 July 1914, Erdmann (ed.), *Riezler*, 188–90.

[68] Tel. Bethmann Hollweg to Pourtalès (no. 128, urgent), 26 July 1914 (D 7.15 p.m.), *DD* I, no. 219; for the news from St Petersburg see tel. vice versa (no. 158), 26 July 1914 (D 3.25 p.m., R 7.01 p.m.), *ibid.*, no. 216; also tel. Chelius to Wilhelm II, 25 July 1914, G. von Lambsdorff, *Die Militärbevollmächtigten Kaiser Wilhelm II. am Zarenhofe, 1904–1914* (Berlin, 1937), 433.

the greater as Berchtold had already given guarantees respecting Serbian territory. Since Austria-Hungary was defending her vital interest, Berlin could not interfere in the dispute. If, however, it widened into an Austro-Russian quarrel, then 'we would support energetically all efforts by other Powers to mediate'. But in the last resort, Germany would fight alongside her ally: 'Only if forced shall we draw the sword, but then quietly conscious that we bear no guilt for the unspeakable disaster that a war would bring for the peoples of Europe.' Ultimately, the instructions were never sent, as a '*Cessat* [cancelled]' in Stumm's hand indicates.[69]

Bethmann's draft telegram to the senior German ambassadors abroad is nevertheless suggestive of the line that the chancellor was pursuing in the aftermath of Giesl's departure from Belgrade. He still hoped to localize the conflict in the Balkans with the aim of buttressing Austria-Hungary's position among the Powers. If the conflict could be contained, then closer arrangements with either Britain or Russia might be possible in the future; with the former because of repeated joint crisis management and the recent understanding on the Near East, and with the latter in light of French and British reluctance to support her in the Serbian crisis. To that end Britain and France had to be forced to restrain Russia. Even so, as the various precautions, including Bethmann's reaching out to the leadership of the Social Democrats, indicated, a continental war now hove into view.

There is further evidence to suggest that the Wilhelmstrasse continued to believe that a display of resolution on the part of Germany and her allies would yield the desired result. Jagow impressed upon Lichnowsky that the unity of the *Dreibund* alliance offered the best guarantee of a satisfactory solution of the crisis.[70] In conversation with the journalist Theodor Wolff, Stumm, the political director of the Auswärtiges Amt, remained optimistic that Berlin would somehow 'get out of it', and insisted that there was no alternative to what he called 'quiet perseverance'.[71] This was also the line Stumm took in his talks with the representatives of the smaller German states. Stumm was confident, the Württemberg envoy reported home, that Britain not only desired peace but would take energetic steps in that sense at St Petersburg. Russia was not ready for war, and the recent revelations in the French Senate about the mismanagement of the recent armaments programmes would make Paris incline towards peace as well. Berlin had supported the Austro-Hungarian démarche, Stumm

---

[69] Draft instructions for Schoen, Lichnowsky and Pourtalès, 26 July 1914, *DD* I, no. 234.
[70] Tel. Jagow to Lichnowsky (no. 24), 27 July 1914 (D 10 p.m.), *DD* I, no. 273.
[71] T. Wolff, *Der Krieg des Pontius Pilatus* (Zürich, 1934), 331. The book was written in exile, but Wolff drew on his contemporary notes.

explained, because Germany 'could no longer look on as the Austro-Hungarian state was eaten up from the inside by Serbdom'.[72]

The notion of 'quiet perseverance' set the tone of German diplomacy during the next few days. The situation remained unsettled, the chief of staff, General Helmuth von Moltke, was told later that day when he returned from leave at the Bohemian spa town of Karlsbad (now Karlovy Vary). The only fly in the ointment was the uncertain attitude of Italy. Her neutrality would complicate the next diplomatic moves. Moltke, too, insisted on the importance of keeping Rome in the fold of the *Dreibund* alliance. To that end, Bethmann now began to put pressure on the Ballhausplatz. An arrangement with Italy was urgently needed: 'Vienna must not evade this with dubious legal interpretations, but has to decide in accordance with the seriousness of the situation.'[73]

By the end of Sunday, 26 July, a number of different threads had come together. All of them pointed to some form of negotiated settlement; but all of them also implied different routes towards a solution of the crisis. Sazonov had shifted his position the most. Instead of internationalizing the Austro-Serbian dispute, he now favoured negotiations. However, he sent different signals as to whether the negotiations should take the form of direct Austro-Russian talks or whether they should take place under the auspices of the four Powers not directly interested in the dispute between Vienna and Belgrade. This was to sow confusion, and thus complicated matters over the next twenty-four to forty-eight hours. A precondition for Sazonov's policy to be effective, however, was for Berlin to moderate its ally's stance. Implicit in his statements to Szápáry and Pourtalès, moreover, was the hint of his willingness to flex Russia's military muscle to back up his diplomatic moves. Deterrence thus remained at the core of Russian policy.

In contrast to Sazonov's ambiguities, Grey's proposal of mediation under the auspices of the quartet least affected by the Austro-Serbian quarrel had the virtue of being clearly developed. It was flexible enough, however, to be broadened into another ambassadorial conference, backed by the four Powers. To be effective, Grey's scheme of classic conference diplomacy *en miniature* required German participation; and, to that end, it was necessary for Berlin to rein in Vienna as had happened during the

---

[72] Graevenitz to Weizsäcker (no. 1966), 26 July 1914, *DGB* no. 17; see also Schoen to Hertling (no. 400), 26 July 1914, *BayD* no. 29.

[73] Tel. Bethmann Hollweg to Tschirschky (no. 150), 26 July 1914 (D 3 p.m., R 7.10 p.m.), *DD* I, no. 202; for Moltke see A. Mombauer, *Helmuth von Moltke and the Origins of the First World War* (Cambridge, 2002), 196–7.

earlier Balkans crises. All efforts would be for nought, however, if either Austria-Hungary or Russia commenced military operations.

The 'quiet perseverance' advocated at Berlin also had a diplomatic settlement as its ultimate objective. Unlike the ideas advanced by Sazonov and Grey, however, German policy was predicated on localizing the Austro-Serbian conflict. As the more resolute tone emanating from the Wilhelmstrasse indicated, the German leadership was ready to coerce Russia into acquiescing to a settlement on Austro-German terms. This could succeed only if Britain and France acted to restrain Russia. Thus abandoned by her ally, and not supported by London, Bethmann Hollweg reasoned, St Petersburg might eventually become more amenable to the idea of a reconstituted *Dreikaiserbund*, that conservative alliance of the three eastern military monarchies of Bismarck's days. Alternatively, relations with Britain might be strengthened, provided London was persuaded that German diplomacy had cooperated loyally with its crisis management efforts. To an extent, Bethmann's game plan was the mirror image of Sazonov's strategy. His policy, too, was based on an element of deterrence, the threat of German mobilization, with the clear implication that mobilization meant war. Underpinning all of this, however, was the assumption that Russia would not move. If Pourtalès's reports reinforced this belief, it was nevertheless also what the Wilhelmstrasse wanted to believe. It was one of the many absurdities of the July crisis.

The skirmish that never was

On Monday, 27 July, international crisis diplomacy swung into action for the first time. Ostensibly, the most important decision of the day was taken at Vienna, the decision at last to declare war on Serbia. But other developments gathered momentum, developments which were to push the Powers in different directions and so heighten the international crisis.

At Vienna, the Serbian reply to the démarche had caused considerable dismay. That in substance Belgrade's note amounted to a rejection of the Austro-Hungarian demands has already been discussed. Its conciliatory tone, however, made it difficult for the Habsburg government simply to reject it. Certainly, the collective effort of the Serbian ministers had manoeuvred the Dual Monarchy into an awkward position. Nothing would have been achieved, Giesl explained on arrival at the Ballhausplatz, and 'everything would remain as it is, if we were satisfied with the Serbian answer'.[74]

---

[74] [A.] von Musulin, *Das Haus am Ballplatz. Erinnerungen eines österreich-ungarischen Diplomaten* (Munich, 1924), 240. Musulin himself claimed that he favoured aborting the diplomatic action at that point.

It was then left to Musulin, one of the section chiefs at the Ballhausplatz, to compose a rebuttal of Belgrade's note. Working through the night of 26/27 July, Musulin prepared a detailed, point-by-point examination of the Serbian reply. This was then appended to a circular despatch to the Monarchy's representatives abroad, with firm instructions to the heads of mission that the Serbian note had to be treated as 'unsatisfactory'.[75]

The circular despatch and Musulin's textual exegesis were to provide a quasi-legal cover for and moral justification of Austro-Hungarian military action against Serbia. Far more complicated, however, was the issue of mobilization. As seen earlier, the order for 'War Case B', the partial mobilization against Serbia, had been issued to the commanders of the Monarchy's military district at 9.23 p.m. on 25 July, with the order to be published on 27 July, making the following day, Tuesday, 28 July, the first day of mobilization. In mobilizing the armed forces for a conflict with Serbia, the Habsburg leadership faced two difficulties, one political and the other a matter of logistics. Both were inseparably entwined. The weak spot of the Austro-Hungarian mobilization plan lay in the Dual Empire's insufficient transport capacity. The limited number of railway lines, not all of them fully double-tracked and some with different gauges (especially in Bosnia-Herzegovina), increased the importance of certain railway junctions. For the mobilization to run smoothly, the bulk of the troops had to pass through these transport hubs before they could disgorge from the railheads into the deployment areas. In turn, this meant that in order to have the forces needed for the campaign against Serbia fully deployed, a partial mobilization, as had now been ordered, could not easily be reversed if the conflict escalated. Indeed, partial mobilization against Serbia could only be extended to a general mobilization against Russia and Serbia by the eleventh day of mobilization (M +11).[76]

There was thus a zone of considerable danger before Austria-Hungary was able to commence military operations against Serbia. For one thing, Russia's attitude would determine whether the mobilization

---

[75] Berchtold circular, encl. annotated copy of Serbian note, 28 July 1914, and circular tel. Berchtold, 27 July 1914 (D 6 p.m.), ÖUA VIII, nos. 10860 and 10781; Musulin, *Haus am Ballplatz*, 246–7, for the background.

[76] F. Conrad von Hötzendorf, *Aus meiner Dienstzeit* (5 vols., Vienna, 1921–5) IV, 109. For detailed discussions see R. Kizling, 'Die österreichisch-ungarischen Kriegsvorbereitungen und die Mobilisierungsmassnahmen gegen Russland', BMH IV, 3 (1936), 365–77; M. Rauchensteiner, *Der Tod des Doppeladlers. Österreich-Ungarn und der erste Weltkrieg* (Graz, 1993), 88–91; N. Stone, 'Die Mobilmachung der österreichisch-ungarischen Armee 1914', MGM II (1974), 67–95; G. A. Tunstall Jr, *Planning for War against Russia and Serbia: Austro-Hungarian and German Military Strategies, 1871–1914* (Boulder, CO, 1993), 144–6 and 172–4.

along the southern frontier could be completed; for another, moving immediately to general mobilization was guaranteed to force Russia off the fence and to mobilize herself. Finally, the long period of mobilization left the Habsburg Empire vulnerable to a vigorous diplomatic initiative by the other Powers.

Since Sarajevo, the Ballhausplatz had left it to their Germany ally to deal with the Russian aspect of the Monarchy's Serbian problem. Only István Tisza had repeatedly warned of the dangers that could arise from that quarter. And it was the Magyar prime minister who returned to the problem on 26 July. Habsburg diplomacy now had to secure Russia's neutrality by playing the non-annexation card to maximum effect, he wrote to the Hungarian representative at the imperial court, Count István Burián. Russia's attitude was 'very uncertain'. Secure in the knowledge 'that Germany will take action *immediately* as soon as Russia threatens [us] or mobilizes', Austria-Hungary could hang fire for the moment. One day later, he reiterated his warning against any premature preparations against Russia in response to any threats by St Petersburg: 'Economically, we would bleed to death, [we] would stand at the southern frontier with a smaller army without the necessary offensive capacities, and Russia could draw matters out.'[77] This was more a description of the Monarchy's problems than a prescription for their solution. But for the moment it was by no means clear how Russia would react. Burián recorded in his diary that 'Russia's position is still entirely uncertain. We work on Russia in that we promise territorial *désinteressement* with regards to Serbia.'[78]

There was another problem, however. To ensure that the eventual conflict could be localized, Berlin was piling on the pressure to open hostilities at the earliest opportunity since any further delays increased the likelihood of foreign diplomatic or indeed military intervention. It was largely with a view to Berlin's representations and to render impracticable any mediation attempt that Berchtold decided that, coinciding with the first day of mobilization, Austria-Hungary would declare war on Serbia.[79] There were no compelling military reasons for opening hostilities

[77] Tisza to Burián, 26 and 27 July 1914, as quoted in Galántai, *Österreichisch-ungarische Monarchie*, 348.
[78] Burián diary, 27 July 1914, I. Diószegi, 'Aussenminister Stephan Graf Burián. Biographie und Tagebuchstellen', *Annales Universitatis Scientiarum Budapestinensis de Rolando Eötvös nominatae. Sectio Historica* VIII (1966), 207.
[79] Tel. Tschirschky to Auswärtiges Amt (no. 113), 27 July 1914 (D 4.37 p.m.); *DD* I, no. 257. For Berlin's pressing for an early campaign see tel. Szögyény to Berchtold (no. 283, strictly confidential), 25 July 1914 (D 8.45 p.m., R 12.30 p.m.), *ÖUA* VIII, no. 10655; and tel. Tschirschky to Auswärtiges Amt (no. 105, secret), 26 July 1914, *DD* I, no. 213.

immediately. Conrad had always insisted that operations could commence only once deployment was completed, that is on the fifteenth day of mobilization; and he originally favoured delaying a declaration of war until that moment. Now, Berchtold let it be known at Berlin that whilst there was still some further delay, this was to enable Austria-Hungary 'to deliver the decisive strike with full force'.[80]

On that Monday, Emperor Franz Joseph received Giesl at his summer retreat at Ischl for a report on the final day of his Belgrade mission. 'You could not have acted otherwise', he told the envoy: 'I will have to bear this as well now.' While Giesl was with his monarch, Lieutenant-Colonel Otto Gellinek, the military attaché at Belgrade, had a conversation with a member of the Emperor's military entourage. He was optimistic about the forthcoming campaign against Serbia; it would be a case of some 'light marching'.[81] After he had dismissed Giesl, Franz Joseph received Berchtold. The reply by the Pašić administration, the foreign minister explained, had been 'in substance of no value'. But couched in accommodating language it was likely to lead to attempts by what he referred to as the triple entente Powers to mediate between Vienna and Belgrade. A formal declaration of war would clarify the situation. There had already been skirmishes with Serbian troops near Temes-Kubin (now Kovin) on the northern bank of the Danube opposite Smederevo. Hostilities had thus commenced already, and declaring war would provide the necessary international legal framework for the operations of the Habsburg armed forces. 'I approve the appended draft telegram to the Serbian foreign ministry', the monarch wrote underneath Berchtold's memorandum as he sat at his small writing table overlooking the hunting grounds of the Salzkammergut.[82]

The reference to the exchanges of fire between Serbian troops and Habsburg forces across the Danube was excised from the declaration of war as communicated to the Serbian government and the other Powers on 28 July. There was a good reason for this. For the skirmish at Temes-Kubin never occurred. That news of the incident was received at Vienna on 26 July, and that Berchtold was informed of it by the general staff, is well documented, though extensive searches in the Viennese archives have not been able to unearth the document itself. Certainly, at some stage during the morning of 28 July – after the Emperor had signed the declaration of

---

[80] Tel. Berchtold to Szögyény (no. 274), 27 July 1914 (D 11.10 p.m.), ÖUA VIII, no. 10873; see also Conrad, *Aus meiner Dienstzeit* IV, 132.
[81] Giesl, *Zwei Jahrzehnte*, 273; and A. von Margutti, *Kaiser Franz Joseph. Persönliche Erinnerungen* (Vienna, 1924), 423.
[82] Min. Franz Joseph on report Berchtold, 27 July 1914, ÖUA VIII, no. 10855; A. Pieroni, *La gaia apocalisse* (Milan, 1983), 222.

war – Berchtold knew that there had been no engagement with Serbian forces, and he simply struck out the passage referring to Temes-Kubin.[83]

It must remain a matter of speculation whether news of the incident was fabricated – a piece of deliberate diplomatic deception – or whether it rested on a genuine misunderstanding, an over-reaction to guns going off inadvertently in a tense situation. What is not in doubt, however, is the use to which Berchtold and the Ballhausplatz put the 'incident'. It did not trigger the Monarchy's formal declaration of war – political calculations had been decisive here – but it certainly helped to frame the case for Serbia as the true aggressor. Already on 27 July, Shebeko was told by Macchio – Berchtold was still at Ischl – that it would now be well-nigh impossible to avert a conflict 'as a skirmish had already taken place on the Danube in which the Servians had been the aggressors'.[84] This was also the tenor of the Emperor Franz Joseph's telegram to King Carol of Romania, still nominally his ally. Serbian troops, he explained, had 'provoked a skirmish without prior declaration of war'.[85] Berchtold himself made use of Temes-Kubin on the following day to bat away British suggestions of international mediation. Such an effort was useless, he asserted, as in Serbia one was not dealing with a 'civilized nation [*Kulturnation*]'. Besides it was already too late since 'yesterday [27 July] our border troops were fired on from the Serbian side'.[86] The 'incident', of course, was supposed to have taken place the day before, but it was not the first time that Berchtold elided events or was economical with the truth. The Emperor himself was informed of the subsequent excision of the reference to the non-event in the declaration of war only after the fact, on 29 July, though not without reference to another, previously not reported, 'minor skirmish', this time at Gradište (now Bačko Gradište).[87]

[83] R. Kiszling, 'Die Kriegserklärung Österreich-Ungarns an Serbien', *BMH* VIII, 12 (1930), 82, refers to a file in the Vienna *Kriegsarchiv*, but without giving a shelfmark reference; also his 'Die Wahrheit über das Gefecht bei Temes-Kubin', *Österreichische Wehrzeitung*, 3 Feb. 1933, 3; for a further discussion of the matter see Rauchensteiner, *Tod des Doppeladlers*, 92–4.

[84] Tel. de Bunsen to Grey (no. 111), 27 July 1914, *BD* XI, no. 199. Shebeko himself makes no mention of this: see tel. Shebeko to Sazonov (no. 104), 14/27 July 1914, *IBZI* V, no. 139.

[85] Tel. Franz Joseph to Carol, 28 July 1914 (D 1 p.m.), *ÖUA* VIII, no. 10873.

[86] Tel. Berchtold to Mensdorff (no. 179), 28 July 1914 (D 1 p.m.), *ÖUA* VIII, no. 10892. The ambassador made no reference to it in his report: see tel. de Bunsen to Grey (no. 115), 28 July 1914 (D 4.10 p.m., R 9.40 p.m.), *BD* XI, no. 230.

[87] Memo. Berchtold, 29 July 1914, *ÖUA* VIII, no. 11015; see also Rauchensteiner, *Tod des Doppeladlers*, 94.

Since the Emperor had supported a military strike against Serbia from the beginning, Berchtold had no need to fabricate news of an incident to sway the monarch. But certainly the Ballhausplatz accentuated news of developments favourable to its designs. Alek Hoyos, for instance, reported to the Emperor's *chef de cabinet*, Baron Franz von Schiessl, that Theo Russell, counsellor at the British embassy, had impressed upon him that Britain 'did not wish in any way to meddle in our quarrel with Serbia, as long as it remained localized'.[88]

It is perhaps part of the psychology of political crises that greater weight is accorded to positive news than to anything that might contradict established policy preferences and desired outcomes. Hoyos's assessment of Britain's attitude was not wrong, but it was at best only partially accurate.

Sir Edward is irritated

In the morning of 27 July, the Serbian envoy to Britain communicated Belgrade's reply to the Austro-Hungarian démarche. On perusing it, Nicolson concluded that 'it practically concedes all the Austrian demands' and queried how Vienna could possibly open hostilities now 'when Servia has yielded so much'. Information received overnight from Vienna suggested that the concentration of the Austro-Hungarian army along the Serbian frontier would not be completed until about 5 August, the Wednesday of the following week. '[S]o we have a few days ahead of us', Nicolson concluded optimistically.[89] The notion that Belgrade had 'swallow[ed] nearly all the Austrian demands "en bloc"' was gaining currency at the Foreign Office now. Perhaps here, too, the desire for a mediated settlement as the preferred outcome led officials to ignore some of the ambiguities in Belgrade's note. G. R. Clerk, head of the Foreign Office's Eastern Department, thought that such reservations as were made – usually requests for further explanation or proof – were 'quite reasonable'. Only on the sixth point concerning the participation of Habsburg police in investigations on Serbian soil was there a direct refusal, albeit for 'reasons which are good arguments'. The Serbian response, concluded Crowe, was 'reasonable'. If Austria-Hungary expected 'complete compliance with her ultimatum it can

---

[88] Hoyos to Schiessl (private), 26 July 1914, ÖUA VIII, no. 10772; see also Hantsch, *Berchtold* II, 622.

[89] Memo. Nicolson, 27 July 1914, *BD* XI, no. 171; for the information on Austria-Hungary's mobilization see tels. de Bunsen to Grey (nos. 107–8), 26 July 1914 (D 12 p.m., R 9.30 a.m.), *ibid.*, nos. 165–6.

only mean that she wants war'. It was obvious that submitting to it was 'tantamount to accepting a protectorate'.[90]

Crowe's conclusion was entirely accurate. Even so the extent to which it was believed in London that Serbia had accepted Austria-Hungary's demands is remarkable. That Vienna was resolved to act was no longer doubted, however. In the early afternoon, de Bunsen wired that 'Austria-Hungary is fully determined on war with Servia.' Vienna believed the Monarchy's position as a Great Power to be at stake, and the note had therefore been drawn up 'so as to make war inevitable'. The Habsburg leadership was not likely to entertain any proposals for a diplomatic settlement 'until punishment has been inflicted on Servia' and 'guarantees for the future' obtained. The scope for mediation was now narrower than it had appeared even twenty-four hours earlier. But there was another obstacle now, as Crowe realized. Austria-Hungary's non-annexation pledge and promise not to diminish Serbia's independence were all very well, but what other meaning could 'guarantees for the future' have? 'The outlook is bad. All now depends on what line Germany may be prepared to take.'[91]

With Germany's attitude Grey's mediation scheme would stand or fall, that was accepted in London. But Russia's reaction to the impending Austro-Serbian conflict could also scupper its chances of success; and the news from St Petersburg throughout the day was not encouraging. Already, de Bunsen had reported Shebeko's belief that Russia 'will be compelled to act'. Now Buchanan's latest interview with Sazonov earlier that morning cast further light on thinking at St Petersburg. The Russian foreign minister renewed his efforts to persuade Britain to join France and Russia in a united front against the two Germanic Powers. Buchanan stuck rigidly to his instructions. Threatening Germany would be counter-productive, he argued. Only by approaching Berlin 'as a friend anxious to preserve peace' could it be persuaded to moderate Austria-Hungary's next moves. To succeed in this, however, it was essential that Russia did nothing to precipitate matters. Any mobilization on Russia's part had to be deferred for as long as possible, and, if it became necessary, there had to be an intermediate phase between the completion of mobilization and commencement of hostilities. Sazonov did not demur, but his response was not encouraging. If Russian mobilization were deferred for too long, he observed, 'Austria

---

[90] Mins. Clerk and Crowe, 28 July 1914, *BD* XI, no. 171.

[91] Quotes from tel. de Bunsen to Grey (no. 109), 27 July 1914 (D 1 p.m., R 2.45 p.m.), and min. Crowe on same, 27 July 1914, *BD* XI, no. 175; see also T. G. Otte, '"The Pick of Ambassadors": Sir Maurice de Bunsen, Edwardian Ambassador', in T. G. Otte (ed.), *Diplomacy and Power: Studies in Modern Diplomatic Practice: Essays in Honour of Keith Hamilton* (Leiden, 2012), 78–9.

would profit by [the] delay to make her military preparations complete, while Russia could do nothing'. Russia would have to mobilize the moment Austro-Hungarian forces entered Serbian territory, but it might be possible to issue an accompanying declaration that 'troops would be retained on this side of the frontier'.

Sazonov's concession offered no real solution to the crisis, as Crowe observed. The 'real difficulty' now was the question of mobilizations. De Bunsen's telegram suggested that Austria-Hungary was determined on war, and that conflict would be considered a serious menace to Russian interest. Given the slow pace of Russian mobilization, Crowe elaborated on Sazonov's argument: any delay tilted the balance of influence towards the two central European Powers. Austro-Hungarian mobilization, then, was very likely to lead to Russian mobilization – and here lay the problem: 'If Russia mobilizes, we have been warned [by Lichnowsky] Germany will do the same.' It was understood in London that German mobilization plans were directed against France. The latter therefore could not delay her own mobilization 'for even the fraction of a day'. Within twenty-four hours, then, London would be faced with a momentous question: 'whether, in a quarrel so imposed by Austria on an unwilling France, Great Britain will stand idly aside, or take sides'. It was not for a civil servant to offer advice, Crowe noted, only to do just that:

> It is difficult not to remember the position of Prussia in 1805, when she insisted on keeping out of the war which she could not prevent from breaking out between the other Powers over questions not, on their face, of direct interest to Prussia.
>
> The war was waged without Prussia. But in 1806 she fell a victim to the Power [France] that had won in 1805, and no one was ready either to help her or to prevent her political ruin and partition.[92]

It was small wonder, then, that Grey was 'displeased and determined'[93] at his interview with Lichnowsky in the early afternoon of 27 July, which had been arranged at the Foreign Secretary's request. The ambassador opened the conversation with the suggestion that his government would

---

[92] Tel. Buchanan to Grey (no. 173), 27 July 1914 (D 10.06 a.m., R 1.15 p.m.), and min. Crowe on same, 27 July 1914, *BD* XI, no. 170. Crowe, an avid reader of historical works, had read Seeley's *Life of Stein* and Ranke's *Preussische Geschichte* in 1893, and the relvant volumes in the *Cambridge Modern History* in 1912–13, see 'List of Books Read' [the *Lesebuch*], Crowe MSS, Bodl., Ms.Eng.d.2909.

[93] According to Mensdorff, see tel. Mensdorff to Berchtold (no. 113), 27 July 1914 (D 2.12 p.m., R 6.30 p.m.), *ÖUA* VIII, no. 10812.

accept mediation between Austria-Hungary and Russia, but would not sacrifice the alliance with Vienna. As instructed, he pressed Grey to use his influence to restrain St Petersburg so as to keep the conflict localized. In reply, Grey observed that the Serbian note had gone 'further than could have been expected to meet the Austrian demands'. This, he presumed, was the result of Russian intervention at Belgrade. Jagow himself had earlier admitted that some of the Austro-Hungarian demands were unacceptable. It was therefore 'at Vienna that moderating influence was now required', Grey repeatedly stressed. Any Austro-Hungarian move against Serbia would be 'reckless'. Grey conceded that Berlin could not afford to see its ally crushed, but warned that other Powers might become involved for similar reasons if Germany entered the conflict, 'and the war would be the biggest ever known'. For as long as German diplomacy worked towards a peaceful settlement of the Balkan crisis, Berlin could count on Britian's willingness to cooperate.[94]

For the first time since arriving at 9 Carlton House Terrace two years ago, Lichnowsky found Grey 'irritated'. He spoke with great seriousness, the ambassador reported, and expected the Wilhelmstrasse to use its influence at Vienna. During previous periods of Balkan turmoil, Grey explained, he had willingly complied with German requests to give moderating advice at St Petersburg, much to the displeasure of the Russian government. Now, he expected Berlin to reciprocate and rein in its ally. It would be a promising sign for the future, he impressed on Lichnowsky, if London and Berlin once more succeeded 'through our respective influence on our allies to secure the peace of Europe'. If the conflict escalated, the ambassador warned, the German leadership could no longer count on British sympathies. The key lay at Berlin; it was for the Wilhelmstrasse to prevent Austria-Hungary from pursuing, 'as Sir E[dward] Grey puts it, a reckless policy'.[95]

Grey thus continued to press his mediation scheme on Germany, but he had sharpened his tone. Whilst he held out the prospect of further closer cooperation in the future, this could not be one-way traffic. There had to be reciprocity. Britain had proposed some form of international arbitration; it was now for Berlin to ensure that Vienna would accept the

[94] Tel. Grey to Goschen (no. 208), 27 July 1914 (D 3 p.m.), *BD* XI, no. 176; see also Buchanan aide mémoire, 15/28 July 1914, *IBZI* V, no. 161; and tel. Fleuriau to Bienvenu-Martin (no. 149, secret), 27 July 1914 (D 8.42 p.m., R 1.35 a.m.), *DDF* (3) XI, no. 156.
[95] Tel. Lichnowsky to Auswärtiges Amt (no. 164), 27 July 1914 (D 1.31 p.m., R 4.37 p.m.), *DD* I, no. 258. As so often, Lichnowsky's report was very accurate; see also tel. Benckendorff to Sazonov (no. 208), 14/27 July 1914, *IBZI* V, no. 122.

diplomatic route. If it failed to do so, the conflict would escalate to a general European war. His line was sensible enough, and reflected the information at his disposal. It offered mediation and cooperation, but underpinning them was the implied threat of war. Lichnowsky's statement that Berlin would participate in a Four-Power conference, moreover, was encouraging. The ambassador had faithfully executed his instructions.[96] But they were designed to mislead. For neither Jagow nor Bethmann Hollweg favoured an international conference as proposed by Grey. True, the state secretary's instructions to Lichnowsky were unequivocal in support of such a scheme; and true also, Jagow reaffirmed his support for Grey's proposals in conversation with the French ambassador at Berlin, Jules Cambon, in the morning of 27 July. He reiterated that Russian mobilization would be a serious escalation of the crisis, and that Germany would have to respond to it with her own military preparations. Significantly, he suggested that this would not be the case if Russia did not mobilize along the German frontier. Jagow laid particular stress on this point, and asked Cambon to report it to Paris, presumably in the expectation that it would thence be transmitted to St Petersburg. Even so, Jagow's statement calls into question the argument that the military dictated policy at Berlin.

Two further points raised by Jagow in his conversation with the experienced French ambassador are suggestive. In the first place he referred to Grey's proposal as intervention at St Petersburg and Vienna, and further he warned that any precipitate move would ruin the prospect of a diplomatic solution.[97] The former reflected the fact that Lichnowsky's telegram on the conference proposal arrived at about the time that Jagow spoke to the French ambassador. Its contents, however, were to pose a significant problem for German diplomacy. Jagow's concluding warning, meanwhile, was aimed exclusively at Russia. For as seen earlier, he had urged Austria-Hungary to commence military operations against Serbia without too much delay so as to minimize the chances of diplomatic intervention by the Powers.[98]

Belgrade's note was communicated to the Wilhelmstrasse by the Serbian legation in the morning of 27 July. Separately, and as if to

[96] The instructions are in tel. Jagow to Lichnowsky (no. 176), 25 July 1914 (D 11.05 p.m.), DD I, no. 192.
[97] Tel. J. Cambon to Bienvenu-Martin (no. 200), 27 July 1914 (D 12.50 p.m., R 4.25 p.m.), DDF (3) XI, no. 136. There does not seem to be a record by Jagow on this interview.
[98] See tel. Tschirschky to Jagow (no. 105, secret), 26 July 1914 (D 4.50 p.m., R 6.20 p.m.), DD I, no. 213. Lichnowsky's telegram no. 161 arrived at the Auswärtiges Amt at 12.07 p.m. on 27 July, see ibid., no. 236.

underline the lack of communication and coordination between the Ball-hausplatz and the Wilhelmstrasse, Jagow had to request the text of the Serbian reply from Vienna, from where it was transmitted through Tschirschky and then only on 28 July and without Musulin's comments.[99] There was, however, little appetite at Berlin to take cognizance of the Serbian reply. Nor was the chancellor minded to abandon the essence of his localization scheme. If anything, Bethmann Hollweg remained rather hawkish for much of the day, and it was he who was in charge. Around noon he laid down his line of attack. Austro-Hungarian military operations would commence on 12 August, he wired to the Kaiser who at that moment was travelling by train from Kiel to Potsdam. The diplomatic situation remained uncertain. Britain and France wished for peace, and so did Italy, while Russia appeared willing to open direct talks with Austria-Hungary. German diplomacy would continue to press for localization. So far Russia had made no move to mobilize, but St Petersburg had been warned that military measures against Germany would have consequences.[100] Then he instructed Schoen at Paris to explain the need to separate the Austro-Serbian dispute from other questions in his discussions at the Quai d'Orsay. Germany could not consent to mediating in the quarrel between Vienna and Belgrade, but would possibly do so in a dispute between Austria-Hungary and Russia.[101]

In the meantime, Lichnowsky's telegram on his conversation with Nicolson and Tyrrell the previous evening had arrived at the Wilhelmstrasse. In consequence, the chancellor issued fresh instructions for the ambassador in London. Germany could not accept Grey's proposal of a conference à quatre, Bethmann explained, as 'we cannot drag Austria in her Serbian affair before a European court'. Germany would consent to international mediation only in the event of an Austro-Russian crisis. Sazonov's interview with Pourtalès seemed to open up the prospect of direct talks between the two eastern empires, and Lichnowsky was therefore to impress upon Grey 'the necessity and possibility of localization'.[102]

[99] Tel. Jagow to Tschirschky (no. 160), 27 July 1914 (D 11.30 a.m., R 4 p.m.), *DD* I, no. 246, and Tschirschky to Auswärtiges Amt, 28 July 1914, *ibid.* II, no. 347; the Serbian communication is in *ibid.* I, no. 271.

[100] Tel. Bethmann Hollweg to Wilhelm II, 27 July 1914 (D 11.20 a.m., R 1.20 p.m.), *DD* I, no. 245.

[101] Tel. Bethmann Hollweg to Schoen (no. 170), 27 July 1914 (D 11.20 a.m.), *DD* I, no. 247.

[102] Tel. Bethmann Hollweg to Lichnowsky (no. 179), 27 July 1914 (D 1 p.m.), *DD* I, no. 248; cf. tel. Pourtalès to Auswärtiges Amt (no. 163), 26 July 1914 (D 10.10 p.m., R 12.45 a.m.), *ibid.*, no. 238.

Sir Edward makes a statement and Jules Cambon lights a firework

Matters were heading towards a diplomatic impasse, and Grey now took the unusual step of making his mediation proposal public. This, combined with the order of the previous day to keep the fleet assembled at Spithead, should help to advance his proposals, he explained to Benckendorff.[103] In response to a parliamentary question by the leader of the opposition, Andrew Bonar Law, he explained his twin proposals of Four-Power mediation at St Petersburg and Vienna and an ambassadorial conference to be held at London. There had been no time to ascertain whether the proposals would be well-received, he explained: 'But, where matters are so grave and the time so short, the risk of proposing something that is unwelcome or ineffective cannot be avoided.' The Serbian reply ought to be a sufficient basis on which the quartet of Powers 'should be able to arrange a settlement that would be generally acceptable'. It was obvious to any observer, the Foreign Secretary wound up his statement, that if another Great Power became involved in the Austro-Serbian dispute, 'it can but end in the greatest catastrophe that has ever befallen the Continent of Europe at one blow: no-one can say what would be the limit of the issues that might be raised by such a conflict, the consequences of it, direct and indirect, would be incalculable'.[104]

Grey's statement did not differ in substance from the line he had taken so far with the foreign ambassadors, most of whom sat in the Strangers' Gallery above the Commons chamber that afternoon. As before, it was a clear signal to St Petersburg not to take any precipitate action that would antagonize Germany; as before, it was an unambiguous gesture aimed at Berlin that it had to restrain Austria-Hungary. But in making his proposals public, the Foreign Secretary increased the pressure on Germany in particular. Indeed, as the journalist Theodor Wolff later commented, it is remarkable how, at a time when the chancelleries of Europe hid behind the moves, counter-moves and subterfuges of secret diplomacy, Grey stepped out of this darkness and emerged as Europe's only 'man of action'.[105]

During the Cabinet meeting that evening, Lewis 'Lulu' Harcourt, the Colonial Secretary, found Grey 'working hard for peace and not belligerent'.[106] There was, of course, a not inconsiderable risk of failure. The

---

[103] Tel. Benckendorff to Sazonov (no. 208), 14/27 July 1914, *IBZI* v, no. 122.
[104] *Hansard House of Commons* LXV (27 July 1914), cols. 938–9. It is not clear whether the question was planted. Benckendorff's telegram no. 208, *vide supra*, suggests that Grey had very carefully rehearsed the answers to anticipated questions.
[105] Wolff, *Krieg*, 332.
[106] Harcourt Cabinet notes, 27 July 1914, Harcourt MSS, Bodl., no accession number. Harcourt had certain pro-German leanings, and had been involved in colonial talks with

Cabinet, meeting for just about an hour, nevertheless endorsed Grey's line. 'The outlook for war rather serious', noted John Burns, the President of the Board of Trade and the only working-man Liberal in the Cabinet: 'Why 4 great powers should fight over Servia no fellow can understand.'[107] The ministers' mood was sombre, as Herbert Samuel, the President of the Local Government Board, wrote later that night to his wife: 'I am still pessimistic about the outlook, but we are doing our best to localise the conflict. The Irish trouble is not likely to have serious results, but it is impossible to be sure. Fortunately, the P[rime] M[inister, Asquith] & Grey are very fit and in good physical trim – very necessary when we are in a double crisis like this.'[108] 'There is just a chance of peace in the Near East', wrote the Lord Chancellor after the ministerial meeting: 'But everything is very uncertain.'[109]

If the outlook was uncertain, Grey himself was convinced that there was no real alternative to his chosen course. The French government, he learnt from Bertie the next day, was anxious to avoid war. Indeed, Paris should be encouraged, the ambassador suggested, 'to put pressure on the Russian Government not to assume the absurd and obsolete attitude of Russia being the protectress of all Slav States whatever their conduct, for this will lead to war'. Bertie himself doubted that the Kaiser and his ministers had been 'accessories before the fact' to the terms of Vienna's note. Izvolsky, his Russian colleague, was due to arrive back in Paris on 27 July, 'and he is not an element of peace', and Berthelot, the political director at the Quai d'Orsay, was 'not sufficiently *coulant*' with Schoen. Time was therefore of the essence, and he also advised Grey to call the proposed ambassadorial conference 'consultations' as otherwise the Austrians would 'consider that they were being treated as a Balkan Minor State'.[110] All of this was sensible counsel, and it reinforced Grey's decision to persevere

Richard von Kühlmann of the German embassy, see memo. Bertie (on conversation with Elibank), 30 July 1914, Bertie MSS, Add. MSS 63033; see also R. T. B. Langhorne, 'Anglo-German Negotiations concerning the Portuguese Colonies, 1911–1914', *HJ* XIV, 2 (1973), 361–87.

[107] Burns diary, 27 July 1914, Burns MSS, BL, Add. MSS 46326; for a discussion of some of the background see K. R. Robbins, 'The Foreign Secretary, the Cabinet, Parliament and the Parties', Hinsley (ed.), *Foreign Policy*, 3–21; Z. S. Steiner and K. Neilson, *Britain and the Origins of the First World War* (Basingstoke and New York, 2nd rev. edn 2003), 244–8.

[108] Samuel to Beatrice Samuel, 27 July 1914, Samuel MSS, PAL, SAM/A/157/689r.

[109] Haldane to Elizabeth Haldane (his mother), 27 July 1914, Haldane MSS, NLS, MS 5991; S. E. Koss, *Haldane: Scapegoat for Liberalism* (New York and London, 1969), 114–15.

[110] Bertie to Grey (private), 27 July 1914, Bertie MSS, BL, Add. MSS. 63033.

with his mediation proposals. But Bertie, of course, was as ignorant of Paléologue's encouragement of a hard line at St Petersburg as Bienvenu-Martin was.

While the Cabinet met in London, Britain's ambassador at Berlin, Sir Edward Goschen, just returned from leave at home, called on Jagow at the Wilhelmstrasse formally to submit Grey's conference proposal. Jagow prevaricated. A conference was tantamout to 'a court of arbitration' and Vienna would never accept this. Goschen sought to explain the scheme, but in vain. It was not practicable, Jagow decided. Sazonov had hinted at direct talks, and this seemed the best way forward. In the course of the brief meeting with the British ambassador, the state secretary also reiterated his warning that Germany could not leave unanswered any Russian mobilization. As before, in his conversation with Jules Cambon, he added an important qualification: 'if Russia only mobilised in [the] south Germany would not mobilise'. In the event of full mobilization in Russia, Germany would have to follow suit, but Russia's system of mobilization was 'so complicated that it might be difficult exactly to locate her mobilisation. Germany would therefore have to be very careful not to be taken by surprise.'[111]

The French ambassador arrived hot on Goschen's heels. The two diplomats had clearly coordinated their move, but the meeting between Jagow and Cambon was a good deal more uncomfortable for the state secretary. Cambon confronted Jagow with a number of awkward questions. When the latter rejected the conference proposal by trotting out the arbitration argument, Cambon replied that, given the great object Grey had in view with his initiative, 'questions of form' should not matter. What did matter was that the four governments cooperated 'in a work of peace'. Had Jagow not previously complained of divisions among the Powers? Here was his chance to prove that he was inspired by a 'European spirit'. Cambon countered Jagow's hint at Berlin's obligations towards Austria-Hungary by pointing out that, in that case, it was Jagow himself who pitted the two groupings against each other.

Jagow then suggested that Germany would participate in Four-Power intervention in any Austro-Russian conflict, but not in that between Austria-Hungary and her southern neighbour. The one was a consequence of the other, Cambon shot back. The important thing now was to prevent a

---

[111] Tel. Goschen to Grey (no. 96), 27 July 1914 (D 6.17 p.m., R 9 p.m.), *BD* XI, no. 185; also Goschen aide mémoire, 27 July 1914, *DD* II, 304. Although conscientious, Goschen was not particularly effective at Berlin, see Eisendecher to Harcourt, 14 Apr. 1913, Harcourt MSS, Bodl., Ms. Harcourt dep. 443; C. H. D. Howard, 'Introduction', in C. H. D. Howard (ed.), *The Diary of Edward Goschen, 1900–1914* (London, 1980), 60–1.

new situation which would bring about Russia's intervention. When Jagow insisted on Berlin's obligations towards its ally, Cambon asked whether these obligations extended to following Vienna's lead 'blindfolded'. Had he taken cognizance of Serbia's official reply to the démarche? On Jagow's response that he had not had time to study it, Cambon's comment was dripping with sarcasm. It was regrettable, he noted, that he had not done so, for he would see that, 'except for a few points of detail', Belgrade had submitted to the Austro-Hungarian demands. Vienna had thus received satisfaction, and Berlin should be in a position to counsel moderation. Jagow remained silent, and Cambon turned up the heat: did Germany wish for war? This elicited a vigorous denial from Jagow, but Cambon persisted. Germany had to act with a view to the likely consequences: 'When you read the Serbian response, weigh its terms with your conscience, I beg of you in the name of humanity, and do not assume for your person part of the responsibility for the catastrophe which you are letting happen.' Jagow again vehemently protested, but then hinted that he was ready to cooperate with London and Paris, provided the right form for the envisaged intervention could be found. But, in the meantime, direct talks had begun between St Petersburg and Vienna, and he was hopeful of their positive results.

As he left, Cambon ventured a parting shot. Earlier in the morning, he observed, he had thought that all signs pointed towards tensions easing. Now he saw that he had been wrong. But Jagow insisted that matters were making rapid progress. '"Press Austria surreptitiously [Pressez l'Autriche en dessous main]", said I [Cambon]. "Oh", he said, "that is something different and we shall do it".'[112] Cambon's firework display of Cartesian logic versus German metaphysics, albeit a very poor specimen of it, was impressive. It certainly laid bare the inconsistencies of the German position and the practical difficulties Berlin now faced in persisting with its rejectionist attitude.

On Cambon followed Bronevski, the Russian chargé d'affaires, with whom Jagow took a more lenient position. In part, it reflected Bethmann's hopes for some future arrangement with Russia, but it was also dictated by Bronevski opening the discussion with a reference to the private exchanges between Sazonov and Szápáry. Now that these had commenced, Jagow explained, the Habsburg ambassador at St Petersburg might as well

---

[112] J. Cambon to Bienvenu-Martin (no. 435, secret), 27 July 1914, *DDF* (3) XI, no. 167; see also tel. same to same (no. 204), 27 July 1914 (D 6.18 p.m., R. 9.30 p.m.), *ibid.*, no. 148; and tel. Bronevski to Sazonov (no. 135), 14/27 July 1914, *IBZI* V, no. 136. For a useful vignette of Jules Cambon see Comte de Sainte Aulaire, 'Jules Cambon', *RHD* XLIX, 2 (1935), 429–39.

continue the talks, and he promised to instruct Tschirschky at Vienna to encourage the Ballhausplatz in that direction.[113]

No such instructions, it seems, were issued. Direct Austro-Russian talks at St Petersburg were meant to provide a cover until Austria-Hungary had delivered the expected military blow at Serbian pretensions. In the absence of support from France and Britain, St Petersburg would then have to acquiesce, and this might open the path to a settlement with Russia. Whether this was ever a realistic proposition or not, what mattered for the Wilhelmstrasse now was to gain time until the Monarchy was ready to strike. Diplomatic moves were a smokescreen to protect Vienna from the probings of the Powers prior to the opening of hostilities. Berlin's priorities were thus the exact reverse of Grey's. The latter hoped to gain time for diplomacy to find a solution. The Wilhelmstrasse, meanwhile, regarded diplomacy as a means to gain time so that Austria-Hungary could have her localized war in the Balkans.

With a view to this consideration, and after Grey had gone public with his mediation scheme, it was also a tactical necessity now for Berlin to show greater flexibility towards Britain. Later that evening, Lichnowsky returned to the charge. If German diplomacy supported Grey, then 'I will vouch for it that our relations with Great Britain will have for a very long time hence the close and intimate character that marked them out for the past year-and-a-half'. Britain's only interest, he explained, was the maintenance of peace on the basis of the European equilibrium. If Austria-Hungary abandoned her 'stubborn policy of prestige' in the Balkans, London would attribute this to Germany's moderating advice. Conversely, were Berlin to subordinate larger considerations to the special interest of its ally, 'then I believe it will never be possible again to reconnect the threads that bound us [Germany and Britain] together in recent times'. If under these circumstances war ensued, Lichnowsky warned, Britain was likely to view it as a 'test of strength', engineered by Germany, between the German-led group and the Franco-Russian alliance and Britain. In that eventuality, Britain would oppose Germany, more especially so in light of Belgrade's accommodating reply to the Austro-Hungarian démarche.[114]

The ambassador in London carried no great weight with the officials at the Wilhelmstrasse. Too engrained had the notion become that somehow Lichnowsky had 'gone native' in Britain.[115] But his warning that

---

[113] Tel. Bronevski to Sazonov (no. 133), 14/27 July 1914, *IBZI* v, no. 134.
[114] Tel. Lichnowsky to Auswärtiges Amt (no. 166), 27 July 1914 (D 5.08 p.m., R 8.40 p.m.), *DD* I, no. 265.
[115] Zimmermann's minute on Lichnowsky's telegram is instructive: 'What happens to the balance of power, if Austria-Hungary yields?' *DD* I, no. 265.

Berlin's hitherto uncompromising identification with the interests and proceedings of Austria-Hungary would complicate matters had to be taken seriously. Lichnowsky, of course, did not know that Berlin hoped to use diplomacy as cover for Vienna's localized war or at the very least a Habsburg diplomatic triumph. But Bethmann Hollweg appreciated that outright rejection of Grey's mediation proposal would make it more difficult to protect Austria-Hungary against international intervention. Having earlier in the day refused to support the British Foreign Secretary's conference idea, Bethmann wired Tschirschky late at night stating it was now impossible to reject '*a limine*' Grey's suggestion of Four-Power intervention at St Petersburg and Vienna. To do so would make Germany 'responsible for the conflagration before the whole world', thus also wrecking the chancellor's carefully laid plans to cultivate the support of the SPD leadership. Berlin's position was all the more difficult, he warned, as Serbia had seemingly yielded to most of Vienna's demands: 'We can therefore not reject the role of mediator and have to submit the English proposals to the Vienna Cabinet, since London and Paris continually work on Petersburg.'[116]

The instructions to Tschirschky are suggestive of a last-minute effort on the chancellor's part to free Berlin from its dependency on Habsburg diplomacy. But he was reluctant to be seen in London as yielding to British pressure. He could not possibly counsel the Habsburg leadership to accept the Serbian note, he explained to Lichnowsky, but he was prepared to support Grey's initiative of Four-Power mediation between Vienna and St Petersburg. This was a considerable concession on Germany's part, he argued, and Lichnowsky was to emphasize this point in his discussions at the Foreign Office. Whether the Serbian reply had gone 'to the limits of the possible', he could not yet say, but Belgrade's decision to mobilize before the expiry of the ultimatum suggested 'a bad conscience'. Austria-Hungary did not aim at crushing Serbia – the phrase used by Grey. Her non-annexation pledge was sufficient guarantee of that. What she desired was security against pan-Serb activities. This had nothing to do with a 'policy of prestige' – Lichnowsky's suggestion. Bethmann Hollweg wished to cooperate with Britain to maintain European peace, and he hoped for even closer relations in the future, but the other Powers did not have the right to aid Serbian intrigues against Austria-Hungary.[117] The chancellor's instructions

[116] Tel. Bethmann Hollweg to Tschirschky (no. 169), 27 July 1914 (D 11.50 p.m., R 12.45 a.m.), *DD* I, no. 277.
[117] Tel. Bethmann Hollweg to Lichnowsky (no. 184), 28 July 1914 (D 2 a.m.), *DD* II, no. 279; for a critical view see F. Fischer, *Griff nach der Weltmacht. Die Kriegszielpolitik des kaiserlichen Deutschland, 1914–1918* (Düsseldorf, 3rd edn 1964), 83–4.

kept open the options of either a swift localized Austro-Serbian war or a far-reaching diplomatic success for the Habsburg Empire. In the former case, diplomacy was to provide the necessary cover, in the latter it was to furnish the international framework that was required for buttressing the Dual Monarchy's position in south-eastern Europe. In both cases, Anglo-German cooperation was the necessary prerequisite, but from the chancellor's perspective it was equally necessary to make London understand that any cooperation was to be had only on Germany's terms. As international diplomacy swung into action in the course of 27 July, a new 'diplomatic duel' between London and Berlin thus commenced.

That either of Bethmann's two options still appeared to be practicable was reaffirmed by Pourtalès. The ambassador at St Petersburg informed the Wilhelmstrasse of far-reaching military preparations in Russia, but noted that mobilization had not yet been ordered; Sukhomlinov had given him his word of honour. Pourtalès had the impression of 'great nervousness and anxiety' at the Choristers' Bridge: 'Consider desire for peace genuine ... They are visibly aiming to gain time for new negotiations and continuation of armaments programme.' Russia's fragile internal situation also gave cause for concern at St Petersburg. The basic tendency there, the ambassador concluded, was to hope for German mediation, possibly by the Kaiser.[118]

The German monarch himself had returned from his Nordic summer cruise in the afternoon of 27 July, arriving at the Wildpark station outside Potsdam at 3.10 p.m. He had only reluctantly accepted the chancellor's advice not to head to Berlin to avoid any public outpouring of patriotic emotions. The Kaiser was not amused: 'This is getting madder; now that man instructs me that I may not show myself to my people.'[119] But the chancellor had reassuring news to impart at the subsequent conversation at the Neues Palais, scene of Wilhelm's encounter with the Austro-Hungarian ambassador a little over three weeks earlier. It is true, Bethmann handed the Kaiser a file by the ministry of the interior on the administrative measures to be taken in the event of a war. But this was to prepare for all eventualities. The tenor of his advice was different, as Hans von Plessen, the Kaiser's aide-de-camp, noted in his diary: 'The Austrians are not ready for a long time yet! It will take until early August before operations can

---

[118] Tel. Pourtalès to Auswärtiges Amt (no. 165), 27 July 1914 (D 1 a.m., R 2.45 a.m.), *DD* I, no. 242; Pourtalès, *Meine letzten Verhandlungen*, 31–2.

[119] Müller diary, 27 July 1914, W. Görlitz (ed.), *Regierte der Kaiser? Kriegstagebücher, Aufzeichnungen und Briefe des Chefs des Marine-Kabinetts Admiral Georg Alexander von Müller, 1914–1918* (Göttingen, 1959), 35; for the Kaiser's movements see A. von Wegerer, *Der Ausbruch des Weltkrieges 1914* (2 vols., Hamburg, 1939) I, 364–5.

commence. They [the German government] hope to localize the war! England declares that she wishes to remain neutral. I have the impression that nothing much will come of this matter.'[120] Matters would remain somewhat uncertain for another fortnight 'until one can know or say anything for certain', as Moltke wrote to his wife later that day.[121] For all the uncertainty, there was nevertheless still a sense of quiet confidence at Berlin. Britain's calm attitude, noted the chief of the Kaiser's naval entourage, had 'a very cooling' effect on France and Russia. Austria-Hungary would not be ready to commence operations against Serbia until 12 August: 'Tendency of our policy: calm attitude, letting Russia put herself in the wrong – but then, if it has to be, not to shy away from the war.'[122]

The notion of a military showdown with Russia now rather than at a later stage had featured frequently in German strategic calculations before 1914. During the July crisis, however, it was not until Jagow's ruminations in the middle of that month that this scenario gained wider currency again at Berlin. A preventive war, however, was by no means the preferred outcome of the crisis. Arthur Zimmermann summed up current thinking at the Wilhelmstrasse in a conversation with the Belgian envoy, Baron Eugène de Beyens. Germany, the under-secretary explained, had not exercised any influence on Vienna before the démarche. For Austria-Hungary, suppressing the pan-Serb movement was now 'an existential question, of being or not being'. The movement aimed at inciting an insurrection in all the Slav-populated provinces in the Danube basin, and it was necessary that Serbia 'had to receive a severe and salutory lesson by means of a military expedition'. It was thus impossible now to avert an Austro-Serbian conflict. Britain had proposed diplomatic intervention to prevent an Austro-Russian clash, and Germany would support mediation between the two Powers, provided that Austria-Hungary was not prevented from 'inflicting exemplary punishment on Serbia'. If Russia mobilized, then Germany would follow suit, 'and that will be the general war, a war that will engulf all of central Europe and even the Balkan peninsula, for the Romanians, Bulgarians, Greeks and Turks will not be able to resist the temptation to take part fighting each other'. The best course for Serbia would be not to resist an Austro-Hungarian invasion and to concede to all of Vienna's demands

---

[120] Plessen diary, 27 July 1914, *DGB*, 22; for the file on administrative measures in the event of war see Gutsche, *Aufstieg und Fall*, 125, who interprets this as an indication of aggressive intentions.

[121] Moltke to Eliza Moltke, 27 July 1914, Moltke (ed.), *Erinnerungen, Briefe, Dokumente*, 371; see also Mombauer, *Moltke*, 198.

[122] Müller diary, 27 July 1914, Görlitz (ed.), *Müller*, 35–6; see also J. C. G. Röhl, 'Admiral von Müller and the Approach of War, 1911–14', *HJ* XII, 4 (1969), 668–9.

without reservation. If she did not, and a general war ended in victory for the Central Powers, 'Serbia would very likely cease to exist as a nation; she would be scratched out on the map of Europe'.

Zimmermann nevertheless concluded on an optimistic note. A 'general conflagration' would be avoided. The despatches from St Petersburg suggested that Sazonov was disposed to view the situation coolly: 'I hope we shall be able to dissuade him from intervening in favour of Serbia, whose future territorial integrity and independence Austria is resolved to respect, once she has obtained satisfaction'.[123] In his conversation with the Belgian minister, Zimmermann had aired views widely held at the Wilhelmstrasse. For now, Russia would concentrate on diplomatic means 'to deflect the worst away from Serbia', opined Stumm, the head of the political department. The situation would become critical the moment Austro-Hungarian forces entered Serbian territory, but as this was not expected to happen until sometime around 10 or 12 August diplomacy could still isolate the conflict. France, moreover, would do everything to prevent Russia from resorting to warlike measures – here Stumm drew comfort from the recent fall on the Paris *bourse*. Finally, Grey's mediation proposal could now have only one practical object, and that was to assist in localizing the Austro-Serbian quarrel.[124]

Jagow issues a second 'blank cheque'

Bethmann Hollweg's instructions to Tschirschky and Lichnowsky and Zimmermann's statement to the Belgian minister underline the extent to which Berlin's moves in the days after 26 July were focused on insulating the Austro-Serbian quarrel from interference by any of the Powers. Berlin's objectives remained either a successful Austro-Hungarian punitive expedition against Belgrade or Serbia's complete surrender to Habsburg pressure in anticipation of a military strike. The Wilhelmstrasse, however, had no coherent diplomatic strategy. The complex and disparate decision-making structures at Berlin were one complicating factor; the ambitions of different officials were another. While the chancellor sought to stamp his authority on German diplomacy following his return to the capital, the state secretary at the Auswärtiges Amt quietly undermined his influence.

In the evening of 27 July, just before Tschirschky was informed that the German government could no longer reject the British mediation

---

[123] Beyens to Davignon, 27 July 1914, *BelD* suppl. II, no. II/10; see also [E.] de Beyens, *Deux Années à Berlin, 1912–1914* (2 vols., Paris, 1931) II, 246–8.
[124] Lerchenfeld to Hertling (no. 402), 27 July 1914, *BayD* no. 35.

initiative, Jagow had asked the Habsburg ambassador to call upon him for a confidential discussion. Szögyény's resulting telegram is one of the most intriguing documents of the entire July crisis. Jagow alerted Vienna to Grey's suggestions. He made it clear that the German government did not identify themselves with the proposals, but merely passed them on. It was important at the present moment, however, to ensure that London did not join with the Franco-Russian group in blocking Austria-Hungary's campaign against Serbia. The wire to London was not to be severed. Tschirschky had been informed of Grey's initiative, but had not been instructed to submit the proposal to Berchtold.[125]

A small cottage industry has sprung up around this telegram. It is tempting to see in it evidence of Berlin's duplicity towards Grey, that it was an attempt to feign cooperation whilst in reality sabotaging the British Foreign Secretary's initiative.[126] Although a strong interpretation that fits the extant evidence, it fails to answer the question why the German leadership should have thought it necessary to resort to such underhand methods. If it was meant to deceive London, it could do so for no more than twenty-four hours at the most because the Ballhausplatz's next moves would show whether or not Germany had sought to restrain her ally. Given that military operations were not to commence for some time, little tactical advantage was to be gained by such a ruse. Once the deception became apparent, moreover, the adverse political fall-out would be all the more serious, as Lichnowsky had warned. Besides, Bethmann Hollweg himself had already instructed Lichnowsky to explain to Grey Berlin's reluctance to put pressure on Vienna to moderate its stance in the quarrel with Serbia.[127]

Moreover, the Wilhelmstrasse could not assume that Mensdorff, the Austro-Hungarian ambassador at London, would not hear of Grey's initiative either from Grey, who cared little now for formalities, or from Lichnowsky, who was strongly in favour of the British initiative. Indeed, the Foreign Secretary discussed his conference proposal with Mensdorff in the evening of 27 July. He warned Vienna against assuming that Russia would remain a spectator in the event of a military conflict with Serbia: 'Were we able to induce Russia to remain quiet, all would be well and we would have no more to say. If not, the possibilities and dangers are

[125] Tel. Szögyény to Berchtold (no. 307, strictly secret), 27 July 1914, ÖUA VIII, no. 10793.
[126] Most succinctly in L. Albertini, *The Origins of the War of 1914* (3 vols., London, 1953) II, 445–50; Fischer, *Griff nach der Weltmacht*, 83–5.
[127] Tel. Bethmann Hollweg to Lichnowsky (no. 184), 28 July 1914 (D 2 a.m.), DD II, no. 279.

incalculable.' Grey, whom Mensdorff described as 'downcast and worried, but not irritated', hoped to delay any collision between the Powers for as long as possible so as to isolate the Austro-Serbian conflict. In the event of Russian and German mobilization, however, another London conference would be futile. The Foreign Secretary, Mensdorff added in a follow-up telegram, wished to cooperate with Berlin to secure peace. If he ever began to suspect that it had used Austria-Hungary as a cat's paw or indeed wished to provoke a war with Russia, 'he would veer off and, I fear, side much more decisively with Russia'.[128]

For Berlin, then, little could be gained by any attempt to deceive Grey. Revisionist scholars in the inter-war period suggested a different interpretation of Jagow's conversation with the Austro-Hungarian ambassador. The superannuated Szögyény, shortly to be retired at any rate, so the argument runs, had muddled things up in his telegram. Jagow himself later hinted at the ambassador's mental decline and, indeed, denied that the conversation ever took place.[129] True, Szögyény's replacement at Berlin had already been decided upon, but the ambassador was still an effective representative of his Emperor at the German court, as the interviews of 5/6 July had shown. His despatches on conversations with the leading officials at the Wilhelmstrasse, moreover, did not differ in their substance from the corresponding German reports. Far more significant, therefore, is the fact that Jagow himself did not keep a record of the meeting with Szögyény. He did not wish to leave a paper trail at the Wilhelmstrasse, as Albertini rightly surmised.[130]

But this in turn begs the question of who at Berlin was to be kept in ignorance of this counter-move to the British initiative. Jagow was under no obligation to show his telegraphic communications to Goschen or any of the other foreign ambassadors for their perusal. Similarly, there was no need of this elaborate charade for the benefit of the Kaiser, who was not, as a rule, shown copies of diplomatic instructions sent out; nor was the government required to share such information with the parties in the *Reichstag*. This, then, leaves only the

---

[128] Tels. Mensdorff to Berchtold (nos. 114–15), 27 and 28 July 1914 (D 8.05 p.m., R 9 a.m., D 1.55 p.m., R 9 a.m.), *ÖUA* VIII, nos. 10813 and 10893.

[129] Szögyény's retirement was finally confirmed for 19 August, the day after the Emperor's birthday, see tel. Tschirschky to Auswärtiges Amt (no. 121), 28 July 1914 (D 10.30 p.m., R a.m.), *DD* II, no. 324; for Jagow's denial, see his *Ursachen und Ausbruch des Weltkrieges* (Berlin, 1919), 118–19, and n. 1; for some of the contemporary anecdotes of Szögyény's eccentricities see Wolff, *Krieg*, 335.

[130] Albertini, *Origins* II, 449, who however is wrong to implicate Bethmann Hollweg in the move; see also L. Meyer-Arndt, *Die Julikrise 1914. Wie Deutschland in den Ersten Weltkrieg schlitterte* (Cologne, 2006), 127.

chancellor and Jagow's own officials at the Wilhelmstrasse. Jagow's intimation to Szögyény, thus, amounted to a second 'blank cheque', this time to Tschirschky: Vienna was to accept proposals of mediation only if encouraged to do so by the German ambassador. Jagow's intrigue, however, could only work with Tschirschky's cooperation. The ambassador's steps the next day are certainly suggestive of some understanding between him and the state secretary. For at that time, Tschirschky informed Berchtold of the British mediation proposal, and clearly had not urged him to accept it. Berchtold, he wired back to Berlin, was obliged to the German government for transmitting Grey's suggestions, to which he would respond in due course. In the meantime, however, 'the opening of hostilities by Serbia' – a hint at Temes-Kubin – and the now-issued declaration of war meant that the British initiative had come too late. Significantly, he did not report the Habsburg foreign minister's appreciation of Berlin's motives, which the latter instructed Szögyény to express to Jagow.[131]

Tschirschky's hawkishness has already been noted. If he wished to ensure that Vienna declined international mediation, then Jagow was sure to find in the ambassador a likely ally. Why he should wish to take recourse to such subterfuge, however, is more difficult to explain, especially since the move increased, rather than lessened, Berlin's dependence on Vienna. Possibly, Jagow was worried that the chancellor, known at Berlin for his apparent indecisiveness and irresolution, might buckle under pressure, as Bethmann's instructions to Tschirschky may have indicated. Ultimately, Jagow's intrigue only makes sense if he wished Vienna to present the Powers with a fait accompli. That he regretted the slow pace of the Habsburg Monarchy's military preparations and the subsequent delay in commencing operations is a matter of record.[132] If Vienna now dictated facts on the ground by moving against Serbia, then the small war had broken out and the Powers would have to join efforts to localize it, the prospect of a general war acting as a sufficient deterrence against any further escalation. Given Pourtalès's recent reports on Russia's seeming reluctance to mobilize, such calculations made some sense. But there is no denying their utter recklessness. The second 'blank cheque' moreover was to create yet further difficulties.

---

[131] Tel. Tschirschky to Auswärtiges Amt (no. 120, secret), 28 July 1914 (D 4.55 p.m., R 7.25 p.m.), DD II, no. 313; cf. tel. Berchtold to Szögyény (no. 284), 28 July 1914 (D 11.50 p.m.), ÖUA VIII, no. 10865.

[132] See tel. Szögyény to Berchtold (no. 305, strictly secret), 27 July 1914 (D 5.50 p.m., R 3 a.m.), ÖUA VIII, no. 10792.

Sazonov confuses everyone

At the end of 27 July different currents threatened to carry the Powers in different directions. At the Choristers' Bridge Sazonov struck a more conciliatory tone in his conversations with Pourtalès and Szápáry, but underpinning his stance was an assumption that an element of deterrence was required to safeguard Russian interests in the Balkans. Shebeko, now back at Vienna, confirmed him in this assumption. Sazonov's earlier statement that Russia could not remain indifferent in the event of an Austro-Serbian conflict had made an impression at Vienna, where Tschirschky had persuaded officials that St Petersburg would not interfere on Serbia's behalf. The 'enormous danger' of a general war that would be triggered by an Austro-Serbian conflict was the best means of coercing Austria-Hungary to disengage, Shebeko advised.[133]

If this implied the need for signalling clarity of intent, there was nevertheless an element of confusion in Sazonov's statements on that day. Having earlier appeared to indicate his support for Grey's mediation proposal, or at any rate not his opposition to it, by the afternoon he had come to favour direct talks between Vienna and St Petersburg on modifying Austria-Hungary's demands on Serbia. Whether, and if so, how Austro-Russian negotiations were to relate to the Four-Power intervention favoured by Grey remained unclear. 'This is confusing', Nicolson at the Foreign Office minuted: 'In three consecutive days M. Sazonof has made one suggestion and two proposals all differing from each other … One really does not know where one is with M. Sazonof.'[134]

Nor was this the only element of confusion as international diplomacy felt its way towards a solution of the Balkan crisis. Bethmann Hollweg's apparent change of mind in the evening indicated a renewed willingness to explore diplomatic options, though at the root of the chancellor's calculations remained the wish to gain time to shield the Habsburg ally against the interference of the Powers. He left it open whether the diplomatic track would lead to a localized war or a major Austro-Hungarian diplomatic success. Either outcome required a degree of cooperation with Britain. That, however, had been called into question by Jagow's little intrigue in the evening of 27 July and the second 'blank cheque' to Tschirschky. In so doing Jagow had switched the points and the diplomatic

---

[133] Tel. Shebeko (no. 104), 14/27 July 1914, *IBZI* v, no. 139.
[134] Min. Nicolson, n.d. [27 July 1914], on tel. Buchanan to Grey (no. 174), 27 July 1914 (D 2.13 p.m., R 3.45 p.m.), *BD* xi, no. 179. Nicolson told Benckendorff as much, see tel. Benckendorff to Sazonov (no. 211), 14/27 July 1914, *IBZI* v, no. 125.

train was now hurtling towards localization or escalation, though the chancellor himself had no notion of this yet.

The key to a solution, however, still lay with Berlin, as Eyre Crowe wrote to his wife at the end of another long day at the Foreign Office: 'Things here look grave. No sign so far of any relaxation of the political strain. Berlin is still dumb. But she must come out into the open before too long, and that will be the decisive moment. Lichnowsky seems really to be working *with* us. Grey is much worried.'[135]

Count Berchtold sends a telegram to Bucharest

On the following day, Tuesday, 28 July, Vienna once more set the pace of events. Decisions here accelerated the speed of developments, and complicated and confused the efforts of the other Powers to localize the Austro-Serbian conflict or to mediate in it. In the morning, as agreed three days earlier, began the mobilization of the Habsburg army for 'War Case "B"'. It was a partial mobilization, affecting around two-fifths of the armed forces which were to be concentrated and deployed to the south along the Serbian frontier. In addition, one reserve army corps was mobilized. No preparations were made along the Galician salient. This was meant to deny St Petersburg any pretext for intervention. It was Conrad's contribution to localizing the war.[136] And, as agreed on 25 July and sanctioned by Emperor Franz Joseph two days later, at 11 a.m. Berchtold issued Austria-Hungary's declaration of war on Serbia. Following Giesl's departure from Belgrade, there were no more official channels of communication with that country, and the telegraph line had already been cut. Germany had declined to act as Austria-Hungary's messenger at Belgrade, fearing that it might create an impression elsewhere that 'we had driven Austria-Hungary into the war'. There was nothing for it, then, but to issue the declaration by an *en clair* telegram via Bucharest for onward transmission to Niš, to where the Serbian government had been evacuated.[137]

[135] Crowe to Clema Crowe, 27 July 1914, Crowe MSS, Ms.Eng.d.2903. Fortunately for the historian, Lady Crowe had left the capital for the seaside delights of Hunstanton on the north Norfolk coast and so contributed to the production of a series of very useful letters.
[136] Conrad, *Aus meiner Dienstzeit* IV, 134–5; J. H. Maurer, *The Outbreak of the First World War: Strategic Planning, Crisis Decision Making, and Deterrence Failure* (Westport, CT, 1995), 79–88.
[137] Tschirschky to Jagow (secret), 22 July 1914 (R p.m.), and reply (no. 134), 24 July 1914 (D 2.05 p.m., R 6.15 p.m.), *DD* I, nos. 138 and 142. The declaration is in tel.

In deciding simultaneously to mobilize and to declare war, the Habsburg leadership was influenced by diplomatic considerations. Once a state of war existed, international mediation in the Balkan quarrel, it was hoped, would become futile. Calculations of potential political complications, in fact, were given priority until the very last moment.[138] On the same day, Emperor Franz Joseph issued an imperial proclamation, which appeared in all the newspapers and was displayed on public noticeboards across the Monarchy on the following day. 'To my peoples', it read in the Empire's ten different languages, for the past four decades the Emperor had striven to preserve peace and protect his subjects against the burdens and sacrifices of war. Providence, however, had decided otherwise: 'The intrigues of an enemy filled with hatred force me after long years of peace to draw the sword for the maintenance of the honour of my monarchy, for the protection of its prestige and position of power, for securing its possessions.' Pan-Serb terrorist activities transcended the boundaries of Serbia proper and were aimed at shaking the bonds of mutual loyalty between the Emperor and his peoples, and so threatened to undermine public order in the Empire. All other options having been exhausted, and Belgrade having rejected his government's measured and just demands, there was now no alternative but to resort to military force. 'In this solemn hour', the Emperor's personal manifesto concluded,

> I am fully conscious of the full import of My decision and of My responsibility before the Allmighty.
>
> I have probed and weighed everything. With a calm conscience I enter upon the path dictated to me by duty.
>
> I have confidence in My peoples, who in stormy times have always rallied around My throne in unity and loyalty and were always ready to make the heaviest sacrifices for the honour, greatness and power of the fatherland.[139]

The declaration of war on Serbia would be Austria-Hungary's last independent political act. It ended, over four years later, in the collapse of the Habsburg Empire, an entity that had been a permanent feature of European politics for well-nigh seven centuries.

Berchtold to Serbian Ministry for Foreign Affairs (*en clair*), 28 July 1914, ÖUA VIII, no. 10862; Galántai, *Österreichisch-ungarische Monarchie*, 354.
[138] Tel. Tschirschky to Auswärtiges Amt (no. 113), 27 July 1914 (D 3.20 p.m., R 4.37 p.m.), *DD* I, no. 257; on the primacy of diplomatic considerations see also Conrad, *Aus meiner Dienstzeit* IV, 132.
[139] *Wiener Zeitung*, 29 July 1914.

For the Great Powers, with the declaration of war against Serbia began a limited, regional war, the sequel to the last Balkan war. Within a matter of days it escalated into the first general war in Europe since 1815. It was only after the Ballhausplatz telegraphists had begun to tap out the encyphered declaration of war that Berchtold received the foreign ambassadors at Vienna. De Bunsen called first. There was no mystery about the purpose of his visit, nor about Berchtold's likely reply. As Burián, the Magyar representative at the imperial court, wired to Tisza at 12.45 p.m.: 'At this moment the English ambassador is carrying out a mediation effort on Grey's instructions. He will receive the answer, which incidentally Grey acknowledged in his speech of yesterday, that – for as long as it was a matter between Serbia and us – mediation was not called for and that military proceedings could not be delayed.'[140]

The response came as little surprise to the Foreign Office. Already overnight, London had received further intimation – this time via Rome – that Austria-Hungary was not willing to disengage. The upshot of de Bunsen's conversation with Berchtold in the morning of 28 July confirmed this: 'Austria-Hungary cannot delay warlike proceedings.' As instructed, de Bunsen avoided using the term 'mediation', but suggested that the Serbian government had gone far to meet Vienna's demands, and Grey's quartet might now forge a new settlement that would be acceptable to Austria-Hungary. In reply, Berchtold 'said quietly, but firmly' that no further discussions were possible on the basis of Belgrade's reply, and hinted that war would be declared this very day (the telegram had in fact already been sent). There was little for de Bunsen to do now but to impress upon the Habsburg foreign minister the European dimension of the Balkan crisis. Great Britain, he explained on taking his leave, was not unsympathetic with many of the Monarchy's just grievances against Serbia, but 'whereas Austria-Hungary put first her quarrel with Servia, you [Grey] were anxious in the first instance for [the] peace of Europe'.[141]

It was important now, if hostilities could no longer be avoided, to prevent at least the collision of the two armies, de Bunsen further explained, and suggested that Serbian forces might fall back and not offer any military resistance. But Berchtold remained firm. He was mindful of the wider European implications of the current crisis, he assured the ambassador, but the 'European peace could not be saved by the Great Powers standing

---

[140] Tel. Burián to Tisza, 28 July (D 12.45 p.m.), Burián MSS, as quoted in Galántai, *Österreichisch-ungarische Monarchie*, 355.

[141] Tels. de Bunsen to Grey (nos. 114 and 115), 28 July 1914 (D 1.10 and 4.10 p.m., R 7.45 and 9.40 p.m.), *BD* xi, nos. 227 and 230; for San Giuliano's hints see tel. Rodd to Grey (no. 125), 27 July 1914 (D 9.15 p.m., R 28 July, 12 p.m.), *BD* xi, no. 202.

behind Serbia and pressing for her immunity'. Such a settlement could only encourage Serbia to persist in her provocative attitude towards the Habsburg Empire.[142] Berchtold's reference to Grey's statement in the Commons the previous afternoon was a clever, though transparent, attempt to twist the meaning of the Foreign Secretary's initiative. Whereas Grey had suggested that the larger European question should force Vienna to act with restraint, Berchtold countered by asserting that only Russian intervention would turn a regional dispute into a European crisis. It was for St Petersburg, then, to show restraint.

Berchtold remained equally firm in his interview with the Russian ambassador, who had in vain sought a meeting on the previous day. Shebeko argued along similar lines as de Bunsen. Serbia's reply had been accommodating and on that basis a settlement could be found. Russia would gladly assist in the process, and to that end the ambassador suggested that direct talks between Sazonov and Szápáry be continued. Berchtold rejected any suggestion of international mediation between Serbia and the Monarchy. Shebeko explained 'with great eloquence' that any military strike against Serbia would be counter-productive and merely fuel the further growth of Slav animosity against the Habsburg Empire. Berchtold parried this thrust with reference to Austria-Hungary's hitherto patient attitude in the face of years of provocation. Belgrade had rejected Vienna's demands, and had already mobilized before the expiry of Vienna's note. That in itself, he suggested, had been a hostile act – and yet Austria-Hungary had waited for three days. But Serbian troops had opened hostilities along the Hungarian frontier yesterday (again the misleading hint at the skirmish at Temes-Kubin). Thus, 'a thorough but peaceful restoration of our relations with Serbia' was no longer possible, and Austria-Hungary now had to meet the continued provocations by Serbia 'in the only manner ... commensurate with the dignity of the Monarchy'.[143]

The meeting between Berchtold and Shebeko was friendly in tone. Yet there was an edge to it. It was in Austria-Hungary's own interest, the Russian ambassador argued, to come to a settlement that improved her relations with Russia and secured the desired guarantees from Serbia, the implication being that the one could not be had without the other, and that both required moderation on Vienna's part. An 'armed collision' between the Habsburg Empire and Serbia would imperil the peace of Europe.

---

[142] Tel. Berchtold to Mensdorff (no. 179), 28 July 1914 (D 1 p.m.), ÖUA VIII, no. 10892; see also Berchtold's instructions for Mensdorff, in tel. no. 178, 28 July 1914 (D 12.40 p.m.), ibid., no. 10891.

[143] Tel. Berchtold to Szápáry (no. 191), 28 July 1914 (D 11.40 p.m.), ÖUA VIII, no. 10915.

This was, perhaps, a little ambiguous. War, after all, had been declared now, as Berchtold confirmed, but the two armies had not yet engaged each other, and that might provide space for diplomacy to continue its work. Shebeko's suggestion was in line with Sazonov's advice to Belgrade to withdraw its forces in the face of any Habsburg invasion, but it was for Vienna now to show restraint. The ambassador, however, was convinced that Vienna was determined now to strike against Serbia, confident that German support and the pacific inclinations of the other Powers would keep the conflict localized.[144]

Berchtold had been entirely consistent in his conversation with Shebeko, but his categorical refusal to countenance any talks on the Habsburg démarche or Belgrade's reply pulled the rug from underneath Sazonov's direct talks with the Austro-Hungarian ambassador. Any further discussions with Szápáry were now 'obviously inappropriate', the Russian foreign minister decided when news of the declaration of war arrived at St Petersburg in the afternoon of 28 July.[145]

Whether Berchtold intended as much is not clear. However, in the course of 27/28 July, the Ballhausplatz became more alarmed at Russia's likely attitude towards a Serbian war. On 27 July, Szápáry cabled news, derived from open-source intelligence, that mobilization orders for the military districts of Kiev, Warsaw, Odessa and Moscow had been issued, and that preparations prior to mobilization were underway in the districts of St Petersburg and Vilnius.[146] The information itself was partial and, indeed, not wholly accurate, but it was sufficient to alarm the Habsburg leadership. In a moment of self-reflection, Tisza now admitted that it had been illusory to assume that Russia would stay out of an Austro-Serbian conflict at all costs. Even so, he grasped the extent to which conflicting calculations pulled the Tsar's ministers in different directions: 'they feel what a defeat it would be not to protect Serbia just as much as they feel that now they would have to take up the fight under the most adverse circum-stances'.[147] For the Hungarian premier it was now imperative for the Monarchy to open the campaign against Serbia without any further delay, whilst observing all possible caution against Russia. It was not necessary to force Russia to declare her intentions, however. That was a matter for the German ally.

---

[144] Tel. Shebeko to Sazonov (no. 105), 15/28 July 1914, *IBZI* v, no. 188.
[145] Tel. Sazonov to Benckendorff (no. 1538), 15/28 July 1914, *IBZI* v, no. 167.
[146] Tel. Tschirschky to Auswärtiges Amt (no. 115), 27 July 1914 (D 28 July, 1.45 a.m., R 4 a.m.), *DD* ii, no. 281; Kronenbitter, *'Krieg im Frieden'*, 503–4.
[147] Tisza to Burián, 28 July 1914, as quoted in Galántai, *Österreichisch-ungarische Monarchie*, 348–9.

Tisza was not alone in this view. Later that same day, at 4.30 p.m., Berchtold, assisted by Forgách and Macchio, held a meeting at the Ballhausplatz with Stürgkh, the Austrian prime minister, war minister Krobatin, Conrad and Burián to discuss the military situation after the declaration of war. At the insistence of the chief of staff, the officials agreed to mobilize the entire Habsburg navy, largely to put pressure on Montenegro, whose mercurial monarch, King Nikola, had ordered mobilization on that same day without, however, indicating whether he would support Serbia. Beyond that, the meeting is remarkable because it revealed the dysfunctional nature of Habsburg policy-making. Potiorek, as commander of the forces in Bosnia-Herzegovina, was informed that border skirmishes with Serbian units were desirable – no doubt to extract political advantage from them now that Temes-Kubin had turned out to be a canard – but that larger-scale engagements were to be avoided until mobilization was complete. Then Berchtold raised what he called 'the big question': were the Monarchy's forces capable of facing Russia when 400,000 troops were being mobilized against Serbia? As Conrad recorded in his contemporary notes: 'Now that the action against Serbia is in train, this objection appeared rather late.' That Berchtold only now raised the likely impact of Russian intervention underlines the extent to which Habsburg diplomacy had been afflicted by tunnel vision. The humiliation of Serbia, by means of the démarche followed by some kind of punitive expedition, overrode all other considerations. Most disastrously, there had been no proper integration of diplomatic strategy and military planning. Berchtold's belated recognition of the Russian dimension of the Monarchy's Serbian problem was matched by Conrad's political naivety. By 1 August, Conrad informed the assembled ministers and officials, Vienna had to have clarity about Russian intentions. This was the last moment at which the troops earmarked for deployment against Serbia could be diverted north to Galicia. After that day no such switch was possible; all troop transports would then roll towards the Serbian frontier. The decision before them now was momentous – whether to order mobilization and deployment for 'war case "R"', that is against Russia, or against Serbia.[148] If Russia remained quiet, Burián noted in his diary, 'then we shall throw ourselves with full force against Serbia, and thereafter we might be ready for

---

[148] Conrad, *Aus meiner Dienstzeit* IV, 137–8; for the Montenegrin mobilization and the King's prevarication between Austria-Hungary and Serbia, see J. D. Treadway, *The Falcon and the Eagle: Montenegro and Austria-Hungary, 1908–1914* (W. Lafayette, IN, 1983), 189–99.

Russia'. Indeed, Conrad was still confident then that he would be able to defeat Serbia 'with swift blows'.[149]

The Habsburg leadership was thus caught on the horns of a dilemma – a dilemma of its own making. A direct approach to St Petersburg would very likely precipitate Russian intervention, the very thing Vienna wished to avoid. But allowing the present uncertainty as to Russia's intentions to persist entailed the risk of leaving the Habsburg armed forces vulnerable in the event of Russia joining the conflict at a later stage. In this situation, the ministers and officials decided to shift the burden of responsibility for eliciting some clarifying statement from St Petersburg to Germany. There was no need for an ultimatum, as in 1909, Conrad opined – 'a polite despatch' would suffice. Following the meeting, therefore, Szögyény was instructed to make appropriate representations at Berlin. With reference to the reported military measures already taken by the Russian government, it was vital for Austria-Hungary to have clarity as to whether she could throw a strong force against Serbia or whether the bulk of her army had to be deployed in the Galician salient. Berchtold therefore requested Berlin to remind Sazonov 'in a friendly manner' that any mobilization was a threat to Austria-Hungary and thus liable to trigger the Austro-German alliance mechanism. 'Decided language' by Germany, Szögyény was to explain, was the most efficacious means of deterring Russia.[150] It was the exact mirror image of Russian thinking. Somehow the other side was to be deterred by a demonstration of firmness.

Vienna's decision to turn to Berlin for assistance revealed the natural order of things in the Austro-German alliance, though following the two 'blank cheques' it did nothing to restore that order. But it also underlined the fantasy element in Austro-Hungarian policy and its lack of any internal strategic coherence.

There was an additional complication in relations with Germany – Berlin's desire to keep Italy within the fold of the *Dreibund* alliance. Here, too, Vienna had demonstrated remarkable complacency. During the hiatus between the delivery of Vienna's démarche and Giesl's severing of diplomatic relations with Serbia, Flotow, the German ambassador at Rome, had several, often somewhat heated, exchanges with San Giuliano on Italy's likely attitude in the event of an Austro-Serbian war. Rome's active support was not likely to be had, he reported to Bethmann Hollweg after one of his

---

[149] Burián diary, 28 July 1914, Diószegi, 'Aussenminister', 207; Burián to Tisza, 28 July 1914, E. von Wertheimer (ed.), *Graf Stefan Tisza. Briefe (1914–1918)* (2 vols., Berlin, 1928) I, 43.
[150] Tel. Berchtold to Szögyény (no. 282), 28 July 1914 (D 11 p.m.), ÖUA VIII, no. 10863.

talks, but 'prudent behaviour' on Vienna's part might prevent worse. It was 'absolutely necessary', the chancellor and the Kaiser agreed, 'that Austria comes to an understanding with Italy regarding the compensation question'.[151]

Tschirschky duly called on the Ballhausplatz to make urgent representations that – 'for Heaven's sake' – Vienna should arrange matters with the Italian government. Rome would adopt a friendly position only if Austria-Hungary accepted its interpretation of the compensation clause of the triple alliance treaty. The ambassador directed 'a solemn and emphatic appeal' to Berchtold to settle the question. If Italy did not recognize the *casus foederis*, Germany's own military plans would be thrown into disarray, Tschirschky argued. Under such intense pressure, Berchtold decided that he had no choice but to appease the Italians. For Austria-Hungary, he informed Mérey at Rome, was currently engaged in 'a *grand jeu* [a game for high stakes] which already entailed significant difficulties, but which would be wholly impracticable without the firm cohesion of the *Dreibund* Powers'. To that end he agreed to consult with the government in Rome, in the event of Austria-Hungary having to occupy, even if only temporarily, any portion of the Balkans.

What was presented to Tschirschky as a major and gracious concession was in fact minimal. In substance, Austro-Hungarian policy had not changed. As Szögyény was to explain at the Wilhelmstrasse, Vienna would not agree to include the Italophone portions of the Trentino in a compensation package for Italy. Bethmann and Jagow had to understand that 'the question of ceding a portion of the Monarchy could not even be the subject of discussions'.[152] Mérey, the curmudgeonly anti-Italian ambassador at Rome, encouraged Berchtold in this line. The assurances of friendly support given by his Italian colleague at Vienna, the Duke of Avarna, he warned, were nothing but a prelude to compensation claims. Berchtold ought to reject all such claims, and not to enter into 'delicate negotiations or engagements': 'Otherwise we should allow Italy the role of the man who says to his friend who has fallen into the Danube: "*I shall not*

---

[151] Flotow to Bethmann Hollweg, 25 July 1914, and min. Bethmann Hollweg, 27 July 1914, *DD* I, no. 244. Tschirschky was instructed accordingly, see tel. Jagow to Tschirschky (no. 168), 27 July 1914 (D 9 a.m.), *ibid.*, no. 267. The ambassador had, in fact, pressed Macchio and Berchtold to give up the 'academic dispute' about the true meaning of article VII of the triple alliance treaty, and to focus on 'practical decisions', see Tschirschky to Jagow (secret), 26 July 1914, *DD* II, no. 326.

[152] Tels. Berchtold to Mérey and Szögyény (nos. 892 and 280), 28 July 1914 (D 1 p.m.), *ÖUA* VIII, no. 10909; see also tel. Tschirschky to Auswärtiges Amt (no. 122), 28 July 1914 (D 9.10 p.m., R 12.02 a.m.), *DD* II, no. 328.

pull you out. If however you manage to get out on your own, then you will have to pay me compensation".[153]

The question of compensating Italy, as seen before, had always been a sensitive point for Vienna. From the moment Berchtold decided on a forceful response to the Sarajevo assassination, he had sought to keep Italy, still notionally an ally, at arm's length. The 'blank cheque' of 5 July had given him a free hand in his dealings with Italy, but curtailing that country's involvement in the crisis had become more complicated ever since Flotow had lifted the veil on Vienna's true intentions towards Belgrade in mid-July. For as long as the conflict with Serbia could be localized, the Habsburg government need not fear Italian claims for compensation. But if Russia decided to intervene, then Vienna could ill afford to encourage the grievance-mongers at Rome.[154]

The Kaiser decides that there is no need for war

If Vienna accelerated the pace of events with the declaration of war against Serbia, confusion was sown at Berlin on 28 July. Ever since the Hoyos mission had signalled Austria-Hungary's will to war, German diplomacy had consistently striven to isolate the Balkan quarrel and to shield it against foreign diplomatic interference. Indeed, Berlin had pressed its ally to mobilize sooner and to strike a swift and decisive blow against Serbia. In this manner, it was hoped, the conflict could be localized or at least Vienna's complete diplomatic triumph be secured. Now the Kaiser was prepared to retract the offer of unconditional support for Austria-Hungary. The 'blank cheque' was not to be honoured after all.

The protean character of Germany's last Emperor has already been commented upon. In hindsight, his intervention on 28 July reinforces the argument made earlier that the chancellor had every reason to keep his volatile imperial master out of the country for much of July. In the afternoon of the previous day, the Kaiser had returned to Potsdam, not amused at Bethmann's insistence that he stay away from the capital. On the

---

[153] Tel. Mérey to Berchtold (no. 547), 28 July 1914 (D 1.30 a.m., R 12.30 p.m.), *ÖUA* VIII, no. 10912 (original emphasis); see also S. R. Williamson, *Austria-Hungary and the Origins of the First World War* (London, 1991), 209–10.

[154] Anatoli Nikola'evich Krupenski, the Russian ambassador at Rome, came to the same conclusion as Mérey: San Giuliano advocated mediation but on the basis of Serbia's unequivocal acceptance of the Austro-Hungarian note, which would then open the way for Italy to make her demands, to Sazonov (no. 47, confidential), 14/27 July 1914, *IBZI* V, no. 131.

following morning, he was in a better frame of mind. He had been up early, as always, and even before his obligatory morning ride in the park of the Neues Palais at about 7.30 a.m., he had studied the despatches and reports that had arrived during the last few days. There were two despatches from St Petersburg, the first from Pourtalès, the other from Chelius, the Kaiser's military plenipotentiary at the Tsar's court. Both were two days old, but both offered a glimpse into current Russian thinking and both framed the Kaiser's reaction to a third document.

The ambassador reported on a conversation with a highly authoritative source at St Petersburg. Following Vienna's rejection of the earlier Russian suggestion that the ultimatum be extended, St Petersburg had exhausted all diplomatic options. This had made an impression on Pourtalès, who warned that 'the chances of war have increased considerably and we are on the eve of major events'. On the other hand, the ambassador's subsequent conversations with Sazonov on 27 July – the telegraphic reports on which the Kaiser had already seen – suggested that the Russian foreign minister was still exploring diplomatic options. Pourtalès's anonymous source hinted that the Russian government had taken certain military precautions so as not to be caught out later, and he suggested that 'behind the scenes' Germany had encouraged Habsburg belligerence. Without German support the Austro-Hungarian government would never have decided upon a course that had no justification. As so often, the report was richly adorned with the Kaiser's marginalia. The imperial comments on Pourtalès's high personage's concluding observation were succinct: 'swine!' – this in reference to the suggestion that Berlin had pulled the wires in the background – and 'then regicide is a bagatelle' – this on the suggestion that a war against Serbia was not justified.[155]

Chelius's despatch added another dimension. Like his predecessors as the Kaiser's military representative in the Tsar's entourage, his reports on life at the St Petersburg court were cast in vivid and bright colours and with deftly executed, broad brushstrokes. Much of what Chelius had to say about events at Krasnoe Selo reinforced the ambassador's latest report, but there was an abrupt change towards the end of his lengthy despatch. Disgust with the Habsburg Empire was widespread in court circles, he noted, not least because it was feared that Russia might be forced to wage war 'when all of Russia was set ablaze by a rising of the labouring masses'. There had been an expectation that Vienna would strike – 'the guns along the Danube would open up' – immediately on expiry of the ultimatum. As this, however, had not happened, 'the crisis must be over, and the gates

---

[155] Memo. Pourtalès, 13/26 July (R 28 July a.m.), *DD* II, no. 290.

have been opened for mediation. Sazonov is delighted, for the work of the diplomats that had nearly come to an end, can now start afresh ... The view in Russia has been reinforced that "*l'Autriche aboie mais ne mord pas* [Austria barks but she does not bite]".' For good measure, the General added that the Tsar's treatment of Poincaré had been noticeably cool and condescending.[156]

The final piece in the jigsaw was provided by Lichnowsky's telegrams from London, which Bethmann Hollweg had forwarded to the Neues Palais by personal courier in the early hours of 28 July. The chancellor had appended a note in which he emphasized the impossibility of an outright rejection of Grey's conference proposals, 'especially since London and Paris continually work on Petersburg'. Grey's words, as transmitted by Lichnowsky, made an impression on the Kaiser.[157] The telegrams from London and Chelius's report on the latest events at Krasnoe Selo thus framed the Kaiser's reaction to one of the next documents on his desk – a copy of Serbia's official reply to the Austro-Hungarian démarche, which the Serbian chargé d'affaires, Milutin Jovanović, had submitted to the Wilhelmstrasse on 27 July, and which was then sent on to Potsdam. Wilhelm's reaction to the document was ecstatic. Belgrade's response amounted to a humiliating capitulation to Austrian pressure, he decided:

> A brilliant achievement for a deadline of a mere 48 hours! That is more than one could expect!
>
> A great moral victory for Vienna; but it removes every reason for war, and Giesl could have stayed at Belgrade. *I* would never have ordered mobilization in response.

Even Belgrade's equivocal reply to the infamous sixth demand – the participation of Habsburg police in investigations on Serbian soil – could be overcome, the Kaiser decided: 'the legation can just be asked to control it'.[158]

The despatches from St Petersburg thus suggested a diplomatic route out of the crisis, and the German Emperor, whose public bellicose bombast was exceeded only by his private aversion to war, snatched at the

---

[156] Chelius to Wilhelm II, 13/26 July 1914, *DD* II, no. 291; also Lambsdorff (ed.), *Militärbevollmächtigte* no. 6/5.

[157] Bethmann Hollweg to Wilhelm II, 27 July 1914, *DD* II, no. 283; for the effect of Lichnowsky's telegrams see also Plessen diary, 28 July 1914, *DGB*, 23.

[158] Min. Wilhelm II on Serbian note, 28 July 1914, *DD* I, no. 271; for the Kaiser's conviction that the conflict could remain localized see also C. Clark, *Kaiser Wilhelm II: A Life in Power* (London, 2009), 289–92.

chance. In his reaction to the Serbian note the Kaiser, so often so intemperate and unwise in his pronouncements, showed a good deal more common sense, political nous and diplomatic intelligence than his chancellor and the officials at the Wilhelmstrasse. True, he glossed over the ambiguities in Belgrade's reply, perhaps he had never noticed them. But here seemed an opportunity for settling the mounting crisis without any further escalation. Under the influence of the Serbian note and Grey's observations on it, the Kaiser initially concluded that there was now no cause for war, as he explained to Plessen, his aide-de-camp, during their early-morning ride. He was ready, as Plessen noted in his diary, 'to separate himself from the ways of Austria'. He nevertheless accepted his adjutant's argument that 'Austria ought at least lay her hand on a "*Faustpfand* [forfeit]" that would serve as a guarantee for the fulfilment of the concessions.'[159]

The Kaiser saw the practical sense of Plessen's idea. Vienna could not very well be asked to halt the mobilization of eight army corps, let alone demobilize them, without having anything to show for it. It was important, moreover, for Vienna to retain some sort of leverage over the Serbian government lest Belgrade renege on its commitments, as had happened before. Wilhelm decided to act. Plessen was instructed to inform the chief of staff that there would be no war. He himself wrote a lengthy letter to Jagow, in which he outlined what is generally referred to as his 'Halt in Belgrade' proposal. '[B]y and large', he informed the state secretary, Serbia had fulfilled all of Austria-Hungary's demands. The few reservations in the note could be solved through negotiations: 'But in it lies the capitulation of the most humiliating kind, proclaimed *orbi et urbi* [*sic*], and by it every cause for war has gone.' The note would be no more than 'a piece of paper' – the Kaiser observed anticipating a phrase that would cause much controversy later – if Serbia failed to act on her commitments. The Serbs, Wilhelm reminded his minister, were 'Orientals, and thus deceitful, false and masters of procrastination. *Douce violence* must be exercised so that these pretty promises may become reality and facts.' To that end Austria-Hungary should be permitted to occupy the Serbian capital as a 'forfeit', with the duration of the occupation dependent on Serbia's fulfilment of her promises. Austria-Hungary could not be expected to mobilize for a third time without receiving appropriate '*satisfaction d'honneur*'. On that basis, the German monarch was prepared to propose peace mediation to Vienna. Any other proposal would be rejected, 'all the more since everyone is more or less openly appealing to Me to help to preserve peace'. Mediation had to be sensitive to Austria-Hungary's prestige and the 'honour of

[159] Plessen diary, 28 July 1914, *DGB*, 24 and 23.

her arms': 'This is the precondition for My mediation.' Jagow was to approach the Habsburg government with this proposal.[160]

Under the given circumstances, 'Halt in Belgrade' was sensible enough. It offered a realistic framework for settling the Austro-Serbian dispute without any further escalation (the news of Austria-Hungary's declaration of war was not received until the evening).[161] Vienna could not be expected to disengage at this late stage without denting the Monarchy's prestige in the region. But the temporary occupation of Belgrade would offer Austria-Hungary the necessary political and military satisfaction. Serbia was not to be subjected completely – the further talks on the 'few reservations' in the note would see to that. But Belgrade was a secondary consideration now. More important was the anticipated effect on St Petersburg. If Sazonov could be brought to accept the temporary occupation of Belgrade or an equivalent 'forfeit', as seemed likely at some stage,[162] then war could be averted. If the scheme appeared practicable, it was also sanctioned by international precedent, the German occupation of northern France in 1871–3 to secure the full payment of the French war indemnity after the Franco-German War. The difference with 'Halt in Belgrade', of course, was that the earlier occupation was the result of a war, whereas the Kaiser's proposal envisaged occupation as a means of averting a full-blown conflict.

Already before the instructions went out to Jagow, the Kaiser had consulted with the chancellor and the Prussian war minister, General Erich von Falkenhayn. The latter was much perturbed by the Emperor's latest change of heart: 'He makes senseless utterances, that show clearly that he does not want war any longer and is determined, for that prize, even to leave Austria in the lurch.'[163] The Kaiser ignored Falkenhayn's objections, and Wilhelm and the chancellor then pondered the next move. Bethmann himself was all in favour of the initiative. Whilst he had taken a more hawkish stance in recent days, the object of his policy remained a military or diplomatic success for Austria-Hungary. 'Halt in Belgrade' might secure

---

[160] Wilhelm II to Jagow, 28 July 1914 (D 2.10 p.m.), *DD* II, no. 293; for Plessen's instructions see *DGB*, 23; J. Angelow, *Kalkül und Prestige. Der Zweibund am Vorabend des Ersten Weltkrieges* (Vienna, 2000), 459–60.

[161] See tel. Tschirschky to Auswärtiges Amt (no. 118), 28 July 1914 (D 4.10 p.m., R 6.39 p.m.), *DD* II, no. 311.

[162] See tel. Pourtalès to Auswärtiges Amt (no. 192), 30 July 1914 (D 1.01 p.m., R 3.32 p.m.), *DD* II, no. 421.

[163] Falkenhayn diary, 28 July 1914, H. Afflerbach, *Falkenhayn. Politisches Denken und Handeln im Kaiserreich* (Düsseldorf, 1996), 154. The letter to Jagow was despatched at 2. 10 p.m., after the *déjeuner* with Bethmann and Falkenhayn. The Kaiser's late 'breakfasts' (at lunchtime) are the source of some confusion in the literature.

either of them; and another of the St Petersburg telegrams received overnight suggested that the scheme offered a realistic route out of the crisis.
Sazonov, Pourtalès reported, had reciprocated Bethmann's earlier pacific
assurances during an interview late on 27 July. On the basis of Vienna's
non-annexation pledge and given that hostilities had not yet commenced,
Sazonov was ready 'to "build golden bridges" for Austria' in direct
exchanges with Vienna. Serbia deserved to be taught a lesson, he conceded,
provided her sovereign rights were respected. Altogether, the ambassador
observed, the foreign minister's defence of Belgrade was 'far weaker than
two days ago, [and] his language as conciliatory as yesterday [i.e. 26 July]'.

For Bethmann it was clear, then, that 'the wire between Berlin and
Petersburg has not at all been severed', as he explained to the Kaiser.
Sazonov might prove receptive to the 'Halt in Belgrade' idea. But in turn
this meant that Germany must not be too accommodating to Grey's suggestions of international mediation, for Sazonov's lenient attitude was seen
to be the result of German pressure. If 'clumsy' Lichnowsky were told of
the latest news from St Petersburg, he would inform the British Foreign
Secretary, who in turn would then be even more reluctant to restrain
Russia.[164] This was a delicate act of brinkmanship to perform. It meant
that every move had to be carefully calculated and prepared. Any misstep
would have devastating consequences.

Bethmann Hollweg finds Austrian ambiguities intolerable

The Kaiser and Bethmann considered the idea of despatching an official
from the Wilhelmstrasse, most likely Zimmermann, on a special mission to
Vienna – a form of Hoyos mission in reverse – to explain the 'Halt in
Belgrade' scheme but also to establish what Vienna's true objectives
were.[165] That question had bedevilled German diplomacy throughout the
July crisis. On 30 June and 2 July, Tschirschky had urged Vienna to
establish clarity on this point.[166] So far Berlin had not received an answer.
This did not matter much prior to the ultimatum to Serbia. Indeed, ignor-
ance of Vienna's motives had proved convenient for Berlin. Since the

---

[164] Tel. Pourtalès to Auswärtiges Amt (no. 167), 27 July 1914 (D 8.40 p.m., R 4.36
a.m.), and min. Bethmann Hollweg, 28 July 1914, *DD* II, no. 282.
[165] Bach, 'Einleitung', *DGB*, 23–4; A. von Tirpitz, *Politische Dokumente. Deutsche
Ohnmachtspolitik im Weltkriege* (Hamburg, 1926), 4; see also Meyer-Arndt,
Julikrise, 146.
[166] See Tschirschky to Bethmann Hollweg, 30 June 1914, and 2 July 1914 (secret), *DD*
I, nos. 7 and 11.

démarche, however, and with war now impending, that same ignorance complicated matters.

With the 'Halt in Belgrade' scheme in the pipeline at Berlin, it made little sense for the chancellor to comply with Berchtold's request of the previous night to warn off St Petersburg. A 'categorical statement' appeared 'premature' at the present moment. Tschirschky was to suggest at the Ballhausplatz that Szápáry might intimate the likely consequences of a Russian mobilization.[167] This suggestion was perhaps a little disingenuous, for Bethmann understood that Berchtold was reluctant to do anything that would openly antagonize the Russian government. From Berlin's perspective, however, firm language directed at Russia was likely to reduce the chances of Sazonov accepting 'Halt in Belgrade'. Any démarche at St Petersburg, moreover, would ensure that the ship of German diplomacy continued to drift in Austria-Hungary's wake.

The Wilhelmstrasse's disquiet with Vienna grew yet further that afternoon. Within half an hour of the instructions to Tschirschky having been sent, a telegram arrived from London. His colleague Mensdorff and members of the Austro-Hungarian embassy, reported Lichnowsky, had left him in no doubt that Vienna had aimed at 'crushing Serbia' from the outset. News of Belgrade's apparent acceptance of Austria-Hungary's demands had caused consternation amongst Habsburg diplomats in London. Mensdorff had confided to him on the previous evening under the seal of secrecy that 'Vienna absolutely wanted war as Serbia was to be "ironed flat".' He was further told that portions of Serbian territory were to be ceded to Bulgaria and possibly also to Albania.

Lichnowsky's report set alarm bells ringing at Berlin, where Berchtold's previous non-annexationist assurances had been accepted at face value, and had in fact informed statements made to the other Powers. Now Bethmann realized that he had been deceived. 'These ambiguities of Austria are intolerable', the chancellor minuted: 'They deny us information about their programme, say explicitly that the explanations of Count Hoyos which hinted at Serbia's dismemberment had been purely private; in Petersburg they are little lambs that have no evil intentions; and in London their embassy talks of giving Serbian territories as presents to Bulgaria and Albania.'[168] Lichnowsky's revelations were all the more awkward since ten minutes before the London telegram arrived at the Wilhelmstrasse, Bethmann had instructed Pourtalès at St Petersburg to

---

[167] Tel. Bethmann Hollweg to Tschirschky (no. 173, secret), 28 July 1914 (D 3.20 p.m., R 6 p.m.), *DD* II, no. 299. The telegram was drafted by Stumm.

[168] Tel. Lichnowsky to Auswärtiges Amt, 28 July 1914 (D 12.58 p.m., R 3.45 p.m.), and min. Bethmann Hollweg, 28 July 1914, *DD* II, no. 301.

thank Sazonov for his conciliatory attitude so far, and to explain that a diplomatic solution should now be possible on the basis of Vienna's declaration of 'territorial *désintéressement*'.[169]

Clarity of Austria-Hungary's intentions was desirable also in light of a steady trickle of information from Russia. The entrance to the port at Riga on the Baltic coast had been mined and the harbour lights extinguished, reported the consul there. Soldiers were patrolling railway bridges, and freight wagons on the private railways had been requisitioned. The acting consul-general at Moscow wired that mobilization appeared to be underway at Kiev, Vilnius and Warsaw, and large numbers of officers of all branches of the armed forces were leaving from the city's Alexander station, the terminus of the Moscow–Brest railway line. At Odessa, Pourtalès reported, reserve officers appeared to have been called up and field guns concentrated.[170]

Later that same evening the Wilhelmstrasse received news of the declaration of war and Berchtold's subsequent rejection of Grey's mediation proposal.[171] This was an additional complication, but what mattered now was to implement the Kaiser's idea of mediation on the basis of 'Halt in Belgrade'. To that end the chancellor initiated a series of diplomatic moves, further accelerating the pace of events. Lichnowsky was instructed to reiterate to Grey that, as Austria-Hungary's Great Power position was imperilled, Berlin could not advise the Habsburg government to moderate its demands on Serbia. The contemplated action was meant to put a stop to Serbia's intolerable provocations. This was also in the interest of Europe as, over the past five years, Serbia's expansionist ambitions had three times threatened to disrupt the tranquillity of the continent. Indeed, Bethmann wished to assure Grey that Berlin did not regard the Austro-Serbian stand-off as a 'test of strength between the two European groups' and would continue its diplomatic efforts at St Petersburg. Tellingly, in light of Lichnowsky's warnings that afternoon, Zimmermann struck from the original draft a reference to Vienna's earlier pledge to respect Serbia's territorial integrity.[172]

[169] Tel. Bethmann Hollweg to Pourtalès (no. 130), 28 July 1914 (D 3.55 p.m.), *DD* II, no. 300; see also tel. to Tschirschky (no. 172), 28 July 1914 (D 4.10 p.m., R 7.15 p.m.), *DD* II, no. 309.
[170] Tels. Riga consulate to Auswärtiges Amt (no. 2), 28 July 1914 (R 11.55 a.m.), Hauschild to Auswärtiges Amt (no. 4), 27 [*recte* 28] July 1914 (D 12.36 a.m., R 12.10 p.m.), and Pourtalès to Auswärtiges Amt (no. 172), 28 July 1914 (D 12.14 p.m., R 1.04 p.m.), *DD* II, nos. 294–6; cf. tel. Bosanquet [British consul at Riga] to Grey, 28 July 1914 (D 7.43 p.m., R 8.45 p.m.), *BD* XI, no. 228.
[171] Tels. Tschirschky to Auswärtiges Amt (nos. 118 and 120, secret), 28 July 1914 (D 4.10 and 4.55 p.m., R 6.39 and 7.25 p.m.), *DD* II, nos. 311 and 313.
[172] Bethmann Hollweg to Lichnowsky (no. 185), 28 July 1914 (D 8.40 p.m.), *DD* II, no. 314 and n. 4; see also Jarausch, *Enigmatic Chancellor*, 167–8.

To some extent, the chancellor stuck to the line he had pursued during the last few days. He would not interfere in the core dispute of the crisis. And yet the instructions to Lichnowsky signalled a significant concession to London, for Bethmann now associated Germany with international mediation efforts. Later that evening he requested the British ambassador to call upon him at the chancellery. He was anxious, he explained to Goschen, to cooperate with Britain in the interests of peace. He had declined Grey's idea of Four-Power mediation only because it had the 'appearance of an "Areopagus" ... sitting in judgment'. But this did not militate against his desire for effective cooperation with Britain. German diplomacy continued to work at Vienna and St Petersburg 'to get the two Governments to discuss the situation directly with each other and in a friendly way', even though, as he observed later, the 'quarrel with Servia was a purely Austrian concern with which Russia had nothing to do'. As Goschen took his leave, the chancellor reiterated his desire to cooperate with Britain 'and his intention to do his utmost to maintain general peace. "A war between the Great Powers must be avoided" were his last words.'[173]

This, of course, was the familiar line that only Russia could prevent further escalation, with the implication that either singly or in conjunction with other Powers, London had to act to restrain Russian policy. The 'diplomatic duel' between London and Berlin had thus not been terminated. But the German government was clearly now engaged in diplomatic efforts to settle the brewing crisis. At this stage the Wilhelmstrasse had not yet been informed of Berchtold's veto of any direct talks at St Petersburg. But, as will be seen, Bethmann's emphasis on such negotiations would effect a change in British diplomacy.

Bethmann continued to assure the Powers that he was determined to resolve the Balkan turmoil. Pourtalès was instructed to explain at the Choristers' Bridge that Berlin kept pressing the Habsburg government to give assurances to Russia about the object and extent of the operations against Serbia. The declaration of war did not change matters, he suggested.[174]

At around 10 p.m. the latest instructions for Tschirschky, incorporating the 'Halt in Belgrade' scheme, were ready for transmission to Vienna. The plan to despatch Zimmermann or another high-ranking official on a special mission to the Habsburg capital to retract the 'blank cheque' handed to Hoyos, however, was quietly dropped. Regular train

---

[173] Tel. Goschen to Grey (no. 99), 28 July 1914 (D 12 a.m., R 8 a.m.), *BD* xi, no. 249.
[174] Tel. Bethmann Hollweg to Pourtalès (no. 131), 28 July 1914 (D 9 p.m.), *DD* ii, no. 315. The telegram was also circulated to the embassies at Vienna, London and Paris.

connections with Vienna no longer existed, the chancellor was told, and the matter was therefore left in Tschirschky's hands.[175]

This was little more than a convenient excuse. For, in truth, Jagow opposed the Kaiser's mediation proposal. Since 6 July the Wilhelmstrasse had sought to shield Austria-Hungary's planned operation against Serbia from foreign intervention, using Germany's support for the Monarchy as a deterrent. Now, the Kaiser sought to change course and weaken Germany's commitment to Austria-Hungary. As seen earlier, Stumm and other leading officials at the Wilhelmstrasse were still convinced at this stage that Russia would not resort to military force to support Serbia. The Kaiser's scheme therefore threatened to reduce whatever advantages Austria-Hungary could extract from the situation.

There was, however, another problem – Jagow's second 'blank cheque' of the previous evening.[176] The Hoyos mission in reverse bruited by Bethmann and their imperial master threatened to unravel Jagow's little intrigue behind the chancellor's back. The state secretary had always been anxious to avoid later accusations by Austria-Hungary that Berlin did not support her aspirations sufficiently. A special emissary to press 'Halt in Belgrade' upon the Ballhausplatz would surely be resented at Vienna.

Nor was this all. Unbeknown to the Kaiser, key aspects of his mediation proposal were toned down by Jagow and Stumm. The instructions for Tschirschky reflected some of Bethmann Hollweg's irritation with Austro-Hungarian duplicity over the real objectives of the campaign against Serbia, however. Despite repeated enquiries at the Ballhausplatz, the ambassador was told, Berlin had been left in the dark about Vienna's plans. The Kaiser's colourful phrase of Serbia's 'capitulation of the most humiliating kind, proclaimed *orbi et urbi* [*sic*]' had been removed from the text, though Vienna was to be left in no doubt that the Serbian reply had gone far to meet the original demands. Austro-Hungarian intransigence thus threatened to turn European opinion against the Monarchy. Further, since military operations could not commence before 12 August, Berlin was coming under mounting pressure by the other Powers to acquiesce to some form of diplomatic intervention in the Austro-Serbian crisis. If it maintained its 'hitherto reserved attitude towards such proposals it would incur the odium of having caused a world war'. It was 'an imperative necessity' that, if the conflict escalated, Russia should be held responsible for it.

---

[175] Bethmann Hollweg to Wilhelm II, 28 July 1914, *DD* II, no. 308. The Kaiser read the letter at 10.15 p.m., see *DD* II, n. 2.
[176] Tel. Szögyény to Berchtold (no. 307, strictly secret), 27 July 1914, ÖUA VIII, no. 10793. For the notion that Bethmann was responsible for amending the Kaiser's proposals, see *inter alios* Albertini, *Origins* II, 504–5; Mombauer, *Moltke*, 208.

This was nothing but an exposition of the growing strategic dilemma into which the two Germanic Powers had drifted since 5/6 July, Austria-Hungary because of her tunnel vision and Germany because of her abdication of leadership in the *Zweibund* alliance. The instructions then turned to the Kaiser's mediation proposal. Sazonov had acknowledged that Serbia deserved to be taught a lesson, and had taken a more conciliatory stance over the past two days. Vienna therefore had to reaffirm its non-annexation pledge. Given that Austria-Hungary's partial mobilization had already commenced, Sazonov would therefore accept that the 'honour of her arms' demanded that Habsburg forces enter Serbian territory. He would be all the more ready to do so if Vienna gave assurances now that its military campaign aimed solely at the temporary occupation of Belgrade 'and certain other parts of Serbian territory', all of them to be vacated once Austria-Hungary's demands had been fully met.

This had been the essence of the Kaiser's proposal. Stumm, who had drafted the telegram, then added more specific instructions. Tschirschky was to impress upon Berchtold the need for Habsburg diplomacy to take the initiative at St Petersburg. But he was to avoid creating the impression 'as though we wished Austria to hold back' – that of course was precisely what the Kaiser and Bethmann Hollweg wanted. It was rather a question of 'finding the right mode that would allow for the achievement of Austria-Hungary's aims to sever the vital nerve of pan-Serb propaganda, without simultaneously unleashing a world war'. If the latter could not be averted, then a Habsburg diplomatic initiative based on 'Halt in Belgrade' would improve the broader international conditions under which the two Powers would have to wage such a conflict.[177]

The telegram to Tschirschky diluted the Kaiser's mediation proposal. For this Jagow and Stumm were responsible. The instructions, and especially the concluding paragraph, reflected their thinking more than that of the chancellor, let alone the Kaiser. Leaving it to Vienna to initiate a diplomatic move based on the temporary occupation of the Serbian capital as a prelude to a negotiated settlement ensured that the whole scheme remained abortive. Indeed, the final section made sense only if its authors assumed that 'Halt in Belgrade' was either not desirable or not practicable. The extant evidence does not suggest that this was the Emperor's view or that of Bethmann Hollweg – if anything the reverse was true on 28 July. But Jagow's reluctance to restrain Vienna up to this point is well-documented.

---

[177] Tel. Bethmann Hollweg to Tschirschky (no. 174), 28 July 1914, *DD* II, no. 323. The telegram was drafted by Stumm, but despatched in the chancellor's name. For Sazonov's comment on a 'deserved lesson' for Serbia, see tel. Pourtalès to Auswärtiges Amt (no. 167), 27 July 1914 (D 8.40 p.m., R 4.36 a.m.), *DD* II., no. 282.

Even so, the telegram to Tschirschky is significant in the wider context of the July crisis. Whatever their respective differences, the entire German leadership was seized now of the potential risks inherent in the current situation. Much would depend on whether either St Petersburg or Vienna would show restraint.

Instead of a special emissary pressing the Kaiser's case on Berchtold, it was now left to Tschirschky to do so – and the ambassador, of course, had in his pocket a second 'blank cheque'.

Sazonov is clutching at straws

Following Vienna's escalation of the crisis, Russia's reaction would be key to how events unfolded. And without Russian support the Kaiser's 'Halt in Belgrade' proposal was meaningless. After the recent calm and relative optimism, the mood at St Petersburg was ambiguous. In the morning Sukhomlinov, the war minister, attended the Tsar at Peterhof for his regular report on military matters. He found Nicholas listless and curiously detached.[178]

That morning, Sazonov still appeared optimistic, Szápáry wired to Vienna.[179] There was, however, a decided edge to the mood at St Petersburg. Prince Trubetskoy, a member of the Tsar's entourage and a scion of one of the oldest aristocratic families in Russia, sought out Chelius, the German military attaché. It was now incumbent on Austria-Hungary to acknowledge the goodwill Serbia had shown in meeting most of the demands laid down in the ultimatum. Russia could not stand by if Serbia were crushed. St Petersburg hoped – Trubetskoy laid stress on this – that the 'terrible, automatically following clash of the Great Powers' could be averted. 'Oceans of blood' would be spilled if it came after all. The Kaiser, however, had it in his power to give moderating advice to Vienna. It would be useful if the German and Russian monarchs exchanged views by telegram, he suggested.[180]

---

[178] V.A. Sukhomlinov, *Erinnerungen* (Berlin, 1924), 361.
[179] Tel. Szápáry to Berchtold (no. 172), 28 July 1914 (D 1.20 a.m., R 8 p.m.), ÖUA VIII, no. 10916.
[180] Tel. Chelius to Auswärtiges Amt (no. 174), 28 July 1914 (R 29 July 3.42 a.m.), DD II, no. 337. It is not entirely clear which of the many Trubetskoys spoke to Chelius, but it may be assumed that this was Prince Grigori Nikola'evich, who was then a counsellor of the II Department of the foreign ministry (Near East) and Hartwig's designated successor at Belgrade.

Sazonov, too, had become more pessimistic. A perceptive analysis of the situation by Mikhail Nikola'evich de Giers, the ambassador at Constantinople and son of a former foreign minister, throws a revealing light on Russian concerns in the aftermath of the ultimatum. The Balkan wars and the diminution of the Turkish Empire, the ambassador wrote, had shaken the political balance in the Near East to the detriment of the *Dreibund* triplice. Sarajevo had offered an opportunity for Austria-Hungary to restore her former position and prestige in the region. From his conversations with his German colleague at the Bosphorus, Hans Wilhelm von Wangenheim, Giers concluded that Berlin had actively encouraged the Habsburg government in its actions against Serbia. The ultimatum itself, he observed, was 'unique in the history of international relations and aimed at implementing the dangerous principle that the enslavement of smaller states by Great Powers is permissible'. There was no doubt that Vienna hoped to smash Serbia and force her into some form of vassallage. A Habsburg triumph would be a triumph of the three Central Powers, and it would ruin Russia's prestige and position in the Near East. It was necessary, therefore, Giers advised, to place the Black Sea fleet and the army on alert so that Russia would not be found unprepared if and when the moment for action came.[181]

Giers's analysis was no doubt tinted by his Turkish perspective, but it touched a chord with Sazonov – especially the ambassador's insistence on credible deterrence. Indeed, it is one of the many ironies of the July crisis that, while Pourtalès thought that Sazonov was now committed to the diplomatic route, the interviews with the ambassadors of the two Germanic Powers late on 27 and 28 July left the foreign minister depressed. Pourtalès called twice on Sazonov on 28 July, though he only sent one somewhat anodyne report to Berlin. The first encounter in the morning was anything but friendly. Sazonov was irritated, and received the ambassador with the words that he 'now saw through our devious policy'. Berlin had known all along of Vienna's plans; there had, in fact, been 'a conspiracy' between Berlin and Vienna. The interview was going nowhere, and Pourtalès broke off the meeting.

At the embassy, he was confronted with news that Russian police had boarded a German steamer moored at St Petersburg harbour and disabled its wireless telegraphy equipment. The ambassador duly returned to the Choristers' Bridge to lodge a formal protest. On leaving he complained to the assistant foreign minister, Anatol Anatolevich Neratov, about Sazonov's tone during the earlier meeting. No sooner was he back

---

[181] Giers to Sazonov (private), 14/27 July 1914, *IBZI* v, no. 154.

at the embassy than a telephone message arrived from the ministry, asking Pourtalès once more to call upon Sazonov. The latter apologized profusely for his earlier outburst, and the two settled down to a discussion of the Serbian crisis. But the discussion was unproductive. Sazonov repeated his request that Germany join efforts to mediate; the ambassador reiterated his government's refusal to interfere in the Austro-Serbian dispute. Pourtalès warned, however, that an incipient agitation in the St Petersburg press against Germany and Austria-Hungary was 'a clumsy manoeuvre' that would fail to have any effect. He also stressed that reports of Russian military preparations were worrying and increased the inherent danger of the current situation.[182]

Sazonov was in a mellower mood when Szápáry called, but their exchanges were just as sterile as those with Pourtalès. As instructed, the Habsburg ambassador declined to discuss the idea of direct exchanges between the two Eastern Powers. There were, therefore, no talks about talks. But the meeting was by no means unfriendly. The situation was serious, Sazonov observed. Belgrade's reply had been conciliatory, and the dispute between the Habsburg and Serbian governments had now been narrowed to just one point – the absence of the promised official dossier on pan-Serb agitation made it difficult for Szápáry to argue convincingly. The ambassador found Sazonov visibly disappointed at the latest turn of events. Vienna's declaration of territorial disinterestedness made little impression on the Russian foreign minister, but he spoke 'in quite calm and friendly a manner'. Sazonov, 'in his aversion to come into conflict with us, was clutching at straws', Szápáry concluded. In contrast to earlier periods of Austro-Russian tension, morever, Sazonov had not referred to the strength of pan-Slav opinion in Russia or the role of the Orthodox church, but had argued with 'political objectivity throughout' by stressing Russia's strategic interest in preventing Serbia from being reduced to a state of vassallage [*Infeodierung*]' – Giers's warning.

At that point, Austria-Hungary's declaration of war on Serbia was not yet known at St Petersburg, and, not having been instructed to inform Sazonov, Szápáry left him in ignorance. He was certain, however, that the declaration would force Russia to reveal her hand. The diplomatic body at St Petersburg was pessimistic, he reported, and the British and Japanese ambassadors in particular were certain that the Russian government was determined to intervene.[183]

---

[182] Quotes from Pourtalès, *Meine letzten Verhandlungen*, 32–6, and tel. Pourtalès to Auswärtiges Amt (no. 177), 28 July 1914 (D 8.12 p.m., R 6.15 a.m.), *DD* II, no, 338.
[183] Tel. Szápáry to Berchtold (no. 173), 29 July 1914 (D 10 a.m., R 4 p.m.), *ÖUA* VIII, no. 10999. The interview took place in the afternoon of 28 July. Later that afternoon the

Sazonov was dismayed by the interviews, as he told Paléologue: 'Austria does not wish to negotiate.'[184] Indeed, he was certain that Berlin 'rather encourages the irreconcilable attitude of Austria'. He was much disquieted by Germany's attitude and instructed Benckendorff at London to renew his attempts to encourage Grey to exercise more pressure on the German government: 'The key to the situation lies undoubtedly in Berlin.'[185]

After the meeting with Szápáry, Sazonov left for Peterhof, where events would take a decisive turn. For Sazonov and the Tsar's ministers, Berlin held the keys also with regard to the military dimension of the crisis. As seen earlier, for as long as Germany remained passive, it was assumed at St Petersburg that the combination of a firm diplomatic line and lower-level military preparations – Sazonov's diplomacy of deterrence – would enable Russia to safeguard her interests during the crisis.

Two developments now came together that would accelerate the course of events, one internal, the other external. During the past few days, Yanushkevich, the hapless Russian chief of staff who had blithely concurred with Sazonov's plans for a partial mobilization on 25 July, was confronted with awkward advice by his mobilization specialists, most importantly Quartermaster-General Yuri Nikoforovich Danilov, who had been on leave until 27 July, and the head of the general staff's mobilization section, General Sergei Konstantinovich Dobrorolski. They warned that Mobilization Schedule No. 19 was 'a seamless whole, an all-or-nothing operation'.[186] Partial mobilization against Austria-Hungary, whatever its political utility in a Balkan crisis, would leave Russia dangerously exposed if faster-mobilizing Germany were to interfere in the crisis at a later stage. Mobilizing only four military districts would cause havoc with Russia's fragile transport system, so that the plan for general mobilization would lose its coherence and the various armies would be left stranded far away from their designated areas of deployment.

There was, then, no real choice between partial and general mobilization. Crucially, for the course of events over the next few days, Sazonov knew it to be so and had done since 28 July, when Yanushkevich had

---

ambassador submitted Vienna's dossier, Sazápáry to Sazonov, 15/28 July 1914, *IBZI* v, no. 162.

[184] Tel. Paléologue to Bienvenu-Martin (no. 296), 28 July 1914 (D 7.04 p.m., R 9.20 p.m.), *DDF* (3) XI, no. 208.

[185] Tel. Sazonov to Benckendorff (no. 1528), 15/28 July 1914, *IBZI* v, no. 164; copy submitted to Foreign Office: see *BD* XI, no. 210.

[186] B. W. Menning, 'The Mobilization Crises of 1912 and 1914 in Russian Perspective: Overlooked and Neglected Linkages', unpubl. MS, fo. 41.

explained to him the dangers inherent in a partial mobilization.[187] Indeed, the war minister himself had warned the Tsar in late 1912 of the potential pitfalls of partial measures against the Habsburg Empire. In the event of an Austro-Russian confrontation, Germany could remain neutral at the beginning of hostilities: 'This fact cannot be ignored because it is hardly beneficial for us to take the initiative and bare the sword against Germany.' On the other hand, it could not be assumed that 'the occasion of the mobilization of our army can force Austria to fulfil all the demands presented to her'.[188] For now, however, Tsar Nicholas II had asked for two separate mobilization orders to be prepared, one for partial mobilization against Austria-Hungary, and one for general mobilization, on the understanding that one or the other would be implemented depending on circumstances.[189]

And these evolved with speed. In mid-afternoon of 28 July, Spalajković, the Serbian minister, informed the Choristers' Bridge of Vienna's declaration of war.[190] Shortly afterwards, Sazonov saw Paléologue, who assured him of 'France's absolute willingness, if necessary, to fulfil her alliance obligations' towards Russia.[191] As will be seen, in doing so the French ambassador once again exceeded his instructions. But for Sazonov the assurances were welcome news. He was determined not to submit to Austro-Hungarian pressure again. Neither he nor the Tsar had yet decided between partial or general mobilization. Germany, after all, except for a few indirect hints at the dangers entailed in Russian mobilization, was still passive. But all the firm language so far, all entreaties, all conciliatory signals, had neither coaxed nor deterred Austria-Hungary. If anything, matters took on a more ominous aspect when intelligence arrived to the effect that the Habsburg mobilization appeared to be on a larger scale than previously thought. The Danube flotilla was steaming south towards Belgrade, reserve officers had been called up in larger numbers and on 28 July Shebeko reported that eight army corps were being mobilized, half the Austro-Hungarian army.[192] The ambassador's figures were somewhat inflated. But what alarmed the Russian general staff officers was

[187] See Schilling, 'Introduction', in his *How the War Began*, 16–17.
[188] Sukhomlinov to Nicholas II, 12/25 Nov. 1912, RGVIA, f. 200, op. 1, d. 7410, l. 84. I am grateful to Bruce Menning for providing me with a copy of this document.
[189] Dobrorolski to Yanushkevich (no. 3645/668), 13/26 July 1914, *IBZI* v, no. 112 and n. 1.
[190] Spalajković aide mémoire, 15/28 July 1914, *IBZI* v, no. 162.
[191] Schilling daily journal, 15/28 July 1914, *IBZI* v, no. 172.
[192] Menning, 'Mobilization Crises', fos. 43–4, on which the following is based; see also Laporte [French consul-general at Prague] to Bienvenu-Martin (no. 21), 27 July 1914, *DDF* (3) XI, no. 176.

the fact that their own estimates suggested that five to six corps would be a sufficient force to subdue Serbia, even if supported by neighbouring Montenegro. The far larger number reported by Shebeko, concluded staff officers at St Petersburg, could mean only that Austria-Hungary's army was undergoing covert mobilization, and very likely in Galicia, too. In that case the Habsburg forces approaching wartime strength would not be eight but eleven corps, sufficient to ward off a Russian military move against Galicia.

Later that evening, at 6 p.m., the Tsar received Sazonov at Peterhof for a report on the international crisis. The foreign minister, noted the monarch in his diary, 'informed me that today at noon [Belgrade time] Austria declared war on Serbia'.[193] That was all. No wonder Sukhomlinov had earlier found the Tsar strangely detached from the situation in the Balkans. It seems clear, however, that in principle a preliminary decision for general mobilization was taken that evening. Partial mobilization had not yet been discarded, however, and the Tsar signed orders for both variants on the following morning, Wednesday, 29 July.[194] It would be tempting to see in this a sign of confusion at St Petersburg, especially given the incompetence Yanushkevich had displayed on 25 July. But, for now, having both options available purchased the Russian government an additional twenty-four hours, if not two full days, during which to gather further intelligence to complete the picture of the military postures adopted by the two Germanic Powers. This, however, required a degree of diplomatic deception on Sazonov's part – he informed Szápáry the following day of 'mobilization on a considerable scale' as a 'precautionary measure'.[195] At the same time Yanushkevich alerted the commanders of all military districts that mobilization would be ordered on 30 July.[196]

On his return to the Choristers' Bridge later that evening, Sazonov informed the Russian missions at Berlin, Vienna, London, Paris and Rome that partial mobilization would commence on 29 July, confined to the districts of Odessa, Kiev, Moscow and Kazan. Bronevski, the chargé d'affaires at Berlin, was to impress upon the Wilhelmstrasse that Russia harboured no aggressive designs against Germany and that the measures were a response to Austria-Hungary's escalation of the crisis.[197] To

---

[193] Nicholas II diary, 15/28 July 1914, 'Nikolai Romanov v pervykh dynakh voyny', *KA* LXIV (1934), 136 [134–8].
[194] Schilling daily journal, 16/29 July 1914, *IBZI* v, no. 224.
[195] Tel. Szápáry to Berchtold (no. 180), 29 July 1914 (D 11 p.m., R 11 a.m.), *ÖUA* VIII, no. 11003.
[196] Tel. Yanushkevich to commanders of military districts, 15/28 July 1914, *IBZI* v, no. 210.
[197] Tels. Sazonov to Bronevski (no. 1539) and to Shebeko, Izvolsky, Benckendorff and Krupenski (no. 1540), 15/28 July 1914, *IBZI* v, nos. 168–9.

Benckendorff, he wired separate instructions. In consequence of Vienna's declaration of war, any further direct talks with the Austro-Hungarian ambassador at St Petersburg were no longer appropriate. Indeed, from Sazonov's perspective, such exchanges might merely provide cover while Habsburg forces crushed Serbia. Under the altered circumstances, Benckendorff was told, it was now imperative that Britain initiated another mediation attempt on the basis that Vienna suspended any military operations against Serbia.[198]

Sazonov's instructions for the ambassador in London were not incompatible with the 'Halt in Belgrade' plan which the Kaiser and Bethmann Hollweg had developed that same afternoon. Its implementation, of course, would depend on Tschirschky and the Ballhausplatz. But there was still scope for a diplomatic solution. The wiggle room necessary for the diplomats to arrange a mutually acceptable settlement, however, had shrunk further, for at some stage within the next twenty-four to forty-eight hours the Tsar's ministers would have to decide whether to proceed with partial mobilization or to implement the decree for a general mobilization.

Paléologue makes a suggestion

It is impossible to quantify the importance of Paléologue's assurances of absolute French loyalty to the alliance with Russia. But it certainly did nothing to restrain Sazonov in his more anti-Austrian mood during the latter part of 28 July. Moreover, as seen earlier, Paléologue's instructions had been more circumspect and nuanced; and, in associating his government with whatever course of action St Petersburg now decided upon, he had interpreted his instructions somewhat liberally. Naturally, Poincaré's and Viviani's continued absence from Paris gave him greater latitude to pursue his own personal diplomacy at St Petersburg, but he could always claim merely to be acting in the spirit of the president's gushing speech on the final day of his state visit to Russia.

Certainly, Paléologue, like Poincaré, believed in the efficacy of deterrence. After Sazonov's second interview with Pourtalès, the paths of the two ambassadors crossed at the Choristers' Bridge, and Paléologue raised the Austro-Serbian crisis with the Count. 'Allow me to speak freely, my dear colleague', he said to Pourtalès:

> The hour is grave enough and I think that we value each other
> enough to explain ourselves with complete frankness. If in a day, in

---

[198] Tel. Sazonov to Benckendorff (no. 1538), 15/28 July 1914, *IBZI* v, no. 163.

two days at the most, the Austro-Serbian conflict has not been calmed, that will be war, the general war, a catastrophe such as the world cannot perhaps today comprehend. Now, that calamity may still be warded off since the Russian government is pacific, since the British government is pacific, and since your government itself says it is pacific.

Pourtalès concurred. Germany, however, could not and would not abandon her ally. For the past forty-three years, Germany had helped to preserve peace, and now Paléologue was accusing her of wishing to unleash war? 'History will show that we [Germany] [had] the good right on our side and that our conscience had nothing for which to reproach itself.' Under no circumstances could Berlin abandon the Habsburg Empire. And with that – and 'a fierce expression' – the ambassador left.[199]

Paléologue was no stranger to poetic or other licence, and some caution is no doubt called for here. But if he irritated his German colleague, he also did little to calm Sazonov, whom he found 'pale and agitated' when they met in the early afternoon. The interviews with Szápáry and Pourtalès had left a very bad impression on him. Austria-Hungary refused to enter into talks with him – a slight exaggeration of what the Habsburg ambassador had said – and Germany had encouraged her surreptitiously. Pourtalès had repeated that Germany could not abandon her ally: 'But did I demand of her to abandon [Austria-Hungary]? I simply demanded that she aided me to resolve the crisis through peaceful means. As for the rest, Pourtalès could not control himself. He could not find the right words; he stuttered; he gave the impression of being frightened. Why the fright?' Paléologue suggested that the German ambassador was overcome by a growing sense of his own responsibility. After all it was impossible now to make France renounce the Russian alliance, he assured Sazonov. His government was headless while Poincaré and Viviani were still at sea. His responsibility was thus enormous, but would Sazonov engage to agree to whatever Britain and France proposed to preserve peace? After a brief moment's hesitation, the foreign minister replied: 'Ah well. Yes, I accept.'[200]

Paléologue may well have exaggerated Sazonov's reluctance, but the Russian foreign minister, as seen earlier, had concluded that another British mediation effort now offered the best, possibly the only, way

---

[199] Paléologue diary, 28 July 1914, in his *La Russie des Tsars pendant la Grande Guerre* (3 vols., Paris, 1921) I, 31–2.

[200] Paléologue diary, 28 July 1914, *ibid.*, 33–4; see also tel. Paléologue to Bienvenu-Martin (no. 293, urgent), 28 July 1914 (D 1.22 p.m., R 2.30 p.m.), *DDF* (3) XI, no. 192.

forward. That was also the view of the acting French foreign minister, who received Baron Schoen in the afternoon of that day. Germany did not seem to be inclined to restrain Vienna at the moment, Bienvenu-Martin said: 'But a moderate proceeding on the part of Austria was the necessary precondition for any successful negotiation.' The best means for avoiding a general war was to avoid a local conflict. That should be the aim of any mediation; and to that end he suggested that Vienna should receive 'the assurance of guaranties for Serbia's atonement and for her future good behaviour'.[201] This was all very well as an aspiration, but it scarcely mapped a diplomatic route out of the current crisis.

On board the warship *France*, now somewhere in the Danish Straits, Poincaré and Viviani were much impressed by the latest radiograms received during the brief stopover in Copenhagen. Jules Cambon's conversations with officials at the Wilhelmstrasse allowed for only one conclusion, 'that Germany does not seek to discourage Austria'.[202] Under the circumstances, even the hitherto hesitant Viviani insisted on reciprocity: 'Only if Germany made her advice heard at Vienna, might France possibly be able to make a move at St Petersburg to reassure the imperial government with regard to the possible repercussions of the conflict, towards which Russia, far less than other Powers, could not remain indifferent.' Paris would therefore associate itself with Grey's proposal for mediation by the four Powers least interested in the Balkan quarrel. The British Foreign Secretary's idea of intervening in the Austro-Serbian dispute and at St Petersburg, Viviani concluded, offered Berlin now an opportunity, without injury to its dignity, to step back from its previous attempts to isolate the Serbian crisis.[203]

The Foreign Office wants to see practical action

Everything, then, pointed to Britain. Already earlier, at around 3 p.m., after his interviews with Pourtalès and Szápáry, Sazonov had left the British ambassador in no doubt as to what was expected of London. The news received, he explained to Buchanan, was 'disquieting' and he was pessimistic about the situation. Austria-Hungary's two pledges as to Serbia's

---

[201] Schoen to Bethmann Hollweg, 28 July 1914 (R 29 July, p.m.), *DD* II, no. 250; tel. Bienvenu-Martin to J. Cambon (no. 355), 28 July 1914 (D 4.50 p.m.), *DDF* (3) XI, no. 198.

[202] Poincaré notes journalières, 28 July 1914, BN, Bnfr 16027, fo. 122 v.

[203] Tel. Viviani to Bienvenu-Martin (no. 16), 28 July 1914 (D 1.40 p.m.), *DDF* (3) XI, no. 190; see also note P. Cambon, 28 July 1914, *BD* XI, no. 211.

independence and integrity did not satisfy the Russian government any longer. As soon as Habsburg troops crossed the Serbian frontier, Russia would mobilize against Austria-Hungary. The Russian government had no domestic reasons for fearing external conflict. On Buchanan's question as to what steps St Petersburg would be willing to take to prevent any further escalation, Sazonov replied 'that [the] only way to avert war was for His Majesty's Government to let it be clearly known that they would join France and Russia'. The unity of these three Powers would have the necessary deterrent effect. According to Paléologue, Buchanan urged Sazonov to refrain from any measures that were liable to provoke Germany into making military preparations. In a similar vein, the British ambassador impressed upon Pourtalès that it was Germany's turn to rein in Vienna: 'I warned [Pourtalès] that Russia was thoroughly in earnest, and that nothing would avert [a] general war if Austria attacked Servia.'[204]

Buchanan had made these observations to Pourtalès during a small luncheon party at the British embassy. He sought to open his German colleague's eyes to the growing dangers of the situation. It was for Germany now to apply the brakes on Austria-Hungary. In accepting Grey's proposal for a conference *à quatre*, Russia had signalled her pacific intentions, whereas Austria-Hungary had already mobilized. But Pourtalès was not prepared to exceed his instructions. The conflict was solely a matter for Austria-Hungary and Serbia, and Russia 'had to look on quietly and maintain the passive role of a disinterested spectator'. Pourtalès, Buchanan later reflected, was 'personally anxious to avert war ... But his attitude was not calculated to smooth over matters'.[205]

In pushing Grey's conference proposal, Buchanan acted in line with his instructions. For his part, the Foreign Secretary kept other options in view. Under the impression of the news of the previous day, in the early afternoon of 28 July he supported direct exchanges between the Russian and Austro-Hungarian governments as a form of talks about talks. He himself was ready to put forward 'any practical proposal that would facilitate this'. But it was for Sazonov to make progress now. Once the Austro-Russian talks had yielded practical results, the foreign representatives at Belgrade could collectively work on the Serbian government.[206] This, of course, was before news arrived that Sazonov now considered direct talks with Szápáry meaningless.

[204] Tel. Buchanan to Grey (no. 177), 28 July 1914 (D 8.45 p.m., R 1 a.m.), *BD* XI, no. 247; see also Paléologue diary, 28 July 1914, in his *La Russie des Tsars* I, 30.
[205] Sir G. Buchanan, *My Mission to Russia and Other Diplomatic Memories* (2 vols., London, 1923) I, 198–9.
[206] Tel. Grey to Buchanan (no. 388), 28 July 1914 (D 1.25 p.m.), *BD* XI, no. 203.

There was, however, another problem, which became apparent when Benckendorff presented a summary of Sazonov's telegram on his interview with the Austro-Hungarian ambassador on the previous afternoon, when direct exchanges still appeared feasible. Sazonov's opening move in the talks, commented Nicolson, had been clumsy: 'He tells the Austrian Ambassador in fact that part of what Servia has promised she is unable to do, and he asks that Austria should discuss a revision of some points in the Austrian note.' Grey, too, was irritated with his Russian colleague: 'On the very day when I was urging upon the German Government that the Servian note had conceded nearly all that Austria asked … M. Sazonof was telling the Austrian Ambassador that the Servian note was worth much less than its face value!!'[207] Benckendorff subsequently sought to correct the somewhat infelicitous translation of Sazonov's telegram, but the damage had been done. Although Grey accepted the ambassador's explanations, it was clear that the option of direct Austro-Russian talks was fraught with difficulties.

There was an alternative to the exchanges at St Petersburg, however, and Grey was determined not to foreclose on it. In the early afternoon, a telegram from Goschen at Berlin had arrived. The ambassador had talked over recent events with his French and Italian colleagues, Jules Cambon and Ricardo Bollati, and the three diplomats agreed that Berlin's objection to the conference proposal was to its form rather than to its object. Jagow, in fact, had explained to all of them that he wished to cooperate with them in the interest of general peace. Would it not make practical sense, Goschen wondered, to repackage the proposal omitting the word conference or even to invite the state secretary to suggest the lines on which he might be able to cooperate with London? There was 'much sound sense' in this idea, observed Crowe. At the very least, it would force Berlin to explain its position more clearly than it had done so far. 'I am a little tired of these protestations and should like to see some practical action', Nicolson minuted. If direct talks were to take place at St Petersburg, then British diplomacy ought not to confuse matters by making a fresh proposal.[208]

By this time, the telegram to Buchanan encouraging direct Austro-Russian talks in the Russian capital had already been despatched. But Grey was anxious not to close down the option of mediation by the quartet, in whatever form this might prove possible. To that end he informed Goschen that, for now, Sazonov's discussions with the

[207] Mins. Nicolson and Grey, 28 July 1914, on note Benckendorff, 15/28 July 1914, BD XI, no. 207.

[208] Tel. Goschen to Grey (no. 97), 28 July 1914, and mins. Crowe and Nicolson, 28 July 1914 (D 2.03 p.m., R 2.45 p.m.), BD XI, no. 215.

Austro-Hungarian ambassador were 'the most preferable method of all', and for as long as there was a realistic prospect of them continuing he would suspend all other suggestions. But this did not mean that the quartet idea was dead in the water. The construction Goschen had put on the Foreign Secretary's original idea was entirely correct, Grey wired: 'It would not be an arbitration, but a private and informal discussion to ascertain what suggestion could be made for a settlement.' In this manner, as long as the Romanov and Habsburg governments were kept talking, the quartet could strike the necessary accompanying chords. It was not the traditional form of the Great Power concert, but it was a variation on that theme. This could work only if there was an Austro-Russian theme, of course. But for now Grey drew some comfort from Lichnowsky's earlier assurances that the German government had taken action at Vienna.[209] A follow-up telegram to Goschen made clear that the original mediation scheme had not yet been discarded. As Berlin had accepted international mediation in principle, Grey was ready to propose to Jagow that he should suggest the lines 'on which the principle may be applied, but I will keep the idea in reserve till we see how the conversations between Austria and Russia progress'.[210]

The chances of success of these conversations were narrowly balanced. It was, perhaps, also with this in mind that Grey impressed upon Mensdorff that the naval alert in Britain was 'an illustration of the anxiety under which the whole of Europe was placed by Austria's action'. Given the circumstances of the case, this was as much direct pressure as he thought Britain could bring to bear on Austria-Hungary. If it was not much, it was also a reflection of the widely held assumption at the Foreign Office that the road to Vienna ran through Berlin. Hence Grey's repeated emphasis on the 'favourable construction' that ought to be placed upon the lengths to which Belgrade had gone in its reply to the Austro-Hungarian démarche.[211]

There was another glint of sunlight breaking through the darkening horizon that afternoon. The Serbian army, reported Crackanthorpe from Niš, had withdrawn into the interior of the country and was concentrated in the Morava valley, the strategically important north–south axis of Serbia. No attempt would be made to engage Austro-Hungarian forces

---

[209] Tel. Grey to Goschen (no. 218), 28 July 1914 (D 4 p.m.), *BD* XI, no. 218; for Lichnowsky's assurances see Lichnowsky to Grey, 28 July [1914], *BD* XI, no. 236.
[210] Tel. Grey to Goschen (no. 220), 28 July 1914 (D 6.15 p.m.), *BD* XI, no. 223. The view that Grey abandoned the conference proposal, as advanced by C. Ponting, *Thirteen Days: The Road to the First World War* (London, 2002), 184, is difficult to sustain.
[211] Grey to Bertie (no. 508), 28 July 1914, *BD* XI, no. 238.

until they invaded.[212] That should avoid any clash between the two armies, and so provide a window for diplomatic action. It also was compatible with the Kaiser's notion of 'Halt in Belgrade', though that proposal had yet to wend its way to Vienna.

At Rome, too, there was movement. San Giuliano left the cooler climes of the spa town of Fiuggi and returned to the frenzied atmosphere of the capital. Here, Grey's conference proposal had made a 'grand impression', the French ambassador, the long-serving Camille Barrère reported. The Italian foreign minister, moreover, did not hold back in his criticism of the Austro-Hungarian démarche. Belgrade's response, he noted, had been politic and had caused great embarrassment to Austria-Hungary. He left Barrère in no doubt that Italian policy would be dependent on Britain: 'if there is one Power that can push Germany towards pacific action, it is England'.[213]

Indeed, San Giuliano confided to Rodd, the British ambassador, Vienna's démarche could only be regarded as either 'a deliberate provocation to war or else as *le triomphe de l'imbécilité*'.[214] He was anxious to associate himself with any initiative Grey might propose. But there was more bustle than purpose in San Giuliano's moves on 28 July. Serbia's representative at Rome, he informed Rodd, had indicated that Belgrade might yet accept the Austro-Hungarian demands in their entirety, provided that the modalities of a Habsburg police presence on Serbian soil could be settled. It was important, San Giuliano emphasized, that 'discussion should begin at once'. He also launched his own peace initiative, though in practice it was little more than Grey's ambassadorial conference scheme at London, dressed up in the Italian tricolours and on the basis that Serbia ought to concede all of Austria-Hungary's demands and the latter suspend hostilities while the diplomats got to work. Italy's ability to affect the course of events decisively was always limited, and San Giuliano's initiative smacked more of a desire not to offend either Britain or Italy's own two northern allies – Italian ambassadors were

---

[212] Tel. Crackanthorpe to Grey (no no.), 28 July 1914 (D 3.50 p.m., R 4.15 p.m.), *BD* XI, no. 221.

[213] Quotes from tels. Barrère to Bienvenu-Martin (nos. 207 and 210), 27 July 1914 (D 8.35 p.m., R 10.50 p.m., D 11.15 p.m., R 3.40 a.m.), *DDF* (3) XI, nos. 153 and 159. Of course, Rome needed to have good relations with Britain, see R. J. B. Bosworth, 'Britain and Italy's Acquisition of the Dodecanese, 1912–1915', *HJ* XIII, 4 (1970), 683–705.

[214] Rodd diary, 27 July 1914, as quoted in Sir J. R. Rodd, *Social and Diplomatic Memories, 1884–1919* (3 vols., London, 1922–5) III, 204; also R. J. B. Bosworth, *Italy, the Least of the Great Powers: Italian Foreign Policy before the First World War* (Cambridge, 1979), 391.

instructed to accept all proposals on which the British and German governments agreed.[215]

Grey himself may well have understood the latter consideration. At any rate, for as long as Vienna refused to admit international mediation in the Austro-Serbian quarrel, an ambassadorial conference alone could achieve little now.[216] Involving Rome, moreover, risked complicating matters, though its evident desire to preserve peace and to cooperate with Britain to that end might prove useful at a later stage. But for now, the moves of the other Powers would determine whether diplomacy might yet succeed.

There was nevertheless a mood of apprehension in London. The chop and change in Sazonov's policy in recent days had caused some dismay at the Foreign Office, Nicolson, the Permanent Under-secretary, confided to Buchanan. Given the latest twist at St Petersburg, direct talks appeared the best method of averting war at the moment: 'The great hope that we have ... is that Austria will abstain from actually entering Servian territory ... Of course in that case all hope of a peaceful solution will vanish.' Localizing the conflict meant that the Powers would 'hold the ring while Austria quietly strangles Servia'. As for Germany, she had not 'played a very straight game', he observed, though he explicitly excepted Lichnowsky from this criticism. But his chief concern was Russia. The current crisis, Nicolson feared, would be seen at St Petersburg 'as a test of our friendship'. This, of course, had been the constant refrain of Nicolson's advice for some time. Anglo-Russian relations in Asia, he had observed at a time when the Austro-Serbian quarrel was still largely quiescent, were 'approaching a point when we shall have to make up our minds as to whether we should become really intimate and permanent friends, or else diverge into another path'.[217]

---

[215] Tel. Rodd to Grey (no. 127), 28 July 1914 (D 7.30 p.m., R 9.45 p.m.), *BD* xi, no. 231; the reheated conference proposal is in tel. San Giuliano to Imperiali, Avarna, Bollati, Carlotti and Ruspoli (no. 777), 28 July 1914 (D 5 a.m.), *DDI* (4) xii, no. 621. For a critique of San Giuliano's initiative, see Albertini, *Origins* ii, 417–24, but this is based on an exaggerated notion of Italy's influence.

[216] Tel. Grey to Rodd (no. 217), 29 July 1914 (D 12.45 a.m.), *BD* xi, no. 246. It was symptomatic of Italy's low standing that ambassador Imperiali was not seen by Grey but by Nicolson and Tyrrell, see tels. Imperiali to San Giuliano (nos. 859/218 and 6798/223), 28 July 1914 (D 8.10 a.m., R 12.50 p.m., D 9.51 p.m., R 4.29 a.m.), *DDI* (4) xii, nos. 625 and 655.

[217] Quotes from Nicolson to Buchanan (private), 28 and 14 July 1914, Nicolson MSS, TNA (PRO), FO 800/375; the letter from mid-July was in connection with Sazonov's scheme for Britain, Russia and Japan to guarantee the status quo in Asia, Buchanan to Nicolson (private), 9 July 1914, *ibid.*; for the background see Neilson, *Britain and the Last Tsar*, 338.

Even by his own lugubrious standards, Nicolson was profoundly pessimistic. He appeared to have no hope, reported ambassador Imperiali, that 'the terrible crisis could be overcome'.[218] Among Cabinet ministers, optimists and pessimists were evenly balanced. 'Things look a little less threatening', Haldane noted: 'I believe there is no Power that really wants war. The next twenty-four hours will decide. It is to the good that no act of violence has occurred and the Governments have taken time to reflect.'[219] Herbert Samuel, by contrast, considered that the 'situation looks no better'. Vienna's declaration of war – known in London in the early evening – had been

> clearly inevitable. There is a strange silence from Russia, which may mean that she is carrying out the preliminaries to the mobilization without alarming the Germans prematurely. The great difficulty for Russia arises from the vast distance over which her armies have to be brought. The Germans can mobilize much more quickly and may be able to throw all her [sic] weight upon France before Russia is ready to move effectively. The Russians, of course, are fully alive to this and may possibly be refraining from showing their hand as long as possible.[220]

At the end of another gruelling day at the Foreign Office, Crowe reflected that the 'situation abroad is grave'. Little had changed for the better over the past twenty-four hours. 'Austria at the very moment of using soft words at St Petersburg, has declared war on Servia. Unless the Russians now decide to run away – which is always possible – we shall have the general war upon us very soon.' This was no idle speculation. The danger of further escalation was appreciated by the British government, as Crowe knew. Wilson, the chief of staff, had called upon him:

> He had been requested by the Admiralty to give orders that any foreign airship showing itself was to be fired at. He had refused to give such orders without superior authority and accordingly asked the Prime Minister, who is also Secretary of State for War.

---

[218] Tel. Imperiali to San Giuliano (no.859/218), 28 July 1914 (D 8.10 a.m., R 12.50 a.m.), *DDI* (4) XII, no. 625; H. Nicolson, *Sir Arthur Nicolson, Bart., First Lord Carnock: A Study in the Old Diplomacy* (London, 1930), 414–16.

[219] Haldane to Elizabeth Haldane, 28 July 1914, Haldane MSS, NLS, MS 5991; J. A. Spender and C. Asquith, *Life of Herbert Henry Asquith, Lord Oxford and Asquith* (2 vols., London, 1932) II, 80–1.

[220] Samuel to Beatrice Samuel, 28 July 1914, Samuel MSS, PAL, SAM/A/157/689t.

Asquith said: 'Ask Crowe at the Foreign Office. If he says it's all right, you can act!'

I declined to be saddled with this responsibility, but went to Grey who agreed to the order being given.[221]

The episode underlined the extent to which the stakes had been raised in the past three days. Since Baron Giesl's dramatic departure from Belgrade the European Powers had had to confront the growing likelihood of another conflict in the Balkans, itself now a reality following the Austro-Hungarian declaration of war. Until then, it should still have been possible to isolate the Austro-Serbian dispute – either through direct talks between Sazonov and Szápáry at St Petersburg or by adopting Grey's conference proposal – and so allow for the diplomats to get to work. Vienna's next move, however, was to narrow the path towards a peaceful solution yet further.

[221] Crowe to Clema Crowe, 28 July 1914, Crowe MSS, Bodl., Ms.Eng.d.2903.

7 ESCALATION: 29 JULY TO 4 AUGUST

> One afternoon I watched him as he stood
> In the twilight of his wood.
> Among the firs he'd planted, forty years away,
> Tall, and quite still, and almost blind,
> World patience in his face, stood Edward Grey;
> Not listening,
> For it was at the end of summer, when no birds sing:
> Only the bough's faint dirge accompanied his mind
> Absorbed in some Wordsworthian slow self-communing.
>
> SIEGFRIED SASSOON[1]

In the course of 29 July, the other Powers received final confirm-ation of Austria-Hungary's declaration of war on Serbia. With consider-able delay Vienna thus confronted the chancelleries of Europe with the fait accompli that Berchtold had hoped to create in the immediate aftermath of the Sarajevo assassination and that the Wilhelmstrasse had urged upon the Monarchy since 5/6 July. The crisis now reached its decisive phase. Localization and a Habsburg triumph over Serbia, the objective of German diplomacy, could be achieved now only if the other Powers were prepared to bow to Berlin's pressure and Austria-Hungary's intransigence. To avert further escalation, on the other hand, required of the German leadership a softening of its support for Vienna, or for the latter to suspend military operations to allow for a last-minute diplo-matic settlement. How serious the situation had become, and how close to the brink of war Europe had moved, was underlined when, in the afternoon of the previous day, the Netherlands became the first country not directly involved in the Balkan squabble to mobilize its armed forces.[2]

---

[1] S. Sassoon, 'A Fallodon Memory', in Sassoon, *Selected Poems* (London, 1968), 77.
[2] Chilton to Grey (no. 14), 28 July 1914 (D 10.40 a.m., R 2.15 p.m.), *BD* XI, no. 213. For the Dutch mobilization see minutes of ministerial council, 27 July 1914, *BBBP* (3) IV, no. 6; also N. Bosboom, *In moeilijke omstandigheden, Augustus 1914 – Mei 1917*

As during the previous days and weeks, much depended on Vienna's next moves, but even more important were the decisions taken at St Petersburg and Berlin. For the Ballhausplatz, two pressing issues had to be tackled. For weeks Germany had urged Vienna to commence the military campaign against Serbia at the earliest possible moment in order to create facts on the ground. For weeks Vienna had tarried. Now it was ready to strike; and now Berlin sprang its 'Halt in Belgrade' surprise on the Ballhausplatz. Both were interlinked; both were compatible with each other, but either had the potential to sabotage the other.

Berchtold plays Shylock in his own image

The scope for diplomatic action had narrowed, however. In the early hours of 29 July, Austro-Hungarian river gunboats and artillery batteries on the opposite bank of the Danube let loose on the Kalemegdan, the ancient, Ottoman-built fortress that towered over the Serbian capital. Already earlier in the night, Serbian pioneers had blown up the bridge across the Sava river that carried the railway from Belgrade to Semlin and on to Budapest. Contrary to earlier decisions, the Serbian government had resolved to put up some form of resistance, albeit only briefly. Military honour demanded that much, even if the foreign representatives counselled against such a step. There was 'considerable panic' in the capital, as Crackanthorpe wired to London, and a portion of the British legation building had been damaged during the bombardment.[3] The outbreak of hostilities signalled an escalation of the crisis, though given the Austro-Hungarian pronouncements of the past two days it came as no surprise. More importantly, the shelling of the Serbian capital could still be reconciled with the Kaiser's 'Halt in Belgrade' scheme.

The plan itself had obvious practical advantages. Even its name should have resonated with Habsburg sentiments. Ever since Prince Eugene of Savoy had conquered the Turkish citadel for the Emperor in 1717,

---

(Gorinchem, 1933), 1–15; and W. Klinkert, 'De Nederlandse Mobilisatie van 1914', in W. Klinkert, J. W. M. Schulten and L. de Vos (eds.), *Mobilisatie van Nederland en België 1870 – 1914 – 1939* (Amsterdam, 1991), 24–33. The Dutch army was kept at full strength for much of the war: Johnstone to Grey (no. 33), 28 Jan. 1915, TNA (PRO), FO 371/2418/11638.

[3] Tel. Crackanthorpe to Grey (unnumbered), n.d. (R 30 July, 2.20 a.m.), *BD* XI, no. 291; tel. Strandtmann to Sazonov (no. 251), 16/29 July 1914, *IBZI* V, no. 260; F. Conrad von Hötzendorf, *Aus meiner Dienstzeit* (5 vols., Vienna, 1921–5) IV, 142; for an eyewitness account see D. A. Lončarević, *Jugoslaviens Entstehung* (Zürich, 1929), 620–3.

Belgrade had occupied a prominent place in the history of the Monarchy, and the name of Belgrade had a patriotic ring to it. Its occupation would have satisfied Austro-Hungarian military honour and restored Habsburg prestige in the region. With Belgrade as a 'forfeit' in its hands the Monarchy could have exercised strong pressure on Serbia in the future as well as on Russia. Above all it might have furnished a basis on which to negotiate with St Petersburg at a time when the room left to diplomacy could be measured in hours at the most already.

Tschirschky duly called on the Ballhausplatz to submit Berlin's plan. Berchtold, he reported briefly, was willing to reiterate his assurances with regard to Serbia's territorial integrity (no reference was made to her independence). As for the planned military campaign, the foreign minister was unable to give an immediate reply.[4] The Ballhausplatz was stalling, as it had done so often during the July crisis. No doubt, Berchtold had been caught by surprise by Berlin's initiative. It was, in fact, doubly unwelcome. Politically, it threatened to constrain Austria-Hungary at the very moment that pressure on Serbia had reached its peak. But there was another complication – a move against the Serbian capital did not feature in Conrad's plan of campaign! He did not envisage an invasion from the north, across the rivers Sava and Danube to take Belgrade and then to move down the Morava valley, as all other invaders of Serbia had done throughout the ages. Instead, he planned to invade from the west, cutting across all the natural lines of advance – and leaving Belgrade to one side – in order to annihilate the Serb army in the interior of the country. His aim was to devastate Serbia's military capabilities, not to score diplomatic points by occupying her capital. 'Halt in Belgrade', so seductively neat and elegant an answer to the complicated international situation, was thus never a practicable solution.

Switching the military campaign to focus on the capital now, moreover, was well-nigh impossible given that mobilization had already commenced, and the intricate and carefully integrated transport, concentration and deployment schedules could not easily be unpicked again. The Habsburg leadership now had to confront the strategic dilemma that had been inherent in its policy, but that had been masked by the Monarchy's slow decision-making process. Militarily, there were two possible outcomes, as Conrad pointed out to Berchtold. Either Serbia caved in and withdrew her army, in which case Habsburg forces would then occupy the neighbouring kingdom or portions of it. This meant 'no military success, no

---

[4] Tel. Tschirschky to Auswärtiges Amt (no. 133), 29 July 1914 (D 11.50 p.m., R 1.30 a.m.), *DD* ii, no. 388.

manifestation of power by the Monarchy and moreover ... the danger of later [Serbian] traps'. Alternatively, if the Serbs resisted the occupation of the capital, given the insufficient numbers of Austro-Hungarian troops deployed against it, there was the risk of military defeat. In both events, Austria-Hungary's military action would be compromised and both the morale of her armed forces and her military prestige in the Balkans would diminish, with obvious consequences for the Monarchy's strategic position towards the smaller states in the region and towards Russia.

There was, however, a political consideration that weighed with Berchtold, as the foreign minister later reflected. 'Halt in Belgrade' would have been no more than staging a 'military gala manoeuvre [*Schauman-över*]', which would have failed to make any impression on the Serbs. It would have been 'a licence for further uninterrupted agitation' against the Habsburg Empire.[5] Berchtold was not prepared to yield. He had spent the entire month of July steadily and purposefully preparing for the show-down with Serbia, and he was determined not to snatch a short-lived diplomatic triumph – the most ephemeral of all such achievements – now from the jaws of what he expected to be a crushing victory. That the latter could only be had at the price of a war with Russia, and so very likely a general war, had been implicitly accepted at Vienna ever since the minister-ial council meeting of 7 July. Now the Habsburg leadership had to confront that reality.

Leaving aside Berchtold's own ambitions and calculations, there is also the problem of the man who brought the 'Halt in Belgrade' proposal. As seen earlier, Tschirschky had continually pressed Vienna to act swiftly and decisively to crush Serbia. In the days immediately after the Archduke's murder, he had done so surreptitiously. But since 6 July he had openly urged the Ballhausplatz to adopt this course of action, so much so that at Vienna it was an open secret that the German ambassador was 'so identi-fied with [the] extreme anti-Servian and anti-Russian feeling prevalent in Vienna that he is not likely to plead [the] cause of peace with entire sincerity'.[6] Therein, of course, lay the problem, all the more so since Tschirschky was in possession of his own personal 'blank cheque'. Berch-told's report on his interview with Tschirschky is remarkable for its absence

[5] Berchtold, 'Halt in Belgrade', H. Hantsch, *Leopold Graf Berchtold. Grandseigneur und Staatsmann* (2 vols., Graz and Vienna, 1963) II, 632–3; Conrad, *Aus meiner Dienstzeit* IV, 300–4.

[6] Tel. de Bunsen to Grey (no. 135), 30 July 1914 (D 3.50 p.m., R 5 p.m.), *BD* XI, no. 307. The foreign heads of mission at Vienna were unanimous in their denunciations of 'the nefarious influence of M. de Tschirschky on the Ballplatz', tel. Dumaine to Viviani (no. 136), 1 Aug. 1914 (R 11 p.m.), *DDF* (3) XI, no. 539.

of any detail and for its late despatch, either of which is suggestive of his desire not to leave behind too much incriminating evidence. Berchtold's minute would indicate that the ambassador informed him fully of the proposal – now of course somewhat diluted. But having briefly sketched the object which the scheme of the temporary occupation of Belgrade had in view, Tschirschky then stressed that a conciliatory attitude towards St Petersburg would ensure that Russia incurred the odium of having unleashed a world war.[7]

As seen before, since the previous night Berchtold had found out through Szögyény that he was only to act on German mediation proposals if expressly encouraged by Tschirschky to do so. And this the German ambassador had clearly not done. For during the night of 29 July, Berchtold instructed the Habsburg ambassador at Berlin to bring to the attention of the Wilhelmstrasse information received from consular and military intelligence sources that suggested military preparations were in train in western Russia. If the Russian authorities did not suspend their mobilization measures, Austria-Hungary would be forced to order general mobilization. 'As a last attempt to avert a European war', Szögyény was to encourage Berlin to warn Sazonov of 'the serious consequences' if Russia did not disengage. As for the planned strike against Serbia, the ambassador was to explain that 'naturally we shall not be distracted from our warlike action'.[8]

Berchtold never touched on 'Halt in Belgrade' in his reply. The Bosnian annexation crisis of 1908–9 had set the precedent – it was for Germany to deter Russia from escalating a Balkan crisis. In July 1914 Berlin had issued two 'blank cheques', thus removing any restraint from Austro-Hungarian foreign policy. If 'Halt in Belgrade' was a belated attempt to revoke the earlier promise of unconditional support, Jagow's second 'blank cheque' to Tschirschky cancelled this out, and Berchtold was not going to accept any shackles at this late stage.

In a similar manner, Berchtold now also rejected Grey's mediation proposal, which had been transmitted via Berlin on the previous day. Belgrade's reply did not amount to a wholesale acceptance of Vienna's demands, he insisted. On the contrary, the reservations it contained diminished the material value of the assurances given, and he reiterated that the action against Serbia was not aimed at curtailing Russia's influence in the Balkans (that, of course, was precisely one object of Habsburg policy).

---

[7] Berchtold daily report, 29 July 1914, ÖUA VIII, no. 10939.
[8] Tel. Berchtold to Szögyény (no. 291), 29 July 1914 (D 30 July, 1 a.m.), ÖUA VIII, no. 10937; see also G. Kronenbitter, 'Krieg im Frieden': Die Führung der k.u.k. Armee und die Grossmachtpolitik Österreich-Ungarns, 1906–1914 (Munich, 2003), 504–5.

Since a state of war now existed with Serbia, Grey's mediation proposal had become irrelevant, Berchtold decided, but he would welcome any British attempts to moderate Russian policy to allow for the conflict, which had been forced on Austria-Hungary, to remain localized.[9] Clearly, Tschirschky had not made any encouraging noises.

While Berchtold had very much his own way with Berlin, Italy continued to be a nuisance. As seen earlier, the Ballhausplatz was reluctant to admit the validity of Italian claims to any form of compensation under article VII of the *Dreibund* alliance treaty, and sought to deflect German and Italian pressure with promises of talks at a later stage if Austria-Hungary ever found it necessary to occupy Serbian territory. If Tschirschky did not rein in Habsburg belligerence, and indeed encouraged it, he did however press Berchtold and the Ballhausplatz to make whatever concessions were necessary to keep the Italians on board. He was fully seized of the importance of maintaining the unity of the alliance between the three Powers, he wrote to Jagow. He had urged Berchtold and Hoyos, who currently wielded the most influence over the foreign minister, to be practical and to avoid unnecessary disputes about the correct legal interpretation of the contentious article: 'But the Austrians will always be Austrians. Arrogance coupled with insouciance cannot easily and swiftly be overcome! I know them well.' There could be no question of ceding all or portions of the Trentino, he observed. This would only be 'thinkable after a great victorious war, if Austria completely obtained *carte blanche* in the Balkans', the clear implication being that this was not a likely scenario. On his own initiative, Tschirschky had suggested that some offer of compensation should be made in the event that the Monarchy extended its territory in the Balkans.

Conrad was less recalcitrant than the diplomats, and suggested that Italy should occupy Montenegro. But Berchtold was not inclined to accommodate Rome. On 28 July, Tschirschky had breakfasted with Berchtold and Forgách, on which occasion he returned to the charge. At the end of the hour-and-a-half-long meeting, Berchtold signalled his willingness to conciliate Italy: 'I see the situation very clearly. I am Shylock who insists for the sake of appearances but who does not act on it.' There was the problem of the Italophobe Austro-Hungarian ambassador ar Rome, Tschirschky warned, who had described Italy's compensation claims as '*chantage*' (blackmail). But the principal objective

---

[9] Berchtold mémoire, 29 July 1914, *ÖUA* VIII, no. 10941; transmitted by Tschirschky in tel. to Auswärtiges Amt (no. 132), 29 July 1914 (D 30 July, 3 a.m., R 6.50 a.m.), *DD* II, no. 400.

now was 'that the matter is settled for us by papering over the rift between Vienna and Rome'.[10]

Tschirschky's optimism was ill-founded. Later that same day, he learnt that Mérey had been instructed to reiterate Vienna's non-annexationist pledge and offer 'an exchange of views' in the event of any temporary occupation of Serbian territory.[11] Clearly, Berchtold had read Shylock's part differently, and he was determined to keep his pound of flesh. Mérey's interview with San Giuliano on 29 July was even frostier than their previous encounters. Privately, the ambassador had pleaded for some time not to recognize Italy's claims to compensation. These were but the latest instalment of 'a manoeuvre composed of begging, sophistry and *chantage*, an attempt to extort something'. But he equally resented Germany's persistent pressing for concessions to Rome. It was not 'normal or natural that, following the opinion or pressure of a third state my views are thrown in the wastepaper basket and decisions are made in the opposite sense'. Accepting the legitimacy of Italy's claims would lead to further demands by Rome, and it was deplorable, Mérey observed, 'how Germany, under whose tutelage we placed ourselves completely, throws over our interests for her own purposes'.[12] Clearly, the ambassador never grasped that Vienna and Berlin might have a common interest in keeping Italy within the fold of the *Dreibund*.

It was clear that direct talks between San Giuliano and the Habsburg ambassador would lead to an open breach between the two allies, warned Flotow, the German ambassador at Rome. The Italian foreign minister was still holding out for a binding promise of compensation before committing himself to give diplomatic, let alone military, assistance to Austria-Hungary, and he pressed Berlin to act as mediator between the two lesser parties to the *Dreibund*. Time was pressing however, San Giuliano warned, as 'the moment drew nearer where they [the Italians] had to decide whether to move diplomatically for or against Austria'.[13]

The minister reiterated this warning to Mérey in yet another fraught meeting on the following day. Since the *Dreibund* was a defensive alliance, and as Vienna had not consulted with Rome prior to its ultimatum

---

[10] Tschirschky to Jagow (private), 26/28 July 1914, *DD* II, no. 326.
[11] Tel. Tschirschky to Auswärtiges Amt (no. 122), 28 July 1914 (D 9.10 p.m., R 12.02 a.m.), *DD* II, no. 328.
[12] Mérey to Berchtold (private), 29 July 1914, *ÖUA* VIII, no. 10991. Mérey also criticized Vienna for the delay in opening the campaign against Serbia, and urged Berchtold not to settle for a diplomatic compromise.
[13] Tel. Flotow to Auswärtiges Amt (no. 149), 29 July 1914 (D 6.20 p.m., R 8.15 a.m.), *DD* II, no. 363.

against Serbia, Italy was not obligated to support Austria-Hungary. Rome would, however, have to decide whether to join a European conflict or whether to remain neutral. San Giuliano hinted that he favoured entering such a war on the side of Italy's two allies, but much would depend on whether her interests in the Balkans were safeguarded.[14] This, of course, was little more than the mixture of begging and blackmail that so incensed Mérey. San Giuliano's policy was driven by an acute sense of Italy's weak position amongst the other Powers. This could be strengthened only if both her allies and their prospective opponents were left in some doubt as to her likely attitude. San Giuliano's real objective, however, was to be paid in substantial territorial concessions, actual or potential, in advance of making any decision.[15]

To some extent Italy's weakness, and San Giuliano's subsequent attempts to extract concessions from the Powers, contributed to the uncertainties of the July crisis as much as to tensions within the *Dreibund* combination. But the fact that Rome's likely attitude in a Balkan or, indeed, a European conflict had become acute at all, underlines further the lack of any coherent political strategy in Vienna.

Sazonov changes his mind

The shelling of Belgrade by Austro-Hungarian river monitors had escalated the crisis. But Vienna was no longer central to events now. More important were developments at St Petersburg and Berlin.

As seen earlier, in the morning of 29 July Tsar Nicholas signed two mobilization decrees, one ordering partial mobilization against Austria-Hungary and the other calling for general mobilization.[16] Beyond this, the Russian capital was the scene of frantic diplomatic activity throughout that day. At 9.30 a.m., Pourtalès telephoned the Choristers' Bridge to seek an interview with Sazonov. He had positive news to convey, but added: 'Nevertheless, not too much optimism.' Ninety minutes later, the two men met. Berlin sought to moderate the government in Vienna, the ambassador

---

[14] Tel. Mérey to Berchtold (no. 560), 30 July 1914 (D 31 July, 2.30 a.m., R 9 a.m.), ÖUA VIII, no. 11090; see also R. J. B. Bosworth's assessment of San Giuliano's policy, in his *Italy, the Least of the Great Powers: Italian Foreign Policy before the First World War* (Cambridge, 1979), 390–2.

[15] Italian military preparations, by contrast, were based on the assumption that the country would support its two allies, see Szeptycki [military attaché, Rome] to Conrad (no. 6/10), 29 July 1914, ÖUA VIII, no. 10992.

[16] V. A. Sukhomlinov, *Erinnerungen* (Berlin, 1924), 361–2.

explained; the Ballhausplatz had pledged itself to respect Serbia's territorial integrity, and Austro-Hungarian troops had not set foot on Serbian soil. Russia should not undermine Germany's efforts to rein in Austria-Hungary by taking precipitate military measures, which would trigger German mobilization. For his part, Sazonov gave assurances that the measure taken so far, the partial mobilization of the four western military districts, was not aimed at Germany but was dictated by the mobilization of the bulk of the Austro-Hungarian army. To resolve the crisis by peaceful means, the foreign minister now suggested a dual diplomatic track, Grey's Four-Power conference running in parallel with direct exchanges between Vienna and St Petersburg.[17]

Whether this was a serious proposition is not entirely clear. For one thing, already on the previous day Sazonov had tended towards viewing any further talks with Austria-Hungary as no longer practicable, an assessment confirmed by the short meeting with the Habsburg ambassador just before the interview with Pourtalès.[18] For another, he left Pourtalès under the impression that he attached little value to any further discussions with Szápáry. Even so, the German ambassador reported that his statements had made 'a visibly good impression' on Sazonov. There was, however, the problem of Russia's partial mobilization. Pourtalès expressed serious reservations on that score, which Sazonov sought to allay by explaining that mobilization did not mean war: 'if need be, [the] Russian army could be kept at the ready for weeks, without crossing [the] frontier. Russia wished, if at all possible, to avoid war.' Pourtalès then became more explicit. The danger in any military measures lay in the counter-measures the other side might take: 'The idea was obvious that the general staffs of Russia's potential enemies would not want to give up the card of the time-advantage over Russia in mobilization and would press for counter-measures.'[19] Although couched in suitably hypothetical language, this was a clear enough warning to Russia that mobilization would escalate the crisis and lead to German counter-measures.

After Pourtalès had left, Sazonov met with his senior advisers Neratov, Schilling and Trubetskoy to discuss the latest events. Did Berlin

[17] Quotes from Schilling journal, 16/29 July 1914, and tel. Sazonov to Bronevski (no. 1544), 16/29 July 1914, *IBZI* v, nos. 224 and 218. The communication was Bethmann Hollweg's telegram (no. 131), 28 July 1914 (D 9 p.m.), *DD* II, no. 315.
[18] See tel. Szápáry to Berchtold (no. 173), 29 July 1914 (D 10 a.m., R 4 p.m.), *ÖUA* VIII, no. 10999.
[19] Tel. Pourtalès to Auswärtiges Amt (no. 183, urgent), 29 July 1914 (D 1.58 p.m., R 2.52 p.m.), *DD* II, no. 343; see also F. Pourtalès, *Meine letzten Verhandlungen in St Petersburg Ende Juli 1914. Tagesaufzeichnungen und Dokumente* (Berlin, 1927), 38–9.

really wish to restrain Austria-Hungary, they wondered? Or was the ambassador's communication meant to lull Russia into a false sense of security to gain time for the Habsburg Empire in its campaign against Serbia? The general impression was that the route suggested by Pourtalès was not likely to produce anything useful. Even if Germany were sincere in her desire for peace, then Vienna's actions so far suggested that her influence over Habsburg decision-making was now much diminished.[20]

If Sazonov was in two minds about the most suitable way forward, Shebeko's report on his meeting with Berchtold the previous evening provided for greater clarity: Vienna would not continue direct exchanges at St Petersburg.[21] This cast further doubt on the efficacy of relying on Berlin to moderate its Habsburg ally, and it made the case for military measures to signal political resolve all the more compelling. Germany had repeatedly stated that a partial Russian mobilization would not be considered a threat at Berlin, Sazonov explained to Buchanan, and it 'was for this reason that it had been decided not to order the general mobilisation which [the] military authorities had strongly recommended'.

Direct exchanges with the Austro-Hungarian ambassador had run into the quicksand of Vienna's tardy obstructionism. Under these circumstances, only Grey's conference proposal offered any chance of a diplomatic settlement. Sazonov 'was ready to accept almost any arrangement that was approved by France and England'. The room for diplomatic action, however, had shrunk considerably, he warned: 'There was no time to lose, and war could only be averted if you [Grey] could succeed by conversations with [the] Ambassadors either collectively or individually in arriving at some formula which you could get Austria to accept.' Russia would not precipitate matters; the partial mobilization would take a week or more to complete; and Russian troops would not make incursions into the Galician salient or the Bukovina.[22] The Russian government, Sazonov informed Benckendorff in London, left it to Grey's initiative to propose whatever measures he deemed appropriate.[23]

[20] Schilling daily journal, 16/29 July 1914, *IBZI* v, no. 224.
[21] See tel. Shebeko to Sazonov (no. 105), 15/28 July 1914, *IBZI* v, no. 188; and tel. Berchtold to Szápáry (no. 191), 28 July 1914 (D 11.40 p.m.), *ÖUA* viii, no. 10915. For the arrival of Shebeko's telegram after the first meeting with Pourtalès see tel. Sazonov to Benckendorff (no. 1548), 16/29 July 1914, *IBZI* v, no. 219.
[22] Tel. Buchanan to Grey (no. 182), 29 July 1914 (D 8.40 p.m., R 11.30 p.m.), *BD* xi, no. 276.
[23] Tel. Sazonov to Benckendorff (no. 1548), 16/29 July 1914, *IBZI* v, no. 219.

Sazonov changes his mind again

Pourtalès's observations on general staff thinking were more pertinent than the ambassador had cause to know. In the evening of the previous day, the Saxon envoy at Berlin had noted that the mood in the German capital had become more pessimistic. The situation was judged to be 'more critical' now, not least because of persistent rumours of more extensive military preparations on Russia's part.[24]

Around the same time, the chief of the German general staff, General von Moltke, submitted a lengthy memorandum on the current international situation, copies of which reached the Kaiser and Bethmann Hollweg the following morning. A spirit of pessimism breathed through Moltke's memorandum; it was very much written in a minor key. It reflected the conflicting intelligence that had begun to trickle in over the past twenty-four hours about Russian troop movements – there had been thirteen different such reports on 27 July alone.[25] But above all it reflected a deep-seated cultural pessimism that had come to affect so many of Germany's political élite. Austria-Hungary, he opined, was defending the values of Europe against a state that had spread regicide at home and abroad. Vienna was resolved 'with a red-hot iron to cauterize a cancerous growth that constantly threatened to poison the body politic of Europe'. But Russia had now made it plain that she intended to interfere, and Austria-Hungary could not therefore accomplish her mission safely, for she could not 'surrender to the grace or ill-favour of a Russia prepared for war'.

Moltke argued that the whole crisis had been 'neatly staged' by Russia, aided and abetted by France. If Austria-Hungary clashed with Russia, Germany would have to support her ally. The Russians had begun full mobilization whilst pretending to mobilize only part of their forces; France, too, appeared to be readying her army. In this fashion, Moltke reasoned, the two Germanic Powers were to be forced to take the first steps towards an all-out war, thereby relinquishing the moral high ground to France and Russia. Moltke was resigned to this scenario becoming an awful reality: 'Thus things will and must develop unless . . . a miracle happens to avert at the last hour a war which will destroy for decades to come the culture of all of Europe.'

Germany did not desire 'this terrible war', but she had to support her ally, 'the deep-rooted feelings of loyalty [being] one of the most

---

[24] Biedermann to Vitzthum (no. 1906), 28 July 1914, *DGB*, no. 30.
[25] G. A. Tunstall, Jr, *Planning for War against Russia and Serbia: Austro-Hungarian and German Military Strategies, 1871–1914* (Boulder, CO, 1993), 148.

beautiful traits of the German character'. It was imperative now, however, to establish certainty as to whether the Franco-Russian group was prepared to risk war. And time was pressing. The military situation would deteriorate rapidly if Paris and St Petersburg were allowed to complete their preparations unhindered, and this would lead to 'fateful consequences for us'.[26]

There was a certain fatalistic streak in his memorandum, as there was in the character of the German chief of staff, who dabbled in the occult and spiritualism when not composing staff memoranda.[27] He had variously spoken of an inevitable war in the two years before 1914, but he had never made a clear, strategic case for a pre-emptive war. If anything, he had often changed his mind, and throughout the July crisis he did not offer any assessment of the military prospects of any war. He certainly did not advocate a continental war. In the middle of July, he hoped for a swift Austro-Hungarian strike against Serbia: 'Austria should beat the Serbs, then swiftly make peace and insist as the only condition on an Austro-Serbian alliance' just as Bismarck had done after the defeat of Austria in 1866.[28]

Moltke's memorandum, indeed, underlined his ambivalence towards war. If he was resigned to accept the war as inevitable at the end of July, he also feared that with the coming conflict 'will begin the mutual butchering of the European civilized states [*Kulturstaat*].' His hope for a miracle that might avert the catastrophe – a latter-day version of the 'Miracle of the House of Brandenburg' that had saved the Prussian state from extinction during the most perilous phase of the Seven Years' War – reinforced the profound pessimism in Moltke's thinking.

Without question, Moltke's memorandum constituted a significant intervention in the political decision-making process at Berlin. But it was scarcely 'a robust intervention' that hastened on war.[29] Moltke's

[26] Moltke to Bethmann Hollweg, 29 July 1914, *DD* II, no. 349; the classic study of 'cultural pessimism' remains F. Stern, *The Politics of Cultural Despair: A Study in the Rise of the Germanic Ideology* (Berkeley, CA, 1963).

[27] His wife Eliza was the *spiritus movens*: see A. Mombauer, *Helmuth von Moltke and the Origins of the First World War* (Cambridge, 2002), 52–4.

[28] Min. Moltke, n.d., on Kageneck [military attaché, Vienna] to Moltke, 13 July 1914, *JK* I, no. 84, n. 10.

[29] The argument developed by Geiss, *JK* II, 236. Moltke's role remains controversial, though most scholars attribute to him a decisive one: Mombauer, *Moltke*, 182–226, and 'A Reluctant Military Leader? Helmuth von Moltke and the July Crisis of 1914', *WiH* VI, 4 (1999), 417–46; M. Trachtenberg, 'The Coming of the First World War: A Reassessment', in M. Trachtenberg, *History and Strategy* (Princeton, NJ, 1991), 47–99; G. Ritter, 'Der Anteil der Militärs an der Kriegskatastrophe von 1914', *HZ* CXCIII (1961), 72–91.

memorandum did little more than sketch Germany's growing strategic predicament. It offered no reasoned politico-military strategic response to the crisis. Nothing it contained came as a surprise to the chancellor. Nor did the chief of staff force the direction or pace of decision-making.

At a meeting with Bethmann Hollweg in the morning of 29 July, Moltke and war minister Falkenhayn pressed for immediate military precautions. Moltke asked for railway junctions to be placed under army control and troops to be recalled from manoeuvre camps; Falkenhayn demanded that *Kriegsgefahrzustand* (imminent danger of war) be proclaimed, a preparatory stage immediately preceding mobilization. The chancellor refused to budge. With some effort the chief of staff succeeded in winning Bethmann's approval for the recall of the troops on manoeuvres. 'The imperial chancellor wants to avoid anything that might heighten nervousness and escalate the situation', reported the Saxon military plenipotentiary at Berlin.[30]

For now the chancellor remained in control of events at Berlin, but for how much longer depended on the course of events – and these were more difficult to control now. If Russian military preparations continued, Bethmann's policy threatened to unravel; pressure by the general staff might force his hand, and once Germany had begun to mobilize conflict could scarcely be averted. The chancellor was anxious to avoid further escalation, but this did not preclude pressure on Paris and St Petersburg. Only if Russia were prepared to disengage could escalation be prevented. He therefore instructed Pourtalès to warn Sazonov explicitly that 'Russian mobilization measures' would force Germany to do likewise, and that a European war could then no longer be avoided. Similar instructions were despatched to Schoen at Paris, who was to explain that military precautions by France – there had been reports of troops being recalled from manoeuvres – might force Berlin to declare a state of '*Kriegsgefahr*', which would 'increase tensions'.[31] The pressure on Germany's two Great Power neighbours was thus graduated, the warning to St Petersburg being explicit, that to Paris somewhat milder in tone.

Russian military measures were not the only development that had the potential to undo Bethmann's plans. Berchtold's recalcitrance,

---

[30] Leuckart to Carlowitz (no. 77/3515), 29 July 1914 (D 1 p.m.), *DGB*, no. 34; Falkenhayn diary, 29 July 1914, H. Afflerbach, *Falkenhayn: Politisches Denken und Handeln im Kaiserreich* (Düsseldorf, 1996), 155.

[31] Tels. Bethmann Hollweg to Pourtalès (no. 134), and to Schoen (no. 172), both 29 July 1914 (D 12.50 p.m.), *DD* II, nos. 342 and 341; D. Stevenson, *Armaments and the Coming of War: Europe, 1904–1914* (Oxford, 1996), 395.

especially with regard to Italy, further complicated the chancellor's plans. Berlin was in danger of being hoisted on the Habsburg petard. Bethmann's mounting irritation with Vienna has already been noted. In the morning of 29 July he wrote to Jagow calling for a sharply worded reprimand to be addressed to the Habsburg government. Its attitude towards the Italian ally was 'absolutely unsatisfactory', and Vienna therefore bore full responsibility if a general war broke out because *Dreibund* unity had not been maintained. Statements of territorial *désintéressement* made at St Petersburg, moreover, stood in contrast to promises of talks about compensation made to Rome. News of the latter would leak out: 'As allies we cannot support a policy with a false bottom.' Pressure on Vienna was now necessary, Bethmann argued: 'Otherwise we can no longer mediate at St Petersburg and we shall end up on Vienna's tow-line. This I do not want, even at the risk of being accused of wobbling.'[32]

Later that evening instructions went out to Tschirschky. The telegram recounted the different statements made by Austro-Hungarian diplomats in recent days, which Berlin viewed 'with mounting disquiet'. The earlier dismissal of Hoyos's off-the-cuff remark about a possible partition of Serbia was thus clearly 'meant for the gallery', which left only one conclusion – that Vienna had secret plans. The original draft of the telegram was even more sharply worded. At St Petersburg, it ran, 'the chalumeau of peace is played; she [Austria-Hungary] leaves us in the dark about her programme; Rome is fobbed off with meaningless phrases about the compensation question'. The telegram to Tschirschky was a remarkable document, accusing the Austro-Hungarian government of having consciously, deliberately and systematically deceived Berlin about the true nature of the plans. And yet Bethmann – or the Wilhelmstrasse – was still reluctant to put too much pressure on Berchtold. The final paragraph, added for Tschirschky's 'personal orientation', suggested that the ambassador '*for now*' recommend further assurances with regard to Serbian integrity and further explain that Vienna's statements to Italy were 'hardly satisfactory'.[33]

The extant evidence does not allow for unequivocal conclusions as to why Bethmann decided to tone down the instructions for Vienna. His decision may have reflected Jagow's advice – not unlikely given the latter's intrigues with Tschirschky. Indeed, Jagow's deputy had separately signalled

[32] Bethmann Hollweg to Jagow, 29 July 1914, *DD* II, no. 340.
[33] Tel. Bethmann Hollweg to Tschirschky (no. 181), 29 July 1914 (D 8 p.m.), *DD* II, no. 361 (original emphasis). The draft was amended, but not altered in substance, by Jagow and Stumm.

Berlin's approval of Austria-Hungary's line towards Italy.[34] The decision to pull his punches may have been, as one of his biographers observed, a consequence of a personal failing of Bethmann's, his reluctance to put overt pressure on people.[35] Possibly, the chancellor himself, for all his protestations to the contrary, feared that undue pressure on Vienna might lead to a complete Habsburg collapse at the last moment. The insertion of 'for now', which Bethmann had underlined in the original draft, meanwhile suggests a similar graduated approach as was pursued towards France and Russia, with the option still open of increased pressure at a later stage. Whatever the chancellor's motives, it was becoming increasingly clear how difficult it would be to control Vienna without risking either diplomatic defeat or fracturing, if not decoupling, the alliance with Austria-Hungary.

In the early afternoon, Bethmann requested a further interview with Goschen, the British ambassador. Without doubt the chancellor wished to avoid war, hence this latest approach to Britain. Yet for all his sincerity his conduct was clumsy and his policy towards Britain lacked direction. He regretted Vienna's cool and late reply to Grey's mediation proposal. Whilst events had moved on, he emphasized that he still supported the Foreign Secretary's idea and had communicated this to Vienna. He then intimated that Vienna required 'some sure guarantees' of Serbia's full compliance with its demands. The chancellor presumed that the 'hostilities about to be undertaken against Servia had [the] exclusive object of securing such guarantees'. With that in mind, he had impressed upon Berchtold the need for giving further assurances at St Petersburg that Austria-Hungary had no territorial designs on Serbia.

In essence, the chancellor's circumspect and prolix statement was a hint at 'Halt in Belgrade'. Why he was not open about the scheme is perplexing. It was surely in Germany's interest to coopt Grey into it, thus increasing its chances of success; and even if, ultimately, it failed, British neutrality in a continental war would then have been more likely as a consequence. Again, the conclusion suggests itself that, for now, Bethmann feared that Vienna would cave in completely if confronted with strong pressure by all the Powers.

But this was not Bethmann's only clumsiness during the interview with Goschen. Grey, he begged, was not to divulge the German efforts at

---

[34] See tel. Szögyény to Berchtold (no. 317), 29 July 1914 (D 6.15 p.m.), ÖUA VIII, no. 10943.

[35] See E. von Vietsch, *Bethmann Hollweg. Staatsmann zwischen Macht und Ethos* (Boppard, 1969), 185 and 198–9; see also K. H. Jarausch's comments on Bethmann's political style, in his *The Enigmatic Chancellor: Bethmann Hollweg and the Hubris of Imperial Germany* (New Haven, CT, 1973), 150–1.

Vienna to any of the other Powers. Even Lichnowsky had not been told. This, he suggested, was a sign of Bethmann's confidence in Grey and of his desire to cooperate with him 'in the cause of general peace'.[36] This protestation of faith in Anglo-German cooperation could not make up for the lack of candour in Bethmann's opening statement to Goschen. There was nothing to be gained by it. On the contrary, it was made at the cost of undermining Lichnowsky's position with Grey and the Foreign Office. But this, too, was the result of the absence of any real strategic forethought in German policy. How to balance the need to restrain Vienna and yet keep Britain on side was indeed an impossible task.

Nineteen men in Downing Street contemplate the European sphinxes and Grey warns of the greatest catastrophe ever seen

In the course of 29 July, the mood darkened at the Wilhelmstrasse. Zimmermann and other senior officials were now pessimistic about the chances of securing British neutrality in the event of a continental conflict.[37] Indeed, Grey and the British government were now forced to confront the likely prospect of a continental war. In the morning of 29 July, the Foreign Secretary had a further interview with the German ambassador to explore the options of mediation. Grey took a serious view of the situation now. Vienna had declined his conference proposal; and Austro-Russian exchanges, which he still regarded as the preferred method of settling the dispute, were unlikely to succeed now. Grey therefore repeated the invitation to the German government to indicate a solution acceptable to it. There was no question of humiliating Austria-Hungary, but securing the necessary guarantees could not be purchased at the price of humiliating Russia. Serbia might still be ready at this late stage to accept the Austro-Hungarian ultimatum in its entirety – as Rodd had reported from Rome.[38] This might furnish the basis for further talks. But it was vital that Habsburg troops did not enter Serbian territory.

Lichnowsky stuck closely to the official German line. The Austro-Serbian dispute was no concern of Russia's and Vienna harboured no territorial ambitions on Serbia, which elicited a robust response from

---

[36] Tel. Goschen to Grey (no. 100, secret and confidential), 29 July 1914 (D 4.27 p.m., R 5.45 p.m.), *BD* XI, no. 264.

[37] Tel. Szögyény to Berchtold (no. 324, secret), 29 July 1914 (D 11.40 a.m., R 11.30 p.m.), *ÖUA* VIII, no. 10950.

[38] Tel. Rodd to Grey (no. 127), 28 July 1914 (D 7.30 p.m., R 9.45 p.m.), *BD* XI, no. 231.

Grey – annexation was not required to reduce Serbia to a state of vassal-lage. The ambassador read Grey's intentions very accurately, as indeed he had done throughout the July crisis. Unless Vienna was ready to enter into discussions of the Serbian question, 'world war would be unavoidable'. And one could never know, Grey indicated, 'which houses would remain unscathed in such a fire' – even 'tiny Holland' was now mobilizing. This was clear enough, but Grey did not confine himself to issuing a warning. He also made a constructive proposal. It should be possible to agree on some formula to define the 'extent of Austria's military operations and the demands of the Monarchy'.[39] This was not unlike 'Halt in Belgrade', and if linked to Serbia's acceptance of the ultimatum, might have furnished a basis for a diplomatic settlement. But, of course, neither Grey nor Lichnowsky knew of the 'Halt in Belgrade' scheme, and so further valuable time was lost.

Before leaving the Foreign Office, Lichnowsky spoke to Tyrrell, Grey's Private Secretary, who warned him that the prospect of war would tear apart the *Dreibund*; Italy would not lend her support to an Austro-Hungarian campaign against Serbia.[40] As for Grey himself, he reiterated his readiness to use whatever means proved acceptable to the Powers to resolve the crisis: 'The whole idea of mediation or mediating influence was ready to be put into operation by any method that Germany could suggest if mine was not acceptable. In fact, mediation was ready to come into operation by any method that Germany thought possible if only Germany would "press the button" in the interests of peace.'[41]

Grey's first interview with Lichnowsky on 29 July was of a piece with his previous policy towards Germany. Although conciliatory in tone, there had been a clear and unmistakable warning of the incalculable consequences of any further escalation. As for the Serbian crisis itself, Grey was prepared to accept a solution on Germany's terms as long as it provided for a negotiated settlement. He could afford to, for the Balkan quarrel in itself was of little intrinsic interest to Britain. To an extent, then, Grey negotiated from a position of diplomatic strength in relations with Germany. But he did not have an entirely 'free hand'. Domestic consider-ations acted as a restraining factor. Grey had never enjoyed more than the grudging respect of the ruling Liberal party's powerful Radical wing. Its members were little interested in the intricacies of international politics,

---

[39] Tel. Lichnowsky to Auswärtiges Amt (no. 174), 29 July 1914 (D 2.08 p.m., R 5.07 p.m.), *DD* II, no. 357; see also Grey to Goschen (no. 251), 29 July 1914, *BD* XI, no. 284.
[40] Tel. Lichnowsky to Auswärtiges Amt (no. 176), 29 July 1914 (D 2.10 p.m., R 4.34 p.m.), *DD* II, no. 355.
[41] Tel. Grey to Goschen (no. 226), 29 July 1914 (D 4.45 p.m.), *BD* XI, no. 263.

knew even less of them, indeed found them uncongenial, but were all the readier to criticize the Foreign Secretary's policies. Grey's successful handling of the recent Balkan wars had won him a few plaudits and some respite, but any British involvement in a continental conflict would open up internal divisions. It would split the Cabinet and the rank-and-file of the Liberal party in the country. A European war thus entailed the risk of the Asquith government collapsing – an additional reason for securing a peaceful solution to the European crisis. This domestic consideration also explains Grey's reluctance to give assurances of more than diplomatic support to France.

The fissures within the ruling party were laid bare by the discussions in Cabinet on 29 July, at which Grey arrived late, having been delayed by his interview with Lichnowsky. At one level, the ministerial meeting, commencing at 11.30 a.m., was inconclusive. 'It was decided not to decide', as John Burns noted in his diary.[42] Its true significance rather lay in the fact that it revealed how narrowly circumscribed Grey's room for manoeuvre was. Part of the meeting was taken up with the situation in Ulster, but when it came to the European crisis Grey opened discussions 'in his own quiet way', reflected John Morley, the elder statesman of the Liberal party, 'which is none the less impressive for being so simple, and so free from the *cassant* and over-emphatic tone that is Asquith's vice on such occasions'. The ministers had to accept that there was the risk of war, and they had to decide what course to follow in such an eventuality: 'We could no longer defer decision.' No clear view emerged from the discussions, however: 'We rambled, as even the best Cabinets are apt to do, from the cogent riddle that the European Sphinx or Sphinxes had posed, into incidental points and secondary aspects.' Morley's recollections were not entirely accurate, except in one respect. It was not obvious 'in which direction opinion was inclining'.[43]

Cabinets usually think of only one thing at a time, and Grey's circulating of a paper on the subject of the 1839 and 1870 treaties on Belgium's independence and neutrality – consisting largely of extracts from various speeches by Gladstone at the time of the outbreak of the

---

[42] Burns diary, 29 July 1914, Burns MSS, BL, Add. MSS. 46326; Z. S. Steiner and K. Neilson, *Britain and the Origins of the First World War* (Basingstoke and New York, 2nd edn 2003), 245–6.

[43] J. Viscount Morley, *Memorandum on Resignation* (London, 1928), 1–3. 'Honest John' Morley's account needs to be treated with some caution in so far as details are concerned. The extant evidence, for instance, disproves his suggestion that this discussion took place around 24–27 July; the Cabinet did not discuss Belgian neutrality until 29 July: see Harcourt cabinet notes, 29 July 1914, Harcourt MSS, Bodl., no accession number.

Franco-Prussian War and from an August 1870 report by the Law Officers of the Crown – helped to concentrate the ministers' minds. The legal opinion was clear enough. Belgian neutrality had been guaranteed collectively by the Great Powers. If one of the guaranteeing Powers acted in breach of the treaties, the other Powers would not be relieved of their obligations. The neutrality guarantee was not conditional upon unanimity of the European Powers. Thus, if in the event of a continental war, either France or Germany launched their campaign in the west by invading Belgium, Britain would be compelled to assist the latter, if appealed to by Brussels. The form of that assistance was not defined, diplomatic support being deemed sufficient, especially if the Belgian government decided not to resist the onslaught. Ultimately, as Asquith informed the King after the Cabinet meeting, the ministers agreed that the question of Belgian neutrality was thus 'one of policy rather than of legal obligation'.[44] There were, however, difficulties. Efforts to elicit from Paris and Berlin declarations respecting Belgian neutrality 'w[oul]d be notice to Germany of our non-participation – & [be] regarded at this moment by France as an unfriendly act'.[45]

Grey's criticism was directed at Austria-Hungary. Her conduct was one of 'brutal recklessness', and he regarded the situation as 'very grave'. France and Russia expected Britain to join them on the assumption that in their union lay the best means of preserving peace; Germany, by contrast, argued that British neutrality 'alone [would] preserve Peace', recorded J. A. 'Jack' Pease, the President of the Board of Education, in his diary:

> Evidently we could do nothing right, & that we should be liable for anything that happened. The cabinet agreed we must do the best for our own interests, and that was the cause of Peace & was the course to be promoted. All the Powers were now building their hopes of our participation or abstention as suited them best.

And in that the Yorkshire Quaker was entirely correct. Had it not been for his intervention, Grey asserted, the Powers would have 'hopelessly drifted

---

[44] Asquith to George V, 30 July 1914, TNA (PRO), CAB 41/35/21 (the meeting took place on 29 July). The memorandum circulated by Grey is 'Belgian Neutrality in 1870', July 1914, CAB 37/120/95.

In November 1908, an inter-departmental Whitehall committee of the Foreign Office and the Committee of Imperial Defence had looked into the matter; its findings informed the memorandum of July 1914: see memo. Crowe, 'Memorandum respecting Belgian Neutrality and Britain's Obligation to Defend it', 15 Nov. 1908, BD VIII, no. 311.

[45] Harcourt cabinet notes, 29 July, Harcourt MSS, Bodl., no accession number.

into war' already. None of them had any constructive proposals to make, but he 'would continue to urge mediation by as many Powers as he could – and restrain Russia who was mobilizing from doing so opposite the German frontier'. As for France and Germany, the Foreign Secretary proposed to revert to the tactics that had stood his diplomacy in such good stead during earlier Franco-German crises: 'he would say to Cambon Don't count upon our coming in, & to Lichnowsky don't count on our abstention – & neither could then regard our inaction or action respectively as an Act of Treachery. This was assented to.'

The prospect before the ministers was appalling. War would be a 'calamity for civilised nations', Winston Churchill observed, and suggested that the crowned heads of Europe ought to be brought together. But Asquith dismissed the notion of monarchical summitry as a viable solution: 'The Austrian Emperor is bitter ... & we hear that the Czar is violent & they are far apart – no help can be looked for in this direction.' There seemed little for it but for Grey to 'leave nothing undone to promote Peace'. At the same time it was accepted that 'to make no preparations would lose all our influence with all the powers'.[46]

The 'nineteen men round the table at Downing Street' still pinned some hope on a peace party at Berlin 'under the influence of the Emperor and Bethmann Hollweg'. If Germany did not respond to Russia's military preparations, escalation would be avoided, noted Herbert Samuel. But if Germany did hold back, it was understood at Downing Street, she would be placed at a disadvantage against Russia. Samuel himself thought that 'the fuse which has been fired will quickly bring a catastrophic explosion'.[47] Even so, the mood of the ministers was finely balanced. 'The Declaration of War by Austria against Servia has made the situation very critical', wrote the Lord Chancellor: 'There is still hope, however', not least because the Foreign Secretary was working hard to secure a diplomatic settlement: 'Grey is marvellously cool & concentrated.'[48]

Grey needed to be all of these, for the accelerating pace of events over the next forty-eight hours would test him and the other European leaders. The Foreign Secretary was 'certainly indefatigable in his efforts to

---

[46] Pease diary, 29 July 1914, K. M. Wilson, 'The Cabinet Diary of J. A. Pease, 24 July–5 August 1914', *Proceedings of the Leeds Philosophical and Literary Society. Literary and Historical Section* XIX, 3 (1983), 43–5; for Pease see also C. Hazlehurst and C. Woodland (eds.), *A Liberal Chronicle: Journals and Papers of J. A. Pease, 1908–1910* (London, 1994), 1–16.

[47] Samuel to Beatrice Samuel, 29 July 1914, Samuel MSS, PAL, SAM/A/157/691; B. Wasserstein, *Herbert Samuel: A Political Biography* (Oxford, 1992), 160.

[48] Haldane to Elizabeth Haldane, 29 July 1914, Haldane MSS, NLS, MS 5991.

try and keep Germany and Russia quiet', Crowe noted.[49] In the afternoon, following the Cabinet meeting, Grey gave a brief statement on the international situation to the House of Commons. He left the parliamentarians under no illusion that, in consequence of Austria-Hungary's declaration of war on Serbia, the situation was grave. British diplomacy would continue to pursue a peaceful settlement of the crisis and kept in touch with all the Powers, though so far it had 'not been possible for ... [them] to unite in joint action'.[50]

There was no debate afterwards, but the Foreign Secretary's statement was to have a sequel of some political significance. One of the Radical campaign groups in Parliament, the Liberal Foreign Affairs Committee, now intervened. Its members could not support the government in any 'military or naval operations which would carry this country beyond its existing treaty obligations'. They thought that if Paris and St Petersburg were told that Britain 'would not be drawn into a war ... it would have a moderating effect on their policy'.[51] Grey then sought out the group's chairman, Arthur Ponsonby, son of Queen Victoria's Private Secretary and a former diplomat-turned-MP who now revelled in his role as the self-appointed nemesis of the inequities of international diplomacy. Britain was under no obligation to any other Powers, Grey explained to him privately. He could not state in public that the government did not wish to be drawn into a conflict: 'The doubt on this point was useful to him in negotiating.' Affirming Britain's determination to remain neutral would have the opposite effect to the one intended by Ponsonby's group. He promised to discuss the matter with Asquith, but in the meantime asked the group to remain quiet for the rest of the week, while he continued to search for a diplomatic solution. 'Possibly Austria might be content with occupying Belgrade & going no further', he suggested.[52]

The reference to the possible occupation of the Serbian capital is suggestive of the trend of Grey's thinking that day. Already in his interview with Lichnowsky there was a hint at this. But in the course of the afternoon and evening the idea would crystallize and take more distinct shape.

---

[49] Crowe to Clema Crowe, 29 July 1914, Crowe MSS, Bodl., Ms.Eng.d.2903.

[50] *Hansard House of Commons* LXV (30 July 1914), col. 1574.

[51] Ponsonby to Grey, 29 July 1914, Ponsonby MSS, Bodl., Ms.Eng.hist.c.660 (copy in Murray of Elibank MSS, NLS, MS 8805); for some of the background see A. J. A. Morris, *Radicalism against War, 1906–1914* (London, 1972), 408–9; see also R. A. Jones, *Arthur Ponsonby: The Politics of Life* (London, 1989).

[52] Ponsonby, 'Notes of Grey's statement to me on 29 July 1914', Ponsonby MSS, Bodl., Ms.Eng.hist.c.660.

In so far as his critics on the government backbenches were concerned, however, Grey's efforts were wasted on Ponsonby, who on the following day wrote again, this time to the prime minister. The thirty-strong group remained opposed to a war 'in which neither treaty obligations, British interests, British honour or even sentiments of friendship are at present in the remotest degree involved'. Any decision by the Cabinet, he warned, would not only meet with their 'strongest disapproval but with the actual withdrawal of support from the Government'.[53] So there it was, the deep rift within British liberalism that had lain hidden from view since the Boer War, an ideological division on foreign policy and Britain's correct role in international politics. The impact of Ponsonby's letter should not be exaggerated. His flaunting of his liberal conscience did not dictate Grey's and Asquith's policy. But it indicated the exceedingly fine line they had to tread. Almost by the hour, considerations of external and now internal developments narrowed that line yet further.

Back at the department, Grey saw Mensdorff, the Austro-Hungarian ambassador, who had called at last to hand the Foreign Secretary a copy of Vienna's dossier on Serb-sponsored terrorist and subversive activities, parts of which the embassy had already fed to Spender and the *Westminster Gazette*. The interview was sterile at best. Grey refused to enter into a discussion of the merits or otherwise of Vienna's case against the Serbian government. His interest was solely in 'facts and the most important thing: how can a European war still be averted?' He batted away Mensdorff's argument that the Austro-Serbian dispute was a matter for those two governments alone. If the Powers were to urge St Petersburg to remain passive, it would amount to giving Austria-Hungary a 'free hand' to do as she pleased with Serbia: 'Even without territorial acquisitions we [Austria-Hungary] could reduce Serbia to the status of a vassal and so eliminate Russia completely from the Balkans.' The ambassador found Grey 'very pessimistic. "Today St Petersburg is still talking to Berlin; how will it be tomorrow?"' The Foreign Secretary was in touch with Bethmann Hollweg, who was also casting about for a way to mediate between the two Eastern Powers.

Tyrrell, whom Mensdorff saw before returning to the embassy, confirmed that Grey was 'very disturbed' by the events of the past twenty-four hours. The government wished to remain aloof from any conflict, if possible. 'Russian interests leave England cool', Tyrrell explained, but if France's position and so the European equilibrium were threatened, no British government could stay out of the war. 'The absolutely undiminished

---

[53] Ponsonby to Asquith, 30 July 1914, *ibid*.

preservation of France's Great Power position', Mensdorff reiterated in a follow-up despatch, 'is an irrevocable fundamental principle of English policy regardless of party. This has to be kept always in view when assessing England's stance in the great European questions.'[54]

As agreed in Cabinet, Grey then saw Paul Cambon, to whom he explained that in the present dispute in the Balkans, British interests were not directly affected:

> Even if the question became one between Austria and Russia we should not feel called upon to take a hand in it. It would then be a question of the supremacy of Teuton or Slav – a struggle for supremacy in the Balkans; and our idea had always been to avoid being drawn into a war over a Balkan question.

In the event of further escalation, the British Cabinet had not yet made up its mind. France might be obligated to support Russia even at the risk of a continental war. Britain, however, was 'free from engagements, and we should have to decide what British interests required us to do'. Cambon said little in response beyond suggesting that his government anticipated a German demand for France to remain neutral 'while Germany attacked Russia. This assurance France, of course, could not give.'[55]

Grey then saw Lichnowsky. Any further direct talks between St Petersburg and Vienna had been made redundant by the Austro-Hungarian declaration of war. If Bethmann Hollweg succeeded in his purported efforts in the two eastern capitals, all would be well. But Grey did not think this likely. It was all the more important, then, for Berlin to respond to his invitation 'and propose some method by which the four Powers should be able to work together to keep the peace of Europe'. Russia insisted that all military operations be suspended as a precondition for mediation. Grey himself accepted that it was too late now for Austria-Hungary to halt her campaign altogether. Given these circumstances, he proposed his version of 'Halt in Belgrade'. He expected the Austro-Hungarian army to be in occupation of the Serbian capital and the surrounding areas shortly. The Powers could still mediate, he suggested, 'if Austria, while saying that she must hold the occupied territory until she had complete satisfaction from

[54] Quotes from tel. Mensdorff to Berchtold (no. 119), 29 July 1914 (D 4.32 p.m., R 9 a.m.), and despatch (no. 36A), 29 July 1914 (R 1 Aug.), ÖUA VIII, nos. 10973–4; F. R. Bridge, *Great Britain and Austria-Hungary, 1906–1914* (London, 1972), 215–16.
[55] Grey to Bertie (no. 500), 29 July 1914, *BD* XI, no. 283; cf. tel. P. Cambon to Viviani (nos. 157–8, very confidential), 29 July 1914 (D 7.20 p.m., R 7.45 p.m.), *DDF* (3) XI, no. 281.

Servia, stated that she would not advance further, pending an effort of the Powers to mediate between her and Russia'.[56]

This was the only possible basis for mediation now, Grey argued. Austria-Hungary could still secure the guarantees she needed without a European war. Mediation was more urgent than ever now, 'if it was not to come to a European catastrophe'. He then added that their cordial personal relations should not deceive Lichnowsky about British policy in the event of escalation. He hoped to be able to develop further the friendly relations with Berlin. Whilst a war limited to Austria-Hungary and Russia would be of no concern to Britain, the situation would be transformed, however, if France and Germany were dragged into the conflict. The British government would then have to make swift decisions: 'it would not be possible [for Britain] to stand aside and to wait. *"If war breaks out, it will be the greatest catastrophe that the world has ever seen."*'[57]

Grey's second interview with the German ambassador on 29 July has been invested with great significance. It has been asserted that, if his now more explicit warning of British intervention in a European war had been made earlier, Berlin might still have disengaged and a general war thus have been avoided. The criticism is neither new nor particularly original. Already in August 1914, three days into the war, the notion of missed opportunities had begun to circulate in opposition circles in Britain.[58]

However widespread, the criticism is nevertheless ill-founded. In the first place, there was nothing new in what Grey had said on this occasion. True, his previous statements had been couched in more restrained language, but there had been no need to be explicit. Lichnowsky had understood the full import of Grey's words on these earlier occasions and had reported in this sense. Lichnowsky 'took no exception to what I [Grey] had said [on 29 July]; indeed, he told me that it accorded with what he had already given in Berlin as his view of the situation'.[59] But if the Foreign Secretary had full confidence in the accuracy and reliability of the German ambassador, that confidence had received a blow. For just before their second interview, Goschen's report on his conversation with Bethmann Hollweg arrived at the Foreign Office, and it was apparent now that Lichnowsky was only imperfectly informed of Berlin's plans.

[56] Grey to Goschen (no. 252), 29 July 1914, *BD* XI, no. 285.
[57] Tel. Lichnowsky to Auswärtiges Amt (no. 178), 29 July 1914 (D 6.39 p.m., R 9.12 p.m.), *DD* II, no. 368 (highlighted section in English in the original).
[58] Bridgeman to Caroline Bridgeman, 7 Aug. 1914, P. Williamson (ed.), *The Modernisation of Conservative Politics: The Diaries and Letters of William Bridgeman, 1904–1935* (London, 1988), 81.
[59] Grey to Goschen (no. 253), 29 July 1914, *BD* XI, no. 286.

Conversely, it could not be excluded that the ambassador's reports had not been given due consideration at Berlin.[60] With his interlocutor's credibility thus damaged, Grey had to become more explicit if he wanted to ensure that his views were understood at the Wilhelmstrasse.

The blanket criticism of Grey for allegedly failing to warn Berlin is based on a failure to consider the previous conversations in their proper context. As seen earlier, already a few days after the Sarajevo murders, the Foreign Secretary had warned both the Russian and German ambassadors of the dangers of European complications. Under the then prevailing circumstances this was an appropriate response. It was only the recalcitrance of both the two Germanic Powers and the Franco-Russian group that made Britain's role vital now. Until that moment, Grey's previous crisis strategy of studied ambiguity seemed the most sensible course. Until then, as Spender, who saw Grey and Tyrrell daily during the final week of the crisis, reflected shortly after the events, 'G[rey] was determined to keep the free hand till the last moment'. That moment was approaching now. The declaration of war

> brought the situation to the point of acute danger. It was evident by Wednesday [29 July] evening that the situation was slipping out of the hands of the ministers & diplomatists into those of the General Staffs ... all of whom ... were pressing to be allowed to mobilize, lest their opponents should steal a march on them. From this point the only chance was that concessions could be obtained from Austria which would enable Russia to stop the mobilization. Grey threw all his energy into this & implored the Germans to get him something from Austria which he could take to Russia while begging Russia not to extend her mobilization to the north, which would be signal for German mobilization.[61]

But there were yet further twists in the story of the events of 29 July.

'Nicky' and 'Willy' exchange telegrams

The Cabinet discussions of 29 July and the internal debates at the Foreign Office underlined Britain's limited ability to affect the course of events. Indeed, for Grey's officials the most important news of the day was

---

[60] See tel. Goschen to Grey (no. 100, secret and confidential), 29 July 1914 (D 4.27 p.m., R 5.45 p.m.), *BD* XI, no. 264.

[61] Memo. Spender, n.d. [Aug. 1914], Spender MSS, BL, Add. MSS 46932, fos. 172–3.

Bethmann Hollweg's statement, as relayed by Goschen, 'that an exchange of telegrams was taking place between the German Emperor and the Czar'.[62]

In the early hours of that day a telegram had arrived at the Neues Palais in Potsdam. 'In this most serious moment I appeal to you to help me', wired the Tsar to his German cousin. Over the years the two monarchs had frequently exchanged views on political developments in their private correspondence, writing to each other in the language they both preferred, English. The 'Nicky-Willy' correspondence, as it has become known, was part of a legacy of an earlier period when the monarchs of Europe decided over war and peace. Whilst of a private character, the correspondence was thus also intensely political in its nature. It was in part governmental in that it reflected the monarchical form of governance in much of Europe. Yet it was also private in that it was part of the royal prerogative, Tsar Nicholas II for one being something of a martinet when it came to etiquette and established procedural and decision-making hierarchies (more so than cousin 'Willy'). The telegram was very much Nicholas's personal initiative, even though suggestions of an exchange with the Habsburg Emperor or the Kaiser had been made at a number of occasions during the course of the crisis.[63] On the previous day, the Tsar had signed the two mobilization orders, a step which had caused him some agony. Soon he would have to wrestle with an even more difficult decision – which of the two decrees to implement. A telegram to his Berlin cousin, either to complement the official channels of communication or to short-circuit traditional diplomacy, might then provide clarity. '[S]oon I shall be overwhelmed by the pressure brought on me and be forced to take extreme measures which will lead to war. To . . . avoid such a calamity as a European war I beg of you in the name of our old friendship to do what you can to stop your allies from going too far.'[64]

---

[62] Tel. Goschen to Grey (no. 100, secret and confidential), 29 July 1914 (D 4.27 p.m., R 5.45 p.m.), and min. Crowe, 29 July 1914, *BD* XI, no. 264.

[63] See tel. Pourtalès to Auswärtiges Amt (no. 162), 26 July 1914 (D 10.05 p.m.), *DD* i, no. 229, reporting on such suggestions from members of the Tsar's entourage. The Grand Duke Nicholas Mikhailovich, who suspected that Germany was hoping to unleash a war, made similar comments, see tel. Szápáry to Berchtold (no. no), 29 July 1914 (D 1.18 p.m., R 9 a.m.), *ÖUA* VIII, no. 11000.

[64] Tel. Nicholas II to Wilhelm II, 29 July 1914 (D 1 a.m., R 1.10 a.m.), *DD* II, no. 332; see also W. Goetz (ed.), *Briefe Wilhelms II an den Zaren, 1894–1914* (Berlin, 1921); for the view that the correspondence was shaped by their respective governments see M. S. Neiberg, *Dance of the Furies: Europe and the Outbreak of World War I* (Cambridge, MA, 2011), 116.

In yet another ironic twist in a story richly endowed with such warps, the Tsar's telegram crossed one despatched in the other direction. At Bethmann's suggestion, the Kaiser expressed in it 'the gravest concern' at the rising tensions. He appealed to Nicholas's sense of monarchical solidarity just as Pourtalès had done, in vain, with Sazonov. The regicidal spirit still dominated Serbian political life, and the murderers and the wire-pullers in the background needed to be punished: 'In this case politics play no part.' He appreciated the Tsar's difficult position, and given their mutual bond of friendship, he would exert 'my utmost influence to induce the Austrians to deal straightly to arrive at a satisfactory understanding with you. I confidently hope you will help me in my efforts to smoothe [*sic*] over difficulties that may still arise.'[65]

The Kaiser read 'Nicky's' telegram at 7.30 a.m. on 29 July, and as usual adorned it with his marginalia. The telegram, he noted, 'contained a hidden threat! And a request resembling an order to fall into an ally's arm'. His appeal to monarchical solidarity had been trumped by Russian fears of losing influence in the Balkans in the event of Austrian successes against Serbia: 'These can now surely be awaited in their overall effect. There will still be time to negotiate later on.' Instead of summoning him to stop the action against Serbia, the Tsar should turn to the Emperor in Vienna and negotiate with him.[66]

The Kaiser's instinct was to wait for a reply to his earlier telegram. But Jagow counselled otherwise, and, unlike his Russian cousin, 'Willy' accepted. Austria-Hungary was acting in self-defence, he wired back to Peterhof at 6.30 p.m. Vienna entertained no territorial designs on Serbian territory; Russia could therefore remain passive 'without involving Europe in the most horrible war she ever witnessed'. Russian mobilization would 'precipitate a calamity we both wish to avoid' – the original draft warned in more emphatic language that it 'could set the house on fire'. Mobilization, moreover, Wilhelm suggested, would 'jeopardize my position as mediator'.[67] In a similar vein he commented on the latest report from his military representative at the St Petersburg court. The mood of optimism in the Russian capital had given way to a sense of foreboding, wrote Chelius. Austria-Hungary's 'brusque and unjust' proceedings against Serbia proved, it was argued by members of the Tsar's entourage, that

[65] Tel. Wilhelm II to Nicholas II, 28 July 1914 (D 29 July 1.45 a.m.), *DD* II, no. 335. The telegram had been approved by 10.45 p.m. on 28 July; for an earlier, undated draft that only focused on the murder see *ibid.*, no. 233.

[66] Min. Wilhelm II, 29 July 1914 (7.30 a.m.), *DD* II, no. 332.

[67] Tel. Wilhelm II to Nicholas II, 29 July 1914 (D 6.30 p.m.), *DD* II, no. 359; cf. *IBZI* v, no. 238.

Vienna had acted '*mala fide*' (in bad faith) and that it had sought a military confrontation with Belgrade from the beginning. 'They [the Russians] do not want war', the General observed, 'and would like to avoid it and they regret that no Power succeeded in preventing Austria from making this dangerous step'. Wilhelm marked the passage and wrote in the margins of the decrypted telegram 'Yes, we!', and then underlined it twice.[68]

The Kaiser's marginal comments and his reference to his mediating role can only be explained in connection with his 'Halt in Belgrade' scheme. He clearly assumed that Jagow had transmitted the plan to Vienna and that it now formed part of the diplomatic exchanges. Only on that assumption could their curious mixture of conciliation and rejection make sense; they cannot be explained in any other way. As seen earlier, of course, Jagow and Tschirschky had quietly sabotaged the proposal.

When 'Nicky' received 'Willy's' wire in the evening of 29 July, he was prepared to rescind the order for general mobilization. He immediately telephoned Sazonov. The Kaiser had begged him to avoid a war, he told the foreign minister, who pointed out that Pourtalès's language had been less accommodating. The Tsar promised to seek clarification, but authorized further conversations between Sazonov, Sukhomlinov and Yanushkevich about mobilization measures.[69] In his reply the Tsar thanked Wilhelm for his 'conciliatory and friendly' telegram, but noted the discrepancy between his cousin's telegram and the representations made by Pourtalès at the Choristers' Bridge: 'Beg you to explain this divergency [*sic*].' The best way forward now, he suggested, was to submit the Austro-Serbian dispute to the international court of arbitration at The Hague.[70]

The Tsar causes confusion

The Tsar's reference to 'this divergency [*sic*]' was pertinent. He himself had added an element of confusion by entering the idea of arbitration into the debate. But more importantly other forces were now at work at both St Petersburg and Berlin that made this belated attempt at monarchical diplomacy redundant.

[68] Tel. Chelius to Auswärtiges Amt (no. 184), 29 July 1914 (D 2.30 p.m., R 3.15 p.m.) and marginal comment by Wilhelm II, n.d. [29 July], *DD* II, no. 344.
[69] Schilling daily journal, 16/29 July 1914, *IBZI* v, no. 224; see also D. C. B. Lieven, *Nicholas II: Emperor of All the Russias* (London, 1993), 201–2. As so often, Sazonov's suggestion that the Tsar gave up hope of peace on receiving the Kaiser's telegram needs to be taken *cum multis granis*: Sazonov, *Les Années fatales* (Paris, 1927), 218.
[70] Tel. Nicholas II to Wilhelm II, 29 July 1914 (D 8.20 p.m., R 8.42 p.m.), *DD* II, no. 366.

At around 3 p.m., at Sukhomlinov's suggestion, Yanushkevich, the Russian chief of staff, asked Major von Eggeling, the German military attaché, to call on him. He gave him his 'word of honour' – he repeated this and also offered to confirm it in writing – that until that moment there had been no mobilization, 'no draft of a single man or horse'. There had been some preliminary measures, aimed at strengthening forces along the frontiers, but Yanushkevich affirmed that any measures that might be taken were aimed against Austria-Hungary, and hinted that even in the event of war 'no offensive was intended'. For his part, Eggeling was sceptical of the chief of staff's assurances, and warned that the statement was meant to confuse Berlin.[71]

At about the same time, Pourtalès called once more on Sazonov at the minister's request. Vienna had rejected direct talks and Sazonov therefore reverted back to Grey's conference proposal. He laid stress on the fact that he was 'seeking the means of getting out of the current situation, and he was clutching at straws'. There would be mobilization against Austria-Hungary, but this did not mean war, to which Pourtalès replied that Berlin could not regard this 'as other than a grave mistake'.[72] The ambassador returned to the Choristers' Bridge some time between 6 and 7 p.m. to warn Sazonov, as instructed earlier by the chancellor, against mobilizing Russia's armed forces. Since, as seen, some form of partial mobilization had already been decided in principle, the démarche came too late. Certainly, Sazonov confirmed that partial mobilization against Austria-Hungary was planned, and that this was meant to put Russia in a 'state of armed neutrality'. Pourtalès's communication left him visibly agitated. Indeed, the interview grew very heated. 'Now I have no more doubts about the true causes of Austrian intransigence', Sazonov burst out. Pourtalès responded equally sharply: 'I protest with all my power, *M. le Ministre*, against such an offensive assertion.' The two men parted somewhat frostily.[73]

[71] Encl. in tel. Pourtalès to Auswärtiges Amt (no. 186), 29 July 1914 (D 7 p.m., R 9.45 p.m.), *DD* II, no. 370; cf. tel. Szápáry to Berchtold (no. 178), 29 July 1914 (D 4.26 p.m., R 10 p.m.), *ÖUA* VIII, no. 11002.

[72] Tel. Pourtalès to Auswärtiges Amt (no. 185), 29 July 1914 (D 6.10 p.m., R 8.29 p.m.), *DD* II, no. 365; cf. tel. Sazonov to Bronevski (no. 1544), 16/29 July 1914, *IBZI* V, no. 218. Buchanan thought Pourtalès's language not conducive to calming the atmosphere at St Petersburg: see tel. Buchanan to Grey (no. 182), 29 July 1914 (D 8.40 p.m., R 11.30 p.m.), *BD* XI, no. 276.

[73] Quotes from tel. Pourtalès to Auswärtiges Amt (no. 187), 29 July 1914 (D 8 p.m., R 10.55 p.m.), *DD* II, no. 378, and Schilling daily journal, 16/29 July 1914, *IBZI* V, no. 224; also Pourtalès, *Meine letzten Verhandlungen*, 43. The ambassador's accounts are somewhat less colourful; the timings given for the meeting by Schilling are not entirely accurate.

There was an equally fraught encounter with Szápáry shortly afterwards. The minister and the ambassador touched once more on the well-established points either side had advanced in recent days; old, familiar arguments were trotted out again; and the conversation was little more than diplomatic shadow-boxing. Neither man landed a punch, neither suffered a hit. Sazonov hinted at concerns about the nature of Austro-Hungarian military preparations. Even 'a child in military matters', Szápáry countered, could see that 'our southern corps' in Bosnia were no threat to Russia. There was the danger of inadvertent 'military competition [*Lizitieren*] on the basis of false news.' Even so, Sazonov then explained that an imperial *ukase* would be signed today, 'ordering mobilization on a rather large scale' – no decision had in fact been taken yet. No offensive was planned, Sazonov assured the ambassador: 'these troops were not destined to fall upon us; they would only stand at the ready in case Russia's Balkan interests were threatened'. The interview thus meandered to a stalemate, when Sazonov received a telephone report of the bombardment of Belgrade: 'He appeared as if transformed, and sought to take up again all the old arguments in a logic-defying manner ... "You only want to gain time by negotiations, but proceed to shell an unprotected city!" "What else do you want to conquer when you are in control of the capital" and similar such childish utterances ... "Why should we converse if you act in this manner!"' Szápáry left Sazonov 'in an extremely agitated state'.[74]

In the ambassador's analysis, Sazonov was playing a complicated political game. Like the Tsar himself, the minister 'shuns war and ... tries to deny us the fruits [of the Serbian campaign] if possible without war, but were it nonetheless to come to a war, to enter it better prepared'. Mobilization against Austria-Hungary was meant to ensure Romania's drift into Russia's orbit. It would eliminate any German influence in the matter and so allow Russia to harrass Austria-Hungary during her Serbian campaign, 'and as soon as our operations have led to some success, to undertake the rescue of Serbia by Russia'. If the other Balkan states sought to join with the Monarchy, then St Petersburg would use Bucharest as a cat's paw in the defence of the 1913 Balkan peace settlement, and Romania would fight alongside Russia in a European war. Conversely, if Austria-Hungary and Germany precipitated matters, Russia 'would stand attacked and would have better prospects of dragging in France and possibly even England'. Sazonov sought to protect Russia's Balkan interests by means of this

---

[74] Tel. Szápáry to Berchtold (no. 180), 29 July 1914 (D 11 p.m., R 11 a.m.), *ÖUA* VIII, no. 11003. Geiss, *JK* II, 757, suggests that the meeting with Szápáry took place before the third interview with Pourtalès, but internal evidence of the various reports suggests otherwise.

complicated game that was meant to stop short of war. But Szápáry warned that 'military circles', presumably around the Grand Duke Nikolai Nikola'evich, were at work 'to reduce this complicated political calculation ... to a simpler formula and ... to precipitate events as far as possible'.[75]

Szápáry's analysis was perceptive, except that the ambassador underestimated Sazonov's hawkishness at that point. After the interviews with the two ambassadors, Sazonov conferred with the war minister and the chief of staff in Yanushkevich's office. Also on hand were Danilov, the Quartermaster-General, General Nikolai Avgustovich Monkewitz, and Sazonov's deputy *chef de cabinet*, Nikolai Aleksandrovich Basili, to draft submissions to the Tsar in accordance with any proposals the three men might make. The conference was interrupted twice, the first time by the Tsar telephoning to inform Sazonov of the Kaiser's telegram. Then a telegram arrived from Strandtmann, now at Niš where the Serbian government had fled: 'The last hopes are gone. Belgrade has been shelled and the Sava bridge blown up.'[76] Given that Szápáry also claimed that the report arrived during his interview with Sazonov, it is possible that the foreign minister arranged the second arrival during the conference for special effect. Whatever the truth of the matter, after further discussion the two ministers and the chief of staff decided that 'given the low probability of avoiding war with Germany it was necessary to prepare for it in every way, and that therefore the risk could not be accepted of postponing a later general mobilization by carrying out a partial mobilization now'. The Tsar was then informed of this recommendation by telephone, and the monarch authorized the necessary decrees.[77] This, of course, did not mean immediate mobilization, for this could not happen without the Tsar's signature. Sukhomlinov, the war minister, however, was certain: '*Cette fois nous marcherons*' ('This time we shall march'), he said on hearing the news from Belgrade.[78]

In so far as Sazonov was concerned, the events of the past twenty-four hours had dispelled what hopes he still had of a peaceful outcome. Two factors came together and made a compelling case for a harder line. The news of the bombardment of Belgrade confirmed the minister's

[75] Tel. Szápáry to Berchtold (no. 181), 30 July 1914 (D 1 a.m., R 3.15 p.m.), ÖUA VIII, no. 11094.

[76] Tel. Strandtmann to Sazonov (no. 243), 16/29 July 1914, *IBZI* v, no. 257; for the arrival of the telegram see Schilling daily journal, 16/29 July 1914, *ibid.*, no. 224.

[77] Schilling daily journal, 16/29 July 1914, *IBZI* v, no. 224.

[78] R. R. Rosen, *Forty Years of Diplomacy* (2 vols., London, 1922) II, 163. Rosen was present at a dinner when Sukhomlinov made the statement.

suspicions that the Habsburg leadership had been bent on war from the start. Pourtalès's warnings in the course of 29 July, and their latest somewhat heated exchanges, reinforced him in this belief – the ambassador's statements were too reminiscent of Berlin's thinly disguised ultimatum of March 1909, and Sazonov was determined not to be caught in the same position as his predecessor at the Choristers' Bridge. Mobilizing now was of one piece with his diplomatic strategy based on credible deterrence. The risks, however, were significant. General mobilization presented Germany with the choice of either drawing back or escalating a regional conflict to an all-out European war. The former would result in a significant political setback, possibly accelerating the further disintegration of the *Dreibund* combination. The consequences of the latter were incalculable, but because they were incalculable they might prove preferable, for being less immediate, than the certainties entailed in a diplomatic defeat. Partial mobilization, even if this had been logistically possible, equally raised the stakes. Given that Austria-Hungary was already committed to the campaign against Serbia, it would again be left to Germany to provide cover for the Habsburg Empire, and the balance of options available to Berlin was not much different than in the case of full mobilization.

But there was an alternative, and it is difficult not to conclude that, having dithered at the beginning of the crisis, Sazonov now erred in the opposite direction. Certainly, there was no reason for rushing into the decision to mobilize. The shelling of Belgrade and even the limited occupation of Serbian territory were undoubtedly awkward for Russia, but it was clear to Russian military analysts that Austria-Hungary would not be ready for a major offensive against Serbia for another ten or twelve days at least. For as long as Germany remained quiescent, there was no need for Russia to force the pace of events, unless he feared that the French government might retract Paléologue's assurances of support. The preliminary preparations were enough to allow Russia to move to mobilization at a later stage if the situation demanded it. For now, there was still time for the diplomats to get to work, possibly on the basis of something akin to 'Halt in Belgrade'. Even if the Kaiser's initiative had sunk without much trace, Grey's latest proposals indicated that the scheme, or some version of it, was not dead yet. The risk, of course, from Sazonov's perspective, was that international diplomacy might do no more than provide a cover for Austria-Hungary to complete her mobilization unimpeded. Some pressure, then, was necessary to force Vienna to suspend her military movements. But any form of Russian mobilization was always likely to be the wrong choice.

Immediately after the conference, Sazonov wired instructions to Izvolsky at Paris – who had been the foreign minister at the time of the

Bosnian crisis – and to Benckendorff in London. Both were to inform the governments there of the decision to mobilize. The former was to express St Petersburg's gratitude for Paléologue's assurances of France's absolute loyalty to Russia; the latter was to urge Grey 'to join France and Russia, without delay, for it is only thus possible to prevent a dangerous disruption of the European equilibrium'.[79]

If Sazonov had hardened his stance, the Tsar now decided that general mobilization was too risky. As before at Berlin, so now at St Petersburg – at the decisive moment the monarchs showed greater sense than their ministers. Still, what now followed in the Russian capital was little short of farcical. Dobrorolski, the mobilization expert, had scurried around the capital collecting the required signatures for the mobilization decree. He was about to set off for the general telegraph office to despatch the necessary alert telegram, when at 9.30 p.m. Yanushkevich telephoned him to order him to stay put. Shortly afterwards a staff officer, Colonel Tugan-Baranowski, turned up with orders from the Tsar not to proceed with the order for general mobilization. 'I will not be responsible for a monstrous slaughter', Nicholas had explained. At 11 p.m. Sukhomlinov telephoned Sazonov to inform him of the latest turn of events. Preparations for a general mobilization were to be stopped, though the war minister was not slow to notice that the Tsar had not rescinded the earlier order for general mobilization – uncertain as to the right course he had asked not to go ahead with it.[80] For Nicholas II, cousin 'Willy's' assurances rang true. 'War would be disastrous for the world and once it had broken out it would be difficult to stop', he told Bark, the finance minister: 'The German Emperor had frequently assured him of his sincere desire to safeguard the peace of Europe and it had always been possible to come to an agreement with him, even in serious cases.'[81]

There was some confusion at St Petersburg following the Tsar's intervention that night. While the first steps of partial mobilization were implemented, the general staff, it seems, decided to proceed with parallel preparations for full mobilization. That at any rate was the advice Basili imparted to the French ambassador when he called upon him sometime around 11 p.m. Thirteen army corps would be mobilized that same night to operate against Austria-Hungary, and general mobilization would

---

[79] Tel. Sazonov to Izvolsky (no. 1551), 16/29 July 1914, *IBZI* v, no. 221; communicated by Benckendorff to the Foreign Office on 30 July, *BD* xi, no. 300.
[80] Sukhomlinov, *Erinnerungen*, 364; S. Dobrorolski, *Die Mobilmachung der russischen Armee* (Berlin, 1922), 25–6; L. C. F. Turner, 'The Russian Mobilization in 1914', *JCH* iii, 1 (1968), 87–8.
[81] Bark memoirs, as quoted in Lieven, *Nicholas II*, 199–200.

commence in secret.[82] News of Russia's partial mobilization came as no surprise to Paléologue. Already in the evening of that day, he had reported as much to the Quai d'Orsay, where Viviani was now once more installed, though it was really President Poincaré who had set the tone of French policy since the return of the two men earlier that morning.[83] Berchtold having declined any further talks, Russia would mobilize troops against the Habsburg Empire, and in the meantime Sazonov supported Grey's idea of a Four-Power conference. Later in the evening, after the foreign minister's third meeting with Pourtalès, Paléologue wired to Paris that the tone of the German ambassador's communication had persuaded the Russian government to order the mobilization against Austria-Hungary. Paléologue's original draft of the second telegram also alerted Paris to the decision to commence general mobilization surreptitiously. Things, however, had changed in the meantime following the Tsar's intervention. At the last moment, shortly before despatching the encyphered text, the embassy counsellor, Charles Pineton de Chambrun, was alerted to the annulment of the general mobilization decree and so struck out all mention of it.[84]

At no stage that evening did Paléologue seek to dissuade Sazonov from his chosen course. If his Italian colleague, Carlotti, is to be believed, the French ambassador had come to the conclusion that, at its core, the current crisis was no longer an Austro-Serbian quarrel but a Russo-German one which was not amenable to any efforts at conciliation – that, in fact, war with the two Germanic Powers was imminent.[85] In consequence, neither on 29 July nor on the following days, did Paléologue take any steps to moderate Russian policy.

There was one more sequel to the frantic events at St Petersburg that night. At midnight Sazonov telephoned Pourtalès and asked him to call upon him once more, for the fourth time that day.[86] Their conversation

[82] Paléologue diary, 29 July 1914, in his *Russie des Tsars* I, 35; see also N. A. de Basily, *Diplomat in Imperial Russia, 1903–1917* (Stanford, CA, 1973), 96.
[83] The President was resolved to assume responsibility for foreign policy, see Poincaré notes journalières, 29 July 1914, Papiers de Poincaré, BN, Bnfr 16027, here fo. 124 v.
[84] See tel. Paléologue to Viviani (no. 304), 29 July 1914 (D 9.09 p.m.), *DDF* (3) XI, no. 283, n. 5; also J. Stengers, '1914: The Safety of Ciphers and the Outbreak of the First World War', C. Andrew (ed.), *Intelligence and International Relations* (Exeter, 1987), 43. The earlier report on partial mobilization is in tel. Paléologue to Viviani (no. 302), 29 July 1914 (D 6.14 p.m., R 8.40 p.m.), *DDF* (3) XI, no. 274.
[85] See tel. Carlotti to San Giuliano (no. 824/11), 26 July 1914 (D 12.40 a.m.), *DDI* (4) XII, no. 537.
[86] Thus Pourtalès, *Meine letzten Verhandlungen*, 43; Schilling daily journal, 16/29 July 1914, *IBZI* v, no. 224, claims that Pourtalès telephoned to request a meeting, though this seems unlikely as against usual diplomatic practice.

lasted for some ninety minutes, and the ambassador found Sazonov in a calmer frame of mind than earlier in the evening. He confirmed that partial mobilization had now been ordered, and then suggested that Germany join the quartet to induce Vienna 'in the friendliest manner to drop the demands infringing upon Serbia's sovereignty'. Pourtalès was pessimistic. Diplomatic intervention appeared difficult, if not impossible, 'now that Russia had decided upon the fatal step of mobilization'. Austria-Hungary's declaration of territorial *désintéressement* was a significant concession to Russia's interests, and the question of how best to safeguard Serbia's sovereign rights was best left to the eventual peace negotiations. Pourtalès warned of the 'danger of a European conflagration', but Sazonov refused to budge. Russia could not leave Serbia to her fate at the hands of Austria-Hungary, and now that the latter had mobilized it was impossible to rescind the decree for partial mobilization. It was a vital Russian interest that Serbia was not reduced to a 'vassal state of Austria-Hungary'; she was not to become a Balkans 'Bokhara', he insisted – a reference to one of the central Asian khanates that fell under Russian influence in the 1860s before eventually being absorbed by that empire. Only Germany was in a position to restrain Austria-Hungary. The latter's pledge respecting Serbian integrity and independence 'cannot satisfy us', Sazonov warned. The telegraphic exchanges between the imperial cousins at Berlin and St Petersburg had not failed to make an impression on Sazonov, Pourtalès sensed, but he warned that the foreign minister would work on the Tsar to remain firm.[87]

Berlin contemplates the great *Kladderadatsch* and Bethmann Hollweg makes a bid

In Germany, too, events moved at a frantic pace. In the late afternoon, commencing at about 4.40 p.m., a series of meetings took place at Potsdam and Berlin between the Kaiser and the heads of the civilian and military leadership. Falkenhayn, the war minister, pressed for an immediate declaration of *Kriegsgefahrzustand*. The chancellor demurred. Such a step would mark a significant escalation. He was anxious to gain time for further talks; and there had, of course, been no answer yet to the 'Halt in Belgrade' idea. Bethmann Hollweg and, much to Falkenhayn's amazement, Moltke, too, would agree to no more than minimal security precautions, mostly to place railway bridges and installations under military guard. The war minister was not wholly opposed to this decision: 'for he who still believes in peace,

---

[87] Tels. Pourtalès to Auswärtiges Amt (nos. 189, urgent, and 190), 30 July 1914 (D 4.30 a.m., R 7.10 a.m., D 9.30 a.m., R 12.13 p.m.), *DD* II, nos. 401 and 412; also Pourtalès, *Meine letzten Verhandlungen*, 45.

or at least wishes it, cannot urge the declaration of imminent danger of war here'. There was the risk of placing Germany at a disadvantage militarily, 'but if Moltke is able to justify this, I cannot resist it'.[88] The military had not yet seized control of German decision-making.

It was not unusual for the chief of staff to make self-contradictory statements. But in his moderate stance on 29 July, Moltke may well have been influenced by the latest intelligence reports compiled by the general staff that day. In western Europe, Dutch mobilization continued apace, while at Brussels a call-up of reservists was contemplated. There had been no such recall as yet in France, though railway rolling stock was being set aside in the marshalling yards around Paris and other railway materials stockpiled. The arming of the strategically important fortress at Belfort in the Franche Comté continued. Similarly, rolling stock on the Russian railways was being marshalled. Border guards had been strengthened, and in some areas horses requisitioned. But there were as yet no indications of mobilization in the Vilnius and Warsaw military districts.[89]

As for Bethmann, his line appears to have been the one he developed on the following day at a meeting of the Prussian government (under Germany's 1871 constitution the positions of German chancellor and Prussian minister-president were held in conjunction): declaring the immediate danger of war was tantamount to announcing mobilization, and this could only mean war. In the meantime, diplomatic moves and military preparations could not run in parallel.[90]

What is remarkable about the meetings at Potsdam on 29 July is that at no stage did either the Kaiser or the chancellor raise Moltke's memorandum of the previous evening; nor, it seems, did Moltke press the matter himself. For the moment the chancellor had prevailed, even though he left the meeting 'crimson-faced'. But it was apparent now that there were 'sharply contrasting opinions' held by the civilian and the military leaderships, as the Württemberg envoy at Berlin was told, with Bethmann favouring further talks and senior military officials arguing for military preparations to be made.[91]

---

[88] Falkenhayn diary, 29 July 1914, as quoted in Afflerbach, *Falkenhayn*, 155–6; see also *JK* II, no. 674; A. von Wegerer, *Der Ausbruch des Weltkrieges 1914* (2 vols., Hamburg, 1939) II, 112.

[89] General Staff Report No. 3, 29 July 1914 (*c.* 4 p.m.), *DD* II, no. 372.

[90] Minutes of the Meeting of the Royal Prussian State Ministry, 30 July 1914, *DD* II, no. 456.

[91] Quotes from Müller diary, 29 July 1914, W. Görlitz (ed.), *Regierte der Kaiser? Aus den Kriegstagebücher des Chefs des Marinekabinetts im ersten Weltkrieg Admiral Georg von Müller* (Göttingen, 1959), 36; Varnbühler to Weizsäcker (no. 1991), 30 July 1914, *DGB* no. 52.

Around 6 p.m. the Kaiser received navy minister Tirpitz and other members of his naval entourage. He informed them of his brother's encounter with King George V, and he was satisfied that British neutrality seemed certain: 'I have the word of a king; that is enough for me.' That the King had no decisive say in the matter, his German cousin blithely ignored, and went on in a similar vein to explain his telegraphic exchanges with the Tsar: 'It would be madness if it came to a general war because of that [the Austro-Serbian quarrel].' The Kaiser added a number of revealing observations. Despite Vienna's non-annexation pledge, 'he did not know what the Austrians wanted. He ... had therefore meant to despatch a gentleman from the Auswärtiges Amt to Vienna, but the trains had been stopped.' Tschirschky had been instructed to make enquiries at Vienna: 'The Serbs had really conceded everything except for a few bagatelles. He could understand that the Austrian army needed satisfaction, having three times mobilized in vain, but for that a *Faustpfand* [forfeit] would suffice.' He also said that when Szögyény and Hoyos asked for German support, he had assumed that Austria-Hungary would launch an immediate military strike against Serbia.[92] The Kaiser's comments throw another light on his motivations in early July; they underline that, at the end of the month, he remained convinced that his 'Halt in Belgrade' scheme was still current; but they also highlight once more the dysfunctional nature of the German governmental system. The monarch was in utter ignorance that his mediation scheme had been quietly ditched, nor was Bethmann any better informed.

When the chancellor emerged from the Potsdam meeting 'crimson-faced', he had nevertheless retained control over the central question of whether or not to mobilize. By the time he had returned to the Wilhelmstrasse sometime around 6 p.m., his diplomatic strategy was on the verge of collapse. In the late afternoon, Sergei Nikola'evich Sverbe'ev, the Russian ambassador, who had returned to Berlin that day, called on Jagow at the Auswärtiges Amt. During their conversation, the state secretary received news of Russian military preparations, which the ambassador confirmed meant the mobilization of the four western military districts – a curious parallel with Sazonov receiving the news of the shelling of Belgrade while Szápáry was with him. Jagow responded to the ambassador's statement 'with strong emotion'. The Russian move changed the situation; it brought to an end all diplomatic efforts. There was no chance now of averting a European war. This was a remarkable suggestion, for on previous

---

[92] Tirpitz notes, 29 July 1914, A. von Tirpitz, *Politische Dokumente. Deutsche Ohnmachtspolitik im Weltkriege* (Hamburg, 1926), 2–4.

occasions Jagow had made it plain that partial mobilization by Russia would not trigger German counter-measures, as Sverbe'ev pointed out to him.[93] For Jagow the news of Russia's partial mobilization did indeed change everything, because until now he had assumed that a hard line by the Austro-German group would be sufficient to deter Russia – hence his second 'blank cheque' to Tschirschky. Now it would no longer be possible for Austria-Hungary to wage a successful limited war against Serbia and so restore her prestige in the Balkans. All his calculations had proved wrong; his policy had failed. Little wonder that he reacted 'with strong emotion' to Sverbe'ev's communication.

Bethmann's reaction to the news from Russia is not recorded. That same evening, he had a further conference with Moltke and Falkenhayn, with Jagow in attendance. The war minister pressed for immediate mobilization, which suggestion the chancellor rejected 'against *quiet, very quiet* resistance from Moltke'. Russia's mobilization did not necessarily mean war, and the *casus foederis* was thus not yet given. It would be better, Bethmann pointed out, if Russia 'unleashed the furies of war by attacking Austria and so bore the guilt for the great *Kladderadatsch* [crash]'. Falkenhayn disagreed but kept his views to himself, for 'it is not my job to guide the politicians'. Besides, a few hours' wait would not make much difference to Germany's military prospects.[94] There was no question, then, of the military assuming power at Berlin. Although no military measures were to be taken, as a precaution a draft ultimatum was drawn up and despatched to the German minister at Brussels, in a double-sealed envelope, to be presented to the Belgian government but with firm instructions to do so only if ordered by Berlin.[95]

Russian neutrality in an Austro-Serbian conflict had been one key assumption underpinning German policy during the July crisis. There was a sense of shock and incipient panic at the Wilhelmstrasse. As he passed the two sphinxes in the foyer of the foreign ministry, Theodor Wolff sensed a change in the mood at the Wilhelmstrasse. It was an atmosphere as in a casino when, as dawn approaches, nervous gamblers placed their dwindled stock of chips on a last throw of the dice. There was – literally – a whiff of Dutch courage wafting down the corridors of the Auswärtiges Amt:

---

[93] Tel. Sverbe'ev to Sazonov (no. 140), 16/29 July 1914, *IBZI* v, no. 241. For Jagow's earlier statement to Jules Cambon, see tel. Bronevski to Sazonov (no. 134), 14/27 July 1914, *ibid.*, no. 135.

[94] Falkenhayn diary, 29 July 1914, Afflerbach, *Falkenhayn*, 157–8 (original emphasis).

[95] Jagow to Below-Saleske, 29 July 1914, encl. ultimatum, 29 July 1914, *DD* II, nos. 375–6. The ultimatum was based on an earlier draft by Moltke of 26 July: *ibid.*, no. 376, n. 1.

'Shrugging their shoulders they feigned *sang froid*, they hid their fear behind masks, they returned from the club ... where they had revived their fortitude with brandy, to find despatches, every one of which reveal the rising of the tide.'[96]

Goschen, the British ambassador – more prosaic than the journalist Wolff – found Jagow 'very depressed' that evening. He was 'much troubled' by Russian mobilization and preparatory measures taken by France. No mention was made of the British naval alert, but Goschen noted that it had caused instability on the German money markets, shares in the major German shipping lines dropping by several points. From Berlin's perspective, in light of the latest news from Russia, cooperation with Britain acquired renewed importance. And here Grey's invitation for Germany 'to make any suggestion' and to '"press the button" in the interests of peace' offered an opening. Jagow tried to resurrect Grey's quartet scheme and combine it with 'Halt in Belgrade', which he had earlier tried to sink. It occurred to him, he explained to Goschen, that when Austro-Hungarian troops had entered Serbian territory, and Habsburg military prestige had thus been satisfied, the moment might have come for the four disinterested Powers 'to discuss [the] situation and come forward with suggestions for preventing graver complications'.[97]

Whatever their surreptitious differences so far, adversity threw Jagow and the chancellor together. Late at night, Bethmann asked Goschen to call upon him at the chancellery – some 500 yards from the British embassy along the Wilhelmstrasse – to make 'the following strong bid for British neutrality', the ambassador reported. An attack by Russia on Austria-Hungary now seemed likely, and this would mean war, 'a European conflagration'. Would Britain remain neutral? The chancellor appreciated that London could not tolerate France being crushed for balance of power reasons. 'Such a result was not contemplated', however, and he offered assurances that, were Germany to be victorious, she would not seek to secure 'territorial acquisitions at the expense of France'.[98] Goschen was shrewd enough to ask whether the guarantee covered French colonies – it did not – but the chancellor was ready to guarantee that the neutrality of

---

[96] T. Wolff, *Der Krieg des Pontius Pilatus* (Zürich, 1934), 337.
[97] Tel. Goschen to Grey (no. 101), 29 July 1914 (D 11.20 p.m., R 12 a.m.), *BD* XI, no. 281. Grey's invitation is in tel. Lichnowsky to Auswärtiges Amt (no. 174), 29 July 1914 (D 2.08 p.m., R 5.07 p.m.), *DD* II, no. 357; and tel. Grey to Goschen (no. 226), 29 July 1914 (D 4.45 p.m.), *BD* XI, no. 263.
[98] The draft ultimatum to Belgium offered 'to accommodate in the most benevolent manner possible compensation claims on the part of the kingdom [Belgium] at the expense of France' in return for allowing free passage to German troops, draft ultimatum, 29 July 1914, *DD* II, no. 376.

the Netherlands would be respected. This was a clumsy move on Bethmann's part, for it triggered the obvious counter-question as to Germany's attitude towards Belgium. The chancellor hid behind vague yet transparent phrases. He 'could not tell to what operations Germany might be forced by the action of France', but affirmed that Belgium's 'integrity would be respected after the conclusion of the war'. This was as good an admission as any that German troops would invade neighbouring Belgium in any campaign in the west, as Goschen duly noted. The chancellor was angling for some neutrality agreement with Britain – during the earlier meeting with the Kaiser he had broached the subject – but Goschen stuck to the official line: the British government would 'retain full liberty of action'.[99]

Bethmann's bid for British neutrality was a crass manoeuvre, especially by the chancellor's own standards and given that similar attempts to secure a neutrality agreement with Britain had failed repeatedly between 1909 and 1912. It seems that, at the moment of his interview with Goschen – Lichnowsky's telegram no. 178 arrived at 9.12 p.m. at the Wilhelmstrasse but still needed to be decyphered – he had no knowledge of Grey's explicit warning. Even so, his maladroit manoeuvre was counter-productive and did little more than to convince London of Germany's willingness to go to war. 'The only comment that need be made on these astounding proposals', minuted Crowe, 'is that they reflect discredit on the statesman who makes them'. The one 'restraining influence' on Berlin so far had been the fear of British intervention in the event of a continental war.[100] On the night of 29 July, Crowe wrote to his wife that the 'Austrians have refused to discuss anything with anybody. They are singularly stupid and ill-inspired'. With Germany so far not having restrained Austria-Hungary and Russia beginning to mobilize, the 'only remaining hope at the moment is that the Emperor of Russia is in communication with the German Emperor'.[101]

Bethmann sends several telegrams and the Kaiser sees Germany squirming in the net

Goschen and Wolff were not the only visitors to the Wilhelmstrasse who sensed a change of the prevailing mood there. Hitherto, reported Szögyény on 30 July, officials at Berlin had viewed the prospect of European

---

[99] Tel. Goschen to Grey (no. 102, secret), 29 July 1914 (D 30 July, 1.20 a.m., R 9 a.m.), BD xi, no. 293; Bethmann's notes are in DD ii, no. 373. Goschen drafted the telegram in the chancellor's presence, and the latter made a few amendments to it.
[100] Min. Crowe, 30 July 1914, BD xi, no. 293.
[101] Crowe to Clema Crowe, 29 July 1914, Crowe MSS, Bodl., Ms.Eng.d.2903.

complications with calm. Now, he noted that 'in recent days a nervousness has gripped them', a mood-swing that he attributed in equal measure to the prospect of war and Berlin's failure to force the Habsburg government to appease Italian expectations of territorial gain as a reward for not abandoning the alliance of the Central Powers.[102]

Berlin was, in fact, in the grip of confusion and panic following the news of Russia's partial mobilization and Grey's explicit warnings. The two main planks on which Germany's ill-conceived policy had been erected had snapped. Unless the Austro-Hungarian campaign against Serbia – Berlin still did not know of Conrad's planned attack from the west – could be limited, Russian intervention in the conflict could scarcely be prevented now. If Russia entered the war in the Balkans, the Franco-Russian and Austro-German alliances made a continental war all but certain. And now Grey's latest statement had made clear that British neutrality was not likely either.

During the night of 29/30 July, the chancellor launched several initiatives aimed at St Petersburg, London and Vienna. It was a last-minute attempt to stave off a European war, and it was a desperate gamble to defend his own position at Berlin before the military logic of the deteriorating international situation started dictating the next moves. He was, in fact, prepared to throw German policy into reverse gear. Grey's version of 'Halt in Belgrade', as developed in conversation with Lichnowsky earlier on 29 July, seemed to offer a way out of the crisis; and on this basis Bethmann was prepared to negotiate. With that in view, Pourtalès was instructed to warn Sazonov that Russian mobilization along the Habsburg frontier would trigger Austro-Hungarian counter-measures: 'It is difficult to say how far the stones that have thus begun to roll can still be stopped, and I fear that Herr Sazonov's pacific aims can now no longer be realized.' Berlin sought to moderate Austro-Hungarian policy to avert a general war. A temporary occupation of some Serbian territory coupled to a formal pledge not to annex any portions of it should satisfy both Russia and Austria-Hungary. Serbia would have been taught the 'deserved lesson', which even Sazonov had admitted was necessary, and Vienna would secure the guarantees it needed. It was necessary therefore for Russia to avoid any measures that would precipitate an Austro-Russian conflict. It is an

---

[102] Tel. Szögyény to Berchtold (no. 328), 30 July 1914 (D 5.30 p.m., R 7.20 p.m.), ÖUA VIII, no. 11030; see also B. W. Bülow, *Die Krise. Die Grundlinie der diplomatischen Verhandlungen bei Kriegsausbruch* (Berlin, 1922), 125, who speaks of 'headlessness' at Berlin. Jules Cambon, by contrast, thought that Goschen's vague declarations were not enough to dispel Berlin's illusions as to British neutrality, see tel. J. Cambon to Viviani (no. 220), 30 July 1914 (D 2.05 p.m., R 3.50 p.m.), DDF (3) XI, no. 326.

indication of the extreme sense of urgency with which the chancellor acted that, in a follow-up telegram in the small hours of 30 July, the ambassador was instructed to impress upon Sazonov that Berlin continued to work on Vienna.[103]

Similar instructions were wired to Lichnowsky in London at 2.55 a.m. German diplomacy continued mediating at Vienna, and urged the Habsburg leadership to accept Grey's latest proposals.[104] This was, in fact, true – or, at least, Bethmann hoped that it would be by the time Pourtalès and Lichnowsky acted on their instructions. Now at last, the chancellor and Jagow sought to put Vienna on a short leash. Two telegrams were despatched to Tschirschky shortly after midnight. In the first Grey's version of 'Halt in Belgrade' was transmitted with express instructions to the ambassador to impress upon Berchtold that the German government regarded this an appropriate basis for negotiations. In a second telegram Vienna was reminded that Russian mobilization did not necessarily imply war, and that St Petersburg had complained of the uncommunicative nature of Austro-Hungarian diplomacy in recent days: 'To avoid a general catastrophe, or at least to put Russia in the wrong, we must urge that Vienna ... continues conversations.'[105] Tellingly, the reference to avoiding 'a general catastophe' was inserted in the final draft by Jagow. That Tschirschky was now to 'urge' Berchtold to accept also went a good deal further than previous instructions. Of course, the telegram also indicated an alternative outcome – war, in which case Russia had to be shown to be the aggressor. But as the reference to avoiding the 'general catastrophe' under-lines, this was very much the least preferred outcome. It was an attempt to reassert German influence over the alliance partner and so to regain control over events.

Jagow and Bethmann were prepared to go further still. They now sought to revoke the 'blank cheque'. The fresh instructions to Tschirschky, sent at 2.55 and 3 a.m., were intended to be 'the sharpest notes which diplomatic form made acceptable' and the telegrams were 'very peremp-tory', as Jagow later reflected. But having effectively equipped Tschirschky with a second 'blank cheque' he found it difficult now to ensure that this time the ambassador acted on his instructions. To lend greater emphasis to 'our standpoint', Jagow decided to have the telegraphic instructions to

---

[103] Tels. Bethmann Hollweg to Pourtalès (nos. 139, urgent, and 142), 29 July 1914 (D 11.05 p.m.) and 30 July (D 2.55 a.m.), *DD* II, nos. 380 and 392.
[104] Tel. Bethmann Hollweg to Lichnowsky (no. 188), 30 July 1914 (D 2.55 a.m.), *DD* II, no. 393.
[105] Tels. Bethmann Hollweg to Tschirschky (nos. 190 and 187), 29 July 1914 (D 12.30 a.m.), *DD* II, nos. 384 and 385 (quote from latter). The final drafts are in Jagow's hand.

Tschirschky signed by Bethmann Hollweg. With that in mind, he walked across the gardens behind the Wilhelmstrasse to the chancellor palais. It was nearly midnight by now, and the rear door to the chancellor's residence was already locked. There was still light in one of the ground-floor offices, however, and Jagow pushed open one of the windows, climbed through and then walked up to Bethmann's rooms, where he found him already asleep: 'He signed the note in his bed' (he also made a number of smaller amendments to the texts).

Because of Berchtold's 'stubborn reluctance', Jagow observed in unpublished post-war reflections on the July crisis, valuable time had been lost,

> which might have irritated Sazonov yet more and might have driven him to wrest full mobilization from the Tsar. Sazonov as well as the Tsar knew that this meant war. I believed firmly that, if the negotiations between Vienna and Petersburg, already initiated, were resumed – Grey after all referred to them as "the best means" – with our efforts an arrangement could have been achieved.[106]

If there was something of a cloak-and-dagger operation about Jagow's late-night breaking and entering of the chancellor's residence, it underlined the sense of panic and urgency at Berlin. The message to the Ballhausplatz to be conveyed by Tschirschky was sharply worded, indeed. The first telegram forwarded Lichnowsky's last telegram, containing Grey's explicit warning. Austria-Hungary's refusal to accept any form of mediation was now likely to lead to 'a conflagration'. With Britain not likely to remain neutral, and Italy and Romania unlikely to support the Austro-German combination, the main burden of the war would fall on Germany – 'we would stand 2 against 4 Great Powers'. In these circumstances, Germany pressed Vienna 'urgently and emphatically' to accept mediation 'under honourable conditions', including the occupation of Belgrade or other places in Serbia. With the 'humiliation of Serbia' thus secured, the Habsburg Empire would enhance its prestige 'in the Balkans as well as against Russia'.[107]

The second telegram was more explicit still. It contained an abridged version of Pourtalès's telegram of the previous evening – abridged

---

[106] Jagow, 'Julikrise und Kriegsausbruch', Nachlass Jagow, TNA (PRO), GFM 25/16, fos. 17–18.
[107] Tel. Bethmann Hollweg to Tschirschky (no. 192, urgent), 30 July 1914 (D 2.55 a.m., R ? p.m.), DD II, no. 395. For the view that Bethmann only wished to give the appearance of restraining Vienna see F. Fischer, *Der Krieg der Illusionen. Die deutsche Politik von 1911 bis 1914* (Düsseldorf, 1969), 712–13.

in that it omitted all reference to Sazonov 'clutching at straws'. Berchtold was requested to confirm whether Szápáry had been instructed not to continue talks at St Petersburg, as alleged by the Russian foreign minister. This was another attempt to obtain clarity on Vienna's aims. Tschirschky was to explain 'with all emphasis and great seriousness' that, whilst Austria-Hungary could not be expected to negotiate directly with Serbia, it would be a grave mistake to reject any exchange of views with the Russian government – 'it would rather provoke Russia's military intervention'. To avoid this ought to be Vienna's principal interest, the chancellor argued, and then finished with a bang: 'We are quite prepared to fulfil our alliance obligations, but we must refuse being dragged by Vienna, recklessly and without consideration of our advice, into a world inferno [*Weltenbrand*]. In the Italian question as well Vienna appears to ignore our advice.'[108] Effectively, this was a threat to revoke the *casus foederis*, though Jagow himself did not make this explicit in his own conversation with Szögyény later on 30 July.[109]

In line with this attempted course correction, Jagow called upon Goschen at the British embassy in the morning of 30 July, apparently the only such visit during the crisis. Germany was mediating at Vienna on the basis of 'Halt in Belgrade' or a variant thereof, he explained. Mobilization in Russia's south-western districts complicated matters, and he asked Grey to intercede with St Petersburg to persuade it to accept this as the basis for an arrangement. In the meantime, it was important that Russia took no steps 'which might be regarded as an act of aggression against Austria'. For as long as that did not happen 'he still sees some chance that European peace may be preserved'.

This was straightforward enough. As for his dealings with Britain, his call on Goschen was, in part, also an attempt to repair some of the damage the chancellor's nocturnal musings on a war in the west and Belgian neutrality might have done. Had Bethmann known of Lichnowsky's latest conversation with Grey, in which the Foreign Secretary had warned of Britain's intervention, 'the Chancellor would, of course, not have spoken to me in [the] way he had done'. There was still the hint of a threat, however. Germany herself was caught in an awkward position, and the measures taken by Russia, and possibly by France

[108] Tel. Bethmann Hollweg to Tschirschky (no. 193), 30 July 1914 (D 3 a.m., R 10 a.m.), *DD* II, no. 396; F. Fischer, *Weltmacht oder Niedergang. Deutschland im ersten Weltkrieg* (Frankfurt, 2nd edn 1968), 58–9.
[109] See tel. Szögyény to Berchtold (no. 327), 30 July 1914 (D 5.15 p.m., R 8 p.m.), *ÖUA* VIII, no. 11029.

too, would force her to respond in kind: 'He [Jagow] regretted this …
but it would be a military necessity.'[110]

Jagow's reference to aggressive measures by Russia against the
Habsburg Empire was ambiguous at best, though Bethmann's instructions
to Lichnowsky later that morning suggest that he hoped British pressure
might yet prevent the deployment of Russian forces along the Galician
frontier.[111] If they were deployed there, it would, of course, increase the
pressure on Austria-Hungary, and, conversely, increase the damage to the
Austro-German alliance if Vienna decided to give in to such pressure
because German support was insufficient. There was, then, still an only
half-articulated hope that London might somehow still pull Berlin's already
scorched chestnuts out of the fire. If Britain asserted her influence to secure
Vienna the guarantees it sought, on the basis of the temporary occupation
of Belgrade, 'then this would be a possible satisfaction for Austria'.[112]

At the same time, Stumm, the Wilhelmstrasse's British expert
whose certain predictions of British neutrality had disproved his claims to
expertise on the subject, approached the Berlin correspondent of Spender's
Westminster Gazette with a slightly abridged version of the third of the
late-night telegrams to Tschirschky and requested that this 'telegram of the
highest importance' be published in the London paper. Stumm's motives
are not entirely clear. Certainly, the news, if printed, was calculated to win
Berlin some sympathy in Britain, especially perhaps amongst the doubters,
pacificists and sceptics on the Liberal backbenches. But it would also have
increased the pressure on Vienna to reciprocate in kind to what, in practice,
would then be a joint Anglo-German mediation proposal. Either way
greater publicity could only be to Berlin's benefit. Spender 'cabled at once
that I would & put it straight into the paper, but my cable was not
delivered', leaving Stumm angry and embittered at the hitherto seemingly
so pro-German editor's non-reply.[113]

Whether the publication of the abridged telegram would have
made any difference, it is idle to speculate. Even if it had, there is no
denying that Berlin had left it far too late to rein in the Habsburg ally.

---

[110] Tel. Goschen to Grey (no. 103), 30 July 1914 (D 1.45 p.m., R 3.35 p.m.), *BD* xi,
no. 305; for Jagow's visit see Wegerer, *Ausbruch* ii, 106.
[111] Tel. Bethmann Hollweg to Lichnowsky (no. 191), 30 July 1914 (D 11.30 a.m.),
DD ii, no. 409.
[112] Bethmann to Wilhelm II, 30 July 1914 (D 11.15 a.m.), *DD* ii, no. 407. The letter was
drafted by Jagow; the Kaiser was not informed of the apocalyptic warnings contained in
the final telegram to Tschirschky.
[113] Memo. Spender, n.d. [Aug. 1914], Spender MSS, BL, Add. MSS. 46392, fo. 172;
also H. Kantorowicz, *Gutachten zur Kriegsschuldtage 1914*, ed. I. Geiss (Frankfurt,
1967), 94.

And, of course, there was the problem of the hawkish ambassador at Vienna, who had in his possession a personal 'blank cheque'. That Tschirschky conveyed Berlin's change of heart is beyond doubt. As Hugo Ganz, the correspondent of the *Frankfurter Zeitung* and Tschirschky's oft-employed go-between at Vienna, later testified, he found the ambassador in sombre mood on 30 July, and about to call on Berchtold with whom he was to have lunch. Tschirschky was 'in unaccustomed official dress and had a portfolio under his arm'. Knowing, presumably from the ambassador himself, that Berlin now sought to restrain Austria-Hungary, Ganz said 'jestingly ... in the words of Frundsberg to Luther: "Little monk, thou goest on a hard journey." He answered: "God knows I do."' On his return to the embassy Tschirschky said: 'Thank God, Berchtold gave way.'[114]

According to Berchtold's notes, Tschirschky had, indeed, acted in accordance with his instructions. Having explained the recent exchanges at London and St Petersburg, he suggested that 'Austria-Hungary could thus secure guarantees for the future without unleashing a world war'. Vienna ought to accept the mediation proposals 'under the given honourable conditions'.[115] Tschirschky had acted as instructed, but the Ballhausplatz's response was not encouraging. Szápáry, Tschirschky reported to Berlin, had been instructed to open discussions with Sazonov on the Serbian note and to receive any further suggestions the Russian foreign minister might make concerning the Serbian dispute or any other questions pertaining to Austro-Russian relations – a curious statement, considering that any of this fell into the remit of an ambassador's ordinary duties. The Russian government would be given further assurances that the mobilization of eight army corps reflected Austro-Hungarian intelligence estimates which put the strength of the Serbian army at *c.* 400,000 men. Meanwhile, Szápáry at St Petersburg and Berchtold himself in his conversations with Shebeko, would reiterate Austria-Hungary's non-annexation pledge. Any temporary occupation of Serbian territory after a peace had been signed was meant to ensure that Belgrade fulfilled the terms of the treaty. '*Au fur et à mesure*', that is, to the degree to which they had been fulfilled, the occupied areas would then be evacuated. 'Pretty much my proposal', minuted the Kaiser later that afternoon: 'accepted and thus enacted, as I telegraphed my views to the Tsar. *Good*.'[116]

---

[114] Deposition Ganz, 17 Dec. 1919, *OGD* I, no. 10. Ganz mistakenly gives 31 July as the date of the meeting.

[115] Berchtold daily report, 30 July 1914, *ÖUA* VIII, no. 11025.

[116] Tel. Tschirschky to Auswärtiges Amt (no. 135), 30 July 1914, and marginal comment by Wilhelm II, n.d. [30 July], *DD* II, no. 433 (Kaiser's emphasis).

Except all was not well. For what Berchtold had signalled was not talks with Russia on the basis of 'Halt in Belgrade', but merely further explanations on the Serbian note and a promise to act in the spirit of the scheme when it came to signing the peace treaty. As with the German proposal regarding Italian claims for compensation, Berchtold had settled for his own version of Shylock, this time making concessions 'for the sake of appearances' but without actually conceding anything at all.[117] Vienna's reply to Berlin's latest representations had been carefully worded, and it is difficult to avoid the conclusion that Tschirschky and Berchtold had colluded in the matter.

Tschirschky's handling of the instructions contained in the fourth of the night-time telegrams provides further evidence. The telegram was received at the embassy sometime between 10 a.m. and noon, just as Tschirschky was about to leave for the Ballhausplatz. Dietrich von Bethmann Hollweg, the chancellor's cousin and second embassy secretary at Vienna, deciphered it and then personally delivered it to Tschirschky at the Ballhausplatz. As he later recounted to Josef Redlich: '[Dietrich] Bethmann sat next to Berchtold, when he read the telegram that Tschirschky had handed him, and he noticed that he turned deathly pale.'[118] And well he might, for this was the telegram that threatened to revoke the 'blank cheque' and refuse German support unless Vienna accepted some form of mediation. The foreign minister's account of the luncheon with Tschirschky differs slightly from the embassy secretary's recollections, but adds a further piece of evidence. The ambassador, Berchtold wrote, having twice read out the urgent telegram, 'resembled a man from underneath whom had been pulled the plank on which he stood'. Previously Tschirschky had urged Vienna to persist and not to yield. Now Berlin instructed him to argue the opposite case. Even so, as Berchtold put it, 'we met in the idea that this new suggestion need not cause the slightest concern. Rejection nevertheless ought to be avoided, and an accommodating formula be chosen.'[119] In other words, Berchtold and Tschirschky agreed not to take heed of Berlin's warnings of a world war and to ignore the explicit threat to revoke the *casus foederis*.

In consequence, the ambassador wired back to Berlin Berchtold's assurances that he had not rejected direct Austro-Russian talks as part of a

---

[117] Tschirschky to Jagow (private), 26/28 July 1914, *DD* II, no. 326.

[118] Redlich diary, 13 June 1915, F. Fellner (ed.), *Schicksalsjahre Österreichs, 1908–1919. Das politische Tagebuch Josef Redlichs* (2 vols., Graz and Cologne, 1954) II, 43. The telegram in the German files gives 10 a.m. as the time of receipt; Dietrich Bethmann suggested that it was nearer noon.

[119] Berchtold, 'Halt in Belgrade', Hantsch, *Berchtold* II, 633–4.

wider mediation effort, and that Szápáry had already been issued with fresh instructions.[120] In a follow-up telegram, Tschirschky reported that he had acted in the sense of his latest instructions, and that he had given Berchtold and Forgách, who took notes, the telegram to read, but added that 'a restriction of the already commenced military operations scarcely appeared possible'.[121]

Clearly, however, this was a deliberate deception, practised jointly on the Wilhelmstrasse by the Habsburg minister and the German ambassador. As seen before, the latter had long identified himself with Habsburg interests and the 'anti-Servian and anti-Russian feeling prevalent in Vienna', as the British ambassador observed on that same day. Indeed, according to the later recollections of de Bunsen's French colleague, Alfred Dumaine, Tschirschky 'constantly proclaimed himself an irreconcilable adversary of Serbia ... One day he said to me: "I am so convinced of the necessity of crushing the Serbs that I should not fear to outstep my Government's instructions in order to make Austria decide to act."'[122] If Tschirschky arrogated for himself the authority to decide which instructions to execute, or which parts of them, then Jagow's second 'blank cheque', personal to the ambassador, had done nothing to restrain Tschirschky's arrogance.

Indeed, the ambassador's act of disobedience passed almost unnoticed, Jagow merely forwarding his latest telegram to Lichnowsky 'for information'.[123] By now, Berlin was preoccupied with Russia's mobilization. In the early hours of 30 July Pourtalès was instructed to inform Sazonov that Berlin continued to mediate, but that Russia had to refrain from 'any hostilities' against Austria-Hungary. This was a precondition of any German efforts in that direction.[124] As with Jagow's statement to the British ambassador that same morning, the instructions to Pourtalès lacked precision. Sazonov had already declared that, on mobilization, Russian troops would not cross into Austro-Hungarian territory. Was mobilization against Austria-Hungary already a hostile act? Quite possibly the imprecision was meant to generate yet more pressure on St Petersburg.

[120] Tel. Tschirschky to Auswärtiges Amt (no. 141), 30 July 1914 (D 8.50 p.m., R 10.25 p.m.), *DD* II, no. 448.
[121] Tel. Tschirschky to Auswärtiges Amt (no. 142), 30 July 1914 (D 31 July, 1.35 a.m., R 4.35 a.m.), *DD* II, no. 465.
[122] Quotes from tel. de Bunsen to Grey (no. 135), 30 July 1914, *BD* XI, no. 307; and Dumaine's recollections as quoted in L. Albertini, *The Origins of the War of 1914* (3 vols., London, 1953) II, 153.
[123] See *DD* II, no. 448, n. 2.
[124] Tel. Bethmann Hollweg to Pourtalès (no. 142), 30 July 1914 (D 2.55 a.m.), *DD* II, no. 392.

Conversely, Berlin itself was beginning to feel the impact of Russia's partial mobilization. In the morning of 30 July, the Tsar's reply to the Kaiser's latest telegram arrived at the Neues Palais. The military measures which had now come into force, Nicholas wired, had been decided upon on 25 July, and had been dictated by Austria-Hungary's military preparations. He hoped that the steps 'won't in any way interfere with your part as mediator ... We need your strong pressure on Austria to come to an understanding with us.' This was sensible enough, though it tilted the balance of influence in Russia's favour. It was, in fact, in line with Bethmann's and Jagow's latest attempts to moderate Habsburg policy. But it was not the way to talk to the German Emperor. He regarded the revelation of the Russian decision of 25 July, that is before the Tsar's appeal to him, as a personal affront. Russia had thus gained nearly a week's time for preparations. This, of course, was not entirely correct, for there had been no mobilization measures yet, but an impression to that effect was beginning to form at Berlin. Meanwhile, Austria-Hungary had no intention of attacking Russia. Why, then, had Russia decided on measures against the Habsburg Empire? The Tsar, Wilhelm concluded, had called upon him to mediate and yet had begun to mobilize 'behind my back. It is just a manoeuvre to play us along and so to increase the gain already made.' Under these circumstances, he could no longer act as mediator: 'My job is done.'[125]

Impetuous as the Kaiser was in his reactions, he was also usually ready to accept his chancellor's wiser counsel. On no account was the Emperor to indicate that his mediating efforts had run their course, Bethmann urged, not at least until there was clarity on Vienna's response to Anglo-German mediation proposals. The Kaiser's response to Tsar Nicholas's telegram was thus more measured in tone, but it was unyielding in the matter of Russia's military preparations. Austro-Hungarian measures were aimed only against Serbia, he reiterated, and mobilization on Russia's part thus 'endangered if not ruined' his efforts at mediation. 'The whole weight of the decision lies solely on you[r] shoulders', he warned his cousin at St Petersburg. Nicholas now bore 'the responsibility for Peace or War'.[126]

The Kaiser had done as his chancellor had requested him to do, but there was a subtle shift now in the discussions at Berlin. Localization was no longer part of the calculations there. However measured his reply to

---

[125] Nicholas II to Wilhelm II, 30 July 1914 (D 1.20 a.m., R 1.45 a.m.), and marginal comments by Wilhelm II, 30 July 1914, *DD* II, no. 390.
[126] Tel. Wilhelm II to Nicholas II, 30 July 1914 (D 3.30 p.m.), *DD* II, no. 420.

Tsar Nicholas II, in private Wilhelm considered his role as mediator over. In one of his earlier telegrams, the Russian Emperor had expressed his hope that military measures on Russia's part would not lead to a European war. Responsibility for any such conflict thus rested with the Tsar, the Kaiser informed his chancellor in the evening of 30 July. 'He [Nicholas II] simply lied to me', and his personal appeal to the Kaiser was calculated 'to push us onto the muck heap'.[127]

At around the same time, the Kaiser also read Pourtalès's account of his midnight interview with Sazonov. Wilhelm was beginning to feel the pressure of the deteriorating situation, and, as so often, vitriolic language acted as a safety valve. He doubted the Tsar's word that the Russian mobilization decree could not be rescinded. 'Frivolity and weakness are to plunge the world into the terrible war, which ultimately aims at the destruction of Germany', he fulminated. London, Paris and St Petersburg had conspired to use the Austro-Serbian quarrel as a pretext 'for waging a war of annihilation against us'. Indeed, his ire was chiefly directed against Britain:

> Thus the stupidity and ineptitude of our ally is turned into a noose for us. So the famous '*encirclement*' has become an accomplished fact. The net has suddenly been pulled together over our head and sneeringly England reaps the most brilliant success of her stubbornly pursued purely *anti-German world policy*, against which we are powerless, while she twists the noose of our political and economic destruction, as we squirm *isolated* in the net ... Edward VII is stronger after death than am I who am still alive!![128]

And so on. The vitriol that poured forth from Wilhelm's pen on this occasion was perhaps as much a reflection of the German Emperor's sense of inadequacy to his high office as of the growing pressure on him and on the German leadership. No doubt, Germany's ally had shown great ineptitude, but so had Berlin. That German diplomacy found itself squirming in a net was entirely the result of recklessness at the imperial palace and negligence at the Wilhelmstrasse. Now, however, the focus of Berlin's policy calculations was firmly on Russia.

---

[127] Marginalia by Wilhelm II (7 p.m.) on Bethmann Hollweg to Wilhelm II, 30 July 1914, *DD* II, no. 399.
[128] Marginalia by Wilhelm II, 30 July 1914 (7 p.m.), on tel. Pourtalès to Auswärtiges Amt (no. 189, urgent), 30 July 1914 (D 4.30 a.m., R 7.10 a.m.), *DD* II, no. 401 (Kaiser's emphasis).

Pierre de Margerie is alarmed

The Russian decision for partial mobilization knocked one of the intellectual props from beneath Germany's policy during the July crisis, the assumption that, as in previous Balkan crises, St Petersburg would not enter the fray. The political effect of Russia's military measures was not confined to the two Germanic Powers, but it affected the other Powers in different ways. Most immediately affected was France.

As seen earlier, during the night of 29 July, Sazonov informed ambassador Izvolsky of Pourtalès's warning that Germany would have to mobilize unless Russia stopped her own preparations. Unable to yield to such pressure, St Petersburg had no alternative 'but to hasten our own military preparations and to accept the inevitability of war'.[129] Sazonov's telegram arrived at 3 a.m., and despite the unsociable hour the ambassador took the telegram immediately to the Quai d'Orsay, with a simultaneous communication being made to the French war minister, Adolphe Messimy.[130]

This was the first indication received at Paris that Russia was stepping up military preparations. For the previous four days, Paléologue had kept the Quai in the dark about the state of affairs at St Petersburg. He had portrayed Sazonov as amenable to a compromise solution, and his German colleague as a bully. He had not, for instance, reported on Pourtalès's attempts to encourage direct exchanges between Vienna and St Petersburg. His telegram alerting his government to Russia's partial mobilization did not reach Paris until around midnight and, as seen earlier, it contained no hint that general mobilization had even been discussed by the Tsar's ministers.[131] On the contrary, during the night of 29/30 July, he informed his government of intelligence received by the Russian general staff to the effect that Germany would declare general mobilization on 30 July. As will be seen, reports of German troop movements had indeed been received, but the ambassador's statement was a good deal more conclusive than the intelligence allowed.[132]

The reference in Izvolsky's note to an imminent war was alarming enough. But something else caused consternation at Paris. Pierre de

---

[129] Tel. Sazonov to Izvolsky (no. 1551), 16/29 July 1914, *IBZI* v, no. 221.
[130] Tel. Izvolsky to Sazonov (no. 208), 17/30 July 1914, *DD* II, no. 289; note Izvolsky, 30 July 1914, *DDF* (3) XI, no. 301; also tel. Ignatiev [military attaché] to Danilov (no. 227), 17/30 July 1914, *IBZI* v, no. 293.
[131] See tel. Paléologue to Viviani (no. 304), 29 July 1914 (D 9.09 p.m., R 11.45 p.m.), *DDF* (3) XI, no. 283; cf. Paléologue diary, 29 July 1914, in his *Russie des Tsars* I, 35.
[132] Tel. Paléologue to Viviani (no. 306), 30 July 1914 (D 1.45 a.m., R 3.40 a.m.), *DDF* (3) XI, no. 302; see also Basily, *Memoirs*, 98 n.

Margerie, the political director at the Quai d'Orsay, who received Sazonov's telegram from Izvolsky, was perturbed to read in it of St Petersburg's gratitude for the French government's assurances of absolute support to Russia. Clearly, Paléologue had exceeded his instructions. Margerie immediately woke Viviani, and drafted fresh instructions for the ambassador at St Petersburg. These were then discussed at a hastily convened conference between Poincaré, Viviani and Messimy at the Elysée Palace at 4 a.m.[133] The telegram to Paléologue was carefully worded. France was resolved to fulfil all her obligations towards Russia under the alliance, but at the same time Paris was equally determined 'not to neglect any efforts towards a solution of the conflict in the interest of universal peace'. The ambassador was therefore to advise the Russian government against taking any step 'which may offer Germany a pretext for a general or partial mobilization of her forces'.[134]

Undoubtedly, Margerie and Viviani wished to restrain Russia, if they could. But the decision for some degree of mobilization presented the French government with a dilemma. During the 1912 Balkan turmoil, Poincaré had effectively and unilaterally tightened the terms of the Franco-Russian alliance; and, although not authorized to do so, Paléologue had gone very far in his assurances of support for Russia in the current crisis, as Margerie and the premier only now began to realize. Whether and, if so, how to row back from this position was not at all clear. As for Poincaré, having earlier complained of Sazonov's apparent lack of firmness, he was not likely now to seek to soften Russia's response to the escalating crisis. That he agreed to Margerie's draft was in part dictated by the need to placate his head of government. But there was another consideration that weighed certainly with the president, and possibly with Messimy and Viviani, too. In his diary Poincaré prefaced his summary of the instructions to St Petersburg with the words 'On account of the ambiguous attitude of England, we let it be known at St Petersburg ...'[135] And, indeed, Paul Cambon, the ambassador in London, was not only informed of Izvolsky's communication, he was also instructed to remind Sir Edward Grey of the exchange of letters between the ambassador and the Foreign

---

[133] Poincaré, notes journalières, 30 July 1914, Papiers de Poincaré, BN, Bnfr 16027, fo. 125 r.; for Margerie's role in drafting the telegram, see M. B. Hayne, *The French Foreign Office and the Origins of the First World War* (Oxford, 1993), 287–8.

[134] Tel. Viviani to Paléologue and P. Cambon (nos. 453 and 373–4, confidential), 30 July 1914 (D 7 and 7.10 a.m.), *DDF* (3) XI, no. 305.

[135] Poincaré, notes journalières, 30 July 1914, Papiers de Poincaré, BN, Bnfr 16027, fo. 125 r.; for the importance of Britain for Poincaré see also S. Schmidt, *Frankreichs Aussenpolitik in der Julikrise 1914. Ein Beitrag zur Geschichte des Ausbruchs des Ersten Weltkrieges* (Munich, 2009), 322.

Secretary about possible Anglo-French naval cooperation in the event of European complications.[136]

For Poincaré at least, advising Russia not to precipitate matters – Paléologue was instructed to do no more than advise – was dictated by the perceived necessity of having to carry Britain with the Franco-Russian group. But Paris would not interfere in Russian decision-making, as Messimy made clear to the Russian military attaché, Colonel Count Aleksei Alekse′evich Ignatiev. 'With respect to the higher interests of peace', Russia might even slow up her preparations and avoid mass transports of troops for the moment, without stopping the measures altogether.[137] A note by Abel Ferry, the under-secretary for foreign affairs, made after a brief cabinet meeting at 9.30 a.m., throws further light on French calculations: '1. For the sake of public opinion, the Germans must put themselves in the wrong. 2. Do not stop Russian mobilization. Mobilize but do not concentrate.'[138] Presumably, this was meant to allow for the call-up of reservists. It would at any rate explain why Paris never reacted to Paléologue's report late that night that St Petersburg was 'resolved to proceed secretly to the first measures of general mobilization'.[139]

Neither Poincaré nor the French cabinet was prepared to exercise any kind of moderating influence at St Petersburg. Nothing was done at Paris to prevent war. What mattered now was to frame a case against Germany, without hindering Russian preparations for a war. If, in fact, conflict was now likely, it was all the more important that such preparations commenced sooner rather than later. Only if Russia were able to put pressure on Germany's eastern frontiers would France be able to repel the first wave of the expected German onslaught in the west. These considerations also shaped France's own military measures that day. Marshal Joseph Joffre, the Chief of the General Staff, argued for preparatory measures to be taken. But the ministers were reluctant to allow anything that could later be construed as a provocation. Certain precautions were made, but French troops were not to be mobilized as yet, reservists were not to be called-up and forces were to be kept at a ten-kilometre distance from the

[136] Tel. Viviani to P. Cambon (nos. 373–4, confidential), 30 July 1914 (D 7.10 a.m.), *DDF* (3) XI, no. 305.
[137] Tels. Izvolsky to Sazonov (no. 210), 17/30 July 1914, and Ignatiev to Danilov (no. 227), 17/30 July 1914, *IBZI* v, nos. 291 and 293.
[138] Note Ferry, 30 July 1914 (but misdated Friday), Papiers de Ferry, MAE, PA-AP 181/1; partly also in Schmidt, *Aussenpolitik*, 326; and, albeit partially misquoted, in C. Ponting, *Thirteen Days: The Road to the First World War* (London, 2002), 216.
[139] Tel. Paléologue to Viviani (no. 315, secret), 30 July 1914 (D 9.15 p.m., R 11.25 p.m.), *DDF* (3) XI, no. 359; J. Doise and M. Vaïsse, *Politique étrangère de la France. Diplomatie et outil militaire* (Paris, 1987), 237–45.

German frontier. In taking these measures, at the risk of losing ground during the opening rounds of any conflict, the French government had no other reason 'than to show to the English public and government that France, like Russia, would not be the first to fire'.[140]

One final point needs to be borne in mind. Although French diplomacy took no steps to rein in its Russian ally, it is doubtful whether anything that Paléologue could have said at St Petersburg would have made much difference now. The ambassador's instructions, which stressed 'the interests of universal peace', were despatched at 7 a.m. Later in the day, after his interview with Sazonov and the British ambassador at around 11 a.m., Paléologue reported back to Paris that he had acted as instructed and impressed upon the foreign minister the need to avoid offering Germany a pretext for mobilizing.[141] This, however, seems unlikely. For one thing, Buchanan's report on the meeting did not record any such statement by the French ambassador; and for another, Paléologue's diary suggests that the telegram from Paris did not arrive at St Petersburg until 6 p.m.[142]

Whatever reasons Paléologue may have had for misleading the Quai d'Orsay on this point, it is clear that he did not have the instructions to hand when he saw Sazonov. Nor is it likely that he would have acted on them had they arrived in time. Certainly, when Sazonov later in the day revealed to him that it had now been decided to order general mobilization, the ambassador did not counsel against such a step.[143] This was all the more remarkable since, under the terms of the Franco-Russian alliance, either party had the right to be consulted before the other ordered general mobilization. That he refrained even from commenting underlines the degree to which the ambassador and Poincaré, whose views he thought he represented, prioritized alliance unity over all other considerations.

If French diplomacy exercised no direct influence over Russian decisions on 30 July, either by inadvertance (because Viviani's 7 a.m. telegram had not arrived in time) or by choice (Paléologue was determined to prevent Paris from restraining Russia), France nevertheless played a

[140] Tel. Ferry to P. Cambon (no. 377), 30 July 1914 (D 2.10 p.m.), *DDF* (3) XI, no. 316; see also tel. Joffre to Messimy (no. 10), 30 July 1914 (D 10.45 a.m., R 12.30 p.m.), and memo. Dupont [General Staff], 30 July 1914 (2 p.m.), *ibid.*, nos. 313 and 315.
[141] Tel. Paléologue to Viviani (no. 311, very confidential), 30 July 1914 (D 4.31 p.m., R 6.51 p.m.), *DDF* (3) XI, no. 342.
[142] See tel. Buchanan to Grey (no. 185), 30 July 1914 (D 1.15 p.m., R 3.15 p.m.), *BD* XI, no. 302; Paléologue diary, 30 July 1914, in his *Russie des Tsars* I, 39. There is a further element of confusion in that Baron Schilling's journal suggests that Sazonov met with Paléologue at 3 p.m., see Schilling daily journal, 17/30 July 1914, *IBZI* V, no. 284.
[143] Tel. Paléologue to Viviani (no. 315, secret), 30 July 1914 (D 9.15 p.m., R 11.25 p.m.), *DDF* (3) XI, no. 359.

significant role. After all, since 24 July, Paléologue had repeatedly assured Sazonov of his country's unconditional support. Against the backdrop of such assurances, the foreign minister pressed for the reversal of the Tsar's last-minute decision of the previous night to rescind the order for general mobilization.

Yanushkevich wants to smash his telephone, Sazonov suggests a formula and the Tsar swims in the sea

The confusion of that night reflected the disjuncture between the Tsar, his ministers and the general staff. That confusion at the heart of Russian policy-making persisted until the late afternoon of 30 July. As seen earlier, Sazonov's initial preference had been for some form of partial mobilization as means of signalling seriousness of intent towards Vienna. Given the now apparent organizational and logistical difficulties which partial mobilization placed in the way of general mobilization – if this were to become necessary at a later stage – a military posture poised against the Habsburg rival in the Balkans alone was now too risky.

Two factors had come together in less than twenty-four hours on 29/30 July to convince Sazonov that there was now no alternative but to order general mobilization. One was diplomatic, the other a matter of military intelligence. Pourtalès's rather strident tone during their midnight encounter had dashed any lingering hopes that Germany might remain aloof from the Balkan fray if the dispute between Vienna and Belgrade escalated into an Austro-Russian war. The ambassador had made a pointed reference to 'the automatic effect that the mobilization here [in Russia] would cause with us [Germany] in consequence of the German-Austrian alliance'. For his part, Sazonov had asserted that 'a retraction of the mobilization order was no longer possible'.[144] If this was brinkmanship, then both sides had little room for manoeuvre left now. They would either have to disengage under pressure, and so accept diplomatic defeat, or they had to accept the likelihood of a general war.

Sazonov was not prepared to yield to German coercion. If the diplomatic signals made for gloomy prognostications, then military intelligence, however partial in nature, complemented such assessments. There was information from the military attaché at Athens, who on returning to

---

[144] Tel. Pourtalès to Auswärtiges Amt (no. 189, urgent), 30 July 1914 (D 4.30 a.m., R 7.10 a.m.), *DD* II, no. 401. Intriguingly, Buchanan had observed that Pourtalès's tone made matters difficult, see tel. Buchanan to Grey (no. 182), 29 July 1914 (D 8.40 p.m., R 11.30 p.m.), *BD* XI, no. 276.

his post via Berlin reported on increased military traffic on the German railways. Ignatiev, the military attaché at Paris, provided supporting evidence. One of his agents in Germany reported troop movements in the eastern provinces of Posen (Poznan) and East Prussia. Six classes of reservists had been called up; all reservists of the post-1902 cohorts currently in France had been ordered back to Germany; frontier positions had been reinforced and fortresses put on alert; railways were under military guard, border crossings barricaded and travellers being interrogated.[145]

None of this was conclusive, but combined it pointed towards a hardening of Germany's attitude. At 10 a.m., Sazonov met Krivoshein, the influential and hawkish minister of agriculture, whom he urged to request an audience with the Tsar in order to remove the monarch's reservations about mobilization. An hour later, the foreign minister visited the headquarters of the general staff, where he found Sukhomlinov and Yanushkevich in a state of considerable anxiety on account of the latest intelligence. It was urgently necessary, they argued, 'to prepare for a serious war without any further loss of time'. Given the practical impossibility of partial mobilization – in train for a good twelve hours now – this meant mobilizing for a general war. The Tsar's decision of the previous night to rescind the general mobilization decree had to be reversed. Sukhomlinov and Yanushkevich telephoned Nicholas II at Peterhof, but the Emperor refused to change his mind and threatened to break off the conversation. There was just enough time for Yanushkevich, who then held the receiver, to ask if Sazonov might call upon the Tsar for an audience: 'There followed a silent pause, after which the Emperor indicated his concurrence.' Sazonov was to come for 3 p.m.

Yanushkevich was on the verge of panic. The Tsar had to authorize general mobilization, otherwise Russia would be caught in a dangerous position if the crisis escalated further, 'as the successful completion of a general mobilization would be compromised by prior partial mobilization'. Yanushkevich begged Sazonov to telephone him as soon as he had secured the Tsar's agreement to general mobilization. 'Afterwards', said Yanushkevich, 'I shall go away, smash my telephone and take steps so that I cannot be found, in case one wants to give me opposite orders in the sense of a retraction of general mobilization'.[146]

---

[145] Tels. Ignatiev to Danilov (nos. 229 and 232), 17/30 July 1914, *IBZI* v, no. 294–5; for the importance of the intelligence dimension see also B. W. Menning, 'The Mobilization Crises of 1912 and 1914 in Russian Perspective: Overlooked and Neglected Linkages', unpubl. MS, fos. 47–8.
[146] Schilling daily journal, 17/30 July 1914, *IBZI* v, no. 284; see also Sukhomlinov, *Erinnerungen*, 365, though the timing given here varies somewhat from Schilling's journal.

There then followed another interview with the German ambassador, who had called to inform Sazonov, as instructed, of his government's ongoing efforts to mediate at Vienna. On Pourtalès's probings, Sazonov reaffirmed that Austria-Hungary's declaration of a territorial disinterestedness would not satisfy the Russian government. Neither Berlin nor St Petersburg seemed prepared to yield. Russo-German diplomatic exchanges had thus reached a stalemate. As Habsburg forces were already committed, the ambassador was casting about for a compromise solution and invited Sazonov to suggest a formula that might prove acceptable to Russia and Austria-Hungary. The minister took up a pencil, tore a page out of his little, squared notebook, and wrote on it: 'If Austria, recognising that her conflict with Serbia has assumed the character of a question of European interest, declares herself ready to eliminate from her ultimatum the points that touch on the sovereign rights of Serbia, Russia engages herself to cease all military preparations.'

Pourtalès himself was sceptical whether this formula would be acceptable to Vienna.[147] Yet Sazonov had not insisted on Austria-Hungary halting her expedition against Serbia, as he had done on earlier occasions. The demand for Vienna to eliminate the contentious parts from its ultimatum would be a bitter pill for the Ballhausplatz to swallow without either Germany offering a sweetener or forcing that pill down Vienna's throat. Nevertheless the formula seemed to indicate a possible route out of the crisis. It was not beyond the wit of Europe's diplomats to incorporate it in some version of 'Halt in Belgrade', as the German chancellor minuted on Pourtalès's report: 'Which points of the Austrian ultimatum did Serbia really reject? To my knowledge only the participation of Austrian officials in court proceedings. Austria could forgo this participation on condition that she will keep occupied parts of Serbia till the completion of negotiations.'[148] The opening question may not have been entirely rhetorical – further evidence of the lack of a coherent strategy at Berlin – but the minute underlines that Bethmann Hollweg understood the diplomatic utility of the Sazonov formula. According to Paléologue, Sazonov himself regarded his formula as, 'by way of a logical corollary, the overture to deliberations by the Powers in London'.[149]

[147] Tel. Pourtalès to Auswärtiges Amt (no. 192), 30 July 1914 (D 1.01 p.m., R 3.32 p.m.), *DD* II, no. 421; tels. Sazonov to Sverbe'ev (nos. 1554, parts 1 and 2, very urgent), 17/30 July 1914, *IBZI* v, no. 277–8. A facsimile of Sazonov's text is in Pourtalès, *Meine letzten Verhandlungen*, 16; see also 46–8 for the interview.

[148] Min. Bethmann Hollweg, 30 July 1914, *DD* II, no. 421, n. 2.

[149] Tels. Paléologue to Viviani (nos. 307–8), 30 July 1914 (D 1.32 and 1.30 p.m., R 4 and 5.25 p.m.), *DDF* (3) XI, no. 328. For the argument that this was a cynical ploy by

If the formula provided the conceptual basis for a compromise settlement, what was needed now was time for its details to be negotiated. It was for Berlin to respond to the formula as a matter of urgency, as Sazonov wired to Sverbe'ev, again assuming that only the German government could force Austria-Hungary to accept an international settlement of the dispute with Serbia. Russia was ready 'to do the utmost for a peaceful outcome of the question'. But the government at St Petersburg would not stand by if further talks were merely a means to gain time for Austria-Hungary and Germany to complete their respective military preparations.[150]

This was also the line Sazonov took with Buchanan and Paléologue, who arrived at the Choristers' Bridge after the German ambassador. There were indications of German preparations, especially in the direction of the Gulf of Finland, he claimed. Partial mobilization of Russian forces had been ordered last night, to commence this morning, but preparations for general mobilization would proceed in parallel. He then produced his formula, which he described as 'a last straw'. If Vienna rejected the compromise formula, general mobilization would commence 'and European war will be inevitable'.[151]

And yet, Sazonov's next action brought the prospect of war closer. Far from lifting the baton for the first bar of a London conference overture, he was determined to deny diplomacy more time. At 12.30 he lunched privately with Krivoshein and Schilling at St Petersburg's Donon's restaurant. The mood of the three men was pessimistic, and their conversation revolved exclusively around the need for swift general mobilization. War with Germany, they were convinced, was inevitable. Krivoshein, who had not been granted an audience by the Tsar, could only hope that the foreign minister would be able to persuade the monarch, 'as otherwise … we drifted towards certain catastrophe'.

Around 2 p.m., Sazonov left for the Alexander Palace at Peterhof, accompanied by General Ilya Leonidovich Tatishchev, the Tsar's military plenipotentiary at the imperial court at Berlin. The audience began a little

Sazonov, see S. McMeekin, *The Russian Origins of the First World War* (Cambridge, MA, 2011), 74. However, *pace* McMeekin, Sazonov continually referred to Grey's conference proposal since the route of direct exchanges with Szápáry no longer seemed practicable.

[150] Tel. Sazonov to Sverbe'ev (no. 1554), 17/30 July 1914, *IBZI* v, no. 277.

[151] Tel. Buchanan to Grey (no. 185, urgent, very confidential), 30 July 1914 (D 1.15 p.m., R 3.15 p.m.), *BD* xi, no. 302. There is a persistent belief among some writers that Buchanan was continually misled by Sazonov, but a closer examination of the source material makes clear that this was not so; for such a view see Ponting, *Thirteen Days*, 223; McMeekin, *Russian Origins*, 69–72.

over an hour later. The foreign minister, it seems, dominated the meeting. Germany was resolved on war, he argued – why else had Berlin rejected all earlier proposals for a settlement? It was better now to prepare for war than to be caught by surprise later. The Tsar demurred. He felt the weight of the responsibility that lay on his shoulders; and, like his cousin 'Willy', he responded with 'uncharacteristic irritability'. When after one of Sazonov's lengthy monologues, Nicholas fell silent, Tatishchev, who had so far not interfered in the discussion, ventured that the decision was a complex one, the Tsar responded 'sharply and angrily: "I shall decide."' Eventually, the Emperor gave in to Sazonov, and authorized general mobilization.

With the concession wrung from the Tsar, Sazonov walked down to the telephone cabin in the vestibule of the palace to place the promised call to Yanushkevich. Having passed on the anxiously awaited news, the minister concluded the call with the words: 'Now you may smash the telephone.' As he replaced the receiver the clock struck 4 p.m., as he later recalled to Paléologue.[152] While Dobrorolski hurried off to collect the necessary signatures, the Tsar's ministers met at the Mari'inski Palace, the reddish-brown sandstone pile in St Petersburg that housed the Imperial State Council. Sazonov explained to the ministers assembled there that war could scarcely be averted now, if 'our threat of armed neutrality' against Austria-Hungary failed to have the desired effect. Nerves were frayed, and it nearly came to a fight between Krivoshein and the minister of the interior, the reactionary Nikolai Alekse'evich Maklakov. Even so, in the end, Sazonov carried the day.[153]

Despite his obvious hesitation to authorize general mobilization, it is not clear whether Nicholas II had fully grasped the significance of his decision. It was a fateful decision in the true sense of the word. Not only did it escalate the crisis, it would also seal his own fate and that of his family and dynasty. Nicholas's diary entry for 30 July betrays little sense of the gravity of the situation: 'After lunch Sazonov and Tatishchev with me. I went for a walk on my own. The weather was warm ... Bathed with delight in the sea. Olga [Aleksandrovna Romanova, his sister] ate with us and we spent the evening together.' Pourtalès, who was received by Nicholas on the following day, found the Tsar distant and not fully alive to the dangers of the situation.[154]

[152] Schilling daily journal, 17/30 July 1914, *IBZI* v, no. 284; Paléologue diary, 30 July, in his *Russie des Tsars* I, 39; see also Sazonov's colourful account in his *Années fatales*, 216–20.
[153] Sukhomlinov, *Erinnerungen*, 362–3; R. Pearson, *The Russian Moderates and the Crisis of Tsarism, 1914–1917* (London, 1977), 12–13.
[154] Nicholas II diary, 17/30 July 1914, 'Nikolai Romanov', 135; and Pourtalès, *Meine letzten Verhandlungen*, 59–61.

Sazonov's position was crucial in the Tsar's renewed change of mind. The arguments made by Sukhomlinov and Yanushkevich had made little or no impact on him, and without the foreign minister's insistence on the urgent necessity of general mobilization he might well have continued to resist. But he now faced a united front of the civilian and military leadership, all pressing him to agree to general mobilization. According to Sazonov's later account of the events of that day, the Tsar seemed rather more concerned with any threat the Austro-Hungarian military preparations might pose to Russia. If St Petersburg now yielded to German pressure and halted mobilization, 'we would be disarmed against Austria'.[155] Considering that at that moment the Habsburg campaign was entirely focused on Serbia and no preparations had been made along the Galician salient, the Tsar's statement appears remarkable. In fact, it reflected the consistent overestimation of Habsburg military capabilities that characterized Russian intelligence assessments of Austria-Hungary in the years before 1914. The unease at the mobilization of eight army corps against Serbia when six were considered sufficient by Russia's staff, has already been noted. Whether or not the larger number of corps meant a secret shift to near-full, if not general, mobilization, it certainly increased the chances of swift annihilation of the Serbian army, after which it would be difficult for Russian diplomacy to salvage the situation. But, undoubtedly, there was a tendency to read all intelligence as confirming established interpretations, the classic failing of all intelligence work.[156]

Nicholas II himself had not yet written off the chances of finding some '*modus* to prevent that general mobilization [which] would be an irrevocable cause for war'. For that reason he continued the telegraphic exchanges with the Kaiser. It would be '*technically* impossible to stop our military preparations', he wired to Wilhelm on the following day. Russia did not wish war; as long as talks continued, 'my troops shall not make [*sic*] any *provocative* action. I give you my solemn word for this.'[157]

For Sazonov's part, the Austro-Hungarian declaration of war, followed by the shelling of Belgrade, the hardening of Pourtalès's stance, and various snippets of intelligence were sufficient to convince him that mobilization was now necessary. A telegram from Sverbe'ev announcing

[155] Sazonov, *Années fatales*, 218.
[156] See Menning, 'Mobilization Crises', *passim*; D. C. B. Lieven, *Russia and the Origins of the First World War* (London, 1983), 148–9; C. Clark, *The Sleepwalkers: How Europe Went to War in 1914* (London, 2012), 514–15.
[157] Quotes from Schilling daily journal, 17/30 July 1914, *IBZI* v, no. 284; and tel. Nicholas II to Wilhelm II, 31 July 1914 (D 2.55 p.m., R 2.52 p.m.), *DD* III, no. 487 (Tsar's emphasis).

that German mobilization was imminent may well have confirmed what Sazonov suspected, but it was not decisive. As it turned out, the ambassador's report was erroneous, based on a note in the Berlin *Lokalanzeiger* which announced that the order to mobilize would come into effect that same day. It seems that the paper decided to print a special edition in anticipation of such a decision, and that copies of it then somehow got into circulation. The German authorities immediately impounded all copies of the paper still in circulation, an official statement was issued denying that any military preparations had been made, and Jagow himself telephoned Sverbe'ev to assure him that Germany's armed forces had not been mobilized. The ambassador retracted his warnings once he had realized his mistake. This was sometime around 2.40 p.m., Berlin time. By then, Sazonov had already obtained from the Tsar the authorization for general mobilization.[158]

But there was another decisive consideration that weighed with Sazonov, the idea that for Russia mobilization did not mean war. This, of course, was an illusion. That Germany would not remain passive if Russia mobilized – that she would not accept the risk of the Russian army at full strength on her frontiers – he had been told by Pourtalès and Buchanan. But Sazonov chose to ignore them. Equally illusory was his assumption that mobilization could be carried out in secret, though how it should be kept a secret once the red mobilization notices had been posted up in public places up and down the Russian Empire seems puzzling to say the least. Even so, it was not until the following day, Friday 31 July, that Sazonov and his officials at the Choristers' Bridge realized that to maintain secrecy was 'technically impossible' once the decree, printed on red paper, appeared in the streets, calling reservists to the colours.[159] In ignoring the warnings of the German and British ambassadors and in his ignorance of the practicalities of mobilizing the Russian army, Sazonov was just as reckless as Berchtold or Jagow had been.

---

[158] Tels. Sverbe'ev to Sazonov (nos. 142, unnumbered and 143), 17/30 July 1914, *IBZI* v, nos. 301–3; also Rimski-Korsakov to Navy Staff (no. 38), 17/30 July 1914, *ibid.*, no. 306, and tels. J. Cambon to Viviani (nos. 225–6, secret), 30 July 1914 (D 4.52 and 5.15 p.m., R 6.10 and 6.20 p.m.), *DDF* (3) xi, no. 339; and Sverbe'ev's notes in Sukhomlinov, *Erinnerungen*, 366–7; see also B. N. de Strandtmann, 'Vospominania', unpubl. TS, CUBA, Sviatopolk-Mirskii Collection, fos. 432–5.

The first telegram may well have been the source of Paléologue's tel. (no. 306, very urgent), 30 July 1914 (D 1.45 p.m., R 3.40 p.m.), *DDF* (3) xi, no. 302.

[159] Schilling daily journal, 18/31 July 1914, *IBZI* v, no. 349. The notes went up at 6 a.m.: see Paléologue interview, H. R. Madol [pseudo. G. Salomon], *Gespräche mit Verantwortlichen* (Berlin, 1933), 44.

Later in the afternoon, on his return from Peterhof, Sazonov met with the French ambassador. He told the latter that the mobilization decree had been issued at 5 p.m. Having earlier in the afternoon untruthfully informed the Quai d'Orsay that he had urged Sazonov to avoid any provocative measures, Paléologue now delayed communicating the latest news until 9.15 p.m. Even then he reported only that, on receipt of 'unsettling pieces of information' about German preparations, Russia was now 'resolved secretly to proceed to the first measures of general mobilization'. Sazonov, he wrote, had assured him: 'I shall negotiate until the last moment.'[160] And until the last moment, Paléologue continued his practice of feeding Paris carefully calibrated half-truths with the aim of preventing any attempt by the French government to restrain Russia.

Count Berchtold escalates the situation

Russia was not the first country in Europe to order general mobilization – the Netherlands had already begun the process on 28 July. But the decision by a Great Power to mobilize its entire armed forces marked a significant escalation of the crisis. To that extent the Tsar's decision in the afternoon of 30 July, however hesitant and half-hearted, to give the 'green light' for general mobilization, was one of the most consequential decisions of the entire July crisis.

It has often been argued that Russia's decision to mobilize made war inevitable. It is difficult to refute this argument entirely, especially so in light of what followed.[161] No doubt, in terms of professional competence, the Russian military leadership left much to be desired. The conceptual confusion at St Petersburg about the practical implications of partial mobilization added a further element of uncertainty to an already volatile situation. On the other hand, it is difficult to see how else Russia could have deterred Austria-Hungary from commencing operations against Serbia. After all, even after 31 July, Vienna was not prepared to abort the Serbian

[160] Tel. Paléologue to Viviani (no. 315, secret), 30 July 1914 (D 9.15 p.m., R 11.25 p.m.), *DDF* (3) XI, no. 359. Paléologue's own diary leaves no doubt that he knew that general mobilization had been ordered, diary, 30 July 1914, in his *Russie des Tsars* I, 39. For an eyewitness account of the events on that day see R. Ullrich, 'Herrn Paléologues Meldung der russischen Mobilmachung', *BMH* XI, 8 (1933), 781–3. Dr Richard Ullrich was the Russia correspondent of the *Kölnische Zeitung*.
[161] Turner, 'Russian Mobilization', 87–8; M. Trachtenberg, 'The Meaning of Mobilization', S. E. Miller *et al.* (eds.), *Military Strategy and the Origins of the First World War* (Princeton, NJ, 1991), 195–225; G. Frantz, *Russlands Eintritt in den Weltkrieg. Der Ausbau der russischen Wehrmacht und ihr Einsatz bei Kriegsausbruch* (Berlin, 1924).

campaign, and instead switched to general mobilization. Perhaps Buchanan, Britain's ambassador, unjustly maligned by some scholars, had shown the right instinct long before there was even talk of the Archduke Franz Ferdinand paying a visit to Bosnia-Herzegovina. In his annual report for 1913, he warned that the Powers had grown used to strong Russian statements being followed by weak, indeed if any, actions; but past indecision on the part of St Petersburg was no guide as to its future behaviour.[162] This time, Russia's leaders were determined not to repeat that mistake.

Russian mobilization changed the direction of travel towards war. But St Petersburg was not alone in hardening its stance on 30 July. At the Ballhausplatz, too, Berchtold was preparing to mount a diplomatic offensive that would further escalate the crisis. As already seen, encouraged by Tschirschky, Berchtold had decided to parry Bethmann Hollweg's belated attempt to revoke the 'blank cheque'; nor was he ready to yield to German pressure to appease Italy.[163]

In the afternoon of 30 July, at Berchtold's request, Shebeko called on the Ballhausplatz. Their long conversation was of 'a most friendly character', the ambassador reported back to the Choristers' Bridge. Shebeko gave assurances that Russia did not at all seek to diminish Habsburg prestige in south-eastern Europe or to encourage any anti-Habsburg agitation in Serbia. For his part, the minister signalled his willingness to resume talks at St Petersburg. Certainly, Berchtold's dulcet tones left Shebeko with the impression that 'he really wishes to come to an arrangement with us, but that he is of the opinion that it would be impossible for Austria to halt her operations against Serbia without having received full satisfaction and serious guarantees for the future'. Just as he had sought to mislead Berlin, so Berchtold deceived Shebeko about the nature of the renewed talks. For he had not, in fact, offered anything of substance, but merely general exchanges of views. If the ambassador had failed to notice this, he did not fail to report, however, Berchtold's explicit warning. In consequence of Russia's mobilization – Vienna still assumed this to be partial – Austria-Hungary would be forced to take adequate precautions and mobilize her own troops in Galicia as well.[164]

[162] Buchanan to Grey (no. 60), 4 Mar. 1914, TNA (PRO), FO 371/2092/10333.
[163] Min. Zimmermann, 30 July 1914 (p.m.), DD II, no. 425.
[164] Tel. Shebeko to Sazonov (no. 122), 17/30 July 1914, IBZI v, no. 307; and tel. Berchtold to Szápáry (no. 202), 30 July 1914 (D 31 July, 1.40 a.m.), ÖUA VIII, no. 11093; see also tel. de Bunsen to Grey (no. 127), 30 July 1914 (D 9 p.m.), BD XI, no. 311; see also S. R. Williamson, 'Leopold Count Berchtold: The Man who Could have Prevented the Great War', G. Bischof, F. Plasser and P. Berger (eds.), From Empire to Republic: Post-World War I Austria (New Orleans, 2010), 37–8.

However much Berchtold emphasized that he did not wish to coerce Russia or that he harboured no aggressive designs on her, this was an attempt to increase pressure on St Petersburg. Stripped of its friendly verbiage, it was a threat to meet Russia's partial mobilization with full mobilization on the part of the Habsburg Empire. The offer of resuming talks, of course, was also meant to deflect Berlin's recent pressure on Vienna by signalling an apparent willingness to conciliate Russia – Berchtold was acting his own version of Shylock again.

Indeed, Berchtold sought to reverse the balance of influence in the Austro-German group once more. In the afternoon of 30 July, Szögyény appeared at the Wilhelmstrasse to explain that mobilization in the military districts of Kazan, Kiev, Moscow and Odessa would have to be met with full mobilization by Austria-Hungary. 'As a last step, to preserve the peace of Europe', the Vienna government suggested a joint démarche at St Petersburg to force it to halt its military preparations. Jagow declined, and left it to Vienna to act on its own.[165] From Berlin's perspective, this was entirely logical. The German ambassador at St Petersburg had already warned Sazonov of the dangers of mobilization, and there appeared to be no need to repeat the exercise. Joint action by Szápáry and Pourtalès, moreover, would have discredited assurances that Berlin was seeking to moderate Vienna's stance, and would have convinced Sazonov – if he needed any further convincing – that the two Germanic Powers had colluded from the beginning. But it would also have reinforced Germany's growing dependence on Austria-Hungary. This, of course, was precisely Berchtold's object in making the proposal of a joint démarche. Militarily, there was no need to respond to Russia's mobilization against Austria-Hungary for a few more days. But the overnight telegrams to Tschirschky indicated very clearly to the Habsburg foreign minister that there was every chance now of Berlin buckling under pressure. Joint representations at St Petersburg, the joint threat of general mobilization, was meant to make it impossible for the German leadership not to honour the 'blank cheque'.

But Berchtold was ready to go further still and to present Berlin with a fait accompli to allow it no way out of the crisis. He did not wait to hear from Szögyény before he warned Shebeko that general mobilization would be ordered if Russia continued her preparations.[166] While the Austro-Hungarian foreign minister escalated the crisis with remarkable insouciance, he was nevertheless plagued by doubts. Would the Monarchy

---

[165] Min. Jagow, 30 July 1914 (p.m.), and tel. Jagow to Tschirschky (no. 201), 30 July 1914 (D 9 p.m.), *DD* II, nos. 429 and 442.
[166] Tel. Szögyény to Berchtold (no. 332), 31 July 1914 (D 12.38 a.m., R 5 a.m.), *ÖUA* VIII, no. 11126.

withstand the financial pressures of war, he wondered in conversation with Conrad and Stürgkh, the Austrian prime minister? Not if it meant waging war against Serbia and Russia simultaneously, warned the latter. Such considerations, Conrad interposed, 'must be dropped, for they come too late; our situation was such that we had no other way out'.[167] It was a remarkable admission of strategic bankruptcy at the heart of the Habsburg Monarchy.

In the afternoon, presumably after Berchtold's meeting with Shebeko, the foreign minister, accompanied by Conrad and Krobatin, the war minister, drove out to Schönbrunn palace to call on Emperor Franz Joseph. They were determined to secure his agreement to a general mobilization order. A significant part of the discussion at the palace appears to have revolved around one of Bethmann Hollweg's night-time telegrams to Tschirschky, in which he explained that Berlin now regarded the temporary occupation of Belgrade or other places in Serbia as 'a suitable basis for negotiations'.

The two ministers and Conrad were not prepared to assent to anything of this kind. On the contrary, Belgrade had to accept the ultimatum in full and compensate Austria-Hungary for the costs of mobilization. In line with his earlier comments and irrespective of Magyar opposition, Conrad also pressed for annexing Serbian territory: 'Belgrade and Šabac and their environs for the erection of extensive fortifications, the costs of which Serbia also would have to bear.' Belgrade would never accept this, the Emperor suggested, nor would Tisza agree to the incorporation of further Slav territories, observed Berchtold. The chief of staff 'interposed that, now that everything was in train, we could not suspend the hostilities against Serbia'. If Russia mobilized, then Austria-Hungary had to follow suit. Berchtold again raised the costs of general mobilization, but Conrad batted this away with the words: 'The Monarchy is at stake.' Berchtold then argued that deploying the army in Galicia would lead to war with Russia:

> I [Conrad] replied that if the Russians do not touch us, we did not have to touch them. The situation was not desperate if our own mobilization was ordered in good time; to begin with there would then be 27½ of our infantry divisions against 33 Russian ones.

---

[167] Conrad, *Aus meiner Dienstzeit* IV, 148; J. H. Maurer, 'Field Marshal Conrad von Hötzendorf and the Outbreak of the First World War', T. G. Otte and C. A. Pagedas (eds.), *Personalities, War and Diplomacy: Essays in International History* (London, 1997), 51–9.

> It would have appeared to me irresponsible, in view of the undoubted Russia mobilization, to fold our hands and to fail to mobilize. The consequence of such an omission would be the invasion of the Monarchy – the road to Budapest and Vienna would lie open to the Russian armies.

It was remarkable, indeed, that Berchtold, who had blithely risked a European war in his quest for 'settling the score' with Serbia, now sought refuge behind the likely financial costs of the military operations. Conrad brushed aside any objections. The meeting concluded that the campaign against Serbia would continue. Britain's mediation proposal 'would be answered in a very accommodating form, without accepting it on its merits'. General mobilization was to be ordered on 31 July, with 4 August as the first day of mobilization.

Earlier in the day, the Habsburg liaison officer with the German general staff, Colonel Moritz Fleischmann von Theissruck, reported that Moltke did not regard Russia's partial mobilization a sufficient cause for German counter-measures. In sharp contrast to the 'already customary Russian mobilizations and demobilizations', Fleischmann advised, German mobilization would inevitably mean war.[168] Full mobilization of the Habsburg armed forces would thus raise the spectre of the *casus foederis*. There would be no way back for Germany now; she would be firmly tied to the Monarchy.

In the meantime, Tschirschky continued along the path upon which he and Berchtold had agreed at lunchtime – he kept misleading the Wilhelmstrasse. He had carried out his instructions emphatically, he reported. Berchtold would reply later.[169] There was not a word in his report about the impending decision to switch from mobilizing against Serbia to general mobilization. Given the prolonged official silence at Vienna and Tschirschky's brief and opaque telegram in the afternoon, Stumm was instructed to place a telephone call through to the Vienna embassy. This time, it seems, the ambassador was more forthcoming. He divulged that general mobilization would be ordered in the Habsburg Empire, but added that it was merely a counter-measure to Russian preparations. Vienna's reply to Bethmann Hollweg's proposals, Stumm understood Tschirschky to say, 'would not necessarily be a rejection'.[170]

---

[168] *Ibid.*, 150–2; for Bethmann's telegram (no. 190) see *DD* II, no. 384; also Kronenbitter, '*Krieg im Frieden*', 509–10.
[169] Tel. Tschirschky to Auswärtiges Amt (no. 137), 30 July 1914 (D 5.20 p.m., R 5.56 p.m.), *DD* II, no. 434.
[170] Min. Stumm, 31 July 1914 (p.m.), *DD* II, no. 468.

Just as the French ambassador at St Petersburg sought to shield the government there against attempts by his own government to restrain it, so Tschirschky did the same at Vienna. Stirred by the telephone call, he sent another telegram in the early hours of 31 July. He had acted on his instructions and pressed on Berchtold, Forgách and Hoyos 'Halt in Belgrade' followed by international talks, but none of them thought it possible now to restrict the operations already underway against Serbia. Conrad, Tschirschky confirmed, had requested authorization for general mobilization – he knew already that it had been granted – and closed his message with an astounding sentence: 'They are not entirely clear whether in the present situation mobilization was still required.'[171] If Tschirschky had previously been selective in his reporting, he now actively dissimulated. Regardless of Berchtold's last-minute wobble, Vienna had decided to escalate the situation to prevent its German ally from disengaging – and the German ambassador had connived in this manoeuvre.

During the morning of the following day, Friday, 31 July, the Habsburg ministerial council reassembled formally to sanction the decisions of the previous evening. There was no real disagreement among the ministers and officials. Berchtold, who once more presided over the proceedings, informed his colleagues of Tschirschky's revelations of the previous afternoon. A reply had not been finalized, but the draft text was guided by three considerations: that the operations against Serbia had to be continued; that there could be no discussions of the British proposal unless Russia ceased mobilizing; and, finally, that Serbia had to accept the demands made of her without any reservations. Berchtold's ministerial colleagues agreed.

International mediation, the foreign minister warned, tended to dilute essential conditions, and in the event of another London conference, the German ambassador was not likely to prove a help: 'Of Prince Lichnowsky everything was to be expected except that he would warmly support our interests.' As seen, Berchtold's assessment was not far of the mark. It was a curious statement to make nonetheless. It was not Lichnowsky's job to protect Habsburg interests; he was not, after all, the Austro-German ambassador to Britain. But Berchtold's comments are suggestive of the growing suspicions and tensions between Vienna and Berlin at the height of the July crisis. A conference, Berchtold continued, would produce little more than 'star dust [Flitterwerk]'. 'Halt in Belgrade' would not serve Austro-Hungarian interests. Russia would then emerge as the

---

[171] Tel. Tschirschky to Auswärtiges Amt (no. 142), 30 July 1914 (D 31 July, 1.35 a.m., R 4.35 a.m.), DD II, no. 465.

saviour of Serbia; the Serbian army would remain intact; and in three years' time it would be in a stronger position to take the offensive against the Monarchy.

Biliński, the common finance minister, concurred. Austria-Hungary's mobilization, moreover, had created new circumstances, and proposals that might have been acceptable at an earlier point could no longer be countenanced now – a clear reference also to financial compensation for the costs of mobilizing the army. Tisza was remarkably hawkish. The military operations could not be stopped, he confirmed. But he suggested that London should be told that the Monarchy was prepared, in principle, to accept a conference on condition that the campaign against Serbia would continue while Russia's mobilization was halted. Stürgkh and Biliński supported this notion. In practice, of course, it amounted to a rejection, but such was the desire to avoid a repetition of the 1912–13 London ambassadorial conference – of 'ghastly memory' – that Grey's proposal held no attractions for the Habsburg leadership.

There then followed a lengthy discussion of the Italian problem. Biliński's was a lone voice here. The 'impending great struggle was a struggle for survival of the Monarchy', he warned, and appeared ready to 'purchase' Italian support. But the other ministers were determined to keep any price to be paid for Italy's dubious loyalty at a minimum. Rome should be offered the prospect of talks about compensation and, if circumstances required it, be offered Valona on the Central Albanian coast as a sop, with northern Albania reserved as an Austro-Hungarian sphere.[172]

It is difficult to avoid the impression that the Habsburg ministers merely went through the motions. There was no discussion of the Dual Monarchy's strategic situation. If anything the escalation of the crisis in recent days had merely reinforced their intransigence. The near prospect of conflict had strengthened the Habsburg leadership's audacity of despair.

Thus, at 12.23 p.m. on 31 July, Conrad's general staff received final authorization for mobilizing the entire Habsburg armed forces. Forty-three minutes later, Szápáry's telegram with the news of the Tsar's mobilization order reached the Ballhausplatz.[173] Berchtold let another three hours pass before he replied to London's mediation proposal as transmitted by Tschirschky. The response was couched in the most exquisite diplomatese. Grey's desire to avert further complications was gratefully

[172] Minutes of Ministerial Council Meeting, 31 July 1914, M. Komjáthy (ed.), *Protokolle des Gemeinsamen Ministerrates der Österreichisch-Ungarischen Monarchie, 1914–1918* (Budapest, 1966), no. 3.

[173] Conrad, *Aus meiner Dienstzeit* IV, 155; tel. Szápáry to Berchtold (no. 183), 31 July 1914 (D 11.25 a.m., R 1.09 p.m.), *ÖUA* VIII, no. 11175.

acknowledged. Despite 'the altered situation caused by Russia's mobilization', Vienna would be willing 'to enter more closely' into the Foreign
Secretary's proposals. But the essential preconditions were that the military
campaign against Serbia would continue 'for the time being' and that
Russia halted her mobilization, in which case Austria-Hungary would
'reverse the defensive military counter-measures' in Galicia.[174]

The decision to mobilize the entire Habsburg armed forces had
marked a considerable escalation of the crisis; the reply to London
further exacerbated the international situation. Tardy even by Vienna's
standards, it closed down all practicable diplomatic options. Neither
'Halt in Belgrade' nor St Petersburg's suggestions – let alone Sazonov's
formula – had been touched upon. Any solution, then, had to be on
Austria-Hungary's terms, and this made a solution short of war all but
impossible. Vienna wanted everything, but was not prepared to make
any concessions.

There was one further quirk in the proceedings at Vienna. Despite
the decision for general mobilization, Conrad continued with the deployment against Serbia, in accordance with the mobilization scheme under
Plan 'B'. His original planning had always envisaged 1 August as the day by
which the 2nd Army deployed against Serbia could still be sent to Galicia
without any significant loss of time. In practice, however, he did little to
redirect troops north- and eastwards. Troop trains continued rolling
towards the Serbian frontier. Halting them, Conrad later reasoned, would
have allowed the Serbian army to invade Habsburg territory while the bulk
of the armed forces was engaged against Russia. But his decision to continue the deployment in the south was also dictated by logistics and
transport constraints. It would be preferable, the railway directorate
advised, to proceed with the deployment against Serbia and then to
re-embark the troops at the railheads in the south for final deployment in
Galicia. The subsequent confusion in the mobilization schedules – aided by
Conrad's failure to alert Potiorek, now in command of the forces in the
south – and the resulting gridlock on the railways complicated the campaign against Serbia and ensured that the Habsburg armies came close to
annihilation in Galicia in September.[175]

---

[174] Tel. Berchtold to Mensdorff (no. 194), Szögyény (no. 308) and Szápáry (no. 208),
31 July 1914 (D 3.45 p.m.), ÖUA VIII, no. 11155; cf. tel. de Bunsen to Grey (no. 129),
31 July 1914 (D 4.16 p.m., R 10.45 p.m.), BD XI, no. 360.
[175] Conrad, Aus meiner Dienstzeit IV, 156–8; for detailed discussions see R. Kiszling,
'Die Mobilmachung der europäischen Mächte im Sommer 1914. Österreich-Ungarn',
BMH XIV, 2 (1936), 189–224; N. Stone, 'Die Mobilmachung der österreichisch-
ungarischen Armee 1914', MGM II (1974), 77–95.

'Nicky' and 'Willy' send further telegrams and Bethmann Hollweg caves in

However inept, Habsburg military proceedings, and the decision to put the Empire on full war alert, escalated the crisis. Berchtold's communications on 30 and 31 July had not only rebuffed the various proposals made by London and St Petersburg, he had also sought to ensure that Berlin remained attached to the Habsburg guide-rope. Stumm's telephone call on the evening of 30 July was an indication of the anxiety at the Wilhelmstrasse caused by the continued ignorance of Vienna's ultimate objectives and the growing realization of Germany's dependence on Austria-Hungary. The one reinforced the other, but the German leadership's willingness to rein in the Habsburg ally weakened in the course of 30/31 July.

In the evening of 30 July, the Kaiser issued a direct appeal to the Habsburg Emperor. He had willingly accepted Nicholas II's personal request to mediate so as 'to avert a global inferno and to maintain world peace'. Negotiations on the basis of Austria-Hungary's temporary occupation of Belgrade and other places, as explained by Tschirschky, offered a way out of the crisis. Would Franz Joseph let him know his decision very soon?[176] No doubt, the Kaiser's sense of propriety might well have baulked at the idea of putting overt pressure on the aged fellow-monarch at Vienna. Even so, there was no suggestion that Berlin expected its ally to accept the mediation proposal. The Kaiser's telegram at any rate arrived too late, after the Schönbrunn conference between Franz Joseph, Berchtold and Conrad, at which it had been decided to proceed to full mobilization and to ditch Grey's suggestions. The reply arrived in the afternoon of the following day. It was not promising. He was fully conscious of his grave responsibilities towards his Empire and its peoples, the Emperor said. Military preparations were not to be interrupted by 'the threatening and provocative attitude of Russia'. Mediation – here he used Berchtold's argument – would mean 'another rescue of Serbia by Russia's intervention', and this would have 'the most serious consequences for my dominions'. He could therefore not countenance any diplomatic intervention. 'I am alive to the full consequences of my decisions', Franz Joseph concluded, 'and I took them trusting in God's mercy and confident in that your armed forces will stand by my empire and the *Dreibund* in unshakeable fidelity'.[177]

Even within the constraints of telegraphic communication, this was more a personal manifesto of the kind that Franz Joseph had addressed

---

[176] Tel. Wilhelm II to Franz Joseph, 30 July 1914 (D 7.15 p.m.), *DD* II, no. 437.
[177] Tel. Franz Joseph to Wilhelm II, 31 July 1914 (D 1 p.m.), *ÖUA* VIII, no. 11118; S. Beller, *Francis Joseph* (London, 1996), 216–19.

to his peoples on 26 July than a reasoned strategic discussion with the head of state of the Monarchy's most important ally. It underscored Vienna's intransigence, but it is also suggestive of the limits of monarchical diplomacy during an international crisis. The Kaiser himself had not given up on royal channels to keep a diplomatic solution before the chancelleries of Europe. At his instigation, Prince Heinrich despatched a private telegram to King George V, whom he had seen in person only five days earlier. His brother, the Kaiser, was working hard for peace. Germany had taken no military measures as yet, but might be forced to do so soon. If the King wished to prevent a war, Britain ought to use her influence to keep France and Russia neutral. This would be 'the only chance to maintain the peace of Europe', Heinrich urged: 'I may add that now more than ever Germany and England should lend each other mutual help to prevent a terrible catastrophe, which otherwise seems unavoidable.'[178]

All of this was no doubt true. But the telegram did not address a number of difficulties that complicated the situation, the principal one being the various mobilizations already in train. Russia, after all, could remain neutral yet mobilize at the same time – and this would be problematic for the two Germanic Powers. But there was also the issue of Germany's restraining influence over Vienna. Without any effort to moderate Austro-Hungarian policy no mediation was possible. The King's reply was more practical. War would be an 'irreparable disaster', he wrote. London would do all it could on the basis of 'Halt in Belgrade' while the other Powers suspended their military preparations. He hoped that the Kaiser would use 'his great influence' at Vienna to persuade the Habsburg leadership to accept this proposal. It would prove, he concluded, that Britain and Germany 'are working together to prevent what would be an international catastrophe'.[179]

This last flurry of royal diplomatic exchanges came too late and underlined the much reduced political significance of Europe's crowned heads on the eve of the First World War. Besides, the focus of German calculations was now on events in Russia. Russia had begun general mobilization, Wilhelm II complained to his cousin in London, and 'Nicky' had not even 'awaited the results of my mediation'. He would now leave for Berlin 'to take measures for ensuring safety of my eastern frontiers where strong Russian troops are already posted'.[180]

---

[178] Tel. Prince Heinrich of Prussia to George V, 30 July 1914 (D 2.15 p.m.), *DD* II, no. 417.
[179] Tel. George V to Prince Heinrich of Prussia, 30 July 1914 (D 8.54 p.m., R 11.08 p.m.), *DD* II, no. 452.
[180] Tel. Wilhelm II to George V, 31 July 1914 (D 12.55 p.m.), *DD* II, no. 477.

On the previous evening, at a meeting of the Prussian government, Bethmann Hollweg had still argued firmly against any military preparations on Germany's part while diplomatic options were still being explored. At that stage, the chancellor was still hoping to persuade Vienna of the merits of 'Halt in Belgrade'. The telegraphic exchanges between the Kaiser and the Tsar were still in full swing, and London and Berlin had 'taken all steps to avert a European war'. Russia's mobilization posed no immediate threat as her troops could remain mobilized for any period of time. The declaration of *Kriegsgefahrzustand*, by contrast, would mean mobilization and this would lead to war. Bethmann Hollweg concluded that the peoples of Europe were pacific, 'but direction had been lost and the stone had begun to roll. As a politician he would not abandon hope and efforts to keep the peace as long as his démarche in Vienna had not been rejected.'[181]

The chancellor's comment on the absence of direction and leadership was revealing. Above all it applied to Bethmann himself. While the Prussian cabinet met, Tschirschky's two telegrams arrived at the Wilhelmstrasse, announcing that Berchtold was not opposed to direct talks at St Petersburg and a proper reply to the mediation proposals would be sent later.[182] Although the hint at further Austro-Russian talks, however carefully couched, held out the prospect of some settlement, Stumm's telephone conversation with Tschirschky at around 8 p.m. seems to have convinced Bethmann that Vienna would reject the British proposals. Immediately afterwards, the chancellor sent fresh instructions to the ambassador at Vienna. He now foregrounded the need to present Russia as the guilty party in the event of a European conflict. The Kaiser was determined to continue with his mediation effort. Russian mobilization against Austria-Hungary complicated the situation, but London had offered – as had King George – to use its influence to persuade France and Russia to suspend their military preparations. If Grey were successful, 'while Vienna rejects everything, then Vienna gives proof that it absolutely wants war, into which we would be drawn, while Russia remains free of guilt'. It would place the German government in 'an untenable situation' before its own nation. He therefore urgently counselled the Ballhausplatz 'to accept the Grey proposal, which protects Austria's position in every respect'. Tschirschky was to explain this to Berchtold 'in the most emphatic language', but also to Tisza.[183]

[181] Minutes of the meeting of the Prussian state ministry, 30 July 1914, *DD* II, no. 456; Jarausch, *Enigmatic Chancellor*, 172–3.
[182] Tels. Tschirschky to Auswärtiges Amt (nos. 135 and 137), 30 July 1914 (D 2.30 and 5.20 p.m., R 5.25 and 5.56 p.m.), *DD* II, nos. 433–4.
[183] Tel. Bethmann Hollweg to Auswärtiges Amt (no. 200, urgent), 30 July 1914 (D 9 p.m., R 3 a.m.), *DD* II, no. 441.

If the latest instructions were a little less strongly worded than the four telegrams of the previous night, there can nevertheless be no doubt about Bethmann's intention. He still hoped to restrain Vienna; Berchtold was expected to accept Grey's mediation without delay or reservations. The instruction for Tschirschky to see the Magyar prime minister – so far thought to be sceptical of a Serbian war – was meant to increase the pressure on Berchtold significantly. No doubt also, his concerns about the domestic impact of Berlin's 'untenable situation' were quite genuine. The prospect of a divided nation facing a European war, possibly with SPD deputies lambasting the imperial government's failed foreign policy in the *Reichstag* and mass peace demonstrations on the boulevards of Berlin and other big cities, touched on fears about the fragile foundations of Germany's imperial régime. But if anything his domestic worries reinforced the chancellor's urgent attempt to restrain Austria-Hungary.

It was Bethmann's last attempt, and it was short-lived. Not even two-and-a-half hours later, Tschirschky was ordered to ignore the chancellor's telegram no. 200. A second telegram, never despatched, explained the reasons for this latest turnabout. Military preparations 'by our neighbours, especially in the East, necessitate swift decisions if we do not want to be caught by surprise'.[184] Russia, it seemed, had moved to general mobilization. Before the explanatory telegram could be sent, the Kaiser's brother turned up at the Wilhelmstrasse with a copy of King George's telegram. In light of the telegram, the chancellor changed the instructions for Tschirschky again. The ambassador was to inform Berchtold of the telegraphic exchanges. 'A definitive decision by Vienna is urgently desired', he concluded, the implication being that speed was of the essence now rather than the substance of Vienna's decision.[185] The chancellor's suggestion that he cancelled the instructions contained in his telegram no. 200 because of the King's message is puzzling.[186] If anything, the logic of the situation now demanded that those same instructions were executed immediately, if peace was to be preserved. But this would now have meant accepting the risk of a diplomatic defeat given that Russia was apparently mobilizing her entire army. The speed of the chancellor's change of heart thus underlines the impact of Russian mobilization on decision-making at Berlin. It not only

[184] Tel. Bethmann Hollweg to Tschirschky (no. 202, urgent), 30 July 1914 (D 11.20 p.m.), and draft tel. (unnumbered), 30 July 1914 (not despatched), *DD* 11, nos. 450–1 (quote from latter); Stevenson, *Armaments*, 402–3.
[185] Tel. Bethmann Hollweg to Tschirschky (no. 203), 31 July 1914 (D 2.45 a.m., R 9 a.m.), *DD* 11, no. 464. The King's telegram was received at 11.08 p.m., see *ibid.*, no. 452, n. 2.
[186] Albertini, *Origins* 111, 28, suggests that it was not sent in good faith.

killed off all hopes of localizing the Balkan conflict; it also placed Germany at a military disadvantage.

Although doubts have been raised in the scholarly debate about the nature of the so-called 'Schlieffen Plan', German war planning was infused with a sense of the imperative of speedy mobilization and deployment. It was generally understood at Berlin that Russia's mobilization did not necessarily imply an intention to open hostilities, but Germany's own dispositions did not distinguish between deployment and the commencement of operations. Mobilization meant war. Conversely, Germany could not allow the slowly mobilizing Russia to take the initiative for fear of falling behind.[187]

A number of observations need to be made at this point. To an extent the chop-and-change in Bethmann's policy reflected the chancellor's flawed character – a 'markedly unreliable, unsteady, fearful personality', in the judgement of the leader of the Prussian conservatives.[188] The absence of direction about which Bethmann Hollweg had complained at the Prussian cabinet meeting that same evening was also a self-indictment. The chancellor did not lead, even within the narrow constraints of his office; he was being buffeted by events. More importantly, he had now abdicated control to the military. Later during the night Moltke and Falkenhayn called upon the chancellor. There was a heated exchange between Bethmann and the chief of staff. 'The chancellor and his people apparently still hope for a miracle', Falkenhayn recorded in his diary. But the two senior officers eventually ground down Bethmann and extracted an important concession from him: 'the decision on a declaration of "imminent danger of war" must be made by noon tomorrow at the latest. Moltke spoke up for war in a very determined manner *sans phrase*. His mood-changes can scarcely be explained or not at all.'[189]

---

[187] Tel. Moltke to Conrad, 30 July 1914, Conrad, *Aus meiner Dienstzeit* IV, 151–2; see G. Ritter, *Der Schlieffenplan. Kritik eines Mythos* (Munich, 1956). For the recent debate about the nature of the plan see T. Zuber, *Inventing the Schlieffen Plan: German War Planning, 1871–1914* (Oxford, 2002) and his 'The Schlieffen Plan Reconsidered', *WiH* VI, 3 (1999), 262–305; R. Foley, 'The Origins of the Schlieffen Plan', *ibid.* X, 2 (2003), 222–32; T. Holmes, 'Asking Schlieffen: A Further Reply to Terence Zuber', *ibid.* X, 4 (2003), 464–79; and the contributions to H. Ehlert, M. Epkenhans and G. P. Gross (eds.), *Der Schlieffenplan. Analysen und Dokumente* (Paderborn, 2006).
[188] Heydebrand to Westarp, 20 Dec. 1913, as quoted in D. Groh, *Negative Integration und revolutionärer Attentismus. Die deutsche Sozialdemokratie am Vorabend des Ersten Weltkrieges* (Frankfurt, 1973), 519; for further contemporary comments see K. Hildebrand, *Kanzler ohne Eigenschaften? Urteile der Geschichtsschreibung* (Düsseldorf, 2nd edn 1970), 20–2; see also G. Eley, 'The Wilhelmine Right: How it Changed', R. J. Evans (ed.), *Society and Politics in Wilhelmine Germany* (London, 1978), 128–9.
[189] Falkenhayn diary, 30 July 1914, Afflerbach, *Falkenhayn*, 158–9.

Finally, the chancellor's latest about-turn removed the disjuncture at the core of German policy-making. From now on Bethmann and Jagow pulled in the same direction. For while the former had sought to restrain Vienna until the evening of 30 July, the latter had begun to move in the opposite direction again. When Sverbe'ev, the Russian ambassador, called to discuss Sazonov's formula in the afternoon of 30 July, Jagow dismissed it as 'unacceptable' for Austria-Hungary and hid behind Szápáry's resumption of talks at St Petersburg.[190] Indeed, the compromise formula was not even forwarded to Tschirschky for information. The state secretary was resigned to accept a continental war as the most likely outcome of the crisis now. Localization was no longer possible, and any diplomatic settlement would have to be based on an initiative made by one of the other Powers, since Berlin had previously refrained from initiating any mediation itself. Throughout the crisis, Jagow had seen the Austro-Serbian quarrel in binary terms: it would end either in the Habsburg Empire crushing the neighbouring kingdom or in a continental war. Of the two, only the latter was now possible.

News of Russian military preparations in the course of 29/30 July hardened not only Jagow's but also Zimmermann's attitude. The latter had suggested rescinding the chancellor's telegram no. 200 to Tschirschky, and Jagow and Bethmann readily accepted. It did not require Moltke and Falkenhayn to step in and dictate the next steps. The civilian leadership had already begun to give priority to the military aspects of the situation. Jagow said as much to Sverbe'ev when the latter called on him at the Wilhelmstrasse early on 31 July. He repeatedly raised rumours pointing to Russian military preparations and barely engaged in a discussion of possible diplomatic moves, much to Sverbe'ev's consternation, the latter complaining that Berlin and Vienna had done little to facilitate a diplomatic settlement. Altogether, the ambassador found Jagow in 'an extremely gloomy mood'.[191]

There had been a steady trickle of news of Russian troop movements over the past twenty-four hours. Partial mobilization of the four south-western and central military districts was officially confirmed on the morning of 30 July. At the same time, there was activity in other districts as well. The garrison at Kovno (now Kaunas) had been moved towards the German frontier; and from Warsaw it was reported that in Russian Poland the railways had been placed under military control, advance positions along the long Polish salient had been evacuated, and banks no longer accepted cheques issued by other financial institutions.[192]

---

[190] Tel. Sverbe'ev to Sazonov (no. 146), 17/30 July 1914, *IBZI* v, no. 305.
[191] Tel. Sverbe'ev to Sazonov (no. 149, urgent), 31 July 1914, *IBZI* v, no. 359.
[192] Pourtalès to Auswärtiges Amt (no. 191, urgent), 30 July 1914 (D 11 a.m., R 11.50 a.m.), Bülow [acting consul Kovno] to Auswärtiges Amt, 29 July 1914 (R 30 July, a.m.),

All of these were straws in the wind. Certainly, by the evening of 30 July Moltke, the chief of staff, had come to anticipate war. Early the next morning he was given further, though as yet uncorroborated, intelligence about Russian troop transports in Poland. Moltke was very nervous, Falkenhayn noted in his diary. The self-imposed deadline for declaring the 'imminent danger of war' was midday on 31 July, but military intelligence officers at Berlin were by no means certain about the situation in Russia. Around noon, Moltke and Falkenhayn returned to the chancellor's office for a further conference. While they were discussing the information available, a messenger from the foreign ministry next door burst in with a telegram from Pourtalès reporting that general mobilization of the Russian army and navy had been ordered with effect on that same day. The meeting then decided to ask the Kaiser to declare *Kriegsgefahrzustand* as the required preparatory measure for general mobilization. It was also resolved, as Stumm who was in attendance later recollected, 'to address the well-known ultimatum to Russia, summoning her to suspend her military measures'. On his return to his desk at the Auswärtiges Amt, Stumm received a telephone call from Dietrich von Bethmann Hollweg, the chancellor's cousin at the Vienna embassy, with news of Vienna's reply to Grey's proposal. Stumm cut him short – 'this question had become outdated on account of the mobilization of the whole Russian army'.[193]

The declaration of 'imminent danger of war' required the Kaiser's signature. Until that morning Wilhelm still appeared hopeful of a peaceful outcome to the crisis. Early in the morning he read the latest report by Chelius, his military representative at St Petersburg. Pro-German circles at the Tsar's court had expressed the hope that some Russo-German arrangement might be come to on the basis of Austro-Hungarian guarantees not to smash Serbia. For the Russian military, mobilization did not mean war as there was an intermediate step between mobilizing the armed forces and commencing operations. The General had formed the impression that 'here they have mobilized out of fear of impending events but without aggressive designs and now they are aghast at what they have done'. This was also the Kaiser's view: 'Right – so it is.'[194]

and Brück [consul-general Warsaw] to Auswärtiges Amt, 29 July 1914 (R 30 July, p.m.), *DD* II, nos. 410, 404 and 422.

[193] As quoted in Albertini, *Origins* III, 29; tel. Pourtalès to Auswärtiges Amt (no. 199), 31 July 1914 (D 10.20 a.m., R 11.40 a.m.), *DD* II, no. 473. For Moltke, see Mombauer, *Moltke*, 205–6.

[194] Tel. Chelius to Auswärtiges Amt (no. 195), 30 July 1914 (D 5.46 p.m., R 10.05 p.m.), and marginal comments by Wilhelm II, 31 July 1914, *DD* II, no. 445.

But now the chancellor called him to return to the Schloss at Berlin, where he arrived in the early afternoon. The news from St Petersburg meant that the game was up. Germany would have to declare *Kriegsgefahr*. Aware of the risk entailed in such a move, Bethmann and Jagow were still anxious to do everything possible to ensure British neutrality, and therefore decided to give ambassador Goschen advance warning of the impending declaration. The ambassador was not amused. Did Jagow not realize, he spluttered when a telephone call came through from the Wilhelmstrasse requesting his immediate presence there, 'that I am having lunch, that I am having boiled chicken and rice, my favourite dish?' On his arrival at the foreign ministry, Jagow explained that Russia's general mobilization forced Germany to prepare for mobilization herself, but assured the ambassador that Berlin continued to advise the Austro-Hungarian government 'to do something to reassure Russia'.[195]

The Kaiser required no persuasion. Following Russia's general mobilization his mood veered towards the bellicose. Between 2 and 3 p.m., he received the military leadership for a meeting in the *Sternensaal*, the star chamber, of his Berlin residence. The proceedings, as so often at the highest level of Wilhelmine politics, were characterized by an odd mixture of the pathetic and the casual. The monarch held forth at some length about the news from Russia and blamed everything on the government at St Petersburg. 'His posture and language were worthy of a German emperor! Worthy of a Prussian king! The order for imminent danger of war, which I hold in my hand, is signed [by the Emperor] while standing.' For good measure this was followed by a near-altercation between Bethmann and the Kaiser because the monarch had allowed his senior military adviser to draft a declaration to the German people, which the chancellor considered to be a matter for the civilian government.[196]

With the proclamation of *Kriegsgefahr*, a host of measures took effect. Germany was now under martial law; the press was subject to military censorship; railways were placed under military guard; and all troops had to return to their barracks. Covering forces moved into position in the frontier districts, and private road traffic there was prohibited. The declaration confirmed now the supremacy of the military over the civilian leadership. It answered Berchtold's flippant, but not altogether inappropriate question: 'Who governs [at Berlin]: Moltke or Bethmann?'[197]

---

[195] Quotes from Sir F. Oppenheimer, *Stranger Within* (London, 1960), 229, and tel. Goschen to Grey (no. 110), 31 July 1914 (D 3.50 p.m., R 5.35 p.m.), *BD* XI, no. 349. Sir Francis Oppenheimer was the commercial attaché for central Europe, then based at Berlin.
[196] Falkenhayn diary, 31 July 1914, Afflerbach, *Falkenhayn*, 160.
[197] On 31 July as quoted in Conrad, *Aus meiner Dienstzeit* IV, 153.

With the declaration of *Kriegsgefahr*, Germany had also taken a big step towards general mobilization, though the latter did not automatically follow from the former. It still required a separate decision to ready the armed forces for war. Even so, the fear that by mobilizing first Russia had stolen a march on Germany concentrated minds at Berlin now. There was the danger, as Pašić – of all people – ruminated, that 'Russia is now talking and drawing out the negotiations to gain time for the mobilization and concentration of her army. When that is complete she will declare war on Austria.'[198]

The German leadership was not prepared to allow for that to happen. Once the proclamation on the imminent danger of war had been signed, the diplomatic missions abroad were informed of this step. Pourtalès and Schoen were instructed to obtain clarification on the attitude of the Russian and French governments. Pourtalès was to inform the Choristers' Bridge that 'unless Russia halted every war-measure against us and Austria-Hungary within the next twelve hours and gave a definite statement thereon', Germany would be forced to mobilize herself. If not in its form, then in its substance this was an ultimatum. In 1909 it had proved sufficient to coerce Russia. Now, there was no prospect of this happening. Just as the Ballhausplatz had been certain that Belgrade would reject its démarche, so the German leadership had no illusions that a Russo-German war was, potentially, imminent. Similar instructions were despatched to Schoen at Paris. The French government was given eighteen hours, that is until 4 p.m., central European time, the next day to declare its intentions. If, as was not expected, France did declare herself neutral after all, Schoen was to demand the temporary cession of the fortresses of Toul and Verdun as guarantee of a French pledge of neutrality.[199]

There was nothing subtle about the demand on France. It was an ultimatum tossed by a mailed fist inside an iron-clad glove. To some extent Berlin was going through the motions now. The logic of military necessity dictated its policy. There was something else that was now required. Whilst it had suited Berlin to feign ignorance of Vienna's objectives against Serbia, the imminence of war required that the governments now coordinated a joint military strategy. For at that moment, Habsburg troop trains were still rolling south, towards Serbia, whereas the German campaign plans required substantial Austro-Hungarian support along the Polish salient while the bulk of Germany's forces was engaged in a massive move swinging through

---

[198] Pašić to Putnik, 31 July 1914, as quoted in B. E. Schmitt, *The Coming of the War* (2 vols., New York, 1930) II, 314–15; also Albertini, *Origins* III, 59.

[199] Tels. Bethmann Hollweg to Pourtalès (no. 153, urgent), and Schoen (no. 180, urgent), both 31 July 1914 (both D 3.30 p.m., R 11.10 p.m.), *DD* III, nos. 490–1.

Belgium to envelop the French army. To begin the process of coordination, the Kaiser addressed an urgent telegram to the Emperor Franz Joseph. Just as at the beginning of the July crisis the German monarch had shown a remarkable ability to misjudge the political situation, so now his ability to be tactless had not deserted him. Compelled to answer Russia's general mobilization by mobilizing Germany's army and navy, the Kaiser affirmed that he was 'ready, in fulfilment of my alliance duties, to begin the war against Russia and France'. The existing alliance treaty between the two countries contained no such obligation. Germany was pledged to support Austria-Hungary in the event of a Russian attack on the Dual Monarchy, but there was no obligation to make war on Russia and France because Vienna had decided to fight a regional war. Wilhelm left the Emperor in no doubt what was now expected of Austria-Hungary:

> In this difficult struggle it is of the greatest importance that Austria throws her main force against Russia and that she does not dissipate it by a simultaneous offensive against Serbia ... In this gigantic contest, in which we stand shoulder to shoulder, Serbia plays a quite secondary role that will require only the absolutely necessary defensive measures. Success in this war and thus the maintenance of our monarchies can only be hoped for if we both meet the new powerful enemy with all our force.

Vienna, moreover, had to do its utmost to conciliate Italy to secure the unity of the *Dreibund* alliance. Ironically, the Wilhelmstrasse had drafted a much more anodyne telegram in which Russia was blamed for the failure of international mediation efforts and for forcing Germany now to mobilize. There was no talk of war, except for an appeal in the concluding paragraph to stand 'shoulder to shoulder in a war forced upon us'.[200]

The effect of the Kaiser's telegram on Vienna was electrifying. No doubt, there was something monstrous about the wording of the Kaiser's telegram, a 'total disregard for the interests of the alliance partner' if not indeed 'a betrayal' of the latter's interests.[201] If so, it was no more than the interest Vienna now had to pay for its own self-delusions and the deceptions it had practised on Berlin. Having shown a cavalier disregard for Germany's position during much of the July crisis, and having escalated it

[200] Quotes from tels. Wilhelm II to Franz Joseph, 31 July 1914, ÖUA VIII, no. 11125 (transmitted by German embassy that evening), and draft of same by Stumm, 31 July 1914, DD III, no. 502.
[201] See Fritz Fellner's posthumous outrage in his 'Austria-Hungary', K. M. Wilson (ed.), *Decisions for War 1914* (London, 1995), 22–3 [9–26].

through a mixture of insouciance and recklessness, the Habsburg leadership found itself in a situation in which its self-proclaimed struggle for survival against Serbia was subsumed under a much larger struggle, one in which it had no stake and over which it could exercise but little influence.

The Kaiser's tactless telegram had nevertheless achieved one thing – it restored the natural hierarchy in the Austro-German alliance. Yet it still took some considerable time before the two countries coordinated their respective strategies. It was not until 3 August, and only after persistent German pressure applied via Szögyény and Tschirschky, that Berchtold agreed to declare war on Russia. Even then, it was not to be presented to the Choristers' Bridge until 5 August at the earliest.[202] And all the while Conrad was scrambling to correct his mistakes since 25 July. Plan B had to be rescinded, leaving only a skeletal force of three corps for a slower and smaller-scale Serbian campaign and redeploying a total of thirteen army corps against Russia in the Galician salient. To an extent, Berchtold's reluctance to submit to Berlin's pressure and declare war on Russia soon was a reflection of the chaos that now engulfed the Austro-Hungarian railways as the troops originally destined for the Serbian front had to detrain and re-embark for trains heading north. Indeed, when fighting began in earnest along the Galician frontier on 23 August, only nine corps had been deployed, assisted by a few reserve and *Landsturm* militia formations.[203]

Haldane finds things trembling in the balance and Grey tries to keep the two sides talking

Whilst the military element was in the ascendant, diplomacy had not yet run its course. Its function, however, had changed. If until 30 July localization or some form of negotiated settlement had been the principal object of the continental Powers, they now sought to shift the blame for any conflict on their opponents. For the British Cabinet, meanwhile, two problems now arose – how to limit any warlike complications and whether to enter a continental war, if the former proved impossible. At this point, then, two currents pulled the Powers in different directions. While Sir Edward Grey continued his efforts to keep the door open for diplomacy, what had begun

[202] See tel. Tschirschky to Auswärtiges Amt (no. 162), 3 Aug. 1914 (D 5.30 p.m., R 7.17 p.m.), *DD* IV, no. 772; cf. tel. Szögyény to Berchtold (no. 362), 2 Aug. 1914 (D 2 p.m., R 6.40 p.m.), *DA* III, no. 105.
[203] See Tunstall, *Planning for War*, 178–9; L. Sondhaus, *Franz Conrad von Hötzendorf: Architect of the Apocalypse* (Boston and Leiden, 2000), 146–8.

as an Austro-Serbian quarrel had been transformed into a rapidly escalating Russo-German crisis. And this now threatened to engulf the continent.

Grey's manoeuvres on 31 July and 1 August are put in their proper context by the events since 30 July. In London, the German chancellor's crude bid for British neutrality on the evening of 29 July had caused some consternation. The European situation was 'at least one degree worse than it was yesterday, and the 'prospect [is] very black to-day', wrote the Prime Minister to Venetia Stanley, his confidante and platonic enamorata, while the Lord Chancellor thought that '[t]hings are trembling in the balance[;] today or tomorrow will decide'.[204] Berlin, the Foreign Office clerk Eyre Crowe informed his wife, had made a 'most cynical and dishonourable proposal, offering all sorts of inducements to us in future if we allow France to stand alone'. It was distressing to see 'what the German gov[ernmen]t thinks us capable of'. If Germany was determined on war, then war would come. Even so,

> I cannot say that all hope of a peaceful issue has vanished. A slight glimmering of hope there still is, seeing that Germany is obviously rather nervous about the danger of our joining in. Join in we undoubtedly shall have to, on pain of losing the respect and goodwill of every Power, as well as our self-respect. The gov[ernmen]t are still undecided, but I think they are mistaken in believing that they will have any choice when the moment comes.[205]

If there was dismay at Bethmann's bold bid, the attitude of British ministers and officials was nevertheless a curious mixture of detachment and foreboding. To an extent, of course, the events at Sarajevo had happened in a faraway country and British interests were not directly affected. 'Events are marching swiftly along the path that has been traced', wrote Herbert Samuel with his usual acuity. Berlin and St Petersburg seemed 'most reluctant to go to war. But the headstrong recklessness of Austria is too much for them. Austria, which is really embarking on war in order to prevent the break-up of her own dominions, is utterly selfish and cares nothing at all whom else she involves . . . It will be the most horrible catastrophe since the

---

[204] Asquith to Venetia Stanley, 30 July 1914, M. and E. Brock (eds.), *Asquith: Letters to Venetia Stanley* (Oxford, 1985 (pb)), 136; Haldane to Elizabeth Haldane, 30 July 1914, Haldane MSS, NLS, MS 5991; R. Jenkins, *Asquith* (London, 1967 (pb)), 366–7.
[205] Crowe to Clema Crowe, 30 July 1914, Crowe MSS, Bodl., Ms.Eng.d.2903; tel. Goschen to Grey (no. 102, secret), 29 July 1914 (D 30 July, 1.20 a.m., R 9 a.m.), *BD* XI, no. 293.

abominations of the Napoleonic time.' It was marvellous, Samuel noted, 'how serene, and indeed cheerful, he [Grey] keeps; cheerful that is, in his demeanour, not in his outlook.'[206]

There was nothing unusual in Grey's unruffled exterior, but it was just as well that the strain of the crisis was not telling on him. In the afternoon of 30 July, he sent an official reply to the German chancellor's approach. His proposal could not 'for a moment be entertained'. It was in Britain's material interest to preserve France as a factor in the European equilibrium. But beyond this strategic calculation, there was a moral dimension. To enter into the kind of bargain Bethmann Hollweg had offered 'would be a disgrace from which the good name of this country would never recover'. Then there were Britain's international obligations towards Belgium, he warned: 'We could not entertain that bargain either.' The British government would reserve their full freedom to act as circumstances required.

This was in line with his handling of previous crises and the decisions of the Cabinet on 29 July. It also reinforced Grey's explicit warning to Lichnowsky on the previous evening. But there was still that tender plant of Anglo-German détente, and Grey held out the prospect of better relations in the future – it is significant here that, given that Lichnowsky's position had been compromised by Bethmann's clumsy communication, the gesture was made via Goschen. Cooperation between the two countries to preserve peace, Grey stressed, would be the best way of maintaining good relations: 'if we succeed in this object, the mutual relations of Germany and England will . . . be *ipso facto* improved and strengthened'. But the Foreign Secretary was ready to offer something more tangible still. If the crisis could 'be safely passed' he would work for a general settlement,

> some arrangement to which Germany could be party, by which she would be assured that no hostile or aggressive policy would be pursued against her or her allies by France, Russia, and ourselves, jointly or separately. I have desired this and worked for it, as far as I could, through the last Balkan crisis, and, Germany having a corresponding object, our relations sensibly improved.

If the idea of such an arrangement had hitherto been 'too Utopian', the imminence of war had concentrated minds sufficiently for it to be practicable now.[207]

---

[206] Samuel to Beatrice Samuel, 30 July 1914, Samuel MSS, PAL, SAM/A/157/692; [H.] Viscount Samuel, *Memoirs* (London, 1945), 101–2.

[207] Tel. Grey to Goschen (no. 231), 30 July 1914 (D 3.30 p.m.), *BD* XI, no. 303; see also aide mémoire by Goschen, 31 July 1914, *DD* III, no. 497. Lichnowsky learnt of Grey's

Five minutes after the telegram had been despatched to Berlin, Goschen's report on Jagow's grovelling apology for Bethmann's approach arrived at the Foreign Office. But Jagow also suggested that mediation on the basis of 'Halt in Belgrade' was still feasible, provided Berlin and London worked simultaneously on the Habsburg and Romanov governments.[208] This coincided with Grey's own suggestion of the previous evening, and he was ready to pursue this line further. In the early evening, he met Lichnowsky, with whom he discussed the latest instructions for Buchanan at St Petersburg. There could be discussions of Serbia's obligations towards Vienna, provided that the latter suspended any further military operations once its forces had occupied places in the frontier region. At Lichnowsky's suggestion Grey dropped any reference to the word 'ultimatum'. Instead he suggested that the Sazonov formula be amended, obliging Vienna to accept 'Halt in Belgrade' to be followed by the Powers examining 'how Servia could fully satisfy Austria without impairing Servian sovereign rights or independence'. The German ambassador found Grey 'absolutely calm and [he] appeared not to have given up all hope'. But the chances of preserving peace were 'slender' now, the Foreign Secretary wired to Buchanan. If Berlin and St Petersburg could not arrange matters, then his latest proposal was the only way forward. Meanwhile, Bertie was instructed to make similar representations at Paris.[209]

Grey's latest proposal provided a perfectly practicable solution to the crisis. But it was already too late to implement his plan. As seen earlier, by the time the instructions to Buchanan were sent, Sazonov had already won the Tsar's approval for general mobilization; and although the red notices would not go up until early the following morning, with the Russian chief of staff prepared to smash his telephone, it was not likely that the order would be retracted again.

King George's telegram of that same evening contained a version of Grey's proposal, and this may well explain the delay at Berlin in taking the next decisions. But here, too, military considerations had moved to the fore. As seen, that evening Moltke and Falkenhayn forced the chancellor to

post-crisis plans from one of the Foreign Secretary's aides, presumably Tyrrell, see tel. Lichnowsky to Auswärtiges Amt (no. 184), 30 July 1914, *ibid.* II, no. 435.

[208] Tel. Goschen to Grey (no. 103), 30 July 1914 (D 1.45 p.m., R 3.35 p.m.), *BD* XI, no. 305.

[209] Quotes from tel. Lichnowsky to Auswärtiges Amt (no. 189), 30 July 1914 (D 6.10 p.m., R 8.45 p.m.), *DD* II, no. 439; and tel. Grey to Buchanan (no. 412), 30 July 1914 (D 7.35 p.m.), *BD* XI, no. 309. Lichnowsky transmitted a copy of the telegram to Buchanan later that evening, see tel. (no. 192), 30 July 1914 (D 9.56 p.m., R 12.52 a.m.), *DD* II, no. 460.

concede that by noon of Friday, 31 July, a decision would have to be taken on whether to take the first preparatory steps towards mobilization.

The slow speed of telegraphic communications at the height of the crisis was another complication. Possibly because the central European telegraph cables were now no longer considered to be entirely safe, telegrams to and from St Petersburg were sent by a circuitous route via Aden. The volume of telegraphic traffic caused delays in transmission; encyphering and decrypting further delayed communications. Whatever the precise reasons, Buchanan did not receive Grey's telegram no. 412 until much later on 31 July, and so did not act on it until the evening of that day.[210] By then, general mobilization in Russia and the declaration of *Kriegsgefahrzustand* in Germany had created an entirely different situation. News of these measures did not reach London until later in the afternoon of 31 July. At 4.45 p.m., Lichnowsky reported that the Foreign Office had no information on the full mobilization of Russia's army and navy. Indeed, at precisely that time a telegram arrived from Goschen, announcing the Kaiser's proclamation of 'imminent danger of war', but without any further explanations.[211] These were not to arrive for another fifty minutes, when a more detailed report was received that placed the German decision in the context of the proclamation of Russia's general mobilization. Just before then, Buchanan had wired news of the Russian move.[212] In fact, it was the German embassy that first alerted the Foreign Office to the latest developments at St Petersburg and Berlin, as Asquith confirmed at 5 p.m. in the House of Commons: 'We have just heard – not from St Petersburg but from Germany – that Russia has proclaimed a general mobilisation of her army and fleet.'[213]

Whatever the cause of the late despatch of Buchanan's telegram, the government in Paris was equally in the dark about the events in Russia. Only here the reason was obvious. Anxious to reduce any chances of interference by his own government, Paléologue had delayed informing his government. True, his telegram no. 318, marked 'very urgent', was

---

[210] Tel. Buchanan to Grey (no. 193), 31 July 1914 (D 1 Aug., 12.15 a.m., R 11 a.m.), *BD* XI, no. 393. For the Aden cable see *ibid.*, no. 347 n. The French embassy at Vienna sent its telegrams via Milan: see *DDF* (3) XI, no. 539.

[211] Tel. Lichnowsky to Auswärtiges Amt (no. 200), 31 July 1914 (D 4.45 p.m., R 10.30 p.m.), *DD* III, no. 518; tel. Goschen to Grey (no. 111), 31 July 1914 (D 3.09 p.m., R 4.45 p.m.), *BD* XI, no. 346.

[212] Tels. Goschen to Grey (no. 110), 31 July 1914 (D 3.50 p.m., R 5.35 p.m.), and Buchanan to Grey (unnumbered), 31 July 1914 (D 6.40 p.m., R 5.20 p.m.), *BD* XI, nos. 349 and 347.

[213] *Hansard House of Commons* LXV (31 July 1914), cols. 1787–8; min. Tyrrell, 31 July 1914, *BD* XI, no. 344.

apparently despatched at 10.43 a.m. But he chose the more circuitous Scandinavian route rather than the German cable, and the telegram did not arrive until 8.30 p.m.[214] Other representatives had begun to use the Scandinavian line from 30 July, but in Paléologue's case concerns about cypher security are not likely to have played a role. News of the general mobilization of France's ally should have been transmitted as a matter of urgency. Given that the red notices had been plastered all over St Petersburg it was scarcely a secret, and there was no need now even for encyphering the telegram.

Paléologue need have had no concerns about a possible diplomatic intervention by Paris at this stage. At 6.30 p.m. Schoen, the German ambassador, called on the Quai d'Orsay to inform Viviani of the proclamation of *Kriegsgefahrzustand* in response to Russian general mobilization, and to enquire how the French government would respond to a Russo-German conflict. Viviani refused to give an immediate answer, but promised to do so by 1 p.m. the following day.[215] In a telegram to Paléologue, Viviani made clear that he would give no answer at all. He asked for confirmation of Russia's general mobilization and reiterated his earlier advice that, 'in the superior interests of peace', Russia ought to avoid anything that might 'open up the crisis'. But there was no real attempt to restrain St Petersburg. Indeed, later that night, in conversation with the Russian ambassador, the war minister, Messimy, 'declared in solemn and cordial tones the [French] government to be firmly resolved to war'.[216]

With the hardening of the French position, Grey's chances of success were even more 'slender' than he realized. As it was, from London's perspective the morning of 31 July looked promising enough, at least for a few hours. Overnight de Bunsen's telegram on Shebeko's 'quite friendly' conversation with Berchtold had arrived at the Foreign Office. As seen, Berchtold had described Austria-Hungary's mobilization as a precaution and had indicated that he had no objections to further talks between Sazonov and Szápáry.

[214] Tel. Paléologue to Viviani (no. 318, extreme urgency), 31 July 1914 (D 10.43 a.m., R 8.30 p.m.), *DDF* (3) XI, no. 432; for a different view see Hayne, *French Foreign Office*, 300–1, who claims that the telegram was not sent until *c.* 6 p.m. For the use of the Scandinavian route see Stengers, 'Safety of Ciphers', 37.

[215] Min. Berthelot, 31 July 1914, *DDF* (3) XI, no. 417; tel. Schoen to Auswärtiges Amt (no. 237), 31 July 1914 (D 8.17 p.m., R 12.30 a.m.), *DD* III, no. 528.

[216] Tels. Viviani to Paléologue (nos. 483–4, very urgent), 31 July 1914 (D 9 and 9.20 p.m.), *DDF* (3) XI, no. 438, and Izvolsky to Sazonov (no. 216), 18/31 July 1914, *IBZI* v, no. 356; P. Miquel, *La Grande Guerre* (Paris, 1983), 72–3.

The latest news from Vienna, noted Crowe, 'looks at last as if some German pressure were making itself felt' there.[217]

That morning, Grey once more saw the German ambassador. Neither man, of course, knew then of Russia's mobilization. But their ignorance of this latest turn of events throws into sharper relief the nature of Grey's diplomacy. Under the impression that Szápáry and Sazonov were about to resume their talks in the Russian capital, Grey sought to bring the quartet into being again. The chief obstacle so far had been Vienna's mistrust of Serbian assurances and St Petersburg's suspicions of Habsburg designs on Serbia. Lest the talks break down on that score again, he suggested that the quartet 'undertake ... that she [Austria-Hungary] obtained full satisfaction of her demands on Servia ... [and] prevent[ed] Austrian demands going the length of impairing Servian sovereignty and integrity'. In the meantime, the Powers had to suspend 'further military operations or preparations'. In essence, what he offered was an internationally guaranteed settlement rather like the 1913 Treaty of London, but based on 'Halt in Belgrade' and incorporating the Sazonov formula.

The Foreign Secretary went a step further, and held out the prospect of British neutrality in a continental war, provided Berlin and Vienna 'could get any reasonable proposal put forward which made it clear that [they] were striving to preserve European peace'. If it were rejected by France and Russia, Britain would remain aloof and 'have nothing more to do with the consequences'. At the same time, he left Lichnowsky under no doubt that a German attack on France would draw Britain in.[218]

The naval preparations in train since the previous Sunday were a clear enough signal of intent, as Lichnowsky well understood. The ambassador had nevertheless formed the impression – for the first time, as he reported to Berlin – that in consequence of the recent improvement in Anglo-German relations, 'England might adopt a waiting attitude' in a continental war. But for that to happen it was indispensible that Vienna offered more than merely 'formal concessions' to Grey's mediation proposals. The Foreign Secretary had in fact suggested that any concession on the part of Austria-Hungary had to be such as 'to place Russia in the wrong' so that British diplomacy could then exercise greater pressure on France and Russia. But for any of this to work, as Lichnowsky repeatedly

---

[217] Min. Crowe, 31 July 1914 on tel. de Bunsen to Grey (no. 127), 30 July 1914 (D 9 p.m.), *BD* xi, no. 311; F. R. Bridge, 'The British Declaration of War on Austria-Hungary in 1914', *SEER* xlvii, 3 (1969), 410–11 [401–22].

[218] Tel. Grey to Goschen (no. 241), 31 July 1914 (D 11.40 a.m., R 1.40 p.m.), *BD* xi, no. 340.

stressed, it required 'energetic pressure applied by Berlin' on Berchtold.[219] The ambassador, his Austro-Hungarian colleague, noted, 'tears his hair out and wishes that we [Austria-Hungary] give in at the last moment'.[220]

With his proposal of a far-reaching settlement, guaranteed by the quartet, Grey offered Berlin a diplomatic triumph on a silver salver. If it accepted, the Russian government would have had to acquiesce in more extensive Serbian concessions to Vienna. All the German leadership had to do was gratefully accept Grey's latest proposal, implement Bethmann Hollweg's late-night instructions to Tschirschky of 29/30 July, and avoid taking any military measures themselves. But there, of course, lay the problem now.

As for Grey, there is no reason to doubt his genuine intentions. The Prime Minister took a gloomier view of the European situation. He 'had no hope that there was an idea that things were better', he explained to his wife at 11 a.m., and with that he went downstairs to chair a Cabinet meeting. The most pressing concern for Asquith at that moment was a sudden financial panic which had gripped the City of London, and which had led the Bank of England to suspend gold payments. The stock exchange had also closed for the first time in its history.[221]

At the meeting of the Cabinet, Grey developed his thoughts once more for the benefit of his fellow ministers. Britain would not 'bargain treaty obligations away'; there could therefore be no question of accepting Bethmann's brash advance of the previous evening. If Germany wanted peace, Grey affirmed, 'we were working for [the] same end & [he] believed if we could jointly bring it about it would do more to cement good feeling than any abstention now from war'. He would use his good offices to secure 'a (more) permanent understanding & [he] thought that the better relations which had been established c[oul]d be take [sic] definite form'. The ministers, as Jack Pease recorded in his diary, agreed that 'British opinion would not now enable us to support France – a violation of Belgium might alter public opinion, but we could say nothing to which at the moment we could commit ourselves'. Harcourt, the Colonial Secretary, slipped Pease a pencil note during the meeting: 'It is now clear that *this* Cabinet will not join the war.'[222]

---

[219] Tels. Lichnowsky to Auswärtiges Amt (nos. 197 and 196), 31 July 1914 (D 12.13 p.m., R 2.50 p.m., D 12.15 p.m., R 3.25 p.m.), *DD* III, nos. 484 and 489.

[220] Mensdorff diary, 31 July 1914, Nachlass Mensdorff, HHStA, Karton 4.

[221] Margot Asquith diary, 31 July 1914, Asquith MSS, Bodl., Ms.Eng.d.3210; D. Kynaston, *The City of London*, II, *Golden Years, 1890–1914* (London, 1996 (pb)), 600–8.

[222] Pease diary, 31 July 1914, Wilson (ed.), 'Cabinet Diary', 45. Harcourt himself originally was inclined to 'smash our Cabinet before they can commit the crime [of committing Britain to war]', Harcourt Cabinet notes, 30 July 1914, no accession number.

This was true enough, but it was only true under the current circumstances. Even so, there was a strong sense that, in so far as British interests were concerned, a conflict in the east was quite distinct from a continental war. As Harcourt noted, Grey would try to convince Berlin to put pressure on Vienna 'to make some reasonable offer to St Petersburg and *then* if Russia proved *un*reasonable it might give us ground to wash our hands of Russia'.[223] No firm decisions were taken, Samuel told his wife later in the evening: 'nothing untoward happened at the Cabinet today'. By the time he wrote the letter, news of Russia's mobilization and Germany's declaration of 'imminent danger of war' had reached London. It still looked, Samuel wrote, reflecting the mood of that morning's Cabinet meeting, 'as though she [Germany] still had hopes … There is no doubt that the Kaiser is working strenuously to prevent the catastrophe but he is likely to find the Austrians too obstinate for him.'[224] For now ministers pinned their hopes on the assumed peace party at Berlin. As John Burns reasoned, war would end in Germany's military defeat; it 'will end the Hohenzollerns, terminate Junkerdom, finish the Monarchy and inaugurate a Federal German Republic – and may lead to a United States of Europe with Britain the last in the hegemony of emancipated European states'. The only decision ministers took that Friday morning was to stay put in London; they would not disperse, and hold further Cabinet meetings on Saturday and Sunday.[225]

With some of the elements of his latest initiative in place, Grey now needed to sound out the French, and after lunch he met Cambon. The ambassador opened with the familiar line that uncertainty as to London's attitude in the event of a European war encouraged the hardliners at Berlin, and that only Britain's siding openly with the Franco-Russian group would act as a restraint on them. That, of course, was precisely the sort of step that would undermine Grey's mediation strategy; it would also mean a deviation from the line of policy agreed by the Cabinet on 29 July. Besides, Grey's previous statements to Lichnowsky could not have left Berlin under the impression 'that we would not intervene'. The current financial crisis, which had been triggered by the political crisis, threatened 'a complete collapse … and it was possible that our standing aside might be the only means of preventing a complete collapse of European credit'. German aggression in the west, the invasion of Belgium, might justify British

---

[223] Harcourt Cabinet notes, 31 July 1914, Harcourt MSS, Bodl., no accession number (Harcourt's emphasis).
[224] Samuel to Beatrice Samuel, 31 July 1914, Samuel MSS, PAL, SAM/A/157/694.
[225] Burns diary, 31 July 1914, Burns MSS, BL, Add. MSS. 46326; Haldane to Elizabeth Haldane, 31 July 1914, Haldane MSS, NLS, MS 5991 (quote from former).

intervention. But for now, he emphasized, 'we did not feel, and public opinion did not feel, that any treaties or obligations of this country were involved'.[226]

To an extent, public opinion and the financial crisis were a convenient screen behind which to hide. True, divisions within the Liberal party at Westminster and the fragile consensus in the Cabinet constrained Grey's freedom of manoeuvre. But there were also important diplomatic calculations that meant he could not give Cambon the assurances the French ambassador sought. If the latest initiative was to succeed, Berlin had to exercise a decisive influence on the Ballhausplatz – the reports of that day suggested that this was happening – and Russia would have to take steps to de-escalate the situation – this was more likely if the French government acted to restrain its ally. A firm pledge by Britain to join any conflict against Germany would simply remove any incentive Paris and Berlin might have had to act in this sense. As Francis Bertie, the ambassador at Paris, warned, the French, 'instead of putting pressure on the Russian Government to moderate their zeal', expected London to warn off Germany: 'If we gave an assurance of armed assistance to France and Russia now, Russia would become more exacting and France would follow in her wake.'[227]

Even after news of Russia's mobilization and the German premobilization measures reached London, Grey still considered 'that [the] situation is not irretrievable'. He nevertheless now knew that the chances of peace were at best evenly balanced, more especially as the Foreign Office had been informed by the German embassy that unless Russia retracted her mobilization decree, Germany would move to general mobilization herself. A Russo-German if not indeed a continental war thus hove into view, and Grey requested from the French and German government assurances that they would respect Belgium's neutrality.[228] Following Bethmann's bid for British neutrality on 29 July, such an undertaking was not to be expected from the German government, and to that extent Grey tended towards intervention. This was consistent with his policy since succeeding to the Foreign Office in December 1905. It is nevertheless a remarkable testimony to his persistence that he pursued the option of a diplomatic settlement until the very last moment.

---

[226] Grey to Bertie (no. 513), 31 July 1914, *BD* xi, no. 367; cf. tel. Grey to Bertie (no. 290), 31 July 1914 (D 7.30 p.m.), *ibid.*, no. 352, and P. Cambon to Viviani (no. 357), 31 July 1914, *DDF* (3) xi, no. 459.

[227] Bertie to Grey (private), 30 July 1914, Bertie MSS, BL, Add. MSS. 63033.

[228] Tel. Grey to Bertie (no. 287), 31 July 1914 (D 5.30 p.m.), *BD* xi, no. 348; see min. Tyrrell, 31 July 1914, *ibid.*, no. 345.

Grey may well have come to expect war, as his Parliamentary Private Secretary, Arthur Murray, noted in his diary, but he remained calm and would not give up on diplomacy. The two men dined at Brooke's and then played billiards, before Grey returned to Downing Street to drop in on the Asquiths, as Margot Asquith recorded in her diary:

Ed[ward] Grey came in after dinner and played bridge ... he was very grave & silent but in quite good form. In [a] crisis he seems to get right away from himself ... Grey has in some ways an undeveloped schoolboy side to him but he has a strong ethical basis for his opinions ... He 'thinks to scale' ... & is as unpsettable as Henry [Asquith] is.[229]

There was no shortage of advice from senior ministers and officials that Britain should adopt a firmer line. At that morning's Cabinet meeting, Churchill had 'once or twice bec[o]me bellicose and aggressive'. And, later that evening, Edwin Montagu, the Financial Secretary to the Treasury, burst in on a gathering at No. 10 Downing Street, where 'he seized [Margot Asquith] by the arm & in a violent whisper said: "We ought to mobilize tomorrow & declare it! How I wish [Sir John] Simon [the Attorney General] c[oul]d be crushed right out! His influence is most pernicious."'[230]

This was also the view advanced by senior Foreign Office officials. Nicolson, the Permanent Under-secretary, warned that unless Britain mobilized, 'our aid would be too late'. Mobilizing the navy and the small British army would be 'a precautionary and not a provocative measure – and to my mind is essential'. Grey concurred. Preparations were necessary – they would also reinforce the statements made to Lichnowsky without directly threatening Berlin – but any decision to that effect had to be sanctioned by the Cabinet.[231]

Eyre Crowe, Nicolson's designated successor, took the unusual step of interfering in what was the preserve of the Cabinet. He offered 'some simple thoughts ... [on] the grave situation', as he put it. What followed was a robust exposition of a form of British realpolitik that combined the stout defence of British interests with liberal morality. 'The theory that England cannot engage in a big war means her abdication as an independent State', he warned: 'She can be brought to her knees and made

[229] Murray diary, 31 July 1914, Murray of Elibank MSS, NLS, MS 8814; Margot Asquith diary, 31 July 1914, Asquith MSS, Bodl., Ms.Eng.d.3210 (quote from latter).
[230] Pease diary, 31 July 1914, Wilson, 'Cabinet Diary', 45; Margot Asquith diary, 31 July 1914, Asquith MSS, Bodl., Ms.Eng.d.3210.
[231] Mins. Nicolson and Grey, 31 July 1914, BD XI, no. 368.

to obey the behests of any Power or group of Powers who *can* go to war.' Crowe dimissed so-called City opinion as 'pusillanimous', prone to short-term panics, and liable to be influenced by foreign governments. Remaining neutral at all cost would negate the principle of the balance of power, hitherto upheld as the lode star of British foreign policy. A European equilibrium could not be maintained by a state that was incapable of waging war and so carried no weight in international politics. But neutrality now would also make a mockery of Grey's earlier refusal of Bethmann's disreputable offer of a guarantee of Belgium's post-war integrity and independence. At least 'terms were offered which were of some value to France and Belgium. We are apparently now willing to do what we scornfully declined to do yesterday, with the consequence that we lose the compensating advantages accompanying yesterday's offer.'

There were no binding, contractual obligations towards France, Crowe affirmed. But the Anglo-French understanding of 1904 had evolved from the strictly colonial agreement it was at its inception. Repeated German challenges had strengthened and tempered it 'in a manner justifying the belief that a moral bond was being forged'. Expectations of British support had been raised, he argued. Repudiating it now would expose 'our good name to grave criticism'. The matter of British intervention in a continental war was 'a question firstly of right or wrong, and secondly of political expediency'. On both counts, Crowe concluded, the answer pointed towards Britain entering the war.[232]

Crowe took some risk in sending his memorandum to Grey, 'but it may do good', he hoped. The Cabinet appeared to be 'in a panic and it seems doubtful whether they will take the only honourable and absolutely necessary course and declare that they will stand by France if attacked'. The ministers were 'funking' because of the pressure brought to bear by City 'panic mongers'. He was 'pleading hourly with Grey who is undecided and tired'.[233]

For all his incisive political intelligence, Crowe was not a good judge of character. If Grey was undecided, then only in the sense that he did not consider the present moment the right one for a final decision. On the contrary, diplomatic and domestic considerations counselled delay. Later that night, 'masses of F[oreign] O[ffice] boxes drove Grey away' from the Asquiths' card table,[234] and he launched one further diplomatic initiative. A number of developments came together that night, which help to explain

---

[232] Crowe to Grey, 31 July 1914, and memo. Crowe, 31 July 1914, *BD* xi, no. 369.
[233] Crowe to Clema Crowe, 31 July 1914, Crowe MSS, Bodl., Ms.Eng.d.2903. The letter was, in fact, written at 1 a.m. on 1 August.
[234] Margot Asquith diary, 31 July 1914, Asquith MSS, Ms.Eng.d.3210.

London's next move. From Paris, Bertie reported that relations between France and Germany were likely to be severed on the following day on account of Russia's mobilization. The French government, it seemed obvious, had done little to restrain Russia. French mobilization might be ordered any moment, and French military officers had sought out the Paris correspondent of *The Times* to induce him to prepare the British public for a continental conflict. France's military preparations, meanwhile, appeared to be more substantial than previously thought, and troops had taken up covering positions on the previous day with orders to keep at eight kilometres' distance from the frontier.[235] Just before midnight a note from the German embassy arrived, announcing that Germany was compelled to respond to Russian general mobilization 'with serious counter-measures'. The note confirmed that St Petersburg had been requested to cease mobilizing, and enquiries had been made at Paris as to the attitude of France in the event of a Russo-German war.[236]

Russia's mobilization, the absence of any restraining French influence on the Russian government and the counter-measures Berlin was about to take threatened to undermine British diplomacy. Once Germany mobilized, previous German pronouncements left no room for doubt that war could no longer be averted. If diplomacy was to have any chance at all now, then St Petersburg had to be persuaded that it had to suspend the mobilization decree. And if France proved unwilling or unable now to exercise sufficient influence on the Russian government, then Britain had to approach Russia directly. The telegraphic exchanges between the Kaiser and the Tsar, and, more recently, between the Kaiser's brother and King George, suggested that only monarchical diplomacy now offered the prospect of unblocking the official diplomatic channels. Grey thus sent Tyrrell, his ubiquitous Private Secretary, across to No. 10 Downing Street, where he, Asquith and Maurice Bonham-Carter, the Prime Minister's Private Secretary, drafted a direct appeal from the King to the Tsar. With some difficulty Tyrrell and Asquith then flagged down a taxi and headed to Buckingham Palace, where they roused the monarch, who had already turned in for the night. George V received his Prime Minister and Grey's Private Secretary in his dressing gown, but offered no objections to the proposed telegram, which was then despatched at 2 a.m. The telegram was a direct appeal from 'Georgie' to 'Nicky'. There had to be a

[235] Tels. Bertie to Grey (nos. 99 and 97, confidential, 100 and 101), all 31 July 1914 (D 8.35 p.m., 6.10 p.m., 8.35 p.m., 9.20 p.m., R 9.46 p.m., 8.15 p.m., 10.10 p.m., 11 p.m.), *BD* xi, nos. 357, 353, 358 and 363.
[236] Note by German embassy, 31 July 1914, *BD* xi, no. 372; cf. tel. Bethmann Hollweg to Lichnowsky (no. 199), 31 July 1914, *DD* iii, no. 513.

misunderstanding, the King suggested, and it was for the Tsar to remove it now. He had to stop the mobilization of the Russian armed forces so as to allow negotiations to continue. He himself would do what he could 'to assist in reopening the interrupted conversations between the Powers [i.e. Austria-Hungary and Russia] concerned'.[237] This left open the question of the basis of which of the various proposals Austro-Russian exchanges should resume on. But the important consideration for now was to keep the two sides talking.

'*Vorsprung in der Mobilisierung*': Count Pourtalès goes to Peterhof

In the broader context of the July crisis, the British effort at monarchical diplomacy came too late, and the belief in the efficacy of royal channels to alter decisions elsewhere was perhaps a sign of desperation. But its true significance lies in the fact that it was made at all. Clearly, Asquith and Grey remained committed to exploring all remaining diplomatic options. They were in no doubt as to what was required of Britain in the event of a continental war. But for now, they had not committed to France, let alone to Russia.

That same night two meetings took place, at St Petersburg and Berlin, which would soon force the British government to face the decision they had so far been able to avoid. Earlier that evening, at his own request, Pourtalès had been received by the Tsar in his small study at the Alexander Palace at Peterhof. The ambassador spoke earnestly of the dangers inherent in Russia's general mobilization. It was 'a threat and a provocation', more especially so as the Kaiser personally still sought a negotiated settlement. The Tsar's attitude remained friendly throughout the Count's explanations, but appeared somewhat detached from the situation. He interrupted the ambassador with an occasional 'Vous croyez vraiment?' ('Do you really think so'), and only later suggested that strong German pressure at Vienna – he emphasized the point with a suggestive hand gesture – alone could avert a catastrophe now. This was clearly the line Sazonov had taken on the previous evening, and Pourtalès batted the argument aside with a reference to Germany's position in Europe, which did not allow her to alienate her only reliable ally. His words of caution nevertheless failed to have the desired effect, as he reported to Berlin: 'Despite my very earnest language,

[237] Tel. George V to Nicholas II, 1 Aug. 1914, *IBZI* v, no. 397; and tel. Grey to Buchanan (no. 423), 1 Aug. 1914 (D 3.30 a.m.), *BD* xi, no. 384. Bonham-Carter informed Lichnowsky of this, see tel. Lichnowsky to Auswärtiges Amt (no. 203), 1 Aug. 1914, *DD* iii, no. 537.

I could not but form the impression that His Majesty was not fully conscious of the full severity of the situation.' As he left the palace Pourtalès was intercepted by Baron Vladimir Borisovich Fredericksz, the Tsar's long-serving minister of the imperial household. This cavalry general with pro-German leanings was deeply moved by the ambassador's account of what had passed during his audience with the Tsar. He could 'scarcely suppress his tears' and offered to do whatever was possible to persuade the Tsar of the need to retract the mobilization order.[238]

It was only at 11.10 p.m. that Pourtalès received Bethmann's latest instructions. Accordingly he once more requested an urgent meeting with Sazonov and set off for the Choristers' Bridge for another midnight interview with the minister. Unless St Petersburg gave an undertaking within the next twelve hours to halt mobilization against Germany and Austria-Hungary, the German government had no alternative but to mobilize, he explained to the foreign minister. Was mobilization equivalent to war, Sazonov enquired? The ambassador did not think so, but impressed upon the minister that 'we were very close to war'.[239] According to the ambassador's account, during their hour-long conversation, Sazonov once again pointed out the 'technical impossibility' of rescinding the mobilization decree, and sought to assuage German fears about the extent and direction of Russia's military measures. Mobilization did not mean war; the Tsar had given 'his word of honour'. But such assurances were not enough for Germany. Pourtalès asked openly whether Sazonov was able to give a guarantee that Russia was willing to maintain peace even if no Austro-Russian settlement was possible. As the foreign minister was not able to do so, Pourtalès left with the warning that 'one should not blame us for not being willing to allow Russia a further head-start in mobilization [*Vorsprung in der Mobilisierung*]'. If Russia wished to preserve peace, she had to stop mobilizing, thereby removing the implicit threat against Germany. The ambassador returned to the embassy with the 'firm impression', as he later recalled, that St Petersburg was 'resolved to let matters come to extremes'.[240]

---

[238] Quotes from tel. Pourtalès to Auswärtiges Amt (no. 204), 31 July 1914 (D 7.45 p.m., R 5.45 a.m.), *DD* III, no. 535, and Pourtalès, *Meine letzten Verhandlungen*, 59–62. For Fredericksz's version, which dovetails with the ambassador's account, see L. Magrini, *Il dramma di Seraievo* (Milan, 1929), 249–51.
[239] Tel. Sazonov to Izvolsky and Benckendorff (no. 1601), 19 July/1 Aug. 1914, *IBZI* v, no. 385.
[240] Quotes from tel. Pourtalès to Auswärtiges Amt (no. 209), 1 Aug. 1914 (D 1 a.m.), *DD* III, no. 536, and Pourtalès, *Meine letzten Verhandlungen*, 64–6. Communicated by the Russian government in London in the morning of 1 August, see min. Crowe, 1 Aug. 1914, *BD* XI, no. 398.

Under the impression of Fredericksz's offer of help, and as a last resort, Pourtalès despatched one of his attachés, Dankward Christian von Bülow, to Peterhof with a personal letter to the Baron. It was a direct appeal to the minister to persuade the Tsar to retract the mobilization order. It was also a measure of the ambassador's desperation now that nothing could apparently be achieved through Sazonov. The situation was very serious, he wrote, and he was 'searching everywhere for means of preventing a calamity. For war would pose an enormous danger for all monarchies.' The two countries were now a 'finger's breadth from war', he warned: 'I know how difficult it is to stop the machine that has already been set in motion. But in this respect the Emperor of Russia is all-powerful. I implore you to do what you can to avert a calamity.' Fredericksz received the attaché with the words 'Thank God, you have come. In 10 minutes I am to report to the Tsar.'[241]

Jagow thinks Russia has spoilt everything

At about the same time that Pourtalès called on Sazonov, the second crucial meeting during the night of 31 July/1 August took place – at Berlin between Goschen, the British ambassador at Berlin, and Jagow. The outcome of the hour-long interview was not reassuring. As instructed by Grey, Goschen sought to obtain a commitment from the German government pledging them to respect Belgian neutrality. Jagow was reluctant to give any such assurances, promised a fuller statement shortly and hinted privately that any answer to that question might 'have the undesirable effect of disclosing to a certain extent part of their plan of campaign'. This was as good an admission as any that the German onslaught in the west entailed an incursion into Belgium. The problem, of course, was all the more acute for Berlin as there was only one plan of campaign. It was a problem of Germany's own making.

Goschen also sought to convince Jagow to accept Grey's latest proposal and 'make another effort to prevent [the] terrible catastrophe of a European war'. Jagow was sympathetic to the Foreign Secretary's initiative, but insisted on Russia immediately countermanding her mobilization as a precondition to all further talks. He admitted Germany's demand in this respect 'had the form of an ultimatum'. Berlin's hand, however, had been forced, he argued. If St Petersburg gave a satisfactory answer, Grey's

---

[241] Quotes from Pourtalès to Fredericksz, 1 Aug. 1914, *DD* III, no. 539, and Pourtalès, *Meine letzten Verhandlungen*, 67–8.

proposal 'merited favourable consideration'. Berlin had sought to restrain Vienna, and the latest communications from there 'had been of a promising nature – but Russia's mobilization had spoilt everything'.[242]

It was still not too late to explore this latest initiative. Full mobilization after all had not yet been decided upon, and would at any rate not come into effect for another forty-eight hours. That Jagow did not reciprocate the latest British move was a reflection of the rigidity of German military planning. Given the intricate nature of German mobilization plans, the de facto ultimatum to Russia demanding the immediate cessation of Russian mobilization was meant to produce the clarification of Russia's objectives that Moltke and the military leadership had demanded. As for Britain's likely attitude in a continental war, Zimmermann, previously so certain that London would wish to remain neutral, was now equally certain that Britain would 'move at once against Germany and Austria-Hungary, if a military conflict with France and Russia broke out'.[243]

Berchtold makes a late concession and ponders the manifold follies of Russia

Jagow's and Sazonov's statements indicated the extent to which the governments at Berlin and St Petersburg were now concerned with ensuring that the blame for a European conflagration fell on the other. The room for a diplomatic solution had become narrower still, but it had not vanished entirely, as the exchanges between Sazonov and Szápáry at St Petersburg and Shebeko and Berchtold at Vienna indicated. Szápáry called on the Choristers' Bridge early in the morning of 1 August. Whatever the impact of Russia's general mobilization, the ambassador declared that his foreign minister would 'not only be ready to negotiate with Russia on the broadest basis, but was also especially inclined to make our note [to Serbia] the subject of discussions in so far as it concerns its interpretation'. This, of course, was little more than the previous offer by Berchtold to explain the nature of Austria-Hungary's demand. There was 'a certain discrepancy', Szápáry conceded – Sazonov wished to modify the demands – but he thought that 'in essence' the two proposals were the same. That indicated a significant concession, as the Russian foreign minister readily acknowledged, and 'the matter might be directed onto the terrain that he had had in mind from the beginning'. Sazonov admitted Vienna's goodwill, and

[242] Tels. Goschen to Grey (nos. 114 and 113), 31 July 1914 (D 2 a.m., 2 a.m., R 3.30 a.m., 3.45 a.m.), BD XI, nos. 383 and 385; min. Jagow, 31 July 1914, DD III, no. 522.
[243] Tel. Szögyény to Berchtold (no. 333), 31 July 1914 (D 12.35 a.m., R 9.10 a.m.), ÖUA VIII, no. 11127.

suggested that talks had better take place 'on the neutral ground of London'. There was something surreal about the conversation, Szápáry reflected. He himself was without instructions that took into account the fact of Russia's general mobilization, while Sazonov avoided the question of 'what should be done about the military operations [against Serbia] during any negotiations'. Sazonov, indeed, appeared to attach too much importance to his statement, the ambassador reported back to Vienna. He had made his explanations, Szápáry observed, because it seemed important to him that Habsburg diplomacy had made one more effort 'that could be described as the most extreme in conciliatoriness'. On the other hand, he suggested that if Berchtold still thought talks 'practicable or opportune' after Russia's mobilization, his latest interview afforded a basis for another attempt at a negotiated settlement.[244]

At about the same time, a meeting took place at the Ballhausplatz between Berchtold and Shebeko. It was almost the mirror image of the encounter between Sazonov and the Austro-Hungarian envoy at St Petersburg. Shebeko sought to induce the minister to define precisely Vienna's objectives towards Serbia. After some gentle linguistic fencing over the matter, Berchtold suggested that following the declaration of war on Serbia any further discussions of the ultimatum had become redundant. Whilst Shebeko had failed to elicit from the foreign minister any precise answer to his question, he concluded that 'Austria would not be disinclined to accept a proposal that offers her the chance to extract herself from the present situation without damage to her *amour propre* and her prestige in the Balkans and in the interior of the country.'[245] There was also the possibility, Avarna, the Italian ambassador, suggested to Shebeko, that after the first Habsburg successes against Serbia, Vienna might be content with Belgrade's reply to the ultimatum, subject to an unofficial Russian guarantee.[246]

According to Berchtold's record, the Russian ambassador reaffirmed that mobilization did not mean war and also raised the possibility of relocating the talks to London. For his part, the foreign minister avoided discussing specifics, but widened the discussion by touching on 'the manifold follies of the Russian Balkan policy'. There was 'a far broader basis for exchanges' between the two countries, he averred, if only St Petersburg could bring itself to see the bigger picture and not always to prioritize the interests of the Balkan states. Shebeko reciprocated

[244] Tel. Szápáry to Berchtold (no. 190), 1 Aug. 1914 (D 10.45 a.m., R 1 p.m.), *DA* III, no. 97.
[245] Tel. Shebeko to Sazonov (no. 135), 19 July/1 Aug. 1914, *IBZI* v, no. 418.
[246] Tel. Shebeko to Sazonov (no. 136), 19 July/ 1 Aug. 1914, *IBZI* v, no. 419.

Berchtold's sentiments. He made a vague reference to Russia's 'manifold obligations as an orthodox and Slavic state', hinted at 'a certain sentimental inclination of the Russian people', and observed that 'the whole thing was a great misapprehension between us [Austria-Hungary] and Russia'. Alfred Dumaine, the French ambassador, made similar comments. A formula could and should be found that 'took account of our justified expectations, satisfied Russia's interest in Serbia and opened the way to peace'.[247]

Pourtalès returns to the Choristers' Bridge and declares war

If the latest Austro-Russian discussions came too late, they nevertheless indicated the scope for a diplomatic solution that still existed, had it not been for Vienna's recklessness in declaring war on Serbia and St Petersburg's precipitating matters by decreeing a general mobilization. As it was, the friendly sentiments evinced by Sazonov and Berchtold on these occasions counted for nought. Events at St Petersburg overtook them.

At 2 p.m., Fredericksz called Pourtalès from Peterhof to inform him of the contents of another telegram the Tsar had addressed to his cousin in Berlin, which he hoped might still avert war. In it Nicholas accepted that the Kaiser was now compelled to mobilize, but requested from him the same guarantee that he had given him – that mobilization did not mean war and that talks would continue irrespective of the ongoing mobilization measures on both sides: 'Our long proved friendship must succeed, with God's help, in avoiding bloodshed.'[248]

Neither monarchical amity nor divine assistence was of any avail, however. The Tsar's telegram offered little of substance, and cousin 'Willy' at any rate was not willing to yield. 'Immediate affirmative clear and unmistakable answer from your government is the only way to avoid endless misery', he wired back in response. Unless Russian mobilization was halted, there could be no further discussions. Indeed, the Kaiser added a further request to the draft text of his reply, asking the Tsar to ensure that on no account did Russian troops cross the German frontier.[249] The latest round of telegraphic exchanges between 'Nicky' and 'Willy' came too late. Indeed, the Kaiser's additional demand underlined the degree to which the German leadership was now exercised by the prospect of Russia having stolen a march on them by mobilizing earlier.

---

[247] Berchtold daily report (no. 3737), 1 Aug. 1914, *DA* III, no. 99.
[248] Tel. Nicholas II to Wilhelm II, 1 Aug. 1914 (D 2.06 p.m., R 2.05 p.m.), *DD* III, no. 546; Pourtalès, *Meine letzten Verhandlungen*, 69–70; Magrini, *Il dramma*, 250.
[249] Tel. Wilhelm II to Nicholas II (D 10.45 p.m.), *DD* III, no. 600.

At 5.45 p.m., St Petersburg time, Pourtalès received an urgent telegram from Berlin. It contained Germany's declaration of war, which he was to hand to Sazonov in the event of the Russian government having failed to give a satisfactory reply to the earlier ultimatum by 5 p.m., central European time, i.e. 7 p.m. in St Petersburg. The document provided for two alternative scenarios – either that St Petersburg had not given an answer to Pourtalès's démarche or that it had declined to do so. The difference was infinitesimal, the outcome the same – war. Depending on Sazonov's response the ambassador was expected to hand him a note that matched the response. It was no doubt the proper procedure for such an occasion. Time, however, was short, all the more so since the telegram from Berlin was not decyphered until 6.45 p.m. Pourtalès therefore decided to deliver the required declaration orally, and later to submit Germany's declaration of war in its precise wording as an aide mémoire.

At the stroke of 7 p.m., the ambassador was admitted to the great cabinet at the Choristers' Bridge, where Sazonov received him. In a curious parallel with Giesl's meeting with Pašić, the two men stood during the exchange. There were few pleasantries. Sazonov himself was under no illusions as to the purpose of Pourtalès's call: 'He is probably bringing the declaration of war', he quipped. What followed next is not entirely clear. The Russian and German accounts differ on a number of points. According to Schilling's journal, the German ambassador asked whether Sazonov was in a position to give a positive reply to his note of the previous evening. Sazonov said that he could not, but added that, whilst mobilization could not be halted now, Russia had not rejected further talks to reach a negotiated settlement. Pourtalès, who had appeared depressed on arrival at the ministry, grew more agitated and emphasized the grave consequences of Russia's refusal to suspend the mobilization order. Three times he asked whether St Petersburg would halt its military measures; three times Sazonov replied in the same sense. 'I have no other answer to give to you', he said. On this, 'deeply moved, breathing heavily', as Schilling noted, the ambassador said: 'In that case, M. le Ministre, I am charged by my government to submit to you this note.' And with shaking hands he handed Sazonov the document, which still contained the reference to the two alternative scenarios.

That Pourtalès repeated his question three times is confirmed by his own account of his final interview with the Russian foreign minister. Having explained the nature of his instructions, he asked Sazonov to accept his statement as an oral declaration rather than a formal note. It was only at Sazonov's request that the ambassador signed the text. It was an unusual procedure – the Russian wartime Orange Book claimed that in his agitation Pourtalès handed over the wrong document – but the whole incident was a quibble over a few words. What is not in doubt, however, is that the meeting was highly charged. Schilling observed that, having made his declaration, Pourtalès 'lost all self-command, stepped towards the window, put a hand to his head, burst into tears and said: "I could never believe that I should leave Petersburg under such circumstances." He then embraced the minister and left.' In the ambassador's version of events, it was Sazonov who lost all control over himself. On Pourtalès explaining that he had always been a firm adherent of the closest Russo-German relations and that he had striven throughout the July crisis to prevent an open breach between Berlin and St Petersburg, the foreign minister broke down: 'Croyez-moi nous vous reverrons' (Believe me, we shall meet again), he cried out. Sazonov made 'a quite helpless impression' on the ambassador; he was a man, he reflected, who 'during the final phase of the crisis was carried along by the currents and allowed himself to be made the willing tool of the warmongers'.[250]

In all likelihood, both men were very agitated. Neither could be in any doubt about the immensity of what had just happened. The first ever Russo-German war had just begun (if, that is, one does not take into account the Seven Years' War, during much of which Russia fought against Prussia). Pourtalès, his embassy staff and a number of German subjects, some eighty persons all told, left St Petersburg at 8 a.m. the next day, Sunday, 2 August, from the Finland station to return to Germany via Åbo and Stockholm, nearly the same route that Poincaré and Viviani had travelled nine days previously. An age had passed since then.

Following the meeting with the German ambassador, Sazonov telegraphed Sverbe'ev that Germany had declared war, and that he and his staff were to return to St Petersburg forthwith. Shebeko at Vienna was instructed to remain at his post, for so far relations with Austria-Hungary had not been severed.[251] The minister also telephoned Buchanan to inform him of the German declaration. True to his previous form, Paléologue delayed informing his own government. It was not until the early hours of the following morning that he despatched a brief telegram to Paris at 1.19 a.m.; it did not arrive there until 2 p.m.[252] A little over twenty-four

[250] Quotes from Schilling journal, 19 July/1 Aug. 1914, *IBZI* v, no. 396, and Pourtalès, *Meine letzten Verhandlungen*, 70–4. The declaration of war is in tel. Jagow to Pourtalès (no. 159, urgent), 1 Aug. 1914 (D 12.52 p.m.), *DD* iii, no. 542; for Pourtalès's official report, which refers to Sazonov's thrice denial, see his tel. (no. 214), 1 Aug. 1914 (D 8 p.m.), *ibid.*, no. 588.

[251] Tels. Sazonov to Sverbe'ev (unnumbered), and Shebeko (no. 1622), 19 July/1 Aug. 1914, *IBZI* v, nos. 393–4.

[252] Tel. Paléologue to Viviani (no. 333), 2 Aug. 1914 (D 1.19 a.m., R 2 p.m.), *DDF* (3) xi, no. 583; for a vivid account of Sazonov's interview with Pourtalès see Paléologue

hours earlier, just before 1 p.m. on 1 August, one of the ambassador's misleading telegrams had arrived at the Quai d'Orsay, announcing that Pourtalès had seen Sazonov to inform him that the German government would order general mobilization that same day.[253] His German colleague had made no such communication, of course. In all likelihood, it was but the latest effort to prevent any last-minute interference on the part of Paris. He need not have feared any such move by his government. Earlier in the morning, at 9 a.m., the French cabinet had met and unanimously decided to begin mobilization. The official notices would be posted at 4 p.m. that same day, with the first day of mobilization fixed for the following day. French troops would be kept at a ten-kilometre distance so as to avoid any border incidents.[254] If this was meant to avoid any untoward events, there was nevertheless no intention at Paris to exercise any moderating influence on the Russian government. On the contrary, Messimy, the war minister, expressed his desire for Serbia and Russia to commence operations at the earliest opportunity. And when Izvolsky informed Poincaré of the German declaration of war, the president reaffirmed France's commitment to the alliance with Russia 'in a very categorical manner', though he stressed that it would be politically convenient for the French government if Germany declared war on France first.[255]

Indeed, when Schoen, the German ambassador, called on Viviani at 11 a.m. to enquire as to whether France would remain neutral in the event of a Russo-German war, the prime minister decided to obfuscate. He answered after some hesitation: 'France will do what her interests demand.' Viviani's account of events differed somewhat from Schoen's report. France, he argued, had consistently worked for a peaceful settlement of the crisis that satisfied the interests of all parties concerned. Germany, by contrast, had escalated the crisis. In the midst of Grey's mediation proposal, which envisaged the suspension of military measures, Germany had addressed an ultimatum to Russia and intimated to France that Franco-German relations were about to be broken off. Paris would continue to work towards conciliation but would have to take whatever military precautions were necessary to prevent Germany from gaining an advantage

---

diary, 1 Aug. 1914, in his *Russie des Tsars* 1, 42–4. Buchanan's telegram arrived much sooner – see his tel. (no. 201), 1 Aug. 1914 (D 1.20 p.m., R 11.15 p.m.), *BD* xi, no. 445.
[253] Tel. Paléologue to Viviani (no. 323), 1 Aug. 1914 (D 4.25 a.m., R 12.50 p.m.), *DDF* (3) xi, no. 490.
[254] Poincaré notes journalières, 1 Aug. 1914, Papiers de Poincaré, BN, Bnfr 16027, fo. 138 r. The order is in circular tel. (extremely urgent), 1 Aug. 1914 (D 3.55 p.m.), *DDF* (3) xi, no. 507.
[255] Tels. Izvolsky to Sazonov (nos. 221 and 222), 19 July/1 Aug. 1914, *IBZI* v, nos. 408–9.

through her early military preparations. The concluding paragraph was written already with a view to publication in the event of a war. It was also somewhat misleading. Germany had not yet mobilized, but the French government had already committed to mobilization. Viviani did not mention this, nor did he admit France's tacit approval of Russia's decision to start the scramble for mobilization.[256]

That Germany would declare war on France first, French ministers may well have expected. But they were also confident that, in that case, Britain would join the war. 'I do not despair', Poincaré noted in his diary at the end of the day: 'the [British] Foreign Office is well disposed in our favour; Asquith too; the English are slow to decide, methodical, deliberate, but they know where they are going'.[257]

King George thinks there must be a misunderstanding

Meanwhile at Berlin, the German leadership was anxiously awaiting news from St Petersburg. By noon, when the twelve-hour deadline had expired, only Pourtalès's telegram on his latest midnight interview with Sazonov had been received at the German foreign ministry, and with it the Russian foreign minister's implicit indication that mobilization would not be suspended.[258] Although Pourtalès wired to Berlin at 8 p.m., confirming that a state of war now existed between Germany and Russia, his report never reached the Wilhelmstrasse. The Russians had already cut the telegraph line.

By 4 p.m., with no Russian reply to Pourtalès's démarche received, war minister Falkenhayn called on Bethmann Hollweg to urge him to ask the Kaiser to sign the order for general mobilization. The chancellor initially resisted. Mobilizing, as he well understood, meant war, and this was tantamount to declaring bankrupt his entire strategy throughout the July crisis. In the end he yielded. As he did so, the Kaiser himself telephoned to request the chancellor and war minister to report to him immediately and to submit to him the mobilization decree for signature. The two men

---

[256] Quotes from tel. Schoen to Auswärtiges Amt (no. 239), 1 Aug. 1914 (D 1.05 p.m., R 6.10 p.m.), *DD* III, no. 571, and Viviani circular tel. (very urgent), 1 Aug. 1914 (D 3 p.m.), *DDF* (3) XI, no. 505; see also Poincaré, notes journalières, 1 Aug. 1914, Papiers de Poincaré, BN, Bnfr 16027, fo. 137 r.

[257] Poincaré, notes journalières, 1 Aug. 1914, Papiers de Poincaré, BN, Bnfr 16027, fo. 139 v.

[258] See tel. Pourtalès to Auswärtiges Amt (no. 209), 1 Aug. 1914 (D 1 a.m., R ? p.m.), *DD* III, no. 536.

immediately set off for the Schloss. In front of it a large crowd had begun to gather, and they had to force their way through the heaving mass amidst cheers and patriotic songs. At 5 p.m., surrounded by his senior military and naval advisers, Kaiser Wilhelm II signed the mobilization 'at a table made from the wood of Nelson's *Victory'*. Falkenhayn said: '"May God bless Your Majesty and your arms, may God protect our beloved fatherland." The Kaiser held my hand for some time; there were tears in the eyes of both of us.'[259] Outside the Schloss, as the proclamation of general mobilization was posted, the crowd spontaneously burst into 'Now let us all thank God' – a Lutheran chorale that had become an unofficial anthem in Prussia ever since Frederick the Great's soldiers, bloodied but victorious, had sung it after one of the soldier-king's most famous victories on the battlefield.[260] The Kaiser himself appeared on the balcony to address the vast crowd. 'If war comes, there will be no more parties; we shall just be German brothers', he declared. The monarch's appeal to patriotism across the parties, and including the Social Democrats, was meant to rally support for the often beleaguered imperial régime in the face of external adversity. It was the beginning of the *Burgfrieden* (or party truce) that was confirmed four days later when the SPD voted for the war credits requested by the government.[261]

General mobilization was thus declared before any official Russian reply to the démarche of the previous night had been received; and with mobilization war with Russia was now only a formality. After all, four hours earlier, Pourtalès had been instructed to present Sazonov with a formal declaration of war. The Kaiser's flamboyant signature underneath the document had barely dried, when Bethmann Hollweg and Jagow burst in on the assembled military men, brandishing a telegram from Lichnowsky. The news it contained was 'like a bomb-shell'.[262]

And like a bomb-shell it stunned the key actors and caused a great deal of confusion on that day and, indeed, amongst historians later on. In London, Jagow's carefully hedged reply to Goschen's request for German assurances in respect of Belgian neutrality was rightly viewed as suggestive of Germany's campaign plans in the west. 'France will respect Belgian

[259] Falkenhayn diary, 1 Aug. 1914, as quoted in Afflerbach, *Falkenhayn*, 162.

[260] B. Tuchman, *The Guns of August 1914* (New York, 1962), 96.

[261] For the Kaiser's address see E. Johann (ed.), *Reden des Kaisers. Ansprachen, Predigten und Trinksprüche* (Munich, 1966), no. 55; for discussions of the *Burgfrieden* see S. Miller, *Burgfrieden und Klassenkampf. Die deutsche Sozialdemokratie im Ersten Weltkrieg* (Düsseldorf, 1974); J. Verhey, *The Spirit of 1914: Militarism, Myth and Mobilization in Germany* (Cambridge, 2000).

[262] Lyncker diary, 1 Aug. 1914, *DGB*, 39.

neutrality, Germany will not', minuted Crowe: 'But Germany will delay a definite answer until it is too late for England to act effectively.'[263] However it was for the Cabinet to decide, and the ministers were to re-assemble at 11 a.m. that Saturday. Half-an-hour before the appointed time Haldane and Grey, who had sought refuge in the Lord Chancellor's house at 28 Queen Anne's Gate during the final week of the crisis, went to see Asquith for a pre-Cabinet discussion of the international situation. 'Things look black', Haldane wrote to his mother before setting off for Downing Street, 'but it is possible, though not probable that the struggle may be limited & short'. The three men were making 'every preparation which can make peace likely & avert peril'.[264]

What precisely they discussed is not clear. What is not in doubt is that they were under the impression of the deep divisions amongst their ministerial colleagues. It is also likely that they took into consideration the general consensus that had emerged at the last two Cabinet meetings that France had not acted as restraint on Russia in a faraway Balkan quarrel which appeared to be of no intrinsic strategic interest to Britain. That Saturday morning the ministers sat together for two-and-a-half hours. Opinion remained finely balanced. The Cabinet was 'serious, united for the day, but no decision [was taken] as in all our minds there rested the belief and hope for agreement', noted John Burns.[265] The staunchest proponent of war was Churchill, the First Lord of the Admiralty, whom Asquith and Harcourt described as 'very bellicose' and 'very violent', with a tendency to dominate proceedings.[266] The ministers rejected Churchill's suggestion of the immediate mobilization of the Royal Navy, but this did not stop him. He afterwards won Asquith's tacit approval, and then ordered the Navy to mobilize. The Prime Minister, Churchill later wrote, had looked at him 'with a hard stare and gave a sort of grunt. I did not

[263] Min. Crowe, 1 Aug. 1914, on tel. Bertie to Grey (no. 104), 1 Aug. 1914 (D 1.12 a.m., R 2.15 a.m.), *BD* XI, no. 382; Jagow's reply is in tel. Goschen to Grey (no. 114), 31 July 1914 (D 2 a.m., R 3.30 a.m.), *ibid.*, no. 383.
[264] Haldane to Elizabeth Haldane, 1 Aug. 1914 (first letter under that date), Haldane MSS, NLS, MS 5992; R. B. Haldane, *An Autobiography* (London, 1929), 270. This statement rather contradicts the argument by K. M. Wilson that Haldane merely wished to delay a decision for war so as to allow the British Expeditionary Force more time to prepare for war: see 'Understanding the "Misunderstanding" of 1 August 1914', *HJ* XXVII, 4 (1994), 885–9.
[265] Burns diary, 1 Aug. 1914, Burns MSS, BL, Add. MSS. 46326; W. Kent, *John Burns: Labour's Lost Leader* (London, 1951), 237.
[266] Asquith to Venetia Stanley, 1 Aug. 1914, Brock and Brock (eds.), *Asquith Letters*, 140; and Harcourt Cabinet notes, 1 Aug. 1914, Harcourt MSS, Bodl., no accession number.

require anything else.'[267] There was, however, to be no mobilization of Britain's small army.

At the other end of the spectrum was the Chancellor of the Exchequer, David Lloyd George, leader of the party's Radicals and Churchill's one-time mentor during the latter's fling with Radicalism. He seemed 'all for peace', or at any rate for 'keeping the position still open'. There were moments that morning, Asquith wrote to Venetia Stanley, when 'we came ... near the parting of the ways', though in the end the meeting broke up 'in a fairly amicable mood'.[268] Certainly, Lloyd George had his finger on the pulse of political Liberalism, and he knew, if Churchill did not, that a forced vote on entering a continental war against Germany at the present moment would split the Cabinet and the parliamentary party down the middle. As the debate raged back and forth across the Cabinet table, he slipped a hastily scrawled pencil note to Churchill: 'if patience prevails and you do not press us too hard we might come together'.[269] Herbert Samuel captured the uncertainties of the day when he wrote to his wife that '[h]ope of peace [is] not quite abandoned', only later on in the same letter to suggest that '[w]e may be brought in under certain eventualities'. He himself, he reflected, was now 'less hopeful than yesterday of our being able to keep out of it'.[270]

Over lunch with Grey, Haldane and Walter Runciman, the President of the Board of Agriculture, Burns '[u]rged him [Grey] to press for the triumphs of Peace rather than the laurels of war. The one [is] everlasting, the other withers and fades.'[271] And press Grey did – or rather someone did in his name. The so-called 'misunderstanding' of 1 August, a series of communications by Lichnowsky and between the ambassador and Grey, has generated a debate within the wider debate on the origins of the war. In the absence of complete and continuous documentation, and given the contradictory nature of the extant evidence, students of the July crisis have offered disparate interpretations of the events and the motivations of the people involved – itself suggestive of the innate difficulties of making sense of the events of July 1914 in general.

---

[267] W. S. Churchill, *Great Contemporaries* (London, 1952), 109.
[268] Asquith to Venetia Stanley, 1 Aug. 1914, Brock and Brock (eds.), *Asquith Letters*, 140.
[269] Lloyd George to Churchill, 1 Aug. 1914, Lloyd George MSS, PAL, C/14; also Ponting, *July 1914*, 255.
[270] Samuel to Beatrice Samuel, 1 Aug. 1914, Samuel MSS, PAL, SAM/A/157/696; J. Bowle, *Viscount Samuel: A Biography* (London, 1957), 118–19.
[271] Burns diary, 1 Aug. 1914, Burns MSS, BL, Add. MSS. 46326.

It is nevertheless possible to unravel what evidence there is, and to offer a different reading of the events of that day in London. Central to the initiative were Lichnowsky and Grey's Private Secretary, Tyrrell. During the second half of July, the ambassador had been sidelined by the Wilhelmstrasse; indeed he had been practically disavowed by his superiors. Critical of Berlin's attachment to the Habsburg Empire, he had been an ardent supporter of a rapprochement with Britain ever since his appointment in 1912; and during his eighteen months at Prussia House he had sought to build on the recent détente in Anglo-German relations. War would destroy his life's work. Tyrrell – secretive, subtle and surreptitious – was in constant touch with the German ambassador, as already seen. By 1913/14 he had become an 'advocate of a rapprochement' with Germany, an objective that both he and Grey shared, as Lichnowsky later wrote. It was common currency at the Foreign Office during the war that Tyrrell had grown sceptical of the value of cooperation with Russia, that, in fact, he 'was at the crisis ... for neutrality'.[272] The harder lines taken by some of the London papers at the end of July, he confessed in one of the few letters that this otherwise ink-shy official penned, 'make me fairly sick'.[273]

What is beyond doubt is that at 11.14 a.m. on that Saturday, Lichnowsky telegraphed to Berlin that Tyrrell had asked him to call on Grey in the afternoon. Grey would make a proposal that might help 'to avert the catastrophe'. He hinted that, provided Germany did not attack France, Britain would remain neutral and might guarantee 'France's passivity' as well. Tyrrell urged the ambassador that it was vital that German troops did not encroach upon French territory, just as French forces had been pulled away from the frontier. 'Everything depended on it', he emphasized. According to Lichnowsky, Grey himself then telephoned to enquire whether the ambassador could give assurances that, if France did not interfere in a Russo-German war, Germany would not open hostilities in the west. Lichnowsky thought that he could. In a further telegram, he reported that Tyrrell had indicated that British neutrality might be possible even in the event of a continental war.[274]

---

[272] Quotes from K. M. von Lichnowsky, *Auf dem Weg zum Abgrund. Londoner Berichte, Erinnerungen und sonstige Schriften* (2 vols., Dresden, 1927) I, 125–6, and Temperley diary, 28 Mar. 1918, Temperley MSS, private.
[273] Tyrrell to Ponsonby, 31 July 1914, Ponsonby MSS, Bodl., Ms.Eng.his.c.660; for some of the background see *History of The Times* (4 vols., London, 1920–52) IV, 204–9.
[274] Tels. Lichnowsky to Auswärtiges Amt (nos. 205 and 209), 1 Aug. 1914 (D 11.14 a.m. and 2.10 p.m., R 4.23 p.m. and 6.04 p.m.), *DD* III, nos. 562 and 570 (quotes from former).

This was the 'bomb-shell' Lyncker's diary recorded. Lichnowsky's first telegram arrived at 4.23 p.m., and had been decyphered into plain text some ten minutes after the Kaiser had signed the general mobilization order. The news was received with 'great but joyous surprise!', Admiral von Müller noted. And well it might.[275] A major triumph, it seemed, had been snatched from the jaws of the political bankruptcy which had just been declared with the order for general mobilization. What was on offer, it seemed, exceeded the previous goal of a localized Austro-Serbian war. Now, it seemed that, with British and French neutrality guaranteed, Russia could be coerced into submission. The much-feared triple entente, more a product of German imagination than a political reality, had been destroyed. Either Russia disengaged or she faced the risk of defeat in a war in the east. Whichever St Petersburg chose, there was now the prospect of a new Russo-German arrangement in eastern Europe, one largely on Germany's terms.

The Kaiser was exultant, and even the usually reserved chancellor joined in the celebrations. The monarch was all in favour of accepting any such proposal – none had been made, of course – and of halting the deployment of troops in the west. The jubilation was short-lived. There now followed a heated clash of opinion between the Kaiser and the chancellor on the one hand, and Moltke on the other. 'Well now we simply march the entire army to the east', the Kaiser said to Moltke.[276] Much to everyone's surprise, as Lyncker recorded, the chief of staff now declared that deployment in the west could no longer be stopped and 'that despite everything France had to be attacked'. A violent dispute now ensued in which the chief of staff remained isolated: 'Moltke, very agitated, with trembling lips, insisted on his position.'[277]

The problem for Moltke was that the preparations now in train were based on the scenario of a war on two fronts. Stopping the deployment of seven-eighths of the German forces in the west, as envisaged in the latest version of the 'Schlieffen Plan', would cause chaos, Moltke warned, and 'deprive us of any chance of success'. Besides, advance troops had already crossed into Luxemburg – strategically vital on account of the railway junction there which had to be secured against a French *coup de main* – and the 16th Division at Trier was about to follow. 'Now all we need is that Russia also snaps off', he burst out.[278] Halting general mobilization now, he warned, would leave Germany without an army ready to

[275] Müller diary, 1 Aug. 1914, Görlitz (ed.), *Regierte?*, 38.
[276] H. von Moltke, 'Betrachtungen und Erinnerungen', in his *Erinnerungen*, 19.
[277] Lyncker diary, 1 Aug. 1914, *DGB*, 39.
[278] Müller diary, 1 Aug. 1914, Görlitz (ed.), *Regierte?*, 39.

strike. Instead there would be 'a mass of orderless armed men without provisions'. The Kaiser grew intemperate: 'Your uncle [the elder Moltke] would have given me a different answer', a cutting remark that hurt the less-distinguished nephew very much.[279]

Moltke's argument was somewhat disingenuous. At this stage, general mobilization with the main thrust planned in the west, after all, had only just been ordered; and contrary to his explanations, German troops had not yet occupied Luxemburg – this did not occur until the following morning. The problem Moltke now faced was one of his own making. He had ruled out any alternative to the deployment of forces in the west, followed by the swift capture of Liège and the sweep through Belgium. The intricate meshing of railway timetables and mobilization schedules could not now easily be unpicked, though Moltke himself admitted that after mobilization was complete, any number of troops could be diverted to the east. And yet plans for an *Ostaufmarsch*, the deployment in the east, had been revised every year, the last time in 1913. It would have been a challenge to implement this now, but it would not have been impossible. There would have been some confusion, and the German staff would have lost a few days. But this would have been of no great strategic consequence as the redirected troops could then be deployed more advantageously against an enemy whose own dispositions would by then have become more clearly discernible.[280]

At the root of Moltke's inflexibility was a combination of his own character flaws – he lacked decisiveness and doubted his own abilities – and a deeper strategic malaise in Germany. What, after all, was the strategic objective now? Was it to assist the Habsburg ally in a Balkan war or was it to secure a decisive victory over Russia? If it were the former, then the bulk of the German army had to be deployed in the east to shield Austria-Hungary against a Russian offensive in Galicia, and it would undoubtedly have prevented the Habsburg defeats there in September and the loss of the fortress of Lemberg (now Lviv). If it were the latter, geography and the vastness of Russia stood against it, and the basic premise of the Schlieffen Plan, whatever its inherent risks and practical flaws, was the correct one. It was this strategic confusion at the heart of German decision-making that explains the violent dispute between the Kaiser and Moltke. Wilhelm's wounding comparison between his chief of staff and his illustrious uncle

---

[279] Moltke, *Erinnerungen*, 20; L. Cecil, *Wilhelm II* (2 vols., Chapel Hill, NC, 1996) II, 206–7.

[280] For this argument see W. Groener, *Lebenserinnerungen. Jugend, Generalstab, Weltkrieg*, ed. F. Hiller von Gaertringen (Göttingen, 1957), 145–6; for an exposition of Moltke's thinking, see Mombauer, *Moltke*, 220–3.

may well have contained a grain of truth. But the Kaiser conveniently forgot that his own grandfather and Bismarck would never have placed the elder Moltke in such an awkward situation.

In the end, Falkenhayn intervened in the raging debate, and drew Moltke aside to console him. A compromise was then agreed. Mobilization would continue, but the advance on Luxemburg by the 16th Division was to be halted. The chancellor and Jagow, in the presence of Falkenhayn and Moltke, drafted a reply to Lichnowsky. Germany was ready to accept London's proposal on the understanding that Britain guaranteed, 'with her entire armed forces', French neutrality for the full duration of a Russo-German conflict – a precaution against a later French entry into the war to prevent a Russian defeat. It was for Germany alone to determine when that conflict had been brought to a conclusion. For the moment, German mobilization could not be halted, Lichnowsky was told, but Bethmann guaranteed that no troops would cross into French territory before 7 p.m. on Monday, 3 August, by which time British acceptance was required – a precaution against losing the competitive advantage of Germany's swifter pace of mobilization.[281] Moltke demanded the temporary cession of the fortresses of Toul and Verdun as an additional guarantee of French neutrality, but this was rejected by the others as 'a vote of no-confidence in England' – a curiously late recognition of the impossible nature of the idea; after all Schoen had already been instructed to make the same demand.[282]

Berlin proceeded along parallel tracks. A separate telegram was despatched by the Kaiser to King George. The British government, it stated, had 'offer[ed] french [sic] neutrality under guarantee of Great Britain'. For 'technical reasons' the mobilization had to proceed as prepared, but if Britain kept France out of the war, then Germany would not strike in the west. 'I hope that France will not become nervous', the Kaiser added: 'The troops on my frontier are in the act of being stopped by telegraph and telephon[e] from crossing into France.'[283] There was an element of dissimulation in the concluding sentence. For the German war plans did not provide for a direct attack on France, and the 16th Division, whose advance had been halted, of course, was destined for Luxemburg and not France.

At that moment, at around 7 p.m., Lichnowsky's second telegram arrived at the Schloss, promising, it seemed, British neutrality in a

---

[281] Tel. Bethmann Hollweg to Lichnowsky (no. 204), 1 Aug. 1914 (D 7.15 p.m.), *DD* III, no. 578.
[282] Moltke, *Erinnerungen*, 21.
[283] Tel. Wilhelm II to George V, 1 Aug. 1914 (D 7.02 p.m.), *DD* III, no. 575.

continental war, even if this involved France. If the earlier telegram had come as a pleasant surprise, this one was the cause of jubilation. 'What a fabulous change!', recorded Müller in his diary: 'The Kaiser was very happy and ordered champagne'.[284] As the champagne corks popped, Moltke left the Schloss, a defeated and broken man. The Kaiser had always been the one incalculable risk factor in his military planning; his meddling in matters he did not fully understand presented a potential danger. 'I want to wage war against the French and the Russians, but not against such a Kaiser', he complained bitterly to one of his officers.[285] Indeed, it seems that the chief of staff suffered some sort of collapse that evening, either a minor stroke, as his wife suspected, or a nervous breakdown. 'It is impossible to describe the mood in which I arrived at home', Moltke later wrote: 'I was as if broken and shed tears of despair.'[286]

The Kaiser, meanwhile, was in an exultant mood. The Austro-Hungarian ambassador, who had been asked to call on Wilhelm late that evening at around 10 p.m., found him in the small garden of the Schloss, surrounded by his family. Grey had offered British neutrality; France appeared terrified by Germany's mobilization; and it was now necessary to carry on 'with calm, but with great determination' along the lines already agreed. Indeed, he was hopeful that Italy would remain loyal to the *Dreibund* alliance now, and that Bulgaria, Greece and Romania were moving in the right direction – the pre-crisis objective of a diplomatic realignment in the Balkans. The monarch was also full of praise for his chancellor, his 'manly attitude' and his 'correct execution of his intentions'.[287]

The jubilations at the Schloss and the Wilhelmstrasse were not of long duration, however. A little after 10 p.m., around the time 'gypsy' Szögyény was with the Kaiser, Lichnowsky's final telegram arrived, the long-awaited report on his 3.30 p.m. interview with the Foreign Secretary. Grey had told the ambassador that Germany's earlier equivocal statement on Belgian neutrality was 'a matter of very great regret'. If Berlin were able to match the French pledge, 'it would materially contribute to relieving anxiety and tension here'. If, on the other hand, Germany violated Belgium's neutrality, Britain was not likely to remain aloof. Lichnowsky

---

[284] Müller diary, 1 Aug. 1914, Görlitz (ed.), *Regierte?*, 39. Lichnowsky's second telegram was received at the Wilhelmstrasse at 6.04 p.m., but still had to be decyphered, hence the delay.

[285] As quoted in Mombauer, *Moltke*, 223.

[286] Moltke, *Erinnerungen*, 22; for the suspicion of a slight stroke, see Mombauer, *Moltke*, 222.

[287] Tel. Szögyény to Berchtold (no. 362), 2 Aug. 1914 (D 2 p.m., R 6.40 p.m.), *DA* iii, no. 105.

then asked openly whether Britain would remain neutral if Germany gave a pledge to respect that Belgian neutrality. Grey declined to give such an assurance, as Britain had to keep a free hand – the familiar refrain of his previous statements. Belgium, however, would play a significant role. Would it not be possible, he speculated, for France and Germany to face each other, fully mobilized but without commencing military operations? Would France agree to such a pact, Lichnowsky countered? For Germany might accept it, if it were offered. Grey promised to make enquiries. Lichnowsky's impression was 'that here they want to keep out of the war, if at all possible'.[288]

This was far less than Lichnowsky's afternoon telegram had promised. Worse was to come. King George's reply to the Kaiser's latest wire arrived sometime later that night:

> [T]here must be some misunderstanding as to a suggestion that passed in [a] friendly conversation between Prince Lichnowsky and Sir Edward Grey this afternoon when they were discussing how actual fighting between [the] German and French armies might be avoided while there is still a chance of some agreement between Austria and Russia. Sir Edward will arrange to see Prince Lichnowsky early tomorrow morning to ascertain whether there is a misunderstanding.[289]

The ambassador, too, now beat a retreat. There had been 'no positive English proposal' after all, he wired later that night, and no further action was therefore required. The matter was now finished, he reaffirmed in the early hours of the following morning. Grey's 'suggestions' had been made in ignorance of French mobilization and without consulting France.[290]

Lichnowsky's three telegrams were curiously vague and are suggestive of an attempt to cover his own tracks. Had he misunderstood what Tyrrell and Grey told him? This was the accepted view at Berlin, and the Prince did little to correct it then or later.[291] Or had Grey, in fact, made the offer, largely because he was under pressure from the Cabinet, a substantial

---

[288] Tel. Lichnowsky to Auswärtiges Amt (no. 212), 1 Aug. 1914 (D 5.47 p.m., R 10.02 p.m.), *DD* III, no. 596.

[289] Tel. George V to Wilhelm II, 1 Aug. 1914 (no time of despatch), *DD* III, no. 612.

[290] Tels. Lichnowsky to Auswärtiges Amt (nos. 214, unnumbered and 217), 1 Aug. 1914 (D 8.26 p.m., R 11.10 p.m.) and 2 Aug. (D 5 a.m. and 6.28 a.m., R 8.52 a.m. and 8.55 a.m.), *DD* III, nos. 603, 630 and 631.

[291] See e.g. T. von Bethmann Hollweg, *Betrachtungen zum Weltkrieg* (2 vols., Berlin, 1919–21) I, 183; Lichnowsky, *Abgrund* II, 285 n.; Young, *Lichnowsky*, 115–17.

section of whose members would not support war? Or did he throw out the offer knowing that the Cabinet would remain opposed to entering a continental conflict, but hoping that the promise of neutrality offered the chance of extracting some concessions from Berlin?[292]

In fact, it is very likely that there was no misunderstanding at all, but unravelling the origins of the initiative is more complex. No doubt, Grey was under intense pressure at that time. The final position of the Cabinet remained uncertain, and on it might depend the survival of the Asquith administration, possibly even of the Liberal Party as a whole. The physical and mental strain on the Foreign Secretary was enormous. But there is no evidence to suggest that he had succumbed to such pressures. On the contrary, a number of eyewitnesses described him as 'very fit and in good physical trim' and 'in quite good form'.[293] Given, moreover, that Grey had so far stuck very closely to the line of policy which he had pursued since 1905, and which the Cabinet had endorsed as recently as the previous day, it seems improbable that Grey should now have offered British neutrality. In fact, it would have been out of character.

What was not out of character, however, was for the Foreign Secretary to leave Tyrrell considerable leeway. As seen earlier, Tyrrell had proved a smooth and silky diplomatic operator during his mission to Washington at the end of 1913. Grey could rely on his absolute discretion and on his ability to defuse international complications, even if they could not be resolved. The suggestions transmitted by Lichnowsky in the morning and early afternoon of 1 August had something of that oblique originality and elegant ambiguity that was so characteristic of Tyrrell and so unlike Grey's sobre and straightforward pragmatism.

It is significant that Lichnowsky identified Tyrrell as the person who approached him that morning. Whether, in fact, the scheme originated solely with Grey's Private Secretary may be doubted. The scheme itself was of a kind that also appealed to Lichnowsky's mind. By 1 August, the ambassador was a desperate man, who saw before him the collapse of everything he had worked for. But that, of course, was also true of Tyrrell, and the two men may well have concocted the scheme together. Certainly,

---

[292] For these arguments see H. F. Young, 'The Misunderstanding of August 1, 1914', *JMH* XLVIII, 4 (1976), 644–65; and S. J. Valone, '"There Must be Some Misunderstanding": Sir Edward Grey's Diplomacy of 1 August 1914', *JBS* XXVII, 4 (1988), 405–24.
[293] Quotes from Samuel to Beatrice Samuel, 27 July 1914, Samuel MSS, PAL, SAM/A/157/689r, and Margot Asquith diary, 31 July 1914, Asquith MSS, Bodl., Ms.Eng. d.3210. Grey himself noted the pressure on ministers, see his *Twenty-Five Years, 1892–1916* (2 vols., New York, 1925) II, 11; for the suggestion that Grey began to buckle under pressure, see Clark, *Sleepwalkers*, 535.

it is – if not impossible – at any rate doubtful that the Foreign Secretary telephoned Lichnowsky just before 11 a.m., as the ambassador claimed in his first telegram. For, as seen earlier, Grey and Haldane had set off for 10 Downing Street where they were ensconced in a meeting with Asquith by 10.30 a.m. It seems much more likely, then, that Lichnowsky, knowing of the Wilhelmstrasse's suspicions of himself, advanced as Grey's initiative what was in fact his and Tyrrell's. That the two remained in contact throughout the day is confirmed by Lichnowsky's second telegram. But there is further circumstantial evidence to support this, in the shape of one of Haldane's daily letters to his aged mother that served him as an *ersatz* diary. 'At 2 o'clock there was just a chance of peace – a bare chance, for things are very bad', he wrote that night.[294] At precisely that moment, Lichnowsky sent his second telegram on Tyrrell's further explanations.[295]

This would certainly suggest that Haldane and Grey were cognizant of the Tyrrell-Lichnowsky scheme, even though three weeks into the war Grey suggested that the whole episode originated with the ambassador.[296] In the course of the day, indeed, the ambassador sent a note to Grey: 'I have immediately communicated the contents of our letter to Berlin and hope that the result may prove satisfactory. If we succeed once more in avoiding European war, it will, I feel sure, be due essentially to your help and statesmanship.'[297] What that 'letter' was is not clear, but Lichnowsky's only substantive communications with the Wilhelmstrasse on that Saturday were the telegrams on Britain's possible neutrality under certain circumstances. Finally, in essence, what had been suggested was not that dissimilar to Grey's earlier proposals to use the time-gap between mobilization and commencement of hostilities to find a negotiated settlement, and to protect that window through pledges by the Powers concerned not to start operations once talks had been initiated. That was the core also of the Tyrrell-Lichnowsky proposal, and it dovetailed neatly with Grey's own views. At that moment, despite the Russian mobilization and the imminent move by Germany to follow suit, his mediation proposal based on some variant of 'Halt in Belgrade' had not been formally rejected by any of the Powers – nor would it be later – and Sazonov had accepted a revised compromise formula. Grey himself was determined to abstain from anything that was liable to 'precipitate matters . . . Things cannot be hopeless while Russia and Austria are ready to converse.'[298]

[294] Haldane to Elizabeth Haldane, 1 Aug. 1914, Haldane MSS, NLS, MS 5992.
[295] It was despatched at 2.10 p.m.: see *DD* III, no. 570, n. 2.
[296] *Hansard House of Commons* LXVI (28 Aug. 1914), cols 264–5.
[297] Lichnowsky to Grey, 'Saturday' [1 Aug. 1914], Grey, *Twenty-Five Years* II, 238.
[298] Tel. Grey to Goschen (nos. 250 and 252), 1 Aug. 1914 (D 3.10 and 5 p.m.), *BD* XI, nos. 411 and 417 (quote from former).

For that reason, he had raised with Lichnowsky the possibility of the French and German armies remaining mobilized without 'crossing the frontier as long as the other did not do so'. Under such circumstances, Britain would remain neutral if Germany remained on the defensive. There were two problems, however. For one thing, the Foreign Office did not have any precise knowledge of the terms of the Franco-Russian alliance. This was not a sign of a weak grasp on political realities, but one of those realities. Britain, after all, was not party to the alliance, and London was to remain in ignorance of its precise terms until after the outbreak of the war. Grey did not know whether the idea of mobilized passivity 'would be consistent with French obligations under her alliance'.[299]

Furthermore, the German conception of mobilization militated against the viability of the scheme. For the German military high command, mobilization, once authorized, implied the need to open the military campaign without any delay. At the Foreign Office it had been assumed that this was so, but Berlin's pronouncements on the matter during the July crisis had allowed for a different interpretation, for instance in the context of Russia's partial mobilization. Any doubts on this score were removed only on the following day, Sunday, 2 August. Germany could not remain mobilized for any period of time, Jagow had confirmed to Goschen during the night. Germany 'had speed and Russia had the numbers, and the safety of the German Empire forbade that Germany should allow Russia time to bring up masses of troops from all parts of her dominions'.[300]

In practice, this meant that there was no window for diplomacy. A further complication was the attitude of France. Paris had shown no appetite for restraining its Russian ally, and had in fact mobilized an hour before Germany moved from the state of *Kriegsgefahr* to general mobilization. Adhering to his established line of constructive ambiguity, Grey had 'definitely refused all overtures to give Germany any promise of neutrality' beyond advancing the idea of mobilized passivity.[301] In a similar vein, he explained to the French ambassador that, at that moment, there could be no question of sending a British Expeditionary Force to the continent. The current situation differed substantially from the two Moroccan crises of 1905 and 1911, which affected Britain's obligations towards France under the 1904 colonial understanding. Now, he explained to a nonplussed Cambon, 'the position was that Germany would agree not to attack France if France remained neutral in the event of war between Russia and Germany'. If Paris could not take advantage of this development, then this was

[299] Tel. Grey to Bertie (no. 297), 1 Aug. 1914 (D 5.25 p.m.), *BD* xi, no. 419.
[300] Tel. Goschen to Grey (no. 121), 1 Aug. 1914 (D 2 Aug., 1.32 a.m., R 6.30 a.m.), *BD* xi, no. 458.
[301] Tel. Grey to Bertie (no. 297), 1 Aug. 1914 (D 5.25 p.m.), *BD* xi, no. 419.

because of her obligations towards Russia under the Franco-Russian alliance, 'to which we were not parties, and of which we did not know the terms'. This did not mean that Britain would not under any circumstances support France – he indicated that a German invasion of Belgium or a naval attack on the French coast might change matters – but he refused to commit the government to any definite course of action.[302]

Cambon's own report depicted Grey as somewhat more supportive. But his evidence needs to be taken with some caution. The ambassador, although resident at Albert Gate since 1898, never really understood the country to which he was accredited – he did not even speak its language. Like his superiors at the Quai d'Orsay, he assumed that for Britain the 1904 entente served the same purposes for which Paris sought to use the arrangement with Britain, as a means of containing Germany. That for Britain the colonial barter served the rather more complex interests of her sprawling global imperial possessions, he never fully grasped – or rather he ignored this inconvenient fact. Indeed, when Grey explained to him the decision of the Cabinet of 1 August not to send a British force to the continent, the ambassador informed him that 'he could not transmit this reply to his Government, and he asked me to authorise him to say that the British Cabinet had not yet taken any decision'. Despite Grey's protestation that a decision had been come to, this was the thrust of Cambon's official report.[303] Like all French diplomats, and unlike the British, Cambon thought continentally, and would not report in any other sense to the Quai.

Privately, Cambon, who left the meeting 'white and speechless' and close to tears, was convinced at this stage that Britain would drop France, as he put it ('*Ils vont nous lâcher*'). He warned Grey that, if Britain refused to aid France, no matter what the outcome of any military contest, 'the *entente* would disappear; and ... our situation at the end of the war would be very uncomfortable'.[304] Grey admitted the force of this argument. To avert this danger, of course, had been the purpose of his diplomatic strategy so far, which had deployed a carefully calibrated mixture of cautious diplomatic support for France and subtle warnings to Germany, offset by suggestions of possible cooperation with her. If this was no longer

---

[302] Tel. Grey to Bertie (no. 299), 1 Aug. 1914 (D 8.20 p.m.), *BD* XI, no. 426.

[303] Tel. Grey to Bertie (no. 299), 1 Aug. 1914 (D 8.20 p.m.), *BD* XI, no. 426; tel. P. Cambon to Viviani (nos. 171–2), 1 Aug. 1914 (D 6.24, 6.40 p.m., R 10.05 and 10 p.m.), *DDF* (3) XI, no. 532; W. Marquis d'Ormesson, 'Deux grandes figures de la diplomatie française. Paul et Jules Cambon', *RHD* LVII, 1 (1943–5), 33–71.

[304] Grey to Bertie (no. 518), 1 Aug. 1914, *BD* XI, no. 447; Nicolson, *Lord Carnock*, 419.

sufficient to persuade Paris to restrain Russia, then offering the kind of support that Cambon was asking for would certainly not achieve that end.

Under the circumstances of 1 August, perhaps, Grey's policy, previously so successful, had reached the end of the road. There was no more room for constructive ambiguity. In the event of a war between Russia and the two Germanic Powers, Bertie telegraphed, he could not 'imagine that ... it would be consistent with French obligations towards Russia for [the] French to remain quiescent ... Am I to enquire precisely what are the obligations of the French under [the] Franco-Russian Alliance?'[305] There was nothing impertinent about Bertie's telegram. It merely reflected the uncertainties under which British foreign policy had to operate.

What made Grey abort the initiative was the Kaiser's telegram to the King, in which the German monarch indicated that Grey had suggested a British guarantee of French neutrality in a Russo-German war, something that Bethmann Hollweg's instructions to Lichnowsky explicitly demanded. The Kaiser's 'revelation' did not matter so much in terms of the King's relations with his ministers. But it was awkward in that it went far beyond what Grey himself had indicated as possible during his interview with Lichnowsky in the afternoon; and if a British advance guarantee of French neutrality was the expected starting point for Berlin, it would be impossible to persuade it to settle for something less. Grey thus suggested that Lichnowsky had misunderstood what had been said during the afternoon meeting, even though the Kaiser's telegram did not refer to it; and the King's reply was drafted accordingly in that sense. It was the one slipperiness Grey allowed himself.

With the 'misunderstanding' of 1 August thus disposed of, matters now took their course. 'The force of circumstances', Eyre Crowe wrote to his wife, was 'driving the government where they ought to have gone spontaneously'. With Luxemburg already under German occupation, the invasion of Belgium could 'only be a question of hours. It looks therefore like war definitely, and the dice seems [sic] cast.'[306]

Across St James's Park, at 9 Carlton House Terrace, Lichnowsky may well have anticipated what was to follow. He was a broken man. Early

---

[305] Tel. Bertie to Grey (no. 116), 1 Aug. 1914 (D 2 Aug., 1.15 a.m., R 4.30 a.m.), *BD* XI, no. 453; for the view that Bertie's telegram was an 'impertinent' criticism of Grey, see Wilson, '"Misunderstanding"', 888, but this is based on a somewhat wilful reading of the evidence; see also K. Neilson, '"Control the Whirlwind": Sir Edward Grey as Foreign Secretary', T. G. Otte (ed.), *The Makers of British Foreign Policy: From Pitt to Thatcher* (Basingstoke and New York, 2002), 137–8.
[306] Crowe to Clema Crowe, 2 Aug. 1914, Crowe MSS, Bodl., Ms.Eng.e.3020.

the next morning, he called on the Prime Minister at 10 Downing Street. The ambassador was 'very émotionné', Asquith later recalled,

> and implored me not to side with France. He said that Germany, with her army cut in two between France & Russia, was far more likely to be crushed than France. He was very agitated poor man & wept. I told him that we had no desire to intervene, and that it rested largely with Germany to make intervention impossible, if she would (1) not invade Belgium, and (2) not send her fleet into the Channel to attack the unprotected North Coast of France. He was bitter about the policy of his Government in not restraining Austria, & seemed quite broken-hearted.[307]

The Prime Minister's wife later called on the Lichnowskys while Asquith chaired the Cabinet meeting that morning. She found the princess prostrate on a sofa, crying: 'he was walking up & down in silence. He caught me by the hand & said "Oh, say there is *not* going to be war? (pronouncing it like far). Dear, dear Mrs Asquith can we not stop it (wringing his hands)[?"] I put my arms round Mechtild on the sofa while we both cried.'[308]

What is not in doubt is the reaction to the latest turn of events at Berlin. Grey was 'a false rascal', the Kaiser fulminated: 'The fellow is mad or an idiot.' If the ambassador thought that Grey wished to keep Britain out of a war, the Kaiser's 'impression is that Herr Grey is a false dog who is afraid of his own baseness and false policy, but who does not wish openly to take position against us'.[309] As so often, violent language was a safety valve for the Kaiser's mood-swings. Exuberant only a few hours earlier, he was now plunged into despondence and apathy. While Moltke sat brooding at home, he was called back to the Schloss at 11 p.m., and admitted to the Kaiser's bed-chamber. He found the monarch in an agitated state of mind. Wilhelm pointed to the King's telegram. The whole matter had been an error; Lichnowsky had misunderstood. 'Now you can do what you want' – and with that the Kaiser concluded the meeting.[310]

---

[307] Asquith to Venetia Stanley, 2 Aug. 1914, Brock and Brock (eds.), *Asquith Letters*, 146; see also Harcourt Cabinet notes, 2 Aug. 1914, Harcourt MSS, Bodl., no accession number. According to the US ambassador, Lichnowsky suffered a nervous breakdown after 1 August, or was close to one: see B. H. Hendrick, *The Life and Letters of Walter H. Page* (3 vols., London, 1923) I, 324.

[308] Margot Asquith diary, 2 Aug. 1914, Asquith MSS, Bodl., Ms.Eng.d.3210; see also Young, *Lichnowsky*, 117.

[309] Marginal comments Wilhelm II, 2 Aug. 1914, *DD* III, no. 596.

[310] Moltke, *Erinnerungen*, 23.

Baron Schoen leaves his card

German mobilization continued. Moltke had won. On 2 August German troops took control of Luxemburg. The role of German diplomacy was now merely to pave the way for the German army. The envoy at Brussels, Claus von Below-Saleske, was instructed to explain to the Belgian government that French assurances in respect of Belgium's neutrality were false and to request the unhindered passage through Belgium for the advancing German troops. The Belgian government was advised to withdraw its army to Antwerp and to put up no more than token resistance. An answer was expected by 2 p.m. the following day, which Below was to forward by telegraph to Berlin and also by motorized courier to the German frontier.[311]

With the troop trains now rolling towards the western frontiers Berlin considered it necessary to declare war on France. On 2 August, Bethmann Hollweg and Moltke were still hopeful that France would attack Germany first, so relieving Berlin of the need to make the first move.[312] But with the French troops kept at a distance from the German frontier, no untoward border skirmishes occurred. In a curious parallel with the 'skirmish' at Temes-Kubin, news now reached Berlin of French officers entering Germany in disguise via Holland. A French doctor was arrested at Metz, the capital of Lorraine, on suspicion of having tried to poison wells with cholera bacili; he was executed by a firing squad. There were reports of French troops having crossed the frontier into Alsace and enemy aircraft having entered German airspace in attempted sorties on railway depots at Wesel near the Dutch border and Karlsruhe and Nuremberg in the south.[313] No such incidents, certainly not the latter, actually occurred. Collective war hysteria had already gripped Germany, and the reports provided a convenient pretext for the Wilhelmstrasse to place France in the wrong. With the incursions on sovereign German territory and the bombing raids, 'France has placed us in a state of war', ambassador Schoen at Paris was informed in the afternoon of 3 August.

---

[311] Tel. Jagow to Below-Saleske (no. 42, urgent), 2 Aug. 1914 (D 2.05 p.m.), *DD* III, no. 648; Beyens to Davignon, 2 Aug. 1914, *BelD* suppl. vol. II, 22.

[312] Bethmann Hollweg to Wilhelm II, and Moltke to Auswärtiges Amt, both 2 Aug. 1914, *DD* III, nos. 629 and 662.

[313] See *inter alia* tels. Jagow to Lichnowsky (nos. 214 and 217), both 3 Aug. 1914 (D 6.45 and 10.15 a.m.), *DD* III, nos. 710 and 725; see also tel. Goschen to Grey (no. 132), 3 Aug. 1914 (D 11.42 p.m., R 10.30 a.m.), *BD* XI, no. 575. For the attempt by eighty officers to cross the German-Dutch frontier at Walbeck, see Commanding Officer 8th Army Corps to General Staff, 2 Aug. 1914 (R 3.01 p.m.), *ibid.*, no. 670.

The ambassador was to ask for his passports and formally declare war on France by 6 p.m. that same day. Under the intense pressures of the hectic pace of diplomatic activity, either the cyphering clerks at Berlin or the embassy official in charge of decyphering incoming telegrams made a mess of the communication, and large sections of the declaration of war were garbled, though Schoen's instructions were clear enough.[314] The ambassador twice wired an urgent request for the telegram to be re-sent, first *en clair* and then in cypher. His second request did not reach Berlin until 4 August, by which time it had long become redundant.[315]

Without further instructions, and with the appointed hour already passed, Schoen left the embassy for the Quai d'Orsay at 6.15 p.m. His instructions had been unequivocal, even if the text of the declaration had to be reconstructed as best he could. The document left with Viviani thus included references to the alleged French incursions and air attacks. A falsehood had now become part of Germany's justification for war. 'As my diplomatic mission has thus come to an end', the declaration ended, 'it is left to me to ask Your Excellency to provide me with my passports and to take the measures which you judge appropriate to assure my return to Germany with the personnel of the embassy'.[316]

Irrespective of the document's dignified, diplomatic language, Schoen himself was considerably rattled by the time he appeared at the French foreign ministry. There had been an incident outside the embassy. As in Germany, so at least in Paris, if not all across France, war fever had broken out. A hostile crowd had gathered there, and Schoen had to be protected by gendarmes who happened to be posted on a street corner. Two men, in fact, had jumped on the running board of Schoen's motorcar – shades of Sarajevo – made abusive and threatening gestures, and used strong language. Three secret service officers then placed the car under armed protection and guided it to the Quai d'Orsay. Viviani received Schoen's declaration without any signs of emotion. He accompanied him out of the building, where the two men bowed before the ambassador left. Like his colleagues at St Petersburg and London, Schoen was a broken man. He regarded the war that was about to commence 'as the greatest misfortune that could befall civilized mankind'. Before returning to the

---

[314] Tel. Bethmann Hollweg to Schoen (no. 193), 3 Aug. 1914 (D 1.05 p.m.), and encl. declaration of war, *DD* III, nos. 734 and 734a.

[315] Tels. Schoen to Auswärtiges Amt (unnumbered *en clair* and no. 246), both 3 Aug. 1914 (D 3.10 and 2.45 p.m.), *DD* IV, nos. 776 and 809.

[316] German declaration of war as submitted to French government, 3 Aug. 1914, *DD* III, no. 734b.

embassy he left his *carte de visite* with Viviani. On its back he wrote: 'C'est le suicide de l'Europe.'[317]

Forty-eight hours after Germany had declared war on Russia, she was now also at war with France. The continental war had begun. Not everyone at Paris shared Schoen's sense of foreboding. Poincaré for one welcomed the latest development: 'Never has a declaration of war been welcomed with such satisfaction', he recorded in his diary: 'It was indispensable that Germany, who was entirely responsible for the aggression, should be led into publicly announcing her intentions. It would have been foolish for us to declare war.'[318]

The lamps are going out

The French President's observation reflected France's general strategic posture within the framework of the Franco-Russian alliance, combining an offensive stance through Russia with a passive disposition in the west. But it also reflected Poincaré's ongoing preoccupation with Britain; and in this respect his concluding comment was entirely correct. Declaring war on Germany would have made British intervention in the continental conflict all but impossible. Late at night on 1 August, Eyre Crowe wrote a despairing letter to his wife. The government had 'finally decided to run away, and to desert France in the hour of need'. There was a widespread feeling of revulsion at the Foreign Office at 'such a government of dishonourable cowards'; Crowe himself had prevented five officials from resigning their posts. Even so, he doubted 'whether we shall after all be able to keep out of the war. But Germany has achieved her first great success by keeping us out, and if we are dragged in later, it will be under a severe handicap ... This is the worst day I have lived through for many years.'[319] Horace Rumbold, Goschen's deputy at the Berlin embassy, was resigned to a general war now: 'The whole thing is, to me, a gigantic nightmare, and I keep on wondering whether I am in a sane world.'[320]

---

[317] Quotes from W. von Schoen, *Erlebtes. Beiträge zur Geschichte der neuesten Zeit* (Stuttgart, 1921), 186, and E. Rosenstock-Huessy, *Soziologie* (2 vols., Stuttgart, 1958) II, 140; see also tel. Szécsen to Berchtold (no. 154), 3 Aug. 1914 (D 8.20 p.m., R 5 a.m.), *DA* III, no. 120.

[318] Poincaré, notes journalières, 3 Aug. 1914, Papiers de Poincaré, BN, Bnfr 16027, fo. 144 r.

[319] Crowe to Clema Crowe, 1 Aug. 1914, Crowe MSS, Bodl., Ms.Eng.e.3020.

[320] Rumbold to Louisa Rumbold, 2 Aug. 1914, Rumbold MSS, Bodl., Ms. Rumbold dep. 16; M. Gilbert, *Sir Horace Rumbold: Portrait of a Diplomat, 1869–1941* (London, 1973), 118–19.

Whether a sane world or not, it was subject to competing currents, and these posed significant challenges to Asquith and Grey. Like other senior Foreign Office officials, Crowe paid little attention to the pressures from within the government. The leaders of the Unionist opposition in Parliament, Andrew Bonar Law and F. E. Smith, posed no serious threat. Churchill, the renegade Tory, had already stretched out feelers to them, and they signalled their support for the government in the event of a war.[321] There was even some vague talk of forming a national coalition.

While Grey met Cambon and Lichnowsky on a daily basis, the real struggle was between Asquith and Grey on the one hand and the non-interventionists in the Cabinet on the other. 'We have beaten you [Churchill and the interventionists] after all', Morley, the superannuated torchbearer of Gladstonian little Englanderism and leading non-interventionist, crowed at one of the Cabinet meetings in late July.[322] But opinion was shifting. Until 1 August, Grey himself had kept open the option of some arrangement with Germany. But the events of the previous afternoon convinced him that the German chancellor and the civilian leadership had lost out to the military. This was the latest version of the well-established perception of the internal dynamics at Berlin in terms of a 'peace' and a 'war party', of doves and hawks. 'Jagow did nothing', he thought half-a-year into war; 'Bethmann-Hollweg trifled and the military intended war and forced it.'[323] Over the next four days, this view came to be widely shared. Even Sir John Simon, who resigned from the government in protest against the decision to join the war, and Lloyd George, hitherto the standard-bearer of the pacifist Radicals, agreed that the 'war party' at Berlin had gained the ascendancy. As C. P. Scott, the venerable editor of the *Manchester Guardian*, the mouthpiece of Radicalism, recorded on 4 August:

> [Simon] began at once by saying he had been entirely deceived
> about Germany and ... that the evidence was overwhelming that
> the party which had got control of the direction of affairs
> throughout the crisis had deliberately played for and provoked the
> war ... Beyond question Germany could have held Austria in check

---

[321] The First Lord of the Admiralty had arranged a dinner in the evening of 1 August to discuss matters, see Churchill to Grey, 1 Aug. 1914, Murray of Elibank MSS, NLS, MS 8805; Chamberlain to Lansdowne, 2 Aug. 1914, Lansdowne MSS, BL, Add. Mss. 88906.

[322] Morley, *Memorandum*, 4–5.

[323] Grey to Rodd (private), 6 Mar. 1915, Grey MSS, TNA (PRO), FO 800/65; see also M. G. Ekstein and Z. S. Steiner, 'The Sarajevo Crisis', F. H. Hinsley (ed.), *British Foreign Policy under Sir Edward Grey* (Cambridge, 1977), 403.

and moderated her demands had she wished to do so, but the party in power did not wish to do so ... [Lloyd George] confirmed ... unwillingness of the German Emperor personally to enter upon the war ... He confirmed also the secrecy and deliberation with which the war had been prepared for by the German military camarilla. The German ambassador ... had been entirely deceived and he believed intentionally in order that he might deceive us.[324]

Simon's case was, perhaps, the oddest of all – he resigned in the end, as one of his colleagues noted, because 'he pretended to a special and personal abhorrence of killing in any shape'.[325] But the intense anguish caused by the question before the nineteen men around the Cabinet table at 10 Downing Street was genuine enough. Haldane, the Lord Chancellor, reflected the views of Asquith and Grey and many of the Liberal mainstream: 'The ideas that on the one hand we can wholly disinterest ourselves and on the other that we ought to rush in are both wrong. And the real course, that of being ready to intervene if at a decisive moment we are called on, is difficult to formulate in clear terms. Yet I think this is what we must attempt.'[326]

The Cabinet reconvened in the morning of Sunday, 2 August. At 10.15 a.m., some forty-five minutes before the Cabinet meeting was to take place, a small conclave of non-interventionist ministers met at Lloyd George's residence at 11 Downing Street. The six men – the Earl of Beauchamp, the First Commissioner of Works, Harcourt, Pease, Sir Walter Runciman, the President of the Board of Agriculture, Simon and the Chancellor of the Exchequer – held an informal discussion of the situation and agreed that 'we were not prepared to go into war now'.

At the Cabinet meeting Grey opened the discussions with the observation that 'the time had come for plain speaking'. Cambon, he said, had 'twice wept over our statement that we were not committed & that up to now the French could not rely on our definite help'. As for his own part, he regarded Britain's obligation to uphold Belgian neutrality 'as binding'. He also indicated that he would resign from the government if the German navy were allowed into the Channel to attack the French coast. '[W]ar will come', he suggested, and Britain could not afford to see French power

[324] Scott diary, 4 Aug. 1914, T. Wilson (ed.), *The Political Diaries of C. P. Scott, 1911–1928* (London, 1970), 96–8.
[325] Hobhouse diary, 3 Aug. 1914, E. David (ed.), *Inside Asquith's Cabinet: From the Diaries of Charles Hobhouse* (London, 1977), 180.
[326] Haldane to Elizabeth S. Haldane [his sister], 2 Aug. 1914, Haldane MSS, NLS, MS 6012; Steiner and Neilson, *Britain*, 250–3.

crushed. Both Grey and the Prime Minister suggested that, privately, Lichnowsky had indicted his own government and 'said things against his own Government which would not stand repetition'. Asquith explained that he had told Lichnowsky that morning that British abstention from the conflict was dependent entirely on the non-violation of Belgian territory and on Germany refraining from hostile operations in the Channel. After about an hour-and-a-half, Grey, as Pease noted, became 'more pro-war – Winston also'.[327]

Morley threatened to resign, but he had developed the unfortunate habit of threatening to do so, as one of the younger ministers noted, 'about once a month for 3 years, [so] no one took this very seriously'.[328] Besides, Morley was now 'so old that the views he expresses are sadly inconsequent and incoherent', as Herbert Samuel noted. Nevertheless, the tensions were palpable. The discussions that morning 'almost resulted in a political crisis to be super-imposed on the international and financial crises'. Grey's view was not supported by the majority of the ministers. The Foreign Secretary, Samuel thought, 'was outraged by the way in which Germany and Austria have played with the most vital interests of civilisation, have put aside all attempts at accommodation made by himself and others and, while continuing to negotiate, have marched steadily to war'. Samuel himself sided with the majority of his colleagues against war 'for the sake of our goodwill for France or for maintaining the strength of France and Russia against Germany and Austria'. The invasion of Belgium or the bombardment of the French coastline would change matters, however, and make British intervention inevitable.[329]

The 'dissolution of the Ministry was that afternoon in full view', Morley reflected; and in order to avert the collapse of the Asquith administration, he let himself be persuaded to stay on for now. Indeed, a majority

---

[327] Pease diary, 2 Aug. 1914, Wilson, 'Cabinet Diary', 46–7; Riddell diary, 2 Aug. 1914, [G. A.] Lord Riddell, *Lord Riddell's War Diary, 1914–1918* (London, 1933), 3–4; Harcourt Cabinet notes, 2 Aug. 1914, Harcourt MSS, no accession number; for Asquith's conversation with the German ambassador see tel. Lichnowsky to Auswärtiges Amt (no. 221), 2 Aug. 1914 (D 1.23 p.m., R 6.48 p.m.), *DD* III, no. 676. According to Lichnowsky, Asquith was in tears and repeatedly said 'A war between our two countries is quite unthinkable'.

[328] Hobhouse diary, 2 Aug. 1914, David (ed.), *Inside Asquith's Cabinet*, 180; D. A. Hamer, *John Morley: Liberal Intellectual in Politics* (Oxford, 1968), 368–9; M. L. Dockrill, 'Lloyd George and Foreign Policy before 1914', A. J. P. Taylor (ed.), *Lloyd George: Twelve Essays* (London, 1971), 28–30.

[329] Samuel to Beatrice Samuel, 2 Aug. 1914, Samuel MSS, PAL, SAM/A/157/697; K. M. Wilson, 'The British Cabinet's Decision for War, 2 August 1914', *BJIS* I, 2 (1975), 154–5.

of the ministers thought that 'we should stick together as long as we could'. They knew only too well that if this government collapsed, its successor would either be a pro-war coalition or a Unionist minority government. Only John Burns, the working-class Liberal, was determined to resign and did so. But he had always been a marginal figure in the Cabinet, and had long sought to leave front-line politics.[330]

Later that evening, at 6.30 p.m., the ministers reconvened: 'we had a friendly cabinet for 1½ hours & no discordant note [was] struck & we agreed on [a] line of policy'.[331] The meetings of that day had established two possible war scenarios. The first *casus belli* involved the violation of Belgian neutrality, the second a German naval attack on the French channel coast. The former arose out of Britain's international obligations under the 1839 Treaty of London that guaranteed the neutrality and integrity of Belgium. The latter was presented as an implied moral commitment towards France on account of the 1912 naval arrangements under which French naval forces had been concentrated in the Mediterranean, effectively denuding the French channel coast of any meaningful maritime defence. Cambon, of course, had made much of the assumed obligation on Britain's part, and most Cabinet ministers tended to accept that such liability existed. The different strands of Edwardian Liberalism, as Michael Ekstein and Zara Steiner have rightly commented, 'made for loose thinking' on international relations. 'Idealistic, pacificist and underpinned by assumptions of natural law, it [i.e. Liberalism] encouraged the attitude that pessimistic reasoning was cynicism.'[332] In turn this explains why Asquith and Grey laid particular stress on Britain's obligations under international law or in terms of international morality. In an attempt, clearly coordinated with Asquith and Grey, to keep the Radical wing of the parliamentary party on board, Churchill had developed the argument more fully to Arthur Ponsonby on 31 July:

> So long as no treaty obligation or true British interest is involved, I am of your opinion that we should remain neutral. Balkan

---

[330] Quotes from Morley, *Memorandum*, 17, and Pease diary, 2 Aug. 1914, Wilson (ed.), 'Cabinet Diary', 47. For Burns's decisions to resign see Burns to Asquith, 2 Aug. 1914, Burns MSS, BL, Add. MSS. 46282; Kent, *Burns*, 237–8. He had first speculated about leaving the Cabinet in 1911, see Burns diary, 28 Jan. 1911, Burns MSS, BL, Add. MSS. 46333, and again diary, 31 Jan. 1914, *ibid.*, Add. MSS 46336.

[331] Pease diary, 2 Aug. 1914, Wilson (ed.), 'Cabinet Diary', 48; Harcourt Cabinet notes, 2 Aug. 1914, Harcourt MSS, Bodl., no accession number; S. E. Koss, *Asquith* (London, 1976), 159.

[332] Ekstein and Steiner, 'Sarajevo Crisis', 408–9; M. Bentley, *The Climax of Liberal Politics: British Liberalism in Theory and Practice, 1868–1918* (London, 1987), 121–2.

quarrels are no vital concern of ours. We have done our best to keep the peace & shall continue so to do to the end. But the march of events is sinister. The extension of the conflict by a German attack upon France or Belgium w[oul]d raise other issues than those which now exist, and it w[oul]d be wrong at this moment to pronounce finally one way or the other as to our duty or our interests.[333]

The notion of some dual obligation was thus firmly established in the political discourse within the ruling Liberal party. As Herbert Samuel argued at the end of 2 August, '[i]f Germany chooses to tear up that treaty [on Belgian neutrality] she must bear the blame for the consequences'.[334] Grey himself spent much of the night of 2–3 August drafting the speech he was expected to give in the House of Commons that afternoon. That Monday was a bank holiday, and while the rest of the nation flocked to the seaside or promenaded in the public parks of the bigger cities, Westminster was alive with feverish activity. The Cabinet met at 11.15 a.m. Asquith announced that Burns had resigned on the previous evening. Now Beauchamp, Morley and Simon also tendered their resignations. The other ministers decided to stay on. News of Germany's ultimatum to Belgium, and the Belgian government's dignified rejection of the demands had arrived that morning, and so had the news of German troops being massed on the Belgian frontier. Grey placed the information before the Cabinet, and it made a profound impression on the ministers. By all accounts, the Cabinet meeting was an emotional occasion. Grey, recorded Pease, 'said he felt some responsibility for the resignations & felt it acutely & broke down'. The occasion, Samuel wrote to his wife afterwards, 'was very moving. Most of us could hardly speak at all for emotion. The Prime Minister goes on out of a sheer sense of duty.'[335] With Burns having resigned already, and Beauchamp, Morley and Simon about to do so, Asquith conceded that the Cabinet's authority was 'much shattered … in time of great stress'. Under different circumstances, he himself 'w[oul]d

---

[333] Churchill to Ponsonby (private), 31 July 1914, Ponsonby MSS, Bodl., Ms.Eng.his. c.660.

[334] Samuel to Beatrice Samuel, 2 Aug. 1914, Samuel MSS, PAL, SAM/A/157/697. For the importance of Belgium in British discussion see also J. F. V. Keiger, 'Britain's "Union Sacrée"', J.-J. Becker and S. Audoin-Rouzeau (eds.), *Les Sociétés européennes et la guerre de 1914–1918* (Paris, 1990), 48–50.

[335] Pease diary, 3 Aug. 1914, Wilson (ed.), 'Cabinet Diary', 48; Samuel to Beatrice Samuel, 3 Aug. 1914, Samuel MSS, PAL, SAM/A/157/698. For the German ultimatum and Davignon's response see *BD* XI, nos. 514 and 515.

have resigned, but [there would be] no Gov[ernmen]t with a majority in the H[ouse] of C[ommons] – dislikes and abhors a coalition – experiment none w[oul]d like to see repeated'. He would not separate from Grey and was resolved to remain in office 'in [the] best interest of the country. Asq[uith:] "most thankless task to me to go on".'[336] Even so, a sense of 'calmness & decision' had descended upon the assembled ministers. As Haldane reflected: 'Things are now going their course. I doubt whether in the end we shall not be dragged in. We are making all preparations. If we fail in nerve it may be our turn next, & if we are firm we may bring things to a close.'[337]

This was very much also the tenor of Grey's statement to a packed and sombre House of Commons that afternoon. It was a carefully constructed, brilliantly judged speech – the most important of his career, and his most successful. It was quietly dignified, and very personal in its tone. Even at their rhetorical best, few if any, of Gladstone's speeches are readable today, but no-one reading Grey's speech of 3 August can escape the calm moral authority the Foreign Secretary exuded on that occasion.[338] It was a finely crafted appeal to moral sentiment and calculations of British interest, just as Churchill had done in his letter to Ponsonby. And yet the speech was also oblique. Grey did not examine who might be responsible for the war; he did not, as might be expected, exploit Bethmann's ill-judged attempt to bribe Britain into neutrality. There had been a 'disposition … to force things', he observed, and Russia and Germany had declared war upon each other – only the latter of course had done so. Britain had earnestly striven to maintain the peace of Europe, but it was now no longer possible to do so. Grey impressed upon the Commons the need to approach the European crisis 'from the point of view of British interests, British honour, and British obligations'. The British government, and therefore Parliament also, was free from any binding obligations towards France. But there had grown up 'a long-standing friendship with France', and it was now for every member 'to look into his own heart, and his own feelings, and construe the extent of the obligation for himself', just as Grey had done for himself – this was a carefully dosaged drop of emotion that was always going to appeal to the Commons.

[336] Harcourt Cabinet notes, 3 Aug. 1914, Harcourt MSS, Bodl., no accession number.
[337] Haldane to Elizabeth Haldane, 3 Aug. 1914, Haldane MSS, NLS, MS 5992; Spender and Asquith, *Asquith* II, 83–5.
[338] For its effect on MPs see the reflections of Grey's Parliamentary Private Secretary, A. C. Murray, *Master and Brother: The Murrays of Elibank* (London, 1945), 123–4.

The French fleet, Grey continued, was now concentrated in the Mediterranean on account of the naval arrangement of November 1912. It left her Channel and Atlantic coasts 'absolutely undefended, at the mercy of the German fleet coming down the Channel'. Could Britain stand aside? She could, but the consequences were incalculable. The French fleet might be withdrawn from the Mediterranean, and Italy might feel emboldened to join the war on the side of Germany and Austria-Hungary. Britain would then be forced to join the war because 'our trade routes in the Mediterranean [are] vital to this country'. He then turned to 'the more serious consideration – becoming more serious every hour ... the question of the neutrality of Belgium'. Britain – he had made his obeisances here to the Liberal Gladstone-Granville adminis-tration in 1870 – had guaranteed the independence and neutrality of that country. Faced with a German ultimatum, its King had appealed to Britain for assistance. London had intervened diplomatically during the preceding weeks:

> What can diplomatic intervention do now? We have great and vital interests in the independence – and integrity is the least part – of Belgium. If Belgium is compelled to submit to allow her neutrality to be violated, of course the situation is clear ... The smaller States in that region of Europe ask but one thing. Their one desire is that they should be left alone and independent. The one thing they fear is ... that their independence should be interfered with.

If Belgium yielded to pressure and allowed her neutrality to be breached, her independence would be gone; and if Belgian independence were lost, that of the neighbouring Netherlands would soon follow. From the point of view of British interests, Grey asked the Commons to consider the likely consequences of such developments: 'If France is beaten in a struggle of life and death, beaten to her knees, loses her position as a Great Power, becomes subordinate to the will and power of one greater than herself ... if Belgium fell under the same dominating influence, and then Holland and then Denmark, then ... just opposite to us there would be a common interest against the unmeasured aggrandisement of any Power', as Glad-stone had warned – again the nod to the Liberal icon.

As for Britain, with her unrivalled naval capabilities she had 'to protect our commerce, to protect our shores, and to protect our interests'. Britain would suffer 'but little more than we shall suffer if we stand aside'. Grey struck a sombre note: 'We are going to suffer, I am afraid, terribly in this war whether we are in it or whether we stand aside.' But if Britain did the latter, 'we should ... sacrifice our respect and good name and reputation before the world, and should not escape the most serious and grave economic consequences'.[339]

There was one bright spot, Grey had observed at the close of the speech – the prospect of civil strife in Ireland had vanished in the face of a looming European war. It was a sentiment Asquith echoed later that evening: '"God moves in a mysterious way his wonders to perform"', he said to Jack Pease.[340] There were a few inside Parliament and without it, who objected to 'the idiotic Grey speech' or who accused him of behaving 'like the Jingo boys' and having 'besmirched everything'.[341] But these were isolated voices. Indeed, Grey had achieved something quite remarkable. He had fashioned a narrative that legitimated and so helped to sustain the British war effort, one of 'a long-standing friendship with France', of the vital importance of Belgium, and of the threat posed by German domination of the continent. The reference to Ireland also underlines the extent to which Grey succeeded in binding together the disparate elements in the government, in the different parties and in the wider British public in a British *Burgfrieden*.

Just as Churchill had done in his letter to Ponsonby, the leader of the backbench non-interventionists, so Grey also stressed the importance of Britain's 'true interests'. Preserving Belgium's neutrality was not merely a question of moral or legal obligation. It had been an axiom of British policy since Elizabethan times to prevent the Low Countries, and the Rhine delta and the Scheldt estuary in particular, from falling under the control of a major military Power. By the same token, remaining neutral while the continental Powers were embroiled in a war meant that Britain would have no say in the final outcome of this struggle. If, on the one hand, France were crushed, Germany would establish her dominance on the continent, and Russia would either have to make a separate peace or fight on until either exhaustion or defeat forced her to submit to a triumphant Germany. If, on the other hand, France and Russia vanquished the two Germanic Powers,

---

[339] Grey speech, House of Commons, 3 Aug. 1914, *Hansard House of Commons Debates* LXV (3 Aug. 1914), cols. 1809–32; also repr. in P. Knaplund (ed.), *Sir Edward Grey: Speeches on Foreign Affairs, 1904-1914* (London, 1931), 297–315. The various references to the serious economic consequences may have reflected Grey's reading of Norman Angell's work, see N. A. Lambert, *Planning Armageddon: British Economic Warfare and the First World War* (Cambridge, MA, 2012), 126–8.

[340] Pease diary, 3 Aug. 1914, Wilson (ed.), 'Cabinet Diary', 49; P. Jalland and J. Stubbs, 'The Irish Question after the Outbreak of War in 1914: Some Unfinished Party Business', *EHR* XCVI, 4 (1981), 778–81; Koss, *Asquith*, 159–60.

[341] Quotes from Violet Paget to Ponsonby, 4 Aug. [1914], and Barbara Hammond to Ponsonby, 5 Aug. 1914, Ponsonby MSS, Bodl., Ms.Eng.his.c.660; see also S. A. Weaver, *The Hammonds: A Marriage in History* (Stanford, CA, 1997), 109–13.

the former would dominate much of western Europe and the latter the eastern-central portions of the continent and probably the Near East, too. Whichever side emerged victorious from the war would be implacably opposed to Britain; and even if the contest ended in a stalemate, the belligerent Powers would be united in their enmity against Britain, and London would be marginalized in the peace talks. Entering the war, as Bertie emphasized, 'would give us [Britain] a locus standi to determine the conditions of peace'.[342]

To a large extent the debate triggered by some historians about the respective roles of the German and Russian factors in the British decision for war in 1914 is thus misleading. True, there were senior diplomats who argued that Russia was 'a formidable factor in European politics' now and that Britain could not afford to antagonize her. 'I only pray', wrote George Buchanan on 3 August, 'that England will prove true to herself and to her friends, as if she deserts them in their hour of need she will find herself isolated after the war; and the hours of our Empire will be numbered'.[343] But Britain did not go to war because of a potential future Russian threat to the country's far-flung imperial possessions. The dichotomy in some of the scholarly literature between a continental, equilibrist security paradigm and a global imperial one is not only exaggerated, it is a fallacy. Both paradigms were interconnected because Britain was both a European and an overseas Power. In August 1914, the reality of a continental war meant that Germany was an immediate threat to British interests. But Britain's wider interests meant it was imperative to cooperate with Russia so as to contain this potential competitor. The connection between the two was well-appreciated in London, as the earlier quoted analysis by Eyre Crowe underscored:

> Should war come, and England stand aside, one of two things must happen:-
>
> (a.) Either Germany and Austria win, crush France and humiliate Russia. With the French fleet gone, Germany in occupation of

---

[342] Bertie to Grey (private and confidential), 3 Aug. 1914, Bertie MSS, BL, Add. MSS. 63033.
[343] Nicolson to Goschen (private), 11 Mar. 1913, and Buchanan to Nicolson (private), 3 Aug. 1914, Nicolson MSS, TNA (PRO), FO 800/364 and 375. The argument that Britain went to war because of a fear of Russia is made most prominently by K. M. Wilson, *The Policy of the Entente: Essays on the Determinants of British Foreign Policy, 1904–1914* (Cambridge, 1985), 'The Making and Putative Implementation of a British Foreign Policy of Gesture, December 1905 to August 1914: The Anglo-French Entente Revisited', *CJH* XXXI, 2 (1996), 227–55, and 'Imperial Interests in the British Decision for War, 1914: The Defence of India in Central Asia', *RIS* X, 3 (1989), 189–203.

the Channel, with the willing or unwilling cooperation of Holland and Belgium, what will be the position of friendless England?

(b.) Or France and Russia win. What would be their attitude towards England? What about India and the Mediterranean?[344]

As a global Power with global reach and global interests, Britain had a global security paradigm. The inherent logic of her geopolitical position meant that, under the circumstances as they were in July 1914, Britain had to enter the war and do so against Germany and Austria-Hungary.

But to return to the events of 3–4 August, there were of course other motivations at work as well. The Cabinet was driven by a complex of different factors – calculations of strategic interests, a sense of moral obligation and party-political considerations. A desire to maintain party unity remained strong. Many took the line the chairman of Arthur Ponsonby's constituency association recommended to him. The majority of the local party were 'keen peace men', he observed, 'but ... now that we are into war it is our duty to support the Government and do everything in our power that will in any degree help to secure victory'.[345] When the German army invaded Belgium, it not only trampled underfoot Germany's own obligations as one of the guarantors of that country's neutrality, it also crushed the comforting, if naive and illusory, internationalist beliefs of many Liberal ministers. It also delivered Lloyd George, the supreme opportunist, of his personal political nightmare of having to pretend that there was any other international reality than realpolitik. 'This is not my crowd', he said to Herbert Samuel as the two made their way along Whitehall, thronging with cheering crowds: 'I never wanted to be cheered by a war crowd.'[346] But the chancellor was never one to place such sentiments above cool-headed calculations of personal advantage.[347]

---

[344] Min. Crowe, 25 July 1914, on tel. Buchanan to Grey (no. 166, urgent), 24 July 1914, *BD* XI, no. 101.

[345] Robertson [chairman, Stirling Burghs Liberal Association] to Ponsonby, 5 Aug. 1914, Ponsonby MSS, Bodl., Ms.Eng.his.c.660.

[346] Samuel to Beatrice Samuel, 3 Aug. 1914, Samuel MSS, PAL, SAM/A/157/698; see also Wasserstein, *Samuel*, 164; for Lloyd George's position see C. Hazlehurst, *Politicians at War, July 1914 to May 1915: A Prologue to the Triumph of Lloyd George* (London, 1971), 54–65; M. G. Fry, *Lloyd George and Foreign Policy: The Education of a Statesman* (Montreal and London, 1977), 192–213; D. M. Cregier, *Bounder from Wales: Lloyd George's Career before the First World War* (Columbia, MI, 1976), 240–54.

[347] It seems, however, as if Lloyd George kept in view until the last moment the possibility that Germany would not invade Belgium. On 4 August, some twelve hours

There was a brief meeting of the ministers at 10 Downing Street in the morning of Tuesday, 4 August. During the previous night, German troops had commenced their assault in the west. The invasion of Belgium had begun. That evening Grey was standing at a window of his room at the Foreign Office. It was dusk, and the lamps were being lit along Birdcage Walk. J. A. Spender, the editor of the *Westminster Gazette*, was with him at that moment. 'The lamps are going out all over Europe', he recorded the Foreign Secretary as saying, 'we shall not see them lit again in our life-time'.[348]

At the Cabinet meeting, ministers signed off final instructions for Sir Edward Goschen. He was to protest against the violation of the Treaty of London, to which Germany herself was party, and demand that Berlin halted the assault on Belgium. 'You should ask for an immediate reply.' A follow-up telegram, despatched at 2 p.m., specified that, if no satisfactory reply was received from the German government by midnight – the telegram did not make explicit whether this was central European or Greenwich time – the ambassador was to break off relations. Britain would then 'take all steps in [her] power to uphold the neutrality of Belgium'.[349] The telegram was couched in somewhat ambiguous and elastic language, to some extent conditioned by domestic considerations – the non-interventionist faction in Parliament was still strong, if now shell-shocked. Even so, there could be no doubt about its meaning. It was a British ultimatum to Germany to halt military operations in the west. There could also be no doubt that this was now a mere formality. 'It's war at 12 tonight', Eyre Crowe informed his wife. 'The Germans have invaded Belgium, which we are engaged by Treaty to defend'. Haldane wrote: 'We are preparing for war. It is an awful calamity and sorrow.'[350] That morning Margot Asquith called once more on the Lichnowskys at the German embassy. The ambassador saw her 'a moment alone ... and said "So it is all over – you will declare war tonight, & you knew we *must* go thro[ugh] Belgium – there is no other way. We never counted [on] that old old treaty.

---

after the declaration of war, he asked one of the former members of the Berlin embassy whether Germany might still respect that country's neutrality. '[T]hey will stick at nothing', was the reply, Oppenheimer diary, 4 Aug. 1914, Oppenheimer MSS, Bodl., box 1.

[348] Grey, *Twenty-Five Years* II, 20; H. W. Harris, *J. A. Spender* (London, 1946), 159.

[349] Tels. Grey to Goschen (nos. 266 and 270), both 4 Aug. 1914 (D 9.30 a.m. and 2 p.m.), *BD* XI, nos. 573 and 594; for the domestic considerations see also Pease diary, 4 Aug. 1914, Wilson (ed.), 'Cabinet Diary', 49.

[350] Quotes from Crowe to Clema Crowe, 4 Aug. 1914, Crowe MSS, Bodl., Ms.Eng. e.3020, and Haldane to Elizabeth Haldane, 4 Aug. 1914, Haldane MSS, NLS, MS 5992.

Oh dear! oh dear! don't go to war. Just wait! holding my hands. I felt too sad to speak – we sat & cried on the green sofa.'[351]

There were more tears to flow at Berlin that afternoon. Goschen attended a session of the *Reichstag* during which the chancellor set out Germany's case. War had been forced upon her by the actions of the other Powers, he declared in an impassioned speech:

> [W]e are now in a position of self-defence [*Notwehr*], and necessity [*Not*] knows no law ... So we were forced to set aside the justified protests of the Luxemburg and Belgian governments ... The wrong – I speak openly – the wrong that we are thus doing we will make good again as soon as our military objective has been attained ... He who is as imperilled as we are, and who fights for everything that is dear to him, he must think only of how he can hack his way out [wie er sich durchhaut].[352]

Afterwards, at around 4 p.m., Goschen sought an interview with Jagow at the Wilhelmstrasse, though this did not take place until 7 p.m., when the ambassador presented his demands. Jagow's hands, of course, were tied. The civilian leadership had submitted to the diktat of the military on 1 August, and the clock could not be turned back. The operation underway, Jagow explained, 'was [a] military necessity and [a] matter of life and death for [the German] Empire'. There was nothing now for Goschen to do but to demand his passports. Relations between London and Berlin had thus been severed.[353] At around the same time the journalist Victor Naumann, Tschirschky's occasional go-between at Vienna, had called on Stumm at the Wilhelmstrasse, when Jagow came into the room, looking very pale and distraught, to call Stumm out. When the latter returned, he too was 'pale and said: "England has declared war on us"'[354] – something that Stumm had always declared to be impossible.

[351] Margot Asquith diary, 4 Aug. 1914, Asquith MSS, Bodl., Ms.Eng.d.3210. On 3 August, after Grey's speech, Lichnowsky had still been hopeful that a German assurance of Belgian *post-bellum* integrity would suffice to ensure British neutrality, tel. (no. 244), 3 Aug. 1914 (D 10 p.m., R 4.09 a.m.), *DD* IV, no. 801.

[352] *Verhandlungen des deutschen Reichstages. Stenographische Berichte. Legislaturperiode XIII, 2. Session (1914–6)* CCVI (Berlin, 1914), 5–7; for Goschen's attendance of the session see also H. de Manneville, 'Les derniers jours de l'ambassade de M. Jules Cambon à Berlin', *RHD* XLIX, 2 (1935), 453.

[353] Tel. Goschen to Grey (no. 136), 4 Aug. 1914 (R 13 Aug.), *BD* XI, no. 666; see also Goschen to Jagow, 4 Aug. 1914, *DD* IV, no. 863.

[354] V. Naumann, *Dokumente und Argumente* (Berlin, 1928), 25.

Technically, this was not true, for so far Goschen had only broken off relations between the two countries. War, however, was only a matter of hours away. Before leaving the Wilhelmstrasse, Goschen asked to see the chancellor, 'as it might be ... the last time I should have an opportunity of seeing him'. The meeting took place immediately afterwards in Bethmann's rooms at the chancellery next door to the foreign ministry, and lasted for about twenty minutes. The encounter 'was very painful'. It began with a 'harrangue' by Bethmann. Germany was fighting for her 'life against two assailants', and Britain joining the war was 'like striking a man from behind'. Could he not accept that Britain was honour-bound to preserve Belgium's neutrality, Goschen interposed? 'But at what price!', the chancellor replied.

London's decision was 'terrible to a degree; just for a word – "neutrality", a word which in war-time had so often been disregarded – just for a scrap of paper Great Britain was going to make war on a kindred nation who desired nothing better than to be friends with her'. The consequences would be catastrophic, Bethmann predicted: 'at what price will that compact [Treaty of London] have been kept? Has the British Government thought of that?' At this point Goschen decided to take his leave. Bethmann was 'so excited, so evidently overcome by the news of our action, and so little disposed to hear reason that I refrained from adding fuel to the flame by further argument'.[355] Bethmann's dismissal of the Belgian treaty as 'a scrap of paper' – it seems certain that he said it in English – was remarkable. Only a few hours earlier, he had referred to Germany's violation of Belgium's neutrality as 'the wrong that we are thus doing'. To the end, then, the chancellor was unsteady.

No doubt, Bethmann was overwrought by the events that were now unfolding. But so was Goschen. When he entered the chancellor's study he was in 'a state of deep inner agitation', and he grew more agitated during the interview. According to Bethmann's account, Goschen 'burst into tears and asked for permission to remain in my ante-chamber for a while, because he did not wish to show himself in this condition to the chancellery personnel'.[356] Horace Rumbold, Goschen's embassy

---

[355] Quotes from tel. Goschen to Grey (no. 137), 4 Aug. 1914 (R 13 Aug.), *BD* XI, no. 667, and Goschen to Grey (no. 309), 6 Aug. 1914, TNA (PRO), FO 371/2164/41041. For some sleuthing as to who said what and in which language, and for the further history of Goschen's despatch, see my, 'A "German Paperchase": The "Scrap of Paper" Controversy and the Problem of Myth and Memory in International History', *D&S* XVIII, no. 1 (2007), 53–87.

[356] Bethmann Hollweg, 'Aufzeichnung', 4 Oct. 1914, PAAA, Akten des Auswärtigen Amtes im Grossen Hauptquartier 26, varia, Bd. I; also his *Betrachtungen* I, 180 n.

counsellor, later confirmed that the ambassador 'returned from the crisis very much upset'.[357] Few politicians and officials in the European capitals had any illusions about what the war might mean. Their tears were telling. The crowd that had begun to gather outside the British embassy, meanwhile, relieved its emotions by pelting the building with stones and breaking several windows before mounted police cleared the Wilhelmstrasse of the mob.[358]

In London, meanwhile, it was expected that Berlin would not formally reply to the ultimatum. No communications were received from Goschen after 7.50 p.m. – the telegraph lines had already been disrupted. Later, Asquith, Grey, Churchill, Haldane and Lloyd George and later Harcourt sat in around the Cabinet table at 10 Downing Street. It felt like a wake. Margot Asquith saw the Prime Minister briefly earlier in the evening: '"So it is all up?" "Yes, it is all up" – he had tears in his eyes.'[359]

Sometime between 9 and 10 p.m. a false news agency report suggested that Germany had declared war on Britain. At the Foreign Office the clerks were 'working at full pressure under the blaze of countless electric lights'. Under the impression of the reported German declaration of war, the text of Britain's own declaration now was hastily redrafted. The original text merely stated that following Goschen's communication at Berlin, 'a state of war exists between the two countries from today as of 11 o'clock P.M.' – again the confusion about the precise expiry of the ultimatum. The next document made specific reference to Germany having declared war on Britain. It was placed in a sealed envelope along with Lichnowsky's passports and delivered to the German embassy by Lancelot Oliphant, then a clerk in the Eastern Department and a quarter of a century later, at the time of the next German invasion of Belgium, Britain's ambassador at Brussels.

Less than forty-five minutes later, the Foreign Office discovered that the news of Germany's declaration of war was based on a wireless message alerting German merchant vessels to the imminence of war with Britain, intercepted and misinterpreted by the Admiralty. It was an embarrassing mistake, and it was decided to retrieve the 'wrong' declaration of war and to substitute it with the correct document. The task fell to Arthur Nicolson's son, Harold, then a junior clerk at the Foreign Office. 'Grasping

---

[357] Rumbold to Gaselee, 6 June 1924, TNA (PRO), FO 370/200/2269; Otte, 'A "German Paperchase"', 75.
[358] Sir H. Rumbold, *The War Crisis in Berlin, July–August 1914* (London, 1940), 323–5.
[359] Margot Asquith diary, 4 Aug. 1914, Asquith MSS, Bodl., Ms.Eng.d.3210; Harcourt Cabinet notes, 4 Aug. 1914, Harcourt MSS, Bodl., no accession number; Grey, *Twenty-Five Years* II, 18.

the correct document in a nervous hand', young Nicolson walked across Horse Guards Parade and up the Duke of York steps to call on the German embassy:

> After much ringing a footman appeared. He stated that Prince Lichnowsky had gone to bed. The bearer of the missive insisted on seeing His Excellency and advised the footman to summon the butler. The latter appeared and stated that His Highness had given instructions that he was under no circumstances to be disturbed. The Foreign Office clerk stated that he was the bearer of a communication of the utmost importance from Sir Edward Grey. The butler, at that, opened the door and left young Nicolson in the basement ... On his return he asked Sir Edward Grey's emissary to follow him and walked majestically to the third floor and then proceeded along a pile-carpeted passage. The butler knocked at a door.

Nicolson was then admitted to the ambassador's bedroom, and explained that there had been a slight error in the document, which he now wished to replace with the correct one: 'Prince Lichnowsky indicated the writing table in the window. "You will find it there", he said. The envelope had been but half-opened, and the passports protruded. It did not appear that the Ambassador had read the communication or opened the letter.' He had known what was to happen. Nicolson had to ask for a receipt to be signed. This done, 'Prince Lichnowsky turned out the pink lamp beside his bed, and then feeling he had perhaps been uncivil he again lighted it. "Give my best regards," he said, "to your father. I shall not in all probability see him before my departure."'[360]

The delivery of the wrong declaration of war was the last in a long chain of inadvertent incidents that characterized the events during Europe's last summer of peace. By now all the Great Powers were at war. The first general war since the defeat of Napoleon Bonaparte ninety-nine years previously had begun. Only Austria-Hungary, whose insouciant and reckless leadership had brought about this war, was at war only with Serbia.

---

[360] See Nicolson, *Lord Carnock*, 423–6. The correct document is Grey to Lichnowsky, 4 Aug. 1914, *BD* XI, no. 643; Young, *Lichnowsky*, 125–7.

CONCLUSION

Nescis, mi fili, quantilla sapientia mundus regatur?

AXEL GUSTAFSON OXENSTIERNA (1648)

Historia scribitur ad narrandum, non ad probandum, but if it does prove something on account of its accurate depiction, then it has even more value.

JACOB BURCKHARDT (1864)[1]

And further, by these, my sonne, be admonished: of making many bookes there is no end, and much studie is a wearinesse of the flesh.

ECCLESIASTES 12:12 (1611 KING JAMES BIBLE)

The 'Bogey has come at last', noted the Sussex solicitor and poly-math, Edward Heron-Allen, in his diary at midnight on 3 August 1914. During his thirty years as a professional lawyer, he reflected, 'when people consulted their legal and financial advisers about the highest classes of "gilt-edged" investments, they always asked the stereotypical question "Is it perfectly safe?" and we always shrugged our shoulders and replied "Unless there is a European war!" – meaning that this was utterly beyond the possibility of belief'.[2]

The bogey had come. But the Great Powers had not somehow 'slithered over the brink' without apprehension as if in a fit of absentmind-edness, as Lloyd George put it so evocatively in his war memoirs.[3] War had come as a result of individual decisions and a rapid series of moves and countermoves by the chancelleries of Europe, and set against the backdrop

---

[1] As quoted in K. Loewenstein, 'Historiker und Publizist', H. Tramer (ed.), *Robert Weltsch zum 70. Geburtstag* (Tel Aviv, 1961), 81.

[2] Heron-Allen diary, 3 Aug. 1914, B. W. Harvey and C. Fitzgerald (eds.), *Edward Heron-Allen's Journal of the Great War: From Sussex Shore to Flanders Fields* (Chichester, 2002), 3. Heron-Allen was more than a county town solicitor; he was a distinguished zoologist and Fellow of the Royal Society, a Persian scholar – he translated *The Rubaiyat of Omar Khayam* (1908) – and the author of a classic study of violin-making; he also wrote an early form of science fiction, mostly under the pseudonym of 'Christopher Blayre'.

[3] D. Lloyd George, *War Memoirs* (2 vols., London, new edn 1938) I, 32.

of recent shifts in the international landscape and anticipated further changes in the years to come. The Powers did not operate in a vacuum. If, in 1914, there was no formal and largely institutionalized framework of international politics of the kind that exists today at different levels, there was nevertheless a system of Great Power politics – the European concert, with its norms of behaviour, accepted rules of conduct, and conflict-solution mechanisms. It is true, the understandings that underpinned Great Power politics in the long nineteenth century had become a little threadbare by 1914, and the tools with which they operated to settle international disputes somewhat worn and perhaps a little blunt, too, from frequent use. Even so, each of the Powers acted with explicit reference to this system and its norms; and it is against these that their actions need to be judged.

The system of Great Power politics was not so much a 'real-life phenomenon', a vast impersonal force that directed the actions of the statesmen of Europe in accordance with its own ineffable internal logic. It was rather an informal nexus of often unspoken assumptions and at best half-articulated ones about the norms of international behaviour and the accepted mechanisms of accommodating the interests of the greater and the smaller Powers. The pre-1914 international system, then, consisted of shared understandings of the 'rules of the game', what the Powers were and were not permitted to do, and what tools they could use and under what circumstances.[4]

Abstract concepts, such as the 'balance of power' or the 'alliance system' did not cause Europe's descent into war. Nor did states in the abstract propel the Powers along the path towards war. As this re-examination of the decision-making processes has shown, individuals acting in response to external and internal stimuli, and to perceived opportunities and threats, were central to the developments in July 1914. Their hawkish or dovish views on the perceived realities of international politics, and how they manoeuvred in the space given to them within the existing political arrangements in their respective countries, hold the key to understanding how and why Europe descended into world war.

There can be no serious dispute about the profound consequences of this conflict for Europe and for the wider world, consequences that to varying degrees are still felt a century after Sarajevo. But the causes of the

---

[4] For further thoughts on this see F. H. Hinsley, *Power and the Pursuit of Peace: Theory and Practice in the History of Relations between States* (Cambridge, repr. 1967); E. V. Gulick, *Europe's Classical Balance of Power* (New York and London, 1967); P. W. Schroeder, '"System" and Systemic Thinking in International History', *IHR* xv, 1 (1993), here esp. 133–4; and the individual contributions to E. R. May, R. Rosecrance and Z. S. Steiner (eds.), *History and Neorealism* (Cambridge, 2010).

war were less profound (it would be a logical fallacy to derive conclusions as to the causes of any action from the nature of its consequences). This is not to suggest yet another version of some form of 'chaos theory', of the shockwaves of Prinčip's two bullets unleashing the torrents of war. Such an argument would be as flimsy as the butterfly's wings that supposedly carry this theory. The causes of the war of 1914–18 are at one and the same time more mundane and more profound than the standard arguments about the deeper forces determining Europe's ineluctable progress towards war would suggest. They are to be found in the near-collective failure of statecraft by the rulers of Europe.

When the news of Sarajevo broke, few in Europe seem to have apprehended serious complications. The victim of the crime was perhaps too unlikely an object of public sympathy for one thing. As the Viennese novelist Arthur Schnitzler noted in his diary on that day: 'After the final shock, F[ranz] F[erdinand]'s murder had no strong effect. His immense unpopularity.'[5] The location and the timing of the murder help to explain the prevailing sense of security. There had been crises and regicide in the Balkans very recently, and the Powers had somehow safely steered around these rapids. The fact that, by the fourth week of July, Austria-Hungary had not resorted to force also seemed to guarantee a non-violent outcome of the dispute. Measured against the experiences with earlier Great Power crises and wars, it seemed almost too late to go to war in late July or August. The Crimean and the 1877 Russo-Turkish wars had broken out in the spring, and so had the Franco-Austrian War of 1859. The preliminary peace agreement of Villafranca, which brought that conflict to a conclusion, indeed, was signed on 11–12 July. The 1864 German-Danish War was largely fought in April, with some mopping-up operations in June and July after the brief diplomatic interlude of the London conference. Prussia's subsequent war with Austria in 1866 was effectively over by 3 July; and, in the case of the 1870 Franco-German conflict, the French decision for war was taken on 12–13 July. Though not at all conclusive, such considerations help to explain the absence of any urgent sense of imminent danger in July 1914. But this was also one of the symptoms of an age that had come to feel secure in the blessings of a century of unparalleled material and political progress. The horrors that were to come were too inconceivable.

And while Europe had not 'unexpectedly plunged'[6] into conflict, the Powers were not destined to descend into a general war, as this re-examination of the diplomatic manoeuvres of the summer of 1914 has

---

[5] Schnitzler diary, 28 June 1914, W. Welzig (ed.), *Arthur Schnitzler. Tagebuch, 1913–1916* (Vienna, 1983), 123.
[6] *Ibid.*

shown. Indeed, it has offered a powerful antidote to assumptions of 'inevitability'. It has demonstrated that the martial undercurrents often emphasized by historians in fact played no significant role for much of the crisis – and where they did, they delayed developments more than they accelerated them; they were a force for constraint more than a stimulus for aggression. Military factors did not dictate the course of events, at least not until the very end of July. Even then, the interlocking nature of different mobilizations can be exaggerated. Military factors did, however, shape general assumptions: Grey and Bethmann Hollweg, Sazonov and Poincaré all thought that the prospect of war would have a sufficient deterrent effect on the other Powers and so prevent them from taking matters to extremes. They thus attempted to use the spectre of conflict to gain leverage over their counterparts and so extract advantages for their own countries. In that assumption they were quite wrong.

The Powers also sought to apply deterrence in different ways. Poincaré and Sazonov regarded 'clarity of intention' as the best means of ensuring that the two Germanic Powers disengaged.[7] The success of Grey's diplomacy since 1905, by contrast, had lain in his studied ambiguity about Britain's intentions, but in 1914 this was not sufficient to restrain either Vienna or Berlin or to force moderation on St Petersburg and Paris. And here we come to perhaps the most perplexing aspect of the July crisis. To some extent, all the Powers, with the exception of Britain, were driven by a sense of weakness, which made it difficult for them to pull back from the brink even when they were already staring into the abyss of war. The certainty of diplomatic defeat, and its foreseeable adverse effects in the short term, proved a more powerful spur not to compromise than the incalculable, because more distant, consequences of military conflict. The existing alliances, indeed, reinforced this sense of weakness. Officials at the Wilhelmstrasse were anxious for their one reliable ally, Austria-Hungary, to reassert her declining regional influence lest this sprawling multi-ethnic empire disintegrate, leaving Germany isolated and vulnerable. Vienna thus wielded a form of negative power over Berlin; and, in consequence, there was no appetite there for restraining Austria-Hungary until the very end of the crisis when a continental war began to loom. Even then that prospect was not sufficiently powerful to bring about a change of course.

At the Ballhausplatz, recent events had engendered an audacity of despair. Firm action against Serbia was considered a panacea for the

---

[7] For this argument see J. H. Maurer, *The Outbreak of the First World War: Strategic Planning, Crisis Decision Making and Deterrence Failure* (Westport, CT, 1995), 109–28; H. Strachan, *The First World War*, I, *The Call to Arms* (Oxford, 2001), 100.

Habsburg Monarchy's internal nationalities problem and its mounting external difficulties in the wider Balkans region. It was also regarded as a means of re-energizing the *Zweibund* partner in Berlin who, they thought, had not given proper support for the Empire in recent years; and reasserting Habsburg influence in south-eastern Europe, it was expected, would keep the Italian *Dreibund* ally in its proper place, unable to make unacceptable demands on the Monarchy for territorial compensation.

At the same time, leading French politicians considered the alliance with Russia as indispensable for France's national security. Failure to support St Petersburg in the unfolding Austro-Serb crisis, it was feared, would ultimately convince the Tsar and his ministers that reverting to the traditional Russo-German alliance offered a better chance of securing Russian interests in the longer term. For their part, Russian officials were adamant that Russian power and prestige could not survive another climb-down over the latest Balkans stand-off.

At the distance of a century, and when seen against the broader backdrop of Great Power politics during the long nineteenth century, what is striking is the extent to which the field of vision of the continental Powers had narrowed. In every case, it was an indication of that pervading sense of weakness. Officials at the Ballhausplatz had long ceased to think like the representatives of a Great Power. By 1914, Austria-Hungary had become a greater regional Power, and her policy was essentially *Balkanpolitik*. For Berlin, the key concern until the last few days of the July crisis was to prop up the Habsburg ally. Whereas Vienna pursued *Balkanpolitik*, the Wilhelmstrasse followed *Allianzpolitik*. Narrow alliance calculations were central also to French thinking during the crisis, albeit with an important variation. Whatever their differences in other respects, Poincaré, Paléologue and Viviani wanted to support Russia, but at the same time they were driven by a perceived need to demonstrate to Russia that France, herself, was alliance-worthy. Russian policy was both narrower and broader. Sazonov was anxious to reassert Russia's power in order to demonstrate that she was still a Great Power. At the same time, however, Russian diplomacy also aimed at preserving the balance of power in Europe.[8] In contrast to the continental Powers, Britain's policy was the broadest of all. In part this reflected the global interests and outlook of the British foreign policy élite; and in part it was rooted in the pursuit of a policy of 'enlightened self-interest' in that the maintenance of the European status quo suited British interests.

---

[8] See M. E. Soroka, *Britain, Russia and the Road to the First World War: The Fateful Embassy of Count Aleksandr Benckendorff, 1903–1916* (Farnham and Burlington, VT, 2011), 240–53.

Yet however much the Powers depended upon their respective allies or partners, there was little systematic coordination of policy between any of them. If anything, what is striking is the element of mistrust among allies. Jagow's complaint about the '*k.u.k. Schlampigkeitskrämerei*' in Austria-Hungary was matched by Vienna's condescending '*Katzelmacher*' attitude towards Rome and Poincaré's suspicions of Russia's perceived lack of steadfastness or Sazonov's lack of statesmanship. And as for Britain, although she was not party to any of the continental alliances, her ties with France and Russia on account of the colonial and imperial arrangements with these two Powers had grown more distant on the eve of the Sarajevo murders. Talk of the alliance 'system' as one of the contributing factors to the war, then, is exaggerated.

If there were divergent practices using deterrence as an instrument of foreign policy, there was also no consensus among the chancelleries of Europe as to how best to manage the apparent decay of Austria-Hungary. The decline of old-established empires was not a new phenomenon, of course. Attuned to Social Darwinian notions of the rise and fall of nations, it seemed to have fallen to this generation to deal with the fall-out of the collapse of two such empires. The Ottoman realm was already in an advanced stage of dissolution, having been expelled from almost all of Europe as a consequence of the two Balkans wars and clinging on precariously to its toehold on the Bosphorus. But the problems this created could be contained in the geopolitical periphery of Europe. The demise of the Habsburg Empire, if and when it came, posed challenges of a different kind, challenges that touched on the core relations in Europe, most notably those between Germany and Russia. How to manage the process of Austro-Hungarian decline was one of the unsolved questions of Great Power politics on the eve of the First World War.

Linked to this was another inconsistency in Great Power practice. For much of the long nineteenth century there had been a clear appreciation of the respective roles, rights and responsibilities of the Great Powers and the smaller powers. This understanding had become more brittle by 1914. Thus, Sazonov and Poincaré, and to some extent Grey, too, insisted that any Austro-Hungarian demands on Belgrade had to respect Serbian sovereignty and independence. At the same time, the Powers did little to establish effective limits for Serbia's undoubted provocations of Austria-Hungary and the pan-Serb agitation that was aimed at undermining the internal cohesion of one of the existing Great Powers. At the beginning of the nineteenth century, Tsar Alexander I and Talleyrand would not have tolerated such an explicit challenge to the predominance of the Great Powers and the established international order.

In all of this, the role of individuals in July 1914 was critical. Until the end of the July crisis diplomats and politicians held the strings in their hands, although it is one of its peculiarities that key decisions were taken by junior or middle-ranking officials, especially so during the early stages of the crisis. For much of that month, for instance, Russia was represented by chargés d'affaires at Paris, Berlin, Vienna and Belgrade. Similarly, the heads of the British missions to Germany and Serbia were absent for the entire period or a substantial part of it. The German chancellor was away from the capital until late July, and the foreign minister had been on his honeymoon when Hoyos and Szögyény extracted the 'blank cheque' from the Kaiser.

To emphasize the role of individuals also raises broader questions. One of these concerns the governmental structures within which the statesmen of 1914 operated, and which to a degree constrained them in their actions.[9] What is remarkable about the July crisis was the poor intellectual quality of the decision-making, and the haphazard policy-making processes with their endless capacity for unreality. This problem was particularly acute in the three eastern military monarchies. During the heyday of the debate on the origins of the First World War in the wake of Fritz Fischer's *Griff nach der Weltmacht* it had become fashionable to posit domestic factors as the driving force behind foreign policy decisions. Arno J. Mayer argued, for instance, that the underlying causes of the war were rooted in a general crisis of European society at the end of the long nineteenth century. War, he and others asserted, was regarded as a means of avoiding revolution: 'The decision for war and the design of warfare were forged in what was a crisis in the politics and policy of Europe's ruling and governing classes.'[10]

Yet, as seen in this re-examination of the events of the summer of 1914, domestic considerations, while clearly present in the calculations of the decision-makers, were not at the forefront of their deliberations. Bethmann Hollweg and Sazonov were wary of the power of the force of nationalism. As has been shown neither man was an advocate of pan-Germanism or pan-Slavism; nor did either make himself an instrument of the wilder fantasies propagated by the adherents of these types of ultra-nationalism. Indeed, it is not possible to pinpoint domestic factors as one of

[9] For some pertinent thoughts on this see J. Joll, 'Politicians and the Freedom to Choose: The Case of July 1914', A. Ryan (ed.), *The Idea of Freedom: Essays in Honour of Isaiah Berlin* (Oxford, 1979), 99–114.

[10] A. J. Mayer, 'Internal Crises and War since 1870', C. L. Bertrand (ed.), *Revolutionary Situations in Europe* (Montreal, 1977), 231; and Mayer's *The Persistence of the Old Regime: Europe to the Great War* (New York, 1981), 303–29.

the forces that made for war. If anything, the certainty of economic ruin and social and political unrest, if not revolution, acted as restraints on the statesmen during Europe's final crisis. The problem was not, as Mayer and others have argued, that a crisis of the capitalist system erupted in global war. Rather it was that conflict was to no small degree the result of a crisis of governance in the three eastern monarchies. These gigantic empires staggered under the vast weight of their pre-modern constitutional arrangements that could not meet the needs of the modern state. The existence of different power centres, frequently in competition with each other, and the absence of responsible governments, in the sense of an executive responsible to the public or parliament for its actions, prevented the formulation of coherent foreign policy strategies at Vienna, Berlin and St Petersburg.

The 1867 dualist *Ausgleich*, that wondrous mechanism with its 'multitude of wheels and levers' designed to protect the interests of the Magyar magnates, not only elevated Hungary to the status of a Great Power on the back of traditionally dominant Austria;[11] it also slowed 'common' decision-making, that is joint decisions by the two governments in Vienna and Budapest, to a snail's pace and so robbed the Dual Monarchy of the chance of resolving the Sarajevo crisis on Habsburg terms in the immediate aftermath of the crime. But the dualist constitutional arrangements also meant that the 'common' decisions were based on the lowest common denominator. They could only be achieved through a carefully calibrated balance of mutually tolerable dissatisfaction. No doubt, this kept the Habsburg Empire together. But the semblance of internal cohesion was bought at the price of its leadership's inability to formulate a coherent foreign policy strategy. The decisions that were eventually agreed on in July 1914 neither permitted Berchtold to launch the rapid punitive response he advocated nor allowed for the larger re-orientation of Habsburg diplomacy in the Balkans favoured by Tisza. The absence of a coherent strategy was an even more serious shortcoming in 1914 because the Monarchy was now operating in a more hostile international environment. Until the Balkan wars of 1912–13, Habsburg diplomacy had remained wedded to the status quo. This did not require Franz-Joseph's ministers to make any significant decisions – administering the status quo rarely does. But the two regional wars had destroyed the status quo, and Austria-Hungary now sought to change the emerging post-war settlement in the region herself. But for that she had no strategy, and her representatives could not communicate any sense of her priorities or objectives to the

---

[11] L. B. Namier, *Vanished Supremacies: Essays on European History, 1812–1918* (London, 1962 (pb)), 147.

other Powers. Thus, when Tschirschky, the German ambassador, enquired at the Ballhausplatz as to what the Monarchy's leaders intended to do, how far they were prepared to go and what 'firmly defined plan of action' they had, he asked questions that were impossible for the Habsburg ministers to answer.[12]

Nor were the arrangements much better at St Petersburg and Berlin. In Russia the attempts of the previous prime minister, Pyotr Stolypin, to overcome the diffusion of power at St Petersburg and to tighten decision-making by creating a form of 'united government', had begun to unravel again following his assassination in 1911, and the Tsar had succeeded in clawing back some of his powers.[13] The ministerial council provided a forum for strategic decision-making, but its meetings in July 1914 were overshadowed by the events of the day, and its decisions were taken on an ad hoc basis without much reference to longer-term strategic interests. In 1914, the situation was exacerbated by a weak prime minister and a volatile Tsar. Goremykin's ineffectiveness and Nicholas II's vacillations allowed the hawks, Krivoshein and Sazonov, to carry the day. The Byzantine system at Berlin, meanwhile, gave influence to many, but no-one shouldered responsibility, least of all for formulating a coherent strategic approach to Germany's foreign policy problems. The peculiar proceedings at Potsdam on 5 July underlined this powerfully. And as was seen in the final chapter, Germany had a war plan, but the leadership at Berlin had no clear idea what kind of war they meant to fight, and for what objectives. And that fundamental confusion also affected the vagaries of German diplomacy during the July crisis. When, a few weeks into the war, chancellor Bethmann Hollweg was asked to explain how it had come about, he replied wearily: 'Ja, wer das wüsste! (Well, who can know!)'.[14] It was an admission of personal failure. But it also touched upon a deeper truth. Germany did not have a 'road map' during the crisis because the German leadership had no sense of their final destination and an appropriate itinerary.

The three eastern monarchies were all giants with double heads of clay. But the failings at the top were replicated at the lower levels; and this, too, mattered. The degree of professional incompetence displayed at St Petersburg, Berlin and Vienna during July 1914 was striking. The inability of Yanushkevich, the Russian chief of staff, to grasp the details and import of Russia's mobilization plans is surely an egregious example of

---

[12] Berchtold daily report, 3 July 1914, ÖUA VIII, no. 10006.
[13] For a comprehensive discussion of all this see D. M. McDonald, *United Government and Foreign Policy in Russia, 1907–1914* (Cambridge, MA, 1992), 168–98.
[14] B. von Bülow, *Denkwürdigkeiten* (4 vols., Berlin, 1930) III, 148.

military blundering. It is one of the many ironies of the July crisis that Matscheko, who had drafted the original *Denkschrift* that in turn furnished the basis for the document Hoyos took to Berlin, had failed the diplomatic entrance examination in 1902; and also that Dietrich von Bethmann Hollweg, one of the hawks at the German embassy at Vienna, had been appointed to the diplomatic service without the inconvenience of having to pass an examination (he eventually passed it four years later, in 1906). Both joined diplomacy because they were 'good chaps' and came from the right sort of families.[15] Low professional standards also tended to generate group-think, and this helps to explain why Pourtalès's persistent prognostications of Russian neutrality were listened to and Stumm's confident expectation of British abstention in the event of a continental conflict was accepted, while Lichnowsky's perceptive warnings were ignored.[16]

Of the Powers, only Britain, with her seemingly shambolic and prolix Cabinet discussions, produced coherent strategic decisions. If the other foreign ministers showed no real grasp of military matters or the realities of modern warfare – a disjuncture between the diplomatic and military strands most glaring in the cases of Austria-Hungary and Russia – Grey was the exception. A well-established tradition of responsible government and the existence of the Committee of Imperial Defence, as a liaising body between the civilian executive and the military authorities, ensured that the different factors weighing upon the situation were given due consideration. This was more significant than the wider suffrage that existed in France and Germany and even in Austria-Hungary.[17]

But to emphasize the importance of individuals also raises the question of individual culpability. No doubt, by enshrining the responsibility of Germany and the Central Powers for the outbreak of the war in the Paris peace treaties of 1919, and on making the assumption of war guilt the foundation on which the whole structure of the peace settlement rested, the peacemakers of 1919 made sure that the question of culpability remained at the core of the subsequent debate over the origins of the 1914–18 conflict. The search for the 'guilty men' of 1914 was a significant

---

[15] See W. D. Godsey, Jr, *Aristocratic Redoubt: The Austro-Hungarian Foreign Office on the Eve of the First World War* (W. Lafayette, IN, 1999), 45–6; and J. Hürter *et al.* (eds.), *Biographisches Handbuch des deutschen Auswärtigen Dienstes, 1871–1945* (4 vols., Paderborn, 2000–4), I, 140. Dietrich Bethmann had previously served as an army officer, but without having the requisite officer's patent, *ibid.*

[16] Stumm later admitted that his advice misled Bethmann Hollweg on 5 July, see [W.] von Rheinbaben, *Kaiser, Kanzler, Präsidenten, 1895–1934* (Mainz, 1968), 108–9.

[17] Confirmation perhaps of Max Weber's praise of British institutions, see his 'The Profession and Vocation of Politics', P. Lassman and R. Speirs (eds.), *Max Weber: Political Writings* (Cambridge, 1994), 340–4.

part of the controversies of the 1920s and 1930s, and, as Christopher Clark recently observed, 'the blame game has never lost its appeal' since.[18] If during the interwar years the chief motivation was to exculpate the German leadership, the often heated controversy triggered by Fritz Fischer's powerful arguments and the more variegated work of his disciples was driven more by a desire to cement assumptions of German war guilt. The German leadership had willed war, in Fischer's phrase, with the implication of criminal intent, and the decisions of July 1914 were part of a longer continuum of the peculiarities in Germany's historical development that linked the Prussian tradition with the rise of Hitler in the 1930s, the so-called 'Sonderweg'. The Fischer controversy itself is now largely seen as part of post-1945 (West) Germany's tortuous transition to what might pass for Western European normality.[19] Wilhelmine Germany, meanwhile, was no evil empire *avant la lettre*. For all the pre-modern aspects of this quasi-absolutist régime, in many respects the country was in the vanguard of modernity.[20] Fischer's thesis nevertheless still casts a long shadow over much current scholarship.

Throughout the 'long debate' there has been a strong temptation for historians to cast themselves in the role of prosecutors, whether to indict the Central Powers or, more recently, to castigate the policies of Grey or Sazonov – and no doubt they have not always cut convincing figures in this role. Notions of sin and atonement, of course, are deeply rooted in human consciousness, and it may well be argued that in operating with concepts of guilt historians generate more heat than light. It may also be asked how useful the concept of blame is for the purposes of historical analysis. It is after all the definition of a tragedy that a rightful cause clashes with another equally rightful cause. Who is to judge objectively, and on the basis of which criteria, whether Austria-Hungary's ambition to maintain an empire that provided a tolerable framework for the more or less peaceful coexistence of various nationalities had greater validity than Serbia's

---

[18] C. Clark, *The Sleepwalkers: How Europe Went to War in 1914* (London, 2012), 560.
[19] See for instance the articles on the Fischer controversy in the special issue of *JCH* XLVIII, 2 (2013); also H. Böhme, '"Primat" und "Paradigmata". Zur Entwicklung einer bundesdeutschen Zeitgeschichtsforschung am Beispiel des Ersten Weltkrieges', H. Lehmann (ed.), *Historikerkontroversen* (Göttingen, 2000), 87–140; W. J. Mommsen, *Der grosse Krieg und die Historiker. Neue Wege der Geschichtsschreibung über den Ersten Weltkrieg* (Essen, 2002).
[20] T. Nipperdey, *Deutsche Geschichte, 1866–1918*, I, *Arbeitswelt und Bürgergeist* (Munich, 1993), 414–16ff.; see also W. Hardtwig, 'Der deutsche Weg in die Moderne. Die Gleichzeitigkeit des Ungleichzeitigen als Grundproblem der deutschen Geschichte', in W. Hardtwig and H. H. Brandt (eds.), *Deutschlands Weg in die Moderne. Politik, Gesellschaft und Kultur im 19. Jahrhundert* (Munich, 1993), 9–31.

pursuit of a 'Yugoslav' project? And yet, whilst students of the past would be wise to strive for balance and fairness, '*tout comprendre c'est tout pardonner*' is no useful guidance either. It is a form of intellectual surrender and an abdication of the historian's task to examine and to offer a rational judgement on the past.

If historians should be reluctant to put some of the men of 1914 in the dock posthumously or to issue them, in the best head-teacher style and with a raised index finger, with 'end-of-term' report cards, it is nevertheless right to point out their failings. The blasé belligerence at the Ballhausplatz is surely worth noting. Berchtold and his aides, but also Conrad and the aged Emperor at the Hofburg, were all afflicted by 'tunnel vision'. Settling accounts with Serbia trumped all other considerations. Metternich's successors no longer thought like the leaders of a Great Power; the international consequences of the action against Serbia were left to the German ally. There was an incomparable insouciance among the upper echelons at Vienna. 'What could possibly happen to us?', Hoyos was reported to have said during the crisis: 'If it goes badly, then we will lose Bosnia and a piece of Eastern Galicia!'[21] It was recklessness beyond belief; and Berchtold's diplomatic calculations were the political equivalent of fantasy football.

But the Germans were reckless too. Collectively, Wilhelm II, Bethmann Hollweg and Jagow abdicated an independent policy. The Kaiser did so by issuing the 'blank cheque', the chancellor by not retracting it, and Jagow by reinforcing it. Kaiser Wilhelm and his chancellor did not will war. The rapidity with which they were prepared to accept some form of 'Halt in Belgrade' or what they took to be a British offer of neutrality on 1 August 1914 underscored this powerfully. The German monarch, his bellicose bombast and his habit of launching inky thunderbolts at anyone or anything that had attracted his ire, was remarkably unwarlike in the summer of 1914 – as was his cousin, Tsar Nicholas II (and less surprisingly his other cousin, King George V).

The German chancellor merits a closer look. No doubt an honourable man of more than common decency, he nevertheless lacked the political leadership skills and the strategic intelligence to guide German policy through the crisis. His chief failing, however, was his reluctance to assert German influence over the Habsburg Monarchy. When the Austro-Hungarian ambassador at Rome, the cantankerous Count Mérey, complained of his country's intolerable position under German tutelage,

---

[21] H. Graf von Lützow, *Im diplomatischen Dienst der k.u.k. Monarchie*, ed. P. Hohenbalken (Vienna, 1971), 219.

he mistook recent experience for current reality.[22] Following the 'blank cheque' Vienna's and Berlin's respective positions had changed. For Germany, until the Balkan wars the *Zweibund* had been a restraining alliance, imposing moderation on Vienna. In July 1914, the promise of unconditional German support put Bismarck's adage of alliances having a horse and a rider on its head. Now the horse was in the saddle and the rider staggered under the weight of the double-headed Habsburg quadruped.

Bethmann and Jagow were not in the same league as Bismarck. The task of framing and executing a coherent foreign policy that was commensurate with Germany's strengths and weaknesses and that was designed to safeguard her interests was beyond them. Bethmann's ambition to localize the incipient Austro-Serbian conflict was not unreasonable; nor were his calculations entirely without a certain logic. But there was a sort of wilful blindness to the realities of international politics and a refusal to think through the consequences of what was contemplated. During the early weeks of the war, shortly before the battle of the Marne, Kurt Riezler, Bethmann's amanuensis, wrote that the 'chancellor is a clever man [ist doch ein kluger Kopf] and people will at least have to admit that the whole show was put on very well [die Inszenierung doch sehr gut war]. The war, by the way, was not willed, but calculated and broke out at the most advantageous moment.'[23] There was a good deal of *ex post facto* rationalization in Riezler's reflections. As seen, Bethmann had given no thought to a preventive war but had sought to localize the Austro-Serb conflict. But in one respect Riezler was right – Bethmann did not will the war that broke out in August 1914. There was a similar attempt to make sense of what had happened in the comment by the former German ambassador and one-time Kaiser-intimate, Prince Philipp zu Eulenburg in early September 1914, again just before the Marne. Vienna's note to Serbia, he opined, was 'Prussian to the marrow'.[24] There were, no doubt, superficial parallels between Bismarck's Ems telegram of 1870 and the Austro-Hungarian ultimatum. Both were designed to provoke war. But for Bismarck it was a tool of a carefully prepared policy. In 1914 the Austro-Serbian war came

---

[22] Mérey to Berchtold (private), 29 July 1914, *ÖUA* VIII, no. 10991.
[23] Riezler to Käthe Liebermann, Saturday [probably 29 Aug. or 5 Sept. 1914], Riezler MSS, Leo Baeck Institute, New York. I am grateful to Günther Roth for a copy of this important document; for further thoughts on Riezler, see G. Roth, '"Die Schönheit der wilden Bewegung". Kurt Riezlers Briefe 1914 an Käthe Liebermann', *Zeitschrift für Ideengeschichte* VI, 2 (2012), 105–15.
[24] Eulenburg to Putlitz, 9 Sept. 1914, as quoted in J. C. G. Röhl (ed.), *1914: Delusion or Design? The Testimony of Two German Diplomats* (London, 1973), 64; for a similar argument of a deliberate provocation see D. C. Copeland, *The Origins of Major War* (Ithaca, NY, 2000), 79–118.

about because Vienna willed it and, more importantly, because Berlin had relinquished its political leadership in the *Zweibund*. Bismarck knew how to present a reasonable case to the outside world; Bethmann and Jagow did not. Moreover, they were prepared to sacrifice Germany on the altar of the Habsburg Empire's regional interests.

If this was a catastrophic failure of strategic leadership, Bethmann and Jagow were also found wanting in terms of basic statecraft, most of which flowed from their abdication of an independent policy. Having given Austria-Hungary assurances of absolute German support, it was a serious mistake not to insist on being consulted about the next steps. After the war, Sazonov argued that Berlin had somehow forgotten how to make its views known at Vienna.[25] But Berlin had not forgotten; it did not wish its views to be known. What little tactical advantage could be gained from feigning ignorance of the impending Austro-Hungarian note before 23 July was purchased at a considerable political price. By the same token, it was an unconscionable act of folly to allow Austria-Hungary to break off relations with Serbia at a time when the ideal moment for a swift and limited strike against Serbia had long passed. Finally, if the Habsburg ultimatum was, as San Giuliano put it, 'le triomphe de l'imbécilité',[26] then it was trumped by the German declarations of war on Russia and France. In doing so, the Wilhelmstrasse placed Italy and Romania *ex nexu foederis* and so released them from any commitments to Berlin and Vienna. As the *Dreibund* alliance, of which the former was a part and to which the latter was affiliated, was a defensive alliance, Germany's act of aggression relieved Rome and Bucharest of any obligations towards the two Germanic Powers. The invasion of Belgium merely compounded these mistakes.

Jagow and Tschirschky, meanwhile, were reckless in their own ways, too, the state secretary because he issued a second 'blank cheque', thereby wrecking any chances of mediation in the forlorn hope of coercing the other Powers to acquiesce in a localized Austro-Serbian war. Jagow placed his faith in a bluff, that ingenious invention of the mediocre. Resorting to bluff under adverse circumstances, with such catastrophic possible consequences, and without a strong hand to play, was rash and foolhardy. Ambassador Tschirschky was grossly irresponsible in encouraging Habsburg belligerence and in misleading his own government. No doubt, like Bethmann, neither Jagow nor Tschirschky wished to bring about a European conflagration. No-one at Berlin willed war; there was no criminal intent; and Bethmann and the Kaiser were not simply

---

[25] S. D. Sazonov, *Les Années fatales* (Paris, 1927), 255.
[26] Rodd diary, 27 July 1914, as quoted in Sir J. R. Rodd, *Social and Diplomatic Memories, 1884–1919* (3 vols., London, 1922–5) III, 204.

forerunners of Hitler and his movement. But their miscalculations and their reckless blunders brought about this war more than anything else. There is a recklessness that borders on the criminal. Theirs comes very close to it.

The case of Russia was different. There is no clear evidence of aggressive designs on her part. As the analysis of decision-making at St Petersburg presented here has shown, the quart of Russian foreign policy on the eve of the war cannot be squeezed into the half-pint pot of Constantinople and the Turkish Straits.[27] Russia's cumbersome military and political apparatus made the pursuit of offensive schemes well-nigh impossible at any rate. But Sazonov was highly strung and changeable, prone to act under the impressions of the moment; and the chop-and-change that characterized his handling of the crisis – pressing for direct talks with Vienna, then advocating mediation by an international quartet before reverting again to Austro-Russian negotiations – complicated matters. Sazonov's deterrence strategy, combining attempts at some form of mediation with military posturing, was deeply flawed. If, as he always maintained, clarity of intention was key to deterring the two Germanic Powers from committing acts of aggression, he failed to communicate that intent clearly to all parties. Military measures were a prudent precaution to a certain degree. But his violent language towards Pourtalès and the pacific amiability he displayed in his interviews with Szápáry were liable to confuse, given that both ambassadors were likely to compare notes, as indeed they did. No wonder that both men were convinced until the end that Sazonov's tough talk was nothing but a front, and that Russia would not intervene in a Balkans war.[28] The military measures Sazonov forced through at St Petersburg, moreover, had an underhand appearance, and so were liable to counteract any signals of intent. That he seems quite genuinely to have believed that mobilization could be kept secret was a remarkable feat of the imagination, considering that the red call-up notices would be posted in all public places across the whole of the Russian Empire. It underlines the systemic disjuncture between the civilian authorities and the military leadership in Russia. But it was also a failing on Sazonov's part. To move to general mobilization, which came at his urging, undoubtedly escalated the situation; and to that extent Sazonov, too, is guilty of recklessness.

Poincaré and Paléologue also bear a degree of responsibility for escalating the crisis. The rigidity with which the French president and ambassador prioritized sustaining the Franco-Russian alliance over all

---

[27] For assessments of Russia through Turkish lenses see S. McMeekin, *The Russian Origins of the First World War* (Cambridge, MA, 2011).

[28] On being informed of Vienna's ultimatum, Szápáry told Otto Czernin that 'Russia would not stir!!!': Berchtold diary, 15 July 1918, Nachlass Berchtold, Karton 5.

other considerations had left French policy unresponsive to the developments of the last eighteen months before July 1914. As Francis Bertie – no friend of Wilhelmine Germany – noted during the early stages of the July crisis, French policy was 'not sufficiently *coulant*' towards Germany.[29] On the contrary, Poincaré's unilateral tightening of the terms of the alliance and his insistence on an unyielding position towards Berlin contributed to the further narrowing of the wiggle room that is so necessary for diplomacy to succeed.

On reflecting on the events of July 1914, it is perhaps surprising to see Grey emerge as the 'man of action'. He consistently worked for a negotiated settlement of the dispute until the very end. There was nothing half-hearted or meandering about his policy. Could he have warned Germany earlier, as has so often been argued, ever since Lloyd George gave the idea his imprimatur? The argument, in fact, is problematic. For one thing, there were strong political reasons for not doing so, as Grey's Parliamentary Private Secretary, Arthur Murray, explained years later: 'It is not open to doubt ... that if Grey had insisted on sending an ultimatum of this character to Germany, Lloyd George would have led a revolt in the Cabinet; the Cabinet would have dissolved; and the country would have been split from top to bottom.'[30] Grey was entirely justified to seek to avoid this. Divided countries, after all, count for nothing in international politics.

The argument of Grey's failure to warn Berlin is also problematic with respect to the given international circumstances in July 1914. As the evidence presented here has shown, Grey did issue a warning to Berlin and St Petersburg on 6 and 8 July; and it is also clear that Lichnowsky had grasped the full import of what Grey had said. The problem, however, was not what Grey said; the problem was that Berlin did not listen to its own ambassador. Could Grey have been more emphatic and could he have spoken earlier? There were sound diplomatic reasons for Grey to avoid this, and instead to continue working with Germany. Cooperation between London and Berlin had been key to settling the outcome of the two previous rounds of fighting in south-eastern Europe, and all the indicators on the eve of the Sarajevo crisis suggested that Berlin was anxious for such cooperation to continue. Any overt and early warning, beyond what he had said to Lichnowsky, risked closing the door to further cooperation, thereby encouraging German fears of encirclement and so increasing the risk of Berlin deciding to seek salvation in a continental war at a time more advantageous to itself – precisely what Grey wished to avoid. Indeed,

[29] Bertie to Grey (private), 27 July 1914, Bertie MSS, Add. MSS. 63033.
[30] Elibank to the editor, *The Observer* (30 Nov. 1958).

among the key players of the July crisis Grey and Lichnowsky are the two honourable men.

As has been argued in this book, the debate about what Grey could or should have done flows from a later Lloyd Georgeian fabrication, and revolves around a strategic fallacy based on the assumption of a dichotomy between a continental security strategy and a global imperial, 'blue water' school of thought. In reality, no such dichotomy existed; hence, there was no real choice between the Russian and German factors. The two, in fact, were connected because Britain was both a European Power and an overseas Power.[31] As the only truly global Power with global reach and global interests, Britain had a global security paradigm. The British government did not decide to enter the war in August 1914 simply to uphold Britain's interest in the independence of the Low Countries; nor did it opt for war in Europe as the lesser evil as compared with a potential future Russian challenge to British imperial interests in central Asia. However slowly and however reluctantly, ultimately, the ministers decided that British aloofness was not practicable politics. Whatever the outcome of the war, Britain's position as a Great Power would be diminished and so would her ability to defend her interests. If the conflict ended in a victory of the Central Powers, there would be a reordering of the continent of Europe, and with the French fleet and colonies under German control, Germany would emerge as a formidable challenger to British interests. If, by contrast, the war ended in a Franco-Russian triumph, these erstwhile colonial competitors were not likely to show much respect to British interests in the Mediterranean and in the East.[32] The inherent logic of Britain's geopolitical position meant that she had to enter the war and do so against Germany and Austria-Hungary.

Grey nevertheless made mistakes. His suggestion of mediation by the quartet of Powers not directly interested in the Serbian crisis marked a deviation from the previous model of involving all the Great Powers. It was a slimmed-down version of the classic European concert. It was not without its own internal logic – and here the fact that neither Jagow nor Sazonov insisted on the inclusion of Austria-Hungary and Russia would suggest that they understood it. Even so, Grey never explained why he gave up on the full concert, and this gave Austria-Hungary room to pursue her militant

---

[31] For further thoughts on this see the 'twin' pieces by K. Neilson, 'The Russo-Japanese War and British Strategic Foreign Policy', R. Kowner (ed.), *Rethinking the Russo-Japanese War, 1904–5* (2 vols., Folkestone, 2007) I, 307–17, and T. G. Otte, 'The Fragmenting of the Old World Order: Britain, the Great Powers and the War', R. Kowner (ed.), *The Impact of the Russo-Japanese War* (London, 2007), 91–108.

[32] Min. Crowe, 25 July 1914, on tel. Buchanan to Grey (no. 166, urgent), 24 July 1914, *BD* XI, no. 101.

course. Grey also misread Habsburg diplomacy, and he acted on the assumption that talking to Berlin was the surest, and indeed the only, way of influencing Viennese decision-making. It would have been prudent to have a more direct channel of communication with the Monarchy, whether via Mensdorff in London or de Bunsen at Vienna. In later years Grey wondered privately whether it might have been possible to do more to rein in Russia. But it seems doubtful whether British diplomacy could have done more. As Grey himself reflected in 1929, putting pressure on St Petersburg would have led Sazonov to ask for a firm commitment from Britain: 'And to that question he [Grey] could not have given an affirmative answer.'[33] As was shown here, if anything, Sazonov tended towards the view that Britain would not support the Franco-Russian grouping, and yet this did not deter him from mobilizing and so escalating the situation. It seems scarcely credible that he would have decided to disengage if London had sought to restrain him. Indeed, it was French and Russian recalcitrance that forced Grey to utter his explicit warning of a world war on 29 July.

No discussion of culpability can ignore the assassins. The Sarajevo Seven were self-radicalized young men, whose radicalism thrived on carefully nurtured grievances compounded by ideological indoctrination. They were useful idiots, as such disaffected youths often are. They were prepared to become martyr-terrorists, but were controlled by ruthless men around 'Apis' Dimitrijević in Serbia proper, men who were anxious to settle political scores at Belgrade. In their internecine struggle with the government, potential external complications receded into the background, if they were appreciated at all. Possibly none of the assassins understood the consequences of their action. But that is no excuse. The real tragedy, however, is that, just as the European chancelleries had allowed the instability and volatility of Serbian politics to infect relations, such hopeless individuals as Princip and his associates were given the chance to commit their bloody deed, and so allow the old régimes of Europe to prove their incompetence beyond all reasonable doubt. And here Habsburg *Schlamperei* and Potiorek's bungling on the day cannot be ignored. Would, one wonders, the Prince of Wales have been asked by Britain's Chief Secretary for Ireland to visit Dublin or the Falls Road area of Belfast on St Patrick's Day anytime after 1912 in an effort to 'show the flag'? It does not seem very likely.

By moving the actions of individual monarchs, politicians and generals into the foreground, by examining the ethos of the ruling élites with its emphasis on 'honour' and prestige, and by explaining the accelerating dynamic of the unfolding crisis, this book has offered a

---

[33] Temperley interview with Grey, 1929, Temperley MSS, private.

comprehensive and original reassessment of the July crisis of 1914. Such concepts offer a glimpse into the 'unspoken assumptions' that underpinned and informed the actions of the statesmen of Europe and their advisers.[34] But one should not invest them with more meaning than they actually had, nor does it seem appropriate to attach too much significance to Bethmann Hollweg's post-war observation that disengaging and abandoning the Austro-Hungarian ally would have been tantamount to 'Selbstentmannung' (self-castration).[35] No doubt this reflected certain Social Darwinian notions, then prevalent in political discourse, about thriving and declining nations. But further elaborate constructions have been hung upon this particular peg, revolving around assumptions of a fin-de-siècle crisis of masculinity.[36] Much of this seems irrelevant. Bethmann's observation touched on the political core of the human condition – power and power relations as the vital essence of politics. What mattered here was not so much the language in which he couched it, but whether his analysis was correct. It was not.

None of the decision-makers of 1914 desired a continental war. But individually – with the exception of Grey – after a long period of more or less uninterrupted peace, they had lost 'the sense of the tragic', as Henry Kissinger once observed,[37] the sense of the fragility of all human achievement, and of peace and order in particular. And with that loss ninety-nine years of peace came to an end and the self-destruction of Europe as the powerhouse of world politics began. All of the ministers and their advisers would have recoiled at what unfolded in August 1914. Grey and Lichnowsky, who did understand the dangers throughout the crisis, suffered a mental breakdown of some kind, Lichnowsky after 1 August, Grey after the declaration of war.[38] The lachrymose endings of the embassies of Pourtalès, Schoen, Goschen or Mensdorff are further eloquent

---

[34] For discussions of this see J. Joll, 'The Unspoken Assumptions', H. W. Koch (ed.), *The Origins of the First World War* (London, repr. 1977), 307–28; T. G. Otte, *The Foreign Office Mind: The Making of British Foreign Policy, 1865–1914* (Cambridge, 2011).
[35] T. von Bethmann Hollweg, *Betrachtungen zum Weltkriege* (2 vols., Berlin, 1919) I, 133.
[36] For masculinity-centred interpretations see S. Levsen, 'Constructing Elite Identities: University Students, Military Masculinity and the Consequences of the Great War in Britain and Germany', *P&P* no. 198 (2008), 46–63; for the Social Darwinian aspects see F. Stern, 'Bethmann Hollweg and the War: The Limits of Responsibility', in F. Stern and L. Krieger (eds.), *The Responsibility of Power: Essays in Honor of Hajo Holborn* (New York, 1967), 267.
[37] H. A. Kissinger, *A World Restored: Metternich, Castlereagh and the Problems of Peace, 1812–22* (London, 1957), 6.
[38] Crowe to Clema Crowe, 6 Aug. 1914, Crowe MSS. Ms.Eng.e.3020.

testimony that these men knew that an era was passing. When Berchtold had long left office, he was continually plagued by nightmares and haunted by 'black thoughts about my political activities in 1914'. Hoyos, one of the chief hawks at the Ballhausplatz, apparently contemplated committing suicide in 1919, unable to come to terms with his role in the events of the July crisis.[39]

The events of the summer of 1914 are no quaint Edwardian period drama, replete with stiff collars and quivering moustaches. It would be a form of crass presentism to suggest that the July crisis, or any other past occurrence for that matter, offers neat 'lessons of history'. And yet, in many ways, the concerns and events of that year and the years preceding it are more immediate to us today than the seemingly closer events of the 1970s or 1980s. At the beginning of the twenty-first century, as multiple power centres compete for economic, military and political influence and when suicide bombers have become a feature of modern life, the contours of the international landscape of 1914 look more familiar now than those of the era of Nixon, Brezhnev and Carter. And as the leading international players today are entangled in global financial and regional political crises, each with its own complex internal logic and each beset with enormous risks, yet suggestive of strategic opportunities, the attempts of the decision-makers of 1914 to avert war but to extract advantages for themselves no longer look so different from the challenges to crisis management today.

Of course, the men of 1914 acted in circumstances that were not of their choosing and that cannot be replicated today. Their actions were shaped by their recent experiences in international politics. To that extent the past was a prologue to their decisions in the summer of 1914. Impelled by a conviction of the rightness of their chosen course and impervious to the inherent risks of their actions, they found themselves impaled on their own faulty calculations. In that sense, theirs was a tragedy because they had lost the sense of the tragic.

At the beginning of the twenty-first century we are still dealing with the after-effects of the Great War. If this re-examination of the events that led to its outbreak has made a small contribution towards helping to heighten sensibility of the broader sweep of history, to sharpen an understanding of the importance of strategic thinking and to increase awareness of the frailties of human judgement in politics, then it will have achieved something. To appreciate this is, perhaps, the only pertinent lesson to be learnt from history.

---

[39] Berchtold diary, 15 Apr. 1940, Nachlass Berchtold, Karton 5 (see also entries for 13, 14 and 22 Oct. 1940); for Hoyos see E. U. Cormons [pseudo. E. Urbas], *Schicksale und Schatten. Eine österreichische Autobiographie* (Salzburg, 1951), 158.

INDEX